Heidegger and Sartre

HEIDEGGER
AND
SARTRE

An Essay on Being and Place

Joseph P. Fell

New York COLUMBIA UNIVERSITY PRESS

The author and publisher gratefully acknowledge the generous
support given them by the National Endowment for the Humanities.
Research leading to this book was funded by a Younger Scholars'
Fellowship, and publication has been assisted by a further grant
from the Endowment.
The Andrew W. Mellon Foundation, through a special grant, has also
assisted the Press in publishing this volume.

Library of Congress Cataloging in Publication Data

Fell, Joseph P
  Heidegger and Sartre.

  Bibliography: p.
  Includes index.
  1. Heidegger, Martin, 1889–1976—Ontology.   2. Sartre,
Jean Paul, 1905–   —Ontology.   3. Ontology.   4. Phenomenology.
I. Title.
B3279.H49F39   110   78-27437
ISBN 0–231–04554–9 (cloth)
ISBN 0–231–04555–7 (paper)

Clothbound editions of Columbia University Press books are Smyth-sewn
and printed on permanent and durable acid-free paper.

To
Cynthia
John
Caroline

Contents

Preface   ix

Acknowledgments   xix

Abbreviations   xx

1   The Problem of Phenomenological Ontology   1

Part I   The Quest for the Nature of Being   29

2   Dasein, Ground, and Time in *Sein und Zeit*   31

3   *L'Être-pour-soi,* Ground, and Time in *L'Être et le
    Néant*   66

Part II   Living with Nothing   95

4   Nothing and World: The Need for the Turn   97

5   The Ethics of Play and Freedom: Conversion   129

6   Humanism: The Lecture and the Letter   152

Part III   The Reorientation   185

7   The Nature of the Place: Earth and Language   188

8   Man's Place in the Fourfold: Beyond Displacement   215

9   Heidegger's Notion of Two Beginnings   244

10   Language, Action, and the Sartrean Beginning   268

11   Sartre's Problem of Action Metaphysically
     Resolved   302

12   Man's Place in the Spiral: Beyond Atomism   332

Part IV   Confrontation and Prospect   361

13   The Ground and Truth of Being   362

14   The Direction of Phenomenological Ontology   401

Notes   427

Bibliography   485

Index   497

Since Copernicus, man has been rolling from the center toward X.

— Nietzsche, *The Will to Power*

Naturally, all these things are the most obvious of the obvious. Must one speak about them, and with so much ado? . . . Are they not constant presuppositions of scientific and, at the highest level, philosophical thinking?

— Husserl, *The Crisis*

Preface

I HAVE WRITTEN this volume in the conviction that a need exists for a confrontation between the thought of Martin Heidegger and that of Jean-Paul Sartre. Of course, there exist many studies of the thought of each. Yet no large-scale study of the relation of their positions has been written, despite the fact that they are generally classed together as 'existentialists' or as 'phenomenologists', despite the fact that Sartre's thought is known to have been heavily indebted to Heidegger, and despite the fact that each is known to have harbored serious reservations about the thought of the other.

One reason such a study has not been written, I believe, is that students of Heidegger's thought tend to regard Sartre as not worth equal time, while students of Sartre's thought tend to hold the complementary view. I myself have found it necessary to take both thinkers seriously, even—perhaps especially—when their ideas conflict most sharply. It may be thought that their orientations are so divergent as not to be comparable at all; and yet, as chapter 1 will show, they share in large part a common philosophical ancestry and a common preoccupation with a very particular ontological problem. If their respective solutions to this problem do diverge sharply, this may be taken as a sign of the importance of considering them together. They represent two fundamental directions or alternative routes that their common philosophical inheritance makes possible at the present time. To consider them together, then, is a way of assessing the present situation and prospects of ontology. In their divergent responses to their philosophical predecessors, whom both regard as presenting us with a crisis requiring a revolutionary response, they vie for our allegiance in the future reform of our philosophical inheritance. It is no exaggeration to say that the apparently abstract intricacies of their ontological investigations eventuate in the critical question of the future orientation of our civilization.

I shall place primary stress upon Heidegger and Sartre as ontologists. 'Ontology' can provisionally be defined as study of the real, fundamental, or essential nature of beings, both human and nonhuman, and of the interrelation between human and nonhuman beings. It was by interpreting the notion of 'Being' (*Sein, l'être*) in its relation to the human being that each of them sought to work out his fundamental stance as a thinker. Their respective interpretations of Being provided the criteria in terms of which they treated all other philosophical problems—metaphysical, epistemological, aesthetic, ethical, and social. To isolate the core of their thinking, then, is to isolate their interpretations of Being. And to establish the genuinely fundamental differences between their orientations is to contrast their ontologies.

This study is not limited to Heidegger's and Sartre's earlier and better known ontological investigations in *Sein und Zeit* and *L'Être et le Néant*, since one of the most significant characteristics of their ontologies is a reorientation that occurs for both thinkers in mid-career. My theme is therefore broad, for it concerns two thinkers rather than one, and it explores the development of their thought rather than one phase of it. Given its scope, the reader will be able to spot certain aspects of the topic that cry out for a detailed treatment they do not here receive. These lacunae are justified if this volume succeeds in offering an interpretation of Heidegger's and Sartre's ontologies, and their interrelation, that facilitates further study of particular aspects of their thought such as death, facticity, or art. The treatment of the two ontologies together will be justified if each can be used to shed light on the other. It will be further justified if differences between them can help us to understand better the nature and problems of contemporary European ontological investigation, which is, of course, a vital concern of Heidegger and Sartre themselves. This study therefore concludes with a chapter outlining certain principles that emerge from the work of Heidegger and Sartre, and from the confrontation between the two, as possible guidelines for future ontological inquiry insofar as that inquiry is phenomenological in orientation.

There are two widespread interpretations of the relation between Heidegger and Sartre. One, advanced by a number of introductory handbooks on existentialism, grants them joint membership in something called "the existentialist movement" or, alternatively, "existential phenomenology." This judgment must be tested in two ways. The first is by careful consideration of the real extent of divergence between Heidegger and Sartre, to which the present volume devotes much attention, concluding that existentialism and phenomenology are not only distinct but in certain respects incompatible. The second, which is important but beyond the scope of my study, is by careful consideration of the interrelation of present continental thought and Anglo-American thought, for the purpose of ascertaining whether or not there is some global philosophic tendency shared by Heidegger and Sartre despite all their differences. This subject has begun to receive serious attention,[1] and it has even been suggested that in restrospect continental and Anglo-American philosophy may come to be regarded as two aspects of a single philosophic tendency.[2]

The other interpretation of their relation, taking its cue from Heidegger's own assessment of his relation to Sartre in *Brief über den Humanismus*,[3] finds the two thinkers to be different in all essentials, even antithetical in their thinking. But it is not clear that Sartre would subscribe to Heidegger's estimate of their relation; although Sartre has critized Heidegger,[4] he has not answered the *Brief über den Humanismus* in kind. We should not, therefore, uncritically take over Heidegger's assessment. Part of my effort will be to see each thinker through the eyes of the other in order finally to ascertain the degree to which their ontologies are compatible.

The attitudes and life-styles of Heidegger and Sartre are in important respects antithetical. Heidegger was, from early life onward, profoundly attached to theology—despite Sartre's misunderstanding of this attachment.[5] In *Les Mots*, Sartre wrote of his own lifelong struggle to sustain a consistent atheism.[6] Heidegger, aside from a brief public association with National Socialism in 1933–34, was a man detached from the immediate sociopolitical issues of the day, as symbolized by his frequent meditative withdrawals to Todtnauberg. Sartre seemed the very model of the "committed" man, as citizen of metropolitan Paris, as editor of a journal (*Les Temps Modernes*) whose tone became increasingly political, as popular playwright, as would-be founder of a new political party, as war-crimes tribunalist and editor of *La Cause du peuple*. The "soft" and seemingly mystical tones of Heidegger's later essays and lectures contrast vividly with the often mercilessly direct charges laid by Sartre

against his political adversaries.[7] Sartre demanded immediate sociopolitical change, while Heidegger appeared preoccupied with
both the distant past and the distant future.[8]

Can we dismiss these differences of attitude and life-style as
philosophically irrelevant? Is there more than superficial irony in
the fact that the philosophy of the committed Sartre has been in an
important sense a philosophy of withdrawal, while the thought of
the withdrawn Heidegger has been in an essential respect a reminder of our inevitable commitment?

Such questions must be entertained, because a philosophy is not
propounded in a vacuum but by a particular person in a particular
historical situation. In the course of their careers, and despite their
differences, both Heidegger and Sartre become increasingly sensitized to what may be called the compulsion of history. Both, in retrospect, find their early philosophical efforts insufficiently attuned
to the concealed force of history that had oriented those philosophical efforts. The subtitle of this volume is intended to suggest a
correlation between ontology and the environment in which it is
proposed—a correlation that both thinkers are driven to make. Does
this disclosure of the relativity of ontology to its circumstances
demonstrate the lack of autonomy and the inefficacy of thought?
Curiously, the activist Sartre came to despair of thought's making a
practical difference,[9] while the disengaged Heidegger found
thought to be the ultimate determinant of praxis.[10] These differences, however, will be considered here only so much as the theme of
ontology requires.

In order not to force a comparison between Heidegger and Sartre
by building more common ground between them than is really
there, I will in most of the chapters of Parts I–III treat them alternately and on their own terms. Except for chapter 6, each of these
chapters forms a more or less self-contained study of a particular
aspect or phase of Heidegger's or Sartre's work that is preparatory
to a final confrontation between the two in Part IV. While this technique of oscillating back and forth between Heidegger and Sartre
may seem to deflect the line of the book's development, I believe
the attentive reader will sense the emerging outlines of the final
confrontation in the course of Parts I–III. In each chapter, the
themes treated and the manner of their treatment have been selected partly in order to isolate the basic orientations of Heidegger

and Sartre and partly in order to elicit essential interrelations and points of conflict between the two orientations.

In my effort to reach what is ontologically basic in their thinking, I have intentionally overlooked much that they say in common. One could compile a long list of parallels between *Sein und Zeit* and *L'Être et le Néant*. Such an endeavor could show that Sartre is indebted to *Sein und Zeit* not only for some basic themes but also for a multitude of terms, distinctions, and analyses. But what is in question here is the extent to which Sartre takes over notions from *Sein und Zeit* in the sense in which they were intended by Heidegger. It is entirely possible for two thinkers to use the same terms but to mean quite different things; everything hangs on grasping the context or "ambience" within which a term occurs or an assertion is made. But that is what is hardest to grasp and most important to grasp, and it is what necessitates that Heidegger and Sartre be treated alternately until each of their orientations is sufficiently explored. Whether I have succeeded in articulating these orientations, the reader (whom I assume to be independently familiar with at least the early and long-available writings of Heidegger and Sartre) will have to decide.

I have quite consciously run two risks that seem potentially valuable enough to warrant taking them. First, I have attempted to write about both thinkers as simply and directly as possible, with no more recourse to highly technical terms than is absolutely necessary. For example, I have often opted for traditional philosophical terminology in characterizing Heidegger's thought. Given Heidegger's progressive abandonment of such terminology, the danger of serious distortion is obvious. But the possibility of new understanding—especially of Heidegger's relation to the modern ontological tradition—may, I hope, also be granted. The second risk, related to the first, is that at a number of points (perhaps especially in chapter 2) I have attempted to be provocative where I might have, more pedantically and more prosaically, played it safe. Chief among these provocations are: a very broad definition of the phenomenological movement, designed in part to point to a positive relation between Hegel and Heidegger; a questioning of the rather usual judgment that the later Heidegger has gone beyond phenomenological ontology; the teasing of a largely implicit theory of actuality and an implicit ethics out of *L'Être et le Néant*; an attempt to infer a theory of language from Sartre's writings; above all, an attempt to employ the notions of 'familiarity', 'community of nature', and 'place' as primary ontological categories in interpreting the fundamental significance of Heidegger's and Sartre's ontologies. I take seriously Heidegger's notion of the value of "violence" in interpretation and translation,[11] and I have often turned this dangerous technique back upon Heidegger himself, as well as upon Sartre. At the same time, I wanted to counterbalance the dangers inherent in both these risks by massive quotation from Heidegger and Sartre. Rather than immediately fusing my interpretation and their own argument in a gray and possibly distorting paraphrase, I have purposely moved back and forth between my interpretations and their own words.

There is yet another oscillation in this study: between difficult passages and simple, quite obvious passages. The subject matter itself requires this. It is characteristic of phenomenological ontology (and of much of analytic philosophy) to test the obvious and simple by complex interpretation and to test complex interpretation by the obvious and simple. This happens because, as I shall try to establish, phenomenological ontology is interested in a certain vindication of *the familiar* that requires a complex critical interpretation of (*a*) the reasons for the relative lack of ontological commitment to the familiar in much of modern thought and (*b*) the *ground* on which the familiar could be validated. This effort at adequation of the familiar and its ground exists, to be sure, prior to phenomenology—notably in Aristotle—but it attains a new urgency in post-Copernican thought, especially in German Idealism. It is an acute problem in the later writings of Husserl,[12] which form the immediate and insistent background of the work of Heidegger and Sartre.

A brief introduction to each of the four parts of the study is provided to show how the chapters of that part fit into the overall design of the work. The design is roughly chronological. Chapter 1, which precedes Part I, presents a selective sketch of certain developments in post-Copernican ontology designed to show the sorts of ontological problems facing Heidegger and Sartre at the beginning of their careers. It attempts to show how and why phenomenological ontology arises and to formulate three ontological questions that Heidegger and Sartre face as immediate heirs of Husserl.

Part I offers interpretations of the early phenomenological ontologies of Heidegger and Sartre—their initial responses to the ontological legacy outlined in chapter 1, including Sartre's early response to Heidegger's ontology. Part II seeks to ascertain why both
these ontologies require a form of supplementation or revision—for
Heidegger, a "turn," for Sartre, a "conversion." This part concludes
with an important episode of the mid-forties: Sartre's implication of
Heidegger in existentialist humanism in L'Existentialisme est un humanisme and Heidegger's response to this implication in Brief über
den Humanismus, in which some basic features of Heidegger's later
ontological orientation become visible. Part III shows first how Heidegger and then how Sartre reformulated their earlier ontologies in
their later thought—in both cases by reconsidering the relation of
Being to historical time and the relation of their ontologies to metaphysics. This part also attempts to infer a Sartrean theory of language and a Sartrean critique of the later Heidegger, both of which
are essential for the confrontation but neither of which was ever
fully elaborated in Sartre's publications. The concluding Part IV
brings the two ontologies into more direct confrontation, primarily by asking about the ground on which each claims to be true.
The ability of each to answer satisfactorily the ontological problems
first posed in chapter 1—that of the beginning, of metaphysics, and
of unity—is here assessed. Finally, the question whether either has
accomplished the original aims of a phenomenological ontology is
answered and a provisional characterization of the ontological
legacy of Heidegger and Sartre is offered.

In the notes, which follow chapter 14, page numbers given in parentheses refer to the English translation of the work cited, where a
translation existed at the time of writing. The translation referred to
is listed in the bibliography following the entry for the German or
French original. Where the translation used is my own rather than
that cited in the bibliography, I have adopted the convention of
italicizing the parenthesized page numbers of the published translation. In all cases where no parenthesized page numbers are given,
the translation is my own. A list of abbreviations used for
frequently cited works of Heidegger and Sartre is given opposite
the first page of the text. In cases where the essays in the original
text have not appeared in an integral translation but have rather

been separated into two or more English volumes, the bibliography shows which pages of the original text are to be found in each of the English volumes.

If I have often resorted to my own translations despite the availability of published translations, the chief reason has been terminological consistency. I have learned much from the translations made by others, even when I have not quoted them. I should warn the reader of one inconsistency: the term 'being' will sometimes be capitalized, sometimes not, following existing conventions of translation and what I take to be the intentions of Heidegger and Sartre themselves. Further explanation of my capitalization strategy can be found in the notes. My italicization strategy in quotations also calls for comment. In addition to adding italics to stress the relation of a term or phrase to my argument, I have in some cases deleted all or part of Heidegger's or Sartre's own italics, where these italics make sense only in the context of the surrounding pages that are not quoted. In each case, the addition or deletion of italics is acknowedged in the notes, following citation of the page or pages from which the quotation was taken, so that the reader can readily check my translation against Heidegger's or Sartre's original text. It should also be noted that I have in all cases transliterated Greek terms.

I want to record the names of those who have aided me in this work, while absolving them of all responsibility for its final shape. For invaluable philosophical discussions when the book's basic themes were first being formulated, I thank Heribert Boeder, John Macquarrie, and especially Werner Marx. Professor Marx also kindly put the facilities of the Philosophisches Seminar I at the University in Freiburg at my disposal. I am grateful to Robert D. Cumming, Ernest Keen, and F. David Martin for extensive criticism of a draft of the work. For criticism of individual chapters, I am indebted to Peter D. Hertz, John D. Kirkland, Frank Wilson, and the late J. Glenn Gray. Detailed stylistic advice was offered by Gladys Cook, Cynthia Fell, Jon Loveland, and Mildred Martin. Many substantive comments on drafts of the work were made by my former students Ilan Bizberg, Scott Churchill, Kenneth Lambert, Gerald Mercure, Dennis Schmidt, and David Weinberger. Elinor Bryant, Nancy Johnson, and Jean Machamer were my capable and long-suffering typists. The staff of Columbia University Press brought order out of chaos more often than I care to admit, and no author could have greater good fortune than to have editors like John D. Moore and Karen Mitchell.

Initial research for this volume was supported by a Younger Scholars' Fellowship from the National Endowment for the Humanities. Bucknell University generously supported the writing of several chapters through a semester's leave and a summer research grant.

I owe a special debt to John William Miller of Williams College, under whose keen tutelage I first studied Heidegger and Sartre.

J.P.F.

Freedom, New Hampshire
March 1979

Acknowledgments

Grateful acknowledgment is made to the following publishers for permission to use excerpts from the material cited:

Jean-Paul Sartre, *L'Être et le Néant*, 1943: Éditions Gallimard, Paris; Philosophical Library, New York; and Methuen & Co. Ltd, London.

Jean-Paul Sartre, *Critique de la raison dialectique*, 1960: Éditions Gallimard, Paris, and New Left Books, London.

Jean-Paul Sartre, *L'Idiot de la famille*, I, 1971: Éditions Gallimard, Paris, and The University of Chicago Press, Chicago.

Jean-Paul Sartre, *Literary and Philosophical Essays*, translated by Annette Michelson, 1955: Hutchinson Publishing Group Ltd, London.

Jean-Paul Sartre, *Search for a Method*, translated by Hazel E. Barnes: Copyright © 1963 by Alfred A. Knopf, Inc., New York.

Martin Heidegger, *Being and Time*, translated by J. Macquarrie and E. Robinson, 1962: Basil Blackwell, Oxford.

Martin Heidegger, *Vorträge und Aufsätze*, 1954: Verlag Günther Neske, Pfullingen.

Martin Heidegger, *Poetry, Language, Thought*, translated by Albert Hofstadter, 1971; Harper & Row, Publishers, Inc , New York.

Martin Heidegger, *Wegmarken*, 1967: Vittorio Klostermann, Frankfurt am Main.

J. P. Fell, "Heidegger's Notion of Two Beginnings": originally published in *The Review of Metaphysics*, 25, no. 2 (1971); reprinted with permission.

J. P. Fell, "Sartre as Existentialist and Marxist": originally published in *Bucknell Review*, 12, no. 3 (1965); excerpted with the permission of Associated University Presses, Inc., Cranbury, N.J.

J. P. Fell, "Sartre's *Words*: An Existential Self-Analysis": originally published in *The Psychoanalytic Review*, 55, no. 3 (1968), reprinted through the courtesy of the Editors and the Publisher, National Psychological Association for Psychoanalysis, New York, N.Y.

Grateful acknowledgment is also made to Elfride Heidegger, Freiburg, for permission to quote from personal correspondence by Martin Heidegger.

Abbreviations of Heidegger's Works Most Frequently Cited

BH	Brief über den Humanismus (in H)
EHD	Erläuterungen zu Hölderlins Dichtung
EM	Einführung in die Metaphysik
H	Holzwege
HEH	Hölderlins Erde und Himmel
ID	Identität und Differenz
KPM	Kant und das Problem der Metaphysik
N	Nietzsche I, II
SD	Zur Sache des Denkens
SG	Der Satz vom Grund
SZ	Sein und Zeit
TK	Die Technik und die Kehre
US	Unterwegs zur Sprache
VA	Vorträge und Aufsätze
W	Wegmarken
WG	Vom Wesen des Grundes
WHD	Was heisst Denken?
WM	Was ist Metaphysik?
WW	Vom Wesen der Wahrheit

Abbreviations of Sartre's Works Most Frequently Cited

AR	Aller et retour (in S, I)
CRD	Critique de la raison dialectique
EH	L'Existentialisme est un humanisme
EN	L'Être et le Néant
HC	L'Homme et les choses (in S, I)
I	L'Imaginaire
IF	L'Idiot de la famille
M	Les Mots
PH	Une Idée fondamentale de la phénoménologie de Husserl (in S, I)
QL	Qu'est-ce que la littérature? (in S, II)
QM	Question de méthode (in CRD)
S	Situations, I–X
SGCM	Saint Genet comédien et martyr
SM	Search for a Method (translation of QM)
TE	La Transcendence de l'ego

Heidegger and Sartre

1

The Problem of Phenomenological Ontology

But if at length we are persuaded that there are no points in the universe that are really immovable, as will presently be shown to be probable, we shall conclude that there is nothing that has a permanent place except in so far as it is fixed by our thought.

—Descartes, *Principles of Philosophy*, II.13

I

IRIS MURDOCH, in the course of an admirable essay on Sartre, offers a succinct and just characterization of the present ontological situation:

> For many reasons, the chief of which is that science has altered our societies and our key concepts with a dreadful speed, it seems now impossible for us either to live unreflectively or to express a view of what we are in any systematic terms which will satisfy the mind. We can no longer formulate a general truth about ourselves which shall encompass us like a house. . . . But what we hold in common, whatever our solution, is a sense of a broken totality, a divided being. What we accuse each other of is 'metaphysical dualism.' All modern philosophies are philosophies of the third way.[1]

We inherit an ontological bifurcation, "a broken totality, a divided being." This bifurcation is regarded not as natural and inevitable but as a problem to be solved by means of "a third way." What, then, are the two ways that need to be superseded by a third way? Murdoch characterizes them as "total freedom or total immersion, empty reflexion or silence."[2] I conceive Heidegger and Sartre as developing in the course of their careers two versions of a third way—even though Heidegger has in effect criticized Sartre for following the way of total freedom and empty reflection, and Sartre has criticized Heidegger for following the way of total immersion and silence.

Murdoch's analysis implies that the two unsatisfying options presently available to us are ways of impaling ourselves on either horn, subjectivist or objectivist, of a dualistic dilemma. To embrace the subjectivist horn is to gain freedom or subjective being at the cost of objective reality. To embrace the objectivist horn is to gain identity with the world, "immersion," at the cost of subjective reality. Kierkegaard is sometimes regarded as opting for the former way, Hegel as opting for the latter way. The "totality," which Murdoch claims necessitates a third way, would mean a genuine unity in which both subjective being and objective being are integrated, without loss of either, in a nondualistic ontology. But before I undertake to show how Heidegger and Sartre seek such a third way, it is necessary in this initial chapter to define the present ontological problem more specifically by sketching out its main roots in modern philosophy and science. What sorts of ontological problems do Heidegger and Sartre inherit? Why are they both attracted to the idea of an ontology that is phenomenological? Their thought will have maximum plausibility, and the conflict between them will seem genuinely important, only if we patiently trace and formulate the development of the modern ontological problem to which they address themselves.

II

The thought of Copernicus and Galileo provides a—if not the—decisive impetus to the development of an ontological problem in modern times. For direct experience, nothing could be more obviously the case than that the sun orbits a stationary earth. In advancing the heliocentric theory, Copernicus initiated a revolution that far transcends the fields of physics and astronomy. It is frequently said that the broad cultural effect of the Copernican revolution is to deprive man of his privileged geocentric and anthropocentric position—to displace him from his home at the center of the cosmos.[3]

I think one may formulate the largest effect of the Copernican revolution as follows. The world of ordinary experience progressively loses its right to serve as a reference point, a justifiable orienting center. The familiar and the obvious are no longer self-evidently true. For if even the most obvious of all experiences—that the sun moves about a stationary earth—is questionable, the whole fabric of ordinary experience and traditional codifications of this experience become questionable. What first appears, the phenomenal, may be *mere* appearance. Truth is not a given, but a result, an achievement. Aristotle had maintained that "by starting from what is inadequately known, but familiar to us, we can learn to know what is intrinsically intelligible, using what we do know . . . to guide us."[4] It must now be maintained, on the contrary, that truth arises not from guiding or orienting oneself by the familiar and already "known" but rather from the formulation of hypotheses that challenge the familiar and overthrow it. It is one thing, for which there is ample precedent from Thales forward, to go beyond the familiar in order to know more about its constitution or origin; it is quite another to propose that the familiar does not provide the subject matter that is to be inquired into. The Copernican revolution provokes the protracted effort at *displacement* of ordinary experience and its replacement by hypothetical and theoretical truth.

There is, of course, ancient precedent for this modern displacement of the world of familiar and ordinary experience; the monistic thought of Parmenides offers an example. But while the predominant effort of Parmenides' successors was to adjust his thought so that it would accord with the familiar, with the world of qualitative diversity, the predominant thrust of post-Copernican thought has been progressively and cumulatively to challenge the claims of the familiar. The main instrument facilitating this challenge, which was not available to the ancient investigator, is a mathematical physics.

In Galileo's work the Copernican revolution explicitly becomes the key to a new conception of nature as such. Edmund Husserl, the phenomenological precursor of Heidegger and Sartre, found in Galileo an idealization of man's environment. Summarizing Husserl's treatment of Galileo in his *The Crisis of the European Sciences and Transcendental Phenomenology*, Walter Biemel writes:

> The purpose of the central paragraphs concerning Galileo is to show by what process of idealization Galileo achieved a scientific conception of nature, a nature thoroughly determined by causality and capable of being calculated and reduced to formulae. Insofar as Galileo was not aware of this transformation as

such, he was at the same time responsible for concealing this primordial world, this life-world which is necessarily presupposed by this transformation. [Husserl writes:] "Galileo . . . the consummate discoverer of physics, i.e., physical nature, is a genius who *discovers* and at the same time *conceals*." [5]

Husserl's point is that the world of ordinary experience (the life-world) is displaced by an interpretation of it that tends to conceal the very world that is being interpreted. This tendency is confirmed by the philosophy of Descartes.

Descartes is usually said to have founded modern ontological dualism. He taught that the human mind or spirit, through suspension of inherited belief and through methodic self-discipline, has the independent being requisite for it to serve as an impartial judge of—and source of—criteria of reality and truth. The independence of mind from body is guaranteed first by an original and certain intuition of the independent being of thinking (*res cogitans*),[6] second by the certain intuition of the absolute distinction in nature between mind and body,[7] and third by demonstration of the existence of such a body (*res corporea, res extensa*).[8] The mind is enabled to intuit the nature of bodily or material being truly and independently insofar as it is able to be free of reliance on bodily affects (passions, sensations).[9] This means that the true nature of body is distinct from the shifting and relative properties appearing in ordinary sense perception. Rather, body is to be understood as (*a*) pure nonrelative externality that (*b*) remains constant despite experienced change and that (*c*) is truly described by mathematical calculation rather than by the experience and terminology of ordinary sense perception. The external world is in actuality insensible particles[10] and is thus reached by methodic reflection and calculation rather than being immediately given in ordinary premethodic experience.

Descartes is specifically concerned with the question of the ground or foundation (*fundamentum*) of science. The foundation which he criticizes is that of ordinary experience, which is an undifferentiated complex of mental and sensory, active and passive elements. He seeks to separate this undifferentiated complex into its mental and sensory elements in order to reach a purely nonrelative, or "absolute" and "unshakable" foundation, which is what is immediately "present to the mind" in nonsensory intuition.[11] The complex, undifferentiated, and relative ground is thus replaced by a purely mental ground, the ego or subject. If ordinary experience is an unreliable ground because it is a relative admixture of mental and sensory elements, the ego's intellectual or nonsensory intuition is the true and absolute ground because it is simple and irreducible, restricting itself to what is immediately present to the mind and thus certain. As a result, the true world is present to thought rather than to experience, or the true world is reached by circumventing ordinary experience. There is ontological dualism in the sense that where there had been an uncritical amalgam or union of thought and sensation, of mind and body, mind and body are now held distinct and recognized as mutually exclusive. The actual or external world is present only to the intellect, and in essentially mathematical form. The ordinary world of indiscriminately and unmethodically mixed qualities or properties is purified and simplified so as to become the world of intellectually identified physical properties.

Thus Descartes holds that physics is the "trunk" of the tree of knowledge, the other sciences the "branches" springing out of this trunk.[12] Mathematical physics specifies the true object of knowledge as the object of intellect or noumenon lying behind mere appearance or phenomenon. The thing does not show itself in ordinary experience, but is grasped behind appearances by pure intellect. Therefore, in addition to the dualism of mind and body, there is a dualism between the world of phenomenal experience and the world of intellectual intuition. It is with this latter form of dualism that we can associate Murdoch's distinction between the ways of freedom or immersion, "reflexion" or silence. For Descartes there is freedom, self-mastery, and mastery of nature in reflexive purification; the way of unreflective immersion is the way of ignorance of the true distinction between mind and body and hence loss of both self and world.

I have noted that Cartesian thought requires the circumvention of phenomena by a pure or nonsensory intellectual intuition that isolates and knows pure noumena: ego, external body, and (if Descartes's theological demonstrations are to be taken seriously) God. Such nonsensory or nonphenomenal intuition is generally called "metaphysical" knowledge. Descartes's contemporary Hobbes and his successors, most importantly Hume, elaborate a critique of the very possibility of nonphenomenal, metaphysical knowledge. Knowledge requires the evidence of direct sensory experience, which therefore may not be circumvented. The attempt to circumvent it results, in Murdoch's phrase, in *empty* reflexion.

One might therefore suppose that the movement of British empiricism consists in a return to pre-Copernican and pre-Cartesian ordinary experience, but such is not the case. I have defined ordinary experience as an immediate union of thought and sensation, of activity and passivity. It has naïve and unreflective confidence in its ability to know the world directly and as it really is. Appearance is reality, if not all reality. The British empiricists, however, share in the post-Copernican crisis of confidence in the validity of ordinary experience: what appears is not the thing itself but at best our only evidence of the thing itself. What is experienced is not the thing but an image, idea, or impression of it. The British empiricists accept the assumption that the thing itself is to be defined by its pure unqualified externality. Sensation, as a relative process dependent upon a medium (the sense organs), cannot be said to be a neutral or transparent medium through which the thing shows itself as it is— especially since we have no way of comparing the thing *as sensed* with the thing *in and by itself* (*substantia*). The consequence is limitation of knowledge to appearances and denial of the possibility of metaphysical (i.e., metaphenomenal) knowledge. Empiricism accepts the view that "there is nothing in the intellect that was not first in sensation": all ideas, or all legitimate ideas, are derived from what happens to occur in sensation. If experience has any order and regularity, this is a brute happening for which no reason can be given. Phenomena and the order of phenomena are only signs of or surrogates for an inaccessible reality, an "I know not what" (Locke).

Kant affirms the empiricist critique of the possibility of metaphysical knowledge by pure nonsensory intuition and/or demonstration, but with a reservation that is decisive for the subsequent development of phenomenology and phenomenological ontology. Kant is unwilling to settle for the essential unintelligibility of the world of the empiricists, yet he regards the empiricist restriction of knowledge to appearances as sound. Restriction of knowledge to appearances means the inevitable relativity of the thing known to the knower. The thing can be for us only under the "conditions" of its appearances to us. But Kant sees that there are at least two possible attitudes one may take regarding these conditions. The first attitude is evident in Book I of Hume's *Treatise of Human Nature*: the subjective conditions of the knowing process represent a permanent bar to neutral knowledge of the world and an invitation to skepticism and pessimism. The second attitude is implicit in the balance of Hume's *Treatise*: if one reconciles oneself to and affirms these same subjective and relative conditions, one finds that one's phenomenal world can be regarded for all practical purposes as real, orderly, and sufficient to one's needs.[13]

Kant sees that there is here, in germ, a new kind of reality: *the relative absolute*. Although the unconditioned and nonrelative entity or "thing-in-itself" is forever unknowable, and because it is unknowable, the thing as it appears may legitimately be regarded as the real. Through this revolution in attitude, Kant is able to accord the phenomenon the title "substance"—*substantia phaenomenon*[14]—which would otherwise have to be reserved for the unconditioned thing in itself.

(I pause here long enough to note the striking effect of fundamental shifts in attitude in the history of thought. Heidegger refers to them as the essential decisions of our history,[15] implying that the historical direction of thought is at critical points at least as much a function of attitude toward "facts" or "data" as it is a function of these facts themselves. Later we shall find significant mid-career shifts in attitude in the thought of both Heidegger and Sartre.)

In regarding the phenomenon as real and as substance despite the fact that it represents the thing-in-itself only in conditioned form, Kant says in effect that experience is a process analogous to the one Husserl attributes to Galileo: a discovering that is at the same time a concealing. The price of a thing's showing itself is that it also conceals itself. It appears under multiple conditions (space and time, hence perspective; categories, schemata) that at once constitute the possibility of the thing's revealing itself and the impossibility of its appearing as it would to a nonfinite being or God.[16] A considerable part of the history of philosophy and culture after Kant and to the present time has been given over to the task of either assimilating or seeking to circumvent this Kantian restriction of knowledge to relative and finite conditions. There are signs that it was unpalatable even to Kant, and the magnitude of the preoccupation with it can be taken as an index of its revolutionary and even threatening character. The necessity to postulate nonrelative and nonphenomenal being (the free ego, God, immortality) to orient or to situate and guide human beings who are epistemologically limited to a phenomenal place is an insistent theme for Kant.

Kant's affirmation of the phenomenal world as a region of reality and truth is, of course, not an affirmation of the nonrational and fundamentally unintelligible world of empiricism. The mental categories and schemata relative to which phenomena appear are not empirically conditioned psychological habits or dispositions that simply happen to happen. They are rational or logical preconditions, of transcendental origin, for the uniformity and intelligibility of experience of phenomena. This transcendentally legislative achievement of the human mind is a central theme of both Kantian and post-Kantian idealism, including the phenomenological idealism of Husserl. It means that human thought both has and exercises the free transcendental power to constitute, delimit, and identify the "empirically real" (but it alone) through conditions that are "transcendentally ideal." [17] This means in turn that ideality and reality are not experientially distinct or antithetical: the phenomenon is what it is as an immediate unity of "idea" and "matter." Experience of the world is therefore in part experience of oneself. It is not a matter of a previously separate idea and matter coming together at some point in the course of one's experience; experientially, idea and matter are always already a union (the phenomenon), so that the effort to distinguish between pure idea and pure matter is an effort to factor into its elements a prior unity.

It might seem at first as if the problem of which Murdoch has spoken were here definitively resolved. Rather than a dualism of mind and body, or of idea and matter, phenomenal experience would seem to represent a genuine third way—a marriage of thought and its environment that is not a "broken totality" or "divided being" and that avoids the twin dangers of free but inefficacious thought on the one hand and loss of self through immersion in one's environment on the other. Such, in fact, was the conviction of German idealism, but in retrospect German idealism is generally regarded as having alternately succumbed to one or the other of these very dangers.

The attitude of post-Kantian German thought to Kant is much like the attitude of post-Parmenidean Greek thought to Parmenides.

It is an uneasy mixture of enormous indebtedness and enormous dissatisfaction. Like the thought of Parmenides, that of Kant presented itself as an inescapable fatality. That transcendental thought participates in the constitution of its objects is undeniable. That this must be the key to the occurrence and validation of an intelligible environment for man is undeniable. Yet in Fichte, in Schelling, in Hegel, and in Husserl is found the conviction that Kant was not radical enough. To understand why, one must note the *quasi-theological* power of thought in Kant's philosophy. Although the efficacy of thought for Kant is restricted to the empirical and practical spheres, within these spheres its rightful[18] legislative power is awesome. In the order of formal cause (essence, nature, definition, intelligible form) the mind has the godlike spontaneous transcendental power to form a world—though not to create it in the order of material or efficient cause, nor to design it in the order of final cause. And yet the design and even the existence of God are for Kant as unknown, and unknowable, as is the thing-in-itself. There exists then in Kant's thought a tension between the transcendental power of man and the blunt limitation of this power and of the aspirations to which it gives rise. In this sense there remains a broken totality.

Might not the quasi-theological power of human reason be a sign of human participation in the divine nature? Insofar as human thought transcends and forms its natural conditions, may that thought not be seen as approaching, approximating, and finally becoming identical with God's forming of nature? If that were the case, man's progressive discovery of his world could be seen as God's progressive forming of the world—assuming that the world was not fully actualized at the beginning but is progressively actualized in history. This view would enable one to envisage phenomenal experience as the progressive unification of mind and matter or the progressive appearing of the thing as it is in itself. The phenomenon as a revealing *and concealing* of the thing-in-itself would represent only a stage in the historical process by which the thing-in-itself becomes *fully* revealed in all its perspectives. Such a view would respect Kant's limitation of knowledge to finite spatio-temporal experience and yet see this limitation as progressively self-canceling. The Kantian phenomenon as union of idea and matter, as *substantia phaenomenon*, as revolutionary redefinition of the being of the thing as not simply external and material but as also ideally constituted, is not only preserved but carried further. In the end the phenomenon is not simply the peculiarly limited form in which the thing can appear to a finite being. It is the appearance of the thing as it is in itself because (*a*) idea or formal cause belongs to the very nature of the thing and (*b*) the marriage of the transcendentally ideal with matter is God's self-externalizing of himself in the world through man, God's descent into the flesh in order that the world may become divine.[19]

Such, in broadest outline, is Hegel's effort to assimilate and to radicalize Kant's thought. It represents a "phenomenological ontology" in a more radical sense than does Kant's thought. The Kantian thing has an irrevocably dual being—phenomenal and noumenal. Phenomenal or spatiotemporal and categorial-schematic being, while real and substantial, is nonetheless a necessary privation of noumenal being. Hegel, on the other hand, finally takes Being altogether into space, time, and ideation, so that ultimately Being becomes entirely phenomenal or entirely reveals itself—with the proviso that the spatiotemporal ultimately coincides with the eternal, and human ideation ultimately coincides with divine ideation. The history of phenomena—"phenomenology" in Hegel's sense—is the actualization of Being as phenomenal without remainder. The "broken totality" of which Murdoch speaks is for Hegel a necessary stage, but only a stage, in a *totalization* in which all ontological dualities or oppositions serve to reveal distinct but mutually complementary aspects, elements, and perspectives of an emerging synthesis, union, or identity.

Commenting on Descartes, Hegel wrote, "This identity of Being and Thought . . . constitutes the most interesting idea of modern times."[20] The idea will play an important role throughout my study of the ontologies of Heidegger and Sartre. By way of working out its implications, I shall in some cases speak of it as "the identity of thought and beings" or "the identity of thought and being," rather than as "the identity of thought and Being." By the first two locutions, I mean to stress an identity of thought and entities themselves (entities as thought or as meant, i.e., phenomena). By the third locution, I mean to stress an identity of thought and the nature of entities. (In Heidegger's terms, the first two locutions mean the identity of thought and "the ontic," while the third locution means the identity of thought and "the ontological.") What this identity means when applied to Heidegger or to Sartre may, of course, differ significantly from what it means when applied to Descartes, or to Hegel himself. It may imply a realism, an idealism, or neither. It may imply an identity that always exists (an original identity), an identity that exists only at the end of a historical development, or an identity that is an unachievable ideal. It represents a provocative general idea that is susceptible to a range of particular interpretations or variations. Nevertheless, all these interpretations are variations on a single theme—that thought and its referents, even its material referents, are not simply different in kind.

It seems the fate of post-Cartesian thought to work out the consequences of total acceptance, limited acceptance, or total rejection of this "most interesting idea." It is not always as happy a fate as for Hegel, for whom thought can be identified with the divine. But the notion that Being is available to man only as thought, or as qualified by thought, that the object is present only in subjective form, that there is a de facto if not de jure "identity" or fusion of Being and thought—this notion is seldom far from the center of the modern philosophical stage. If thought constitutes or forms or qualifies Being with either divine right or the right of self-evidence, i.e., with "ground" or "reason," it is a saving thought, for the resulting union of thought and Being is a phenomenon that can be called real, true, substance. If, however, thought constitutes, forms, or qualifies Being without specifiable ground or reason, the resulting union of thought and Being is a phenomenon that is called irrational, illusory, subjective, virtual, relativistic, conventional, circular, or anthropomorphic. If, in the words of William James, "the trail of the human serpent is . . . over everything,"[21] is this the condition for the appearance of Being or the condition for the obscuring of Being? I suggest provisionally that the answer given depends on the way in which *ground* is construed: what is the ground of, basis of, reason for, or justification of the phenomenon as a unity of idea and matter, subject and object, thought and Being? Is this union a marriage made in heaven or in hell?

The dominant ground in post-Cartesian philosophy has been the thought of the cogito, ego, or subject. Whatever happens or fails to happen in experience, there is thought. Thought is the universal constant. It is the orienting center or reference point relative to which all experience is had, to which, for which, and in terms of which there is an environing world. It is the inevitable arbiter of the meaning and validity of its experience. Therefore everything hangs on the establishment of the ego's access to criteria of judgment that are universal and necessary. Otherwise human judgments may be arbitrary, psychological, and idiosyncratic. Nineteenth- and twentieth-century man has been made acutely aware of this danger by research in comparative anthropology and clinical psychology. But philosophical thought has itself contributed to a doubt that the subject as ground has or can have the ontological unity with divine reason that Hegel assigns to it. Both Kierkegaard and Nietzsche make this point in their own quite different ways.

That the subject is inevitably the arbiter of the meaning and validity of his experience is indisputable for Kierkegaard. However, this subject is not a *universal* one but an individual or "existing" subject with no access to self-evident or divinely guaranteed criteria of judgment. Rather than being a grounded ground, he is a groundless ground. That is, the criteria he employs in deciding—as he must—the meaning of his finite and phenomenal experience have only the authority that his decision accords to them. The individual plugs the abyss—the absence of ground (*Abgrund*)—with himself. The price of genuine decision, as opposed to Cartesian involuntary compulsion by the rationally self-evident, is the absence of evidence. The guarantee of one's decision is psychological or affective—the degree of one's resoluteness—rather than logical or evidential. Hegel is right that the only sufficient reason or ground for holding finite spatiotemporal phenomenal experience to be experience of truth is a divine guarantee of the identity of thought and Being; Hegel is wrong that we have such a guarantee. Hegel argued that union, unity, identity, or totality is achieved by the dialectical interplay of opposites through time. A primitive and naïve union or totality breaks apart into its elements, which first appear to be irreconcilably antithetical and ununifiable, but which prove in the course of history to require each other. The goal of history is a reflective and justified reunion in place of an originally unreflective and unjustified union, a reestablishment of identity out of its own differences. In other words, the analytical movement of explicit differentiation of the elements of which experience is composed (e.g., idea and matter) is at once the "death" of ontological unity and a necessary "moment" in the now-legitimated reunification or synthetic movement by which ontological unity is explicitly reclaimed.

Kierkegaard stands solidly within the Hegelian orientation in committing himself to characterization of the analytic *elements* of a once-and-future ontological unity precisely in Hegelian terms: existence/essence, actuality/ideality, possibility/necessity, nonbeing/being, moment/eternal, contingent/absolute. But Kierkegaard attributes the breaking of ontological totality into these antitheses to the Fall, and he denies all possibility of their dialectical reconciliation and all possibility of the achievement of totality within finite spatiotemporal experience or history. "Contradictions" inherent in human finite experience ("existence") cannot be resolved by appeal to any allegedly knowable original or final cause:

> The contradictions of existence are explained by positing a *prae* as needed (because of an earlier state the individual has come into his present otherwise inexplicable situation); or by positing a *post* as needed (on another planet the individual is to be placed in a more favorable situation, in view of which his present state is not inexplicable).[22]

Any such variant of the Greek doctrine of recollection (including Hegel's) appeals to an unknowable "whence" and "whither" to illuminate the dark horizon that surrounds the inexplicable and contradictory present. Kierkegaard fully subscribes to Kant's rejection of the possibility of metaphysical knowledge as well as to Kant's view that this limitation makes room for faith. But the stress in Kierkegaard falls on the anxiety of groundless decision rather than on the rational constitution of a limited but intelligible finite space and time; existence and essence, or being and thought, in no way form a coherent union for Kierkegaard. One might express this by saying that for Kierkegaard there is no ontology of the phenomenal, only onticity: so far as we can know, the phenomenon is bare existence without legitimizable meaning or 'essence'. The legitimating ground is missing. But temperamentally, Kierkegaard had no stake in finitude, in time or history.

Nietzsche, temperamentally, had an absolute stake in finitude and time that expresses itself in his notion of *amor fati*. He is similar to Kierkegaard both in his acceptance of the Kantian limitation of knowledge to the region of phenomena and in his rejection of

Hegelian rational history. But he is close to Hegel (and to Spinoza) in his effort to understand the secular as sacred. For Nietzsche, as for Hegel, this can only be accomplished if the traditional distance between the secular and the sacred is abolished. For Hegel this required the dialectical recombining of what the Platonic-Christian tradition had taken as sacred on the one hand and secular on the other: transcendent being and immanent being. But Nietzsche undertakes a thoroughgoing critique of the possibility of metaphysical transcendence: the "meta-" or "over and beyond" is always for him to be understood in terms of the "under" as he pits against metaphysics what might be called "hypo-physics." This new "topology," or sense of place, has in common with Schopenhauer and Freud the search for the meaning of what is above in terms of what lies below, the light in terms of the dark, the heavens in terms of the recesses of the earth. Nietzsche sees this reorientation as a sort of recentering on the place of early Greek experience and philosophy, displaced by the Platonic-Christian centering of ontology in the meta-physical. He thus sees the preponderant part of the philosophical and theological tradition as ec-centric and tries to think through this displacement of the true center in terms of "decadence" and its consequence, "nihilism."[23]

Reorientation around the true center requires a massive assault on the false center, in which one pushes to its bitterest extreme, by insistently calling attention to it, the nihilism that inheres in a transcendentally oriented ontology. The reason why a transcendentally oriented ontology in the end disvalues everything is that, out of lack of strength (decadence) to face mundane experience on its own terms, it posits a metaphysical Being as compensatory inversion of everything that experience is felt to lack. The transcendental Being of philosophy and theology provides a metaphysical solace to which even Nietzsche, as a self-admitted decadent, feels himself drawn and must struggle against. This Being compensates finite beings whose finite, or phenomenal, experience and fate are not affirmable on their own terms. It erects a Being as eternal ground of the spatio-temporal and phenomenal—a transcendental origin, meaning, and goal (prae and post, "whence" and "whither") by reference to which all the vicissitudes and liabilities of mortal existence are either justified or rectified. But the greater this Being, the greater the devaluation of finite and phenomenal experience by comparison. The less the phenomenal world is experienced as self-centering, the greater and higher must be the transcendental metaphysical center, but the greater the transcendental center, the lesser the phenomenal world—and so on, until the phenomenal world of itself is entirely valueless and meaningless.

Nietzsche's task is that of a great cultural deconditioning. The precondition for the rehabilitation of the phenomenal world as self-centering or self-grounding is a critical destruction of metaphysical Being that leaves, as remainder, Nothing—the *nihil*, absolute nihilism. This is only a matter of calling attention to a historical development already far advanced, which Nietzsche sometimes characterizes as the killing of God. Man has "killed God"—that is, the act of divorcing the sacred from the secular, Being from Time, has as its inevitable consequence the banishment of Being to a region to which there is no human access. There is no access because this region is defined precisely as lacking all those phenomenal predicates in terms of which alone it could have any evidential meaning or practical effectiveness for us.[24] Pure Being, as Hegel saw, is pure nothingness. What Nietzsche sees as necessary is an inversion of the original inversion: if Being becomes nothingness, then nothingness becomes Being; if the metaphysical region by reference to which the phenomenal world is reduced to nothingness is itself reduced to nothingness, only the phenomenal world then remains as a possible site of Being.

In fact, it then becomes possible to see that the mundane world was really the source of Being all along: Nietzsche argues that the real source of meaning and value has always been man, "the esteemer,"[25] but this source has dissimulated itself in order to make the source of meaning and value appear absolute rather than relative. Man must own up to the inevitable circularity of meaning and valuing. There is meaning and value insofar as man means and values. But man *is* the meaner and valuer. Thus in the act of owning up to what he is ("Become who you are!"),[26] he affirms the phenomenal world as the true world, the relative-absolute that is the objective embodiment of the meaning and value with which man endows it. Even nothingness is a human meaning, but when one affirms both meaner and meant, when one affirms oneself as valuer and hence one's world as valuable, then becoming has been given the stamp of Being.[27] This is love of fate: to love the phenomenal world is to find it lovable. Nietzsche is a phenomenological ontologist in the broad but important sense that he accords Being to the phenomenon and regards the phenomenon as the disclosure of Being itself. The "true" world is the "apparent" world.[28] The relative is absolute.

For my subsequent study, it is worth bearing in mind that Nietzsche explicitly correlates ontology and attitude: the phenomenon is ontological—Being is in time—only in the attitude of mortal love, the affirmation of one's finite destiny. What destroys Being and brings on nihilism is hatred of time, of mortality, of the earth.

The history of our culture, then, is for Nietzsche the history of the deontologizing of the phenomenon. The near and familiar is no longer ground and center. Being is displaced and misplaced: "we are losing the center of gravity by virtue of which we lived; we are lost for a while." "Since Copernicus man has been rolling from the center toward X." Why? "The development of science resolves the 'familiar' more and more into the unfamiliar. . . ."[29] Perhaps Nietzsche, who often enough speaks of himself as a scientist, himself participates in this resolving of the familiar into the unfamiliar insofar as he posits a will to power underneath the familiar. This hypophysics—or antimetaphysical metaphysics—represents the residual pull on Nietzsche of nihilism, which, however, "represents a pathological transitional stage."[30] The biology of will to power and the teaching of eternal recurrence can be regarded as transitional notions—aspects of the effort at inversion of the inversion—rather than as final truths, just as Zarathustra is not yet the overman. After characterizing the sort of individual who would be strong enough to live without finalities, Nietzsche adds: "How would such a human being even think of the eternal recurrence?"[31] But when Nietzsche traces the phenomenal world to an underlying ground construed according to the biological and energy-quantum models of his time, he is in imperfect accord with his own judgment that "the 'in itself' is even an absurd conception: a 'constitution-in-itself' is nonsense; we possess the concept 'being,' 'thing,' only as a relational concept." "That things possess a constitution in themselves quite apart from interpretation and subjectivity, is a quite idle hypothesis: it presupposes that interpretation and subjectivity are not essential, that a thing freed from relationships would still be a thing." "All unity is unity only as organization and co-operation.

. . ."[32] Nietzsche points to a relational and relative ontology in which there is a union of thought and Being—that is, a rehabilitation of the reality of the phenomenon. And he sees that the price of regarding the phenomenon as reality is giving up all claim of access to a nonrelative absolute or ground:

> The "other," the "unknown" world—very good! But to say "true world" means "to *know* something of it"—that is the *opposite* of the assumption of an "*x*" world—
>
> *In summa:* the world "*x*" could be in every sense more tedious, less human, and less worthy than this world.[33]

Thus in Nietzsche the restriction to an ontology of phenomena that Kant invoked is pushed still further, in that Kant's appeal to noumena as orienting postulates is disallowed as a de facto devaluation of the phenomenal realm itself. But among the noumena disallowed by Nietzsche is Kant's transcendental ego as spontaneous source of universal and necessary rational categories. The categories had made restriction to the phenomenal world bearable, so to speak: if knowledge or a science of phenomena is to be possible, the mind of man must constitute and experience a regular phenomenal order. The world must be relative to universal mind, not to each individual and idiosyncratic mind.

Edmund Husserl argued that if the latter is the case, both philosophy and science are in danger of "psychologism." Psychologism is the tendency to regard laws of thought as no more than general descriptions of the ways in which human beings happen to think. But thought has no authority insofar as it is merely what happens to happen. Nothing prevents it from being arbitrary, situation-relative, or culture-specific. The legislation of thought to objects, like any legislation, is a mode of violence unless it has true grounds or an established right to legislate. Psychologism leaves open the possibility that the order of thought is simply a consequence of environmental conditioning, whether that environment be biological, geographical, or cultural.

Husserl sees that the first step to be taken in challenging psychologism must be to suspend "the natural attitude" by phenomenological reduction. This consists in the explicit disregarding of whatever simply happens contingently, whether it be external events or psychological events. Thought now focuses in intuition on its own formative activity insofar as it is a formal and logical activity. What it isolates is general or abstract forms and formal relations that may be called "essences." The transcendental or nonempirical origination of these essences is indicated not merely by their general or universal nature (as opposed to the individuality or particularity of entities observed in the natural attitude) but by their self-evidence ("apodicticity"). Sometimes Husserl speaks of this immediate intuitive self-evidence as "seeing."[34] That is self-evident to intuition which I see must be the case. It is constitutive for a whole range of individual experiences, all of which presuppose and exemplify it. Thus, for example, the notions 'three', 'both', 'each', 'natural', 'artifactual', 'ideational', 'present', 'absent', 'same', 'real', 'unreal', 'past', 'future'—to select only a few from a vast multiplicity of essences—are a priori conditions for the possibility of encountering and identifying as what it is (in its own mode of being) any particular case of threeness, artifactuality, presence, pastness, etc. These essences are thus ideal and yet constitutive of the real. Husserl confirms Kant's judgment that the empirically real conforms to conditions that are transcendentally ideal, while claiming that the "seeing" of phenomenological intuition succeeds in actually "disclosing" essences that Kant failed to disclose in their true self-evident givenness because he was dependent on a "constructively inferring" method.[35]

Thus the lawfulness of the phenomenal world is guaranteed by the apodicticity of the thought that constitutes the phenomenal order according to self-evident modes of Being (kinds of Being, levels of Being, kinds of relations between beings). Among these constitutive acts or "achievements" is the crucial act of constituting the ego as "absolute here," the ultimate reference-point relative to which all experience is had. Husserl in this notion confirms Descartes's notion of ego as absolute center and arbiter of its world and Kant's notion of the transcendental unity of apperception—all expressions of the modern notion of the ego as ground of its world. In final confirmation of this absolute ground, Husserl seeks to isolate apodictically the transcendental ego itself as spontaneous origin of the constitutive essences isolated by the eidetic reduction.[36] Thus "transcendental subjectivity" is absolute ground or absolute being, to which the being of things is strictly relative.[37]

The question of the validity of this last step into unqualified idealism is one that has separated strict Husserlian phenomenologists from revisionary phenomenologists. It implies that the phenomenon as experienced is not a relative *absolute* but only relative to an absolute that transcends it. "An absolute reality is as valid as a round square."[38] To those who reject this thoroughgoing idealism, the real source of Husserl's mistake is generally seen to lie in the method of reduction: it is no accident that the world appears as entirely relative to consciousness precisely when its independent natural being is reduced or bracketed. But Husserl can answer that the world appears as independent being *only when it is constituted as such* by thought. When a thing appears "in bodily presence" as "evidence," it appears as what it is only if it is actively constituted as such by the essences body, presence, externality, etc. One is therefore confronted by the paradox that the condition of an independent being appearing as such is that it be a dependent being.

Another way of characterizing this radical idealism would be to say that Husserl's phenomenology, which first seemed like a description solely of mental activity and ideas, turns out to be a universal ontology of Being as such. Husserl writes that phenomenology is "the systematic unfolding of the universal logos of all conceivable being. In other words: as developed systematically and fully, transcendental phenomenology would be ipso facto the true and genuine universal ontology. . . ."[39] "True being . . . has significance only as a particular correlate of my own intentionality. . . ."[40]

What, then, is added to the external-object-insofar-as-intended when we return to the unbracketed natural attitude and actually see the particular object? It seems that what is added can only be the *existence* of the intentional entity. Its essence has a transcendental (mental) origin, so that the only factor which distinguishes the observed entity from the thought entity is the embodiment of this entity. This existence would seem to be pure unqualified matter, "X," since the form of the entity is ideal, of transcendental origin. If that is the case, then there seem to be two possibilities: either (1) the external world apart from human thought is void of all forms, distinctions, determinations; or (2) the external world, in and of itself, possesses all the rational formal determinations that the mind concurrently intends it as having. If (1) is true, then essence and existence are in danger of falling apart into a broken totality, or dualism, in which form is mental being and matter is natural being. There would seem no reason not to conclude that the world we think we see is just the projection of ourselves onto a neutral material matrix, a mere circular reflex of ourselves. If (2) rather than (1) is to be true, recourse to God is necessary in order to prove the actual presence of rational distinctions in nature—but this would represent a metaphysical appeal to a ground that is not self-evident, undercutting the notion that the ego is absolute and apodictic ground.

Husserl is no doubt aware of these two problematic consequences, the first of which approximates the idealism of Fichte, the second the metaphysical theology of Descartes's *Meditations*. Husserl himself explicitly formulates the condition for resolving a dualism between two kinds of being as follows: "Can the unity of a whole be unified other than through the essence proper to its parts, and which must accordingly have some *community of essence* instead of essential heterogeneity?"[41] But it seems impossible for Husserl to speak of a real community of essence *between* idea and object precisely because essence belongs solely or originally to idea. Putting the problem differently: if the ego is the absolute constitutive and legislative ground, it is not in a position to be one half of a reciprocal community of equals, the other half of which is nature. And even if it were, why the ego and nature had essences in common would remain wholly unclear.

I am exploring this problem in some detail because I believe it forms the crucial ontological problem inherited by Heidegger and Sartre from Husserl and, through Husserl, from the modern ontological tradition. It can be characterized as the problem of community of natures (or essences) between subject and object. I shall argue that it is the modern form of a long-standing ontological problem of which Aristotle was already aware, and I shall want to ask whether its resolution is possible so long as the modern assertion of the ego as absolute ground prevails.

There remains, however, another aspect of Husserl's thought that has importance for my topic. In his late thought, in which he seeks to come to terms with the *Lebensphilosophie* of Dilthey and perhaps with the earliest work of Heidegger, the notion of the life-world (*Lebenswelt*) comes to prominence. In *The Crisis of European Sciences and Transcendental Phenomenology*, Husserl argues that the ground

of the sciences is the world as lived. Merleau-Ponty has clearly summarized why this is the case:

> All my knowledge of the world, even my scientific knowledge,
> is gained from my own particular point of view, or from some
> experience of the world without which the symbols of science
> would be meaningless. The whole universe of science is built
> upon the world as directly experienced, and if we want to sub-
> ject science itself to rigorous scrutiny and arrive at a precise as-
> sessment of its meaning and scope, we must begin by reawak-
> ening the basic experience of the world of which science is the
> second-order expression. Science has not and never will have,
> by its nature, the same significance *qua* form of being as the
> world which we perceive, for the simple reason that it is a ra-
> tionale or explanation of that world. . . . To return to things
> themselves is to return to that world which precedes knowl-
> edge, of which knowledge always *speaks*, and in relation to
> which every scientific schematization is an abstract and deriva-
> tive sign-language, as is geography in relation to the coun-
> tryside in which we have learnt beforehand what a forest, a
> prairie or a river is.[42]

In Husserl's terms, the various sciences are "regional ontologies"
that explore aspects of the world as lived. The original and final
subject of the sciences is the familiar world relative to which the
most abstract science does and must situate its results. This is what
Galilean-Cartesian science has overlooked, so as to conceal its own
foundation. Merleau-Ponty pushes the notion of the centrality of
the life-world for phenomenology when he writes that "all its
[phenomenology's] efforts are concentrated upon reachieving a
direct and primitive contact with the world, and endowing that
contact with a philosophical status."[43] But this seems to suggest
that the absolute ground is the life-world rather than the transcendental ego. Can the two be reconciled? The life-world is experienced outside the transcendental reduction, in "the natural attitude"; constitutive acts of consciousness are apprehended only
subsequent to a reduction that places out of account all of the "validities" of the natural attitude. How are the two brought together?

It is for Husserl a question of "the *proper* return to the naiveté of
life."[44] If the reduction takes the world-ground from us,[45] it does so

in order finally to justify it. From within the reduction, thought intuits itself in the act of constituting the essential self-evident forms of the life-world itself, the "invariant structures" of the only "apparently incomprehensible 'Heraclitean flux.' "[46] In radical contrast to Descartes and Kant, who regard transcendental thought as establishing the world of knowledge and science (of *epistēmē*) as the real world, phenomenology rehabilitates "the disparaged *doxa*, which now suddenly claims the dignity of a foundation for science, *epistēmē*." This requires treating the life-world "in its neglected relativity."[47] What this means is that the life-world can be justified as the real and necessary ground of the sciences only if it is shown to be *a grounded ground*—grounded in transcendental subjectivity. If the life-world is grounded in the ego, "having arrived at the ego, one becomes aware of standing within a sphere of self-evidence of such a nature that any attempt to inquire behind it would be absurd." The ego is "the last conceivable ground" or "primal source" and its sphere is the sphere of "primordiality."[48] We here encounter the self-evident forms that constitute the life-world as intelligible and as a progressive "teleological" realization of rationality in the course of human history, first initiated by "the Greek primal establishment." Phenomenology must accomplish the "reestablishment" on secure grounds of the Greek "teleological beginning" of the "European spirit."[49]

Husserl's term for "establishment" is *Stiftung*, which connotes founding in the sense of donating or giving. Transcendental phenomenology discloses that the transcendental subject gives itself a world within which things can appear as what they are: "the world that exists for us, that is, our world in its being and being-such, takes its ontic meaning entirely from our intentional life through a priori types of accomplishments. . . ."[50] The life-world is formed essentially by a self-giving that is ordinarily unaware of itself as giving. Analysis of the outward, "projective," or object-centered thrust of intentional thought shows that one is naïvely and unreflectively aware of the object as if it were simply there of its own accord, and only under special conditions (reduction) is one aware of the act of "meaning-endowing" or intending that first gives the object its formal identity and world-setting. The whole tendency of unreflective thought is to dissimulate its own primal grounding activity. It is a self-effacing gift. If in reduction phenomenology shifts focus from the gift to the giver (and hence to the "pure" phenome-non—the gift *as* gift or *noema*, the object-solely-as-intended) this shift is designed to complete the circle by returning one to the securely "reestablished" (re-given) life-world. Thus the expression "the given" no longer means simply "what happens to be there" but more primordially "the gift." It is the gift of a giving that seems to offer the "sufficient reason" (*Grund*) for the fact of the Being of beings called for by Leibniz: " 'Why is there something rather than nothing?' For nothing is simpler and easier than something. Fur-ther, assuming that things must exist, it must be possible to give a reason why they should exist as they do and not otherwise." [51]

There is a world because the universal transcendental ego (not the individual and idiosyncratic psyche) gives a world by perpetual movement beyond itself into matter. The activity by which it gives itself a temporal flow is the same activity that endows the phenom-enal world with time. The activity by which it situates itself relative to space is the same activity that intends the phenomenal world as spatial.[52] The activity by which it spontaneously generates essential forms is the same activity by which the world is essentially formed. We note again the quasi-theological power of this universal ego in Husserl's reappropriation of German idealism. Phenomenological idealism "achieves the possibility of creating a ground for itself through its own powers." [53] Husserl regards phenomenology as realizing the intent of idealism through the reforming doctrines of reduction, intuitive self-evidence, and intentionality rather than through speculative metaphysics; these doctrines appear to es-tablish the real truth of Hegel's assertion that Substance is Subject [54] and to confirm the "identity of Being and Thought," this "most in-teresting idea of modern times."

III

The foregoing must serve as an approximation of the situation in ontology inherited by Heidegger and subsequently, with the addi-tion of Heidegger's early work, by Sartre.[55] I can now formulate the major ontological tendencies that confront Heidegger and Sartre:

1. There exists in modern thought a dualism between two kinds of Being: the Being of the subject and the Being of the object. This dualism is problematic insofar as subject and object are antithet-

ically defined and cannot enter into real relations with each other.

2. There exists in post-Lockean thought a dualism between two modes of Being of the thing—the thing-in-itself (pure externality) and the thing-for-us (phenomenon). Only the latter is held to be knowable. This dualism is problematic insofar as man has a legitimate desire for access to reality in either ordinary experience, the sciences, or both.

3. There exists in post-Copernican thought a tendency to regard the conclusions of the sciences as replacing naïve and familiar ordinary experience. This tendency is problematic insofar as (a) the sciences can no longer be regarded as disclosing the thing-in-itself hidden from ordinary experience, or (b) the sciences unground themselves by progressively replacing the very world they wish to analyze with theoretical entities and theoretical relations.

4. There exists in post-Hegelian thought a tendency to regard ontology as necessarily temporal or historical, so that beings and the relations between beings appear different in nature in successive epochs. This tendency is problematic insofar as no rational principle governing these changing appearances can be isolated with certainty. In this condition, Being (where 'Being' is defined as the ongoing substantial or substantive self-identity of beings) seems no longer specifiable.

5. There exists in post-Kierkegaardian and post-Nietzschean thought the claim that both the essence and the value of existence (where 'existence' may refer to either the object or the subject or both) are cognitively absent and must therefore be supplied without ground by faith or will. This tendency, often referred to as "existentialism," is problematic insofar as there exists a legitimate human desire to preserve and strengthen a coherent social order by reference to self-evidently or demonstrably universal meanings and values. Existentialism raises in acute form the question of the extent to which ontology is a function of attitude and decision.

Given these major ontological tendencies and problems, and given the fact of the early attraction of both Heidegger and Sartre to Husserl's phenomenology, a chief challenge confronting them is that of determining the extent to which phenomenological idealism can resolve these problems. The critical questions to be raised are listed below; they will be with us throughout. In Part IV I shall attempt to assess the relative importance of Heidegger's and Sartre's responses to them in the course of the development of their thought (Parts I, II, III). It will readily be seen that the three questions are intimately interrelated, and that the way I have divided them is somewhat arbitrary. In Parts I–III I shall allow them to arise together, in the particular interrelation that they possess for Heidegger and for Sartre, respectively. I wish, in other words, to let these questions emerge in their characteristic Heideggerian and Sartrean ways rather than risk distorting them by lifting them abruptly out of the contexts in which they occur.

1. *The Question of the Beginning. Where does and can one begin in order to arrive properly at an ontology?* Husserl's method of reaching a "universal ontology" requires a shift in level—from unreflective engagement to reflective disengagement, from natural attitude to reduction—in order that one may reorient oneself ontologically. Yet, especially in light of Husserl's later work, there are *two* beginnings. There is the life-world in which one "factically" begins and to which one must return; there is the reduced world of pure ego-originated phenomena in which philosophy begins. The two beginnings are held together because "the primal Greek establishment" forms *both* our modern life-world and the transcendental region of philosophy. Can one legitimately invoke a philosophy of history in order to insure the coherence of the factical life-world and the world of transcendental universality? To reformulate the question: does phenomenological reduction "repeat" or "reestablish" a transcendental beginning that has already occurred, unnoticed, in the life-world? Or does transcendental philosophy rupture the ontological unity of the life-world, in which case Husserl's "reestablishment" of the Greek beginning would be the reestablishment of a rupture in the life-world rather than a justification of the life-world. To reformulate the question once again: to what has one's beginning in the life-world committed one? Does it secretly orient the very philosophical attitude that seeks to bracket it? Put in its most general terms, the question asks: *on what level* does and can one situate oneself in order to define reality? Is the ground (reference point, basis, criterion) of Being the life-world, the transcendental ego, or both? This question inevitably leads to the next.

2. *The Question of Metaphysics. Can ontology avoid recourse to metaphysics?* We have called attention to the quasi-theological power of man as a recurrent phenomenon in modern thought. In

the modern period, man has been called upon to serve as ground of Being in lieu of God. Man serves as God-surrogate or de facto ground through the exercise of reason, will, or faith. (Sartre argues that man does not escape this grounding function even in faith, since faith is a mode of human choice and the object of faith has only the force which that choice gives it.)[56] Man is needed as ground of Being in lieu of an unknown and indemonstrable God in order to guarantee, since man is restricted to phenomena, that phenomena are a disclosure of Being. That is, man himself must guarantee that phenomena exhibit intelligibility, self-identity, essence, formal order. Otherwise the phenomenon masks Being and there is "nothingness" or "meaninglessness." But Husserl's position betrays all too clearly a problem inherent in the notion of ego as ground: if the ego is the true origin of form, how can the world be anything more than the material reflex of the ego? If that is the case, one has not found reality but only the ego itself. One *finds* meaning only by forgetting that one has put it there. This amounts to the mapping of a metaphysical essence upon a neutral material receptacle rather than real disclosure of environing beings as they are in themselves. Time becomes the moving image of eternity (permanent universal form) rather than itself the locus of reality. Is there any way to *find* (rather than metaphysically *create*) a Being *in* time and history? Or is Being simply a material reflex of a metaphysics of reason, will, or faith? And if the natural base of the phenomenon of the life-world is a matter X for transcendental phenomenology, is not recourse to speculative metaphysics necessary if one is to regard that X as possessing in itself a formal structure which would guarantee that formal structure is more than mental? This question inevitably leads to the next and last.

3. *The Question of Unity. Can the phenomenon be a genuine unity of thought and Being?* This is tantamount to the question: can phenomenological ontology be saved? Is it possible to show that the phenomenon is relative to thought and is at the same time a disclosure of Being? In other words, is the phenomenon a real union of mental and natural being? Can it be shown that the phenomenon is the fundamental reality rather than an unstable and merely virtual conjunction of ontologically inherently discrete beings (i.e., form and matter, mind and nature)? This would seem to require (*a*) that mind not be regarded as the true ground, or nature will be essentially a

reflex of mind; (b) that nature not be regarded as the true ground, or the inevitable inherence of thought in experience and knowledge will mask or distort nature; (c) that mind and nature require each other in their very being, that they be internally and originally rather than externally and derivatively related. This last requirement would seem to be necessary if the sense of a "broken totality" is to be overcome. Would it mean a reversion to Hegelian metaphysics and its notion of the synthesis of opposites by recognition of their mutual dependence upon each other and upon a "third" that incorporates them in an identity without loss of their difference?

Taking these three questions together, they ask: what must the ground of the phenomenon be if the phenomenon is to be a disclosure of Being? This question, which sounds abstract, is not entertained simply out of idle curiosity or a purely theoretical interest. It asks, when expressed more concretely, whether it is possible for contemporary and future man to find his environment intelligible and affirmable. This is the "existential" import of the problem of phenomenological ontology, the point where the strictly ontological and the moral-practical concerns of Heidegger or of Sartre converge.

The Quest for the
Nature of Being

IN 1943 Sartre published a study of "phenomenological ontology" that apparently seeks to rework Heidegger's 1927 study of phenomenological ontology. These volumes have generally been subsumed under two common rubrics: they are both "existentialist" and they are both contributions to "the phenomenological movement." But it is well known that Heidegger in 1946 explicitly dissociated himself from existentialism and argued that his thought was essentially different from that of Sartre. Some critics have argued that Heidegger was less than candid—that SZ was indeed existentialist, and that Heidegger unfairly criticizes Sartre for not understanding the book in the way Heidegger himself only understood it many years later, after his thought had changed. It will become clear that Sartre never intended EN as simply a restatement of the content of SZ or as an updated revision of it. Certain differences between the two works are essential, not marginal, and they stem from Sartre's quite intentional and radical splitting of the unity of Dasein through the introduction of a negating consciousness. Thereby the meaning of Being, man's relation to Being, and the phenomenological program are all modified.

For reasons that will only fully emerge as I proceed, my analyses of the two works will center on the relation of Heidegger's *Dasein* and Sartre's *pour-soi* to their temporal and spatial ground. Whatever their differences in other respects, Heidegger and Sartre both attempt to characterize the Being of man in relational rather than in substantive or entitative terms. In what follows, I shall examine two ways of understanding the Being of man as a relation to a ground. In both cases one is expected to approach an understanding of Being by understanding the Being of man as a certain relation to

Being. In both cases the problem of "the beginning," which I have identified as a critical feature of their philosophical inheritance, is directly responded to: one can properly arrive at an ontology only by beginning with a consideration of the nature or Being of man. The particular ways in which Heidegger and Sartre accomplish this beginning will determine, as subsequent chapters will show, the kind of response they can make to the two remaining critical questions I have raised: can ontology avoid recourse to metaphysics, and can the phenomenon be a genuine unity of thought and Being?

A word should be said about the way *SZ* is interpreted in chapter 2. Heidegger claimed that comprehension of the goal of *SZ* was "rendered difficult" by the fact that "the third division of the first part, 'Zeit und Sein,' was held back." This third division was to exhibit a "reversal" or "turn" (*Kehre*) that was to express "the location of the dimension from which *SZ* is experienced, and indeed experienced from the ground-experience of the forgottenness of Being."[1] This dimension, Heidegger argued, was neither "existentialist" nor "subjectivistic" nor "humanistic." The interpretation of *SZ* in chapter 2 will take Heidegger at his word and will therefore try to show what this dimension might have been. The interpretation offered in chapter 2 should therefore be regarded as a provisional attempt, subject to reexamination and modification in subsequent chapters,[2] to push a nonexistentialist conception of *SZ* as far as it can be pushed.

There are two reasons for beginning with this nonexistentialist interpretation, in addition to the effort to take seriously Heidegger's expressed intention. The first is to achieve at the very start the maximum possible differentiation of Heidegger's thought from that of Sartre; this hermeneutic device will enable us to conduct what Germans call an *Auseinandersetzung* (roughly, a "confrontation") between Heidegger and Sartre, by which I shall seek to establish their genuine relation to each other. The second reason for this interpretation is that it will enable us to judge the validity of Heidegger's claim that *SZ* has been misinterpreted by Sartre as "existentialism."[3] It would be more difficult to assess the validity of this claim if I were to adopt the existentialist interpretation of *SZ* at the outset.

2

Dasein, Ground, and Time in <u>Sein und Zeit</u>

'Dasein' names that which should first be experienced, and then properly thought of, as Place—that is, the locale of the truth of Being.

—Heidegger, *Wegmarken*, p. 202

THIS CHAPTER interprets Heidegger's *Sein und Zeit* as an attempt to heal a broken ontological totality that he inherits from his philosophical predecessors. It considers only those aspects of *SZ* that bear more or less directly on this effort to overcome a divided being; the success of that effort is considered in chapter 4. For the problem of ontological totality, the critical question is the place of man vis-à-vis his environment, and it is the response of Heidegger's and Sartre's early ontological works to this question that the chapters of Part I attempt to elucidate. The question is a *relational* one: is the relation of man to environment such that it can be regarded as an ontological unity? Chapter 1 has argued that this question is inseparable from the question of ground or beginning and from the question of metaphysics. The present chapter moves from the general themes of unity and origin to the specific themes of everydayness, falling, and authenticity as clues to Heidegger's understanding of the ontological relation of man and environment. The questions of ground and metaphysics raised by these themes will occupy us throughout this volume.

I

It is important to establish at the outset that, in Heidegger's understanding of the term, *Dasein* is not 'man'. It is not out of perversity or a penchant for terminological obscurantism that Heidegger speaks of *Dasein*; yet many of his interpreters have felt they could substitute *Mensch* or *la réalité humaine* without loss or change of meaning. One cannot remind oneself too often that 'man' is a term that carries a heavy historical accretion of meanings. For many of us—and not only philosophers—man is a 'subject' in a world of 'objects', where 'subject' and 'object' refer to kinds of beings that are in principle definable without reference to each other because each 'exists' independently of the other. Or it is maintained, alternatively, that 'subject' and 'object' are indeed to be defined relative to each other, but nevertheless in such a way that their relation is that of mutual exclusion: 'subject' is nonobject, and 'object' is nonsubject. But Heidegger warns that "subject and object do not coincide with Dasein and the world."[1] Nor is 'ego' or 'I', common ways of characterizing man as individual, equivalent to Dasein: "Proximally Dasein is 'they', and for the most part it remains so."[2]

Dasein is "man's Being" (*das Sein des Menschen*)[3] or man's essence (*Wesen*) in the verbal sense—man's essential, though long forgotten and hence nonapparent, *way* of being. In the *Letter on Humanism*, Heidegger presupposes this distinction when he speaks of the "*Dasein* which man endures in existing."[4] This means the way of being that any particular man, as a "mode" of this way of being, must stand within in existing. Here we can assume that 'man' means any of the particular ways of being that the essential way of Being (Dasein) *makes possible*. Not that Dasein exists without some particular way of being (without 'man'), but rather that any particular way is essentially one and the same way. 'Way' here means 'path' or 'route'; hence one can say that man walks the temporal path of Dasein, which is the path of *Sein* (Being) insofar as it is *da* (there—that is, situated). Thus Dasein is 'man' insofar as man is temporally (*zeitlich*) situated with respect to Being.

We assume for the moment that Heidegger understands Being as one, as a unity. If this is so, to say that Dasein is man's Being is to say that Dasein *is* Being, though this does not necessarily mean that Da-Sein is all that *Sein* is. If true, this indicates that the commonly heard claim that *SZ* deals only with man and fails to reach Being is doubly wrong. *SZ* deals primarily with Da-Sein and hence with *Sein* insofar as it is *da*.

To be sure, more argument is required in order to buttress the case we are making. This case can be strengthened by means of an analysis of the interrelation of Dasein and phenomenology in *SZ*.

Heidegger, as a student in Freiburg, had asked himself, "If

beings are spoken of with a multiplicity of meanings, what then is the guiding and basic meaning [die leitende Grundbedeutung]? What does it mean to be?"⁵ Heidegger often reminded his readers that this remained the controlling question of his thinking. Its very wording suggests that for him the question of 'Being' is inseparable from the question of 'ground'. So SZ was to be study of Fundamentalontologie—a study of the founding ontology "from which alone all other ontologies can arise."⁶ The word 'can' (können) here is significant. Heidegger thinks of 'ground' as what enables, what makes possible. From his earliest to his last works he associated phenomenology with 'possibility'.⁷ He saw phenomenology as offering a "way back into the ground" in the sense of a way back into the 'single' and 'simple' founding source of all meanings—to all appearances entirely diverse—of "to be." But why? Phenomenology seems, etymologically, a "doctrine of appearances," but it is already in Husserl a doctrine of the constitution of appearances: what phenomena are is understood through understanding how they come to be phenomena. Thus already in Husserl to ask about the nature and meaning of phenomena is to ask about their ground—that is, to ask how they 'can' be or what makes them possible. But the way back into the ground of phenomena must be, for Husserl as for Heidegger, a way that itself reveals phenomena as what they are. We first reveal phenomena as what they are, we first lay bare "the things themselves," precisely when we understand how they come to be. The actuality question is not separable from the possibility question; the 'nature' or 'essence' question is not separable from the 'basis' or 'ground' question.

But it is still not clear why the understanding of what beings are should hang on understanding how they come to be what they are; in what sense, for Heidegger, does Being depend on Time? The answer lies in the reason for the failure of early modern philosophy—which is in turn indebted to what Heidegger calls "the ancient ontology"—to disclose "the things themselves." While prephenomenological philosophers had indeed sought to describe how beings come to be what they are, in two respects they had done so in such a way as to miss "the things themselves." First, they had usually assumed that, once having come into being, beings are self-contained, self-sufficient, and independent of other beings. A being is in-itself. Second, and correlatively, they had considered the interconnection of beings in 'relational' rather than in 'referential' terms, to use the distinction Heidegger makes in SZ.[8] These correlative tendencies both come under attack in the "phenomenology" of Hegel, who is therefore in my view an important precursor of Heideggerian phenomenology.

In the *Phänomenologie des Geistes*, Hegel teaches[9] that a being is not understood as what it is if it is understood in isolation from other beings (in its alleged self-contained and discrete 'immediacy'). More specifically, a being is not understood as it is so long as our understanding of it is regarded as external to the real nature of the being itself. Still more specifically, a being is not understood as it is unless it is understood to be a meaning. Meaning is part and parcel of the "real internal constitution"[10] of the being. In sum, a being is what it is only in its reference to the total field of beings (or meanings) in their reference to man, his thought, and his praxis. Further, time is not accidental to the nature of beings, inasmuch as in its first appearance a being is a range of yet-unrealized possibilities. Thus a being is an achievement across time and a being may not be understood as what it is apart from its past and its future.

In short, Hegel points the way to Heidegger's phenomenology insofar as he works out a thoroughgoing "doctrine of real internal relations,"[11] by taking meaning into the internal constitution of beings. Indebtedness to the doctrine of internal relations is not, of course, restricted to phenomenology. Whitehead writes:

> For each relationship enters into the essence of the event; so that, apart from that relationship, that event would not be itself. This is what is meant by the very notion of internal relations. It has been usual, indeed, universal, to hold that spatio-temporal relations are external. This doctrine is what is here denied.[12]

The doctrine as it occurs in Whitehead is still, in Heidegger's terms, primarily a doctrine of (causal) 'relations' rather than a doctrine of (meaning-) 'references'. In its phenomenological version, the doctrine might best be called a doctrine of "internal references," and it takes priority over any doctrine of causal relations, where 'causal' is understood as referring primarily to material and efficient causation. One might say that Heidegger's notion of 'references' gives formal and final causation a certain priority over material and

efficient causation. All this means is that when material and efficient causation are experienced as such or known, they are actively identified—'intended' or 'meant'—*as* material or efficient
causation. Our being able actively to identify them or establish
their meaning, their 'form', nature, or kind, is the possibility-condition for these kinds of causes' being phenomena—showing themselves as what they are. Any particular material phenomenon, or efficient phenomenon, can appear to us as what it really is only when
we can mean it as referring to kinds of beings whose nature we already understand. It is this 'referential' way of understanding phenomena that enables Heidegger to approach what beings are in
terms of how they come to be, in terms of their 'ground'.

The ground out of which phenomena—the only beings to which
we have access—come to be what they are is a nexus of meanings in
a complex referential structure or 'totality' that Heidegger calls a
'world'. The very nature of a being is to be contextual: its context is
the possibility of its being at all. Thus one corrects what Whitehead
called "the fallacy of simple location"[13] according to which a being
simply is what it is in an allegedly isolated moment of time and
unit of space.

Husserl had seen phenomena as grounded in a transcendental
subject who constitutes the essential structures of that world as invariant essences.[14] Beings ultimately come to be what they are out
of a transcendental constituting. This is Husserl's solution to what I
have called the problem of "the beginning." In this sense, Husserl
remains "Kantian," while Heidegger denies the ego priority over
world and time. This denial requires considerable explanation, in
the course of which we shall need to return to our earlier assertion
that Heidegger understands Being as one, as a unity.

For the moment, we can conclude that an analysis of Being insofar as it is situated (Dasein) requires phenomenology because the
question of the nature or 'Being' of beings is at the same time the
question of the nature of meaning: to speak of beings is to speak of
meaning-beings or phenomena (entities insofar as they mean something or are meant and understood); and meaning-beings are what
they are by virtue of their coming-to-be what they are "relative to"
(with reference to) a totality or nexus or 'world' of meanings. Heidegger's phenomenology attempts to take meaning into the internal
constitution of beings by showing the origin of beings in a totality

of meanings within which alone beings can first be what, as, and how they are. If for Husserl a totality of meanings is found by reduction in transcendental ideas or *cogitationes*, it is found by Heidegger in the world, or referential totality. To intuition Heidegger therefore opposes circumspection.

Intuition is a looking at (*An-schau-ung*), while circumspection is a looking around or about (*Um-sicht*). Heidegger argues that the idea of *intuitus* as a looking at what is present has served as the model for knowing "from the beginnings of Greek ontology until to-day"[15]—meaning right up to and including Husserl. Heidegger attempts to show its derivative, abstractive, and isolating character. Intuition lifts beings out of the context in which they are what they are, treating them as if their Being were an independent, nonrelative substantiality. The circumspection of ordinary practical experience, however, regards beings in their reference to their spatiotemporal environs. That is, circumspection sees by placing, situating, orienting. The place in which it finds beings revealed as what they are, as 'true', is Dasein's own 'clearing', its time, and in this time its space and its world. A condition for the Being of beings as phenomena is thus Dasein's own Being-in-the-world.

Now Dasein's own space-time is a *circular* space-time in which a seemingly separate past, present, and future interpenetrate each other or are internally related. What I now experience in the present is interpreted in the light cast by a prior future-oriented projection. For example, the condition of my now distinguishing between a hammer and the wood of the tree from which it is made is that the world *already* be intended and hence anticipated as a place where there will be both artifactual and natural beings. But this does not mean that in some pure present that is now past a transcendental subject or ego spontaneously intuited the eternal essences 'nature' and 'artifact' and then projected them into an environment that up to that point had been unqualified by human thought. Rather, the experience of entities in that *past* present was in turn interpreted in light of a still prior projection—the very first bases for interpretation being projections handed down to the individual by the tradition he inherits. This means that as far back as one can go, one never finds a point when there is either an object experienced as a pure, unqualified, nonrelative present or a subject experienced as a pure nonrelative present. In other words, one is never in a position to make a clear and sharp distinction between a pure entity in itself and pure transcendental subjective thought about that entity. One's present experience of the entity is conditioned by past thought, which is inextricably a feature of that present entity. And one's present thought about the entity is conditioned by prior experience of such entities.

So it seems that one cannot isolate in pure present intuition intentional essences originated by mind over and above its world (nor can one isolate in pure present sensation a neutral datum that owes nothing to thought). Thus the Being (essence, nature, constitution) of entities cannot be traced to the pure intentions of a transcendental subject. This is not to belittle the function of intentionality, meaning-endowing. It is rather to understand that intentionality has always *already* entered into the phenomena experienced, so that one cannot in any present sharply distinguish what in the experience is owing to the 'object'. Heidegger asserts, "What is decisive for ontology is to prevent the splitting of the phenomenon." [16] If a transcendental, subjective, intentional component can be isolated from an immanent, objective, natural component, the phenomenon is still in danger of splitting. Intentional meanings really belong to the "things themselves" only if they are so inextricably a part of things as not to be traceable back to a transcendental subject in transcendental reduction and pure intuition.

The substitution of Being-in-the-world for the transcendental ego as the essence of man is intended precisely to prevent the splitting of the phenomenon by showing that thought and beings are inextricably fused by the temporality of Dasein's experience. The high price to be paid by phenomenology for avoidance of the splitting of the phenomenon can perhaps best be indicated by a paradox: the price of the real constitutive efficacy of intentionality is that the exact constitutive contribution of intentionality not be ascertainable. There can be no science of immutable transcendental ideas, meanings, essences. Meanings are always already *in the world*. The price of meanings' really belonging to things is that my effort to trace them back to my own mind as their absolute unconditioned source be frustrated. The fundamental force of Heidegger's incessantly repeated expression 'always already' (*immer schon*) is as constant reminder that the union of essence and existence, of idea and entity, that philosophy seeks to construct out of subjective and objective factors is already there in the most ordinary human experience.

Despite this difference between Husserl and Heidegger, for both of them the question of the 'ground' (basis or source) of beings is a crucial one, and exploration of the nature of 'ground' cannot be construed as a retreat by phenomenologists from their announced goal, to go back to "the things themselves." Since phenomena are what they are by reference to their ground, to try to describe phenomena "as what they are" without reference to their ground would be to miss altogether the nature of phenomena. Thus the great enemy of phenomenology is the unmediated being-in-itself, the contextless, placeless entity.[17] If Heidegger sees in Husserl's transcendental ego the last vestige of the unmediated being-in-itself, he challenges Husserl in the name of phenomenology itself and not as an apostate from the genuine phenomenological impulse. When Heidegger insists that phenomenology must be phenomenological ontology,[18] what he means is that phenomena, to be understood as what they àre, must be understood from within *the original oneness of Being*, which is the prior ground of any distinction between ego and nonego, subject and object, or man and thing. To point to this original oneness is Heidegger's purpose, from early to late, and is his basic response to the "question of unity" (chapter 1).

II

SZ, to be sure, approaches this union or original oneness of Being through an aspect of that oneness, Dasein. But this approach "to" the oneness of Being is and must be an approach from within that original oneness, since the approach to Being is made through beings that are already grounded in Being. It is superficial and unhelpful simply to say that in the published divisions of *SZ* Heidegger fails to reach Being. His fundamental point is that that is where we always already are. At this point, it will be helpful to study Heidegger's analysis of how Dasein can come to affirm this ground or place where it always already is. In this connection, great importance should be attached to Heidegger's reference to Nietzsche in section 31, "Become what you are,"[19] and to other references in *SZ* to being or becoming what one (always already) is.[20]

This means recognition of Dasein as Dasein, of one's real ontological situation, of place.

To become what one is is to become 'authentic', in the wording of Macquarrie and Robinson's translation. *Eigentlichkeit* ('authenticity') is probably best translated by 'ownness' or 'reality' and *Uneigentlichkeit* ('inauthenticity') by 'disownedness'. Thus a passage such as "Dasein . . . for the most part remains concealed from itself in its authenticity"[21] might better read "Dasein . . . for the most part remains concealed from itself in its own reality"—that is, in its own true nature or Being, which it already is but which it has not owned up to. Dasein has in each case owned up to itself, disowned itself, or not differentiated between these two ways of being its Being.[22] It should be stressed that if Dasein is disowned, it is its Being in the mode of *not* being it, in the sense that it has not become what it always already is. As owning up to what one already is, "authenticity" cannot be a shift to a new or novel state of being. It can only be a matter of being what one already is with explicit awareness. It is a self-awareness, awareness of one's own real or true being. Therefore we shall sometimes translate *eigentlich* as 'real', 'true', 'own', 'ownmost'.

But what is it that Dasein "always already"[23] is? As a first approximation to an answer, Dasein is its own *existentialia*, those constitutive ways of being that together exhibit its *Existenz*, the way in which Dasein has to be as "thrown possibility." Heidegger emphasizes that to grasp Dasein as it is is to "see through" all the existentialia at once:

> The sight which is related primarily and on the whole to existence we call "transparency" [*Durchsichtigkeit*]. . . . It is not a matter of perceptually tracking down and inspecting a point called the "Self," but rather one of seizing upon the full disclosedness of Being-in-the-world *throughout all* the constitutive items which are essential to it, and doing so with understanding. In existing, entities sight 'themselves' [*sichet "sich"*] only insofar as they have become transparent to themselves with equal primordiality in those items which are constitutive for their existence. . . .[24]

Seeing through all the existentialia is, then, a matter of "seizing upon the full disclosedness of Being-in-the-world." Reading for emphasis, we may say that this means both seizing upon the disclosedness *of* Being and seizing upon this disclosedness *in the world.* This sighting is not, Heidegger reminds us, a Husserlian intuition of pure essences. It is in no way a sighting of transcendental-egological structures; it is not a reflexive sighting of immanent structures of 'self' as distinguished from a bracketed externality. It is a sighting right on through and past all such derivative structures to the world as the realm of the disclosedness of Being. In other words, the being of an ego, or the being of its intentional essences, is, when seen through to its origin (*Ursprung*), originally (*ursprünglich*) a way or mode of Being, where Being is understood as in the world and as disclosedness.

Now Heidegger repeatedly states that worldhood is an existentiale of Dasein. "Dasein, insofar as it *is,* has always submitted itself already to a 'world' which it encounters, and this *submission* belongs essentially to its Being." [25] "Thus Worldhood itself is an *existentiale.* . . . Ontologically, 'world' is not: it is rather a characteristic of Dasein itself." [26] As obvious as this may seem to the reader of *SZ,* he must constantly remind himself of its full meaning because the whole of what Heidegger calls the "ancient ontology," [27] within which we still think, hides its meaning from us. Out of habit—almost out of instinct—we read 'Dasein' as 'man' and we read 'world' as "the external to man." Yet Dasein is not man, and world is not external to Dasein. Here again, the fallacy of simple location must be combatted. The difficulty of combatting it is indicated by the counterintuitive character of asserting that Dasein is a being whose Being is to be there in a world which it itself *is.* Dasein is not simply here where I am as an embodied man at the spot x at the moment y. [28] Dasein is 'there'—wherever there is a world. This means that the boundary of Dasein is the world itself—the world's 'horizons'—and not merely a point within the world. It is true that Dasein may 'individualize' itself within its world, but the world within which it individualizes itself is itself Dasein. Because of this, and speaking loosely now on a derivative and 'human' level, 'I' am more fundamentally 'there' than I am 'here' and can only understand myself as 'here' insofar as I am 'there'. This may sound like a rank idealism that either bloats the self, or ego, to universal size, and so finds all that is within the self, or else reduces all being to the self. But it is neither. Dasein is an original unity that is prior to the distinction between self and environment, or subject and object, or ego and noematic correlate. It is the *ground within which* these distinctions *can* be made or are *possible*. (For this reason, in part, "higher than actuality stands *possibility*.")[29]

If Dasein were understood in accordance with our habits as a 'thing' or 'object', as simply a being at space x and time y, this would wholly negate Heidegger's version of the doctrine of internal relations. This, it will be recalled, is primarily a doctrine of meaning-references between beings that must be understood not primarily as material beings or as substantive beings but rather as meaning-beings. (Whenever Heidegger speaks of 'a being' he means a meaning-being—even where that being might have the meaning 'meaningless'. As we have noted, Heidegger as phenomenologist takes meaning into the "real internal constitution" of the entity, or 'phenomenon'.) Dasein is a meaning-being (having an understanding of itself) that is at the same time a world within which beings mean what they do mean, are what they are.[30] This means, paradoxically, that Dasein finds itself in a world that it itself is: "*That inside which* existing Dasein understands *itself*, is 'there' ["*da*"] along with its factical existence. That inside which one primarily understands oneself has Dasein's kind of Being. Dasein *is* its world existingly."[31] Within this 'there' (in 'world') are all beings other than Dasein. We can now assert that Dasein is not something other than its ground, but it is itself by reference to the ground which it itself also is. This is to say that Dasein is a relation to itself, but not simply in the usual reflexive sense. Dasein sights itself, becomes transparent to itself, when it 'sees through' its 'here' (the usual location of the self) to its own 'there.' Man generally is opaque to himself because he regards himself as simply an immediately intuitable 'here' and does not 'see through' it to his 'there' and thus does not sight himself in his whole nature, or real Being, as original unity. He does not sight himself as Da-sein, that is, as place.

But if world is an existentiale of Dasein, why does Heidegger say that Dasein must submit itself *to* the world? And how is this submission "disclosive"?[32] Are these really two ways of asking the same question?

Dasein must submit itself to the world in the sense that it has in every case "always already" submitted itself to the world. Every human purposive action is grounded in this prior submission: "The mood has already disclosed, *in every case,* Being-in-the-world *as a whole,* and makes it *possible* first of all to direct oneself towards something."[33] 'Mood' is a mode of *Befindlichkeit* ('state of mind' in Macquarrie and Robinson's translation); *sich befinden* can mean "to find oneself somewhere." *Befindlichkeit* really means something like "thrown and tuned situatedness," the condition of being "plugged into" the world in such a way as to be affected by what happens in it. It is one of three equiprimordial (equally foundational) existentialia of Being-in as such[34] and is not to be understood apart from the other two, 'understanding' (*Verstehen*) and 'discourse' (*Rede*). Heidegger is thinking of these three as a unity and summarizing their meaning when he writes, "Dasein is its disclosedness." He explains: " 'Here' ['*Hier*'] and 'yonder' ['*Dort*'] are possible only in a 'there' ['*Da*']—that is to say, only if there is an entity which, as the Being of the 'there', has made a disclosure of spatiality. . . . In the expression 'there' we have in view this essential disclosedness. By reason of this disclosedness, this entity (Dasein) is 'there' for itself, at one with the Da-sein of the world."[35]

This disclosedness is the original event of Dasein, not as a one-time occurrence but rather as an event that has always already happened as the revelation of the 'there' of Dasein. This means that the experience of any moment, of any event, of any entity (including 'man's' experience of 'himself') is intelligible, affecting, and expressible because it is situated within, relative to, and by reference to a prior common ground or context. Heidegger will later call this context "the clearing of Being" or the "Place." All of Heidegger's critiques of the subject-object duality and of the traditional problem of truth as that of somehow establishing a correspondence—a real relation—between subject and object, knower and known, are designed to provoke a remembering of the fact that prior to all such dualities there is an original but long-forgotten unity,[36] such that subject and object, knower and known, man and 'external world' are always already related within a common context, the 'clearing'. In the words of Aristotle, of whom Heidegger was a close student: "interaction between two factors is held to require a precedent community of nature between the factors."[37] Whereas dialectical philosophy (e.g., that of Hegel or of the later Sartre) tries progressively to *compose* a common ground "between" entities that is not originally given, or at first is only potentially given, Heidegger argues that the common ground is already 'there': *"Dasein is the Being* of this 'between.' "[38]

If it is meaningful for modern philosophers to say that subject is situated in relation to object, knower in relation to something known, man in relation to an external world, these polarities are intelligible or meaningful because they are *together* situated within that kind of a field of meaning which is such that there can be polarities, "betweens," relations at all. In what kind of field is it possible for there to "be" (i.e., exist and mean) subjects over against objects? Over against each other in what? Where? It must be remembered that, as phenomena, subjects and objects or men and things are meaning-beings, and only in this way do they appear for us as a meaningful, intelligible pair. That seems possible only if there is some meaning "between" them, only if they share a common context within which it makes sense to distinguish and interrelate them in this way: the sort of world in which subjects and objects are appropriate. But this world is for Heidegger neither subjective nor objective. It is formed neither by subjects nor by objects but rather by a presubjective and preobjective thrown projection— that is, a projection traceable neither to a transcendental subject nor to an external world of entities in and by themselves. The projection *is* traceable to Dasein, but Dasein is neither simply 'here' where one would expect to find a subject nor 'yonder' where one might expect to find an object. Dasein is not simply locatable but is the overall site of any and every particular location. At any given point in time, one is experiencing entities in terms of a prior projection of their kind of being, but this projection is traceable neither to a particular thinker's thought nor to some inherent property of entities in themselves. It is everywhere and nowhere. It is the common source of phenomena, though one that does not appear as such but dissimulates itself because it is not itself a being but rather the Being (ground, locale, place) of beings.

The sense of the whole is always the locus of any local being. This thesis is indebted to German idealism. Yet this whole is not, as in idealism, a whole generated by a transcendental subject or ego, but a whole relative to which any ego could be identified as such, a context by reference to which any subject could find himself a subject. To be 'here' as man is to be 'here' *in* (not over against) what is 'there'; "what there is" is "what is 'there'." What is there for us is what is phenomenal: what is understood, what we find ourselves moved by or attuned to, and what can be discoursed about, what is articulable. Even natural causes are, insofar as we are aware of them, meaning-beings in a nexus of meanings.

What is phenomenal is, in Heidegger's language, what has been cleared (*gelichtet*) in the clearing (*Lichtung*): lighted in the original or originary (what makes possible) lighting or, more simply, located. To locate is to establish on a foundation (*Grund*). Any entity, including man, is like a tree in that it is rooted in (is what it is by reference to) the ground (the basic situation). This original-originary ground of phenomena is the single 'simple' 'event' on which Heidegger's whole thought career, before and after the celebrated "turn," is centered. "The problem of thinking" for Heidegger in 1962 is "clearing and presentness,"[39] a problem essentially the same as his earlier question, "why are there beings at all rather than nothing?"[40] There is presentness (of phenomena) because of the simple originary event of the clearing of a place within which there could be beings present at all. Already in *SZ* Heidegger's thought is centered on this clearing: "To say that it [Dasein] is 'illuminated' ["erleuchtet"] means that *as* Being-in-the-world it is cleared ["gelichet"] in itself, not through any other entity, but in such a way that it *is* itself the clearing. . . . By its very nature, Dasein brings its 'there' along with it."[41]

This does not say that 'man' brings his 'there' along with him, nor does it say that 'man' clears, nor does it say that 'man' is the clearing. It says that Being as 'there' in the world is the clearing such that the entity Dasein is 'illuminated' within the clearing that Dasein as Sein-in-the-world is.[42] Dasein is the self-cleared clearing, or as Heidegger will put it, it is its own "groundless ground." It is illuminated (made intelligible) by its own illumination (making intelligible).

The accompanying diagram pictures Dasein as the field/ ground/clearing within and by reference to which man and nature —or, in modern thought, subject and object, etc.—can arise and be situated. For the ancient ontology and its modern derivatives, the inner circle is all there is. There are only particular discrete beings (the 'ontic'). The area between the inner and outer circles is the forgotten ontological ground of the ontic, the hidden connection between environmental beings and between environmental beings

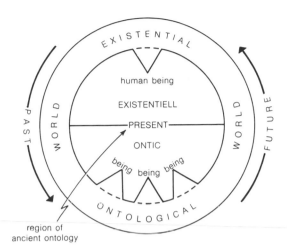

DASEIN AS GROUND

and human being. Dasein is the whole of this outer area, but is also the ontic human being (top). If the inner circle is all there is, the human being is only 'ontic' and only 'existentiell'—that is, its way of being is not transparent to itself in that it has not grasped its 'existential' structure as an 'ek-static' being that is always beyond itself, outside its simple ontic presentness, or "here and now" being. The whole of the outer circle indicates this ekstatic structure. The 'past' arrow at the left is intended to suggest Dasein's prior projection of the kind of being (e.g., present-at-hand, ready-to-hand) that it here and now, at present, encounters in particular environmental beings. The 'future' arrow at the right is intended to suggest that this prior projection is not simply past, is not gone, but instead "comes back" to the entity Dasein as the ground on which beings *about to be* encountered will be intelligible, identifiable, significant. The outer, or existential-ontological, area is an unbroken circle because (*a*) the existential and the ontological are inseparable and interdependent, (*b*) the ontological projection has no absolute beginning but is rather an always-prior basis, (*c*) the ontological projection has no absolute end but is rather always being reappropriated, mostly by a Dasein that has an inexplicit or "pre-ontological understanding of Being."

Taken as a whole, the diagram indicates Dasein as place or site. It indicates that present 'man' and present 'natural beings' are both grounded in something deeper, non-apparent, beyond the present or physically and sensibly tangible, and that this forgotten ground is one and the same ground for both man and nature. Man and nature, subject and object, ego and noematic correlate thus have a prior community that their apparent heterogeneity dissimulates or blocks from view. This always prior community is Dasein, the original unity. Insofar as the 'here' and the 'yonder' are taken solely as separate local entities, or insofar as either is taken to be fundamental, the sense of a unified field, common place, or ground is forgotten. The difference, which is obvious, hides the identity, which is not obvious. The very appearance of beings, as localized entities with clearly delimitable and calculable physical boundaries, dissimulates or covers their original and sustaining ground, and hence dissimulates the original connection of these beings with each other, which is thus 'forgotten' and in need of being 'remembered'. The beings, then, are dissimulated with respect to their ontological essence (Wesen), which is to be found in their source or origin (Ursprung), the event of their coming-into-Being as meaning-beings within a place of intelligibility (Welt, Ort).

Thus Dasein is a locale within which beings are revealed and identified. This locale is fundamentally temporal:

Insofar as Dasein temporalizes itself, a world *is* too. . . . It 'is', with the "outside-of-itself" of the ekstases, 'there' ["da"].[43] The phenomena of the "towards...," the "to...," and the "alongside...," make temporality manifest as the ekstatikon pure and simple. *Temporality is the primordial 'outside-of-itself' in and for itself.*[44]

. . . The *temporalization structure* of temporality . . . reveals itself as the historicality of Dasein.[45]

Dasein is directionality—a way or path through its own temporal and historical field. Because this field is a field of meanings and meaning-beings, Dasein can be temporally and historically near to what is farthest, and far from what is nearest, in a way that is impossible according to the ordinary conception of time in terms of measurable and calculable durations.

On the basis of this temporal structure, Dasein is also spatial:

Dasein understands its "here" [Hier] in terms of its environmental "yonder" [Dort]. . . . Dasein, in accordance with its spatiality, is proximately never here but yonder; and from this "yonder" it comes back to its "here." . . . As Being-in-the-world, Dasein maintains itself essentially in a desevering. . . . *Dasein is essentially de-severance—that is, it is spatial.* . . . As de-severant Being-in, Dasein has likewise the character of *directionality.*[46]

On the basis of its temporal-ekstatic structure, Dasein is a direction through a world that is spatial as well as temporal—a path through its own spatial field. Because of its directional (or teleological) structure, owing to which it is always beyond the present moment, it de-severs (or brings close) beings that lie at great distance. Because Dasein's field is spatial, Dasein can be spatially near to what is farthest, and far from what is nearest, in a way that is impossible according to the ordinary conception of space in terms of measurable and calculable distances.

Dasein is a way or path through its own temporal and spatial field, which is neither past, present, nor future but simultaneously all three, and which is neither here nor yonder but everywhere. Although in SZ Heidegger attempts to ground spatiality in temporality—an attempt he later regarded as untenable[47]—the real intention of SZ in our interpretation is to carry through the phenomenological program by preventing the splitting of the phenomenon, and this requires remembering the long-forgotten fundamental unity or community of the experiencer not only with his finite time but with his total and indivisible mundane environs. For this reason, Place becomes a central notion for Heidegger, as does Earth, and Heidegger writes in SD of "the origin of space in the . . . characteristics of Place."[48] The term 'Place' more concretely evokes the true ground of phenomena than does either the term 'time' or the term 'space.' Heidegger therefore writes in W that ". . . 'Dasein' names that which should first be experienced, and thence properly thought of, as Place—that is, the locale of the truth of Being."[49] This original field, or 'there' of beings, is the clearing or experienced context within which the calculable space and time of man and object as physical are possible.

This field has always already been 'disclosed' in understanding, state of mind, and discourse. This means that Dasein is always attuned to its 'there' in such a way as to understand it, be affected by it, and find it intelligible and articulable. It is intelligible and articulable because it is Dasein's rather than of a different or foreign nature. As Dasein's own field, it is the most familiar of all territories—so utterly familiar and so pervasive as to be taken for granted, and even displaced by the theoretical conceptions of the world that are really abstracted from it—hence 'forgotten'. Intellection and articulation never begin from scratch in a pure present 'here' or 'now,' for they are situated and make sense relative to what has already been understood. The situation of what is present is the field or 'there' to which Dasein has always already submitted and committed itself. In Heidegger's version, intentionality is an always prior 'ekstatic' submission—a being beyond oneself. This primary intentionality cannot be subjective because it is always already *one* with the world within which there could be anything like a subject-object division *of* this oneness; the division will always occur by abstracting out of and by reference to this oneness. Heidegger sometimes expresses this by saying that the past comes to us out of the future, meaning that the situation that is always already 'there' repeats itself as the situation within which the new is experienced. The past is fundamentally not a simple past (what is gone, *vergangen*) but is what keeps coming to us as the situation of the future. This ground-situation, because it is always before us as the locale of what is now coming, comes to us anew as essentially self-same. The situation makes the understanding, the understanding makes the situation, and so on, in a circle that has no beginning in either a pure situationless understanding or a pure situation unqualified by understanding. The true beginning is the always already unified event of the unbreakable circulation or "intro-play"[50] of what are generally, and loosely, called 'man' and 'nature'.

This circular situation orients every particular present situation, and is thus 'primordial', 'original', 'originary'. Dasein is place, and place is orientation.

III

Heidegger argues that "the only way in which entities can be discovered" is by "the prior projection of their state of Being."[51] What now come to us as beings make sense to us insofar as we already understand the nature of such beings, e.g., as ready-to-hand or as present-at-hand. And Heidegger seems to suggest that under certain conditions the prior projection may change in character. An understanding of the character of this categorial projection is crucial for the understanding of Heidegger's early ontology and its relation to the ontology of Sartre. If entities are discovered by a projection of their state of Being, why is this projection not made by a subject? Why is it not the intentional act of a transcendental ego? What else could really account for changes in the character of the projection? It will prove necessary to examine this question at some length in chapter 4. For the moment, we wish to concentrate on those aspects of SZ that indicate Heidegger's intention to prevent the splitting of the phenomenon by pointing to a presubjective and preobjective unity. Specifically, we shall ask how Heidegger's treatment of falling and of authenticity can be seen as compatible with the argument that Dasein's projection is not that of a subject against objects, and not that of a transcendental ego, despite the fact that 'authenticity' might seem to be a liberation of man from his prior 'fallen' unity with his environment.

SZ clearly claims that there is always a prior projection of some sort, so that man is in any present moment already committed by his Dasein to a *particular* understanding of the nature of beings, since the beings he now experiences are understood by reference to a field that is already 'there'. This means that the world and the kinds of entities in it are always already intelligible without and prior to any present act of human will that seeks to *make* them intelligible. Even what may seem utterly novel is understood by its being related to what has already been experienced. What Heidegger calls 'fore-having', 'fore-sight', and 'fore-conception'—three basic aspects of anticipatory understanding and interpretation— cannot be abrogated. Hence: "An interpretation is *never* a presuppositionless apprehending of something presented to us."[52] Heidegger tirelessly stresses this circular, projective, and temporal-historical character of understanding and interpretation:

> *All* interpretation is grounded on understanding. That which has been articulated as such in interpretation and sketched out *beforehand* in the understanding in general as something articulable, is the meaning.[53]

> The intelligibility of something has always been articulated, *even before* there is any appropriative interpretation of it.[54]

. . . As Being-in-the-world it is *already* 'outside' when it understands.[55]

This everyday way in which things *have been* interpreted is one into which Dasein has grown in the first instance, *with never a possibility of extrication.* In it, out of it, and against it, all genuine understanding, interpreting, and communicating, all rediscovering and appropriating anew, are performed. *In no case* is a Dasein, untouched and unseduced by this way in which things have been interpreted, set before the open country of a 'world-in-itself,' so that it just beholds what it encounters.[56]

These passages are decisive for the ontology of *SZ*. They provide important clues for understanding the real interrelation of Division I and Division II of *SZ*. Division II is a 'repetition' or 'retrieve' (*Wiederholung*) of Division I's analysis of everydayness, not an escape from it. It clarifies and reaffirms the 'thrown', 'factical', 'circular', and 'finite' conditions under which, as Division I has shown, there are beings as phenomena. Division II is the second step in a program whose ultimate aim is to show that "The projection of a meaning of Being in general can be accomplished *within the horizon of time.*"[57] This requires that Division II be an 'authentic' (*eigentlich*) repetition of Division I. Despite the fact that Division I has already shown the Being of Dasein—'care'—it has described only *average* everydayness, the 'proximal' condition of Dasein but nevertheless only one of Dasein's possible ways of being its Being (only one particular *existentiell* manner of living its *existential* structures, its caring temporal-ekstatic Being). Division I begins to exhibit the ontologico-existential character of human beings who have not themselves faced and acknowledged their real character. Either their existentiell way of being is inauthentic or they have not differentiated at all between authentic and inauthentic ways of being.[58] Their way of being exhibits the forgetting that is characteristic of "the ancient ontology." Further, their way of being exhibits a 'falling'. In what sense, then, does the authentic repetition in Division II go beyond the undifferentiation or inauthenticity and the falling way of being described in Division I?

Eigentlichkeit, which Macquarrie and Robinson translate as 'authenticity', connotes Dasein's own 'real' or 'true' way of being. It can additionally connote a self-development of its own way of being in which Dasein explicitly "owns up to," or becomes, what it already implicitly understands and is. *Uneigentlichkeit* means Dasein's way of not owning up to its own way of being while at the same time continuing to be it. *Eigentlichkeit*, then, suggests either one's own true, but hidden and not faced, way of being or a form of self-coincidence or coherence in which a human being's particular *existentiell* actions are brought into explicit accord with one's own real *existential* structure, which is the very possibility of those particular actions. This self-coincidence also entails that particular ontic beings be brought into explicit accord with their ontological structure or derivation. In both cases, this means envisaging the actual (event or being) in its relation to the possible, rather than taking the actual as simply actual, as self-standing presentness. To sight the actual in its relation to the possible is to place it in the context of Dasein's own ekstatic-temporal structure—the thrown (prior) projection (future) in which alone the actual can be (appear as present) for the human being. True *(eigentlich)* understanding does not entail changing the actual or present; it entails placing it in the context of Dasein's temporality. Although 'true' understanding is in a sense a 'freeing', the structures that one sights in true understanding—thrownness, projection, facticity, falling, impersonality *(das Man)*, everydayness, making-present—throw the enlightened Dasein right back into its own limited, finite world. So Heidegger warns in two important passages:

> *True Being-one's-Self* does not rest upon an exceptional condition of the subject, a condition that has been detached from the "they"; it is rather an existentiell modification of the "they"—of the "they" as an essential existentiale.[59]

> . . . *True* existence is not something which floats above falling everydayness; existentially, it is only a modified way in which such everydayness is seized upon.[60]

True existence owns up not only to its own Dasein as the possibility of impersonal and falling existence; it owns up as well to its own Dasein as the inevitability of the self-disowning, impersonalizing, and falling tendencies. These tendencies not only have formed but will form the ordinary, usual, "base state" out of which Dasein will always have to wrest the truth of its own nature and the nature of environmental beings. SZ places heavy stress on the powerlessness *(Ohnmacht)* of Dasein to alter fundamentally its basic condition. The mood of one who has owned up to his own true being is neither relief nor faith nor hope; it is 'equanimity'.[61] Equanimity springs from 'resoluteness' or 'resolve'. 'Resolute projection' is an "act of will" only in the sense that it freely owns up to that projection that thrown Dasein has always already thrown ahead of itself. Resolute projection is *submission* to one's present in a 'moment of vision' that sees its inevitability against the whole ground of the world. It is free surrender to the temporal ground as the clearing within which beings or phenomena are possible at all, and it is free surrender to the thrown care (or attunement to and by the ground) that is the necessary condition of all meaning:

> Only in so far as something resistant has been discovered on the basis of the ekstatical temporality of concern can factical Dasein understand itself in its abandonment to a 'world' of which it never becomes master. Even if concern remains restricted to the urgency of everyday needs, it is never a pure making-present, but arises from a retention that awaits; on the basis of such a retention, or as such a 'basis,' Dasein exists in a world.[62]

This basis or ground really has two aspects. The foregoing passage stresses the ontico-existentiell aspect of the ground, its particularity. A particular tool breaks in the midst of a particular project with which I am concerned. My everyday world is like that: as long as I have concerns, I lay myself open to being frustrated by beings that hinder me. If I want to liberate myself from all possibility of being frustrated, I shall have to surrender all my concerns. But the effort to surrender all my concerns would itself be a matter of consuming concern, subjecting me to a new set of frustrations. At most, I can substitute one concern for another, but there is no escape from "the wheel of care." The most I can do is to have an attitude of equanimity springing from resolute projection. I can affirm my limitation, justly balancing my power and my powerlessness. My power consists in my ontological projection, which makes it possible for beings to show themselves. My powerlessness consists in my having to project and in the all-important fact that I can never project from scratch, *de novo*, but must always understand and project on the basis of a prior projection. Hence, for example, "we do not push out from the 'nothing' and come upon some item of equipment which has been presented to us in isolation; in laying hold of an item of equipment, we come back to it from whatever work-world has already been disclosed."[63] The particular aspect of the basis or ground is thus the consequence of its general or onto-logico-existential aspect, care or temporality. My basis can never be simply the general structures of my Being—the existentialia—because the existentialia themselves are only the structures common to all particular or existentiell experiences or actions. Furthermore, the "introplay" of the three dimensions of time seems to preclude the possibility of a present or a future that is not qualified by the particular concerns of the past. The notion of a pure present is both philosophically and personally appealing; if the human being could be free of his past, it would seem that he could know both himself and other beings as they are "now," in themselves and by themselves. And it would seem that his actions could be absolutely self-determined, owing nothing to past preoccupations and commitments. Such is the appeal of the care-less and atemporal ancient ontology. Against this, Heidegger holds that *there is no absolute beginning,* no pure present either for the human being or environmental beings. What we call "free action" and "knowledge of things as they really are" occur under conditions precisely the opposite of those prescribed by the ancient ontology:

> The entity which bears the title "Being-there" [Da-sein] is one that has been 'cleared'. The light which constitutes this clearedness of Dasein is not something ontically present-at-hand as a power or source for a radiant brightness occurring in the entity on occasion. That by which this entity is essentially cleared . . . is what we have defined as "care." . . . Only by this clearedness is any illuminating or illumining, any aware-ness, 'seeing' [*pace* Husserl!], or having of something, made possible. We understand the light of this clearedness only if we are not seeking some power implanted in us and present-at-hand, but are interrogating the whole constitution of Dasein's Being—namely, care—and are interrogating it as to the unitary basis for its existential possibility. *Ekstatical temporality clears the "there" primordially.*[64]

This is Dasein's own true Being. To be 'resolute'—to own up to it—is to surrender all the claims to absolute 'mastery' or 'power' made under the influence of the "ancient ontology." This is the high price to be paid for healing ontological dualism. Immediately following the passage just quoted, Heidegger writes: "We had to assure ourselves in the beginning that the structural unity of this phenomenon [Being-in-the-world] cannot be torn apart. . . . With the aim of protecting this phenomenon from those tendencies to split it up which were the most obvious and therefore the most baleful,"[65] Being-in-the-world in all its factical, thrown, concernful, and existentiell concreteness had to take the place of the ontological dualities man/nature, subject/object, transcendental ego/noematic correlate. To affirm one's true (*eigentlich*) Being is to acknowledge that one is more essentially 'there' than one is 'here' and 'now'—that one is always already "outside" the simple present point where "the self" is allegedly located. Fundamentally the self does not stand over against its world.

IV

The foregoing analysis has quoted *SZ* in a highly selective way and has made no reference to sections 40 and 58, which are *loci classici* for the "existentialist" interpretation of Heidegger. By "existentialist" interpretation we understand one which holds that both the 'essence' and the 'value' of existence (where 'existence' may refer to either human or natural beings) are cognitively absent and must therefore be supplied without ground by a transcendental-subjective faith, will, or choice exercised in independence of any past. Can our interpretation withstand correlation with these "existentialist" sections of *SZ*?

Section 40 treats the relation of anxiety and falling; section 58 treats guilt and nullity. Both sections are obviously indebted to Kierkegaard's *Concept of Dread* (*Angest*). Just prior to section 40, Heidegger has written, "If we are to give an adequate preparation for the question of Being, the phenomenon of *truth* must be ontologically clarified."[66] And Kierkegaard had written against Hegel that "the truth is subjectivity," explaining that "the systematic idea is the identity of subject and object, the unity of thought and being. Existence, on the other hand, is their separation."[67] Yet it would be quite wrong to conclude from this external evidence that Heidegger holds 'anxiety' (*Angst*) to be a splitting of the fallen unity of thought and Being so as to reveal that truth is subjective. What Heidegger is maintaining is in fact very nearly opposite. Nevertheless, a cursory glance at sections 40 and 58 is likely to convince one that Dasein falls away from an unbearable anxiety into an alien everyday world from which it can and should liberate itself through the agency of the "call of conscience." It would appear that the 'call' calls Dasein back to its subjective responsibility, to the truth of its inner guilt as the willful *creator ex nihilo* of its free and chosen acts. The interpretation that follows reads these sections quite differently.

Anxiety is a certain relation of Dasein to its own 'there' so that "That in the face of which one has anxiety is Being-in-the-world as such." [68] Now "Being-in-the-world as such" is the primary unity of Dasein as 'entity' and Dasein as 'world'. This unity, we have seen, is such that the entity and the world occur only with reference to each other. This would seem to mean that any modification of the entity would be a modification of the world, and any modification of the world a modification of the entity:

> Here the disclosure and the disclosed are existentially selfsame in such a way that in the latter the world has been disclosed as world, and Being-in has been disclosed as a potentiality-for-Being which is individualized, pure, and thrown. . . . Anxiety individualizes Dasein and thus discloses it as *'solus ipse'*. But this existential 'solipsism' is so far from the displacement of putting an isolated subject-Thing into the innocuous emptiness of a worldless occurring that in an extreme sense what it does is precisely to bring Dasein face to face with its world as world, and thus bring it face to face with itself as Being-in-the-world. [69]

This means that anxiety takes one out of the "world" (*Umwelt*) with which one is ordinarily and familiarly absorbed, but in so doing situates one in the primary or original world ('world as world'): "as Dasein falls, anxiety brings it back from its absorption in the 'world'. . . . Being-in enters into the existential 'mode' of the *'not-at-home'*." [70] One is then not-at-home in the familiar "world" that is the limited world of entities closest to our present concerns, but rather primarily at home in the world or 'there' that is the place or ground *within which* the familiar world can be and comes to be what it is. In other words, anxiety recalls Dasein from its lost preoccupation with the entities within the world to the ground of these entities, the 'between' itself, Dasein's own world as such. In anxiety, Dasein as entity and Dasein as 'there' show themselves in their primary unity as the original Place among whose beings one *could* lose oneself. This in turn means that Dasein has no world to fall back upon, because it itself *is* its world. Thus, when Dasein falls, it falls from itself into itself; it falls into the midst of the entities of its own world in such a way as to lose track of ('forget') its own world as the site and possibility of these entities. But in anxiety these familiar entities seem alien because they have lost the substantiality or independent, inherent meaning with which familiarity had endowed them. Yet further reflection shows that they are internally related to Dasein's own world.

Thus, it appears that loss of these beings' familiarity is not to be interpreted as nihilistic loss of their meaning. Rather, loss of their routine familiarity is a precondition for reappropriation of their true meaning as *phenomena* within the clearing of Dasein.[71]

This reappropriation of the true meaning of beings as "cleared phenomena" becomes a 'possibility' for Dasein insofar as anxiety "makes manifest in Dasein . . . its *Being-free-for* the freedom of choosing itself and taking hold of itself. . . ."[72] This means to choose—affirm—itself in the whole of its Being, as unity of all its existential structures, or to become what it already is: the 'Being-there' as the always prior context within which entities come to be as what they are. Beings then show themselves as still more 'familiar' than they had seemed to be: they and 'I' emerge from a common context. As revealer of the common ground of all phenomena, the original unity, anxiety is a privileged mood.

Thus the "abandonment of Dasein to itself" that "is shown with primordial concreteness in anxiety" is interpretable as anything but a subjective independence, anything but loss of the world, anything but an "existentialist nihilism." It rather shows that Dasein is "ahead-of-itself-in-already-being-in-a-world,"[73] a world that is its own. Anxiety is explicit awareness of, in Aristotle's terms, "a precedent community of nature between the factors"—between man and the entities of his world.

But if anxiety is a kind of reappropriation of the world, why is it that anxiety is anxious? For an answer we turn to section 58. Here Heidegger asserts: "In uncanniness [i.e., not being at home in what is routinely familiar] Dasein stands together with itself originally. Uncanniness brings this entity face to face with its undisguised nullity. . . ."[74] Why should the original oneness of Da-sein mean 'nullity' (*Nichtigkeit*)? We should recall here that not-being-at-home among familiar entities is being-at-home in the true "home" that is the real ground of these familiar entities, that which makes it possible for beings to be familiar at all. In the uncanniness of anxiety the ground comes to the fore; attention is shifted from foreground beings to their background, their place. Cleared of entities, the clearing stands clear as what it is. But is it the ground one expected or wanted?

Already in his early phase, Heidegger interpreted Western metaphysics as the quest for a secure ground. It is the quest for an ultimate reason, an *ultima ratio rerum*, in answer to the question "why are there beings at all and not rather nothing?" 'Ground' (*Grund*) has meant the ultimate reason and the ultimate reason has meant, for an entity-centered tradition, a first entity that serves as first cause.[75] Knowledge of this ultimate ground/reason/cause is held to be knowledge of the real nature and meaning of what-is as such and as a whole, since the first cause is the ultimate determinant of the nature or 'Being' of what-is. The metaphysical tradition, then, has held that to know what-is as it really is—to know beings in their Being—is to know their ground. This view, Heidegger thought, was not altogether wrong; in fact, we have argued, the phenomenological program presupposes it. But the tradition has mistaken the nature of the ground. The answer to the question why there are beings at all is not a being, a highest or first being, but rather the *event* or coming on of the clearing, not as a one-time beginning but as the always-already unity of Dasein as the original thrown projection and articulation of the ground of beings.

This means that Dasein has itself always already participated in the grounding of beings, including the present being, 'man'. So the quest for the discovery of ultimate reasons always comes too late; Dasein has been there already. The ground lies in human being itself as Da-sein, thrown and projective temporality. But the traditional quest has been precisely for a ground altogether independent of man, such that man could experience himself rooted in solider, more permanent stuff than he appraises himself as being. There seems security in being rooted in the unchanging, the eternal—and when the tradition lost confidence in God as the secure ground, it resorted to an unchanging transcendental ego as secure ground prior to empirical man. (Insofar as phenomenology can be said to be neo-Cartesian or neo-Kantian, the old quest for a secure ground can be said to have invaded the precincts of phenomenology itself, and more than one interpreter of Heidegger has seen him as in effect a neo-Kantian positing a transcendental Dasein as the secure ground.)[76]

In his quest for a ground, we may say, man has sought to hold himself into *Something*. Heidegger, in *KPM*, counters: ". . . Dasein on the basis of its essence holds itself into Nothing. Holding oneself into Nothing is no arbitrary and casual attempt to 'think' about this Nothing but an event which underlies all finding oneself [*Sichbefinden*] in the midst of beings already on hand."[77]

This tells us that prior to the quest for a ground as Something, and as the very possibility of such a quest, Dasein understands itself as grounded in nothing rather than in some-thing. That appears to say no more than that the experience of something as absent is the ground (reason and, perhaps, motive) for having to look for it. Heidegger intends more. It seems that he is in effect asserting the impossibility of the metaphysical quest for a transcendental, nonrelative ground; this quest contradicts itself by being always already grounded in the experience of the absence of a final ground. Any human experience (or alleged experience) of a being as ground will be undercut, since man's essence (his temporal way of Being) has already been there to lay the ground on which a being *could* be experienced as a ground. Thus the true and always-prior ground is the clearing, Dasein's own Being-in-its-world. It is essentially this which has been forgotten and must be remembered. In *KPM* Heidegger writes:

> The finiteness of Dasein—the understanding of Being—lies forgotten. This forgottenness is nothing accidental and temporary but is constantly and necessarily renewed. All fundamental ontological construction . . . must in its projection wrest from forgottenness that which it thus apprehends. The basic, fundamental-ontological act of the metaphysics of Dasein as the laying of the ground of metaphysics is therefore a "remembering" [*Wiedererinnerung*].[78]

The ground-laying of metaphysics of which Heidegger here speaks lays the ground of metaphysics in no-thing rather than in some-thing. It is therefore essentially different from the traditional variety of metaphysical ground-laying, which has forgotten the finite, temporal, thrown-projective character of the understanding of Being. The whole of Heidegger's thinking, early and late, is centrally concerned with the notions of forgetting and remembering. Fundamental ontology (or later: 'thinking', *Denken*) must remember that Dasein has forgotten itself if it is truly to retrieve or repeat its own hidden "understanding of Being."

Here we should recall the injunction "Become what you are!" and our interpretation of its meaning. To 'remember' is in the first instance to remember one's inevitable forgetting as one of the conditions in which there has always already been an "understanding of Being." For Heidegger, the understanding that occurs in falling and forgetting is not simply false, as the following passage shows:

> A specific kind of *forgetting* is essential for the temporality that is constitutive for letting something be involved. The Self must forget itself if, lost in the world of equipment, it is to be able 'actually' to go to work and manipulate something. . . . Letting things be involved is something which we understand existentially as a letting-them-'be' [ein "Sein"-lassen]. On such a basis circumspection can encounter the ready-to-hand *as that being* which it is.[79]

When Dasein brings itself back from falling and forgetting, it does not rise to a new and different region in which fallen experience is shown to have been false or illusory. Fallen, forgetful, average everyday experience is rather shown to be partial, because it has forgotten its context. It has, that is, forgotten its own Place, which is its own true 'Self', Dasein as Being-there. Dasein is the temporal clearing both in the sense of the process or event of clearing and in the sense of the site that is thus cleared. This Self is the very possibility of the actual, ontic beings that everyday experience encounters. It is thus the true ontological ground of beings or phenomena. If it seeks the security of grounding itself in some metaphysical being lying, unknown, beyond the limits of its own time, it disowns its own Being. Dasein has to be as a groundless ground, for "the 'whence' and the 'whither' remain in darkness."[80] This means that no metaphysical being shows itself either as the original ground or as the final ground of one's own being. Beyond the temporal horizons, all is dark; Dasein can push back in time only to its own factical thrownness, and it can push forward in time only to its own death. These horizons are not only the limits of Dasein's possibilities but the limits that make it possible, and necessary, for Dasein itself to be the ground. At most, Dasein can minimize the partiality, relativity, and perspectival character of truth by owning up to the necessarily finite conditions whereby Dasein has already had to submit and abandon itself to the world in order that entities as within-the-world might now be and mean. Dasein then owns up to having been, being, and having to be the groundless ground of its world: "In being a ground . . . Dasein constantly lags behind its possibilities. It is never existent *before* its ground, but only *from it* and *as this ground.* Thus 'Being-a-ground' means *never* to have power over one's ownmost Being from the ground up."[81]

Dasein is 'guilty' in the sense that it has always already been the ground. To be 'guilty' (*schuldig,* 'owing') is to owe what one is and will be to what one has already had to be. It is to be forever outside of mere self-contained presentness (which "the ancient ontology" took to be the criterion of being) as the ekstatic ground of that presentness. The true Self is not a present ego autonomously disengaged from time, having independent, self-contained power and mastery because it depends on neither its past nor its future in order to be what it is. Dasein owes its being to its having been thrown and to its having to project. It is not a matter of an originally autonomous, discrete, and self-contained self losing itself by letting itself be dispersed into time and then needing to regain its autonomy by pulling itself back out of time. Dasein, temporal Being, is rather the original context *within* which any attempt to locate an autonomous present self/subject/ego could be made; therefore any alleged "present self" is grounded (placed, understood, made intelligible) within Dasein's temporal horizons and thus is not self-grounding. The ontology of pure presentness has put the cart before the horse by making the original Self derivative and the derivative self original. Because the present self is derivative, it is not the true Self. 'I' cannot gain power or mastery over my ground, because it is always already beyond 'me' (where 'I' and 'me' refer to present being).

To affirm one's own true (*eigentlich*) Being is, then, to re-cognize—to remember—that one is always already 'outside', 'beyond' one's present being as an entity locatable 'here' and 'now'. One's 'hereness' has dissembled and blocked access to one's 'thereness', in accordance with Heidegger's principle that the true phenomenon is "something that proximally and for the most part does *not* show itself at all: it is something that lies *hidden* . . . but at the same time it is something that belongs to what thus shows itself, and it belongs to it so essentially as to constitute its meaning and its ground."[82] This remembering occurs in what Heidegger calls "the moment of vision" (*Augenblick*) as an 'ekstasis' and a 'rapture'. Both 'ekstasis' and 'rapture' (*Entrückung:* being carried away, being "beside oneself") connote a being beyond one's "present self" which in the moment of vision is also a remembering of the phenomenon beyond the semblance:

> In resoluteness, the Present is not only brought back from distraction with the objects of one's closest concern, but it gets held in the future and in having been. That *Present* which is held in one's own true temporality and which is thus *one's very own*, we call the "moment of vision." This term must be understood in the active sense as an ekstasis. It means the resolute rapture with which Dasein is carried away to whatever possibilities and circumstances are encountered in the Situation as possible objects of concern, but a rapture which is *held* in resoluteness. The moment of vision is a phenomenon which *in principle* can *not* be clarified in terms of the "now."[83]

Not an escape from falling everydayness but rather its reappropriation, resolute rapture affirms the same world into which Dasein hitherto had fallen—the world of particular concerns: "never dwelling anywhere. . . . is the counter-phenomenon at the opposite extreme from the moment of vision."[84] A resolute owning up to oneself, as a becoming what one (always already) is, even affirms forgetting, falling, and disowning as ineradicable characteristics of the human way of being, the inevitable ordinary "base state" on the basis of which remembering, bringing oneself back from falling, and owning up to oneself are possible.[85] The moment of vision is thus intended by Heidegger as a realistic sighting of the human way of being with all of its warts, its powerlessness, its structural tendency to self-dispersal. To sustain this kind of vision surely requires the attitudes of 'resolve' and 'equanimity'. Yet this very vision of the anxious and "manifest burden of Being"[86] is the occasion for "an unshakable joy."[87] There is a certain limited power and mastery in achieving a true estimate of the limits of one's powers, in 'individuating' oneself from one's ordinary loss in the impersonal crowd so as to see clearly how the objects of one's immediate concern are ultimately grounded in Dasein's own caring projection. As we have seen, "In the moment of vision . . . and often just 'for that moment', existence can even gain the mastery over the 'everyday'; but it can never extinguish it."[88] This joyful affirmation of a finite fate that is also an anxious burden is reminiscent of Nietzsche's *amor fati*. If this is not the autonomous transcendental Self, freed from the vicissitudes of time, that one had wanted, nevertheless there is a certain limited power in being able to come to terms with what one is, even to the point of affirming it.

If the moment of vision is thus not an airy transcendence but rather a reconciliation with a Dasein that is always already 'there', this must provide our clue for interpreting what Heidegger calls 'freedom'. Heidegger does not describe freedom as a present power of autonomous or arbitrary choice. He understands it not as a state but verbally, as a "Being-free for."[89] This will have to mean: Being-free for . . . in the way in which one really already is. Being-free for . . . clearly refers to the *future*, which we ordinarily think of as beyond a past that is over and done with. But the future for Heidegger refers to the *past* and its recurrence: "taking over thrownness signifies truly *being* Dasein *as it already was*. Taking over thrownness, however, is possible only in such a way that the futural Dasein can *be* its ownmost 'as-it-already-was'—that is to say, its 'been'."[90]

Being-free for . . . truly is being-free for the future as the coming toward Dasein of its having been in the manner of owning up to it. But in *WG* Heidegger writes: "Freedom as transcendence is . . . not merely one particular 'kind' of ground, but *the origin of ground per se. Freedom is freedom for the ground*."[91] Does this mean, as first appears, that Dasein is that sort of absolute freedom that invents its own ground? Its real meaning is given two pages later: "Transcendence means project of world [*Weltentwurf*] in such a way that the projecting is already attuned to and ruled by the beings [*Seienden*] which it transcends. . . . Transcendence is rooted in the *essence* of time, and that means in its ekstatic-horizonal constitution."[92] Freedom is thus the holding of oneself not simply into an open future but into the threefold ground of time as the 'there' within whose clearing particular possibilities become possible relative to what has already been. This must mean that freedom is the original always-prior event of Dasein as the opening of the clearing. Freedom is the involuntary or prevoluntary (always-already) disclosing of the 'there', the always-prior understanding of an intelligible Place.

But freedom is at the very same time the disclosure of a particular time and space, within which there have already appeared particular beings to which one is attuned and by which one is ruled. In other words, that understanding of world as world that makes particular beings (phenomena) possible is always at the same time attunement to and by those particular beings. 'World as world' is only a way of speaking of the site *of* particular everyday beings— or: Being is always the Being of particular beings, never an empty stage or blank slate. This Being is their disclosure in the time that is 'there'—always a particular time and a particular world.

This peculiar freedom in fact means the impossibility of any essential amelioration or progressive transformation of the human condition and situation, for it is a being-free for a future that is in all essentials the recurrence of what has already been, and one of these essentials is the thrown and factical necessity of having to take over a particular past that one can never make over from the ground up (*ex nihilo*) because it is itself part of the ground. Dasein is 'null' and a 'groundless ground' not because it is faced with a blank future and can thus make present choices *ex nihilo*, but rather because Dasein's whole Being, as Place, is not to its knowledge grounded in anything else, any metaphysical first or final cause. This seems fundamentally different than an existentialist humanism's doctrine of free, autonomous, subjective choice.

V

Heidegger claimed that the project of SZ was not man-centered but Being-centered, not anthropological but ontological, although his intention was widely misread. Now this cannot mean that the human being can be left out of an ontological study, for it is the human being who asks about Being and the human being to whom beings appear as beings, i.e., in their Being. The Being of the human being, his essential nature, is Place, the ground or clearing within which there can be disclosure of beings as what they are, that is, truth. This is the possibility-condition for disclosure of any present being, whether that being is the entity 'man', the entity 'hammer', or the entity 'tree'. Although the published divisions of *SZ* do not claim to answer the question of the meaning of Being in general,[93] it seems possible nevertheless to outline the answer to the question, and to express the fundamental relation of Being to Time, especially since Heidegger goes so far as to define Time explicitly in *SZ:* "we are justified in designating as *original time* the temporality which we have now laid bare."[94]

Past, present, future: each is what it is only by reference to the other two. The relation of 'Being' and 'Time' is that there *are* beings (phenomena) insofar as beings come to pass through the introplay of the three dimensions of time. "To be" (*Sein*) is to come to be present out of and by reference to a ground-time that is the 'there' for an entity that understands itself and all other beings by reference to its 'there'. Being 'is' in temporal ekstasis.

"The Being of beings" means the coming on of the past out of the future as the presencing of the present—that is, the presencing (showing) of beings on the basis of thrown projection. The ground of beings is anticipatory recurrence of what has been. Thus the hammer *is* (now) a hammer as an instrument for the (future) end of hammering, and the hammer already is (past) a member of the class of tools that can be used for this purpose. It *is*, at present, an "in-order-to" because there is precedent for it in a world of beings that are understood in light of Dasein's projects, ultimately Dasein's self-projection or self-understanding. For an ontology restricted to present things, this temporal ground is absent, and the intelligibility ('truth') of things is a miracle. For a temporal ontology and an ontology of meaning-beings, this ground is the source (possibility) of all phenomena, the circumambient field by reference to which they are at all, in the only sense of 'are' that can have significance for us.

Phenomena, including man, dissimulate their rootedness, their common source, their Place, when seen from the standpoint of simple presentness. But the standpoint of simple presentness—of the here and now—has been the standpoint of ordinary ontology. So phenomenology had to ground itself in a revision of ordinary ontology, which had to be an ontology of temporality. And this "new" ontology had to be a true (*eigentlich*) repetition, or remembering retrieve, of the ontology of temporality that has always already and everyday ruled our world. ". . . That which remains hidden in an egregious sense, or which relapses and gets covered up again, or which shows itself only as 'dissembled' ["*verstellt*"], is not just this being or that, but rather the Being of beings. . . . Thus that which demands that it become a phenomenon . . . is what phenomenology has taken into its grasp thematically as its object."[95] Far from being a lapse from phenomenology, *SZ* was the recall to its possibility: the nature of "things themselves" can be truly understood only on the ground of ekstatic time. Far from being the invention of a new system, *SZ* was a way back into the always-prior ground. Far from being an anthropological dead-end, *SZ* seems well on the way to answering the question it poses itself, the question of the meaning of Being as such.

Yet Heidegger came to think that in certain respects *SZ* needed rethinking. Study of Sartre's reappropriation of *SZ* (chapter 3) will help us to ascertain (chapter 4) in what sense *SZ* is misleading and incapable of fully carrying out its own intention. This will enable us to understand the need for a 'turn' (Part II). The famous *Kehre* or 'turn' in Heidegger's thinking will make it possible for Heidegger's later work to carry further his account of "clearing and presentness." The stress and the language will change, but its subject matter will remain the always-prior clearing that was at least partially "wrested from forgottenness" by *SZ*. Heidegger has attempted to retrieve the whole of the situation that is constitutive of the present being by relocating the 'here' and 'now' and the 'yonder' within a dissembled, forgotten 'there'. He treats the phenomenon as being what it is out of its source or ground as original unity of thought and Being; and to do this, I have argued, was the primary goal of phenomenology in its struggle against a dualistic broken totality.

3

L'Être-pour-soi, Ground, and Time in L'Être et le Néant

We cannot take too many precautions in the establishment of our bases.

—Descartes, *The Search After Truth*

SARTRE'S FIRST contact with the thought of Heidegger occurred when a Japanese student of Heidegger's gave him a copy of *SZ*. Simone de Beauvoir records that Sartre spent considerable time reading Heidegger in 1939.[1] With the publication of *L'Être et le Néant* in 1943, the influence of Heidegger on Sartre became apparent. The very title suggests a revision of Heidegger, while the subtitle (*Essai d'ontologie phénoménologique*) suggests that the reading of Heidegger had provoked Sartre to move from the level of his earlier studies—phenomenological psychology—to that of phenomenological ontology. In this chapter, I consider *EN* as I have considered *SZ*, with respect to its treatment of the relation of the nature of man to ground and time, and with an eye on the questions of beginning, metaphysics, and unity that, I have argued, form the essential legacy the modern philosophical tradition hands down to Heidegger and to Sartre.

I

In contrast to the tentativeness with which *SZ* introduces the general question of the nature of Being, the introduction to *EN* immediately offers a conception of being-in-itself as fully positive, contingent, and non-temporal being.[2] To borrow an expression Sartre is fond of, by the time one has read the introduction to *EN*, "les jeux sont faits." But if we expect the fabled French *clarté* from this introduction, we shall be disappointed. It is profoundly ambiguous. Sartre recognizes the ambiguity and offers the hope that the conclusion of the book will resolve it. But when the conclusion is reached the ambiguity remains. What is this profound ambiguity?

The introduction concerns "the pursuit of being" in modern times. It argues that the evolution of modern thought has brought ontology to the phenomenon as the true locus of being (l'être). It would appear that Sartre assents to Heidegger's claim that "only as phenomenology is ontology possible."[3] (We seem already well on the way to the conclusion reached by one of my undergraduate teachers: "L'Être et le Néant is just a rehash of Sein und Zeit.") Only as a doctrine of what does or can show itself to someone is a doctrine of being possible. "Doctrine of being" here means not "doctrine of beings" but rather "doctrine of the being of beings." This will mean, in turn, "doctrine of the being of phenomena." For a phenomenological ontology, being is the being of phenomena. Thus the purpose of EN seems to be the purpose of SZ: to elucidate a general ontology, a general conception of being, of what it means to be. Sartre, like Heidegger, warns us that he is not writing an "anthropology."[4] Yet, as for Heidegger, it is clear that no general theory of being may be elucidated without consideration of the being of man,[5] without which there are no phenomena at all.

Sartre's introduction makes clear that for him, as for Heidegger, working out a phenomenological ontology requires going between the horns of realist and idealist ontologies. The dangers of realism are avoided by asserting that the phenomenon is relative to the being to whom it appears.[6] The dangers of idealism are avoided by asserting that "the being of the phenomenon is not reducible to the phenomenon of being," since the phenomenon "requires in order to be a phenomenon a foundation which is transphenomenal. The phenomenon of being requires the transphenomenality of being."[7]

Now the very phrase "transphenomenality of being" implies that Sartre, like Heidegger, is pointing beyond phenomena to their source, or ground. Sartre's elucidation of the ground of phenomena is a two-step one:

[1] Consciousness . . . is the dimension of transphenomenal being of the subject. . . .[8] We have snatched from the phenomenon its being in order to give it to consciousness, and we

reckoned that consciousness would subsequently restore it to the phenomenon.[9]

[2] . . . The transphenomenality of the being of consciousness . . . itself requires that of the being of the phenomenon. . . .[10] Consciousness is consciousness of something: this means that transcendence is a constitutive structure of consciousness; that is, that consciousness is born *supported by* a being which it is not. We call this the ontological proof.[11]

Sartre here seems to argue for a double transphenomenality. Beyond the phenomenon on one side is consciousness, which is beyond the phenomenon as being conscious *of* the phenomenon. Beyond the phenomenon on the other side is its own being, inasmuch as the very being of consciousness is a being-dependent-upon a being that has its own being beyond consciousness. With reference to Anselm, Sartre calls this "the ontological proof": consciousness "is consciousness of a being, whose essence involves existence; that is, whose appearance makes a claim *of being.*" [12]

But what does this term 'being' mean? It cannot mean 'meaning' if it is to refer to that upon which consciousness is dependent. Sartre's earlier studies of the imaginary[13] had shown that imagination is negation; the imagination posits its object, the image, precisely as unreal, as solely what I make it to be.[14] Yet the imaginary object is meaningful. Since the image is meaningful yet at the same time nonbeing, consciousness of meaning cannot be a proof of consciousness of being. And yet the very fact that the imaginary object is posited as un-real, or as non-being, means that it presupposes a "world":

For the centaur to spring up as unreal, it is necessary that the world be grasped as world-where-the-centaur-is-not, and this can only happen if certain motivations have led consciousness to grasp the world as being precisely such that the centaur has absolutely no place there.[15]

. . . An image, being a negation [*négation*] of the world from a particular point of view, can only appear *on the ground of world* and in relation to this ground.[16]

These passages appear to say that imagination posits the image as a negation of the world, where 'world' means 'the real'. Sartre's view, however, is not that simple. What Sartre calls 'the world' is

already a 'surpassing' of the real: "To be able to imagine, it is sufficient for consciousness to be able to surpass the real in constituting it as world, since the nihilation [néantisation] of the real is
always implied by the constitution of the real in a world."[17]

'World' is the organization of 'the real' as a 'synthetic totality'.[18]
In EN Sartre tells us that "the world is human."[19] The world is a
synthetic fusion or 'syncretic ensemble';[20] it is "the totality of
beings insofar as they exist within the circuit of selfness,"[21] meaning that "it is necessary that I lose myself in the world in order for
the world to exist and in order for me to be able to transcend it."[22]
'World' (le monde) is Sartre's version of Heidegger's Welt: the 'referential totality' that has always already been illuminated by one's
falling concern.

Now in order to understand what Sartre means by the term
'being,' we must understand how the various Sartrean notions we
have just introduced—meaning, the real, the imaginary, the world,
negation—are interrelated. We shall be able to do this only by invoking another Sartrean notion, that of "consciousness (of) self."
And we shall need the help of another passage from L'Imaginaire:
"imagination . . . is the whole of consciousness as it realizes its
freedom; every concrete and real situation of consciousness in the
world is big with the imaginary inasmuch as it always presents itself as a surpassing of the real."[23]

It appears that the image is a surpassing of the 'world' that is in
turn a surpassing of the 'real'. Sartre is arguing that the image can
'surpass' the world (present itself as unreal) only if the world is already understood as itself a surpassing of the real. To 'surpass'
something is for Sartre, to 'negate' it. To surpass something is to
understand that the surpassing is other than (trans-) what is surpassed and the surpassed is other than the surpassing; in Sartre's
terms, there is a relation of 'negation'[24] between the surpassing and
the surpassed.

Thus the 'world' is a 'negation' of the real. This can only mean
that consciousness, as the being by which surpassing comes to be,
understands its world as a perpetual surpassing of the real. The real
has always already been organized from the standpoint of consciousness as a synthetic totality—as a unified structure of meanings, a more or less coherent organization of what we have called
'meaning-beings' or phenomena. Consciousness thus understands

itself in the world which is, as a "human world," *its* world, yet understands itself as *beyond* that world, as consciousness of itself as the standpoint relative to which there is a human world at all, or as the catalyst whereby what is has always already assumed a humanized form.

But if the real has always already been humanized and if "every concrete and real situation of consciousness in the world is big with the imaginary," in what sense is there a 'real' at all? In what sense is there a distinction between the 'real' and the 'imaginary'? Owing to the always-already character of the synthetic 'totalizing' or 'humanizing', the effective unit of experience is the 'phenomenon' and not a neutral given. Sartre even goes out of his way to stress that every concrete situation of consciousness is big with the imaginary and to stress that in order for me to transcend the world I must already have "lost" myself in it. Why not, then, simply equate 'world' and 'real'? What better warrant for this equation could there be than the fact that the 'world' of 'phenomena' is my ever-present situation and that all of my efforts to transcend it presuppose it? Where then is 'the real'? Must we not be as impatient with Sartre's assertion of it as Hegel was with Kant's assertion of the noumenon?

As a phenomenologist, it seems that Sartre must offer an experiential warrant for 'the real'. It will not suffice for him to fall back on tradition and assert that man has always presupposed a reality "behind" his experience.[25] This would be to run the risk of substituting an interpretation of the history of philosophy for a phenomenological description of experience. And it is precisely the specter of the history of philosophy that warns Sartre against taking the Hegelian step; the danger of idealism in all its forms is never far from Sartre's mind. Must he then in effect return to pre-Hegelian ontology? Or has Heidegger offered Sartre a way to save the sense of brute givenness without falling back on the noumenon? What happens is that Sartre, while taking over Heidegger's notion of facticity as an always-prior abandonment to a world, invokes Hegel *against* Heidegger in an effort to banish the specter of idealism.

Sartre notes that Heidegger "has completely avoided recourse to consciousness in his description of Dasein,"[26] meaning that while Heidegger as phenomenologist necessarily accords awareness or understanding (*Verstehen*) a central role in his ontology he refuses to recognize that he is thereby committing himself to the *negativity* of consciousness. Sartre explains:

> Now the characteristic of Heidegger's philosophy is to describe "Dasein" by using positive terms which mask all the implicit negations. Dasein is "beyond itself, in the world," it is "a being of distances," it is "care," it is "its own possibilities," etc. All this amounts to saying that Dasein *"is not"* in itself, that it *"is not"* in immediate proximity to itself, and that it "surpasses" the world inasmuch as it posits itself as *not being* [*n'étant*] *in itself* and as *not being* [*n'étant*] *the world*. In this sense, Hegel is right rather than Heidegger when he declares that Spirit is the negative. But we can put the same question, in slightly different form, to both Hegel and Heidegger. To Hegel one must say: "It is not enough to posit Spirit as mediation and the negative. It is necessary to exhibit *negativity as the structure of being of Spirit*. What must Spirit be in order to be able to constitute itself as negative?" And one can ask Heidegger: "If negation is the primordial structure of transcendence, what must the primordial structure of human reality [*réalité humaine*] be in order for it to be able to transcend the world?" In both cases a negating activity is shown us, yet there is no effort *to ground this activity on a negative being* And Heidegger, moreover, makes Nothingness a kind of intentional correlate of transcendence, without noticing that he has already inserted it into transcendence itself, as its primordial structure.[27]

We are at the heart of Sartre's revision of Heidegger—a revision whose magnitude is sufficient to warn us that *EN* is more than "a rehash of *Sein und Zeit*." While 'understanding' had been for Heidegger one of a number of equiprimordial existentialia of Dasein, understanding, in the sense of awareness of something as other than the awareness itself, becomes for Sartre the defining trait of a being.[28]

II

These considerations will help us to understand what Sartre means by 'the real'. If we now look back to the Sartrean 'world', which Sartre has characterized as a synthetic totality that is always already our 'situation', we can see that this means that 'world', like any totality, incorporates the negative. Consciousness has infected it with its own negativity. The world, Sartre argues, contains an "infinite quantity" of *négatités:* beings "which are inhabited by negation in their internal structure."[29] Sartre offers many examples, among them the *absence* of Pierre from the cafe and the crescent moon as the *lack* or "not yet" of the full moon.[30] William James's human serpent, whose trail lay over everything, has become a worm: "Nothingness . . . is at the womb of being, in its heart, like a worm."[31] It is as if holes had been dug or fissures opened in something, then filled up with human meanings.[32] To dig a hole in the ground is to characterize the prior smooth surface as insufficient; it is to understand it as needing something, which I must supply. Man appears as the poker and filler of holes. He pokes holes only to fill them with himself. The question we are presently raising is: what is the nature of this ground that man digs and fills?

If the ground is infected by negativity, then the ground itself would seem to be positivity. If negativity produces lacks and absences, the ground would seem to be a fullness, a plenitude. Thus we are not surprised to find Satre speaking of "being-in-itself" (*l'être-en-soi*) as a 'positivity', and as a 'plenitude' that is "filled with itself."[33] It is also 'uncreated', "not subject to temporality," and 'undifferentiated'.[34] It is neither possible nor necessary, but rather 'contingent'.[35] It is wholly independent or *selbständig.*[36] It is thus absolutely non-referential. Lacking differentiating predicates, it can only be said to be; "being is."[37]

Being-in-itself is pure existence as such, *existentia.* It cannot be a thing or an ensemble of things. Neither can it be hidden behind things in the manner of the noumenon. It is the being *of* phenomena: that is, the pure existentia, the pure *"that* it is" of things. This is Sartre's reappropriation of Heidegger's assertion that "Being is the transcendens pure and simple."[38] As soon as one speaks of the 'how' or the 'what' of things, one has differentiated and qualified being into beings, into phenomena. We can therefore conclude that the ontological difference between the imaginary and the real is that existentia must be predicated of the latter but not of the former. Thus the 'mode of being' of the imaginary is negation of being, or nonbeing. The phenomenon is 'real' insofar as it is pure otherness to consciousness, pure externality. The difference between a hundred real thalers and a hundred imaginary thalers is, after all, existentia; Sartre has attempted to save the ontological argument from Kant's destruction of it.

What then, is the ontological status of the differentia of phenomena: predicates, identifications, meanings? Has Sartre saved the being of the phenomenon from Husserlian ideality only to abandon all other predicates of phenomena to ideality? Does Sartre offer us an idealism of meaning grounded in a realism of existentia? To be sure, Sartre can hold that the phenomenon, as a synthesis, is an existent that is always *already* meaningful. But can one make a factor analysis of this synthesis, asking what consciousness contributes and what being contributes? What is the source or sources of determination? To put these questions is to generate two problems: (1) If consciousness is solely a negation, how can it contribute anything positive to the world? (2) If being is pure *existentia*, how can it support real predicates or qualities? Sartre's general answer to these questions is that determination is negation.[39] Spelling this out, he writes:

> this negation . . . is entirely ideal. It adds nothing to being and subtracts nothing from it. The being looked upon as "this" is what it is and does not stop being it. It does not become. . . . Negation can come to the *this* only through a being which has to be at once presence to the world of being and to the *this*—that is to say, through an ek-static being. . . . It leaves the *this* intact insofar as it is being in itself . . . it does not accomplish a real synthesis of all the thises in totality. . . . Determination appears as an external negation which is correlative with the radical and ekstatic internal negation which *I* am. This explains the ambiguous character of *the world*, which reveals itself at once as a synthetic totality and as a purely additive collection of all the "thises." Insofar as the world is a totality which is revealed as that on the ground of which the for-itself has to be radically its own nothingness, the world offers itself as *a syncretism of undifferentiation.* But inasmuch as this radical nihilation is always beyond a concrete, present nihilation, the world appears always ready to open like a box to allow the appearance of one or more "thises" which *were already*—in the undifferentiated womb of the ground—what they now are as a differentiated form.[40]

We interpret the meaning of this passage as follows. In losing itself in the world, the for-itself has always already understood the

world as a whole or context. In light of its present concerns or projects, it is explicitly conscious of or attends to particular entities,
which thus stand out as foreground individuals against a background that remains undifferentiated owing to the principle of selective perception or selective attention (which is entailed by the
for-itself's sensory embodiment). In order to attend to *this*, consciousness must relegate to the background ("negate") the remainder of entities in the world. Yet the entity now attended to is
situated, located, understood by reference to the total ground. What
I now attend to is attended to because it bears reference to what I
have recently attended to and to what I *shall* attend to. It is as if the
temporal passage of the for-itself were a narrow beam of light that
traces a path across dark ground where entities wait to be illuminated. (Indeed Sartre often speaks of consciousness as a 'revealing'
and an 'illumining'.)[41] This beam of light can center on *this* only on
condition that it does not illuminate everything. What has been illuminated and what could be illuminated constitute a totality that
could be seen as a mere sum of givens if the beam of light were to
play randomly over the dark ground, or can appear to be internally
related to each other if the light is purposefully seeking its way
from one point to a related point. (Sartre obviously has in mind
Heidegger's distinction between "the whole [sum] of beings" and
"beings in the whole.")[42]

Continuing with our metaphor, this beam of light can never illuminate all beings simultaneously but only selectively and temporally, one after another. It thus perpetually breaks up the totality
even though it shines continuously *amidst* this totality. But this
disintegration is evanescent, for, as the light moves on, what had
been illuminated lapses, unaltered, back into darkness.[43] All that
remains constant is the path or way of the light (consciousness) and
the absent-presence of what is in darkness (being-in-itself). This
continuous light is *not* what it illuminates but is simply the self-effacing condition of things appearing.[44] Its movement adds nothing
but *the sequence* of appearings.

Our interpretive beam-of-light metaphor implies, then, that consciousness is a neutral revealer; it reveals what is as it is, without
alteration. Has Sartre returned us to naïve realism? Sartre's 1939
essay "Une Idée fondamentale de la phénoménologie de Husserl:

l'intentionnalité"[45] suggests that Sartre finds in the principle of intentionality a means of reaffirming a naïve realism as against philosophical realism. And Sartre clearly subscribes to Heidegger's characterization of the goal of phenomenology: "to let that which shows itself be seen from itself in the very way in which it shows itself from itself."[46]

In this early Husserl essay Sartre wrote: "It is things which abruptly unveil themselves to us as hateful, sympathetic, horrible, lovable. . . . Husserl has restored to things their horror and their charm."[47] Can Sartre really mean to say that things are inherently lovable, horrible, etc.? He is clearly too perceptive to have missed the fact that a thing may be horrible to one and not to another; in fact he explicitly takes up the question of perceptual relativism in *EN*, reaching the following conclusion:

> It is, to be sure, a quality of the object that is revealed to me: the warm water *is* cold when I plunge my heated hand into it. A comparison of this objective quality of the water to the equally objective indication given me by the thermometer simply reveals to me a contradiction. This contradiction provokes on my part a free choice of true objectivity. I shall accord the name "subjectivity" to the objectivity which I have not chosen. . . . I intervene here only to the extent that my upsurge into the world gives birth to the *putting into relation* [*mise en rapport*] of objects with one another. As such, they are revealed as *forms*. Scientific objectivity consists in considering the structures separately, *isolating them from the whole:* therefore they appear with other traits. But we in no case get out of an existing world.[48]

This passage is of great help to us, and it returns us to the problem of relations that came to the fore in our analysis of *SZ*. In affirming that "the warm water *is* cold when I plunge my heated hand into it," Sartre subscribes to the phenomenological effort to give ontological status to unanalyzed or "immediate experience." He accomplishes this in a way that is characteristic of Husserl, Heidegger, and Merleau-Ponty: by arguing (1) that the attitude we generally call 'objective' is an analytic dissection of a prior totality; (2) that such analytic dissection presupposes and is grounded in this totality or 'world'; and (3) that this totality or world is a structure of meaning-references that originally illuminate entities as 'phenomena', the sort of intelligible beings that *could* subsequently be analyzed.

Sartre thus appears to grant reality to the phenomenon, and one can find many passages in *EN* that speak explicitly of the 'reality' of the phenomenon.[49] Yet there are certain seeming counterindications in the text that call for consideration. It will be worth listing them at some length:

[1] Space. . . . is a moving relation between beings which have no relation. . . . It is the unique fashion in which beings can reveal themselves as having no relation, can reveal themselves to the being through whom relation comes to the world. . . . The existence of space is the proof that the for-itself by making being *be there* adds *nothing* to being; space is the ideality of the synthesis. . . . Nothing can come to the in-itself through the for-itself except the negation—and this only as a kind of *external relation* which leaves intact what it unites.[50]

[2] The relation determinative of the *this* can . . . belong neither to the *this* nor to the *that*. It surrounds them without touching them, without conferring the least trace of new character on them; it leaves them what they are.[51]

[3] The coincidence of the identical is the true plenitude of being. . . . It is thus a principle constitutive of *external relations*. . . . It does not concern the internal relations of being; inasmuch as they would posit an otherness, these relations do not exist. The principle of identity is the negation of every kind of relation at the womb of being-in-itself. Presence to self, on the contrary, presupposes that an impalpable fissure has slid into being. If it is present to itself, that is because it is not all at once itself. Presence is an immediate *breakdown* of coincidence. . . .[52]

[4] . . . These few remarks run the risk of committing us to Aristotelian "potentiality." This would be to fall . . . into a *magical* conception. Being-in-itself can neither "be in potency" nor "have potentialities." In itself it is what it is in the absolute plenitude of its identity. The cloud is not "potential rain"; in itself it is a certain quantity of water vapor. . . . *The in-itself is in act*. . . . Its relation to a possibility can only be established *from outside*, by a being which stands facing its own possibilities.[53]

[5] . . . This fact "that there is" being is not an internal determination of being—which is what it is—but of negativity.[54]

[6] Since it [negation] leaves the *this* intact insofar as it is being
in itself because it does not achieve a real synthesis of all the
thises in totality, the negation which constitutes *this* is a negation of the *external* kind. The relation of the this to the whole is
a relation of externality.[55]

[7] The for-itself is the foundation of all negativity and of all
relation; *it is relation.*[56]

[8] . . . If I am to be able to *do* anything at all it is necessary
that I act upon beings whose existence is in general *independent*
of my existence and in particular independent of my action. My
action can reveal this other existence to me; *it cannot condition
it.* . . . It can only by its free choice interpret the *meaning* [*sens*]
of their being. It is necessary that they simply be there, altogether brute, in order for there to be freedom.[57]

[9] . . . The given thus *designated* is in no way whatsoever
formed; it is a brute existent, assumed only to be surpassed. . . .
In assuming the *brute given* and in *conferring its meaning* [*sens*]
on it, freedom has at once chosen itself. . . . The *reality-in-itself*
was there, at hand, with its *qualities* and with no distortion or
addition.[58]

[10] Suppose the environment is a field of snow. . . . It represents *pure externality,* radical spatiality; its undifferentiation, its
monotony, and its whiteness manifest the absolute nudity of
substance; it is the in-itself which is only in-itself, *the being of
the phenomenon.* . . . At the same time its *solid* immobility
expresses the permanence and the objective resistance of the
in-itself, its opacity and its impenetrability. . . . That pure in-
itself, like the absolute intelligible *plenum* of Cartesian extension, fascinates me as the pure apparition of the not-me; what I
wish is precisely that this in-itself might by its relation to me
be a relation of emanation while remaining entirely in itself.[59]

[11] In order to maintain my decision [not to smoke], I had to
accomplish a sort of decrystallization. That is, I reduced the
tobacco to being *only itself*—an herb that burns. *I cut its symbolic ties with the world.* . . . At once my regret was disarmed
and quite bearable.[60]

[12] No doubt the "human" meaning [*sens*] of *sticky, slimy,*
etc., does not belong to the in-itself. But neither do potential-

ities . . . belong to it and yet it is these that *constitute the world*. *Material* meanings [*significations*] . . . are just as *real* as the world, no more and no less, and to come into the world is to emerge in the midst of these meanings.[61]

[13] In each apprehension of quality, there is . . . a metaphysical attempt to escape our condition, to pierce the muff of nothingness of the "there is" and to penetrate to the pure in-itself. But obviously we can grasp quality *only as a symbol* of a being which entirely escapes us, even though it be entirely there before us. In short, we can only make being, as revealed, function as a symbol of being-in-itself. . . . This immense universal symbolism . . . is interpreted by our repulsions, hates, sympathies, and attractions to objects whose materiality must, in principle, remain unmeaningful [*non-signifiante*].[62]

These revealing passages, which I have numbered for ease of reference, enable us to draw the following conclusions. If the world, its phenomena, and their qualities are 'real' (9), they are so as *grounded in* an unapprehensible being, which is the 'actual' (4), what exists wholly *in actu* as opposed to what exists *potentialiter* (4, 12). The 'real' is the synthetic fusion of the actual and the potential, of material and meaning (12). The actual is the nontemporal ground of the real, but the occurrence of the real makes the actual inapprehensible, so that it may be grasped only indirectly and symbolically (13): certain reals, such as snow, can be understood as symbolizing the pure otherness or substantiality and *Selbständigkeit* of the actual (10). The substantiality or *Selbständigkeit* of the actual, its completeness without man, guarantees that the for-itself is powerless to alter the actual (1, 2, 3, 8). It is the absent-presence of the actual as ground that makes it possible for the for-itself to move toward the nontemporal ground by stripping off layers of the real (4, 11), but not to reach the ground, since the for-itself is by nature a relation *to* the ground (7) as a temporal path across the ground that disintegrates it in such a way as to make a *human* reintegration of it possible. But the actual stands, mute and obstinate, as a limit to this human reconstruction. "The human world" is not substantial but rather a midworld rising precariously on foreign ground. The for-itself is also a ground of this midworld insofar as it maps relations externally on the actual ground by a magical incantation (4).[63] In contrast to Heidegger, actuality stands higher than possibility as the baseless basis and limit of possibility. The fracturing of non-temporal being by time cannot metamorphose the actual into the real. All determinations float externally across the impassive surface of the actual (5, 6).

If we glance back now to Sartre's discussion of perceptual relativism, it seems that we can express the conclusion he reached there in a new way: the perceptions of the heated hand and of the thermometer are equally *real*, and they can be equally real because of the margin of possibility "added to" the actual by the rise of the for-itself. But neither of the two perceptions is of the *actual*, since "we in no case get out of an existing world."

And yet is there no ontological difference between the perception of the warmed hand and that of the thermometer? Sartre says in the passage to which we are referring that "scientific objectivity consists in considering the structures separately, *isolating them from the whole.* . . ." And we found Sartre saying, "I reduced . . . the tobacco to being only itself—an herb that burns. I cut its symbolic ties with the world." The references in these passages to 'isolating' and 'reducing' both suggest a certain derealization, and in both cases this is accomplished by taking the phenomenon out of its relation to the whole. Thus the cloud "is, in itself, a certain quantity of water vapor" (4). But there are at least two possible ways to interpret this derealization. It may mean that one has thereby reached a closer approximation to actuality, for in cutting the phenomenon's ties with the 'world' one has apparently cut its ties with a world that is merely synthetic. Yet can Sartre subscribe to the occurrence of *worldless* phenomena? Passage 6, above, suggests this possibility: since negation "does not achieve a real synthesis of all the thises in totality," therefore "the relation of the this to the whole is a relation of externality." But there is another possibility, namely, that the reduction has cut the phenomenon from the world that nevertheless remains as the (bracketed) world-ground by reference to which the phenomenon could be *for us* at all.[64]

The difficulty of deciding between these alternatives stems from Sartre's seldom-explicit distinction between the 'actual' and the 'real'. The 'this' is more closely linked to the actual than is the 'whole' or 'totality' or 'world' and its relations. While Sartre insists that the actual or being-in-itself is undifferentiated and that differentiation comes to the in-itself only through consciousness as

negation, he maintains that being-in-itself is the ground of this differentiation. If consciousness is to be a 'revelation' of what is, then
the 'this' and its 'qualities' must not be merely ideal. If consciousness is to reveal a difference between a mountain and a plain, or
between carbon and hydrogen, there must be an 'actual' ground for
this revealed difference. Otherwise one relapses into idealism. Yet
Sartre must tread very carefully here. He ascribes negation strictly
to consciousness, and he ascribes all determination to negation.
Furthermore he ascribes all possibility or potentiality to negation.
As a result of these ascriptions Sartre cannot, in the Aristotelian-
Hegelian manner, think of the actual as an actualizing of its own
potential determinateness (4). Phenomena are 'realizations' of the
actual, but not 'actualizations' of the actual. As a nontemporal plenitude, the actual always already "is what it is" or is fully actual, and
potentiality or possibility comes to it only from the outside, is
mapped upon it externally, and does not actually stick to it. Thus
Sartre cannot say that what he calls 'thises' and their qualities are
realized potentialities of the actual (of being-in-itself). On the other
hand, if he is to carry through the phenomenological program of returning philosophy to "the things themselves," he cannot treat the
phenomenon as less real than its ground.

Thus Sartre must maintain both that the phenomenon is a 'revelation' of what is to which consciousness adds nothing[65] and that
consciousness brings differentiation out of the undifferentiated.[66]
But, as Klaus Hartmann acutely observes, "in view of its identity
with the determinate, it [being-in-itself] cannot be indeterminate."[67] Being-in-itself is at one and the same time determinate
and indeterminate. In the terms in which Sartre has posed it, this
dilemma is insoluble. *So long as the ground of phenomena is fully actual prior to the intervention of understanding, the phenomenological
program cannot be completed.* Either understanding will be reduced
to a purely passive role and one will fall back into all the difficulties
of realism, or understanding will interpose itself between itself and
the actual and one will fall back into all the difficulties of idealism.
Despite Sartre's efforts to go between the horns of realism and idealism, both these positions remain—in uneasy coexistence—in Sartre's philosophy. Owing to Sartre's realism, consciousness is ineffectual; owing to Sartre's idealism, the phenomenal never coincides
with the actual.[68] The irreducible paradox of Sartre's thinking is

that his realism opens up to consciousness the very being from which his idealism cuts him off. Sartre is, of course, aware of this and appears to believe that this paradox more or less coincides with Heidegger's thesis that Being is simultaneously revealed and concealed.[69]

There is therefore no simple way to choose between the two alternative interpretations we advanced. Owing to the ideality of world (as what is *not* being-in-itself) Sartre can indeed speak of cutting the phenomenon's symbolic referential ties with the world in such a way that a 'worldless' phenomenon remains. This means that one is reducing the 'this' to what it is 'revealed' as being, with no addition by consciousness; one strips off the synthetic accretions that an "affective-cognitive synthesis"[70] add to being. One purifies being of imaginative-affective intentionality. In breaking the 'external' ties between the herb that burns and the rest of my world, the phenomenon shows itself as 'what it is': an herb that burns. (Or the threatening cloud shows itself as water vapor.) And yet "we in no case get out of an existing world." I shall henceforth experience situations within the world without my pipe contributing to their flavor, but I shall nevertheless be *affected* by those worldly situations. I shall find that situations are pleasurable even without my pipe, Sartre says.[71] The meaning of things will still be apprehended relative to my particular concerns, relative to my particular illuminating path through the world. I have modified the circuit of selfness, but I have not altogether abrogated it. In cutting one particular external relation or referential tie, I have not cut them all.

It is important to ask how it is possible for the for-itself to cut symbolic ties with the world in such a way as to reduce the phenomenon to 'what it is'. For Sartre two conditions must obtain if one is to accomplish this 'decrystallization'. First, consciousness must be consciousness (of) self. That is, consciousness must be aware of itself if it is to be able to distinguish between the phenomenon and what is added to the phenomenon by the "affective cognitive synthesis." This synthesis ties one phenomenon meaningfully to another and may even partially transform the phenomenon.[72] Second, consciousness must be able to understand the phenomenon as independent of consciousness in its being and self-identical in its being. In order to be able to strip the phenomenon of 'external' or 'synthetic' accretions, one must presuppose the external and self-identical entity as the ideal limit of this process of stripping.

Taking these two conditions together, one can say that the analytic factoring or breaking of a synthesis presupposes that the synthesis is a synthesis of discrete factors; a relationship presupposes relata. The ultimate relata for Sartre are consciousness and being-in-itself. Both are ideal limits of a kind of factor analysis that Sartre calls 'purifying reflection'.[73] But the only real internal relation between these relata is negation—the relation of absolute separation. All other relations between them are synthetic, hence derivative and in principle analytically factorable. Thus what would appear on the synthetic and unreflective level to be real internal relations[74] turn out, when analyzed by purifying reflection, to be external relations—'ties' that can be 'cut'. The cutting of all synthetic ties is, of course, only an ideal limit of reflective analysis, for most experience is of necessity *un*reflective and all experience is temporal experience that moves toward a future desideratum in such a way as to cause phenomena to appear laden with meaning and affectivity relative to one's concerns (one's 'projects'). This is another way of saying that "we in no case get out of an existing world."

Thus for Sartre the very structure of consciousness—as consciousness of (itself as) consciousness of something—poses for consciousness a perpetual threat of the breakdown of its immediate unreflective experience. The relata that consciousness must synthesize in order to experience a meaningful world haunt consciousness in their bare relation of internal negation. This means that for consciousness to maintain the affective power of its unreflective experience it must try to forget the stark antithesis that grounds this synthetic experience. (This forgetting, which Sartre generally calls "the spirit of seriousness,"[75] is part of Sartre's reworking of Heidegger's 'inauthenticity'.) Therefore the ontological structure of consciousness haunts and challenges the authority, power, and efficacy of the unreflective synthesis. The ontological ground of the world and its meaning-references haunts the world as a reminder of its synthetic and virtual character. The ontological structure of things requires that the "horror" and "charm" that Husserl restored to them be perpetually in danger of slipping away from them again. Sartre's application of Heidegger to Husserl means that intentionality is assessed

as falling. And Sartre's application of Heidegger's distinction between what is first in the order of experience and what is first in the
order of ontology[76] means that reflection on the ontological structure of unreflective phenomena will have to challenge the actuality
of these unreflective phenomena. This is to say that while ontological analysis is such as to return phenomena to their primacy on the
unreflective level, it is such as to challenge their primacy on the
reflective level. The very act of showing why phenomena have primacy challenges that primacy. If synthesis is experientially primary,
antithesis is ontologically primary.

III

Ontological analysis therefore requires one to challenge the unreflective experience of time, raising anew Heidegger's question of
the relation between Being and time. One may ask whether the
shift in title from *Being and Time* to *Being and Nothingness* is fortui-
tous or not; how does Sartre's treatment of nothingness and negation revise Heidegger's account of the relation of Being to time?

Being-in-itself, we have noted, is nontemporal. The for-itself is
temporal and the ekstatic source of temporality. Consciousness, as
the "instantaneous nucleus" of the for-itself, is a nucleus that has
always already surpassed its instantaneity in such a way as to have
constituted the for-itself as a totality and the world as a totality at
the same time. That is, in being "consciousness of," consciousness
has always already been an awareness of a past behind it and a future ahead of it in such a way as simultaneously to have surpassed
both its own instantaneity and the nontemporality of the actual.

Because of the primarily unreflective character of consciousness,
time is chiefly apprehended as "the time of the world."[77] But all
consciousness is 'non-thetically' consciousness of itself, i.e., it has
an inexplicit awareness of itself not normally focused upon directly
('thematized'), but nevertheless understood as a "background" or
reference point of all experience of entities in the world. So the
'present' arises as a reference point that both divides past from future and relates past and future. Strictly speaking, the present "is
not,"[78] but is rather a *relation* forward and backward. Thus there
has always already been a totality constituted around the nucleus,
and it is only by reference to this totality that there could be said to

be a nucleus *of* it. We have seen that consciousness traces a path across the surface of being, across the ground. This tracing is both spatial and temporal, both a spatializing and a temporalizing of the actual. Thus we may consider it a dual 'decompression' of an actuality that is in-itself neither spatial nor temporal. Under the moving beam of consciousness the actual appears to be temporal and spatial, to be a coming-on that is in the process of becoming past. Sartre can be said to subscribe to the view developed in the *Timaeus:* time is the moving image of eternity [79] if we regard consciousness as the Demiurge. The for-itself spreads the nontemporal and nonspatial out in time as a before and after, a here and a there, and unreflectively understands and measures itself against this time-space *as if* that time-space were actual. But measured against the ideal of the actual, purifying reflection discovers, this time-space is merely synthetic. Thus all temporal and spatial relations and references within this time-space are synthetic, though the phenomena or reals or 'thises' that are related within this time-space remain 'relative-absolutes' [80] inasmuch as they are merely 're-vealed' by consciousness.

This means that the phenomenological effort to let phenomena show themselves from themselves as they are in themselves is, in Sartre's interpretation, the effort to free phenomena from time. It is the effort to understand things in their revealed self-identity, freed of the external relations that do not constitute the actual even though they form the world within which phenomena can and must first appear to consciousness. Thus "the existing world" is a necessary condition for the appearance of phenomena but is not constitutive of their essence as actual. Indeed, the essence of the actual is dissimulated, covered over, by the synthetic relation of one phenomenon with another; the actual is infected by the possible. The effort to free phenomena from time is the effort to disinfect them of possibility.

What Sartre regards as necessary to complete the phenomenological program is therefore purifying reflection, since to let phenomena be what they are is to turn back on consciousness in an effort to factor out the relata of the unreflective synthesis; what temporal consciousness contributes is to be distinguished from what the nontemporal actual contributes. Stated in a different way, it is the effort to break "the circuit of selfness." Stated in yet a third way, it is the effort to reverse the falling movement of unreflective consciousness.

Purifying reflection is thus the movement from the proximal to the actual ground. The proximal ground is "the existing world" that we, as beings who are proximally and mostly unreflective or 'impurely' reflective,[81] can in no case get out of. The actual ground is nontemporal being-in-itself as revealed by its relatum, consciousness, in internal negation. What purifying reflection finds is a nontemporal plenitude and an instantaneous nucleus that perpetually explodes that plenitude into discrete beings. To reverse the "natural" unreflective movement of falling consciousness is to arrest provisionally the project of consciousness to reconstitute the plenitude that consciousness has itself exploded. It is to attain a vision of a timeless plenitude that, already complete, requires no man to complete it. It is therefore to see man as an "ass" chasing a carrot forever out of reach[82]—trying to reassemble the plenitude that his own nature disperses in space and time. To succeed in this effort would be to escape from the 'world', which we in no case get out of. We shall continue "establishing the circuit of selfness, that is, inserting the world between the for-itself and its being."[83] In other words, we shall continue to try to humanize the actual.

There is a sense, of course, in which man succeeds in humanizing the actual. For Sartre the past of the for-itself is precisely the humanized actual. In "futurizing" the actual, consciousness has caused it to explode into possibilities; these possibilities move into the past as either realized or unrealized possibilities, but in either case as possibilities that are no longer possibilities. If I realized the possibility of writing a topical book in 1970, that book enters the past as both human and actual; if I did not, that project enters the past as an impossible possibility, an actual inpossibility. Thus my past is a mixture of actualized possibilities and actual impossibilities. Is man, then, wholly an "ass"? Cannot the past, as a humanization of the actual, be seen as genuine accomplishment? Sartre does not take this view in EN. The past smells of death; it is finished. Though the past is human, it is also dead and ineffectual, *hors de combat*. As the surpasser of the actual by internal negation, man is quintessentially the possibilizer: man is in his very being "the being of possibilities"[84] while "the past is that which is without any possibility of any kind."[85] "I cannot reenter the past."[86] Since the for-itself is conscious of its past, its relation to the past is that of internal nega-tion.[87] The past is therefore what is perpetually surpassed.[88] For the past to affect me "it is necessary that I *remake it ex nihilo* and freely,"[89] and yet the past, as wholly actual, cannot literally be remade but only added to. The past is a symbol of my own death— my lapse into the unalterable timeless plenitude of being.[90] Here as elsewhere, *consciousness as internal negation renders impossible any other internal relation* and the past falls into externality. I *am* my past in the mode of not being it.[91]

As what I have to be in the mode of not being it, and as what is always surpassed, the past is an essential dimension of time. Sartre reminds us that no one of the three temporal dimensions has any ontological priority over the other two. "Yet in spite of all this," he argues, "it is proper to put the accent on the present ek-stasis—not on the future ek-stasis as Heidegger does. . . ."[92] This remark is at first puzzling. Even though Heidegger indeed asserts that "the fu-ture has a priority in the ekstatical unity of primordial and authen-tic temporality,"[93] how could one possibly lay more stress on the dimension of the future than Sartre does? Is not the Sartrean for-it-self above all a "flight forward"?[94] And does not Heidegger view the present as having "a peculiar importance"?[95] And does not the past for Heidegger retain a kind of efficacy that Sartre denies it? No doubt Sartre's assertion that Heidegger puts the accent on the fu-ture ekstasis is in part to be understood in terms of Sartre's ex-tended critique of Heidegger's "Being towards death."[96] But the inapprehensibility of my own death, of which Sartre reminds Hei-degger, is not the reason Sartre here gives for accenting the present. Instead he writes:

> for it is as revelation *to itself* that the for-itself *is* its Past, as that which it has-to-be-for-itself in a nihilating surpassing. And it is as revelation *to itself* that it is lack and is haunted by its fu-ture, that is to say, by what it is for itself down there, in the distance. The Present . . . is the chasm [*le creux*] of indispens-able nonbeing for the *total synthetic form* of Temporality. . . . The for-itself is the being that has to be its being in the *dia-sporatic* form of Temporality.[97]

Sartre is referring to the relation between time as a synthetic to-tality and consciousness as its instantaneous nucleus in a sort of phantom present reference point. We have seen that for Sartre all totalities have their source in the upsurge of consciousness as an instantaneous nucleus that by negation explodes the plenitude of being into a spatiotemporal totality, a 'diasporatic' totality. And we have seen that the present "is not" but is rather a relation. In other words, the source and reference point relative to which "there is" a past and a future "down there, in the distance" is consciousness (of) self as *other than* past and future, as a relation between past and future, both of which the for-itself "is" in the mode of *not* being them. As instantaneous nucleus that explodes nontemporal plenitude, consciousness is a 'chasm' that divides nontemporal plenitude into a before and an after, a 'detotalized totality'. Consciousness is the relation between past and future across the chasm that is itself. Thus if we come back from the synthetic totality to its source, that source is consciousness (of) self as the nucleus that disperses both itself and the in-itself forward and backward and thus becomes *presence-to-itself* at a distance from itself. Where, but for consciousness, there would simply be being, there is now *"presence* to being."[98] Consciousness of, as presence to, is the primordial source of the past and the future in which consciousness ekstatically loses itself. The future represents the perpetual danger of loss of oneself in unrealizable desire (for which reason the solitary drunkard is more lucid than the leader of nations),[99] and the past represents the perpetual danger of loss of oneself in the actual, the stasis of mere identity. The present is the primary ekstasis in the sense that it refers us more directly to the source of time, to the original event of the explosion of being and its reconstitution as a synthetic totality.

Here as elsewhere Sartre returns us to the negating consciousness that Heidegger is criticized for bypassing. In so doing, Sartre always returns us to the nontemporal being of which that consciousness is the negation and the affirmation, the affirmation-by-negation. "Being and *Time"* becomes "Being and *Nothingness"* because for Sartre being is ontologically prior to time and time first arises out of the 'nothingness' of consciousness as the negation of being. In bypassing consciousness Heidegger has bypassed original negation, which is essentially affirmation of a being that is purely other, purely nontemporal, pure substance, *Selbständigkeit,* pure transphenomenal existentia. This is the ultimate ground. And this is the meaning of being, constantly reaffirmed by the for-itself's flight from it and quest for it.

IV

At the beginning of our analysis of *EN*, I forecast that we would find a profound ambiguity. We have been moving toward it all along and must now focus on it directly. We have found that Sartre on the one hand wants, with Husserl, to return to things their horror and their charm. But on the other hand his method, like Husserl's, requires him to *withdraw* from the unreflective immediacy of ordinary experience. It is in reflexive withdrawal that one analytically isolates the relata that make possible the totalizing syntheses of unreflective immediacy. Now in order that this reflexive withdrawal not commit one to an idealism, as in Husserl, that is unable to reverse the movement of withdrawal and return to brute givenness,[100] one must make two moves, two concessions to realism. First, one must assert the ontological independence of the phenomenon's being, its existentia. Second, one must show that this phenomenon, despite its necessary otherness, can be 'revealed' to consciousness as it is. Sartre is able to make these two moves at once by positing a consciousness that is a negating 'transparency'—a neutral awareness of itself as external to what it is directly aware of. The negation is itself the affirmation of independent being.

But if Sartre were to stop here it would be wholly unclear how phenomena could be experienced as "horrible" or "charming." What accounts for this experience is a version of Heidegger's notion of 'world' that shows how an ekstatic for-itself "loses itself" in order that world may exist.[101] The for-itself fills the gaps between the thises, which are only negatively related to each other, by a falling and ekstatic intentionality that establishes meaningful synthetic relations between the 'thises' relative to the for-itself's projects. Thus the neutral 'thises' are always already humanized, or have their intelligible place in "an existing world." Yet because of the ontological difference between the 'thises' as rooted in the actual and their synthetic relations as human, the 'thises' perpetually threaten to show themselves in their pure *Selbständigkeit*, their unintelligible contingency. The existing world does not collapse—the roots of the chestnut tree in *La Nausée* are still affectively experienced, are horrible—[102] and yet one is reminded of the unstable and synthetic character of the relational ties by which one has tried to humanize the actual.

It is the instability of these relational ties that reveals to us the ambiguity of *EN*. Sartre's reflective and analytic withdrawal has distinguished between four levels of being: the actual (plenitude, being), the real (differentiated plenitude), the virtual (synthetic relatedness), and consciousness (nonbeing). Sartre wishes to restore the efficacy of immediate experience, and yet his analysis is a constant reminder of its synthetic character. The synthesis is achieved, insofar as it can be, by falling, by bad faith, by affectivity, by the spirit of seriousness. It has the character of a patch-up job. One tries to patch all the holes, only to be confronted continually by new ones. The effort to humanize the world is a vain passion, and the solitary drunk who has tried to cut his symbolic ties with the world is more lucid than the leader of nations who is plugged into the world to the hilt.

The analytic withdrawal has opened a moral Pandora's box. What does one want—clouds pregnant with rain, or water vapor? One's pipe, or an herb that burns? A beautiful tree, or an obscene and contingent mass of roots? Vain involvement, or lucid detachment? Sartre's version of the return to things themselves has in fact exposed layers of thinghood among which one must choose. If one now wishes to reverse the movement of withdrawal, to come back to "the world of artists and prophets" toward which Husserl directs us, the world in which "if we love a woman, it is because she is lovable," [103] can one do so without losing oneself? One is perhaps reminded of Santayana's dilemma in *Scepticism and Animal Faith*. If I try to cut my symbolic, synthetic, and virtual ties with the world in order to let the phenomenon show itself from itself as it is in itself, have I not impoverished my world rather than enriched it? In its effort to restore the richness of a human world, Sartre's ontological phenomenology has exposed the ground of the human world as an impassive, undifferentiated, impersonal substance and has made that substance the criterion of actuality. This ground is the specter that haunts and limits the humanizing of the world. Lucid analysis, purifying reflection, leads one to it; must one now flee lucidity, and even flee 'phenomena', in order to have "the world of artists and prophets"?

The ambiguity is between analysis and synthesis. We had thought that reflective analysis of the naïve synthesis of unreflective experience would philosophically justify that naïve synthesis. It has

instead turned synthesis into a moral question. It has done so because ordinary experience has been shown to be a lapse from actuality, even a lapse from reality. Human experience has been measured against the criteria of existentia and substantia and found
wanting: "the for-itself is in no sense an autonomous substance. . . .
The for-itself is an *unselbständig* absolute. . . ." [104] The criterion and
measure of knowledge and of being is independent existentia.
Therefore the final conclusion, "the general theory of being" that
Sartre announced as his goal, cannot be a unified theory reuniting
being and thought, for it must rest upon "the affirmation of the
ontological primacy of the in-itself over the for-itself." [105] Given this
criterion, "the temporalization of consciousness . . . is a surface
runoff. . . ." [106]

If we should have a lingering doubt that Sartre's ontology is an
ontology of *existentia,* a passage from Sartre's conclusion lays this
doubt to rest:

> Should we wish to imagine a synthetic organization such that
> the for-itself would be inseparable from the in-itself and, recip-
> rocally, *such that the in-itself would be indissolubly bound to the
> for-itself,* it would be necessary to imagine this synthesis in
> such a way that the in-itself would receive its *existence* from the
> nihilation which causes there to be consciousness of it. . . . No
> doubt this *ens causa sui* is impossible. . . . [107]

In other words, "in the case of the internal negation for-itself-in-
itself, the relation is not reciprocal. . . ." [108] We recall again Aristotle's assertion that "interaction between two factors is held to
require a precedent community of nature between the factors." [109]
The only precedent community possible between Sartre's fundamental ontological relata is internal negation, and thus the reciprocality of genuine community is ruled out at the start. 'Interaction',
then, can be solely a form of negation, and even this activity is attributable solely to one of the relata, the for-itself. "Nothing can act
on consciousness. . . ." [110] And conversely "this negation . . . is
entirely ideal. It adds nothing to being and subtracts nothing
from it. . . . It leaves the *this* intact insofar as it is being in
itself. . . ." [111]

It is precisely because the *this* is left intact as being in itself that
Sartre can conclude *EN* with "metaphysical hints." [112] One might

argue that Sartre's existential ontology saves the metaphysical from phenomenological idealism as Kant saved the metaphysical from Leibnizian idealism. To be sure, the Leibnizian question "Why is there being at all rather than nothing?" can in a sense be answered *within* the region of phenomenological ontology: " 'There is' being because the for-itself is such that there is being. The character of *phenomenon* comes to being through the for-itself."[113] "There is" (as phenomenon) being rather than nothing precisely because of nothing. Yet this phenomenological answer points beyond phenomenology; in another sense of "there is"—the sense of existentia—there is a being *to which* the phenomenon comes. Now the whole of phenomenological ontology, as a 'description' of the 'structures' of being insofar as being has already fallen prey to the for-itself's negation,[114] occurs after the fact, after the original upsurge of consciousness as negation. But this leaves one vital question unanswered. Why is there an original upsurge of consciousness at all?

This question takes us beyond phenomenology to metaphysics. It asks for the metaphysical ground of phenomena. Phenomenology has been able to show us the "material"[115] ground (being-in-itself) and the efficient ground (the for-itself's negating 'revelation' of 'thises'), but it has not been able to show us the formal and final ground. Seen speculatively from the outside (outside of time and history),[116] one must ask the formal question, what was the proto-original relation of being-in-itself and being-for-itself, and the final question, toward what end is this relation directed? It is here that Sartre toys with the notion of precedent community by asking "What is there in common between the being which is what it is, and the being which is what it is not and which is not what it is?"[117] The answer to this question can only be hypothetical, for in asking it we seek to enter the region of the unconditioned, the region of metaphysical cosmology.

There can be little doubt that Sartre, in asking this question, has Heidegger's definition of metaphysics quite consciously in mind: "Metaphysics is a questioning above and beyond the region of beings for the purpose of reappropriating it as such and in its wholeness for conceptual understanding."[118]

Sartre offers us an hypothetical answer that is inspired by neo-Platonic cosmology. *EN* gives a number of hints at a sort of Plotinian cosmology.[119] One can understand Plotinus as having devoted himself to the Platonic effort to understand the nature of the relation between Parmenides' "Way of Truth" and "Way of Seeming." The way of truth, which mortals can walk only with divine aid, reveals the truth of the cosmos; as an undifferentiated and self-identical plenitude, one can only say of it that "it is." The parallel with Sartre's characterization of being-in-itself strikes us at once.[120] The way of seeming is the way of apparent multiplicity and becoming; it is infected by negativity, nonbeing. But Parmenides offers us no clear account of the *relation* between being and nonbeing, between truth and its dissimulation. Plotinus attempts to explain this relation through emanation out of the One, a descent into multiplicity conditioned by nonbeing. The soul aspires to reverse this descending movement and return to pure being.

A variant of this cosmology appears to haunt Sartre throughout *EN.* Could one not envisage the ontology Sartre has presented as a sort of grand cosmic drama that is inherently meaningful, inherently purposeful? To be sure, "On the ontological level nothing permits one to affirm that, from the beginning and in the very womb of the in-itself, the for-itself means the project to be cause of itself." And yet *everything happens as if* the in-itself, in a project to ground itself, gave itself the modification of for-itself."[121] "Thus everything happens as if the in-itself and the for-itself were presented in a state of *disintegration* in relation to *an ideal synthesis.*"[122] Everything takes place as if what appears to us as "a sharp *duality*"[123] really has its prehistoric source in the ekstatic emanation of consciousness out of the unity of plenitude, this emanation initiating a cosmic spiritual odyssey whose final cause is an ekstatic return to unity that would succeed in an impossible reconciliation of nonbeing and being, *a real synthesis* of consciousness and substance. Consciousness would achieve substantiality without losing itself and substance would achieve consciousness without losing itself. In other words, the cosmos would be inherently intelligible; human meanings would no longer float over the surface of an impervious substance without sticking. Essentia and existentia would therefore coincide.[124] Consciousness would be the articulation of the in-itself's own meaning, the self-realization of substance. Everything happens *as if* the telos of the cosmos were to realize the phenomenological synthesis by healing "a sharp duality."

If metaphysics were to move beyond dualism toward this more

unified view that finds duality to be a duality within a prior and projected unity, then it could "deal with a being which we shall call the *phenomenon*, which will be supplied with two dimensions of being, the dimension in-itself and the dimension for-itself *(from this point of view, there would be only one phenomenon: the world)*—just as in Einstein's physics it has been found advantageous to speak of an *event* that is regarded as having spatial dimensions and a temporal dimension and as determining its place in a space-time. . . ."[125]

This seems to be the conception of the phenomenon that Heidegger is already moving toward in *SZ*. From a Sartrean point of view, this would mean that Heidegger's phenomenology has had to leap into metaphysics in order to reach its goal. From *within* phenomenological ontology, Sartre finds evidence only for a "decapitated" synthesis, "a passage which is not completed, a short circuit."[126] The introduction's quest for the meaning of that being "which includes within itself these two radically split regions of being"[127] turns out to be a quest for a metaphysical ideal. Sartre appears unready to take the leap beyond dualism. He asks, "will it remain preferable, despite all, to preserve the ancient duality 'consciousness-being'?"[128] His answer appears to be yes. And yet he is haunted by the other alternative. We suspect that we have now put our finger on the reason for the unresolved ambiguity between analysis and synthesis in *EN*. The phenomenological program points toward a real synthesis of consciousness and being; but Sartre's analysis of the relata of this synthesis reveals its "made up" character.[129] By isolating existentia and its conscious negation as relata, Sartre saves Husserl from idealism, at a price. The price is the substitution of existentia-lism for the completion of the phenomenological program. Thereby the goal of the phenomenological program recedes into a metaphysical distance, which makes its appeal to Sartre—and, in his view, to man—all the more haunting. Being is a unity only as an ideal. We can now submit that Sartre's ontology mirrors a drive toward the synthesis of truth and seeming, of unity and multiplicity, of being and meaning that has deep and ancient roots in Western culture and of which the phenomenological quest is the most recent exemplification. But in his distinction between experience of the real world and a reflection that purifies this experience, we find echoes of Husserl's distinction between the natural attitude and the reduction that places all its validities out of account. In neither case is the broken totality quite healed.

Living with
Nothing

WE HAVE outlined certain critical features of two versions of phenomenological ontology. Each of the two leaves us in suspense, but each does so for a different reason. Heidegger tells us that the published *SZ* (only its first half) does not reach its announced goal of answering the question of the meaning of Being. Can a further step be taken that 'turns' from *Dasein* into *Sein* as such? Sartre, on the other hand, claims that *EN* has taken us as far as ontology can legitimately go, offering a general theory of being as negated unity. Yet his conclusion suggests, first, that ontology itself leaves open the question of the metaphysical interpretation one makes of that ontology, and second, that an ethics of "salvation" or "radical conversion" may in some sense ameliorate the bleak prospect for man that ontology presents.

It appears that both Heidegger and Sartre call for a turn—Heidegger for a turn *into* (*Einkehr in*) Being, a further step in ontology, Sartre for a turn *around* (*con-version*) in one's meta-ontological attitude toward an ontology already completed. Part II explores the meaning of these two turns, each of which in its own way requires a coming to terms with 'nothing'. Chapters 4 and 5 are limited to a consideration of the respective turns from the standpoint of the two thinkers' early writings: what sorts of turn are either possible or necessary, given the nature of the two ontologies? Is the Sartrean turn premised on a misinterpretation of Heidegger? Is the Heideggerian turn premised on the intention to challenge the sort of ontology that Sartre's turn intends to embrace?

Chapter 6 is devoted to an episode that is crucial for our study: Sartre's implicating Heidegger in his own existentialist humanism and Heidegger's response thereto. Here for the first time we find Sartre taking a wholly explicit ethical stand and

Heidegger explicitly assessing the relation of his own thought to that of Sartre. Occurring at a time when Heidegger's thought had begun to turn dramatically, this episode will ultimately help us to evaluate the real extent of the divergence between the two ontologies.

Part II is centrally concerned with the second of the three critical questions which, I have argued (chapter 1), form Heidegger's and Sartre's problematic ontological inheritance: can ontology avoid recourse to metaphysics? Must it avoid recourse to metaphysics? Does the metaphysical quest for an absent ground eventuate in a nihilism that makes impossible the establishment of a secure ontology? Or does nihilism free man for the construction of a genuinely *human* ontology?

4

Nothing and World:
The Need for the Turn

What problems does the question of the worldhood of the world lay before us?

—Heidegger, SZ, 83 (114)

CHAPTER 2 reached the provisional conclusion that SZ is well on the way to answering the question it posed itself: "if beings are spoken of with a multiplicity of meanings, what is the guiding and basic meaning?" Or, "What does it mean to be?" The general response of SZ is that to be is to be 'there', in such a way that the beings of the 'there' occur in internal temporal and referential relations with each other. This definition holds both for the Being of man and for that of things, with the proviso that the Being of man (Dasein) is requisite for the emergence of a thing as present or ready by reference to a 'world'. That is, no thing, but only Dasein, can locate itself in a world, and this location is requisite for the Being of things, their presentness or readiness. Dasein is that ontic being which has ontological priority over other ontic beings, since there can be no phenomena, no meaning-beings, unless there is already a meaningful field (a world) with reference to which beings could be meaningfully situated/identified as what they are; and Dasein itself has to be this field. The meaningful field, we saw, can be thought of as the 'possibility' or 'ground' of the phenomena. We saw that it has an a priori character, in the sense that, as the ground on which present things can be situated and on which "present man" can situate himself, it is "always already there."

It would appear, then, that Heidegger has in SZ already essentially answered the question of the meaning of Being. What remains to be done? It is well known that Heidegger not only interpreted SZ but also criticized it. He found its language still "metaphysical."[1] He found it, wholly against its own intention, still in danger of consolidating "subjectivity."[2] He found it in effect too voluntaristic.[3] He said that "the foundation of fundamental ontology is no foundation."[4] Yet he claimed, in his preface to the seventh edition (1953), that "the road it has taken remains even today a necessary one. . . ."[5]

In general, I interpret these remarks as meaning that *SZ* succumbed in certain respects to the very same "ancient ontology" it was combating. In other words, *SZ* was not essentially mistaken but rather insufficiently true to its own intention. Looking back with the perspective of further thought, Heidegger came to treat *SZ* almost as if it were the work of a predecessor. He brought to it that same peculiar Heideggerian combination of elucidation and criticism that he brought to the work of Kant, Hegel, or Nietzsche. And to the same end—to free the unspoken thought that the author could not express because of his and his readers' subjection to *Seinsvergessenheit*, that forgottenness of Being that Heidegger attributes to Being's own self-dissimulation.[6] Heidegger, like Sartre, sees his career as a continuing struggle against a sort of deception. But it is indicative of a basic difference in their ways of thinking that Sartre attributes this deception largely to himself, as self-deception, while Heidegger ascribes it to Being.[7]

I

If we are to understand why Heidegger retrospectively finds *SZ* too voluntaristic, its ontology not fundamental, and its intention not fulfilled, we must above all consider the interrelation of 'world' and 'nothing' in Heidegger's early thinking. I venture to suggest that it was out of reconsideration of the relation of 'world' and 'nothing' that Heidegger came to reinterpret the notion of 'ground' or 'foundation' in the 1930s.[8] It is evident from the content of the several publications of 1929—*KPM*, *WG*, and *WM*—that the interrelation of 'world', 'nothing', and 'ground' was a central preoccupation in the years immediately following the publication of *SZ*.

In this chapter I shall try to avoid giving to the years immediately following *SZ* a clarity of direction they probably did not have. The sections of this chapter will have to oscillate back and forth between differing ways of interpreting 'world' and 'nothing' in *SZ* and in the essays of 1929 in order to give anything like an accurate account of the ontological difficulties that then confronted Heidegger's thought. In turning the problem on all sides, I try to see it both from the perspective of chapter 2 and from that of chapter 3. In other words, we want to know to what extent SZ really accomplishes its own ontological intention and to what extent it is liable to a Sartrean or "existentialist" interpretation in which man must supply to 'existence' an 'essence' that it lacks. Unfortunately, the anwer to this question is not unambiguous.

I have (chapter 2) interpreted the experience of 'Nothing' in SZ as the experience of the absence of that sort of initial and/or final ground (a 'whence' and a 'whither') for which the metaphysical tradition has searched—an absence, one might argue, implied by the search itself. In one's search for a ground that is some-thing one finds, instead, no-thing. In other words, one finds no ground beyond Dasein itself, which is therefore a groundless ground. In the "call of conscience" Dasein calls itself to take over being this groundless ground that it always already has been, but to do so "resolutely."[9]

What seems especially noteworthy in this account is the sense of deprivation that pervades it. True resoluteness is difficult to sustain; conscience calls one to what one does not want to hear. Most experience (average everydayness) is a tranquillizing forgetting of something fundamentally disorienting. One does not wish to own up to being a ground. The chief question to be raised is whether this sense of deprivation is constitutive of the human condition or rather historically conditioned. If the latter, it is not necessarily a permanent, inevitable deprivation. But SZ implies that it is indeed an anxiety-producing deprivation to which Dasein is constitutionally liable. As a step in answering this question, we must turn back to SZ and then consider WM.

SZ can be read as suggesting that 'world' is unstable. We have seen, to be sure, that Dasein is always already submitted to a world "of which it never becomes master."[10] As Von Hermann notes, "Although it is Dasein which clears the clearing, the clearing is not Dasein's own property, since Dasein as clearing [als Lichtendes] is always already cleared."[11] Further, this world to which Dasein is already abandoned is a particular world, not simply world as such. "Dasein exists as a potentiality-for-Being that has, in each case, already abandoned itself to definite possibilities."[12] Possibility is always thrown possibility. It would appear that the content and meaning of Dasein's world is beyond Dasein's immediate control. And yet thrown possibility remains *possibility*. But in what sense? Does this mean, along Aristotelian lines, that man inherits given possibilities, yet has the power to decide whether or not these possibilities will be actualized? Notice the interplay of power and powerlessness in the following passage:

> If Dasein, by anticipation, lets death become powerful in itself, then, as free for death, Dasein understands itself in its own *superior power* [*Übermacht*], the power of its finite freedom, so that in this freedom, which 'is' only in its having chosen to make such a choice, it can take over the *powerlessness* [*Ohnmacht*] of abandonment to its having done so. . . .[13]

This means that insofar as Dasein owns up to its thoroughgoing temporality, it also owns up to abiding by the consequences of that choice. To cast one's lot with time is to own up to one's power, projection of the Being of beings, but at the price of having to exercise that power and having to abide by the consequences of having already exercised that power. If, by disowning myself, I seek to trace the Being of beings to an ahistoric Eleatic permanence, I fail to comprehend that the price of understanding beings is participation in the constitution of their Being and thenceforth being subject to that Being. The Stoics understood this when they warned that to love is to risk heartbreak, i.e., to endow a being with a meaning is thenceforth to suffer that meaning. Their response was "Eleatic": do not love. The lasting appeal of Eleatic metaphysics to the Western tradition is that it represents a region beyond risk, beyond compromise, a salvation from the region of finite possibility.[14] (The chief significance of Kant for Heidegger in the late twenties is that he represents the effort—a flawed effort to be sure—to come to terms with finite possibility or 'finite transcendence' as opposed to the ahistoricism of Eleatic metaphysics.)[15]

But to cast one's lot with time and history[16] is of necessity to cast one's lot with others and with a common past rather than simply to take over an individual projection. Heidegger continues:

> But if fateful Dasein, as Being-in-the-world, exists essentially in Being-with Others, its historizing is a co-historizing and is determinative for it as *destiny* [*Geschick*]. This is how we desig-

nate the historizing of the community, of a people. . . . Our fates have already been guided in advance, in our Being with one another in the same world and in our resoluteness for definite possibilities. Only in communicating and in struggling does the power of destiny become free. Dasein's fateful destiny in and with its 'generation' goes to make up the full authentic historizing of Dasein.[17]

Heidegger here analyzes the point of intersection of two existentialia, historicality and Being-with. Their interconnection means that the always-prior world on the basis of which I must live is at the same time the world of others. I find myself not simply in my own world but in a world of which other Daseins are also groundless grounds. We have always conjointly committed ourselves to a group already. Our lot has been cast with others in common projection and interpretation of the world, and it is our common fate to live on the basis of this prior commitment. To acknowledge one's temporality is to acknowledge a common past by reference to which we have always already and shall become what we are. To cast one's lot with time is to be a future-oriented surpassing of-and-on-the-basis-of what we have been. If Dasein *is* the whole temporal stretch between birth and death, it is as present 'man' both in the past and beyond it. Dasein "hands down" to itself its own past (prior projection) as the basis of its making-present of the future. History is not made in a vacuum. The meaning of the future is relative to the past, so that if we own up to what we are really doing, we recognize that in the very act of acting into the future we are reaffirming the past. Yet this does not mean that one is doomed merely to reenact or remake what has already been enacted and made.[18]

> Rather, the repetition makes a *reciprocative rejoinder* to the possibility of that existence which has-been-there. . . . It is made *in a moment of vision.* . . . Resoluteness implies handing oneself down by anticipation to the "there" of the moment of vision; and this handing down we call "fate." . . . From the phenomena of handing down and repeating, which are rooted in the future, it has become plain why *the historizing of authentic history lies preponderantly in having been.*[19]

In interpreting this passage, it is necessary to remember that the existentialia are the essential meanings of particular ('existentiell') events in a life because they are the "possibilizers" of a possible range of particular events or actions. Like entities, events or actions are meaning-beings. They are not what they are without 'understanding' (*Verstehen*); understanding is part of their real internal constitution. But understanding, as we have seen, is the situating and identifying of things by reference to a ground which is the temporal stretch of Being-in-the-world from birth to death. In every thing, event, and person, the whole ground is, so to speak, vicariously present. The writing of a book is not simply a present-time activity. It is the assembling of a particular past and a particular future in a particular present. My particular past is the possibility of a particular book coming to me as my own future. Thus, in writing it, I am repeating my own past as the possibility of my future. This is a particular (existentiell) act that is possible because it has an existential meaning. This means, essentially, that my understanding of my present as being against the whole ground of my past and my future in a particular way—as the coming on of my particular past out of my future—is what makes possible and what limits any present activity of mine. My past is both the possibilizing source and the limiting particularity of my present and future.

Thus when Heidegger speaks of true 'repetition', he means in part that the present act reaffirms and reappropriates its past as the very possibility of this particular present. He also means that every present repeats the same *essential* situation; every situation will always be an actualization of the selfsame existentialia. That is: there is no hope of deliverance from time, a flight to Eleatic Being. Any act is a "meaning-by-reference-to" that necessarily reaffirms the whole referential ground in which alone it can be what it is. (Once again, possibility stands higher than actuality.) Thus, simply in being what I now am, I am reaffirming as constitutive of me the community out of which I became what I am. In acting, I "hand down" that community and "repeat" it as the possibility of my doing what I am about to do.

Summarizing, we can say that Heidegger grounds the historical act in the same way that he grounds the thing or entity—through a doctrine of internal meaning-references that challenges the fallacies of simple location and simple actuality. One consequence is that the 'world' is communal, a world of inherited meanings that are repeated in (reaffirmed by) present actions as the inevitable source and ground of these present actions. Thus we are subject to a common 'destiny'. In speaking of owning up to this our ownmost destiny Heidegger once again implicitly invokes the notion of *amor fati*.

Now this communal world seems stable indeed—until we ask, what is the particular nature of the 'reciprocative rejoinder' that the Self-oriented (*eigentlich*) Dasein makes in a 'moment of vision'? In Sartre's hands, Heidegger's 'moment of vision' (*Augenblick*) becomes the 'instant' (*l'instant*) of 'radical conversion'.[20] Is this what Heidegger had in mind? Or is radical conversion only possible for a being that is in principle separated from its past by a conscious negation? We can elicit Heidegger's own position from the following passage:

> The true repetition of a possibility of existence that has been—the possibility that Dasein may choose its hero—is grounded existentially in anticipatory resoluteness; for it is in resoluteness that one first chooses the choice which makes one free for the struggle of loyally following in the footsteps of that which can be repeated. But. . . . repetition does not let itself be persuaded of something by what is 'past', just in order that this, as something which was formerly actual, may recur. Rather, the repetition makes a *reciprocative rejoinder. . . . in a moment of vision; and as such* it is at the same time a *disavowal* of that which in the "today" is working itself out as the 'past'. Repetition does not abandon itself to that which is past, nor does it aim at progress.[21]

First of all, this means that in committing oneself to time and history (in owning up to one's historicality) one resolutely subscribes to the conditions under which the past can come on out of the future. Second, however, this commitment does not entail, but rather disavows, the view that the present is a necessary result of the past. It rather envisages the past as offering a finite field of possibilities for possible actualization. To take a particularly painful example, the German political, social, and economic past offers Heidegger the choice of affirming or rejecting the National Socialist program, given the fact that Heidegger owns up to his inevitable participation in the making of history as an inherently historical being. The call of conscience requires a decision on the basis of the possibilities offered, and Heidegger chooses his "hero."

In light of this analysis, I am arguing, the 'world' appears relatively unstable. While its existential-ontological structure does not change but rather perpetually makes possible (projects) possibilities, those particular possibilities are subject to historical change on the basis of individual and communal decision. To be sure, Heidegger's fundamental preoccupation is with the abiding existential-ontological structures of the 'there' as such, and a sort of stability is to be found there. Yet these are the very structures that make both possible and necessary[22] the historical variability of the *particular* meanings that 'world' always has. Dasein as temporal clearing is the permanent ground and possibility of the impermanent. The existential fact that Dasein is a groundless ground thus assumes a very particular existentiell meaning: the existentiell, the particular act of a particular being, is ungrounded. Positively, this means that decision is possible (it is possible to be a ground). Negatively, it means that decision is inevitable ('one' is inevitably a ground). But who is this 'one'? In true resoluteness, Heidegger argues, Dasein is "individualized" or freed for its ownmost possibilities.[23] Does Heidegger here fall back into the subjectivism he is fighting? Does true (*eigentlich*) Dasein become the Kierkegaardian subject, stuck between "the despair of possibility" and "the despair of necessity,"[24] forced to choose on the basis of given possibilities, but choosing its response to them on the basis of *nothing?* Is this subjectivism and voluntarism all over again? And is Heidegger here really very far from the position of Sartre and of existentialism? Is this why Heidegger in retrospect found *SZ* still too voluntaristic and lacking a real 'foundation'? And if the particular meanings of innerworldly beings are conditioned by historical decision, does not the 'phenomenon' of phenomenology lose its relative independence and become "subjectivized"? Does the specter of idealism still haunt *SZ?* Does the specter of nihilism haunt *SZ?*

The answer to all of these questions must be an ambiguous yes and no. It must be remembered that Heidegger's fundamental purpose is always to question what it means to be, and that his fundamental answer to the question is always that to be is to be in the "clearing," the always-prior ground of presentness. This notion of the clearing necessarily takes one beyond the traditional view of 'man' as self-contained present subject, for it construes the essence of man as a relation. And, correlatively, it necessarily takes one beyond the traditional view of the 'object' as a self-contained present entity. In effect, Heidegger reappropriates Hegel's doctrine of internal relations while at the same time respecting Kierkegaard's critique of the rational mechanism whereby internal relations progressively actualize a potential rational absolute—Hegel's effort to bring *Sein* into *Zeit* without paying the real price of the temporalization of Being, which is the surrender of its Eleatic rational constancy. Heidegger is in an important sense mediating Hegel and Kierkegaard, tempering Hegel with Kierkegaardian prerational 'possibility' (suspension in the abyss of nothing as the possibility of genuine decision), and tempering Kierkegaard with Hegelian real internal relations "between" 'man' and 'thing' relative to a temporal ground.[25] But does this mediation entail the substitution of a prerational idealism for a rational idealism? (It should be noted that Sartre thinks Heidegger has not succeeded in passing beyond idealism.)[26]

II

It is possible to read *WM* as a response to Heidegger's recognition that the specter of idealism continues to haunt *SZ*. To be sure Heidegger had in *SZ* defended relations against the charge of ideality:

> nor are they merely something thought, first posited in an 'act of thinking.' They are rather relationships in which concernful circumspection as such already dwells. This 'system of Relations,' as something constitutive for worldhood, is so far from volatilizing the Being of the ready-to-hand within-the-world, that the worldhood of the world provides the basis on which such entities can for the first time be discovered as they are 'substantially' 'in themselves.' And only if entities within-the-world can be encountered at all, is it possible, in the field of such entities, to make accessible what is just present-at-hand and no more.[27]

Far from being ideal, worldly reference relationships are precisely the basis upon which traditionally "objective" 'things-in-themselves' can appear. But just because 'the actual' is in this way grounded in 'the possible', Heidegger can elsewhere in *SZ* argue that idealism has a certain priority over realism. While he agrees with realism insofar as he "does not deny that entities within-the-

world are present-at-hand," nevertheless "in realism there is lack of
ontological understanding. Indeed realism tries to explain Reality
ontically by Real connections of interaction between things that are
Real. . . . If what the term 'idealism' says, amounts to the understanding that Being can never be explained by entities but is already that which is 'transcendental' for every entity, then idealism
affords the only correct possibility for a philosophical problematic.
If so, Aristotle was no less an idealist than Kant."[28] Once again
Heidegger rests his case on the always precedent unity of thought
and existence as the unified ground already assumed by any effort
to isolate thought from existence. And he immediately adds a sentence that bears on Sartre's solution to the idealist-realist dilemma:
"But if 'idealism' signifies tracing back every entity to a subject or
consciousness whose sole distinguishing features are that it remains *indefinite* in its Being and is best characterized negatively as
'un-Thing-like,' then this idealism is no less naive in its method
than the most grossly militant realism."[29] In other words, what is
crucial is recognition of the original unity of thought and existence
as the prior ground out of which the 'ideal' and the 'real' get factored by analytic abstraction.

Everything then hangs on recognition of the priority of the temporal ground, the context and source of every entity's Being. This
is, we have seen, Heidegger's fundamental concern, and all his
argument implicitly or explicitly refers back to it. But what happens
to that ground in true resoluteness? Sartre argues that there is a certain "difficulty which generally plagues Heidegger's passage from
the ontological level to the ontic level. . . ."[30] Granted that existentially-ontologically Dasein as clearing is always already the ground,
what happens to that ground in the particular existentiell-ontic situation of true resoluteness? Speaking generally, one can say that
truly resolute Dasein owns up to its inevitable submission to a particular world in which it already is. But *in what way?* We have seen
that authentic resoluteness can be characterized as a "decision" that
can "choose its hero" in such a way that the past becomes a limited
series of options to be chosen from. At the very moment when
Dasein needs guidance from the prior world, that particular world
seems to desolidify into possibilities and present itself as 'nothing'.
This sounds much like the sort of situation in which, as Sartre
would argue, one could reorder one's priorities and order the world

referentially in a new way—that is, a 'radical conversion' in which one could restructure the referential totality by reordering one's intentions. One could change the 'specification' of one's 'project', in Sartre's terms—without, of course, being able to dispense with the referential totality.

What we are asking is whether the ground becomes in effect more *ideal* in the situation of true resoluteness. We shall try to elicit an answer to this question from *WM*. The essay describes what we would ordinarily call a shift in attitude. But it is a shift in which, as in all phenomenological descriptions of attitudinal shifts, experiencer and experienced are simultaneously and correlatively altered. The shift described is that from ordinary everyday preoccupation to "dread" or "anxiety" (*Angst*), a rare "clarity of vision" (*Helle des Blickes*).[31] It might be regarded as a remnant of Husserl's reduction. It is the "transformation" or "reduction" or "conversion of man into his Da-Sein" so that "only the pure Da-Sein . . . is still there."[32] It is not "you" or "I" that "hangs in suspense" but "one"—that is, pure prepersonal Dasein—that witnesses a slipping away of "beings in their totality" (i.e., 'world'). One experiences "a peculiar peace" in which "all things and we ourselves sink into a kind of indifference."[33] Man's ordinary concernful referential attachments to the world are for the moment in abeyance. The resulting situation is not one of instrumental/practical goal-seeking but rather one that "awakens and invites wonder."[34] What one wonders about is beings as a whole, which have slipped away from us in their ordinary familiarity only to "crowd around us in anxiety."[35] Momentarily freed of immediate concerns, one wonders at the pure *that*ness of beings, the unadorned fact that there are beings at all—rather than nothing. It gradually becomes evident to the reader that the essay is an analysis of the Leibnizian question, "Why are there beings at all rather than nothing?", with the explicit mention of which the essay terminates.[36] To wonder is to ask why there are beings at all. That means at the same time that an answer to the central question of metaphysics is lacking; with the first raising of the question, there naturally arises the quest for an answer. The initial raising of the question in anxious wonder is the beginning of metaphysics, and the history of metaphysics is the quest for an answer.[37] Metaphysics is anxiety and the quest to overcome anxiety.

The essay becomes more complex when Heidegger asserts that "in anxiety the nothing comes to pass *at one with* beings as a whole."[38] ". . . Nothing manifests itself as really belonging with and to beings as they are slipping away in their wholeness."[39] "Nothing's nihilating happens in the very Being of beings."[40] The meaning of these assertions can be ascertained only when they are taken together with another passage, which states that "the nothing is what makes it possible for beings to reveal themselves *as such* to human Dasein."[41] This means that beings can show themselves *as* beings only when and if they are understood by Dasein together with nothing, in the context of nothing, against a field of nothingness.

An analogy may help to clarify this difficult idea. The photographs taken of the earth by astronauts on the way to and on the moon have fascinated the world. There is more at the root of this fascination than curiosity over a technological achievement. What fascinates is the appearance of the earth, within a part of which we are normally preoccupied, as a whole standing out in isolation against a field of black and empty nothingness. The way the earth shows itself stands in internal relation with this surrounding nothingness: it is because it is isolated that it can stand out starkly "as such" and "as a whole." And it is because man has been able to transcend the earth by a great distance that he is able to see the earth as a whole, in a sort of moment of vision. But at the same time he is drawn in wonder, fascination, and perhaps anxiety to this retreating home, to which he must soon return and in which he soon loses himself once again.[42]

Phenomena come into being "out of nothing." That is, beings show themselves in their thatness and as a whole only against a field of nothingness. The event of nothing reveals beings "in their full and hitherto hidden strangeness [*verborgenen Befremdlichkeit*] as the absolutely Other—over against nothing."[43] There is not an original dialectic of Being and nothingness, but rather they are originally together as a single event: the event of *Sein* for Da-sein, the coming into Being of beings, which is at the same time the coming into Being of Da-sein. The Being of any and every being is its rise as an entity that is immediately intelligible or identifiable as there *by itself* in itself, as just there, as "a present this" where, but for this, there would be nothing. This, we shall see, is interpretable as the experience of entities as purely "present-at-hand" (vorhanden)—an experience that is not a "proximal and for the most part" (zunächst und zumeist)[44] experience, but one that nevertheless may prove to be ontologically and existentially 'primordial' (in accordance with Heidegger's view that what is first in the order of experience is not first in the order of Being). Anxiety, then, brings Dasein back to its ownmost original experience of beings.

It is at just this point that Heidegger's argument is most problematic. The entity as vorhanden appears to be the entity stripped of any and all relation to Dasein. But Heidegger seems to want to make the opposite point: it is only possible for the entity to show itself in its Being if Dasein is "there" in such a way as to hold the entity in nothingness and experience it as the absolute other to nothingness. This is to say, once again, that Dasein as "the clearing" is the ground-possibility of phenomena. There must be a time-space, a place, within which an entity can be placed. Further, only when that place is free of any other beings beyond beings as a whole can the entity show itself from itself as it is in itself,[45] i.e., in its essentially conditioned, temporal, referential Being. The time-space must be bounded by a nothingness. It is only because entities are originally situated in nothingness that it is possible for historical man to fill in that nothingness with God, or with any of the various historical ontotheological accounts of the ground of beings as a whole. We have seen that "being free for the ground" means existentially-ontologically being always already submitted to the clearing in which phenomena can appear and have appeared. We now see that "being free for the ground" means, equiprimordially, being opened into the open space or nothing that can be filled with 'grounds' or 'reasons' for the Being of beings. Thus Heidegger's assertion in WG that "Freiheit ist . . . Freiheit zum Grunde"[46] is intentionally ambiguous: freedom is submission to the inevitable ground that is at the same time the possibility of giving grounds, giving reasons, answering the metaphysical question why there are beings rather than nothing. Nothing is the 'ground' that is the possibility of 'grounds'. "Dasein's being held within the nothing on the ground of hidden anxiety makes man he who takes the place of nothing."[47] Dasein's own clearing is the place or opening that his-

torical man fills with his quest for a *grounded* place.[48] Metaphysics is
the anxious quest to fill the nothing. It is the will to ground. And
metaphysics "is Dasein itself."[49]

There appears to be a glaring contradiction in the essay, though
Heidegger acknowledges no contradiction. The quest to ground
beings is rendered futile by the very ground that makes the quest
possible. Nothing, as the condition of the quest for grounds, dooms
the quest for grounds in advance. Sartre has, apparently correctly,
read *WM* this way and proceeds explicitly to draw the conclusion
that Heidegger seems to refrain from drawing:

> Every human reality is a passion, since it projects losing itself
> in order to found being and to constitute by the same stroke
> the in-itself which escapes contingency through being its own
> ground, the *Ens causa sui* which religions call 'God'. . . . Man
> sacrifices his humanity in order that God may be born. How-
> ever the very notion of God is contradictory and we lose our-
> selves in vain; man is an unavailing passion.[50]

What is Heidegger's own response to the situation he has outlined? He writes, "The primordiality of nothing is at first and most
of the time dissembled, since in one particular way or another we
altogether lose ourselves amid beings."[51] The antidote is to become
what one is in true resoluteness, which will mean "first, bestowing
space [*das Raumgeben*] for beings in the whole; consequently, releasing oneself into nothing, which means freeing oneself from the
idols we all have and to which we are wont to go cringing; last, letting this suspense range where it will. . . ."[52] It is a question of
taking anxiety upon oneself[53] with lucid courage: "The anxiety of
the courageous. . . . stands . . . in secret union with the serenity
and gentleness of creative longing."[54] The references to the "idols
[*Götzen*] . . . to which we are wont to go cringing" and to "creative
longing" suggest that Heidegger has Nietzsche in mind and that
"true resoluteness" is a reappropriation of the doctrine of *amor fati*.
Amor fati is one's own true metaphysics: love of fate is owning up
to oneself as the inevitable source of metaphysical projections, such
as the projection of God or gods as the source of beings. One disowns oneself if one "idolizes" this projection, suppressing the fact
that it is a finite projection and treating God or gods as if they were
known, secure, absolute grounds. One can claim to discover an ul-

timate and absolute ground only by disowning one's own projection of this ground. But owning up to one's own projection of this "ultimate" ground spoils its absoluteness, for it is a grounded ground rather than an absolute, self-grounding ground. It is Dasein's fate to have to *be* the ground rather than *finding* a ground. Given this interpretation of *WM*, it would appear possible to subscribe to Walter Schulz's characterization of Heidegger's pre-*Kehre* position as "heroic nihilism," bearing in mind Schulz's warning that this position is not a glorification of Dasein's power but rather a coming to terms with Dasein's 'impotence' (*Ohnmacht*).[55]

It is also possible, with the help of *WM*, to argue that the 'phenomenon' of *SZ* turns out to be the present-at-hand (*vorhanden*) being. The following considerations would argue for this peculiar conclusion. The true Being of the ready-to-hand entity seems to be for the most part dissimulated, in accord with Heidegger's assertion that phenomena proximally and for the most part do *not* show themselves as they are in themselves. Why? We have seen in chapter 2 that the encounter with ready-to-hand beings requires a *forgetting* of one's Self.[56] Proximally and for the most part, phenomena are dissimulated because "we completely lose ourselves amid beings."[57] That is, for the most part we have already tried to fill the nothing with grounds and have 'interpreted'[58] entities by reference to those grounds. (For example, if the ground is God's creation, all entities are 'interpreted' as necessary creations, orderable on a scale of values established by scripture. If the ground is "they," entities are interpreted by what "they" do with them and say of them.) But in anxiety, phenomena stand forth in their naked presentness-at-hand. Thus Heidegger speaks of "the insignificance of world disclosed in anxiety." In anxiety "Environmental entities no longer have any involvement. . . . But this does not mean that in anxiety we experience something like the absence of what is present-at-hand within-the-world. The present-at-hand must be encountered in just *such* a way that it does *not* have *any* involvement whatsoever, but can show itself in an empty mercilessness."[59]

Therefore the 'world' is indeed unstable. Its particular historical content (or meaning) is determined by the prevailing answers given by the reigning metaphysics. The referential totality has a history. This explains why Heidegger can say in *SZ* that "Perhaps even readiness-to-hand and equipment have nothing to contribute as ontological clues in interpreting the primitive world"[60] and that "all beings whose kind of Being is of a character other than Dasein's [categorial beings] must be conceived as *unmeaning* [*unsinniges*], essentially devoid of any meaning at all. . . . And only that which is unmeaning can be absurd [*widersinnig*]. The present-at-hand, as Dasein encounters it, can, as it were, assault Dasein's Being; natural events, for instance, can break in upon us and destroy us."[61]

In the foregoing pages we have purposely pushed the existentialist and nihilist implications of Heidegger's pre-*Kehre* thought as far as they can be pushed, culminating in the assertion of a present-at-hand phenomenon by reference to which all meanings would appear merely human and merely ideal. It would appear that we have pushed Heidegger into a position close to that of Sartre, thereby contradicting the characterization of Heidegger's position offered in chapter 2. Furthermore, we seem now to have roughly aligned our interpretation of the early Heidegger with that of Schulz, Löwith, Ott, and other eminent Heidegger scholars.[62] But we have omitted one small consideration that may make a considerable difference: 'nothing' "is" itself 'Being'. Being is not something reached by Heidegger only after "the turn" by passing *beyond* 'nothing'.

III

Nothing does not occur by itself nor does it occur beside beings as if it were a kind of appendage to them. Nothing *makes possible* the revelation of beings as such for human Dasein. Nothing is not first of all the conceptual opposite of beings but rather belongs primordially to essence (Wesen) itself. *It is in the Being of beings that nothing's nihilation happens.*[63]

The Being of beings, I have argued, is for Heidegger their coming to be out of a prior and possibilizing ground. Contrary to the tradition, which seeks the ground of beings in *yet another being* as highest being or first cause, Heidegger argues that "ex nihilo omne ens qua ens fit." ("Every being is as such made out of nothing.")[64] This means that every being is in its Being made out of nothing rather than out of another being. Understood in the context of *WM*, this states that beings are not, as Western thought has generally supposed, traceable to a first, unconditioned, nonfinite, independent

cause. The Being of beings is essentially finite and relative to Dasein: "Only in the nothing of Dasein do beings as a whole become
themselves in accordance with their own possibility—that is, in a
finite way." [65] The ground of beings is finite and temporal; it is the
clearing of Dasein. Hence when metaphysics tries to look beyond
Dasein's own space and time for a ground it finds nothing. *If* Being
is taken to be the unconditioned, then the quest for it begins and
ends in nothing, the absence of Being.

But if Being is itself finite, nothing is not the absence of Being but
is the same as Being. In what sense? From the standpoint of the
tradition, beyond beings there is nothing (an absence of Being).
Heidegger's argument is that it is precisely beyond beings that
Being is to be found. Being is the other to beings. Being 'is' where
beings are not. But where beings are not there is nothing. Thus
Being is where *no-thing* is (where no beings are). Being is to be
found just where science and its implicit metaphysics find nothing.
This is intelligible only if one gives up the ontology of simple presentness in favor of a referential space-time ontology. But to invoke
a referential space-time ontology is precisely to acknowledge the
relativity of Being to Dasein, whose own traits temporality and spatiality are. [66] It is to invoke, as the locale of Being, a time-space that
is understood because Dasein, as a thrown and projective understanding, has always already been *there* as the projective articulation of that time-space. In the context of *WM* this means that beings
always come to be out of a prearticulated time-space which, as
other than those very beings, is nothing from the standpoint of
present-at-hand ontology. Dasein stands out into this nothing as
the being that occupies the place of nothing; this means that Dasein
is always already beyond its own present-at-hand entitativeness as
the prior thrown projection of the world-space within which all entities come to be (are identified and situated).

The 'beyond', or 'meta', of metaphysics refers to nothing as pure
absence only as long as ontology is solely an ontology of the physical entity (or is based upon 'physics'). But when ontology takes into
itself meaning, meaning-references, and prior temporal articulation,
then what had appeared as nothing now presents itself as Being, as
the ground of beings that is beyond and other than beings themselves. If, in other words, meaning and meaning-references are in a
significant sense 'something', then there is 'something' beyond all

beings and ontologically different from them—a something that is indeed not just 'something' additional but 'something' constitutive of the very possibility of the appearance of beings.

Metaphysics to be sure looks beyond beings for their ground but looks only for a ground modeled on the beings it seeks to ground. The chief idol "we all have and to which we are wont to go cringing" is the present-at-hand entity. (So metaphysical theology would like to make even God present-at-hand, a sort of permanent presence.) Heidegger wishes to suggest that, like Aaron, we have all idolized the concrete image and have thereby lost awareness of the source or origin of all concretion. But a true (eigentlich) metaphysics[67] would have to start with the recognition that it is always already grounded in a ground that is (a) ontologically different from beings and (b) relative to man's essence as outside "himself" (as a mere present entity) in a space-time that is always already understood and articulated. This will mean that all phenomena will have finite grounds, and grounds that are beyond entities themselves as conditions of their appearance. Thus every 'disclosing' is a limited (finite) disclosing in which human being participates, and is at the same time a 'closing' such that Dasein is equiprimordially in truth and in untruth.[68]

We can conclude that the 'nothing' of WM is the ground or 'clearing' of SZ. This means that the traditional metaphysical quest for a ground looks right past its own ground, as it must inevitably do so long as 'ground' means yet another entity.

We now ask again whether and in what sense the early Heidegger's position can be thought of as a "heroic nihilism." If 'nihilism' means the experience of the absence of an unconditioned entity as first cause or original and absolute ground, then Heidegger's position is nihilistic—but so, one might argue, is Kant's position in the First Critique. In this sense of 'nihilism', any position that restricts experience and knowledge to the spatiotemporally conditioned will count as nihilism. But if nihilism means the situating of present man such that he must invent meanings ex nihilo in a vain attempt to humanize an environment of beings that are experienced as in their Being devoid of significance, then one may argue that Heidegger's position is not 'nihilistic'. It asserts, on the contrary, that beings are always already significant, bound to man by a "precedent community of nature." Philosophical nihilism is explicable precisely as a forgetting of this precedent community of nature, the prior common ground of both the entity Dasein and all other phenomenal entities.

In what sense, then, can the situation of Dasein call for "heroism"? If Dasein, by virtue of historically forgetting the ontological difference between beings and their Being, has quested for an unconditioned being as a *fundamentum inconcussum* on the basis of which man can free himself from a temporal fate and release himself into an Eleatic permanence, then owning up to his finite situation will inevitably provoke a rebirth of the very anxiety from which he ordinarily seeks release in an unconditioned absolute. To appropriate, rather than flee from, this anxiety requires 'courage'. But it is not the courage of living in sheer groundlessness. It is the courage of owning up to an *historical* ground, a relative and finite ground in which man as Dasein is already participant. As finite, this ground is a "groundless ground"[69]—that is, it is not in turn grounded in the unconditioned. But, as always prior basis, it remains a ground. The absence of an unconditioned ground is what first frees a space for (makes possible) a finite ground. If this position surrenders the quest for an unconditioned ground, it can thereby gain awareness of a precedent community of nature. The price of a meaningful world is 'courageous' renunciation of the view that meaning resides only in the unconditioned. If meaning and value reside only in the unconditioned, all conditioned or historical beings are *ipso facto* devalued. Thus "the struggle against *Vorhandenheit*" must be the struggle against the Eleatic ideal.[70] This struggle is at the same time the return to our ownmost way of being, so that we discover the source of historical nihilism in the forgetfulness of the precedent community of nature. This recognition of the *historical* character of nihilism becomes the prerequisite for passing beyond nihilism.

Is the 'instability' of 'world', to which we have called attention, cancelled by the foregoing considerations? *When judged by the standard of the unconditioned*, world is unstable. But one can equally well say that *when judged by the standard of nihilism*, world is the precedent community of meaning that nihilism has overlooked, and of which nihilism itself is one example. As Nietzsche saw, nihilism and the quest for the unconditioned are two sides of the same coin.[71] The precondition for nihilism is the establishment of the

Eleatic ideal. Renunciation of the Eleatic ideal will mean renunciation of the tendency to judge stability by an ahistoric criterion. One will have to settle for a relative stability. Stability will have to be reconceived as the *relative* linearity of historical inheritance and revision. This will mean, in effect, the liberation of Hegel from the Eleatic remnant that survives in his thinking: there is stability insofar as the past survives as the ground of future reappropriations of it. Heidegger wishes to show that there is a sense in which the past appropriates the future to itself. His notions of 'projection', 'fore-having', 'world', and 'repetition' are ways of delineating a sort of "evolutionary" revision that treads a thin line between static permanence and revolutionary discontinuity.[72]

It is in this frame of reference that Heidegger's treatment of the present-at-hand must be understood. We have seen that it is possible to read the early Heidegger as maintaining that the present-at-hand entity, when it comes explicitly to the fore or "breaks in upon us," shatters the referential totality and proves that world is unstable and 'subjective'. Sartre, among others, seems to have interpreted Heidegger in this way: the present-at-hand has an independence of human meaning such that meanings glide across its surface without sticking.

Now Heidegger, like any recent thinker who is to avoid a rank idealism, must leave room for the dimension of being that Sartre calls "transphenomenality." But we must observe with great care just *how* Heidegger accomplishes this. First of all, as we have seen, he holds that phenomena for the most part do not show themselves as they are in themselves. Since phenomena for the most part show themselves within a concernful referential totality, we might suspect that when phenomena *do* show themselves as they are in themselves, they are freed from concern and from the referential totality and stand forth as purely present-at-hand. But is this what he really intends to say? We take note of the following passages:

> These 'Things' never show themselves proximally as they are for themselves. . . . The more we seize hold of [a tool] and use it, the more primordial does our relation to it become, and the more unveiledly it is encountered as that which it is—as equipment. . . . The kind of Being which equipment possesses—in which it manifests itself in its own right—we call *"readiness-to-hand"* [*Zuhandenheit*]. Only because equipment has *this* 'Being-

in-itself' and does not merely occur, is it manipulable in the broadest sense and at our disposal.[73]

Note Heidegger's dramatic revision of the notion of the in-itself. He places 'Being-in-itself' in inverted commas to show that his usage of the expression differs from ordinary philosophical usage. Yet he intends to say that the phenomenon is internally related to its world in such a way that meaning-references enter into its very nature; its world is "in" it. The ready-to-hand entity "has a usability which belongs to it *essentially*. . . ."[74] Yet proximally and for the most part its Being as ready-to-hand does not force itself upon our attention. The phenomenon dissimulates itself: "The peculiarity of what is proximally ready-to-hand is that, in its readiness-to-hand, it must, as it were, withdraw [*zurückzuziehen*] in order to be ready-to-hand quite authentically. That with which our everyday dealings proximally dwell is not the tools themselves [*die Werkzeuge selbst.*]."[75]

When seen in this way, the phenomenon's showing itself as it is in itself is *not* a loss of its ready-to-hand referentiality. What rather happens is that in certain circumstances attention is called to the entity in such a way that it stands out from its proximal and *essential* subservience to the referential totality. The broken tool shows itself as it is in itself precisely when it breaks down, for it is then that attention is drawn to its referential Being, its essential place and role in a world of concerns.[76] This means that the Being of the ready-to-hand phenomenon appears as such precisely when the entity obtrudes as present-at-hand. The relation between readiness-to-hand and presence-at-hand is not dialectical. The passage from the experience of the ready-to-hand to the experience of the presence-at-hand *of* the ready-to-hand is a passage from the self-dissimulating phenomenon to the manifest phenomenon. The phenomenon is manifest when it *presents itself* (is present-at-hand) *as* an entity that is in its very Being ready-to-hand. In the terminology of *WM*, the manifest phenomenon is what it is "as such" precisely when it is revealed "in the whole" or "totality." Thus phenomenological ontology is in a certain sense the real fulfillment of the metaphysical quest, which Heidegger defines as the "winning back" of beings "as such *and* in the whole."[77] (The entity is present as such, as ready, only in the referential whole.) Heidegger is arguing that phenomenology can understand the phenomenon as what it is, because phenomenology can *bring together* the entity "as such" and the entity "in the whole" in such a way as to show that the entity is what it is "as such" only as it is "in the whole."

IV

The foregoing analysis has, despite all, not yet sufficiently clarified the relation of the ready-to-hand to the present-at-hand. This clarification will require a rather complex analysis if we are to grasp the real extent to which the early Heidegger has saved beings from a "nihilistic" loss of their meaning.

Does not an analysis of artifacts (tools, equipment, hammers, chairs, etc.) leave out the Being of nature? It seems that the artifact has meaning "built into it" in a way that raw nature does not. In *SZ* Heidegger counters:

> "nature" is not to be understood as that which is just present-at-hand, nor as the *power of nature.* The wood is a forest of timber, the mountain a quarry of rock; the river is water-power, the wind is wind 'in the sails.' As the 'environment' is discovered, the 'nature' thus discovered is encountered too. If its kind of Being as ready-to-hand is disregarded, this 'nature' itself can be discovered and defined simply in its pure presence-at-hand. But when this happens, the 'nature' which 'stirs and strives,' which assails us and enthralls us as a landscape, remains hidden. The botanist's plants are not the flowers of the hedgerow; the 'source' which the geographer establishes for a river is not the 'springhead in the dale.' [78]

One is reminded of Sartre's delineation of "the world of artists and prophets" to which Husserl has returned us. I interpret Heidegger as arguing that, from the standpoint of phenomenological ontology, the absoluteness of the distinction between the artifactual and the natural is challenged. Because 'nature' is always already articulated as what it is *in the whole,* natural *phenomena* are original unities. *Out of* these original phenomena one may analytically distinguish a useful "aspect," a material "aspect," etc. But to equate the material aspect of a natural event with its Being is to dissimulate or hide the phenomenon in its Being. Nature is always articulated, identified, located as what it is within the referential

space-time field. ". . . Even Nature is historical."[79] In short, presentness-at-hand is the presentness-at-hand *of* a phenomenon. Presentness-at-hand is a necessary *aspect* of the phenomenon ("only by
reason of something present-at-hand, 'is there' anything ready-to-
hand")[80] but sheer presentness is not sufficient to characterize the
full Being of phenomena as meaning-beings.

Can this interpretation, however, come to terms with Heidegger's
aforementioned assertion that "all entities whose kind of Being is of
a character other than Dasein's must be conceived as *unmeaning* [*unsinniges*], essentially devoid of any meaning at all"? This is one of
the most problematic assertions in the entire Heideggerian corpus.

Looking back to Heidegger's distinction between 'existentialia'
and 'categories', we find that the former refer to "Dasein's characters of Being" and the latter to "characteristics of Being of entities
whose character is not that of Dasein."[81] Heidegger subsequently
distinguishes two types of categorial Being:

> 1. the Being of beings within-the-world which we proximally
> encounter (readiness-to-hand); 2. the Being *of* beings (pres
> ence-at-hand), which is encounterable and determinable by a
> discovering which passes independently through [*in einem
> eigenständig entdeckenden Durchgang*] the entity as proximally
> encountered.[82]

Heidegger's German refers to *both* categories as the "Being of beings" (Sein des Seienden), but in the case of the second category he
italicizes the 'of' (Sein *des* Seienden). We interpret the italicized 'of'
to mean that presence-at-hand is the Being *of* ready-to-hand beings, in the sense that we discover the full Being of the ready-to-
hand entity only when we pass through its initial appearance and
encounter its presentness as such. Its presentness is found to be the
Being *of* its readiness in the sense that no being may be ready-to-
hand without having presentness. So here—as in *WM*—the disclosure of the presentness-at-hand *of* the entity is the coming to the
fore of the sheer thatness *of* the what, the obtrusion of the "as suchness" of beings which are at the same time "in the whole." In the
terminology of *WM*, the whatness-with-reference-to-the-whole of
beings does not disappear, but rather only "recedes" (*wegrückt*)
into the background.[83] But the possibility of the apprehension of an
entity in its pure presentness is that it be already there in its what-

ness, its concrete particularity (as ready-to-hand, as referentially identified).[84] We could not wonder or be anxious about the fact that there are beings at all—their sheer existence or presentness—unless these beings were already familiar to us as beings.

We come back now to our problematic passage: categorial beings are *unmeaning*. The reason Heidegger gives for this assertion is that "meaning is an *existentiale* of Dasein, not a property attaching to entities, lying 'behind' them, or floating somewhere as an 'intermediate domain'."[85] This assertion is altogether unintelligible if Dasein is taken to be 'present man'. Worldhood is an existentiale of Dasein, and beings *are* within this world. The essence of man is not within him as present entity but "beyond" him in the world. Meaning is worldly. But world is not an 'intermediate domain'; it is rather the site of beings themselves that *are* in the world. World is thus "ontologically different" than beings, yet precisely on this account it is a condition of their Being. If meaning were not ontologically different than beings, beings would contain meanings as simple 'properties' and there would be no precedent community of nature between Dasein and categorial beings. Dasein would play no role in their Being. Heidegger argues, on the contrary, that the being comes to be as phenomenon by entering into a space-time field of relations (meaning-references) that are neither things nor free-floating meanings but are the articulation of the nature of beings by reference to other beings. Thus meanings essentially belong to the whole. Meanings are the structure of world, relative to which entities are articulable as what they are. The forest first and only becomes "a forest" (which *is* what it is) when it is articulated *as* a forest by reference to the surrounding plains, rivers, etc. that bound it. "Forest" is "its" assigned and proper meaning, but it is not a *property* of the forest, nor is it something tacked on to the forest from the outside.[86] It is the forest's referential (articulated) Being—and only on the basis of this referential Being can the forest show itself as "a forest in-itself" in its independence *of* other beings. Its independence is precisely independence of the other beings by reference to which it shows itself as what it is. It is "as such" only "within the whole."

Only so, Heidegger is maintaining, can one account for both the intelligibility *and* the independence of the phenomenon. If the phenomenon "has" its meaning as a simple property, it becomes wholly unclear how we could reach that inherent intelligibility without being given divine interpretive clues.[87] And if the meaning were simply "intended" by a present subject it would bear no real (internal) relation to the phenomenon. But if the phenomenon were restricted solely to its present worldly meaning, it would lose its independence and it would be impossible to account for the process of discovery, whereby new traits of the entity are brought to light. How can the wind *be* "wind in the sails" and *also* be the subject of future meteorological and chemical analyses? This is only possible if all phenomena hide themselves in the very process of showing themselves. Heidegger therefore distinguishes between original disclosure and complete disclosure, and in such a way as to show that disclosure need not be complete in order to be 'true'. In fact the original disclosure of the wind as wind, which is a 'true' uncovering, is the very basis and possibility of subsequent uncovering of physicochemical traits *of* the wind. This is simply to say that investigation *of* something presupposes a prior familiarity with that something—a precedent community of nature. In the terminology of *WM*, a being can be both 'familiar' and 'strange', and in such a way that its familiarity masks its strangeness. In the terminology of *KPM*, understanding may at one and the same time be 'valid' and 'finite'.

But if understanding is finite, if the phenomenon is not only revealed but concealed, then the phenomenon essentially surpasses the very meaning that reveals it. Phenomenological ontology "asks about Being itself insofar as Being enters into the intelligibility of Dasein" and yet there is a "legitimate task of grasping the present-at-hand in its essential unintelligibility."[88] Owing to the finitude of understanding and articulation, phenomena essentially surpass the meaning and intelligibility that open them up to us at all. The present-at-hand is not worldless,[89] but neither is it limited to its present worldly appearance. This is only to say that entities surpass their referential Being. This is Heidegger's basic response to the enormously difficult problems of reconciling truth with incompleteness and with relativity.

To summarize, the phenomenon's Being (where 'Being' is understood as source and ground) is dual.[90] Ordinary metaphysical anxiety calls attention to one aspect of this ground, namely the sheer, awesome, strange presentness of the phenomenon as simply 'there' without any reason for being there and as essentially exceeding the meaning and intelligibility Dasein has assigned to it. When this metaphysical anxiety is truly owned up to, however, the other aspect of the phenomenon's ground reappears: Dasein's own world as the condition of both the phenomenon's presence for us and its intelligibility. No phenomenon may be where both conditions do not obtain, and present man's experience is always conditioned already by both aspects of this ground. Dasein is at one and the same time (a) a *general* clearing, site, or 'opening' that "makes room for" or is inherently open to the appearance of the new and the unanticipated;[91] and (b) an ontically *particularized* clearing—a 'world'—in which particular phenomena in a particular referential totality have always occurred already and hence make possible *and* condition the particular meanings man presently and in future experiences. This particular referential totality, we have seen, is not simply individual but rather is communal in its meaning. Thus the "precedent community of nature" is quite literally communal and it is incumbent on true resoluteness to own up to this prior communality.

V

If truly resolute Dasein owns up to this prior communality as a kind of persistence of the past in grounding the future, it must at the same time own up to the historicality of this communal referential totality. This means, we have noted, that the future meaning of the inherited referential totality is modifiable by individual and group decision. In the process of owning up to one's inevitable determination by the inherited world, by prior projection, one may modify one's determination not in such a way as to escape future determination but in such a way as to play a decisive role in the determination that one will in future have to endure. This is to assume one's 'destiny' as a historical being that plays a 'creative' role in laying down (projecting) the very determinations to which it is already and will subsequently be subject. It is a matter of owning up to the limited process of revision to which Dasein's spatiotemporal structure has committed it.

But what, one must ask, is this process of historical revision directed toward? The fact that it is always based in a communal or social inheritance suggests that historical action is not simply the sum of individual projects. Inherited historical projects are communal, although 'individualized' and resolute Dasein must take an individuating stand regarding these inherited projects. Is there a common theme or goal evident in all these projects? Does *SZ*, like *EN*, contain an explicit theory of motivation? Heidegger implies that much human activity serves the goal of escaping anxiety and its revelation of "the manifest burden of Being." [92] But the possibility of a courageous resoluteness in the face of anxiety shows that escape from anxiety is not necessarily a universal motive. Anxiety itself, however, affords the key to motivation: "anxiety discloses Dasein *as Being-possible.*" [93]

Heidegger claims that "historiology will disclose the quiet force [*Kraft*] of the possible." [94] This statement should be associated with another: "everything is haunted by the *enigma of Being*, and . . . by that of motion [*Bewegung*]." [95] The force of the possible is the force of motion, the motive power (*Bewegungskraft*). Motion (*Be-weg-ung*) is one's movement along the way or path (*Weg*). Motive power is what moves one along one's way (*Be*-weg-*ungs*-kraft). One's motive or reason for moving is *Beweggrund*, the ground of action. To be without motive is to be *grundlos*, to have lost the ground on which one must make one's way or path. One makes one's way "in the world"—world and its entities appear to be the ground (*Grund*). But world is an existentiale of Dasein—what Dasein has to be rather than what Dasein has—so that "Dasein is its basis existently" (*Das Dasein ist sein Grund existierend*). [96] This world-ground is as such ("world as world") a nothing. [97] Dasein must lay the ground for its way as it goes. What "moves" it to lay this ground is its understanding that it has to. The primary ekstasis of understanding (*Verstehen*) is the future. [98] But the future is as-yet-nothing, hence it is only possible. In having to lay the very ground on which it will walk, Dasein is condemned to actualize the possible, to fill the nothing with itself, to continue laying the ground that it has always already laid. The answer to the enigma of motion is the quiet force of the possible. Dasein must keep on actualizing the possible as it always has. The remembrance of the past is the awareness of it as the actualization of possibilities that one is fated to keep on actualizing, for history is "the 'recurrence' [*Wiederkehr*] of the possible." [99] *Amor fati* becomes *amor potestatis;* what eternally recurs is the possible. The motive power of history is the portentous power of the possible, and the real future is the fated reappropriation of the possible. The riddle of Being is the same as the riddle of motion, and it is continually answered by the actualizing of the possible.

The form of this motion—at least in our tradition—is the metaphysical quest for an answer to the riddle of Being. "Dasein manifests itself as *in need of* the understanding of Being." [100] "There is" Being rather than nothing because Dasein makes there be Being rather than nothing. Metaphysics (the quest for a ground) is history—Dasein's perpetual self-grounding. History is Dasein's motion on a path across its own ground laid in "creative longing." [101] The motor of history is the anxious longing to sustain Being across time by a continuous creation. Ekstasis is "the pain" of the necessity and "the unshakable joy" [102] of the possibility of finding oneself by losing oneself in the "rapture" of care. The error of the history of metaphysics, owing to forgetting, is that it has sought Being in the one place where finite Dasein cannot find it—in the nontemporal and ahistoric. The tragic irony of the history of metaphysics is that it has quested in the farness of the transcendent unconditioned for what has always been nearest already, the ground of beings. Therefore the history of metaphysics and its ontology must be 'destroyed' in such a way as to prepare for the future 'coming-on' of Being in time, where it has from the beginning always occurred. To destroy the history of metaphysics is therefore to go back into its own ground by remembering that this ground is already there. To destroy the history of metaphysics is in effect to see man as a "bridge"; [103] man goes beyond himself by completing a circle back to his own beginning, coming back into his ownmost Being in time. This is the precondition for Dasein's entering into its "supreme greatness," [104] which it denies itself so long as it seeks 'joy' without 'pain'—that is, Being without time. Thus phenomenological ontology raises the possibility of Dasein's 'homecoming' in its own time. If Dasein as care bears the pain of finitude, Dasein also bears in finite form the divine power of "creating" Being. [105] Dasein is fated to assume part of the power which it has disowned by metaphysically ceding it to an unconditioned being. [106] Heidegger calls upon Dasein to cease the self-abnegating surrender of its own power by remembering that it is powerless to surrender it and has always already exercised it.

It should now be clear how naturally "the turn" (*Kehre*)—which is the turn back (*Rückkehr*) into the ground of metaphysics and thus the turn into (*Einkehr*) Dasein's always prior ground—grows out of Heidegger's early thinking. If the authentic future is a renewed appropriation of inheritance in a repetition that has become resolute, then human history can only go forward appropriately (*eigentlich*) by going back into its beginning. Division II of SZ thus begins this reappropriation by turning back into the historical ground of the present everydayness described in Division I. But there arises in Heidegger's thinking the need to repeat Division II still more primordially (*ursprünglicher*), to bring understanding closer to the origin, the original leap (*Ur-sprung*). So far, everything would lead us to believe that this 'origin' had been reached by the description of primal anxious wonder in WM. But, I suspect, one problem remained to haunt Heidegger, as it has haunted us in this chapter.

That problem is the status of 'world'. Heidegger's treatment of history in Division II shows how intent he is upon retaining for the historical world just as much constancy and persistence as he can—*precisely because* of the vehemence of his assault on ahistoric permanence. In the early Sartre one senses a certain almost masochistic and rather French enjoyment in the volatizing of man's idols, certainties, and alleged modes of stability.[107] Heidegger, however, goes out of his way to warn us that he is not 'volatizing' the world, not 'subjectivizing' the world, not condemning man to the arbitrary.[108] "The steadiness of existence is not interrupted . . . but confirmed in the moment of vision."[109] He is not, he wants to show, condemning us to historicism.[110] These repeated warnings—all to the effect that the temporalizing of Being is not the destruction of constancy—betray, one suspects, a realization that loss of constancy may be precisely the result. As a thinker with great confidence in the historical power of thought,[111] Heidegger was worried by the necessary vehemence of his own assault on the ahistoric. As an early and serious student of theology, he was all too aware of the stake historical man has had in the certitudes and constancies of religion. To attack these metaphysical constancies is to appropriate to oneself the burden of maintaining such stability as can legitimately be maintained. The danger is nihilism—though we have tried to show that this danger is one that the early Heidegger is already trying to combat, rather than casting himself unambiguously into a nihilistic position.[112] The early Heidegger sees Dasein's own self-constancy supplanting a disowning constancy,[113] which tries to drag the past into the present, with true self-maintenance of its inheritance. He even argues that the consequence may be a still greater constancy that renounces the perpetual quest for "the modern" and "the novel."[114] But the danger remains. To move from the 'undifferentiated" way of existing[115] into an explicit awareness of owning up and disowning as possible ways of existing is to run the risk of releasing man into a self-conscious and willful disowning that deliberately seeks to turn its back on the inherited past. Therefore Heidegger must stress that release from unreflective constancy calls Dasein to assume the burden of constancy by owning up to its own collective inheritance. Ironically, Heidegger's own effort to exemplify this reflective assumption of tradition commits him in the Germany of 1933 to a position that appears to confirm the nihilistic danger of his position, and—I suggest without evidence—Heidegger's recognition of this unfortunate irony may well have been the proximate cause of the *Kehre*.[116]

The danger is that world, when anxiety reveals "world as world," will appear as a 'nothing' arbitrarily fillable with anything whatsoever. If the history of metaphysics is a record of the assertion of impossible grounds and idols, does this not reinforce the impression that world is a matrix for the assertion of the arbitrary, or perhaps the conventional? Might not history be the playground for that free exercise of the imagination that Kant is alleged to have feared?[117] In that case, the 'foundation' would indeed be no foundation. *KPM* lends credence to the suspicion that 'world' is an empty space to be imaginatively filled by historical Dasein. "To hold oneself in advance in such a playspace [*Spielraum*] and to form it originally is nothing other than transcendence, which marks all finite comportment with regard to beings."[118] To combat this danger it therefore must be shown that the disowning history of metaphysics was necessary. It was a fated forgetfulness and not an arbitrarily willful series of subjective inventions. But if the inauthentic history of metaphysics was necessary, this suggests that world is 'ruled' by a *particular* 'directive' (*Geschick*) to which Western Dasein has been subject. If such is the case, then may it not be the case that world is always ruled by a particular directive, so that even future Dasein might be subject to a mode of constancy, yet one that might be truly appro-

priated? Where would one look for such a directive? The later Heidegger's thinking will in effect increasingly center on *Rede*, discourse, the least developed and most obscurely treated of the four
fundamental disclosive existentialia of *SZ*, yet perhaps the most important for the question of Being as *meaning*. Heidegger understands *Rede* as "the articulation of intelligibility" underlying both
interpretation and assertion. This articulation gets expressed in and
is existentially 'language' (*Sprache*).[119] This suggests that language
is the way in which the meaningful structure of the world comes to
expression. Heidegger will ask how the meaningful structure of the
world came to expression in the Greek language and 'directed'
subsequent thought. The Greeks express the intelligible structure or
meaning of the world in terms of presentness. *SZ* offers another
expression of the intelligible structure of the world: readiness-to-
hand. But if *SZ* shows that the directive of presentness has overlooked readiness-to-hand as an articulation of the world's intelligibility, it does not show that readiness-to-hand is a universal
or necessary constancy.

"The turn" is a "shift of accent" in a number of interrelated respects.[120] For our study, the most important shift of emphasis is
that by which Heidegger explores the ontological articulation of that
world ground or time-space which, from the standpoint of the ancient ontology, must finally appear as a nothingness. The turn is the
movement through *apparent* nothingness to a "forgotten" and "concealed fullness."[121] This concealment has governed the appearance
of beings as grounded in nothing rather than in a fullness. Being
has dissembled itself as nothing.

If the success of the phenomenological program hangs, as I have
argued, on the constitutive power of internal relations, then a fundamental task of the *Kehre* is to show that internal relations do not
succumb to a nihilism that leaves pure present-at-hand existentia
"essentially devoid of any meaning," as the sole mode of constancy,
freeing Dasein to regard meaning or essentia as a meta-physical creation of the decisive will. The great unresolved danger of *SZ* is that
awareness of the ontological difference between beings and their
Being may be interpreted as awareness of the insufficiency, relativity, and virtuality of meaning by comparison with the sheer existentia or "thatness" of beings that are essentially "unintelligible"
and "devoid of any meaning." If the "projection of world" is, as

WG argues, the "throwing of the projected world over beings,"[122] then the ontological difference is in danger of becoming an ontological dualism. If whatness (essentia) and thatness (existentia) fall asunder, completion of the phenomenological program is impossible.[123]

Another way of characterizing the problem would be to say that, in restricting his case for continuity and stable structure to the existential-ontological level (Dasein's own structures), Heidegger runs the risk of allowing that very sense of continuity and stability to be volatized at the existentiell-ontic level. The existential (structural) always-prior clearing sounds stable; its ontic-existentiell-epochal content sounds variable and volatile.

Yet a third way of stating the problem would be to say that Dasein's having always already thrown itself, in transcendence, 'over' or 'around' beings in the form of world proves to be insufficient for joining meaning to beings so long as Heidegger accords Dasein the 'ownmost' power to reform 'decisively' the significance of the inherited world that surrounds beings that are "essentially unintelligible" and "meaningless."[124]

The presence of this danger in SZ is the chief sign that "the struggle against *Vorhandenheit*" is not yet over. The presence of this residual danger in SZ suggests that Heidegger is not quite free of responsibility for the way in which Sartre reappropriated him. As long as meaning is "thrown over" beings that are inherently meaningless, no real reconciliation of essence and existence, of meaning and entity, of ideality and actuality, is possible. Insofar as SZ is, in accordance with its own principles, historically conditioned, it exhibits the influence of the ancient ontology it challenges.

5

The Ethics of Play
and Freedom:
Conversion

SARTRE WOULD appear, in a general way, to have followed Husserl's path toward "the things themselves." Taking up the drive of "modern thought" toward "the monism of the phenomenon"[1]—the synthesis of appearance and reality, of thought and being—Sartre seeks to ground this synthesis through analytic reflection. The movement of reflexive withdrawal will prepare the way for return to the phenomenon. Yet, as we have seen, analytic reflection isolates ontological relata that resist the movement of return to phenomena; for in the light of analysis, the phenomenon has to be regarded as the unstable fusion of relata that in their antithetical nature resist fusion. A reflexive and lucid awareness of the impossibility of a genuine synthesis thus appears to forfeit the possibility of achieving synthesis except through self-surrender of one's lucidity. Since the analysis that was to ground a new synthesis appears to preclude it, Sartre's thought at the end of *EN* is stuck in reflexive withdrawal—an ironic state of affairs for what has so often been called a "philosophy of engagement" or "commitment."

Sartre concludes *EN* with "metaphysical hints" and "ethical perspectives" in part because the return from reflexive withdrawal has become both a metaphysical and a moral dilemma. Ontological analysis has uncovered an antithesis that can only be bridged, if it can be bridged at all, by a speculative metaphysical leap that might make meaningful cosmic drama out of what ontology has found to be a vain drive toward an impossible synthesis. Ontological analysis has likewise disclosed that man is responsible for the significance of his world, but that this significance is supplied by him without ground. With his situation thus analytically clarified, man is called upon to return to the world by choosing himself, which means to choose at the same time the meaning of the world.[2] The return from reflexive withdrawal becomes a moral decision.

Since phenomenological ontology is purely descriptive, metaphysics exceeds the scope of ontology in requiring a speculative
leap, and ethics exceeds the scope of ontology in requiring a moral
leap. When he asserts that "it is not possible to derive imperatives
from its [ontology's] indicatives,"[3] Sartre has a triple motive: first,
to preserve the traditional distinction between philosophy and
praxis, the region of cognition and the region of decision; second,
to guarantee the possibility of Kierkegaardian ethical decisiveness;[4]
and third, to reprimand Heidegger for allegedly permitting ethical
notions to slip in by the ontological back door, for Sartre had
argued that Heidegger's expressions 'authentic' and 'inauthentic'
"are questionable and not very sincere, owing to their implicit
moral content."[5]

Because Sartre's 'conclusion' consists of delineation of possible
metaphysical and moral leaps beyond ontology, it is, strictly speaking, not the anticipated conclusion at all—the return to the phenomenon—but the confession of ontology's inability to reach the
phenomenon by reflective phenomenological analysis. The return to
the phenomenon is to be accomplished metaphysically or morally.[6]
The 'conclusion' is inconclusive because it in fact presents Sartre
with what will become the decisive problem of his career: *how* to
return to the historical world, since one in any case will do so.
Sartre is already at work on this problem in *EN* itself. To be sure,
the book could be construed as precluding the possibility of resolving the problem. Lacking firm suprahistorical ground from which
one might envisage history as the playing out of a cosmic drama of
attempted reconciliation between in-itself and for-itself, Sartre appears to settle for the historical judgment that man, not the cosmos
itself, is the vain effort to ground himself without losing himself.
Sartre appears to construe Heidegger's assertion that "Metaphysics
. . . is *Dasein* itself"[17] to mean that man is the unrealizable quest
to ground himself. Given this conclusion, it makes no difference
whether one gets drunk alone or becomes a leader of nations—yet
the solitary drunkard is at least lucid. Sartre does not settle for
becoming a solitary drunk, nor does he wish to renounce the lucidity gained by reflective analysis. The problem may therefore be
characterized as that of reentering the world without loss of lucidity. It is a problem already familiar to Nietzsche: "Understanding
kills action, for in order to act we require the veil of illusion."[8]

If *EN* appears to preclude solution of the problem by categorically describing all human action as a passionate sacrifice of lucidity in order that the world might appear meaningful, there are nevertheless certain counterindications. Simone de Beauvoir has implied that the book is not to be construed as a categorical or universal description of human experience.[9] In support of this interpretation one can adduce two famous footnotes:

> this is not to say that one cannot radically escape bad faith. But this implies a reappropriation [*reprise*] of a corrupted being by itself which we shall call authenticity, but whose description has no place here.[10]
>
> These considerations do not rule out the possibility of an ethics of deliverance and salvation. But this can be attained only through a radical conversion of which we cannot speak here.[11]

If these references to a possible moral resolution are scrupulously assigned to footnotes, we can nevertheless locate their real meaning in the descriptive text proper.[12] Sartre speaks of a "conversion" that is "radical," of an "instant" that is "liberating," of a "revolution" that is "reflective," and of a "reflection" that is "purifying." We shall find that all these notions are to be understood in terms of two others: ambiguity and play.

I

We begin with Sartre's analysis of 'the instant'—a notion that recurs with great frequency in *EN*.[13] We have already surmised that it is a notion which represents Sartre's reappropriation of Heidegger's 'moment of vision' (*Augenblick*), the moment when one explicitly owns up to the real ekstatic introplay of the three temporal ekstases in the process of making-present. The instant may be defined as an allegedly discrete segment of time, wholly distinct from prior and future moments of time, thus 'in-itself'. It is what it is. "The instant is . . . non-temporal."[14] Sartre at first appears to reject entirely the notion of the instant; there is "no dissolution of continuity within the flux of temporal unfolding."[15] Rather than a discrete sequence or series of conscious events separated by nothingness, consciousness is continuous, and nothingness is continuous. As there is always consciousness, there is always a "nothing" that is "absolutely impassable" so that "the prior consciousness. . . . is put out of the game and out of the circuit, between parentheses. . . ."[16] This means that "the prior consciousness" is not a discrete unit but is *continuously* surpassed. The past is continuously added to, without a break. Otherwise, Sartre argues, one will be stuck with the insoluble Cartesian problem of trying to put into relation moments of consciousness that are not in relation. The doubting *cogito* is in fact already a temporalizing consciousness that doubts past belief for the sake of the future possibility of removing the doubt.[17]

It is therefore the continuous ekstasis of consciousness that rules out the instant. Consciousness is not first an internal instant that subsequently transcends itself into past and future; consciousness is always already and continuously "beside itself" ("in ecstasy"). We are therefore surprised to read that "in the pure subjectivity of the *instantaneous cogito* . . . we must uncover the original act by which man is to himself his own nothingness." And again, "What . . . must consciousness be, in the *instantaneity* of the pre-reflective *cogito,* if man is to be capable of bad faith?"[18] Are instantaneity and ekstasis compatible after all? We must bear in mind that Sartre says that this "pure subjectivity of the instantaneous *cogito*" is reached by an "analytic regression."[19]

Happily for our study, Sartre's analysis of the instant is developed through criticism of Heidegger's position:

can one even conceive of a truth of the instant? And does not the *cogito* in its own way engage the past and the future? Heidegger is so convinced that Husserl's "I think" is a fascinating and lime-laden snare for larks that he has altogether shunned recourse to consciousness in his description of Dasein. His purpose is to present it immediately as *care*—that is, as escaping from itself in the projection of itself toward the possibilities which it *is*. It is this projection of itself beyond itself which he calls "understanding" (*Verstand*). . . . But this attempt to present *first* Dasein's escape from itself will in turn meet with insurmountable difficulties: one cannot *first* suppress the dimension "consciousness," not even if one intends subsequently to reestablish it. Understanding only has meaning if it is consciousness of understanding. . . . So we are thrown right back towards the cogito![20]

The substance of Sartre's charge is that Heidegger, in his effort to escape subjectivity, has overreacted against both Descartes and Husserl. The passage begins with a question about the 'instant' of the Cartesian cogito. Sartre argues that the cogito ekstatically surpasses its own alleged instantaneity. It is not in-itself. But Heidegger rejects the cogito altogether. Sartre believes Heidegger rightly rejects "Descartes' substantialist illusion"[21] that conceives the cogito on the model of a thing, to which thought is attributable as a property. But Heidegger fails to salvage the legitimate and necessary meaning of the cogito, which Sartre calls "the prereflective cogito." All consciousness is consciousness (of) *itself* in the very process of being consciousness of something *beyond* itself.[22] That is, it is consciousness of itself *as* consciousness of something, or is aware of being aware. Sartre has persuasively argued that without this "self-awareness" it is impossible to understand how the unreflective consciousness could possibly shift to the reflective attitude and impossible to understand our constant awareness of what we are aware of as 'other', as 'there'.[23]

Sartre is maintaining that Heidegger pushes the notion of the ekstasis of understanding so far as not to account for that which the ek-stasis understandingly stands out *from*, namely itself. But if consciousness stands out from itself in the ekstases of time, what is the temporal status of the 'itself' from which it stands out? We find Sartre's answer elsewhere in the text:

> But this flight constitutes in contingency precisely what is fled: the for-itself which is fled is left *in place*. . . . There is never an instant where one can affirm that the for-itself is, precisely because the for-itself never is. To the contrary, temporality wholly temporalizes itself as *refusal of the instant*.[24]

If the for-itself "never is," how can it be left "in place"? What Sartre is maintaining is that the Cartesian *cogito* falsely isolates one aspect of consciousness (its 'immanence' in the instant) and the Heideggerian 'understanding' falsely isolates the other aspect of consciousness (its ekstatic transcendence). Descartes must be used to correct Heidegger and Heidegger must be used to correct Descartes. The meaning of Sartre's expression "refusal of the instant" is therefore that consciousness is neither an immanence nor a transcendence but rather a transcending *of* its immanence, a 'dyad'.[25] In

Husserl's terms, there is an immediate unity or simultaneity of the noetic and noematic. Consciousness is a relation between nothing and something. As awareness *of something*, its content is a transcendent object; as *awareness* of something, it is a neutral openness (a 'nothing') for the object, deferring entirely to the object. Its 'place', then, must be "in-itself" an empty place if it is to be a place in which the object can present itself as *it* is and without addition or distortion. A film cannot record a scene "as it is" unless prior to this exposure it is unexposed, a blank, a nothingness (and it is a commonplace that insofar as we are "filled with ourselves" we are not open to others as they are in themselves). But unlike the camera, consciousness is aware of its own nothingness, of that perpetual deference to the object that Sartre calls "losing oneself" in order that the world may be born.[26] Consciousness is prereflectively aware of the ontological difference between itself and its intentional object.

The instant defers to the temporal ekstases. The nothing defers to something. The instant is precisely the nothingness that is always transcended toward something, "filled up" with something. As a nothingness, the instant "never is." The empty place of the instant is the opening for objects, but since it is always already filled with objects it is only one aspect or pole of a dyad. The nothing-openness-instant is always surpassed in *world* space-time. There "is" a nothing-openness-instant only in the surpassing or transcending of the nothing-openness-instant, so that the nothing-openness-instant is in itself an abstraction that is only isolated by an "analytic regression." And yet "the instant is not a vain invention of philosophers."[27] Consciousness is aware of the nothing-openness-instant as that which is surpassed. Because consciousness is a dyad relation that is aware of being so, consciousness is aware of being beyond itself, being a negated self-identity. Borrowing an expression from psychology that strikes me as entirely apt, consciousness is schizoid. Now there seem three and only three logically possible ways to heal this split: (1) to cancel the nothing-openness-instant pole; (2) to cancel the something-filled-up-time pole; (3) to synthesize the two poles without reduction. Clearly, to accomplish any one of the three would be to destroy the conditions under which there may be presence-to-a-world—hence the 'vanity' of the effort to heal oneself. Insofar as consciousness is aware of the inevitability of its schizoid state, each of these three efforts is in 'bad faith'. In other words, the for-itself can never simply be the instant, can never simply be what it ekstatically encounters in world space-time, and can never simply be the immediate fusion of immanence and transcendence. The for-itself *is* its 'here' in the mode of *not* being it, and *is* its 'there' in the mode of *not* being it. It "is what it is not and is not what it is."[28] Its being is *ambiguity*.[29] Its 'inauthenticity' is flight from ambiguity; its 'authenticity' is owning up to its ambiguity.

II

It is in terms of ambiguity that we can properly proceed to characterize radical conversion, the liberating instant, the reflective revolution, and purifying reflection. First we ask: how does the instant liberate? Sartre writes:

> we are perpetually *threatened by the instant*. . . . We can always make the instant appear as rupture of our ek-static unity. . . . We can produce instants if certain processes spring up with the collapse of prior processes. The instant will then be a beginning *and* an end. . . . The instant must be a beginning that presents itself as the end of a prior project. Therefore it will exist only if we are a beginning and an end to ourselves in the unity of one and the same act. Now this is exactly what happens in the case of a radical modification of our fundamental project.[30]

I interpret this as meaning that since consciousness is aware of itself as a "refusal" or transcending of the instant, it is aware of the perpetual possibility of reappropriating the refused instant in the very act of surpassing it. It is a question of understanding the instant of temporalizing as the temporalizing of the instant. Consciousness is aware, that is, of the "instantaneous nucleus" of its own ekstatic temporalizing as the "place" transcended. As the for-itself ekstatically transcends itself before and behind, into future and past, the locus of the instant surpassed must be *between* the future and the past. It must therefore be the present, which Sartre indeed elsewhere tells us is a "nonbeing"[31] that separates past from future. Another passage supports this interpretation:

The nihilation is pursued continuously . . . and consequently the free and continuous *reappropriation* [*reprise*] of the choice is inevitable. But this reappropriation is not made from *instant to instant* as long as I freely recover my choice, for then there is no instant; the reappropriation is so closely *joined* [across a nothingness] to the totality of the process that it has no instantaneous meaning and can have none. But precisely because it is free and perpetually reappropriated by freedom, my choice has freedom itself as its limit; that is, it is haunted by the specter of the instant. . . . I always have the possibility of positing my immediate past as object. . . . This act of objectifying the immediate past is at one with the new choice of other ends. It contributes to making the instant burst forth as nihilating *rupture* of the temporalization.[32]

In other words, ordinary experience or action is a continuous surpassing of the past by a continuous 'choosing' that "jumps the gap" (refuses the nothing) between past and future or fuses the future to the past by intending the future as a continuation of the past (I continue to pursue the same project). But because the relation between past and future is synthetic, is made to be by 'joining' the two, the for-itself is aware that the relation of the past to the future is not a simple given. Since this 'joining' is *made* to be, it can always be 'ruptured'. To rupture the 'joining' is to bracket the past, to put it explicitly out of the circuit, as in fact it always already is, since it is always surpassed. There arises an abrupt instant in which I no longer let the future surpass the past as a continuation but rather as a new direction, a reorientation. The surpassing continues, the ekstasis continues; the past is not changed, but the meaning of its relation to the future is changed. Like Heidegger's moment of vision, the liberating instant is not sustained; it is merely the beginning of a new way of ekstatic temporalizing ("making present"). It is a readjustment of the interrelation of the inevitable ekstases. It 'liberates' the for-itself not from self-dispersal in ekstasis but rather from enslavement to the ekstasis of the past. It suggests the possibility of "a valid coordination" of facticity and transcendence[33]—that is, of a mode of being that owns up to itself as the baseless basis of the particular way in which it joins an unalterable past to a possible future in surpassing.

As Heidegger's anxiety "individualizes,"[34] so Sartre's instant is associated with individuation:

the *instant* . . . represents abrupt shifts of orientation and the appropriation of a new stance in the face of an immutable past.
. . . Here [in "existential psychoanalysis"] it is a matter of understanding the *individual* and often even the instantaneous.[35]

This passage calls attention to the importance of the instant for "existential psychoanalysis," which is the attempt to reach the *self-transcending* "instantaneous nucleus" of consciousness by an "analytic regression" that Sartre calls "purifying reflection." It is an effort to decipher the 'meaning' of particular acts in a 'fundamental choice.' In terms of the foregoing analysis, it is an effort to 'regress' back from a particular act or series of acts to the instantaneous nucleus that has transcended itself by a particular 'progressive' self-surpassing.[36] It is an effort to regress back to the source of the for-itself's 'progressive', 'ekstatic', or 'diasporatic' self-temporalizing.[37]

The regressive movement of existential psychoanalysis is a "purifying reflection"[38] that is sharply distinguished from ordinary or "impure" reflection, which is in "bad faith."[39] Purifying reflection does not, as one might suppose, aspire to consciousness of the instant: "being conscious (of) self never means being conscious of the instant, for the instant is but one view of the mind and . . . a consciousness which would lay hold of itself in the instant would no longer lay hold of *anything*."[40] On the contrary, "bad faith is instantaneous."[41] As a flight from ambiguity, bad faith is the positing of self-identity in the instant. That is, bad faith tries to fill the nothingness of the instant without ekstasis. In the impurely reflective consciousness this means to experience the self as a simple present, in-itself. Bad faith tries to forget the fact that the past or in-itself is always already surpassed by a futuralizing choosing that refuses the instant, seeking either to maintain or revise the past. Bad faith, in other words, seeks to avoid ekstasis, to pull back from the diaspora, by withdrawing into the instant. Consciousness (of) self is, then, like consciousness of the world in that in both cases one is conscious not of a self-identical present but of a past-being-surpassed, a self-identity continuously denied, a self-identity infected by a nothing that is even now being filled up by our choices-into-the-future. The instant "is but one view of the mind" because it is that aspect of mind which is refused; the other view of the mind is its ekstatic temporality. To view the mind as a *whole*, then, must be precisely to view it as a continuously nihilated whole, a self-identity denied, an immanence transcended—an *ambiguous* being. In achieving this "purified" view of the mind one becomes explicitly aware of the possibility of a liberating instant, a reflective revolution, a radical conversion—all of which refer to the assumption of one's own ambiguity. Authenticity means "living the ambiguity."

This purification is at the same time the possibility of entering the sphere of the moral: "existential psychoanalysis is a *moral description.*" [42] It reveals the ambiguity that must be the major premise of philosophical ethics and of individual moral agency. Philosophically, it uncovers both the essential ambiguity of the for-itself and the general 'project' to surmount that ambiguity. Individually, it uncovers the particular 'specification' of the 'fundamental project', the particular way in which the individual analyzed seeks to realize the fundamental project.[43] Morally, it is a precondition of ethical decisiveness in that it seeks to isolate the real locus of choice—the specification of one's fundamental project—of which all one's actions are exemplifications; the specification of the fundamental project is what is changed in 'radical conversion'.

Here Sartre reappropriates Heidegger's notion of anxiety. As in Heidegger, anxiety is associated with nothingness. Anxiety is the 'mood' in which ambiguity is explicitly disclosed, which means at the same time that it is the explicit reflective apprehension of one's freedom or the disclosure of the future as possibility. Sartre describes it as a *disengagement:*

> Anxiety. . . . springs up from the negation of the appeals of the world; it appears when I disengage myself from the world in which I had engaged myself. . . . Anxiety is opposed to the spirit of seriousness, which understands values as originating in the world and which lives in this tranquilizing and materialist substantialization of values. . . . In anxiety I perceive myself both as totally free and able to make *the meaning of the world* come *only from myself.* [44]

Anxiety discloses man as a "being through whom values exist." [45] As moral description, existential psychoanalysis uncovers the real source of value, which is the ekstasis by which the for-itself has always already intended the world's significance in such a way that the world comes back to the for-itself as "requiring" this action or that. The world is unreflectively presented as a region in which values dwell of themselves. There is an unbroken "circle of interpretation"; the for-itself has lost or surrendered itself in the world in order that the world might mean—in order that value might exist. The analytic regression of existential psychoanalysis is a "disengagement" in that it seeks *to break the circle of interpretation* by analytically distinguishing between the actual and the possible. In this special reflective act the world is disclosed as a merely *virtual* synthesis of the actual and the intentional (meaning, value, possibilities). This is a "reflective *revolution*," since it reverses the unreflective attribution of the source of value, disclosing it as "coming from myself"—as coming from the continuous filling-up of the nothingness of the instantaneous nucleus of consciousness. But "most of the time we flee from anxiety into bad faith."[46] Most of the time we flee from the perpetual 'threat' of the instant by 'refusing' the instant.

Now just as Heidegger distinguishes between anxiety and the "resoluteness which anxiety makes possible,"[47] so Sartre distinguishes between anxiety and the for-itself's response to it. It would appear that the response to anxiety may be either inauthentic or authentic. But is there a Sartrean equivalent of Heidegger's 'resoluteness'? What would "living the ambiguity" be like? We know in general that it must be a "valid coordination" of facticity and transcendence, of instantaneity and ekstasis, of actuality and possibility. Not all 'conversions' will qualify as 'authentic', since the instantaneous change in the 'specification' of one's project may be merely the shift to a new mode of bad faith or a new indulgence in the spirit of seriousness. Rather, the sense of ambiguity must be sustained. One must neither sink into the world in seriousness nor flee from the world. Both are in bad faith. One must neither forget that one's being is in the circle of selfness nor seek escape from the circle of selfness. Rather, one must live in the circle lucidly. One must *progress* synthetically with constant awareness of the results of the psychoanalytic *regression*. One must play.

III

Sartre's first reference to play in *EN* occurs significantly in the context of a description of vertigo at the edge of an abyss. The

description is concrete; a particular man stands at a precipice, diz-
zied by his possible fall. We are inevitably reminded of Heidegger's
references to the abyss[48] and to falling. For Sartre the abyss means
the future ekstasis. The experience is not merely one of vertigo but
also one of anxiety: "If *nothing* forces me to save my life, *nothing*
stops me from throwing myself into the abyss."[49] We have seen
that living the ambiguity means anguished recognition of the nothing of the instant as the "place" where the future supervenes on the
past by the choice of a way of being.[50] The present passage adds to
this general account a description of the for-itself's particular way of
experiencing this anxiety. It is not the experience of a *pure* nothing.
It is the experience of nothing in the form of particular possibilities,
for "when the *cogito* throws us back to its possibles, it drives us
beyond the instant toward what it is in the mode of not being it."[51]
The particular form of the experience of anxiety is play and symbolic realization:

> I approach the precipice, and it is myself that my eyes seek in
> its depths. In this moment, I play with my possibilities. My
> eyes, in traversing the abyss from top to bottom, act out my
> possible fall and realize it symbolically. . . .[52]

I act out my possible future by imaginatively filling the nothing
of the future with myself, completing the circle of selfness. I lie life-
less at the bottom of the abyss, relieved of my anxiety, a suicide. Or
I pull back for the sake of my family's future. The linearity of my
past explodes into contrary options, so that in order for my past to
motivate me now, in order for it to "come to my aid anew, it is necessary that I remake it *ex nihilo* and freely."[53]

Granted that "nothing" determines what I shall do, I shall do
something. The question is whether I can do it without in so doing
lapsing from the authenticity of the moment of anxiety. Can one realize an imaginative possibility without losing the spirit of play?
Since "we cannot be anything without playing at being,"[54] we are
always playing. But generally we play in "the spirit of seriousness,"
a play-acting which suppresses the fact that it is play-acting. If the
spirit of play is to be the antidote to the spirit of seriousness, there
must be a way of playing-and-realizing that remains lucid. We
must turn to Part IV of *EN* for further analysis of play:

There remains one type of activity which seems obviously and wholly gratuitous: the activity of *play*. . . . Play, as opposed to the spirit of seriousness, seems to be the least possessive attitude; *it strips the real of its reality*. . . . All serious thought is condensed by the world and coagulates; it is an abdication of human reality in favor of the world. . . . The serious man . . . is in *bad faith*. . . .

Like Kierkegaardian irony, play liberates subjectivity. What indeed is play but an activity of which man is the first origin, for which he himself makes the rules . . . ? Whenever man perceives himself as free and wants to use his freedom—even if this should mean anxiety—then his activity is play. Man is indeed himself the first principle of play, and through it *he escapes his natural nature*.[55] He himself establishes the value of his acts, makes the rules for his acts, and agrees to play only by the rules that he has set up and defined for himself. *In consequence, there is in a sense "little reality" to the world.* . . .

This particular kind of project, whose ground and goal is freedom, deserves a special investigation. It is radically different from all other projects in that it aspires to a radically different type of being. But such an investigation . . . belongs in an *Ethics*, and it would require . . . taking a position toward the values that haunt the for-itself which can only be a *moral* position.[56]

In linking play to the *Ethics* that he promises at the end of the volume, Sartre implies that "an ethics of deliverance and salvation" would be an ethics of play. And Sartre's use of the adverb 'radically' in this passage suggests a genuinely 'radical' 'conversion'—a passage beyond the 'liberating instant' without loss of liberation, a "reappropriation of a corrupted being by itself."[57] I submit that it is in *lucid play* that Sartre at this time sees 'deliverance', 'salvation', 'liberation', 'radical conversion', and 'purification' from 'corruption'. One cannot miss the religious overtone of these terms—and Sartre himself will later speak of his early writings as a misguided quest for salvation.[58] Since "man is indeed himself the first principle of play," an ethic is to be found in what might be called *the religion of humanism*, whereby the "project of being-God"[59] is metamorphosed into the project of being-man, (being-ambiguous), insofar as this is realizable.

In what sense can one play lucidly in the world? One can do so to the degree that one "strips the real of its reality." As a result, "there is in a sense 'little reality' to the world." The spirit of play owns up to the circle of selfness by taking upon itself the regressive-analytic differentiation of the 'world' into its dual origin: at one pole there is actuality, while at the other pole there is the instantaneous nucleus ekstatically transcending itself. The spirit of play thus treats the world in its genuine ambiguity, its synthetic, virtual, or "made up" character as a perpetually unstable fusion of being and nothingness. The spirit of play approaches the world as a playground whose actuality is existentia and whose meaning and value have their origin in man's own intentionality.

Insofar as the spirit of play takes man as the source of the world's value, it constitutes a religion of humanism that returns to man his rightful portion of the power to make his world—a power traditionally ceded to God or gods in the spirit of seriousness of traditional religions. To this extent, the "project of being-God" is legitimate. As in Heidegger's reading of Kant,[60] man shares in the "divine" power to form his world imaginatively. Yet because actuality is understood as a ground of and a limit to this imaginative creation, the for-itself's imaginative creation remains essentially incomplete and the spirit of play must renounce the desire to ground being, an essential aspect of the "project of being-God." Man is the Demiurge in the form of imagination persuading necessity, but the resulting marriage of imagination and necessity is only symbolic:

> Sport is in reality free transformation of a worldly environment into an element which supports the action. Thus sport is creative, like art. Suppose the environment is a field of snow, an alpine slope. To see it is already to possess it. In itself it is already grasped by sight as a symbol of being. It stands for pure externality, radical spatiality; its undifferentiation, monotony, and whiteness reveal the absolute nakedness of substance; it is the in-itself which is only in-itself, the phenomenon's being, abruptly revealed beyond all phenomena. . . . What I now want is precisely that this in-itself become an emanation of myself while remaining entirely in itself.[61]

To Sartre a field of snow represents an unusually pure symbol of being-in-itself. The field of snow is therefore an ideal test case for the possibility of lucid play. As a pure symbol of otherness, "like the absolute and intelligible *plenum* of Cartesian extension . . . the pure appearance of the not-me,"[62] the field of snow presents itself as an especially clear challenge to my project to ground the world. If lucidity forces me to renounce this project ("I can not take possession of the field"),[63] does there remain any way in which I might act authentically in this field—that is, act without losing myself in a vain effort to ground Being? I can, in the spirit of play, ski, sliding across its supporting surface:

> The snow, which gave in under my weight when I walked and melted into water when I tried to grasp it, solidifies at once under the action of my speed. It supports me. . . . I have a special relation of appropriation with the snow: *sliding*. . . . One thinks of sliding as remaining on the surface, but this is inaccurate. To be sure, I merely skim the surface. . . . Nevertheless I *realize a synthesis* in depth. I feel the bed of snow organizing itself down to its deepest depths in order to support me; the sliding is an action *at a distance* which assures my mastery over the material without my having to sink down into that material and get stuck in it in order to subjugate it. *Sliding is the opposite of taking root.* The root is already half assimilated by the earth which nourishes it; it is a living concretion of the earth. It can utilize the earth only by making itself earth—by submitting itself in a sense to the matter which it wants to utilize. Sliding, on the contrary, realizes a material unity in depth without penetrating the surface; it is like a dreaded master who needs neither to insist nor to raise his voice in order to be obeyed. An estimable picture of power. Hence the familiar admonition: "Slide, mortals, don't bear down!" This does not mean "Be superficial, don't plumb the depths" but rather "Realize syntheses in depth *without compromising yourself*." . . . Sliding realizes a strictly individual relation with matter, an historical relation. . . . I have realized by my passage something which is unique *for me*. The ideal of sliding is therefore a sliding which leaves no trace—sliding on water (with a rowboat, motorboat, or especially with water skis, which . . . represent from this point of view the ideal limit of water sports). Sliding on snow is already less perfect, for there is a trace behind me and I am *compromised*. . . . Sliding on ice, which scratches the ice and encounters matter already organized, is very inferior. . . .
>
> Sliding appears to be assimilable to *a continuous creation*. The

speed is comparable to consciousness and here *symbolizes* consciousness. It gives birth to a deep quality in the material which lives only as long as the speed lasts—a sort of *fusion which conquers the indifferent externality* of the material which then falls back in a diffused spray behind the moving slider.[64]

This passage affords us an especially clear and detailed look into Sartre's understanding of the possibility of an authentic project of the for-itself. Recalling Roquentin-Sartre's special revulsion at roots in *La Nausée*,[65] we find it illustrated here once again and should associate it with Sartre's assertion that in play man "escapes his natural nature."[66] To take root in the earth is to "compromise oneself," to submit to "corruption."[67] It is to dim down the wholly nonnatural "spontaneity" of the instantaneous nucleus of consciousness. It would appear that the "deliverance" of which Sartre speaks is in part deliverance from nature, the "earth" in whose depths I may inauthentically "sink down" in order to ground myself. If I am to have "power" like the "dreaded master" I must approach nature as an "individual"—on my own terms. "Play liberates subjectivity." My own terms are temporal-historical; an authentic relation to nature must be one of movement, a transient sliding that symbolizes my being as a mortal. My authentic moral power consists in the realizing of transient syntheses, syntheses that do not "take root," that leave no trace behind them—that surpass or bracket the past.

To own up to my ownmost instantaneous self-transcending nucleus is to play the role of the artist who continuously creates and continuously surpasses what he creates—to realize and derealize simultaneously. Baconian-Cartesian mastery of nature is authentic insofar as it regards itself as a transient artistry that is playful rather than "serious." It must understand that its historical categories illuminate nature on human terms, and that humanistic salvation can therefore only be individual and transitory. Nature only lends "support" to a synthetic human utilization, not to a permanent assimilation by man. If man takes his categories and names as permanent traits of nature in a spirit of seriousness, nature dooms him to disappointment by surpassing those labels, by slipping through his fingers like the snow when one tries to grasp it.[68] To compromise oneself by such linguistic idealism is to miss the Stoic warning against love and to doom oneself to the pain of discovering that "things are divorced from their names."[69] It is to flee from the synthetic transitoriness of 'world' and its 'significance', only to have nature, in Heidegger's words, "break in upon us and destroy us."[70] Deliverance from vain disappointment comes from being-transient, sliding across the surface and leaving it behind. Like the Plotinian ekstatic emanation into the corrupting region of matter, it must guard itself against loss of its true nature by a purifying ascent or regression to its true immaterial source. One must renounce the self-compromising seriousness of love in favor of the free lucidity of play. To love is to get stuck in the world; to play is to come unstuck.

In sum, one must lucidly own up to the pervasive artifactuality of one's world. Man as artist-demiurge persuades nature to assume the shape of the artifact, but the material ground of the artifact outlasts the artifact itself. Material cause lasts; final cause flees. The profound meaning of the artifact and the deep appeal of the artist's vocation are that they exemplify and symbolize the human effort to transform an alien nature by etching human meaning and value into the depths of material nature, "scratching the ice." Man tries to make his transient meanings assume the permanence of nature and thereby to save himself from temporality. Sartre warns that this attempted synthesis can only be symbolic if it is to be lucid, since being-in-itself is already wholly actual and not a potentiality for synthesis with man. As the artist works an imaginative symbolic synthesis upon a recalcitrant material, so man at large effects syntheses that can be symbolically understood as "the meaning of things." In the act of sliding, speed "symbolizes consciousness," and the impacted surface symbolizes actuality. In the act of sliding there is therefore a symbolic mastery of nature by consciousness, which causes nature to solidify as ground for the play of consciousness. Sartre attributes one's pleasure in sliding to one's understanding of its symbolism as a mastering-and-supporting union, or synthesis of for-itself and in-itself. The world of internal relations is thus to be understood as an array of symbols of synthesis, and history is to be understood as the evanescent play of symbolic syntheses that continually seek to join and rejoin for-itself and in-itself but that remain merely symbolic conjunctions.

Sartre's implicit ethical admonition is to take the world symbolically and playfully, not appropriatively and seriously. Moral action is lucidly playing out symbolic syntheses and letting them go. The moral is identified with the aesthetics of play, its symbolic artistry.[71] Let the earth support you, but don't succumb to the illusion that you can acquire its permanence. The starkness of this outlook, reminiscent of the Hellenistic, is alleviated only by its vision of authenticity as play rather than as duty or refined and passive pleasure.

We can now conclude that if world is ontologically ambiguous, precisely for that reason it is the region of the moral—the playground in which man can symbolically "master" his schizoid being by individuating himself. World is the region of the immoral, of the *terra firma* that loses its solidity when man tries to stop sliding and turns into a watery grave, sticky slime,[72] or a corrupting mud in which one loses oneself as individual. If nihilating consciousness inevitably opens a hole in being, turning the solid and actual into the watery and virtual, then one should become light enough to skim the surface!

Sartre's response to the problem of the virtuality and instability of the historical world is thus a moral one, and it consists in embracing the virtuality as one's own. As one does so, the world gains from the in-itself a limited supportive solidity across which one can make one's transient path, satisfied with a transient mastery that leaves no trace. This is the early Sartre's reappropriation of Heidegger's reappropriation of Nietzsche's *amor fati*. In Sartre's reappropriation, however, Heidegger's notion of the future as a 'repetition' of one's inheritance loses its reverence for the past; in the speed of authentic sliding, the past is left behind, ideally without a trace. It is an outlook that Sartre in retrospective self-criticism will characterize as "a revolutionary and discontinuous catastrophism."[73] It is also an appropriation of Heidegger to which Heidegger's early thought is, as we have seen, inherently liable insofar as the nothingness of 'world', which Sartre traces to the self-transcending instantaneous nucleus of consciousness, is ascribed by Heidegger to Dasein's 'world'.

IV

I began this chapter by suggesting that Sartre would appear, in a general way, to have followed Husserl's path of seeking "the monism of the phenomenon" through the means of analytic reflection. We have already seen that the monism of the phenomenon is, owing to Sartre's analytic reflection, in danger of breaking apart into its dual relata. Yet we saw Sartre hail Husserl for having "restored to things their horror and their charm." There appeared to be a contradiction between the phenomenon as unreflective meaning-being—worlded being—and the reflective disclosure of the virtuality of this synthesis of meaning and being. Drawing upon the conclusions of the present chapter, we can now assert that for Sartre meaning-endowing is inauthentic unless it takes into itself the results of the analytic regression. If Sartre praises Husserl for restoring to 'things' their horror and their charm, everything hangs on how one construes the term 'things'. If thing means "natural entity in-itself," then the restoration of meaning and value to things is an illusion, for Sartre like Husserl subscribes to the gradual regression of meaning into consciousness that the history of philosophy has effected—though not as *in* consciousness, but as ekstatically projected *by* consciousness beyond itself. In either case, consciousness is a source of meaning and value. But if 'thing' means a symbolic synthesis,[74] then one may legitimately 'return' from the reflective regression to 'things'. Phenomena are to be regarded as transient playthings to be cast off at the conclusion of play. Sartre's early Husserl essay then appears in a new light: things can be *authentically* apprehended as "hateful, sympathetic, horrible, lovable" solely on condition that one lucidly understands that they have these properties only when and as long as I play with them. Husserl has indeed "restored to us the world of artists and prophets"[75]—a world where phenomena become understood as artifacts under the hand of man, symbols of the tenuous and transient human quest to fill the human hole in being by an ekstatic endowment of meaning.

For Sartre the proper use of Husserl and Heidegger is to appropriate them for what is in effect the religion of humanism, the quest for deliverance from nature by a reflective lucidity that returns to nature as the supportive ground of a transient symbolic mastery. The religion of humanism is for Sartre equally a religion of art, and in a double sense: both the world and man himself are art works. It is in the "ecstasy" of imaginative creation, in the circuit of selfness, that man shapes himself through shaping phenomena. In a broad sense, the history of culture is the history of man's artistic-ekstatic self-production. History is the passion to create the self through the world. Authentic history is the same passion made aware of its transience, which is not the transience of one's ultimate death but of *the continuous death* [76] which is the continuous surpassing in the refusal of the instantaneous nucleus, the continuous negation of the past. But, Sartre writes, "death is a *boundary* and every boundary . . . is a *Janus bifrons.*" [77] Must not a continuous death be regarded as a continuous rebirth, a continuous purification or deliverance from the corruption of the dead past, the evil matter in which inauthentic man allows himself to sink? [78] This religion of artful play is in fact a variant of the venerable *ars moriendi,* the art of dying. It recommends purification through the monkish art of mortification of the ego, even a sort of mortification of the flesh, a renunciation of beauty, and "renunciation" of the pagan and "degrading" arts of "magic" and "sorcery." [79] The deliverance that can be effected by the purifying reflection of existential psychoanalysis frees one for a symbol-making life that owns up to the freedom that one always already is. The conclusion of *EN* attempts an explicit correlation of deliverance, symbolic life, and freedom:

> Existential psychoanalysis will disclose to man the real goal of his quest, which is being as *a synthetic fusion* of the in-itself with the for-itself; it will confront man with his passion. Many men have in fact practiced this psychoanalysis on themselves. . . . as a means of deliverance and salvation. . . . They renounce the appropriation of things as things and attempt to realize the symbolic appropriation of their being-in-itself. . . .
>
> But ontology and existential psychoanalysis . . . must disclose to the moral agent that he is *the being through whom values exist.* It is then that his freedom will attain consciousness of itself. . . . When the quest for being and the appropriation of the in-itself are disclosed to freedom as *its possibles,* it will perceive by and in anxiety that they are possibles solely on the ground of the possibility of other possibles. Prior to this disclosure, possibles could, to be sure, be chosen and revoked *ad libitum,* but the theme which unified all choices of possibles was the value or ideal presence of the *ens causa sui.* What will become of freedom if it turns against this value? . . . Will freedom have the power to end the reign of this value by simply grasping itself as freedom in relation to itself? . . . A freedom which wills itself as freedom is in fact a being-which-is-not-what-it-is and which-is-what-it-is-not, and which chooses being-what-it-is-not and not-being-what-it-is [i.e., ambi-

guity] as the ideal of being. It thus chooses not to take root in itself but to flee from itself, not to coincide with itself but to be ever at a distance from itself. . . . Will freedom, by taking itself for an end, escape all *situation*? . . . Or will it situate itself all the more precisely and all the more individually as it keeps on projecting itself in anxiety as a conditioned freedom and keeps on reclaiming its responsibility as the existent through whom the world comes into being?[80]

These questions, answerable only in an *Ethics*, push the notions of deliverance and conversion to their ultimate conclusion. Sartre had implied that most play was in the service of the fundamental project,[81] though play settles for a realization of the project that is merely symbolic and transitory. In the passage just cited, Sartre raises the possibility of a still more radical mode of deliverance, which appears to leave behind even the symbolic realization of the fundamental project. Granted that one is always motivated by the futural projection of *some* value, suppose that this value were freedom itself rather than symbolic self-realization as in-itself-for-itself.[82] It what sense would one still be motivated if one were delivered from the fundamental project? What Sartre probably means is that while the "desire to be" is universal and irreducible, and in this sense there is always a fundamental project, in certain cases the desire to be *being* can be transmuted into the desire to be *ambiguous*. This would constitute Sartre's reappropriation of the Nietzschean-Heideggerian notion of "becoming what one is." In Sartre's version it would be a matter of trying to coincide with oneself *as* non-self-coincident, an ongoing struggle against the lure of bad faith. I propose that this is what Sartre has in mind when he asserts that the motive of the man who plays is "to attain to himself as . . . precisely the being who is *in question* in his being."[83] But would this be an escape from all situation, all being-in-the-world? And if it were, would it really solve Sartre's chief problem: how to return to the world without forgetting the hard-won truth about oneself?

EN as a whole shows just how difficult this problem is. The book explores from one angle after another what it calls the 'situation'— the circular affair man has with the world in which he loses himself (or "degrades" himself)[84] in order that the world may come back to him as meaningful, as inscribed with *his* meanings. Lacking internal content, man seeks to fill himself up with the world. By filling

up the world with himself, he fills himself up with the world, gaining himself by losing himself. One gains a meaningful world at the
price of dimming down one's consciousness *of* one's consciousness
as the true source of the meanings and values one wants to find *in*
the world. This seemingly inevitable pursuit of value places one
again and again in bad faith—especially that form of bad faith
called the spirit of seriousness, in which one plugs oneself into the
world and sees *things* as valuable. Being in a 'situation' seems to
presuppose bad faith. Even the playful effort at symbolic self-
realization seems a minimal case of bad faith—but bad faith nevertheless—insofar as its goal remains integrated being, fusion, synthesis. Is then freedom-in-situation, or commitment without
seriousness, a contradiction in terms?

The inevitable pursuit of value casts one into bad faith in every
case but one, the case in which one takes freedom itself as a value.
In all other cases freedom chooses an end incompatible with
freedom—incompatible with man's essential ambiguity. In *QL*
Sartre asserts that "man is alienated by his ends."[85] If man is by
nature a teleological being, what would constitute a nonalienating
teleology of the individual and of history? Freedom itself is the only
lucid value, the sole nonalienating end. Freedom as a value is precisely the systematic quest for purification from all values that ac-
crue from man's unavailing quest for being. Freedom as a value is
therefore a touchstone of admissible value. That is, a value is admissible only insofar as it does not contradict the *source* of value,
which is freedom itself. But freedom is necessarily thrown freedom,
a freedom that temporally-ekstatically surpasses itself toward an
end. What Sartre is therefore proposing is the possibility of taking
freedom rather than being for an end. 'Situation' will then become
nothing other than the pursuit of freedom in the world. The balance
of Sartre's career can be seen as the effort to understand what sort of
'situation', and what sort of 'world', would be compatible with the
pursuit of freedom as an end and a value.[86]

For the moment I rest content with noting certain implications
and problems to which Sartre commits himself in taking freedom as
the only admissible end:

1. Sartre thereby appears to reject decisively the temptation to
understand history metaphysically as the illustration of a cosmic
teleology whose end is the reintegration of being as a genuine syn-

thesis of in-itself and for-itself. To take freedom as an end is to renounce the quest to surmount ambiguity or to gain self-coincidence or self-identity. Will Sartre therefore develop an alternative philosophy of history that takes freedom rather than being as the criterion of historical development? Does not "the religion of humanism" suggest some such philosophy of history?

2. Sartre has argued that all experience is a temporal one that moves toward a future desideratum in such a way as to cause phenomena to appear laden with a project-relative meaning and affectivity that reflective analysis shows to be a virtual synthesis accomplished in bad faith. If this is so, what sort of meaning and affectivity can the world possess for a consciousness whose ekstatic project is freedom? Will lucidity require a world stripped of meaning and of quality?[87] In what sense does the project of freedom remain within the circuit of selfness? Sartre forecasts that "In anxiety . . . we shall perceive our choice . . . as bound to serve as foundation for the totality of significations that constitute reality."[88] In this Sartrean reappropriation of Heidegger's groundless ground of the referential totality, will the project of freedom, or "living the ambiguity," be able in practice to generate a 'world' whose meaning-relations and meaning-beings receive their significance solely from the end of freedom? In sum, in what sense will "the humanization of the actual" remain possible, and in what sense will the quest for the phenomenological synthesis remain possible? EN can be seen as preparing the way for a moral deliverance from the quest for being—a moral "destruction" of the Western ontological ideal that has been delineated as the object of an unavailing passion. Yet this destruction is at the same time premised on an ontology of pure actuality that also may have historical roots. Does the project of freedom as a value mean an appropriation of nihilism, or can the projection of this value singlehandedly vanquish the specter of nihilism?

6

Humanism:
The Lecture and
the Letter

I

IN 1945 SARTRE gave a public lecture, *L'Existentialisme est un humanisme*, that from its title forward explicitly correlates what Gabriel Marcel had called 'existentialism' with humanism. Sartre is clearly out to confound his critics and in so doing to come to terms anew with what we have claimed is his chief problem: how, specifically, to return to the world from analytic-reflective withdrawal. *That* the for-itself must always return to the world is guaranteed by the ekstatic intentionality of consciousness. One is "seized by a whirlwind and thrown back outside."[1] But *how* one will return has become a question of metaphysical and ethical decision. Here once again, the distinction between 'that-being' and 'how-' and 'what-being' rears its problematic head. The lecture's response to this problem is one that we have seen prefigured in the conclusion of *EN*, though the lecture presents it not as a mere possibility but as a moral necessity:

> When I assert that in each concrete circumstance freedom can have no other aim than to will itself, [I mean that] once man has recognized that in his abandonment he posits values, he can thenceforth will only one thing, which is freedom as the ground [*fondement*] of all values. . . . The ultimate signification of the acts of men of good faith is the quest for freedom as such.[2]

This will mean, to those familiar with *EN*, that Sartre is calling for a radical conversion that delivers one from the metaphysical quest for an ideal being. If one is "honest" (lucid), one must quest not for deliverance *from* one's ambiguity but for deliverance *to* it. That Sartre now has full confidence in the possibility of taking freedom as one's end is shown by his blunt condemnation of the "cowards" and "stinkers" who "aim to hide from themselves the complete gratuity and complete freedom of their existence." They have the capacity, Sartre has now concluded, to take freedom as their sole end.[3]

We will not concern ourselves any more than is necessary with the lecture's painfully oversimplified formulation of Sartre's position. What especially interests us is the manner in which Sartre draws Heidegger into complicity with 'existentialism' in three respects.

First, Sartre classes Heidegger among "the atheistic existentialists,"[4] although grounds for this characterization of Heidegger's theological stance are not clearly present in *SZ* or in other early Heideggerian writings available to Sartre.[5] Indeed, Heidegger can be construed as suggesting that were "the Being of God" not understood in terms of the ancient ontology but rather in terms of "an inquiry in which faith is primary," theology might be revitalized.[6] Of course, Sartre was not alone in construing the early Heidegger's position as atheistic, and I surmise that Sartre reached this conclusion on the basis of the fact that *SZ*, as an ontology *of phenomena*, could be interpreted as banishing the subject matter of theology to an extraphenomenal region and handing over to Dasein the grounding role that theology ascribes to God. Given this interpretation, it would be possible to think that Heidegger in *WM* intended to include God among "the idols we all have and to which we are wont to go cringing."[7] Further, Sartre construes Heidegger's term *Überlassenheit* (*délaissement*, 'abandonment') as meaning that "God does not exist."[8] But, unless Sartre's interpretation of this point changed between *EN* and his 1945 lecture, he does not find ascription of "atheism" to Heidegger incompatible with ascribing to him in *EN* a "concern . . . for reconciling his humanism with the religious sense of the transcendent."[9]

Second, Sartre reaffirms in the lecture his aforementioned attribution of "humanism" to Heidegger in *EN*. Sartre sees this humanism as the consequence of man's ekstatic way of being; because man is a "passing-beyond" that is "outside" of itself in the world, "There is no universe but a human universe, the universe of human subjectivity."[10] Therefore, "we are on a plane where there are only men."[11] "Only men" means not gods, and not 'situations' whose meaning and value are determined by a being other than the human being. This 'man' is, by implication, similar to Heidegger's *Dasein*.[12] We have seen that Sartre had criticized Heidegger for placing primary stress on the future ekstasis[13] but had accepted a version of Heidegger's notion of the simultaneity and interdependence of the three ekstases. Yet in the lecture Sartre stresses the future ekstasis almost exclusively, and in such a way that the interdependence of the ekstases is largely lost from view. Sartre appears to revert to the traditional understanding of time as a sequence of separate 'nows':

> Man as the existentialist conceives him is not definable, because *at first* he is nothing. He will be only *afterward*, and he will be such as he makes himself be. . . . Man is not only such as he conceives himself to be, but such as he wills himself to be. And just as he conceives himself *after* existence, so does he will himself *after* this leap into existence.[14]

Sartre, to be sure, qualifies this account by acknowledging that this futural willful projection is governed by an original 'choice', which the lecture also calls a 'plan':

> man will be what he will have projected to be, rather than what he will *will* to be. For what we usually mean by "willing" is a conscious decision, which is generally subsequent to what one has *already* made of oneself . . . a manifestation of a more fundamental and more spontaneous choice. . . .[15]

The distinction here made between choosing or projecting and willing or deciding is rooted in *EN*'s distinction between the involuntary unreflective spontaneity of choice and the voluntary reflective decision that is "deceptive" in presenting itself as voluntary, inasmuch as it is "already" governed by the spontaneous choice that it exemplifies.[16] So in a sense what one wills is governed by a "prior" choice, which would appear to mean that the future is, after all, governed by the past. On the other hand, Sartre had argued in *EN* that purifying reflection shows that the for-itself's fundamental choice does not govern one's will or decisions by pre-existing them and causing them. Rather, each act of will or decision reaffirms or chooses anew the fundamental choice.[17] Impure reflection's belief in horizontal—or sequential—psychic causality must be purified so as to reveal that the relation between choice and decision is vertical:

the choice is "prior" only in the sense of being the *deeper* meaning of the "willed" decision. But if purifying reflection can show that the relation between choice and will is really vertical, then the possibility of a direct and explicit integration of choice and will or decision is raised. In other words, once the for-itself has explicitly pushed back to the instantaneous self-transcending nucleus of consciousness, it has located the real seat and center of decision in consciousness as *continuous* choosing rather than in the past. This means that the for-itself is for the first time in a position to take charge of its willing, which it may not do so long as it regards its will as either "free will" (ungoverned by a deeper choice) or as a will bound by the past. So an "ethics of deliverance and salvation" requires that one understand that consciousness is governed by the past only insofar as consciousness chooses the past anew. Given this understanding, one may at any moment "make the instant appear"[18] as a break in one's ordinary linear behavior and attitudes.

My point is that, in the lecture, Sartre is speaking from the standpoint of purifying reflection, and that from this standpoint he really does mean to say that the future ekstasis, as the continuous supercession or negation of past choice by new choices, has a radical primacy. Thus when Sartre states in the lecture that *"at first* he [man] is nothing. Only *afterward* will he be something,"* he means two things. First, and more obviously, he means that each child at the moment of his *first* choice slips a nothingness between himself and his past in such a way that he must choose "out of nothing" the meaning and weight which that past will have for him.[19] Less obvious, because of the wording of the passage cited, is its second and deeper meaning: that from the standpoint of purifying reflection, this initial situation is thenceforth constant, because the nothing (the correlate of the continuous negation of the past) must be continuously transcended by a continuous choosing that either projects anew or revokes the ongoing linear pattern of one's behavior. Purifying reflection yields the knowledge that the weight and influence of the past are chosen *ex nihilo*.

One can now see what Sartre's attribution of existentialist humanism to Heidegger really means. The impression is given that Heidegger's "human reality" is Sartre's "man," where "man" is thought of from his self-transcending conscious nucleus as a continuously refused instant or self-filling nothingness. This Sartrean, and

allegedly Heideggerian, humanism is "man-centered" in the specific sense of being consciousness-centered.

These considerations lead us to the third notion that the lecture
attributes to Heidegger. Just after listing Heidegger among the existentialists, Sartre explains: "What they have in common is simply
the fact that they think existence precedes essence or, if you wish,
that subjectivity must be the starting point."[20] *EN* has already explained in what sense existence precedes essence: "This *me*, with
its *a priori* and historical content, is the *essence* of man. And anxiety
as the manifestation of freedom in the face of self signifies that man
is always separated from his essence by a nothingness. Here one
must invoke Hegel's dictum: 'Wesen ist was gewesen ist.' Essence
is what has been."[21] Thus "existence precedes essence"[22]—or, as
Sartre misleadingly puts it elsewhere in *EN*, "essence is posterior to
existence"[23]—means not that man has no essence but rather that he
continuously surpasses it. One could equally well say that for Sartre
essence precedes existence; that is the trouble with mottoes and
catch-phrases. Perhaps the least misleading way to express what
Sartre means is to say that the for-itself is an *ambiguous* relation to
its essence. It is its essence in the mode of not being it. This is also
true of the thing, which "does not *possess* its essence as a present
quality. It is even a negation of essence. . . ."[24] For Sartre, the simultaneous coincidence of essence and existence—or resolution of
ambiguity—would be "beauty," the "impossible yet perpetually indicated fusion of essence and existence,"[25] or the self-coincidence of
the temporal ekstases. We have seen that this is Sartre's interpretation of the metaphysical quest for what-is, grasped simultaneously
and synthetically "as such" *and* "in its wholeness." It is being. In
the terms of Sartre's lecture, this synthesis would require the vantage point of the God that atheistic humanism rejects. Therefore, in
associating Heidegger with the thesis that existence is prior to essence—an expression derived, to be sure, from *SZ*[26]—Sartre is implicitly attributing to Heidegger the thesis that being is an impossible metaphysical ideal for the human being.

In the passage I have cited, Sartre adds that "existence precedes
essence" means that "subjectivity must be the starting point." This
means that subjectivity is the starting point for the progressive
totalizing of the for-itself. Therefore, methodologically, philosophy
must regress to that nuclear starting point in order to understand

the for-itself's drive toward totality, which at the same time de-totalizes or nihilates the very totality it vainly seeks to reach. Now it would appear that Heidegger cannot be associated with the thesis that subjectivity is the starting point if this means that a negating consciousness is the starting point, for we have seen Sartre himself criticize Heidegger for *not* interpreting Dasein in this way.

If we look at the way Sartre defines 'subjectivity' in the lecture, we find that he does so by reference to Descartes and in the name of truth:

> At one's point of departure there can be only one tenable truth: *I think, therefore I am.* That is the point where conscious-ness arrives at its own absolute truth. Every theory which con-siders man from a point which is external to this moment in which he arrives at himself is from the start a theory which suppresses the truth, for beyond the Cartesian *cogito* all objects are merely probable, and a doctrine of probability which is not grounded in a truth falls into groundless nothingness [*s'effondre dans le néant*]. In order to define the probable, one must already possess the true. Thus, for there to be any truth whatsoever, there must be an absolute truth. . . .[27]

In defending this thesis Sartre stands shoulder to shoulder with Husserl in the struggle to surmount the modern crisis in the foun-dations of the theory of knowledge, the threat of loss of the tran-scendental ground of knowledge at the hands of psychologism. Sartre retains his judgment of 1939 that "the hermeneutic of exis-tence will be able to ground an anthropology, and this anthropol-ogy will serve as the basis of all psychology."[28] For anthropology to serve as such a basis, it must begin in knowledge of the certain rather than of the merely probable. Certainty is by nature and by definition a characteristic of consciousness. Consciousness may be either consciousness of itself or consciousness of a transcendent ob-ject, an existent. The latter consciousness is aware of an object that exceeds one's consciousness of it; hence knowledge of that object is in principle intermittent and incomplete (dependent on or mediated by the successive temporal appearances of the object), corrigible, and thus probable. But consciousness of itself, or consciousness of being conscious of the object, is constant, immediate or intuitive, and certain. Sartre treats this *conscience (de) soi* as an immediately intuited fact.[29] It is awareness of consciousness as aware of something, not an awareness of consciousness as a separate or egological entity; thus self-awareness must "catch" consciousness "in the act."[30] This "prereflective cogito" or *conscience (de) soi* is not consciousness *as* a self/ego but rather the precondition for consciousness *of* a probable self, which is an *object* of consciousness. Prereflective consciousness is therefore pre-personal or "impersonal."[31] What is *for* consciousness cannot be *in* it, so that everything that consciousness is aware of, except its immediate awareness (of) itself, is beyond it. This inevitable *understood otherness of the object* of consciousness is, of course, the crucial characteristic of consciousness for Sartre, and for several reasons: (1) it guarantees the separation of all entities, natural or social, from consciousness; (2) it guarantees the separation of the ego from consciousness; (3) it commits consciousness to logic, for Sartre with Hegel construes the relation of separation or otherness as negation. If the object of consciousness is understood as other-than-consciousness, it is the 'not-*x*' to the '*x*' of consciousness, and the fundamental and impassable relation of consciousness to any and all of its objects is negation. This is for Sartre (but not for Hegel) an immediate and intrinsic limit to the possibility of all other and derivative relations, most especially that of synthesis.

The commitment of consciousness to logic is of the highest consequence for ontology, for ethics, and for Sartre's position vis-à-vis both Heidegger and the philosophical tradition. It commits ontology to antithetical modes of being. It serves as the basis for committing ethics to the value of honesty or lucidity—avoidance of self-deception. This self-deception is construed as self-contradiction of consciousness by itself, the imaginary-magical-emotional effort to cancel the logical relation of negation by fusing the relata or by canceling one of the relata.

The commitment of consciousness to logic places Sartre in acute opposition to Heidegger at the heart of their respective positions. *WM* seeks to raise a question for thought which, Heidegger argues, the traditional commitment of thinking to logic would rule out: "The commonly cited ground rule of all thinking—the principle that contradiction must be avoided—and common 'logic' rule out the question."[32] But, Heidegger argues, "the very possibility of negation as an act of reason, and consequently reason [*Verstand*] itself, are . . . dependent on nothing."[33] Sartre denies this in *EN*, as we have seen, holding that negation is the source of nothing.[34] Whereas Heidegger concludes: "Nothing is the primordial source of negation, not the other way around. If this breaks the sovereignty of reason in the field of inquiry into nothing and Being, then the fate of the rule of 'logic' in philosophy is thereby decided as well. The very idea of 'logic' loses its footing in the vortex of a more primordial questioning."[35]

I can now speak more precisely about Sartre's implication of Heidegger in the 'subjectivity' of humanism. Sartre's 'subject' is a modification of the Cartesian *cogito* that rejects the *cogito*'s substantiality or nontemporal instantaneous self-inherence but retains its character as an irreducible absolute or *fundamentum inconcussum*.[36] The *cogito* is absolute in the sense that the for-itself constantly *makes* itself a *fundamentum* by ekstatic refusal of its instantaneous nucleus. The notion of the 'subject' is inherently dialectical and logical; the subject is non-object and the object is non-subject. As a dialectical pair, 'subject' and 'object' are notions definable only by each other. Sartre's view is that consciousness is by nature committed to this dialectic. But, as in Hegel, 'subject' and 'substance' are distinguished, although for Sartre the nature of the subject precludes that ultimate Hegelian synthesis whereby subject becomes substance.[37] We can recognize this synthesis as Hegel's effort to accomplish the Western quest for Being—a quest that Sartre acknowledges as man's passion but that he judges to be impossible of realization. Sartre is thus, in the name of traditional logic, rejecting Hegel's reformation of logic.[38] In this respect Sartre's theory of consciousness is profoundly conservative, and Sartre's reappropriation of Heidegger is a deradicalization of Heidegger's position as well as of Hegel's position.

I have argued in chapter 2 that Heidegger's Dasein is intended as an original or primordial unity that is prior to and ground of the distinction between subject and object. I interpreted Heidegger as arguing that this original unity is an always already "precedent community of nature." It is a *prelogical* unity—the prior ground and basis of any logico-analytico-regressive effort to factor this unity into logical relata. It must in fact precede both regression and progression as the ground possibility of either—that is, of either a splitting or a reassembling of the original unity. At the same time, Heidegger must of course account for the possibility of such a splitting, whether the splitting is real or merely apparent. It would seem that for Heidegger the splitting cannot be entirely real, for it will always be grounded in the very unity it attempts to split. If the original unity makes possible such splitting of itself, however, this implies that the unity already contains *in potency* the distinction between subject and object that the splitting actualizes. In other words, if a splitting is to be uncovered or discovered, it must in some sense "be" there already, as in Hegel's notion of a potentially self-factorable immediacy.[39]

Now in chapter 4 we saw that it is possible to construe Heidegger's early position in such a way that it becomes vulnerable to a Sartrean interpretation. This is essentially because anxiety and owning up realize an attitude in which the prior unity appears as having to be freely reappropriated out of nothing, the 'significance' of the world having given way to an apprehension of entities as "essentially devoid of any meaning." This attitude thus realizes a situation in which Dasein, as source of meaning, is indeed sharply distinguished from entities whose character is not that of Dasein. That this attitude can be realized at all implies that Dasein has an awareness, repressed in disowning, of the potential distinctness (factorability) of Dasein as meaningful and of present-at-hand beings as meaningless. An owning up to this repressed awareness, then, means taking over being a groundless ground for the maintenance of meaning-beings in a totality of reference-relationships. It can be argued that so long as the always prior ground can be factored in this way, anxiety and owning up break apart the very unity of the meaning-being that phenomenology had sought to establish, and it becomes the burden of man to maintain a virtual synthesis that perpetually threatens to come apart. Given this interpretation, it is possible for Sartre to regard *Dasein* and *Vorhandensein* as 'subject' and 'object' and as participating in a "precedent community" that is always already potentially disunified by Dasein's awareness of its absolute (though disowned) distinctness from present-at-hand beings. Therefore the phenomenological unity of essence and existence can be maintained only by inauthenticity or by the resolute decision of a being who can be construed as a subject.

Thus Heidegger's retrospective characterizations of his early position as still "too subjectivist" and as "no foundation"[40] point to the features of his early position that make the Sartrean interpretation

possible. Essentially this Sartrean interpretation (or reappropriation) consists in reasoning that if Dasein can, in owning up, realize
a genuine distinction between itself and other entities, that distinction must already be present in the prior unity, which can therefore
be seen not as an immediate or original unity but as a synthesis
which has already been *made to be* by the synthetic fusion of distinct relata.

The foregoing analysis, however, hides a complex ambiguity.
Have I taken sufficiently into account the simultaneous introplay of
the three temporal ekstases, or have I fallen back into the habit of
regarding time as a succession of now-moments? One easily falls
into the trap of thinking of the always-precedent ground as a simple
past, which the futuralizing ekstasis makes present either by re-
newing it or by revising it. On this account, the renewed/revised
ground would then become the past basis of another renew-
ing/revising making-present. But is 'priority' the same as 'pastness'? Kantian 'priority' obviously is not the same as 'pastness', for
the prior ground in Kant is a formal and categorial structure that actively 'anticipates' or 'preforms' the future. This Kantian a priori
structure, however, is not subject to the vicissitudes of time and
history. If in Hegel, as is generally said, "the categories have a history," the vicissitudes of time and history are nevertheless subordi-
nated to a priori rational potencies and become the medium of the
future actualization of these potencies. Heidegger has argued that
Hegel took the wrong turn after Kant in regarding imagination as a
function of pure thought rather than the converse.[41] Heidegger to
be sure stands with Hegel in regarding history as the actualization
of potentialities that are the very structure of the relation between
thought and world. Heidegger, however, sees potentialities as existential facts, not grounded in reason, and as what we have called
"inevitable possibilizers" that make possible a finite range of existentiell-ontic actualizations in such a way that within this range of
finite possibilities the imagination is free. Thus the categories of
reason and "the rule of logic" become one historical way in which
the imagination can bind itself within the range of finite possibilities opened up by Dasein's existential structure. But imagination
necessarily binds itself in *some* existentiell-ontic way, owing to Dasein's ekstatic immanence in its own world. Because this ekstatic
immanence of Dasein in its world is temporal-historical, the imagi-

nation has always already bound itself to a particular existentiell-ontic possibility at any historical moment. In its circularity, this always-prior binding appears to be a double bind, inasmuch as the meaning of Dasein's world is the basis on which Dasein interprets the meaning of that world. That is, Dasein's meaning or interpretation is always already present in the world and conversely the world is always already present in Dasein's meaning. *It is this circularity that accounts for the always-prior unity of the prior ground.*

This means that neither thought nor its environment can be regarded as a source, beginning, or ground of the other—the mistake of idealism and realism, respectively. Neither 'subject' nor 'object', neither meaning nor entity, can be the *fundamentum inconcussum*, since they are always already *one*. There is a prior oneness of the 'human' and the 'natural' such that neither 'humanism' nor 'naturalism' can be taken as fundamental orientations. But at the same time, I have argued, there must be some basis for the rise of the distinctions between the human and the natural, the subject and the object, meaning and entity, interpreter and interpretant. Heidegger locates the basis of these distinctions in Dasein's understanding of itself as an *entity* whose Being is *"mine,"* [42] a being identifiable as an entity with reference to a world in the midst of which it is factically 'thrown' in such a way that there is 'distance' between 'here' and 'yonder' both spatially and temporally. It is Dasein's understanding of itself as a situated entity that is the real ground (possibility) of the distinction between the human and the natural, subject and object, etc.

But this ground does not by itself account for the rise of these distinctions. One must also take into account other, equally primordial existential conditions, especially falling making-present, discursive articulation (*Rede*), and truth. It then becomes possible to argue that the subject-object distinction is an existentiell-ontic modification of the Dasein-world relation in which a selective and partial 'disclosing' (truth) has left 'dissimulated' the prior ontological unity in such a way that entities including Dasein itself are articulated, expressed in language, and made present as simple present entities. This 'fascination' with an ontic present is a forgetting of its ontological condition, the prior unified ground. We have seen that it is anxiety that reveals this prior ground, which is eminently forgettable because it is 'nothing'—i.e., it lacks the physical presentness of the ontic[43] and is "ontologically different" from entities.

But for the early Heidegger anxiety reveals the ground as a 'nothing' not only in the sense of its being *other* than entities but also as an *absence* of ground.[44] In the absence of ground, the entity stands forth in its presence-at-hand as essentially devoid of meaning. If Dasein is thereby reminded that "there are" beings at all only because of Dasein's prior projection of a world, nevertheless anxiety appears to *confirm* Dasein's articulation of entities as objects-in-themselves, inherently meaningless entities! Anxiety is a reminder of the prior ground's role in constituting the significance of the world because in the moment of anxiety this significance is missing. One gains explicit awareness of the existential-ontological ground of significance at the price of loss of existentiell-ontic significance. At just this point Heidegger's notion of ground as a "precedent community of nature" is seriously endangered, since the introplay of the ekstases is here ruptured. In anxiety Dasein is able to view an entity that was meaningful and that may in future be meaningful either through Dasein's resolute making-present or through its self-disowning making-present, but which at the moment shows itself as it is: essentially devoid of meaning. In placing Dasein "in suspense" between a meaningful past and a possibly meaningful future, anxiety in a sense brackets both past and future, ruptures the threefold ekstatic unity, and reduces time in effect to a now-moment, an isolated present.

Of course, anxiety also brings Dasein face to face with its whole temporal stretch, but as a field whose significance is understood as precarious because of the presently anxious experience of the 'nothing.' To be sure, one will either resolutely or irresolutely return to one's ekstatic and caring immersion in the world. Yet this privileged moment of anxiety has revealed the unified ground as splittable, as having to be reunified by a resolute or irresolute fusing of distinct relata: on the one hand, meaning; on the other hand, present-at-hand entity inherently devoid of meaning. The phenomenological unification of meaning and entity, then, is in danger of appearing as a project of the will. In this sense, there are Heideggerian grounds for Sartre's splitting of the temporal unity and his radical stress on the future ekstasis in the lecture. If the a priority of the revelation of beings as present is not challenged by anxiety, nevertheless the a priority of the "precedent community of nature" is challenged, the circle of meaning is cut.

The ambiguity to which I have referred is thus that anxiety allows us to assert what is in effect an irreducible subject-object relation and to challenge the same "precedent community of nature" that was supposed to precede and ground it. Does not anxiety reveal meaningful Dasein and meaningless object as logically distinct relata after all? Do not the human and the natural appear as distinct regions in anxiety? Is not anxiety a *negation* of a prior community and the rise of the project to resynthesize that community *ex nihilo?* Is not *WM* in effect the program for a humanism that enjoins man to take over decisively the burden of synthesizing the entity "as such" with a referential "totality"—this synthesis being the goal of metaphysics—rather than ceding this task, in disownment, to the nonhumanistic idols to which we for the most part go cringing? We must conclude that Sartre's reappropriation of the writings of the early Heidegger as an existentialist humanism of the subject is not exactly arbitrary. Here as before, however, I am distinguishing between the liabilities of Heidegger's early thought and its intention.

II

Heidegger's *Letter on Humanism* (1947) was, unlike many of Heidegger's writings, published soon after its composition.[45] This perhaps suggests a certain urgency, for which there were the best of reasons. Sartre's lecture on humanism had been delivered in 1945, had been published in 1946, and had implicated Heidegger in existentialist humanism. I have argued that in the early writings of Heidegger that were available to Sartre there are some grounds for this implication. But *EN*, in 1943, offers no evidence that Sartre was familiar with *Hölderlin und das Wesen der Dichtung*, published in 1937, in which Heidegger's position has clearly undergone modification, nor does Sartre's lecture on humanism give evidence of any familiarity with *Vom Wesen der Wahrheit* (1943), the epilogue to *Was ist Metaphysik?* (1943), and *Erläuterungen zu Hölderlins Dichtung* (1944)—all crucial indices of Heidegger's reformulation of his earlier position.[46] Is it nevertheless possible that by 1945 Sartre had already formed the judgment of Heidegger's development he expressed to Simone de Beauvoir in 1953?

> He [Sartre] was rather coldly received in Freiburg, where he went to give a lecture. . . . Sartre struck them as too close to Marxism. He paid a visit to Heidegger, perched on his eyrie, and told him how sorry he was about the play Gabriel Marcel had just written about him. That was all they talked about, and Sartre left after half an hour. *Heidegger was going in for mysticism,* Sartre told me; then he added, his eyes wide: "Four thousand students and professors toiling over Heidegger day after day, just think of it!"[47]

If in 1945 Sartre had distinguished Heidegger's position from his own this sharply, he did not publicly say so. We can imagine Heidegger's reaction to what Sartre did say publicly. Living in a retirement decreed by a *Lehrverbot* imposed by the occupation forces,[48] Heidegger was subjected to the spectacle in France of a popularized and suddenly fashionable existentialism, in which "market of public opinion"[49] he himself was implicated, against all his own intentions. If Heidegger himself did not solicit the questions on humanism his friend Jean Beaufret posed him from Paris,[50] Beaufret's inquiry nonetheless provided the best opportunity available to Heidegger for a public clarification of his position and its relation to Sartre's humanism. Indeed, Heidegger's decisive differentiation of his position from Sartre's suggests that *Brief über den Humanismus* is Heidegger's response to *L'Existentialisme est un humanisme*. Together with this letter, which is much more carefully worked out than Sartre's lecture, Heidegger published *Platons Lehre von der Wahrheit,* which has the effect of showing the reader the ancient historical roots of Sartre's humanism and subjectivism in Plato's misunderstanding of the nature of truth: "The beginning of metaphysics in Plato's thinking is at the same time the beginning of 'humanism.' . . . No attempt to ground the essence of disclosedness . . . in any kind of 'subjectivity' can preserve the essence of disclosedness."[51]

The clear impression is given that Sartre has wholly misunderstood Heidegger from *SZ* forward. But Sartre's responsibility for this misunderstanding is lightened by Heidegger's admission that the absence of Division 3 of *SZ* and "the inability of the language of metaphysics" to express the *Kehre* meant that the book's presentation of the "preliminary" preparation for the *Kehre* was handled "clumsily enough." Heidegger even allows that "in *Sein und Zeit* a statement of the relation between essentia and existentia cannot yet be expressed at all."[52] But the essential reason for Sartre's misunderstanding is that he, at one with mankind, is living amid the history of "the forgottenness of the truth of Being."[53]

We have seen that the extent to which the early Heidegger was himself subject to the forgottenness of Being is a problematic question. Heidegger's own retrospective critique of *SZ* implicates him in this forgottenness—though with the proviso that he was already "on the way" out of it. This proviso may certainly be granted if it means that *SZ* was already devoted to a sustained inquiry into the limits of the "ancient ontology." But the early Heidegger, like Sartre, distinguished sharply between ontology and metaphysics; if the ancient ontology misses the ground-Being of Dasein and is therefore "destructible," nevertheless "Metaphysics is the coming to pass of ground [*Grundgeschehen*] in *Da-sein*. It is *Da-sein* itself."[54] This is a concrete indication of the fact that in 1929 Heidegger was still not fully aware of the extent of the forgottenness of Being.

When the *Kehre* in Heidegger's thinking is finally explicitly initiated, his self-critique becomes an essential feature of it. *SZ* and the other pre-*Kehre* writings are themselves taken into the history of Being. The failings of these works become exhibitions of the power of historical forgetting of Being, even over him who is already aware of it. Metaphysics, which had been "Dasein itself," is characterized as an understanding of Being from the standpoint of beings. I suggest that Heidegger retrospectively judges that metaphysics held sway over his early thought in essentially the following ways. First, his early thinking, despite its own announced intention, tends to exempt itself from historical conditioning, judging Dasein's *inevitable* historicity from a transcendental-metaphysical standpoint that nevertheless attempts to isolate permanent defining characteristics (existentialia) of Dasein.[55] The implicit assumption of this metaphysical standpoint is not conducive to comprehension of the extent to which Heidegger's own language and habits of thought are historically conditioned. Second, the implicit assumption of this same metaphysical standpoint traps Heidegger into the admission of an *inherently* meaningless presentness-at-hand that appears to escape historical conditioning and so is dangerously

similar to a permanent metaphysical substrate for historical conditioning. Thus a residual metaphysical permanence is assigned both
to Dasein and to "nature," and the two can be interpreted as irreducible relata. Third, although Heidegger clearly asserts that Being
is always the Being *of* beings,[56] the construing of the ontological
difference in terms of the metaphysical distinction between meaning and entity can be interpreted as in effect a split or dualism between the *source* of meaning and the *receptacle* of meaning. Greater
care is required if the ontological difference is not to lapse into an
ontological dualism of a new type, a dualism between Being and
beings rather than between two kinds of beings. Fourth, once these
latent metaphysical distinctions have been brought to Dasein's explicit attention, Dasein must *will* their recombination through a
'decision' that runs the risk of arbitrariness or else lapses back into
an irresponsible disowning. In both cases—whether Dasin's understanding owns up to or disowns itself—Dasein can be construed as
in effect a transcendental subject, though, to be sure, an ekstatic
one, endowing its world with a transcendental meaning rather than
uncovering an immanent meaning.

These implicit liabilities of the early Heidegger's thinking become overt in *EN*. One way of comprehending Sartre's reappropriation of Heidegger is to suggest that Sartre wears the liabilities of
Heidegger's thought as badges of honor. In other words, it is precisely those latent metaphysical assumptions and distinctions that
are foreign to Heidegger's announced intent that Sartre frees from
their latency and appropriates among the *overt* principles of his
own position. In so doing, Sartre is implicitly enjoining Heidegger
to acknowledge[57] his latent assumptions and distinctions as inevitable structures of philosophical thinking. Once again, Sartre appears as the conserver of certain traditional distinctions.

Just as it has been argued by some that Sartre read Heidegger's
SZ carelessly, it has been argued by some that Heidegger is insufficiently familiar with Sartre's philosophy. Both of these judgments
are, I believe, largely erroneous. It is clear that Sartre read *SZ* both
with care and with a sharp critical eye.[58] If Sartre misinterpreted
Heidegger's thought (e.g., in attributing atheism to him) he was
not alone in so doing; if he misjudged Heidegger's intent, he joins
the company of many of Heidegger's own students.[59]

In any case, *Brief über den Humanismus*, while mentioning Sartre only occasionally, refers throughout to the fundamentals of Sartrean doctrine and may fairly be said to be directed at Sartre in its entirety. It specifically considers not only Sartre's doctrine that "existence precedes essence," and his "humanism," but also his notions of *l'engagement*, action, actuality, project, certainty, cogito, subject/object, being, value, God as highest value, negation, and nothing. In addition Heidegger directly or indirectly considers Sartre's project to write an ethics, his attitude to history, his position on logic, his attribution of atheism to Heidegger, and his charge of covert moralism in Heidegger's notions of 'owning up' and 'disowning'. To be sure, Heidegger is responding to other critics and interpreters in responding to Sartre—and can do so here because he holds Sartre to be sharing with other critics many of the same traditional assumptions.

Heidegger's clarification of his own thinking and its relation to Sartre's position is centered on a single notion—the primacy, or ruling and grounding power, of Being in history through language. The "turn" has in essence consisted in "seeing through" nothing to Being, in comprehending nothing as "the veil of Being,"[60] in regarding nothing as the self-dissimulation of and by Being itself. The apparent emptiness of Being, its appearance as a *nihil* that Sartre can interpret as 'lack', a hole to be plugged by man, is the appearance of Being in the mode of self-dissimulation. The "forgottenness of the truth of Being" is attributable not to a human lapse of memory or to inattention but to a 'fated' closure that is simultaneous with disclosure. Thus the 'ruling' (*Walten*) of Being is 'unobtrusive' (*unaufdringlich*) or 'very secretive' (*geheimnisvoll*).[61] Given that *das Nichts—nihil—*can now be understood as Being's own self-dissimulation, nihilism can be situated as an epoch of the history of Being. Sartre, and the earlier Heidegger, can then be interpreted relative to this epoch of Being. We may say, then, that the "turn" also consists in the development of what would ordinarily be called a "philosophy of history," which is to serve as a basis for situating and evaluating all historical phenomena, including philosophies.

It is therefore owing to Being's self-dissimulation that we *appear* to be, in the words of Sartre's lecture, "on a plane where there are only men."[62] But when the apparent emptiness of 'nothing' is understood as a "concealed fullness,"[63] Heidegger can counter that "we are on a plane where there is primarily Being." Heidegger adds: " 'Being' and 'plane' are the same."[64] That is, Being is 'ground', which is also identifiable as "the clearing itself," as 'Da', and as 'world'.[65]

Metaphysics, now identifiable as exclusive preoccupation with the ontic ('metaphysics' and 'the ancient ontology' thus become virtually identical), is the 'oblivion' or 'forgottenness' of Being. This means that the whole of Sartre's *EN*—rather than only the concluding "metaphysical hints" Sartre hesitated to take—is to be situated within the history of Being as a symptom of the total forgottenness of Being in the epoch of nihilism and humanism. *EN* is not phenomenological description but rather metaphysical interpretation. But this means at the same time that *EN* is ruled by, or is "on the plane" of, Being. If the thinking of Sartre is "unobtrusively" ruled by Being, Sartre's claim to be grounding his thinking in the 'certainty' of a transcendental and 'absolute' *cogito* must be discounted.[66] If Being is original 'truth', then truth is not originally developed by or grounded in a transcendental subject or consciousness. This, of course, inevitably raises the question of the epistemological status of Heidegger's own thinking—a question I shall simply mention here and consider at greater length in chapter 13. The question may be put in the following form: why is Heidegger's interpretation of history not one hypothetical interpretation among others? In what sense, if any, can it be shown to have priority over any and every "metaphysical" interpretation of history? For the moment I restrict my response to these questions to the observation that Heidegger regards the status of his own thought as that of a *remembering*.

'Remembering' (*Andenken*) is a reversal (*Kehre*) of the movement of 'forgetting' such that thought recovers itself as it really always already is—that is, as 'ruled' by Being. If, in 'forgottenness', thinking (e.g., the elaboration of a philosophy of history) appears to itself as a freely and transcendentally generated theory about history, 'remembering' shows that this same thinking inheres in and is ruled by the history of Being: "More primordially thought through, 'there is' [not a history of and for transcendental free thinkers but rather] the history of Being, in which thinking belongs as remembering of this history and as originated and owned by that history itself."[67] *All* thinking—not merely Heidegger's thinking—belongs in this history as, in a sense, a remembering of that history. Sartre's think-

ing, for example, 'remembers' this history in the mode of 'forgetting' it; it 'remembers' that history in the sense that Sartre's thinking is grounded in that history, expresses it, and is 'destined' by
that history itself to forget the rule of Being in that history. So
Heidegger writes: "Neither Husserl nor, as far as I can yet see,
Sartre recognizes the essentially historical character of Being.
. . ."[68] Marx, on the other hand, despite the fact that his thought
is, like Nietzsche's, only an 'inversion' of metaphysics, understands
alienation or estrangement (*Entfremdung*) in its essentially historical
character, and therefore "the Marxian view of history excels all
other historiology."[69] In other words, Marx sees alienation neither
as a permanent structure of the subject-object relation, nor as a
passing *Weltanschauung*, but as the event of man's disownment by a
historical process in which he has unknowingly played out his own
fated alienation but is now called upon to recognize ('remember')
and take over ('own up to') that fate.[70]

Marx reaches this comprehension "through Hegel,"[71] who is for
Heidegger "the single thinker of the West who has *thoughtfully*
[*denkend*] experienced the history of thinking."[72] The reference to
Hegel in Heidegger's letter may carry a subtle sting. Sartre, in making his most fundamental criticism of Heidegger in *EN*, had done
so by invoking Hegel against Heidegger.[73] Heidegger is now able
to invoke Hegel against Sartre. The probable implication is a point-
edly ironic one. Sartre had employed Hegel's notion of Spirit as the
negative to insure the 'transcendence' of consciousness, which
means for Sartre its separation from its past by a 'nothingness'. In
consequence, we have seen, Sartre is able to see the movement of
consciousness as in effect a "flight forward," a continuous supercession of its past. But Heidegger here suggests that this very same
Hegel is, unlike Sartre, a thinker who has understood the real force
of the past in the present and future. Hegel, more than any other
thinker prior to Heidegger himself, 'remembers', whereas even
"Marx's humanism requires no recursion to antiquity, nor does the
humanism which Sartre conceives existentialism to be."[74]

Sartre's "flight forward" in continuous negation projects Being
forward as the impossible future goal of history, whereas 'remembering' locates Being "underneath"[75] the superficies of history as
its continuous self-dissimulating and 'ruling' source. Sartre's early
thinking suggests a ceaseless sliding across the superficies of his-

tory. It is, and wills to be, rootless. It wills alienation as the permanent 'condition' and 'situation' of man—for Sartrean 'radical conversion' is an owning up to man's essential and inalienable alienation. Taking Sartre's thinking into the history of Being, Heidegger argues that self-dissimulating Being "anounces itself at the present moment of the world through the uprooting of all beings."[76] Sartre's thinking is an unwitting organ of Being. Sartre's thinking is "the coming on" or "arrival" of a "lasting" Being[77] with ancient origins—but to apprehend this one must 'repeat' in the sense of "reappropriate" (*wiederholen*) what has been by "turning" the flight forward into a "remembering."[78] Thereby "homeless" man recalls the "home" that he is always already in but proximally and for the most part in the mode of *not* being in it, it being forgotten. Remembering is a matter of "taking over this dwelling"[79] in the "originary [*anfängliche*] dimension of . . . historical abode."[80]

In bringing the notion of ek-sistence against Sartre's existentia, Heidegger is arguing that man is always already outside himself (outside his subjective and entitative being) in this "historical abode" in such a way that his apparently subjective thought is 'ruled' by Being. This applies to Sartre's own notion of existentia, which Heidegger interprets as conforming to its traditional signification: actuality (*Wirklichkeit*).[81] This means that Sartre's thinking is governed from the ground up by the ancient ontology, which is in turn Being's own self dissimulation. Heidegger's characterization of the Sartrean being-for-itself, and not merely being-in-itself, as 'actuality' appears to misconstrue Sartre's own understanding of the for-itself's way of being, inasmuch as Sartre construes the for-itself as an ekstatic transcending of its own nothingness (nucleus). Rather than *an* actuality, the for-itself seems to be a continuous actualizing and deactualizing out of nothingness. It would appear that Heidegger has failed to grasp Sartre's notion of the "refusal of the instant." But what Heidegger has in mind is Sartre's characterization of consciousness as an 'absolute' and a 'starting-point', Sartre's reappropriation of the Cartesian and Husserlian versions of the *cogito* or transcendental subject.

Sartre does to be sure trace the *being*[82] of consciousness to a prior state, in the sense that consciousness 'rises' by an original negation of a prior 'plenum', being-in-itself ('the actual'). But "consciousness *exists* by and through itself."[83] Sartre explains: "That in no way

means that consciousness is the ground of its *being*. On the contrary
. . . the being of consciousness is wholly contingent. We only want
to show (1) that *nothing* [*rien*] is the cause of consciousness; (2) that
consciousness is the cause of its own *manner* of being."[84] Later
Sartre clarifies his usage of 'existence' by saying that the for-itself
"is the ground of its *consciousness-of-being* [*être-conscience*] or *existence*, but on no account is it able to ground its *presence* [*présence*].
Therefore *in no case* can consciousness prevent itself from being."[85]
This means that consciousness must be as "cause-of-itself."[86] These
passages show that in Sartre's terminology 'actuality' applies to
'being' rather than to 'existence'. 'Existence' for Sartre is not 'being'
but the way in which consciousness chooses "to exist" its being, its
manner of being its *given* being. The autonomy of consciousness is
limited to its way of taking over its given presence-to-being. So
regarded, "existence precedes essence" means that because consciousness is choice[87] of *how* (the manner in which) it responds to
its given *that*-ness, it determines its own *what*-ness by continuously
surpassing its past what-ness.

   Thus it is the 'choice', not the being, of the for-itself that is 'absolute', a 'starting-point', a *fundamentum inconcussum*. Since this
choice is separated from actuality by a negation, Sartre saves himself from the charge of treating the *fundamentum inconcussum* as an
absolute substance. And since choice is a negation *of being*, relative
to which consciousness has had to and must continue to situate itself, Sartre saves himself from the charge that he is volatizing the
environment of consciousness by beginning with an environ-
mentless consciousness; consciousness is an 'absolute'[88] that is
nevertheless relative, a free (or 'absolute') reappropriation of its
givenness (or 'being'). As a *relative* absolute, Sartrean consciousness is distinguishable from the *cogito* of Descartes, which is ontologically rather than merely existentially absolute. One might then
say that Sartre argues for a dual *fundamentum:* a foundation of being
and a foundation of existence (the for-itself as having to be). As a
relative absolute—as a relation—consciousness must freely synthesize the two foundations. This synthesis can be free only if the
foundations are separated by a negation, so that the particular manner of synthesizing is undetermined by the being-in-itself to which
consciousness must nevertheless relate. In other words, the 'being'

of consciousness can only be that-being; if it is what-being (essentia), then consciousness is not free to determine its essentia.

This distinction between actuality and possibility, between that-being and what-being, enables Sartre (*a*) to isolate two distinct relata or foundations, two fundamentally distinct kinds of being, and (*b*) hence to account for the absoluteness of consciousness. But because consciousness is for Sartre epistemologically absolute and absolutely distinct from being-in-itself, consciousness and being-in-itself are in effect both existentia, both merely that-being. In this limited sense, for Sartre both being and consciousness are actualities, as Heidegger has suggested, and what-being or essentia can have only a derivative being. Both being-in-itself and consciousness are inherently meaningless, essenceless. It is the question of the source of this logical and linguistic distinction between such pure that-beings and what-beings that Heidegger is really raising in calling attention to the Sartrean way of distinguishing between existentia and essentia. Heidegger had already handled this question explicitly in *KPM:*

> In every being "there is" what-being and that-being, essentia and existentia, possibility and actuality. Has "Being" the same meaning in these expressions? If not, why is it that Being is divided into what-being and that-being? . . . And is not the distinction between what-being and that-being, a distinction whose basis of possibility and mode of necessity remain obscure, entwined with the notion of Being as being-true? [89]

Later, in *Was heisst Denken?*, Heidegger again considers the question of the source of "the distinction between *what* something is, *ti estin*, and *that* it is, *hoti estin*. Later terminology distinguishes between essentia and existentia, between essentiality and factuality. . . . By what authority, and on what grounds, is that distinction made? How and in what way is thinking called to this distinction?" [90]

Heidegger's answer, omnipresent in his later writings, is that the source of this distinction is *language* as "the clearing-concealing arrival of Being itself." [91] In chapter 4 we saw how Heidegger's early thinking was in principle vulnerable to a 'nihilistic' interpretation in which the 'meaning' or 'significance' of world became relativized and in a sense subjectivized by the experience of anxiety. Arguing that this outcome contradicted the intention of Heidegger's phenomenological program, we anticipated that a way out of this dilemma might consist of further investigation of *Rede,* discourse, the least developed of the four fundamental disclosive existentialia of *SZ.* Discourse is the articulation of intelligibility and is existentially 'language' (*Sprache*). In discourse we either succeed in saying or fail to say what we mean. Heidegger allows that he did not quite succeed in saying what he really meant in *SZ*—he failed to articulate overtly and fully his real nonnihilist and nonexistentialist intention. If he were now to develop his hitherto sketchy treatment of linguistic expression, might he not find in the nature of linguistic articulation itself the reason for his failure to say fully what he had meant? Might the nature of language at one and the same time account for the *failure* to say what we mean and for the hidden or dissimulated meaning *of* what we say? Doesn't "saying" often say both more and less than we think we're saying? Isn't saying an ontological commitment rather than just "a manner of speaking"? Conceiving language as both a revealing and a concealing that always means but doesn't always expressly say what it means, one might look to language for (*a*) the source of nihilism as a meaning, (*b*) an underlying constancy of meaning dissimulated in nihilism, and (*c*) a primordial unity prior to, and ground of, the distinction between existentia as devoid of meaning and essentia as meaning. But this development in Heidegger's thinking was only possible once he had been able to understand that the anxious experience of the world and of Being as 'nothing' is an epochal phenomenon rather than a permanent or panhistorical characteristic of Dasein's way of being.

Therefore Heidegger's letter centers its discussion of history, and of Sartre's location within history, upon language as "the house of Being, originally owned [*ereignete*] and pervasively directed [*durchfügte*] by Being." [92] This is going to mean that the Sartrean relata, based on a logico-linguistic distinction between a negatively related that-being and what-being, are a duality grounded in a prior unity, Being, which has dissimulated its unity through an epochal linguistic distinction. What we have called Sartrean 'lucidity' is grounded in 'logic', which is in turn "grounded in *logos*." [93] Heidegger contends that *logos* ('word') has come to exist epochally in the privative mode of *logic*. Thus discourse (*Rede*), to express truly, must be logical. Language must be bound by the laws of logic. Language, when properly used, is itself logical: the *logos* (word) is itself logical. Thus the distinctions of language are meaningful insofar as they are governed by logic. Sartre's discourse is governed by logic and the distinctions of logic—most notably by the notion of negation (as law of consciousness), which implicitly commits his discourse to the notion of identity (as law of the in-itself), the notion of excluded middle (as law of ontological antithesis and impossibility of actual synthesis), and the notion of noncontradiction (as law of ethical lucidity).

Kant, in Heidegger's interpretation, had already retreated in terror before the thought that the universality and necessity of logic and *ratio* might be undermined if they could be traced to a prior source, a faculty of imagination that *happens* to have bound itself historically to logico-categorial distinctions.[94] The liberation of the imagination from its self-restriction to logic has preoccupied post-Kantian thought, and one may interpret Dasein's resolute owning up to itself as 'ground' of its world as one sign of this liberation: it appears that Dasein as groundless ground must *give itself* the grounds/reasons by which it organizes its existence. But at the same time *SZ* remains implicitly bound by certain logical distinctions which, I have argued, Sartre's reappropriation of Heidegger brings into the light of day.

Heidegger's accomplishment of the turn means that he now understands the imagination as bound by the way in which Being is epochally articulated in language. The romantic emancipation of the imagination from the bonds of logic is therefore not the restoration of the imagination to its fundamental absolute freedom, but rather the precondition for discovering that the imagination is always historically bound, but not necessarily always bound in the same way.

It should be noted here that Sartre holds the imagination to be absolutely free, the envisagement of the purely ideal or the unreal. Pure imagination represents man's habitation of a free space, nothingness, in which consciousness is not "degraded" by the effort to "synthesize" itself with perception.[95] Yet even here imagination is bound by logic, for the pure imagination is precisely the *negation* of perception, the positing of a region of pure intentional projection whose relation to the region of perception is dialectical, or antithetical. For Sartre, the effort to synthesize the dialectical relata, perception and imagination, requires a lapse from 'rational' into 'magical' behavior.[96] It is, paradoxically, precisely logic that guarantees for Sartre the freedom of the imagination, for what grounds the free exercise of imagination is the conscious distinction between the region of perception and the region of imagination, together with the power of consciousness to negate the perceptual order in order to inhabit the region of the imaginary. So it would appear that subjective freedom is grounded in, or made possible by, logic—in which case imagination does *not* abrogate the rule of logic.[97]

Therefore Sartrean thinking, even in its freest form, is in Heidegger's sense a "being called by" logic, which 'rules' this thinking. But Sartre's thinking does not 'remember' the self-dissimulated *source* of this logic, *logos* as the priming word that first clears and articulates in a particular way (namely, closing off in the very process of disclosing) the world in which Sartre thinks. That is, Sartre, despite his professed nominalism, treats the philosophical language in which he speaks and thinks as a neutral medium—not as an articulation that reveals selectively and dissimulates or covers its own source. Heidegger wishes to argue that historical language has always already preformed the beings we now encounter. "When we walk . . . through the forest, we are always already walking . . . through the word 'forest'. . . ."[98] The environment is linguistic, and is therefore always already a field of meaning-beings. Present-at-hand being is linguistic being. Being-in-itself is linguistic being. Furthermore, no transcendental-reflective act, be it in *Angst* or in *angoisse,* can analytically isolate a neutral being upon which meanings have been 'conferred'. What reflection can do is to 'remember' the 'source' that 'rules' the meaning-beings that man encounters. In effect, Heidegger recalls Sartre to the historical 'abode' of language in which he has always already 'dwelt', just as Heidegger earlier had had to recall his own early thinking to that abode.

Recalling this abode, it may then be seen that, owing to the "pervasive direction" by Being of the historical course of language, nihilism (as absence of meaning) is a self-dissimulation of and by historical meaning itself. Heidegger characterizes "meaning" (*Sinn*) as "the truth of Being,"[99] without abandoning his early view that Dasein is equiprimordially in 'truth' and in 'untruth'.[100] This means essentially that all of our true 'statements', which are 'true' when they 'correspond' to a factual state of affairs, *can* correspond to a factual state of affairs precisely because there is a prior community of nature between the statement and its factual object or referent. The linguistic statement refers to an "object" that is itself already linguistic. The truth is always already in the environment. Aristotle and Hegel had anticipated this in holding knowledge to be a coming to greater familiarity with the familiar on the basis of what is already familiar.[101] This is perhaps the only legitimate sense of Plato's notion of recollection.

It is on the basis of this linguistic reorientation of the history of thought that Heidegger raises the question of the topology of Sartre's philosophy, which is essentially the topology of the metaphysical tradition. What determines the layout of the distinct regions of philosophy in Sartre's thinking: ontology, metaphysics, axiology, logic, theology, theory, praxis? Heidegger's reorientation of this topology regards metaphysics as the whole, not a region, of philosophy and subsumes all other regions of philosophy under metaphysics. The regions of philosophy thus stand for distinctions whose validity is restricted to metaphysics and challengeable once one has made the turn back into the "ground" of metaphysics, self-dissimulating Being. Heidegger wishes to maintain that man has always already "dwelt" in a primordial 'abode' that is prior to and source of these distinctions, as well as of the distinctions sacred/secular, suprasensory/sensory, and spiritual/nonspiritual.[102] Heidegger's attribution of all of these "metaphysical" distinctions to a dissimulated source relative to which they lose their absolute distinctness is a clear index of the breathtakingly revolutionary implications of his thinking. It should be noted, however, that Heidegger regards this "revolution" (Umkehr) as "conservation" or "preservation" (Rettung) [103] of "tradition" (Überlieferung), in the sense of "saving" man's primordial "home" from the danger of a nihilism to which the self-dissimulation of Being has brought modern man.

Heidegger argues that the regions of philosophy gain the appearance of independence by dissimulating their inherence in the "original dimension of historical abode." For example, we have seen that logic is, but does not seem to be, grounded in logos, or the articulation of world in which understanding-articulation-attunement has always already articulated the world so that we now find it intelligible, articulable—even logically describable.

Similarly, ethics dissimulates its real source in ēthos. The apparent independence of ethics from ontology is indicated by a remark of Sartre's concerning his lecture on existentialism and humanism: "If there's no contradiction between this ethics and our philosophy, nothing more is required."[104] Probably with Sartre in mind, Heidegger writes that "Shortly after *Sein und Zeit* appeared, a young friend asked me, 'When are you going to write an ethics?'"[105] Since *SZ* presents itself as an inquiry that is to be sharply distinguished from ethical (as well as from theological)[106] inquiry, Heidegger's young friend appears to have grounds for assuming Heidegger's commitment to the traditional philosophical topology. Sartre, on the other hand, finds the usual distinction between the descriptive and the ethical already violated in *SZ*. Heidegger's response to his young friend—and to Sartre—consists in challenging the premise on which their comments were made: "But if 'ontology' as well as 'ethics'—along with all thinking in disciplines—were to become untenable and our thinking were thereby to become more disciplined, what would then happen to the question of the relation between these two disciplines of philosophy?"[107]

If the distinction between ethics, logic, and physics has a particular historical starting point in the schools of Plato and Aristotle, a starting point that may have no absolute or self-evident warrant, it may be important to 'remember' back to a more primordial understanding—for example, in Heraclitus.[108] Construing *ēthos* as 'abode', Heidegger translates Fragment DK 119 of Heraclitus (*ēthos anthrōpō daimōn*) as: "Man, insofar as he is man, dwells in the precinct of God."[109] Heidegger thus locates the primal ground not only of ethics but at the same time of theology in an understanding of *physis* (which is also prior to 'physics') as 'abode'. Heraclitus greeted visitors, disappointed at the humbleness and ordinariness of his "abode" and way of life, with the admonition "the gods present themselves even here."[110] This means that neither gods nor ethics are to be sought in a meta-physical *topos*, a separate region, but rather "at this common place" (*an diesem gewöhnlichen Ort*).[111] Here the notion of "owning up" to "everydayness" in *SZ* comes into its own. Heidegger's term *gewöhnlich* is to be associated with *wohnen* (to dwell) and *Wohnung* (dwelling, home). Man's own true dwelling as mortal is a "common place" where he finds a precedent community of nature. The common, the accustomed, the customary—in short, the "everyday"—is the 'proper' (*eigentlich*) home of man. In modern times it has decayed into the "merely" ordinary, from which man seeks meta-physical escape precisely because metaphysics has dis-placed or split off the spiritual, the theological, the ethical, and the aesthetic from the everyday, leaving the everyday impoverished as "the (merely) commonplace."

In stark contrast stands the early Sartre, who exhibits a metaphysical horror of the commonplace. Here certain biographical references of Simone de Beauvoir and of Sartre himself accord perfectly with Sartre's philosophical position. Sartre's feeling of distance from his own (*merely* physical) body[112] is the personal analogue of his philosophical interpretation of emotion as a magical and degrading fall into complicity with the body and also of his interpretation of the synthesis of imagination/affection and perception as a "degradation." Sartre's disaffection with nature and rural settings, and his preference for the artifactual and for cities,[113] is the personal analogue of his philosophical view that "we are on a plane where there are only men." Sartre's personal fear of contingency (the *merely* natural) and his consequent effort to surpass it literally in making himself a destiny and a permanence[114] has its philosophical analogues in *EN*'s description of the project to cancel contingency through synthesis and in purifying reflection's rectification of one's fall into self-deceptive complicity with one's past and with nature. I have called this the religion of humanism. In short, Sartre's personal drive to maintain whatever transcendental purity and lucidity are possible in the face of his ambiguous relation to an alien primeval slime—nature—that constantly threatens to pull him down is the counterpart of his central philosophic view of consciousness as split from actuality by an impassable negation that in principle precludes synthesis.[115]

If Sartre's position therefore appears to stand in the starkest antithesis to Heidegger's post-*Kehre* thought, this means for Heidegger that the apparent opposition dissimulates a common source, since Sartre's metaphysical stance really takes its stand on the same 'ground' to which Heidegger regards his own thought as 'called'. In its treatment of ontology, metaphysics, ethics, aesthetics, and theology, Sartre's philosophical topology forms a coherent whole as an ideal expression of the utmost self-dissimulation of Being in the epoch of nihilism. In the wake of the very Nietzsche whose thought he deplores,[116] Sartre expresses personally and philosophically the last consequence of the metaphysical separation of meaning and *physis*, the progressive devaluation of man's original abode, which is destined by Hellenic language and thought. This destiny rules in utmost self-dissimulation in the thought of Sartre. Since it is a destiny of Being itself, Sartre's thought must be regarded, when properly understood, as a sign of the "abiding . . . arrival" or "coming on" of Being itself.[117] Not a free "engagement," Sartre's thought is "engaged" in a 'directive' (*Geschick*) of Being in language. This means that 'nihilation', which Sartre had criticized Heidegger for tracing to a ground prior to conscious 'negation', must after all be located in Being: "Being nihilates—as Being."[118] That means, in part, that Being closes itself off, and appropriate interpretation of Sartre's thought finds his thought to be, unwittingly, the perfect exemplification of Heidegger's thesis.

Toward the close of his *Letter on Humanism*, Heidegger offers some remarks that are difficult to interpret, that perhaps appear sentimental, and that seem to lend weight to Sartre's later suspicion that Heidegger is "going in for mysticism."[119]

> Together with grace, evil appears in the clearing of Being. The essence of evil does not consist in the mere wickedness of human action; it rests upon the malevolence of violent anger [*des grimmes*]. Both grace and anger, however, can come into Being only insofar as Being itself is struggled for. In it the essential source of nihilation [*des nichten*] hides itself. . . . Every "no" is only the affirmation of the "not." Every affirmation rests in acknowledgment. . . .
>
> It is first and only Being which grants to grace its ascent to favor and drives rage into dis-grace.[120]

With these dark sayings one can associate two passages earlier in the letter:

> the dimension of the holy [*des Heiligen*] . . . remains closed unless the open place of Being is cleared and in its clearing is near to man. Perhaps the distinction of this age consists in the closedness of the dimension of the holy. Perhaps this is the one unique disgrace or disaster [*Unheil*].[121]
>
> To say that there is thought is to say that Being has always, in the form of a particular directive, committed itself to its essence. To commit oneself to a "person" or a "thing" means to love, to be predisposed toward him or it. When thought through more primordially, this predisposition-to means to

grant essence [*das Wesen schenken*]. Such predisposition is the ownmost essence of that enabling power [*Vermögen*] which . . . can let something come out of its source and thus be what it is [*etwas in seiner Her-kunft "wesen," das heisst sein lassen kann*]. . . . This enabling power is the "possible" in its proper sense, whose essence rests in predisposition. . . . Being as the elemental is the "quiet force" of the enabling power that predisposes—that is, the quiet force of the possible. Of course our words 'possible' and 'possibility' are, under the domination of "logic" and "metaphysics," only thought of in contradistinction to "actuality." . . . When I speak of the "quiet force of the possible," I mean . . . Being itself. . . . To empower something here means to preserve [*wahren*] it in its essence, to locate and hold it in its element [*in seinem Element einbehalten*].[122]

In these passages, grace, love, predisposition to, and empowering are to be associated with the openness of the clearing of Being. Disgrace, violent rage, evil, and negation are to be associated with the closure that occurs with all openness, the concealing and dissimulation that occur with all unconcealing. Affirmation and negation are *derivative* phenomena, responses to the openness and the closure of Being itself. If revealing and concealing always occur together, this is the enabling basis for the ability of human history to fixate upon either the revealing or the concealing in the form of affirmation or negation. The history of metaphysics has fixed upon the "violent rage" of negation, progressively 'forgetting' the openness that has been granted it as a kind of "grace." The fact that "there are" beings for man, rather than nothing, is a matter of grace. Heidegger elsewhere, interpreting Nietzsche, thinks of the history of metaphysics, eventuating in nihilism, as "revenge against time." Revenge against time is a violent rage, a willful subjective assertion that seeks to negate "time and its 'it was'."[123] It seeks to free man from his mortal-temporal conditions by negation of an environment now regarded as the merely actual, and to situate him instead in a region of *pure* possibility (transcendent Being, heaven, free thought, pure imagination, etc.). This is all the more necessary the more the environment is reduced to mere presentness-at-hand, bare actuality, an 'abode' unfit for human habitation. In consequence, it is progressively forgotten that the mortal-temporal conditions being negated are the very "possibility" of there being beings rather than nothing. This negation is therefore violence against the ground-possibility of beings—even violence against what makes violence itself possible. Man's present 'disgrace' is his violence against the very source of his world.

The interpretive violence or 'rape' (Raub)[124] for which Heidegger is famous is a kind of counter-violence designed to provoke a 'remembering' of the source of violence in a 'forgotten' 'love'. 'Love' itself ravishes; any being is uncovered at the cost of a certain partiality and a certain forgetting of what escapes one's immediate 'concern'. What is *present* is *privatively revealed*. The vivid attention-seeking present appearance of the object is a privation of the full phenomenon, which exceeds and supports the appearance. What Heidegger had called authentic concernful solicitude[125] tempers the violent partiality of present interest with positive 'care' for the wholeness or integrity of the being that submits or opens itself openly to us. Love is a violent passion that nevertheless 'cares for' or 'preserves' the object of its passion.

Heidegger's effort is to show that negation and nihilism presuppose an openness—the presence of an articulated world—for which they cannot themselves account. Even the presence of a world of mere actuality, a world of beings "essentially devoid of any meaning at all," is the sign of a precedent community of nature to which man has always already committed himself. "There is" no world without man's having named it, articulated it; there is no environment to negate unless it has already been affirmed. The world is now found "meaningless" on the basis of a long history of meanings, the history of metaphysics.[126] The present-at-hand has always already been manhandled. It is not the neutral object of a noninterpretive seeing. The world has submitted to being a playground for a history of varying and often contradictory assertions about its "real meaning"—what it is "as such and as a whole"—and *exceeds* all of these assertions as the ground that makes possible any of these assertions. As man has been concernfully 'predisposed toward' his environment in the quest for its real meaning, the environment has been 'predisposed toward' man in the sense of submitting to and even facilitating these inquiries. This mutual 'predisposition' is the enabling ground of any and every assertion. We may think of it as articulative empathy, and as Heidegger's reappropriation of the 'care' of SZ. Evil is fundamentally the loss of empathy. Before all negative distinction of himself from his environment, man is ekstatically ('lovingly') committed to it, at one with it, in the communal process of its initial disclosure-closure as an articulated place, region, ground, abode. That disclosed 'place' (*Ort*) is the scene and reference point of all subsequent interpretation and analysis. It is a "neutral" place in the sense that it can support ('enable', 'incline toward') a range of interpretations, but it is far from neutral in the sense that it has always already been disclosed-closed as a particular sort of world.

Heideggerian phenomenology[127] is a remembering of the phenomenon, which for the most part does not appear but rather dissimulates itself because of the forgottenness of its ground, its place. The cruel ('malevolent') irony of metaphysics is that it forgets its basic 'debt' to what 'owns' it,[128] biting the hand that feeds it, a hand that is not simply the hand of man. Metaphysics is evil, or impious, insofar as it seeks to dispense with the 'gift' of 'grace' that is a dispensation upon which it absolutely depends.[129]

There is little doubt that Heidegger sees all violence as grounded in the forgetting of a fundamental community, and the overcoming of violence as requiring a remembering return to this primary loving empathy dissimulated by a reductive objectivity and a willful individual subjectivity. This is the real reason for his sympathetic treatment of Marx in the *Letter on Humanism*. It is not that Marx reached an understanding of the precedent community of nature in Heidegger's sense, but rather that he was "on the way" toward it.[130]

I can now assert what has no doubt by now become obvious: for Heidegger, Sartre's grounding of the understanding of Being in negation is violence. His "flight forward" is "revenge against time and its 'it was'." His humanism is a subjective voluntarism that does not understand the real historical (*not* individual) root of human alienation and hence the possibility *within* history of an essential amelioration of that alienation. His 'play' is a resigned and "Hellenistic" sliding over the ground he is really rooted in. In short, Sartre's rage for the future leaves no time for remembering the essential past that 'comes on' or 'arrives' as man's essential future. There is no possibility for Sartrean thought to "become what it is," to return to and accord with its ground, for it has lost all sense of *amor fati*, that is, of loving inclination toward the ground that sustains it. The primordial event for Sartre is separation-by-negation from the ground and this is freedom from fate.

III

Sartre will later write of his published work: "If the critics now find it bad, they may wound me perhaps, but in six months I will be coming round to their opinion."[131] Sartre's thought soon underwent considerable transformation, and it is possible that Heidegger's letter played a limited role in that transformation. We must leave open the question whether Heidegger's critique of Sartre's reappropriation of *SZ* is fair in expecting Sartre to recognize Heideggerian intentions that only became publicly clear after the *Kehre* had explicitly begun. In Sartre's judgment, "Heidegger has no character."[132] But Sartre utters this harsh judgment in the course of defending the autonomy of Heidegger's thinking against critics who tried to discount it by seeing in it merely an expression of Heidegger's personal politics. If Sartre defends Heidegger's thought on the basis of a traditional distinction between the autonomy of thought and the person, does Heidegger's critique of Sartre undermine that distinction by making thought the unwitting expression of a historical fate? Does Sartre come to deny the autonomy of his own thought and insert it within history?

In any case, we shall not find Sartre appropriating Heidegger's notion of Being. In 1961 Sartre could still write that "it is for man to give Being to beings." Sartre says this in the course of an expression of inquietude over the extent to which Merleau-Ponty's later thought approached that of Heidegger: "Being is the only concern of the German philosopher. And in spite of a philosophy which they at times share, Merleau's principal concern remained man. When the former speaks of 'the opening to Being,' I scent alienation." While reassuring the reader that Merleau "never ceased being a humanist," Sartre nevertheless finds it necessary to address one last admonition to his late friend: "It is a pity that a man can still write today that the absolute is not man."[133] It is clear that a chief issue emerging between Heidegger and Sartre is that of the nature of alienation, and it is equally clear that their conflicting interpretations of alienation depend upon how they interpret history. Is history primarily the history of Being or the history of man?

The Reorientation

FOR BOTH Heidegger and Sartre the need arises for a reassessment of the place of their thought in history. As early as *SZ* Heidegger had, to be sure, explicitly situated Dasein in history. Although Heidegger formally situates his own thought *about* Dasein within history and within "the circle of interpretation,"[1] it is likely that the consequence of this historical situating of his thought did not become wholly clear to him until "the turn" commenced. The turn ironically and concretely confirmed his earlier formal situating of his thought within history, for it showed his early thinking to have been historically conditioned—by "the history of metaphysics"—in a manner he had not altogether anticipated.

Sartre's early thought appears to effect a *de facto* disjunction between temporality and historicality. While finding being-for-itself a temporal activity, *EN* contains no systematic treatment of historicality. This lacuna is perhaps attributable to Sartre's interpretation of consciousness. This interpretation both (*a*) retains the transcendental-metaphysical vantage point of the Cartesian *cogito*, which appears to afford Sartre's own thought an essentially suprahistorical standpoint from which to describe permanent structures of the human way of being, apart from the vicissitudes of history, and (*b*) effects by negation, and by the purifying reflection that explicitly grasps that negation, a radical break with the past and the conditioning of thought by the past.[2]

But Sartre is going to find it both personally and philosophically necessary to situate his own thought within history—a move which my references to his autobiography have already anticipated. The shock of discovery experienced by Sartre and de Beauvoir is a shock also experienced by Heidegger: the discovery that history was going on behind their backs. I regard this as a critical point in the thinking of both Heidegger and Sartre. If, as both thinkers now discover, even the most reflective philosophy has missed the fundamental historical conditions which that philosophy itself expresses, what legitimate role remains for philosophy in the future? If history conditions thought, in what sense can thought either guide history or impartially describe history? More technically, if the doctrine of internal relations is going to mean that thought is itself internally related to history, in what sense can the autonomy of thought that philosophy has traditionally presupposed be salvaged? Hegel's thought survives its insertion in history only because for him there is a precedent community of nature—in his case, a rational absolute common to both thought and history. But thinking which is inserted in a history that is no longer characterizable as rational would appear to be a thinking which cannot validate its own assertions as impartial, objective, neutral, disinterested. The thought of Nietzsche is a classic illustration of this dilemma, for Nietzsche's description of thought as a vicissitude of its environment deprives this very description itself (and any other "description") of its validity.[3]

Hegel argued that in the thought of Descartes "Philosophy has regained its own ground—that thought starts from thought as what is certain in itself, and not from something external. . . ."[4] It is partly in order to preserve the ground for his own assertions that Sartre, with Husserl, conserves the transcendental *cogito*. Can Heidegger write ontological descriptions without it? Does he covertly presuppose it, as Sartre would argue? Will Sartre himself, in the face of the claims of history, have to surrender it?

Chapters 7 and 8 attempt to understand the process of thought by which Heidegger comes ultimately to ground and account for his thought in an "original Event" or "beginning" that "directs" all subsequent thought. Chapter 9 shows how this beginning "dissimulates" itself in such a way as to give rise to the appearance that thought is free and groundless, provoking the metaphysical quest for a ground. The fundamental role of language in this grounding and ungrounding process is traced, and it is shown how the role now given to language by Heidegger enables him to surmount the danger of nihilism to which I have found his early thought liable.

Chapter 10 attempts to infer from Sartre's writings a critique of Heidegger's interpretation of the beginning and of the function of language—a sustained response to Heidegger's critique of Sartre (chapter 6) that Sartre himself has never given. The resulting view of the relation of being-in-itself to human language, logic, conceptuality, and action raises certain problems to which Sartre's later thought (chapters 11 and 12) must respond. Chapter 11 traces a "shift of level" whereby the later Sartre resituates his earlier thought in a history of "praxis" or socioeconomic action, thereby resolving the chief ontological problem of his early philosophy. Chapter 12 seeks to show how, given this shift of level, Sartre thinks being and action can be reconciled in history.

Overall, the chapters of Part III present the two thinkers' mature judgment about the nature and interrelation of Being and time, and the relation of thought to history. These chapters show that, despite their common grappling with history, Heidegger and Sartre in their later works were even more dramatically opposed than in their early writings. On this basis, Part IV can undertake a final confrontation of the two ontologies—an assessment of their ground and truth—and a tentative assessment of the legacy they leave to future ontological inquiry.

7

The Nature of the Place: Earth and Language

I HAVE interpreted Heidegger as attempting to carry through the phenomenological program by locating phenomena relative to that sort of ground which will circumvent the necessity of composing phenomena out of discrete and antithetical relata— physical and metaphysical, objective and subjective, meaningless and meaningful, atomic and relational, natural and artifactual. For if phenomena are "composed of" discrete and antithetical components or relata, the phenomenon or "object of experience" is constantly threatened by an analytic factoring that reveals its fundamentally synthetic character, in the sense that the phenomenon is then apprehended as a merely virtual totality. The effect of such factoring is essentially the same, for Heidegger, whether it takes the form of a Democritean analysis into atomic and sensible components or an analysis by epochē into necessary a priori and contingent a posteriori components. The analysis in *SZ*—in its distinctions between existential and existentiell, existential and categorial, ontological and ontic—was at least residually still under the influence of this analytic-factorial way of thinking.[1]

For Heidegger this phenomenological problem is inseparable from the ontological program to determine "the basic meaning" that guides the "multiplicity of meanings" with which beings are spoken of. One may take as evidence for this inseparability the fact that so long as ontologically Being appears as 'nothing', the phenomenon fails to appear in its primordial unity. But when 'nothing' is understood as self-dissimulated Being, the factorial splitting of the unity of the phenomenon (into existential and essential, or objective and subjective, relata) can be understood as a forgetting and a dissimulation of a unity at a deeper level. In short, I have argued, the phenomenological program depends upon an ontological precedent community of nature.

In *SZ* a chief notion for expressing this prior community of nature is that of 'the circle'. The circle is characteristic both of Dasein's way of being and of interpretation of that way of being. To interpret properly is to "reenter" resolutely a circle that the interpreter is always already within. Because one is always *already* within the circle, the Cartesian notion of an absolute starting point for interpretation in the *present* is held to be invalid. The circle is "a remarkable 'relatedness backward or forward' "[2] (Heidegger means both "backward" *and* "forward")—while for Descartes interpretation proceeds properly ("methodically") precisely when it renounces relating backward (to one's prior and inherited presuppositions) and relates only forward, from an absolute new beginning. In effect, one tries to abrogate a prior community of nature that was methodologically ungrounded and naïve. There remains a vestige of this Cartesian procedure, one might argue, in Heidegger's effort to 'repeat' more truly "the average understanding of Being"[3] precisely because it is only average. Yet this repetition is not a new beginning but a "way *back*" (*Rückgang*) into an always prior and primordial understanding whose origin is not attributable to any present. 'Repetition' (*Wiederholung*) means to catch (*holen*) this prior understanding once again (*wieder*) by a 'reappropriation' or 'owning up to' one's ownmost ground.

By 1954, however, Heidegger states that "talk of a circle always remains superficial" and not "originary."[4] The circle, Heidegger's notion for understanding and interpretation, has given way to a more "originary" notion, that of the 'Fourfold' (*Geviert*)[5] whose four members are earth, heavens, mortals, and gods. If we can, in this chapter and chapter 8, ascertain why the circle gives way to the Fourfold, we shall better understand man's relation to history in Heidegger's later thought. The present chapter considers how and why Heidegger introduces the notion of 'earth' and what might be called the notion of a "linguistic ontology" and then shows how these two notions inform his ontologically crucial notion of 'place'. Treatment of Heidegger's subsequent notion of the Fourfold is reserved for chapters 8 and 9.

I

Why does Heidegger rethink the notion of circularity and, in so doing, introduce the notion of earth? Heidegger's account of the

meaning of the circle in the thought of Kant provides a clue to the
need for thinking back behind the circle. In explicating the *Critique
of Pure Reason* A737/B765 in *Die Frage nach dem Ding* Heidegger
writes: "Experience is in itself a circular happening through which
what lies within the circle becomes exposed [*eröffnet*]. This open
[*Offene*], however, is nothing other than the between [*Zwischen*]—
between us and the thing." [6] Two facets of this account should be
noted. First, Heidegger credits Kant with anticipating the notion of
the 'clearing' as the 'open' place within which beings can be articulated and identified, hence can appear. This circle–open place–
clearing–world is a relational place; it does not, like an empty con-
tainer, preexist man and things but is precisely the relation *between*
man and things. Nor, it would appear, do man and things preexist
this open place, since it is the place of relation in which man and
things come to be as they are. It would appear that man, clearing,
and thing are 'equiprimordial' or 'contemporaneous', and that entities do not precede the relations between them—another way of
expressing the "doctrine of internal relations" that, I have argued,
governs phenomenology in both its Hegelian beginning and its
Heideggerian outcome. This relational doctrine challenges the
thesis that one can begin with polar relata and subsequently bring
them into relation with each other.

But there is a second facet of the passage I have quoted that
stands in tension with the first. The 'between' is still "between us
and the thing," meaning that the circle still has two "poles." However much Heidegger pushes the ultimate implications of Kant's account, there remain for Kant two poles that preexist and ground the
'between': noumenal ego and noumenal "thing." Therefore Heidegger must all the more stress "that this *between* is not like a rope
stretching from the thing to man, but that this *between* as an anticipation [*Vorgriff*] reaches beyond the thing, and similarly back behind us. Reaching-before [*Vor-griff*] means thrown back [*Rück-
wurf*]." [7]

This passage seems to argue that the 'between' does after all
preexist both the 'thing' and 'us'. Indeed Heidegger writes that "the
question of the thing is a historical one" and that "The question
'What is a thing?' is the question 'Who is man?' " [8] These assertions
imply that 'man' and 'thing' are phenomena that correlatively
evolve and change historically within the framework of a prior

'clearing'. Yet the 'clearing' is a clearing *between* man and thing. What Heidegger seems to mean is that whatever 'man' and 'thing' have meant at any particular historical juncture,[9] they have always been identified relative to each other and at the same time relative to an inherited past and prior correlative identification of man and thing. So Heidegger is not arguing that there is first a clearing and *then* man and thing, but rather that at any historical point man and thing have to be identified and understood not from scratch (or from an absolute new beginning) but relative to the past man-clearing-thing articulation in and from which present man thinks and experiences.

This line of thought may suggest that it is part of Heidegger's intention to challenge the man-thing polarity by reducing it to the succession of its historical appearances, but many passages speak against this sort of reduction. For example, elsewhere in *Die Frage nach dem Ding*, Heidegger writes that when we think in terms of the progress of science and technology we find that "an original reference to things is missing, that it is only simulated by the progress of discoveries and technical successes."[10] The word 'simulated' (*vorgetäuscht*) can be interpreted as indicating that the historical succession of appearances is just that—a series of semblances of phenomena whose nature is more original or primordial. To characterize these phenomena Heidegger explicitly evokes the phenomenological expression 'things themselves', which refers to what "must constantly be presupposed as that which the physiological-physical inquiry breaks up and reinterprets."[11] Kant too has "disregarded what is manifest [*das Offenbare*]."[12] "Like the tradition before and after him, he skips that sphere of things in which we know ourselves immediately at home, i.e., things as the artist depicts them for us. . . ."[13] Here Heidegger appeals, against the ancient ontology and its modern representatives, to human experience of a phenomenon that is always already articulated in relation to man, and that always exceeds and grounds (is presupposed by) any "physiological-physical" analysis of it. In other words, the 'thing' is primordially the 'phenomenon' as it occurs within the 'circle', as relative to man's understanding and articulation of it *before* analytic inquiry. Similarly and correlatively, the ground of the successive historical-analytic interpretations of 'man' is a series of semblances that dissimulate the phenomenon of man's essence, i.e., Dasein.[14]

Furthermore, the two series of semblances—the history of interpretations of 'things' and the history of interpretations of 'man'—are
functions of each other, since they appear within the same 'circle'
and are 'ruled' by the same ontological assumptions (i.e., by the
same 'directive' of Being).

Thus the notion of the man-'between'-thing circle, when understood as the Dasein-clearing-phenomenon circle, implies neither
the reduction of the man-thing distinction to a prior clearing nor
the reduction of the clearing or 'between' or 'world' to a synthetic
product of the present-time interaction between man and thing. It
is the latter danger that still resides in Kant's position.

But even with this revision of Kant, the circle remains an insufficient notion for Heidegger. The problem is that "the affair" (*die
Sache*) of the circle is still 'between' man and thing. The notion is
inherently bipolar, suggesting a dialectic 'between' man and thing.
Now if Dasein, while exhibiting through history the same existentialia, is empowered precisely by these existentialia to 'decide' by
historical revision the meaning of the between, thereby putting
meaningful flesh on the bones of inherently meaningless entities,
then one has lapsed back into a view that in effect holds the 'between' to be a variable constituted by the interaction of two con-
stants, Dasein and entities inherently devoid of any meaning at all.
By 1935 Heidegger has obviated this danger of *SZ* insofar as he now
explicitly interprets the truly apprehended phenomenon not as an
entity inherently devoid of meaning but as an entity whose own
meaning is *dissimulated as* meaningless.

It is important to note that *SZ* was written at a time when Heidegger was engaged in differentiating his thought from that of the
neo-Kantians by whom he was surrounded and to whom he finds
Husserl's philosophy still too close. He accomplishes this differentiation in part by the effort, in *KPM*, to reappropriate Kant on a
deeper level than the neo-Kantians had been able to do. But Heidegger's chief thrust at the neo-Kantians lies in his delineation of
the experience of anxiety, for it is in anxiety that the allegedly universal and necessary meanings of entities are ripped away, leaving
an inherently meaningless entity that must then become the bearer
of meanings through historical decision (resolute projection), rather
than through a universal and necessary positing of transcendental a
priori reason. For Kant all phenomena are intelligible, ordered,

rule-following, and meaningful. Anxiety abrogates that intelligible order; the entity can, figuratively and literally, "break in upon us and destroy us."[15] One cannot, as the neo-Kantians seek to do, bypass the Hegelian-Marxian encounter with history and the Kierkegaardian encounter with decision. But the price of this most decisive break with the neo-Kantians is, we have seen, an endangering of the phenomenological program to which, despite its affinities with Kant's revision of rationalism, Heidegger is also committed.

There is a significant shift of accent between Heidegger's critique of Kant in 1929 and in 1935. In *KPM*, what is stressed is that Kant does not face up to pre-rational imagination as the hidden ground of reason. In 1935 Heidegger instead stresses that Kant disregards "the manifest," i.e., the primary experience of phenomena that precedes and grounds the rational interpretation of phenomena. Furthermore, Heidegger can call this ordinary pre-analytic experience of phenomena the experience of *things themselves*. It is not difficult to see what this shift of stress is intended to accomplish. It is an effort to guard against the danger, inherent in *SZ*, that the phenomenon may fall apart into "that-being" and "what-being," existentia and essentia, in such a way as to suggest an idealism of meaning based on a realism of existence. The seeming experience of inherent meaninglessness has become a forgetting of the precedent community of nature. Heidegger, then, returns to a modified version of the Kantian view that all phenomena are essentially meaningful. The metaphysical anxiety of *WM* is taken into history as an *epochal* experience of the *apparent* absence of a ground of meaning in the epoch of nihilism.[16] If man must depend on reason, or any other meta-physical source, for the meaning of his world, then there will be a perennial threat of the anxiety from which Kant fled, But if meaning can be located at a deeper and epochally forgotten level, then metaphysical anxiety may turn out to be epochal rather than perennial. This does not mean that in a post-metaphysical time there would be no anxiety, for there would remain a region of the unknown and unfathomable and a mortal precariousness. It rather means that once having surrendered the quest for an absolute unconditional ground as a precondition for "inherent meaning," one could affirm phenomena as meaningful under finite and relative conditions.

Anxiety would, so to speak, be sublimated; it would be an indication of the conditionality of meaning rather than of the absence of meaning. For the same reason, one might say that in a post-metaphysical time, nihilism would be sublimated rather than simply canceled.

But this shift inherent in the *Kehre* raises in turn a new problem. If all phenomena are inherently meaningful, is one not forced to reassert the noumenon behind the phenomenon? In other words, if one finds all phenomena meaningful, must one still not account for brute nature insofar as it does not fall within the phenomenal experience of man? Otherwise the post-*Kehre* unification of that-being and what-being, existence and essence, will mean that what had been in effect an idealism of meaning based upon a realism of existence will become an idealism both of meaning *and* of existence. The key to solution of this problem ought to lie in the experience of the early Greeks, i.e., prior to the metaphysical separation of that-being and what-being. There, indeed, Heidegger finds the experience of "nature" as *physis*.[17] In Heidegger's interpretation of the process of *physis*, phenomena emerge from, and subsequently return into, a dark and uncognizable source or ground—which the subsequent history of metaphysics will unsuccessfully try to fathom and illuminate. 'Mortal' man is aware of this dark source as the limit and boundary of his understanding, out of which he himself comes and back into which he returns.[18] But at the same time, in emerging from darkness into the 'light' (*Licht*) of the clearing (*Lichtung*), phenomena come into an articulated or meaningful 'presence'.

The region of phenomena is also the region of the gods. For Heraclitus "The gods present themselves even here." This can be construed to mean that the dark source of phenomena is not a region that takes metaphysical precedence over phenomena in the sense of being the transcendent repository of their "real" meaning and nature. Clearly and frankly 'mortal' rather than fallen from a meta-physical realm, early Greek man experiences the phenomenal world as his ownmost 'abode' and affirms his 'fate' in that world. Confronted by the obvious fact of meaning, he regards his mortal compresence with entities that are also finite as a 'gift', though to be sure one fraught with terror as well as with wonder.

What Heidegger sees in *physis*, then, is a process of origination that does not discount the reality, meaning, or value of phenomena.

All these are functions of a finite articulation ('lighting') that holds open a clearing or world in which beings come to present themselves as familiar to man but not as originated by man or by any other being. *Physis* is a process that supports an intelligible phenomenon in its full phenomenal reality. This is opposed to a metaphysical ground that can support an intelligible phenomenon only if that ground is itself known, since metaphysics takes the phenomenon as initially and directly experienced to be *a problem*, to be lacking in an intelligibility that must therefore be supplied from beyond (meta-) the phenomenon. One may say that it is precisely by remaining dark and uncognizable that the source of *physis* lets the phenomenon be what it presents *itself* as being. This appears to mean that the price of reaching things themselves—that is, carrying out the phenomenological program—is that the ground of phenomena remain hidden and unintelligible. Otherwise, there is initiated that endless rage for knowledge of causes and grounds, and for mastery of causes and grounds, whose real result is the ironic loss of phenomenal reality in the very quest for its meta-phenomenal source. This result is nihilism. As soon as meaning and intelligibility require a metaphysical guarantee that is in principle unavailable, the history of metaphysics and its consummation in nihilism are 'fated' to occur.

The ground of *physis* that lets the phenomenon be what it is *by* remaining hidden Heidegger calls 'earth'.[19] It is not a reversion to Kant's noumenon, for the simple reason that it is not the thing-in-itself, the pure entity knowable to God under nonfinite conditions. Though Kant regards the phenomenal as 'real' and as 'substance',[20] the noumenal remains as a limit to and frustration of the metaphysical quest of pure reason—for things as they *actually* are—and is speculatively and regulatively posited as a metaphysical ground.[21] Heidegger accedes to the Kantian assertion of the finitude of human knowledge while purifying Kant of the metaphysical drive to compensate for this finitude by the regulative use of reason. This drive for compensation signals that for Kant the finite and phenomenal realm cannot yet be wholly affirmed in *amor fati*. Kant remains meta-physical, although Heidegger sees Kant as taking the first decisive step toward the destruction of metaphysics as a precondition for the affirmation of finitude.

At the same time—roughly 1935—Heidegger pairs 'earth' with

'world' in a kind of strife reminiscent of Heraclitean *polemos*. *Physis* is the strife of earth and world.[22] The notion of 'strife' indicates that articulation is won from a region that exceeds that articulation and supports it only for a mortal span and on terms that cannot be counted upon. What is important for our present analysis is that world here gains a nonmetaphysical support: the Dasein-clearing-phenomenon circle is in effect enlarged so that "the affair" is no longer ultimately 'between' Dasein and thing, but is at least as much between earth and world. In reading *SZ*, one easily falls into the habit of picturing 'world' as a sort of evanescent field that Dasein has always already projected over an inherently meaningless environment. By 1935, world is picturable as supported by the earth, as the finite articulation *of* earth. 'Ground' is no longer simply Dasein's Being-in-the-world. It is now to be construed more literally, as the solid and supportive earth, the fundamentum of world.

If world is the articulation *of* earth and if earth is the fundamentum *of* world, then the notion of a precedent community *of nature* can be construed quite literally. The 'world' of *SZ* still has an "artifactual" quality; it is a prior community, to be sure, for it has already joined Dasein's meanings to entities, but it is one that can be interpreted as having to be metaphysically maintained over a nature that reveals itself to anxiety as *alien*. In anxiety Dasein is "not at home."[23] While the prior community is a fact and a necessity, it is still liable to interpretation as an ongoing effort to make a home, by resolute projection of meaning, out of an essentially alien nature into which Dasein is "thrown" and "abandoned." There is not yet a community of *nature* but only a community of *natures* that remain essentially opposed. We have seen that the Sartrean distinction between in-itself and for-itself capitalizes on this distinction between essentially opposed natures, between which any community can only be "synthetic" or "artifactual."

For the later Heidegger, however, man always already *belongs to* "nature," as is implied by the term 'earth' (as opposed to 'nature' in the sense of 'the physical' or 'the material'). In accord with the standing debt of much of phenomenology to *Lebensphilosophie*, earth is "lived nature," a "dwelling-place," i.e., a partially articulated or "worlded" nature. Earth is not a category, nor is it advanced by Heidegger as a speculative ground. It is intended con-

cretely, as an experienced place. Here the philosophical term
'ground' ceases to be metaphorical; its original, literal, root meaning is recalled. But even in 1935 this understanding of man's community with "nature" is not fully realized.[24] In the notion of strife
between world and earth there remains a residue of the man-thing
polarity, an echo of dialectical or synthetic community as distinct
from "natural" community.[25] Heidegger's reponse to this residue is
to concentrate anew on the relation between unity and multiplicity,
identity and difference, in their relation to *language,* in such a way
that the stress falls increasingly on 'oneness' and 'simplicity'.

II

I have noted in chapter 4 that *Rede* (discourse) is the least developed of the four fundamental disclosive existentialia in *SZ* although
it is perhaps the most important for the problem of meaning and
the phenomenological quest for the unification of meaning and
Being as phenomenon.[26] We should, at this point, consider the interrelation of discourse, articulation, and language in *SZ*. This will
help us to see how Heidegger's thinking moves from what might be
called a prelinguistic ground to a linguistic ground.

> Discourse is existentially equiprimordial with state-of-mind
> and understanding. The intelligibility of something has always
> been articulated, even before there is any appropriative in-
> terpretation of it. Discourse is the articulation of intelligibility.
> Therefore it underlies both interpretation and assertion. That
> which can be articulated in interpretation, and thus even more
> primordially in discourse, is what we have called "meaning."
> That which gets articulated as such in discursive articulation,
> we call the "totality of significations" [Bedeutungsganze]. This
> can be dissolved or broken up into significations. Significa-
> tions, as what has been articulated from that which can be ar-
> ticulated, always carry meaning. . . . discourse [is] the artic-
> ulation of the intelligibility of the "there. . . ."[27]

Owing to Dasein's prior projection of meaning, the "there" has
meaning, makes sense, is intelligible. Individual items in the world
can make sense only because they mean something to Dasein and
have some significant reference to other items in the world. Human
discourse not only makes distinctions (articulations) between these

significant items but articulates them as a more or less coherent whole. 'Articulation' means primarily the joining, organizing, or grouping of entities as or within a structured whole, a unity. It means internal relatedness. This original articulation as a unity-of-the-distinct foreshadows Heidegger's later notion of 'gathering' (*Versammlung*) as the original forming of a 'juncture' (*Fuge*) that 'enjoins' (*fügt* or *bestimmt*) man.[28] This juncture is the ground-possibility of a disjunctive or analytic separating-out or factoring of relata, components, "atomic" entities. Analytic interpretation and assertion 'dissemble' insofar as they present the individual entity as isolated, and are "valid" if and only if they succeed in "letting something be seen in its *togetherness* [*Beisammen*] with something—letting it be seen *as* something."[29] Dissembling is a disjoining of a prior juncture. Thus 'in-itself' means "in the whole" rather than "all by itself." Valid interpretation is a "relating" (in the sense of retelling or recounting) of a prior relatedness.

The primary articulation appears to be prior to language, for language is in *SZ* "the way in which [articulative] discourse gets *expressed*."[30] This implies, as Stephen Erickson has noted, a rather sharp distinction between meaning and referential totality on the one hand and language on the other.[31] Discourse is in *SZ* "the *fundamentum* of language."[32] Nevertheless, Heidegger asserts that "Discourse is existentially language"[33] and that "The Greeks had no word for 'language'; they understood this phenomenon 'in the first instance' as discourse."[34]

If the relative primordiality of language is thus left unclarified in *SZ*, Heidegger does make clear that language provides the possibility of dissembling in at least three ways. (1) As an ensemble of words, language is itself a kind of entity "which we may come across as ready-to-hand,"[35] in which case language can appear as a tool among other tools rather than as an environment to which we are always already submitted and *within* which we think. (2) "Language can be broken up into word-things which are present-at-hand."[36] In this case the relation of the word to its linguistic context is hidden,[37] or the relation of the word to the referential totality is hidden. Thus in 'idle talk', 'curiosity', and 'ambiguity', falling Dasein loses itself in an apparently isolated present that hides its relation to a unified temporal ground. (3) Although the tenses of language are grounded in the "ekstatical unity of temporality,"[38] their very distinctness and the ability of Dasein to choose its tenses in speech and thought enables Dasein to lose itself—for example, in the "rapture"[39] of the future (as do the young), or in the rapture of the past (as do the aged). In summary, language tends to isolate Dasein from other entities, isolate entities from their referential totality, and isolate any of the three dimensions of time from their primordial unity. Language in *SZ* may seem to be primarily the *enemy* of internal relatedness, of a prior articulation, though it is at the same time the possibility of an explicit reappropriation of that prior articulation in "apophantic" assertion.[40]

We are now in a position to see that Heidegger's early treatment of language stands in the most intimate relation with the "nihilistic" interpretation to which I have found *SZ* inherently liable. There are two reasons for this. First, if articulation is inherently pre-linguistic, language as the 'expression' of articulation will have the task of expressing a ground that is *essentially foreign* to it. In other words, there will be no precedent community of nature between language and articulation such that in expressing articulation language would be a returning to its ownmost locale. Articulation will therefore have the status of a meta-physical ground of language, i.e., a ground which must be posited *behind* language and which, as essentially foreign in nature to language, will appear from the standpoint of language as 'nothing'. It is difficult if not impossible to comprehend what a region of meaning and intelligibility that is prior to language would be like. Would it not, in fact, present itself as a region "essentially devoid of any meaning at all"? Furthermore, if the phenomenon is a meaning-being and meaning is prior to language, will not the consequence be the Sartrean experience that "things are divorced from their names?"[41] In that case, the linguistic world will succumb to a nominalism that, aware of the arbitrariness of names, will regard language as a barrier between man and 'things themselves' and also as manipulable by human will and 'decision'.

I do not mean to say that these consequences are part of Heidegger's intention. To the contrary, his intention in distinguishing between discursive articulation and language was probably to save phenomena from a linguistic idealism that reduces entities to what is said *about* them. A phenomenon liberated from its everyday accretion of categories and labels is no doubt a phenomenon before which one may experience afresh the wonder that it is at all, rather than nothing. But it remains unclear how Dasein as an existentially linguistic being could find this prelinguistic region either intelligible or meaningful. Could it then be that Heidegger's early distinction between meaning/intelligibility and language is itself an analytic factoring of a prior unity or 'junction'? If so, could one rejoin thing and name, while still allowing for and accounting for the possibility that language may alienate man from the same entities that it articulates?

Thus once again we are brought back to the latent tension in *SZ* between man's groundedness in an always already meaningful ground and the breakup of this ground in the experience of anxiety. The net effect of overt anxiety is to bring to the fore 'world as world', as ontologico-existentially constitutive, at the price of emptying out the world's particular ontico-existentiell meaning. Heidegger "saves" ontico-existentiell meaning only by asserting that this fleeting overt anxiety will inevitably be surpassed by a renewed 'rapture' that will either simply find meaning by forgetting its own role in projecting meaning or, in explicit care, cast itself resolutely into the "throwing of the projected world over beings."[42] Meaning is "saved" in the sense that there will be meaning of some sort, while the primordial unity of meaning and existence is infected by the awareness that continued meaning for truly resolute Dasein depends on an act of will, since Dasein is the meta-physical ground of meaning.

Now Heidegger's turn to "worlded earth" as ground is at the same time the turn from a prelinguistic ground to a linguistic ground. This is a double simplification: just as the implicit polarity between Dasein's clearing and the essentially meaningless thing is undercut by regarding the clearing as the clearing *of* earth, so the implicit polarity between primordial articulation and language is undercut by regarding the primordial articulation as itself linguistic. The two turns are correlative, for it is precisely by regarding world as *named earth* that both the danger of a nominalism of language and the danger of inherent meaninglessness are combated. Put differently, 'world' loses its abstractness, artifactuality, and virtuality precisely when it is seen as the precedent and lasting linguistic articulation of the earth. Thereby the last residues of an idealism of world projected over a realism of entities are expunged.

In other words, it is the *Kehre's* rapprochement between language and earth that at last guarantees the precedent community of nature on which the success of the phenomenological program depends. The grand scope of this simplification deserves stress. The precedent community of nature means that all the following distinctions are now to be regarded as semblances of prior unities rather than as independent 'natures' or polar 'natures':

existentia	essentia
that-being	what-being
'is'	'as'
referent	name
in-itself	for-itself
secular	sacred
material	spiritual
natural	historical/artifactual
particular	universal
real	nominal/ideal
permanence	temporality
perception	meaning

The ambitious scope of these various correlations is of Hegelian scale. That is no accident. As the initiator of the phenomenological program, as I have broadly defined it, Hegel saw that if the phenomenon were not a real unity of the opposites or factors into which it is analyzable, phenomenology would be impossible. Hegel saw that were these opposites or factors not *internally* related to each other *from the beginning* (for Hegel, in potency, or implicitly), the unity of opposites would be merely virtual. Hegel saw that history presents this unity in a state of disunity, fragmentation, or alienation, so that a "philosophy of history" is required to show that this disunity is grounded in the very unity it dissembles.[43] Hegel saw that unless knowledge is grounded in a prior 'familiarity', its object will retreat to the far side of an epistemological gulf that is by nature and by definition impassable. Hegel saw, finally, that if such a prior unity and prior familiarity is implicit in the origin of history, the goal of history must be a reappropriation of this prior unity and prior familiarity, a future that is the "coming on" of the past.

In each of these respects Heidegger's completion of the phenomenological program conforms to its Hegelian beginning. There are, of course, decisive differences between Hegel's thought and Heidegger's, as the latter has clearly shown. Hegel must be liberated from the 'onto-theo-logical' assumptions that prevent the implementation of his program and require him to resort to a rational Absolute that is metaphysical.[44] But what must now concern us is Heidegger's reappropriation of the Hegelian requirement of a "philosophy of history"—not, to be sure, as a *philosophy* of history but as a "remembering" of the past as the essential future.

III

The first task of any effort at radical simplification of history is an explanation of the apparent complexity, pluralism, and heterogeneity of history. It is a cardinal tenet of Heidegger's interpretation of history that everything conspires to separate, divide, and hence cause one to forget, an "original unity," "original relationship," or "intrinsic togetherness," which is owing to "the primal gathering principle."[45] This happens because of Dasein's inherent tendency to "make present" solely in the self-disowning sense,[46] which means primarily to preoccupy and guide itself by what appears to lie nearest to it. What appears to lie nearest to commonsensical Dasein is what is "present" in the sense of being "at hand"—that is, what can be sensed, what is tangible. Alternatively, what often appears to lie closest to philosophical and scientific Dasein (Descartes is a case in point) is what is or can be made wholly present *to thought*, without remainder. It is then both clear (wholly transparent) and distinct (separable from all else). An essential tendency of Western history is the dissimulation of Being—which rules and organizes both the tangible and the present thought—as merely the tangible, or as merely the presently thinkable, and beyond that, nothing. Therefore the essential struggle of phenomenology for the intangible aspect of both the ground of appearances and the temporal constitution of ideas is "the struggle against *Vorhandenheit*"[47]—i.e., the struggle against the tangible or sensible, or against what appears "nearest" to either a commonsensical or a philosophical thinking that has reduced the full phenomenon to only one of its aspects, its physical or its ideational presentness. This struggle against *Vorhandenheit* is, as the struggle against the discrete separateness of appearances, precisely the struggle for the notion of internal relations that recalls thought to the nonapparent "essential relations"[48] between "discrete" appearances. That is to say, thought needs to 'remember' the context, situation, or situatedness of an appearance. So Heidegger writes in EM that "what counts is the context."[49]

This context is implicitly invoked by the apparently innocuous verb 'is', which always means 'is as. . . .'[50] As we really use it, the verb 'is' never merely refers to an appearance but implicitly situates it where it is, or presupposes and means an appearance as what it is *in its relations* not simply with the class of ontologically similar beings (e.g., other tools, other men, other images, other molecules) but more fundamentally in its relations with beings as a whole. 'Is' *appears* to say only 'exists', making no further ontological claims and no contextual or relational claims. So understood, 'is' appears merely transitive and transitional, mere copula, dissimulating its ontological claim. But even if we admit that 'is' implicitly invokes a multiplicity of *'ases'* ("is as" tool, man, image, molecule), we may fail to take the further step of seeing that "a single determinate trait runs through them all. It directs our contemplation of 'being' ["*sein*"] to a definite horizon, in which understanding is effected."[51] This 'horizon' is of course the 'clearing', which is always 'definite'—i.e., not a mere empty open space ('nothing') but an open space that has been understood in a particular way.

But if the horizon is always 'de-finite', always bounded and determined by the implicit understanding of 'is', this seems possible only because 'is' is essentially *indefinite*. It clears the space for a multiplicity of *possible* 'ases': "Only because the 'is' remains intrinsically indeterminate and devoid of meaning can it be ready for such diverse uses, can it fulfill and determine itself 'as the circumstances require.' . . . in order to be determinable Being must be indeterminate."[52] Here the argument of SZ and of WM is being recapitulated. The horizon appears as 'nothing' and entities correlatively appear as "essentially devoid of any meaning," hence open to a multiplicity of *possible* meanings.

"*Yet*"—and here the *Kehre* enters—"a single determinate trait runs through them all," that is, through all the 'ases' of Western history: "a determinateness which has . . . dominated our historical Dasein since antiquity."[53] This means a single determinate trait that has determined "our historical Dasein" by its self-dissimulation as *mere* 'isness', bare existentia. *The dissimulation of Being is the hiding of the 'as. . . .' and its singleness, its simplicity, its intangible determination of the tangible.* In "is as . . . ," 'is' has come to mean 'existence' and 'as' has come to mean 'essence'. The two are originally together, so that "is as . . ." means "exists in its essence" (*west*), where essence (*Wesen*) means coming to be in its place, in its relatedness. But insofar as the 'as' is not attended to, the existent dissimulates its essence, meaning that it appears essenceless, that is, placeless, relationless. Appearance is first and foremost displacement, which dissimulates the placement whereby the appearance originally becomes what it is. Placement is meaning, i.e., locating, de-fining, de-limiting, or identifying a thing by reference to its place, its boundaries. Articulation is the original understanding of the whole or place in which a thing is emplaced and from which it can be displaced. 'Possibility' is fundamentally the articulation of this place within which beings can be identified, can dissimulate themselves, hence can subsequently be traced back to their place.

This means that Heidegger believes he can locate a single "primal gathering principle" or "junction" that at one and the same time accounts for unity *and* disunity, relation *and* disrelation, togetherness *and* discreteness. This "primal gathering principle" or "event" (*Ereignis*) is the original understanding of place, clearing, abode, home, whole, or totality, "worlded" earth, ground—all of which mean fundamentally the same.

Metaphysics is dis-placement, for it regards the ground or place as to be supplied or made present by ontotheological inquiry, and it does so because it has forgotten that the ground/place *already is* as the place in which the beings about whose ground metaphysics inquires have already been identified as the beings they are.

To be is to appear in place.[54]

Nihilism, as the end or last consequence of metaphysics, is appearance in space, i.e., in nothing. Beings appear as independent of place, as standing in and by themselves (*selb-ständig*). Beings appear to stand either in the space of a neutral present thought or in an otherwise empty physical space. The *Kehre* is the "turn" of space (dissimulated place) "into" place, which it originally and always is. When ontology is able to take meaning into Being, space is then filled with meaning, i.e., becomes place.[55] Stated differently, the space around beings appears empty (beings appear as groundless) only so long as perceptual tangibility and/or mental graspability (*Vorhandenheit*) is the criterion of Being. Phenomenology is a remarriage of meaning and perception through relocation of the ground of their unity; perception is meaningful placement in an already intelligible place.

The epochs of western history mark the successive stages of the working out of the 'consequences'[56] of the displacement that occurred at or near its beginning. This progressive realization of displacement takes a multiplicity of apparently independent forms, which are in fact "ruled" by "a single determinate trait." That trait is displacement into a 'meta-' beyond 'the physical' (perceptual-tangible) that denies them the "reality" of the physical. This *metabasis eis allo genos* is the forgetting of the precedent community of nature in a number of respects that Heidegger enumerates in *EM*: (*a*) Dasein becomes man over against nature; (*b*) *physis* becomes idea over against nature; (*c*) meaning becomes thinking over against nature; (*d*) presence becomes appearance over against reality; (*e*) Being becomes permanence over against becoming; (*f*) order and norm become value over against contingency.[57] In each case "what is held apart in them belonged originally together."[58] In each case a distinction-within-a-unity becomes a polarity. In each case members of a prior community become relata. In each case the power of words to separate and to isolate dissembles (apparently disassembles) an original assembling that is also owing to the power of the word. In each case the unity that is the very possibility of the disunification is obscured. In each case the unity of the beginning is therefore projected as a future goal; the meaning of Western history is the movement to reunite man and nature, thinking and its referent, appearance and reality, becoming and permanence, meaning and object, subject and substance, value and contingency.

It is in effect this historical quest that Sartre in *EN* judged to be a vain passion. It is no less a vain passion for Heidegger. Heidegger and the early Sartre share the judgment that the metaphysical quest for a unification of opposites which have no common nature is impossible. In this sense their reading of the philosophical history of the West is similar. The critical difference between them is that while Sartre takes the polarities to be irreducible, Heidegger reads them as semblances. In Heidegger's judgment Sartre does not, in his "flight forward," see the necessity of "the turn," of reversing the direction of thought so that it becomes a way back into the ground of the metaphysical polarities, a remembering. If it is true that the key to the realization of the necessity of this reversal lies in the problem of language, then Sartre's decisive deficiency is what he calls his "espousal of nominalism."[59] We shall therefore need to examine Sartre's theory of language (chapter 10). It will also be important to see how the later Sartre modifies his earlier treatment of both logical opposition and metaphysics (chapters 11 and 12).

IV

Where, then, are we? What is the nature of the place? Western history presents itself to Heidegger as a progressive displacement, through a turn in his thinking which reverses that progression (forgetting) or regresses (remembers) back into the source of the displacement, which is the place itself. The place shows itself to be a linguistic place, and the event of displacement shows itself to be a linguistic event. The linguistic event of displacement is the source of the apparent absoluteness of a multiplicity of polar distinctions that are now discovered to be united at their source. Source or origin (Ursprung) is always a unity or oneness (Einheit) for Heidegger, although not one being or a One, and he sees in Heraclitus and Parmenides a certain understanding of the source of multiplicity in oneness. Yet it is not the sort of oneness that reduces all multiplicity to mere appearance but rather a oneness that is the "remaining" (bleibend) common ground or context of multiplicity (the phenomenal) itself.

This unified ground or field (Feld) through which man makes his mortal way (Weg) along a path through the field (Feldweg)[60] presents itself to Heidegger in the thirties as what I have called "worlded earth." The earth is "worlded" insofar as it is disclosed in naming or articulating; yet it is also understood by man as a source and support that does not wholly disclose itself to finite beings. I have suggested that Heidegger thus preserves Kant's understanding of phenomena as disclosures that are partial owing to the spatio-temporal finitude of man. These phenomena are going to become the 'things' (Dinge) revealed in the "Fourfold" (Geviert) to beings whose earthly finitude will be expressed by calling them "the mortals" (die Sterblichen), those who understand that the earth is their place, a temporal place, bounded by birth and death. The place of man (from which metaphysics displaces him) is the timespace of worlded earth—a region of limited but genuine intelligibility. Worlded earth is a place of physis.[61] In metaphysics or displacement physis becomes nature, mere earth, allegedly unworlded earth (nature as actual rather than as phenomenal), and world eventually becomes the subjective world of the individual, to be bracketed if one is to know nature as it is objectively in itself.

The "single" and "simple" goal of Heidegger's thinking for the rest of his career will be to 'remember' adequately the character of this place which has been so forgotten in displacement that it now appears as 'nothing'. Place dissembles itself as a vacuum in which "we are suspended,"[62] the "night" of nihilism[63] in which the metaphysical topology breaks down for lack of a common ground (topos) in which to root its branches (ontology, theology, logic, epistemology, axiology):

—ontology as astrophysics and microphysics speeds away from the earth with increasing momentum, seeking the source of being in the supertelescopic origin of the cosmos, and seeking the nature of being in submicroscopic particles—while the earth itself is left in ecological crisis;
—theology encounters "the death of God";
—the rule of logic is challenged by systematic exploration of the prerational and irrational;
—epistemology appears to encounter its own limit in the Uncertainty Principle and in the notion of the relativity of experimental results to the situation of the experimenter;
—axiology confronts the problem of "the subjectivity" of aesthetic and ethical values and norms.

Are these more or less simultaneous and contemporary problems the sign of a common displacement from a common place? If so, is that common place simply a tradition that had no real ground to stand on and that we are thus well rid of? Or does the tradition now appear as groundless because of the dissimulation of its own real ground? Heidegger characterizes the present epoch, the epoch of Com-position (Ge-stell), as the utmost dissimulation of, and displacement from, a ground that nevertheless remains. The success of this characterization of the present epoch hangs on Heidegger's ability to characterize compellingly the nature of this ground, its constancy, and its power to dissimulate its presence altogether. A phrase from Heidegger's essay "Andenken" perfectly expresses his passion: "describing that which remains. . . ."[64]

The characterization of this ground-place has in one sense remained the same ever since the *Kehre* and has in another sense evolved. What has remained the same is Heidegger's characterization of this place as the locus of an original disclosure of a 'world', or lighting-of-a-clearing (*Lichtung*), in which all phenomena 'come into presence'. But the *Kehre* is perhaps best understood as a continuing event, a protracted process of 'remembering' the place displaced.

It should be noted in passing that the term 'remembering' is misleading if it is construed as recalling to mind an event that is simply past. "The way back into the ground" is, to be sure, a remembering of an ancient and original ground, but because this ground remains, this remembering is just as much a recall to where we always already are, and hence are now. If Heidegger's 'remembering' appears to be a reversion to early Greek experience, that is only because he tries to reverse the process of forgetting by tracing it back to its ancient 'start' (*Beginn*), at which time the place that has been displaced had not yet been so thoroughly dissimulated. 'Remembering' is for Heidegger always to be understood as a recall to 'what remains' (*das Bleibende*).

The characterization of the original and originary place of the disclosure of phenomena as worlded earth is provisional and only a stage in Heidegger's protracted process of remembering. Why did it prove to be an insufficient characterization? It is clear that intensive meditation on the poetry of Hölderlin contributed decisively to the development of the Fourfold.[65] Indeed, the "influence" of Hölderlin on Heidegger has been waggishly summarized in the standing joke that Hölderlin is "Heidegger's ventriloquist." Heidegger's real relation to Hölderlin is perhaps best characterized in words of Heidegger's own: "the genuine ability to hear is an original retelling of what is heard, not a mere repeating of it."[66] Heidegger cares not at all for originality in the sense of novelty, inasmuch as his real care is for what remains; "the poets establish what remains,"[67] and Hölderlin is such a poet.

What remains is the place. Heidegger's whole care is for the place. He must be taken at his word when he tells us repeatedly that his thought is centered on something 'single' and 'simple'.[68] If he increasingly speaks and writes like a seer, it is because he shares the seer's care for seeing through novelty, change, and multiplicity to the remaining and the simple, which grounds the very change and multiplicity that hide it from view. In *EHD* Heidegger asks, "Who apprehends, amid the temporal torrent, something which remains . . . ?"[69] The seer-like singleness and simplicity of Heidegger's concern deserve constant stress, for if one does not bear them constantly in mind one sees neither the unity of his thought, early and late, nor what he takes to be the unity amid the "temporal torrent," Western history.

What is the unity of his thought? The answer to his early, and only, question about what is *common* to the *manifold* uses of the word 'Being' is precisely his later meditation on the 'single', 'simple', and 'remaining' place, the common place where every being is 'as' it is.

What is the unity of Western history? Heidegger's early thought, we know, situates Being relative to Time. This also requires, however, a "reversal" that situates Time relative to Being.[70] What does this mean? *SZ* can be interpreted as "throwing" man "resolutely" into the torrent of time so that he has no meta-physical recourse, no possible salvation from time and finitude. If *SZ* does not establish the general relation between Being and Time, it does seem to establish the relation between Dasein's Being and Time. But the later essays ask about the unity or simplicity of this temporal torrent into which man has now been thrown. Interpreting Hölderlin's many references to "streams" (especially the Rhine and the Danube) as references to the "course" of history, Heidegger asks about the unity of this historical streaming, from its small and apparently insignificant 'source' (*Quelle*), or the 'original' site of its 'springing forth' (*Ur-sprung*),[71] to its ultimate self-dissipation in the open sea. The poetic "sailors" who travel from their "home" downstream into a "foreign land" evoke Western man and his historical exploration of the distant (*Ferne*), his search for the real and the true in the novel and hitherto unseen.[72] I have found that *SZ* is liable to an interpretation that casts the sailor (man) out into this temporal torrent (historical time) with no re-course and no terminus in solid ground. There is only ceaseless exploration (the ekstasis of possibility)—

a flight forward—whose sole personal terminus is death and whose sole historical terminus is an anxious nihilism (loss in a "foreign land" or self-dissipation in the sea). This interpretation of man's relation to time was, I have argued, probably far from Heidegger's intention.

In any case, Hölderlin's "sailor" turns back (rück-kehrt) from the "foreign land" and journeys "home," to "dwell" "near the source."[73] This marks a turn homeward in Hölderlin's life and thought, the turning of Heidegger's thinking, and an anticipated turn in the thought of historical man.

It is at this point that Heidegger is accused of turning toward mysticism. This accusation is unfounded; the appropriate image for mysticism would be self-dissipation in the sea rather than the turn back to man's *historical* origin. Heidegger's thinking remains historical and "mundane." Heidegger asks about the unity of history (of the temporal torrent)—not about a unity that cancels it.[74] But turning back and traveling upstream to the source might suggest, if the stream represents historical time, the reversibility of time: rather than a "flight forward," a "flight backward." Heidegger has indeed been interpreted this way—as recommending a simple return to ancient modes of thinking. However, he does not think that time can be reversed but rather that "in the whole of its essence . . . time rests."[75] This does not mean that the movement of time or history is an illusion. That *would* be mysticism.

What is meant by saying that "in the whole of its essence . . . time rests"? Heidegger associates 'rest' (Ruhe) with what remains.[76] It is not a matter of stasis. It is a matter of the "essencing" of time, movement, becoming, history themselves when seen "whole." This 'remaining' essence is itself a movement or 'course' (Gang): "Remaining in one's own and proper place is [itself] the course to the source. It is the origin or original spring which all dwelling of the sons of Earth springs from, away, and to. Remaining is a going into the neighborhood of the original spring."[77]

Elsewhere Heidegger writes that "all is way."[78] To explicate these difficult but crucial passages I return to Hölderlin's sailor on the stream—that is, man's historical journey. The sailor's journey takes time, and it brings him to the new and the foreign. The price of this discovery of the new and the foreign appears to be departure from, even estrangement from, his home or starting point: the modern situation is not the ancient, for science and technology have opened up "new worlds." Modern man searches for "new values" appropriate to a time when one journeys to the moon as well as down the Rhine or the Danube. This appears to be a course away from the source. We shall journey as far as it is possible to travel. What is possible for man to do seems to him what it is imperative that he do, no matter what the cost. The present is understood as what is to be improved or revised. The past is understood as what has been improved or revised. There is no rest, and what simply remains is what has yet to be improved or revised, or else a standing stock of raw material available for use in revision and improvement.[79] Nietzsche finds everything moving away "from the center toward X,"[80] and for Yeats "the centre cannot hold."[81] This situation appears to confirm Sartre's conception of the for-itself as a 'flight forward' by 'negation' of its past, whose goal is the final coincidence of the actual and the possible: 'beauty', 'value', and 'Being'. On this view, the course springs *away* from the source because history originates in the explosion of the actual into the possible, the shattering of unity into multiplicity, and the goal of history can only be the *overcoming* of its origin, the healing of the split between Being and Nothingness with which history begins. But if history begins in the infecting of Being by Nothingness, the explosion of the unity of the actual into the virtual multiplicity of the 'real' as in *EN*, then the only cure for this infection may indeed be mysticism—the radical cancellation of phenomenal multiplicity by return into undifferentiated unity or Oneness.

Now it should be noted that this historical springing away from the source or origin is and remains 'governed' or 'ruled' by the source. The nature of the origin determines the nature of the goal. Because the origin of history is for Sartre a rupture of Being by negation, the goal of history is the healing of this rupture. In Sartrean terms, man's project is the 'plugging' of the 'hole' in Being. Nor is this 'hole' in Being one created in ancient times and subsequently simply inherited by man. Each for-itself continuously repeats its origin—each act of consciousness repeats the ceremony of its birth by an ever-renewed negation of Being. Hence the origin "remains." It is the essential meaning of the whole course, for Sartre as well as for Heidegger. Furthermore, there is a sense in which for Sartre, as for Heidegger, this process of origination 'dissimulates' itself, or is 'forgotten': the 'center' of the 'springing forth' of consciousness is 'the instant', which is 'refused' by consciousness in its flight forward. And Sartre, like Heidegger, intends to remind man of this forgotten originative 'center'.

But here all similarity between Heidegger's and Sartre's views of the nature of the process of origination abruptly ends. Sartrean origination is 'humanistic'—it is self-origination. The originative center is consciousness as original negation of Being. Consciousness originates its own time-space by explosive or diasporatic negation of the actual, and the 'strife' is between consciousness and the actual. What 'remains' is only this perpetual negation of the actual. There is no 'rest'. Heidegger, to the contrary, regards the origin not only as a place of 'rest' but as 'the homeland'. [82] It is what the sailor seeks in his journey into a foreign land, yet, in the words of Hölderlin, "What you seek is near and already befalls you." [83] What you seek is near no matter where you are. No matter where you are, you are essentially in the same place. You are there in that place in the foreign land, but you were also there when at home. Yet you are perhaps less likely to recognize that place in the foreign land, because you left home out of failure to recognize the place.[84] In other words, because the place originally seemed far when it was near, one seeks to bring it near by journeying far. But because the nature of the place is to be everywhere the same (it "remains" or "rests"), historical movement *toward* it as toward something new shows that one has misunderstood its ubiquitous nature. It is not therefore first to be found in future time or distant place. Metaphysics, the ever-future exploratory quest for a new place, the real and true ground, can seek the ground in the spatiotemporal distance only because it has failed to recognize its ubiquity. Because it perpetually pushes into the future the very ground on which it always walks, metaphysics is the ass chasing a carrot forever out of reach.[85] This means that metaphysics perpetually ungrounds or continually displaces itself; its quest for a ground has no ground on which to base its quest. Its orientation and its standpoint are sought, not given. Or so it would appear. Metaphysics appears to stand in *nothing*—yet it must stand someplace in order to be able to quest at all.[86] A quest must start somewhere, must take its bearings. Heidegger wants to argue that the metaphysical quest secretly orients itself in the very ground it seeks.

Thus what metaphysics seeks is near and already befalls it. Because in the whole of its essence time rests, what metaphysics seeks in the future is always already, and remains, there.

It may therefore seem puzzling that Heidegger finds metaphysics more than a mistake. It appears that he has not altogether retreated from his early assertion that "Metaphysics. . . . is Da-sein itself."[87] The reason for this is that he must do justice to, or take adequate account of, the *transcendental* aspect of human experience and understanding. The stress in his later writings on rootedness in a finite place must not occur at the expense of man's obvious transcendence of the moment and the immediate spot—in language, memory, anticipation of future possibility, imagination, or envisagement of events and circumstances other than those he finds immediately surrounding him. In fact, man's understanding of himself *as* rooted in a finite place presupposes an understanding that can distinguish between rootedness and rootlessness, between the finite and the infinite, between time and eternity, between the present and the absent. Human understanding identifies the immediate location in which it now is by ranging beyond it, by situating that immediate location within a whole, a 'world'. If there is no transcendence without finitude, there is also no finitude without transcendence.

Heidegger's ultimate characterization of the relation between transcendence and finitude must be such as to show their community of nature. Kant's account of finite transcendence, acute though it is, still characterizes human experience *dialectically*, relative to two poles. Man is between God (pure transcendence) and animal (pure finitude in the sense of pure immanence). Phenomenal experience is situated between two noumena: transcendental ego and external thing-in-itself. Kant is "on the way" to the phenomenological orientation in pointing to the phenomenon as a community of subject and object—but it remains a community *of* subject and object. Human experience is in effect a compromise between two poles and is understood as such. Experience is evaluated relative to these two poles, and in this sense the poles or relata have priority. If these pure poles are never experienced, they are nevertheless thought of as what experience lies between. They therefore represent a standard relative to which experience is judged as insufficient; there is a need to posit these meta-physical poles as the regulative and normative orientation for a human experience that is insufficient or disoriented without them. Thus the place in which man situates or orients himself is in the end for Kant a metaphysical place. Kant therefore does not quite escape the displacement characteristic of the metaphysical tradition.

It then becomes clear that bringing an end to displacement will require a radical *critique of dialectical reasoning*. It will require, that is, a critique of the historical habit of understanding and accounting for human experience and its situation as the relation (by antithesis and/or synthesis) of poles or relata that preexist this relation. This must be done by showing not that these relata have no experiential warrant whatsoever, but rather that these allegedly original and foundational poles are grounded in and situated relative to a prior unity or 'juncture'. But this prior unity must at the same time be such as not to discount the reality of experiential distinctions. The prior unity must not be meta-physical; if it is, metaphysical dualism will be replaced by metaphysical monism rather than by phenomenology, and the displacement will be maintained.

Furthermore, the account of this prior unity cannot simply reject or cancel the displacement by a stroke of the pen, for the displacement is a pervasive feature of historical experience; the prior unity must be such as to account for its own displacement. Heidegger's account of forgottenness and self-dissimulation attempts to come to terms with this pervasive self-displacing aspect of the original place. Far from being able to cancel this displacement in favor of an original emplacement, Heidegger, looking ahead, asserts that "metaphysics may persist."[88] The place of prior community, then, is a self-displacing place. In other words, it is "the ground *of* metaphysics," not a substitute for metaphysics or an alternative metaphysics. It must be the place of displacement, the "hidden" ground within which metaphysics, which typically regards itself as self-orienting, really orients itself. It must be the locale of all historical phenomena: "the field of all regions,"[89] the common-place of all beings of any description or kind (of any 'as'—"physical" or "metaphysical"), the place of the Being of all beings.

8

Man's Place in the Fourfold: Beyond Displacement

In this change of the essence of truth, a shift of the place of truth takes place at the same time.
—*Platons Lehre von der Wahrheit*, p. 136 (265)

THIS CHAPTER and chapter 9 will be primarily devoted to consideration of Heidegger's Fourfold, which will be interpreted as the farthest point reached by Heidegger's protracted effort to remember the hidden ground of metaphysics and the culmination of his original ontological investigations. The present chapter shows how the Fourfold is reached, how it is related to language and to Heidegger's notion of 'Event', and how it takes up once again Heidegger's early themes of 'death' and 'nothing' as well as the theme of 'love' that briefly figured in the *Letter on Humanism*. While the themes of language, death, nothing, and love are also Sartrean themes, each of these themes has a different significance for Heidegger than for Sartre, for Heidegger situates them in a different place than Sartre does. The overall interpretation centers on Heidegger's understanding of 'Place'.

I

Having established in chapter 7 the general requirements for "the place," it is now possible to see why "worlded earth" was an insufficient characterization of it. Worlded earth is still a residually bipolar or dialectical notion and so turns out to be only a stage in a continuing turn, not its completion. Inasmuch as I am attempting to describe the topology [1] of the field or place of Being, I shall try to situate worlded earth topographically between Heidegger's initial topology and his last topology.

We have seen in chapter 2 that the "field" of SZ is Dasein, thought of as a circle. Because Dasein is ekstatically outside the present-at-hand spatiotemporal location of man as traditionally conceived, in effect it encounters itself everywhere. Its world is its own. But this unity is endangered by anxiety, for the effect of anxiety is to present the environment as inherently devoid of meaning, in which case the prior community of nature is fractured into an unstable synthesis of opposed natures—Dasein as meaningful, entities of other kinds as meaningless. Although Dasein's ekstatic-circular relation with its environment will not cease, we saw in chapter 4 that the anxiety-enforced distinction between two essentially opposed types of Being has the effect of seeming to restore to primacy the man-nature and subject-object polarities. Thus Heidegger's intention to locate the single, guiding, and grounding meaning of all beings[2] is temporarily frustrated by the anxious recursion to the traditional duality of 'the physical' (entities inherently devoid of meaning) and 'the meta-physical' (now seen as Dasein itself, that is, the quest for the unification of Being and meaning). *In effect,* and despite Heidegger's insistence that presence-at-hand is reached on the basis of a proximal experience of ready-to-hand (relational) beings, anxiety is reversion to the traditional meaning of the Being of entities as external (nonrelational) presence. Thus apprehended, the everyday Being of entities is supplanted by a nothingness that man has to fill with his own meanings or metaphysical interpretations of "the meaning of the whole" (see *Topos 1*).

Thus anxiety effectively splits the unified place of ordinary experience into two places, *topoi,* or regions of Being. We now move directly to Heidegger's first topology following the initiation of the 'turn' (see *Topos 2*).

Here my topography seeks to show the primacy Heidegger gives to 'world' and 'earth' which, as 'worlded earth', constitutes the place within which both Dasein and phenomenon occur as what they are. As an answer to the question about the single, grounding, and guiding meaning of Being, Heidegger's new delineation suggests that 'to be' means to be present, in any possible sense of 'presence', in worlded earth. 'Earth' *alone* would suggest mere material or 'physical' presence; 'world' *alone* would suggest mere immaterial, verbal or ideational—i.e., meta-physical—presence. Instead, they are given together. "World and earth are essentially

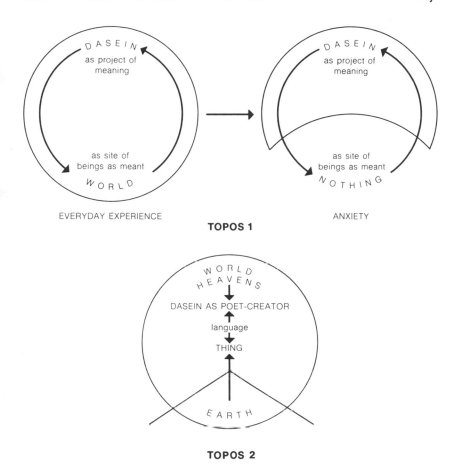

TOPOS 1

TOPOS 2

different from one another, yet are never separated. The world grounds itself on the earth, and earth rises up through [*durchragt*] the world."[3]

At work here is a notion of crucial importance for Heidegger's whole project: *unmediated difference* (or original identity *and* difference). A notion foreshadowed by the notion of 'equiprimordiality' in *SZ*, it challenges the assumptions that distinctions can always be traced to a prior source or cause, that distinctions arise in a "linear" manner, one after the other, and that distinctions are mutually exclusive, "opposites." In a nonphenomenological account of the origin of the distinctions 'world' and 'earth', one would say that first there was earth as the physical precondition of a subsequent human world, and therefore that the physical precedes and grounds the metaphysical, the natural precedes and grounds the human, the material has ontological priority over the immaterial, mental, ideational, or linguistic, and so forth. This account is diachronic rather than synchronic or contemporaneous. And, as Heidegger would say, it is 'right'. But phenomenologically it is derivative, not originary and 'true'. Thinking back to the true origin of the distinction, "there is" earth only when "there is" world. Experientially there is earth *for us*—earth understood *as* earth, earth actually entering into experience as what it is—only when there is world. "Only when there is world" means: only when an articulated, intelligible, comprehensible environment occurs to man, which is the same moment that man as man comes into being.

This original Event (*Ereignis*), which is the original occurrence of "the place," is the primary subject of Heidegger's thinking. It is the Event of lighting or clearing (*Lichtung*), or the place cleared (also *Lichtung*).[4] It is the original happening of Being—that is, the original coming into presence of things *as* what they are, that is, as nameable and intelligible to an understander. It is the original bringing of things "out of hiddenness" (*a-lētheia*) into "unhiddenness" (*Unverborgenheit*) or "presence" (*Anwesenheit*) *to* a being who can identify them as what they are. It is the original "showing" (*phainesthai*) of phenomena.[5] It is the originative leap (*Ursprung*) out of the darkness and muteness of unintelligibility into comprehension and articulation. Because it is the source of all distinctively human experience, the *sine qua non* of human history, yet not originated by an act of man, Heidegger will call it "a favor" for which man owes "thanks."[6] Because of the transcendence or "meta-physical" power to grasp (com-prehend) things and events *as* what they are and *as* a whole—*as* a "world"—that happens to man in this Event, Heidegger will characterize 'world' as 'the heavens' (*Himmel*).[7] This signifies that since man transcends the mere moment in com-prehending an overarching whole (past, present, future; what is revealed and what is still unrevealed), he occupies a place "between heaven and earth." This new way of speaking of finite transcendence does not mean that man is half animal and half god, but rather that man understands his mortality as rootedness in an earth that is what it is *by contrast with* heaven or the heavens and that is what it is *in light of* the heavens. The contrast is between the light, clarity, and openness of the heavens and the darkness, solidity, and impenetrability of the eartn. The earth is both literally and figuratively lighted by the heavens.

We should pause a moment to comment on this Heideggerian fusion of literal and figurative meaning. Is Heidegger not confusing, or collapsing the distinction between, the actual physical process whereby the sun lights the earth and the merely figurative or metaphorical notion of intelligibility as "seeing the light" or "shedding light on"—a clarification or elucidation of that which was previously "obscure," that about which one was previously "in the dark"? Is this not a case of Heidegger's notorious "poetic" thinking? One must ask why the light and darkness found in nature have been persistently associated in human culture with transcendence and immanence, with knowledge and ignorance or intelligibility and unintelligibility, with life and death. Is this only a metaphorical or poetic association? Is it a case of taking a prior experience of *nature* and transferring it to the *human* sphere? The Heideggerian approach to these questions consists in remembering the original relation of the two, and this will be understood as a relation that still rules even if it is now dissimulated by our forgetting the 'identity' that is present in the 'difference' between the two.

The original Event whereby earth and heaven are named and understood as such and man is understood as a mortal or earthly being is the original Event of intelligibility, light, clarity. There is to be sure a *difference* between the sun lighting the earth and the mind understanding its environment. But the time when the mind understands its environment is the very time when *for us* the sun lights the earth. Nature occurs to man as nature, as what it is—or *means* nature—only in the event of understanding or intelligibility. Thus there is a contemporaneity and an *identity* between the phenomenal occurrence of nature and the occurrence of intelligibility. Nature 'is' nature only in the light of understanding, only in being named as what it is. This original togetherness—or community of nature— between "nature as such" and "understanding as such" is the precondition for any subsequent separation of 'nature' and 'understanding' into "separate" spheres. But because "nature as such" can

only be "nature for us" (nature as understood and named) the separation between them can never be completed. It is only "for us"
that nature can be "in itself."

But this is precisely to say that beings "are" only as "meaning-
beings." Thus the Being of earth and the heavens is Being as meaning. The light and darkness of nature are an intelligibilized and
named light and darkness. There can be an ontological *difference* between a being and its meaning only if that being is first meant
(named, understood, identified)—that is, only if there is an original
identity of a being and its meaning. The 'fateful' event of Western
philosophical history has been the dissimulation of the 'identity' by
the 'difference', a forgetting of the real nature of the difference. This
occurs under the dominance of a logic which is "right" and yet incomplete—a logic which holds that identity and difference cannot
occur together, are mutually exclusive.

'Worlded earth,' then, means at one and the same time the region
of nature and the region of intelligibility. They are the same and
different. Only if nature is intelligible can one distinguish between
nature and intelligibility. There can be a distinction or difference
between a thing and our idea of it, or between a thing and its
name, or between a thing and its essence, *only if* the thing and its
idea, name, and essence are an original identity. Heidegger's project is that of remembering back through the difference to the identity, while not discounting the difference. It is because he discovers
that the name is not accidental to the Being of the thing that his terminology shifts in the *Kehre*. A language that allegedly speaks of
beings as such must be turned back into its origins as a language
that speaks of meaning-beings.

> . . . The discussion of Being as Being still speaks an inade-
> quate language insofar as the continually named Being itself is
> expressed with that name which ever and again speaks *away*
> from [*wegspricht*] Being as such.
>   Precisely when we notice this, the suspicion arises that
> Being—thought of as such—may no longer be called 'Being.'[8]
>   Instead of 'Sein und Zeit,' does the title of the problem for
> thought then read: Clearing and Presentness?[9]

The continuing *Kehre* is the progressive turn of language back
into its 'remaining' compresence with beings in the 'original' clear-

ing. This progressive turning is evoked by "thought" (*Denken*) in the form of "remembering" (*Andenken, Erinnerung*). The farthest point reached by Heidegger in this continuing turn is his evocation of the Fourfold. The evocation of the Fourfold is the ultimate result of Heidegger's strenuous effort to express what "Clearing and Presentness" mean. Here 'Clearing' (*Lichtung*) must be thought of both verbally and nominally. This is to say that *Lichtung* means at once both the original event and the original place. It is the place of the event and the event of the place. Thus Heidegger's terms 'Event' (*Ereignis*) and 'Place' (*Ort*) mean "the same." *Ursprung* is to be construed both as 'originative leap' or 'spring' (event) and as 'source' (place). There is an inner necessity that the verbal and the nominative here be equiprimordial. If the place preexists the event that articulates it, it will be bare *existentia* or non-phenomenological; [10] if the event of articulation precedes the place articulated, that place will be merely ideal, or merely verbal, or merely linguistic, or merely mythical. Thus the relation between Event and Place must be that of "unmediated difference" or identity-and-difference. Otherwise either Event or Place will be meta-physical, and there will be no "belonging-together of Being and man." [11] There will, in other words, be no original-and-remaining community of nature. Hence the Event of clearing-intelligibility ("world as world") is the coming into presence of the natural environment as what it is ("Earth as Earth"). Phenomenologically they are not two separate events, one mental, the other physical, one figurative, the other literal. The event of understanding *is* the event of "nature as nature."

II

The position I have described as Topos 2 approaches, but does not yet sufficiently evoke, the place of the event, or event of the place (for short, "the placing"). Heidegger writes that "the relation of Being and human being . . . is unsuitably conceived even in this version. . . ." [12] We may better understand why if we now look at Topos 3.

How in particular does Topos 3 revise Topos 2? (1) A "four-factor" layout replaces the earlier "two-factor" layout; (2) 'Thing' is central—the assembly point, focus, or catalyst around which and by reference to which the clearing, or World, takes place; (3) the 'strife'

TOPOS 3

between Earth and World does not appear, for Earth is now but one of four 'members' who 'play' while World is the whole 'place'; (4) World is no longer identified with the Heavens; (5) the Divine explicitly becomes a member of the *topos,* it would appear, at the expense of Mortals, who now lack the earlier centrality of Dasein or Dasein's lonely and anxious total responsibility for "its" World, a remnant of which remained in Heidegger's characterization of man in *EM* as an adventurous creator, a 'violent' imaginative interpreter of Being.[13] This emphasis on creative violence is moderated as the stress on the 'strife' of world and earth is moderated.

What do these changes mean? We note immediately that the *topos* has taken on a "religious" cast. There is a 'heaven' or 'heavens', and the 'divine' or 'divinities' (*die Göttlichen*). Presumably these notions are somehow relatable to Heidegger's many references to the holy (*das Heilige*), to saving (*retten, Rettung*), to grace (*Gunst*), to gift (*Geschenck*), to restoration or redemption (*Heil*), to release (*Gelassenheit*), rest (*Ruhe*), renunciation (*Verzicht*) and serenity (*Heiterkeit*). Knowing the importance of Heidegger for the theologians Bultmann, Tillich, and Ott, one is tempted to suspect that Heidegger is trying to revitalize the Christian faith. That is not Heidegger's intention; it is at most a possible side-effect, so to speak, of Heidegger's thinking. The nature of this thinking is misconstrued if one regards it as moving from one area of experience and thought—the philosophical-scientific or secular—into another area of experience and thought—the theological-religious or sacred. Heidegger tries to think behind this usual topology to the Place of all such areas of experience and thought (*Bereich aller Bereiche*) or the Relation common to all relations between regions of experience and thought (*Verhältnis aller Verhältnisses*). This common-place is a 'holy' place: "the gods present themselves even here."[14] The transition from the "secular" SZ to the "sacred" cast of the latter essays must be regarded as necessary for the completion of Heidegger's original phenomenological program rather than as an arbitrary and personal turn toward religion. This phenomenological program, I have argued, seeks the Being of all beings in the sense of the site of all phenomena.

The usual view of the site of all phenomena it that it is "physical." It is therefore physics, astrophysics, and physical and historical geology that tell us about the nature of this site. And that view, of course, is 'right'. But it is nevertheless 'deficient' or 'privative'; it is 'governed' (*gewaltet*) or 'directed' (*geschickt*) by the 'ruling' (*waltend*) ontology of *Vorhandenheit*. For this ontology, what exists are nonreferential entities-in-themselves and, beyond that, nothing.[15] Personal meanings, such as religious meanings, are posited to fill that 'nothing' as a metaphysical complement to the physical. The physical is the actual in the sense of the merely given; the metaphysical is the merely possible in the sense of what may or may not be arbitrarily posited by the will or whim of a subject, depending on how "poetic" or "religious" or "imaginative" he is. But even this poetic-religious-imaginative disposition may be traced ultimately to (grounded in) an actual physical state, thus establishing anew that meta-physical Being is not Being at all but rather nothing at all, nonexistent. There is only existence and nothingness. What exists is precisely the non-holy—what is 'given', in the sense of available, at man's disposal as a ready stock or standing inventory of elements or materials for use (*Bestand*). This view is, for Heidegger, "the danger."[16] Among its manifestations are materialism, positivism, utilitarianism, pragmatism, voluntarism—all governed by a single directive (*Geschick*). It is the consummation (*Vollendung*)[17] of the self-displacement of the Place that initiated and still 'directs' (*schickt*) the 'course' of Western 'history' (*Ge-schichte*). This course is a "dis-course" in a double sense: (1) it is a course that dissembles its own original-and-remaining source; (2) it is governed by a *linguistic* Event that originates and sustains the course.

In other words, our traditional or long-standing way of thinking and speaking (thinking is now construed by Heidegger as silent saying—that is, it is not prelinguistic) cannot express the course it is on. Hence we regard language itself as a pragmatic means of expression and intercourse, something useful, and not as 'directive' or formative. Thus Heidegger writes, in a passage from *Hebel der Hausfreund* important enough to be quoted at length:

> We must to be sure admit that ordinary language seems to be a means or medium [*Mittel*] of becoming informed and is used as such a means in the customary relationships of our lives. But there are other relationships [*Verhältnisse*] beyond the customary ones. Goethe calls these other relations the "deeper" ones and says of language:
>
> "In ordinary living we make do with language by designating relations which are only superficial. But another language, the poetic, steps in as soon as the discourse is about deeper relations."
>
> Johann Peter Hebel speaks of these deeper relations of human Dasein when at one point he writes:
>
> "We are plants which—whether or not we like to admit it— have to grow out of the earth in which they are rooted in order to be able to blossom in the ether and bear fruit."
>
> The word 'earth' in Hebel's statement names everything that sustains and surrounds us, excites us and reassures us, as visible or audible or palpable: the sensible or perceptible.
>
> The word 'ether' (the heavens) in Hebel's statement names everything that we become aware of by means other than the sense organs: the imperceptible, mind or understanding, the spirit.
>
> *But the course and bridge between the depths of the wholly sensible and the heights of the boldest spirit is language.*
>
> How? The word of language tones and nuances in the way it sounds; it gives light and illuminates or clarifies in a script. Sound and script are to be sure sensible, but sensible in that in each a sense of meaning is announced and becomes manifest. As the sensible sense, the word traverses the whole expanse of the play-space between earth and the heavens. Language holds open the Place in which man inhabits the house of World on the earth under the heavens.[18]

The Event of language is the event of World, Fourfold, Place, and Truth. This is what language originally and fundamentally is. It can only appear as a useful means and a medium of communication because it has already founded or established the place in which there can be useful means and media of communication.[19] Unless the environment is intelligible, it cannot be talked about. Articulation in the sense of talk about, or ordinary communication, is *rearticulation* of an original articulation. One can make sense when talking about the environment only if, and only because, the environment makes sense. The environment makes sense because it is always already linguistic, for it is always already a juncture (*Fuge*) of the imperceptible and the perceptible, and in naming language accomplishes this juncture. The 'thing' is a meaning-being—an intelligible being or 'phenomenon'—because it is named, or is a linguistic being. The difference between a thing and its name dissimulates an original identity. Thus there is a prior community of nature between thing and name. The thing is a community of the perceptible and the imperceptible, the material and the mental or spiritual, the immanent and the transcendental—i.e., of earth and the heavens. Hölderlin calls it "the wedding of earth and the heavens."[20] It is the original introplay of "matter" and "mind" that happens in what Heidegger had, earlier in his career, called "finite transcendence."

Whether it is realized or not, and generally it is not, language belongs to the internal constitution of the things about which language speaks. The phenomenon is by nature linguistic. The entity 'intended' or 'meant' is already "intelligibilized," so to speak, or it could be neither meant nor recognized as such when it turns up anew. The word or name "applies to" or "fits" the thing only because the thing is itself a word-thing, a name-thing. Thus "the transcendental"—or "discursive"—is *in* the perceptible thing, the, "physical" or "natural" thing. The difference between transcendence and immanence, between the mental and the physical, dissimulates a "deeper" identity. The "deeper" relation, Goethe writes, is "poetic." In the term 'poetic' we must hear the Greek verb *poiein*: to make, fashion, create, render (so and so), to appoint, install, or establish, and to play. Without and prior to our willing it so, "there is" (*es gibt*)[21] without any specifiable reason (*ohne Warum*)[22] a linguistic play that establishes the thing, renders it such as it is, appoints it "as such" "in the whole" (World) in which it could be what it is.

To be human is to be a linguistic being in a world of linguistic beings—that is, to inhabit a world lighted (*gelichtet*) by intelligibility. This is the source and precondition for everything that is distinctively human: culture, history, science, art. Thus everything distinctively human is owed to the original linguistic lighting that "opens" up the world of beings as intelligible, as the beings they are. The possibility of human reasoning is owing to the originary Event that is "without reason," a "play" that "happens to happen" (*es gibt*). That is why Heidegger speaks of 'wonder'—the wonder of all wonders, that there are beings rather than nothing.[23] That is why he speaks of the 'mystery' or 'secret', and why he speaks of the 'gift' for which man owes thanks. And that is why he speaks of 'the holy'. It is not at all a matter of Heidegger going tender-minded in mid-career, indulging a temperamental penchant for religious conversion. It is rather a matter of following out to its ultimate conclusion the disciplined and hard-won insight of his early thought—that "higher than the actual stands the possible" in its "silent force."[24] What makes possible the entirety of human being-in-the-world is the Event of the open Place in language.

What makes everything possible is precisely what is worthy of reverence, what is *holy*. Heidegger's talk of 'the holy' is in no way dreamy talk of some hoped-for other world. It designates where we really are, our own natural community. By 'release' he means letting oneself go into that place which one is already in, and by 'saving' he refers to the possible consequences of owning up to one's ownmost Place—the turn out of displacement into the Place that 'remains' and 'rests'. What is 'holy' is the intelligible time-play-space as the constant condition for everything man values. It is the real ground, which cannot be reached by willing or by positing because it is simply 'there' already. "Reaching" it in the future can only be a matter of coming back to where we have always already been. Hence the proper future is the 'advent' or 'coming-on' or 'arrival' (*Ankunft, Ankommen*) of what has been.[25] "What counts is the context," which is dissimulated by the present foreground entity and by the metaphysical quest for a context. Against the apparent dominion of what lies 'before' us (as *vor-der-gründig*, as *Vor-stellung*, etc.), Heidegger repeatedly calls us 'back' (*zurück, rück-*) to the Place as the "eternal" background which, as is characteristic of backgrounds, is recessive, dissimulates itself, and is easily forgotten.

This is the time-play-space. As place, it 'remains'; as time, it 'rests'. "In the whole of its essence . . . time itself rests."[26] This means that the *essential* future is the same as the past. Novelty is *vor-der-gründig*, standing in front of and hiding the essential sameness. In essence the future is past, and in essence the past is future. The whole of time 'times' (*zeitigt*) together, contemporaneously. This means in part that the Place we inhabit is not simply a present place in present time; it is instead a 'stretch' or 'course' or 'way'.[27] As a finite transcendence we really understand ourselves and things as situated relative to both past and future, and this is what it means "to be present." The present thus is what it is only in its relation to past and future: the past and future enter into the internal constitution of the present. As foreground, the present is a moment; as background, in its essence, it is a relation. All beings that are present in time are relational beings, and none is a self-existing (*existentia*) absolute. "We have left behind us the presumption of all unconditionedness."[28]

Is Heidegger, as seer, simply saying that "there is nothing new under the sun"? Yes, in the sense that the novel is merely foreground and man's place, in the whole of its essence, rests and remains "eternally" the same. No, in the sense that Heidegger is not defining the novel out of existence but rather only placing it in the constant context within which alone it is possible for the novel to come into being *as* what it is. The new *is* new in its relation to the old; the novel is what it is in contrast to what is the same, what remains. Without the constant Place, nothing is either new or old, either present or past or future. The continued 'coming-on' of this constant Place is the ground-possibility of a human future. I should like now to show how the character of this place can be evoked by what might be called "the language of death and love."

III

Man plays within and against this ground as 'a mortal'. Commenting on Hölderlin's saying that "Living is death, and death is also a living," Heidegger writes that "when death comes, it disappears. Mortals die their death in living. In death mortals become im-mortal."[29] Clearly Heidegger agrees with Sartre's assertion that man does not experience his own death, in the sense of his actual termination; we experience only the termination of others. Yet man understands himself as him who must die. My death is a future that enters into the internal constitution of my present. My present is what it essentially is owing to my understanding that such presents are finite. The poignancy, beauty, and value of the present moment of a life, or the frustration over one's misuse of the present moment, are due to its being an understood transiency. For the same reason, the remembering of one's past is a treasuring and a regretting. Death establishes the quality of life.

All this is old, obvious, and perhaps sentimental, the stuff of poetry. It is common-place. Hence it is easily passed over in the habit of thinking that, taking novelty as a test of what is worth saying, says "that's nothing new." What remains is for us largely an embarrassment. But phenomenology is description of and recall to what is common-place, the 'essences' (ways of being) that 'remain'. There must be a reappropriation of the old and the obvious. The old and the obvious are, in Heidegger's words, "the farthest of the near." Phenomenology is, in one of its possible senses, the 'logos' of 'phenomena'—the statement of the obvious, what shows itself or appears. But 'logos' can also connote 'the essential', and the essence of the obvious or the essentiality of the obvious may not be obvious at all: "a phenomenon. . . . is something that proximally and for the most part does *not* show itself at all: it is something that lies *hidden*. . . ."[30] It is the burden of the phenomenologist, owing to his peculiar subject matter, to be constantly in danger of crossing the delicate line that separates the essential from the trivial, and to have to face constantly the accusation that what he takes to be essential is in fact trivially obvious. (This is perhaps one of the reasons for the disinterest in, or disenchantment with, Heidegger expressed by philosophers who pattern their inquiry after that of scientific discovery. Heidegger is "a throwback" to the "old" notion of philosophy as wisdom, and that is an embarrassment.)

So part of what Heidegger means is that human death, anticipatorily understood as what it is by a being who can and must situate himself relative to what is presently absent, turns back on life to constitute it as what it is. One's own death is for every mortal an "absent presence" that testifies to the power of the imperceptible (*das Nicht-Sinnliche*) to enter into the very nature of the perceptible and present-at-hand. All presence is conditioned by an absence.

This absence is not merely a "no more" and a "not yet," for what is absent is present in its own way (see chapter 9) as the Place of the present. To say that mortals are members of the 'Fourfold' who play in constituting the Place is in part to say that man's comprehension of his mortality is not simply a "subjective" experience but one that contributes to the very being of phenomena and the phenomenal field. 'To be' is to come into presence in a time-space which, understood as such, is the ground-possibility of the new, the transitory, and the lasting. It is mortals' care to 'preserve' that Place, which is what it is in part because mortals have always already cared for it— that is, have always already in understanding constituted it as the scene of their finite endeavors. The 'true' and 'anticipatorily resolute' 'care' of *SZ* has become the notion of preserving the Place, "within which we mortals dwell lifelong." [31] "Lifelong" means, in a finite stretch understood as such relative to death.

Heidegger also intends to say that dying is what it is understood to be over against or in contrast to the undying (*die Unsterblichen*). What is dying is precisely what is not immortal. Dying is understood as such only by a transcendental imagination that understands it as a privation or absence of the immortal. Heidegger writes that "Man as man has always already measured himself over against and together with something heavenly." [32] "Over against" invokes the difference; "together with" invokes the identity. Here as elsewhere for Heidegger the difference hides an identity. Man has measured himself over against something heavenly *because* he is together with something heavenly. As ekstatic being, man is with what he is over against: Da-sein, we have seen, is more fundamentally 'there' than 'here'. What Da-sein is 'here' depends on how it understands the 'there'—"what there is," that is, "what is there." Part of what is there, for an ontology that does not restrict itself in advance to the physical or *vor-handen*, is the imperceptible, or roughly what has come to be thought of as the region of human imagination, whose existence is owing to the power of human thought to envisage alternatives to "what-is"—for Sartre it is the region of pure inexistence, of negation of what-is. It is the region of the mythic, the legendary, the fictive or fictional, the cosmological, the speculative, the ideal, the rational, the theoretical, and the hypothetical. It is said to be "meta-physical." In its effort to be rigorously faithful to "the empirical," modern thought has often tried to avoid it. "Hypotheses non fingo," wrote Newton. If one seeks to understand man in terms of his history, as for both Heidegger and Sartre one must, one finds this history returning again and again to the theme of spiritual ascent: in Parmenides, Pythagoras, Plato, Plotinus, Augustine, Petrarch, in the biblical literature, and, as we have seen in chapter 3, in Sartre's Plotinian tendencies. Whether as soft imagination (myth, fiction) or as hard imagination (hypothesis, theory), man's understanding of the actual has been pervasively affected by the possible, "the free air of the high heavens, the open region of the mind or spirit." [33]

Much of recent thought recognizes that in the past man's understanding of the actual has indeed been affected by the possible, but it seeks in the name of empiricism and objectivity to purify the actual of the possible so that man may know the actual as it is in itself. This effort is based on the belief that the "physical" and the "meta-physical" are by nature two discrete regions; therefore the physical may be isolated from, and purified of contamination by, the meta-physical. This belief, in other words, holds that the real relation between the physical and the meta-physical is solely difference, and not also identity. Heidegger contests this belief because he finds that there is always already a community of nature between "the physical" and the "meta-physical," hence the real 'relation' between the two regions is not pure difference—negation or contrariety—but rather "identity *and* difference." Hegel's ontology and "logic of becoming" are already moving in this direction in positing what Hegel[34] calls a "union of union and non-union"—an original implicit experiential union of the physical and metaphysical that history breaks apart into disunity in order to resynthesize it explicitly and as knowledge. Negation in Hegel ceases to be an operation of what Sartre calls an "analytic reason"[35] which holds regions that are spoken of by language as opposites or contraries to be by nature simply external to each other. The operation of dialectic in history shows that what language and analytic reason speak of as opposites over against each other are, when seen in the whole or in context, internally related to each other. There is a hidden unity that history brings into the open by breaking it apart and reassembling it. A proponent of the primacy of analytic reason would hold this alleged unity to be a confusion and would support this claim in part by pointing to the distinctions, differences, or oppositions legislated by the same ordinary language in which we think. It is no accident that Sartre, in championing dialectical reason against analytic reason, comes down on the side of nominalism (see chapter 10). Language misleads. Heidegger also holds that language misleads, and yet he is not a nominalist. That is because of Heidegger's notion of a linguistic identity *and* difference: language disunifies and dissimulates the very relations of unity it itself originally establishes.

Heidegger's interpretation of the function of language is crucial for his attempt to establish the prior unity of the physical and the meta-physical, the perceptible and the imperceptible, the "earthly" and the "heavenly." His point is that originally language unifies but that it more or less systematically dissimulates this original-and-remaining unity (community). If language incorporates in itself the mental-spiritual-imperceptible, and if 'things' themselves are always meaning-beings or linguistic-things, then language always bonds the 'heavenly' to the 'earthly'. Not seeing this original and inevitable linguistic bond, nihilism regards beings as inherently devoid of meaning. Nihilism is a function of metaphysics, which, displacing meaning into a pure beyond, naturally finds no mundane meaning. The place of truth becomes absent, transcendent, meta-physical, a goal. This shift is essentially accomplished in Platonism. What nihilism does not see is that the difference between the heavens and the earth hides an original and originary togetherness or 'identity'. The 'phenomenon' of phenomenology occurs as precisely this original togetherness; both Earth and the Heavens "play" in it, enter into its internal constitution.

For example, the tree we see is rooted in the earth and blossoms in "the ether" in a double sense (which we would ordinarily call the 'literal' and the 'figurative' senses). As a physical entity, part of it is literally in the soil, another part literally in the air. But it is this for us only when identified in language as what it is. This identification understands the tree as *more than* the identification—as over against and surpassing our understanding of it, as 'existent'. But this identification also finds the tree identifiable, intelligible, knowable because the "entity" has "accepted" our name-and-notion of it—it is *'a tree'* and *'an* oak'. In this originary naming, the tree first becomes what it is, *an* oak tree; a non-sensible or imperceptible universality is at play in its very being *as* an oak tree. If it lacks this linguistic and 'heavenly' way of being, it is in Heidegger's terms 'concealed' in the dark recesses of Earth (not yet 'wedded' to the Heavens, not yet 'present' in the 'light'). Thus the tree as phenomenon stands "on the earth under the heavens,"[36] and in a double sense. It does so in a double sense because, in the words of Hebel, we are ourselves "plants": we exist as thrown and rooted *and* we understand, or are finite transcendences that have always already understood entities by their participation in the same original 'wedding' of perceptible and imperceptible, tangible and intangible, perishable and lasting, that makes us what we are.

This original union does not rule out but rather makes possible a subsequent analysis of the phenomenon into its natural and linguistic-notional elements. But it is to be noted that in such analysis (1) the linguistic-notion is abstracted *out of* a thing to which it *belongs*—a thing that is not what it is without it. Therefore (2) the "stripping-off" of the linguistic-notion does not leave a nonlinguistic entity. What it leaves is an entity that now presents itself in another mode of linguistic-notional being (for example, the oak tree now presents itself as a society of molecules). Therefore (3) both the linguistic-notion as such and the existent tree as such are abstracted out of, and hence grounded in, an original unity and a remaining unity. The tree as phenomenon *remains* the ground for saying, for example, "that is what 'tree' (linguistically, or as notion or essence) is," or "it (sc. 'the tree') is really a society of molecules."

"Poetically" put, Heidegger says that the thing 'assembles' or 'gathers' Earth and the Heavens. Or: the thing assembles the Fourfold. Or: the Fourfold plays in the assembling of the thing. Or: the Fourfold is 'centered' on the thing. Or: the thing is 'worlded', or 'world worlds' (*Welt weltet*) in the thing. Or: the 'thing things' (*Ding dingt*) World. Or: the originary saying (*Sage*) of language is the Event (*Ereignis*) of the thing. At his most poetic, Heidegger writes that "Out of the mirror-play of the ringing of the ring eventuates the thinging of the thing."[37] All of these say "the same." All refer to the original uniting union (*einigende Eine*) of "the self-united Fourfold,"[38] which I interpret as Heidegger's final characterization of the precedent community of nature.

We may seem to have wandered from the question of the mortality of mortals to the "different" question of the nature of the heavens and the still different questions of the nature of language and the nature of the 'thing'. We did not wander but were driven: Heidegger writes that when we evoke (sagen) any one of the members of the Fourfold, "we are already thinking the other three together with it."[39] So we have not wandered far enough, inasmuch as to evoke mortals is to evoke not only the heavens but the earth and the divinities as well.

We need to discuss 'the mortals' further, however, before asking about Heidegger's treatment of 'the divinities'. We must try to show how Heidegger turns the usual understanding of human existence—"life" as opposed to death—into the understanding of human existence as "dwelling," an original unity of life and death. Heidegger writes:

> Death is the shrine of nothingness, namely of that which is in every respect never something simply existing, but which nevertheless comes to be [west], even as the secret of Being itself. As the shrine of nothingness, death conceals in itself the event [das Wesende] of Being. . . . Mortals are . . . the occurring of the relation to Being as Being.[40]

Heidegger's word for 'shrine' (Schrein) also means 'cabinet', 'closet', or 'casket'. It evokes a dark recess. This passage itself appears dark—the saying of a seer. Dark is the opposite of light.[41] The notion of light evokes the lighting of the clearing (Lichtung) that Heidegger calls the opening—as opposed to the closedness or recessiveness of darkness, what is "under cover of darkness." The notion of closedness evokes Heidegger's ubiquitous notion of the simultaneity of dis-closure and closure, of revealing and concealing, of truth and untruth. But he also puts all this another way. The event of clearing is the event of Being—of something coming into presence as what it is (wesend)—and there is an original identity-and-difference of Being and Nothing that Heidegger sometimes characterizes as 'Sein'.[42] By 'lighting' Heidegger means both the Event and the Place of intelligibility. Darkness connotes unintelligibility, unfathomability, the illimitable. The pairing of light and darkness, a unity, suggests that intelligibility is purchased at the cost of unintelligibility—or that what is intelligible presents itself against a background or context that is not wholly intelligible, or that intelligibility is essentially (wesentlich) limited. Mortals ultimately bump up against that which is "secretive" (geheimnisvoll)

or "without explanation" (*ohne Warum*). Inasmuch as all our understanding and knowledge is relational, none of it is knowledge of a
non-relational Absolute. Truth is finite (but nonetheless true on that
account). Man "dwells" in a light bounded and de-termined by
darkness. The darkness determines the light not only by terminat-
ing it (in death, in unintelligibility), but also by entering into the
light's internal constitution (which is to say that nothingness enters
into the very nature of Being: 'Sein'). Beings are what they are
owing to their boundaries, and their boundaries are grasped by
beings who understand nothingness not only as it affects themselves
but as it affects other beings. Heidegger here reappropriates Hegel's
notion of the "portentous power of the negative," but he understands this power as primarily an ontological power on which the
logical power of negation is grounded. Being itself "nothings." This
means that beings present themselves only as coming *into* and
going *out of* presence, as being of limited span in space and time,
that is, as doomed to displacement. Again I risk the trivial: "all that
lives must die." Here Heidegger meditates on the 'and' of "Being
and Time" together with the ancient saying of Anaximander: "Each
pays penalty to the other according to the dispensation of time." [43]
Beings "occur in the boundary (*peras*)." [44] Heidegger explains: "The
presently occurring does not lie like a cut-off piece between the absent. When the presently occurring once stands in view, everything
occurs together, one brings the other along with itself, one lets the
other go its way." [45]

Heidegger is not simply saying the obvious, that to die is to make
room for others. He is asserting that what is (presently occurring or
"being") is what it is only "in the whole" and further, that the
whole is limited or bounded, and further, that what lies beyond
the limit enters into the nature of what appears within the limit.
"Even the absent is present and *as* absenting itself from the present,
is present in disclosure." [46] "The seer [*Seher*] stands face to face
with the present in its disclosure, which has at the same time
lighted the closure of the absent *as* the absent." [47] Heidegger here
continues the struggle against the habit of thinking which holds
that only the *vor-handen* is real and efficacious; what has Being is
whatever is disclosed, even if only disclosed as absent, hidden, or
unintelligible. Thus, against Parmenides, past and future *are*. To be
is not to rest self-identical in a present moment but to "sojourn"

(*weilen*) or "tarry for a while." Sojourning is a "passage" (*Übergang*).[48] A passage *is* a passage only in relation to its termini, where it came from and where it is going. The termini of the mortal passage are birth and death—there is a silence, or darkness, and an unintelligibility both before and after. A present-at-hand ontology thinks of human existence as 'life' (*Leben*), existing, as does the *Lebensphilosophie* that Heidegger inherits and revises. Heidegger develops what might be called a *Wohnensdenken:*[49] to "dwell" (*wohnen*) or "sojourn" (*weilen*) means to live death, to live one's limits, to value the gift of and beauty of the light *because of* the darkness, to affirm one's limit as one's fate.

At this point the importance for Heidegger of Nietzsche's reappropriation of the Greek outlook manifests itself. The precondition for loving one's mortal existence and its setting is the affirmation of limits. When Heidegger says "we have left behind us the presumption of all unconditionedness," he means that he decisively rejects the metaphysical impulse to measure his way of being, his dwelling, by reference to a nontemporal Absolute lying beyond (meta-) that dwelling. To affirm death as death and the beyond *as* genuine darkness, genuine absence, genuine unintelligibility—this is to be one's own being, to become what one is. To try to compensate for dwelling, living one's death, by canceling death (eternal salvation), to try to compensate for finite truth by extending it indefinitely (infinitely)—this is to hate, the one true evil, or to demand "revenge against time."[50] Hatred of finite conditions (of limited possibility) is the one true Evil because it devalues the Place wherein man does and must live. Love of finite conditions is affirmation of the one true Good because it cares for and sustains the Place wherein man does and must live. This love of Place (not of oneself), being "centered" on the Place, is the condition of both Truth and Beauty. It is the condition of Truth because if one holds the presence of unintelligibility and error (*Irre*) to be solely signs of failure to reach the true, then truth is dis-placed into the future as that which is always yet to be attained—the object of an endless striving, the carrot chased by the ass. Metaphysics is "the quest for what-is as such and as a whole" where "as a whole" or "in totality" means that man will know the truth only when he "gets to the bottom of things," only when his knowledge is total and absolute. Here Heidegger departs from Hegel, who begins the "consummation" (*Vol-*

lendung) of metaphysics[51] in holding that "the truth is the whole" as the object of "absolute knowledge." To "get to the bottom of things" is to leave nothing in the dark, to un-cover everything. Yet we live in the age of Gödel, Einstein, and Heisenberg—the time when man encounters essential limits to what may be known. This is the time of 'danger'. If knowledge of "the nature" of the environment and of man requires completeness and objectivity, and if man has staked the meaning of his existence on this quest for absolute completeness and objectivity, while he finds his knowledge to be *essentially* incomplete and *essentially* relative to his standpoint, then he finds his essential purpose checked. But the time of danger is for Heidegger also precisely the time of opportunity.[52] The time when man is forced to encounter his own limits is the time when it first becomes possible to reassess at the deepest level the nature and origin of man's historical quest for "what is as such and as a whole."

Against this striving for the absolute ground (*Gründenwollen*) Heidegger counsels 'resignation' (*Verzicht*) in the sense of love of limit, love of time and place, of the time-play-space. This is not an ethical by-way of phenomenology but the carrying out of the original phenomenological program, for the phenomenon is the real or is 'true' only when it is not a mere-present-appearance that remains to be deciphered by a metaphysical key (the science of astrophysics, the science of microphysics, the science of microbiology, or the science of theology).

Love of Place is the condition of Beauty as well as of Truth. To regard mortality and its setting as deficient relative to what it lacks is to displace beauty into the beyond. There is, for example, the well-known type of person who cannot love anything mortal because it dies—the monk who places a skull on his desk as a *memento mori*, or the man who insists on calling up the image of a skull underneath the fair and blossoming skin of a young woman ("that is what she *really* is!"). Merleau-Ponty comments on this very sort of attitude in Pascal:

> Nothing is more pessimistic or skeptical than the famous text in which Pascal, asking himself what it is to love, remarks that one does not love a woman for her beauty, which is perishable, or for her mind, which she can lose, and then suddenly concludes: "one never loves anybody; one loves only qualities." Pascal is proceeding like a skeptic who asks *if* the world exists,

remarks that the table is only a sum of sensations, the chair another sum of sensations, and finally concludes: one never sees anything; one sees only sensations. . . . In order to safeguard the ideal unity of love, Pascal breaks human life into fragments at will and reduces the person to a discontinuous series of states. The absolute which he looks for beyond our experience is implied in it.[53]

Pascal's attitude is a good example of the metaphysical attitude that Heidegger is challenging, and Merleau-Ponty's critique of Pascal is in the Heideggerian spirit. Being really happens in time. It is the understanding of what lives as fragile, as but briefly given, which makes it precious and beautiful; to elevate beauty into a timeless transcendent ideal is to displace "the near," in Heidegger's terms, into "the far." Is this obvious and trivial, or obvious and supremely important? When Heidegger claims that the future is the coming-on of the past,[54] this means in part that what is "old" and "obvious" and "ordinary" is what we essentially have to look forward to. If, in the spirit of metaphysics, we look forward essentially to something else—to deliverance from the old and obvious into the novel, the revolutionary, or "the wholly other"—then we simply discount the conditions under which we do and must dwell. That is what Heidegger calls 'disownment' (Uneigentlichkeit). Meditating on human history as befits a seer, Heidegger sees what might be called the masochism of culture. Metaphysics is the masochism of culture; our culture has a more or less systematic tendency to mistrust its own conditions. e. e. cummings writes satirically of this tendency, "listen:there's a hell of a good universe next door;let's go."[55] If there's a hell of a good universe next door, then this one is a lack. Truth, Beauty, and Goodness lie elsewhere. Value is then the lacked, as Sartre has argued.

We can now, at last, explain why death is "the shrine of Nothingness" and why Being and Nothing are "the same" or "together in their difference." A shrine is a place of mystery, of awe, of reverence, a place where something of rare importance is encountered. Death is worthy of awe, and is of rare importance, because it is here that one encounters the possibility (possibilizing ground) or condition for Truth, Beauty, and Goodness. It is in the acceptance of death as death, as final and unchallengeable, that one finds Truth and Beauty to be present. What comes into presence is 'holy' precisely when it is taken as the only possible region of meaning, when one has left the presumption of all unconditionedness behind one. "Death is the yet unrealized measure of the unmeasurable." [56] Man has yet to contemplate seriously the real function of his understanding of death in establishing the boundaries of the Place. It is in light of what is possible and what is not possible that the 'actual' lights up as true (intelligible in its own finite setting) and as beautiful (as lovable, admirable, valuable). Man dwells *amid* truth and beauty insofar as he understands that beings are finite and relative to a finite place—that is, insofar as he understands that Being and Nothingness go together in Time. To be is to be bound and determined by time. One values the light only if it is *not* eternal and *not* everywhere, only if it is a fragile and fleeting gift on an Earth amid an enclosing darkness. If one demands that it be eternal and everywhere, it will turn out to be nowhere. When man becomes the mortal he is, earth is affirmed as a limit that empowers; as shrine of nothingness, the unfathomable darkness of death makes one's time and place the true site of meaning. This is how I interpret Heidegger's conversion of nihilism into its origin; nothingness is remembered as an essential condition of Being itself.

It should now be clearer how the mortal, in his understanding of his mortality, plays as a member in the Place of the Fourfold. What of the divinities? Is it an accident that they keep eluding us—and Heidegger? If to evoke any member of the Fourfold is at the same time to evoke the other three, how then does evoking mortals evoke the divinities? Heidegger has been less "clear" about this member of the Fourfold than about the other three. Is that Heidegger's fault, or the fault of the times in which we live, or is it necessary, given the nature of divinity itself? One can, as I did with the Heavens, refer to the pervasiveness of the notions of gods and God in history; the history of religion repeatedly presents us with beings who rule as mortal man cannot, beings who seem in various respects inversions of man, endowed with precisely those traits and powers that man understands himself as lacking, yet related to man nonetheless. Is this characterization an important one?

Man places himself, Heidegger has argued, relative to absences that are "present" in the sense that they are understood *as* being absent, are taken into account in their absence. It is characteristic of phenomenological ontology to give ontological status to that which is not *vorhanden*, and in such a way as to try to establish that the being of the *vor-handen* is dependent on the being of what is not *vor-handen;* the being of the perceptible is dependent on the imperceptible; the being of the physical is dependent on the linguistic; and so forth. This is the case not because there is a dialectic between these kinds of being, but rather because they are originally together. What lies "between" (*zwischen*) beings or regions of being is not formed subsequent to these beings (for example, by free imagination or speculative interrelating). The "between" is original. This will mean, in the case now before us, that the mortal "affair" has always been an affair between man and the gods because in some way they belong together in an original community. This must be in some way a unity of the present and the absent. For a present-at-hand ontology the absence of God or gods means either their nonexistence (a ground for atheism), or ignorance about their existence (a ground for agnosticism). But Heidegger holds that the absence of the divinities *is* their ownmost way of being. Commenting on Hölderlin's understanding of the gods, Heidegger writes: "The god is unknown and is nevertheless the measure. Not only this but the god who remains unknown must, in showing *himself* as he who he is, appear precisely as the one who remains unknown."[57]

One is perhaps reminded of the famous closing lines of Schweitzer's *The Quest of the Historical Jesus.* Schweitzer concludes that the sustained efforts of nineteenth-century investigators to uncover the real Jesus leave him unknown: "He comes to us as One unknown. . . ."[58] Were he known, he would not be a god. It is of the essence of the divine to be radically other. It is *the distance* between man and god, mortal and immortal, that makes gods gods (and man man). The gods' proper mode of presence is distance. But if they must by nature be and remain unknown, how can they possibly be "the measure"? Is that not an invitation to the arbitrary assertion of measures or standards? Neither Hölderlin nor Heidegger, however, says "measures," but rather "*the* measure." It appears that it is not a question of particular codes of conduct or ethical guidelines. It is a question of a more "basic" measure of the "dimension" of the "between"—the original establishing of the dimension, the measurements, the boundaries of the cleared site or Place:

The essence of the dimension is the lighted and thus measurable apportionment of the between: up *to* the Heavens and down *to* the Earth. . . . In the words of Hölderlin, man takes the measure of the dimension by measuring himself against the heavenly. Man does not undertake this measuring incidentally; only in such measure-taking is man man at all. Therefore he can obstruct, foreshorten, and deform this measurement, but he cannot escape it.[59]

Mortals understand and acknowledge their mortality or conditionality in understanding and acknowledging that they are not gods, that there is unbridgeable distance between themselves and gods. How? According to Hölderlin, the god shows himself as the unknown through the heavens.[60] The heavens are the region of openness, of distance—an expanse. For a present-at-hand ontology, it is empty space or "the void" or the vast cosmic "wastes." As such it presents itself as an appeal, as a gap or void to be filled by astrophysical research or by astronauts. In accord with Heidegger's judgment that "everything happens together"[61] and hence that mortals and heavens are defined together by the same 'directive', when man regards himself as a quest for universal knowledge, the heavens present themselves as the not-*yet*-known and the to-*be*-known. When man regards himself as the quest for a human environment, the environment at large presents itself as what-is-to-be-humanized. All this can equally well be seen the other way around. It is when the environment at large appears as the calculable and measurable that man regards himself as the calculator. It is when the environment appears primarily as tappable resources or raw materials that man regards himself primarily as user and consumer.

In modern thought—in the period of humanism, of progress, of universal exploration—there arises the view that the light can be indefinitely extended. Darkness is provisional, the yet-to-be-illuminated. The Greek notion of limit strikes us as stultifying—a bar to enterprise. The man who knows his limits is probably the man who has set his sights too low. We are much given to breaking records and tend to feel unfulfilled when not doing so. The old notion of inherent limits to human knowledge simply held back human progress. We are driven by the desire to extend ourselves indefinitely in space and in time. The time-play-space in which we play appears in principle unlimited. Each new present surpasses the past. The past is the more primitive. Though we are fond of saying we can and should learn from the past, we do not really believe it, for the past has been surpassed and "history never repeats itself." There are no grounds for satisfaction with the present because it is in process of being superceded.

We seem to be on the way to godhood. Sartre holds that the profound meaning of human existence is the attempt to be God. Man has always measured himself against something heavenly, writes Heidegger.[62] The goal of humanism is man as master, disposer, arbiter, judge. We read everywhere that man has unlimited potential, profound reserves and yet-untapped powers to reshape his natural and social environments, and to reshape himself. The limit of our ambition is the actualization of our *un*limited potential for change, development, improvement, progress. This implies that there is no conceivable finite limit. No state could be reached that would be recognizable as the fulfillment of human ambitions. Expressed differently, if our goal is the unlimited transformation of finite conditions, our aim is in effect the ultimate cancellation of finite conditions; only this could be recognized as grounds for satisfaction and rest. Thus there is no rest, it appears, in "the temporal torrent."[63] The will to a recognizable limit is replaced by "the will to will."[64] The god recedes indefinitely, in-terminably, un-conditionally. "The god is unknown and is nevertheless the measure. Not only this, but the god who remains unknown must, in showing *himself* as he who he is, appear precisely as the one who remains unknown." Thus God represents the compensatory inversion of all that man lacks. He will so appear until and unless man himself attains godhood.

The quest of present man appears to be self-fulfillment by self-cancellation—the goal of the mystic! Far from advocating mysticism, Heidegger is arguing for the 'turn into' or 'con-version' into the affirmation of the conditioned, the finite, by a 'simple' act of 'remembering' or re-cognition. This re-cognition of something 'old' is at the same time the understanding of the present epoch as 'the danger'. It is the recognition of what 'remains' and 'rests' as 'the same'. What remains? It is "the way," the spatiotemporal course itself. To recognize that the future means the coming-on of finite, mortal conditions "eternally" is to leave "behind us the presumption of all unconditionedness." It is to remember that the essential conditions under which we are at all—'the possible'—cannot be the conditions we seek to cancel. That is disownment and displacement. When man becomes 'the mortal' who he always already is, then God first becomes the God he is—the god who *remains* unknown. To cede to God his radical transcendence is contemporaneously to own up to our own finite transcendence and to be genuinely contemporary. The heart of human religion is not metaphysical theology but the deferential recognition of man's finite transcendence, of his mortality, of the illimitable darkness surrounding the gift of light, and of the lighted Place as 'holy'. This recognition could make possible the "saving" message of a god neither theologically idolized nor humanistically rejected. Such a god would presumably be neither old nor new, but the coming on anew of the sense of a Power beyond mortal powers that "measures" by placing human powers in perspective, thereby saving mortals from their own excessive pride and their revenge against time.

When man 'turns into' his own essence, his finite Place presents itself as the holy, and as to be 'preserved'. This one *topos* is the hidden ground of all philosophical *topoi*: logic, ethics, aesthetics, metaphysics, philosophy of religion, philosophy of science, social philosophy. The crisis of the ground in each of these areas (the loss of objectivity, the threat of subjectivism, the danger of relativism) signals the utter displacement of the true ground. The return of the true ground comes as love or 'care', which remembers the original Good. The original Good can only be the necessary Good, namely, the conditions under which alone everything man values has come to be, Place and Lighting. The original Truth can only be the necessary Truth—the world always already understood is the precondition, basis, and reference point of all our particular truths or assertions.[65] The original Beauty can only be the necessary Beauty—the appearance of things and mortals as in our care in a transient and valuable moment which is ultimately without explanation but which 'gives itself' as the wonder of all wonders—that there are beings at all.[66] What is necessary is what has and will, if we shepherd it, make possible.

All of this is the simple consequence of Heidegger's notion of the phenomenon as an original and originary unity or precedent community of nature. All our linguistic and analytic habits conspire against its re-cognition, for we think and say we understand by separating things into their original elements, most especially their "objective" nature as distinct from their "subjective" appearance.

But the object is the privative mode of 'the thing', the thing only *allegedly* freed of its "subjective" elements. We understand not originally by separating but by 'ekstasis', 'ek-sistence', or 'care', by truly being-*in*-the-world. We—our thought, our language—are originally *in* the thing and thus originally joined with the thing. "We are, in the strict sense of the word," Heidegger says, "die Be-Ding-ten."[67] This expression means both "conditioned" in general and, more literally, "thinged." In Hebel's terms, we are plants, rooted in the earth. Heidegger's original notion of the circle—that we are conditioned by what we condition, and hence that there is between us a prior and remaining community of nature—leads to the notion of the round-dance or Fourfold as the time-play-space displaced by the ontology of *Vorhandenheit*. This is the outcome of reappropriating the "greatness" of German idealism as the beginning of the phenomenological movement—Hegel held that "This identity of Being and Thought . . . constitutes the most interesting idea of modern times," and Heidegger works out a nonsubjectivist and nonmetaphysical version of this most interesting idea.[68] The Fourfold is also the outcome of "radicalizing" Husserl's notion of intentionality by showing that it means the inherence of an allegedly transcendental ego in a prior community of nature.

The language of ontology has become mortal language—the homely language of death and love. In other words, the Being of beings is now remembered as having always been a coming-to-be in language under mortal conditions—a preserving of beings for a while in a fragile light surrounded by darkness. To remember this is to renounce the metaphysical goal of vanquishing darkness by ascending to absolute, unconditioned, and eternal truth. Ontology returns to its original nature and affirms its fate. This is Heidegger's final resolution of the interrelated problems of the beginning, of unity, and of metaphysics that formed the core of his philosophical inheritance.

9

Heidegger's Notion of Two Beginnings

> Everything depends on our seeing how what is designated in the
> first signification of *phainomenon* ('phenomenon' as that which
> shows itself) and what is designated in the second ('phenomenon'
> as semblance) are structurally interconnected. . . . 'Semblance'
> . . . is the privative modification of 'phenomenon.'
>
> —Heidegger, *SZ*, p. 29 (51)

I

THE REMEMBERING of the Fourfold is the culmination of
Heidegger's long effort to resolve the inherited problems of the
beginning, of unity, and of metaphysics: the true beginning is a
non- or pre-metaphysical unity.[1] This beginning is retrieved by
taking the way back into the original ground of metaphysics—a 'destruction' of the history of philosophical ontology that recalls the
deeply veiled source of that ontology. This source is a Place that has
been displaced. This displacement, I shall argue, must be seen as a
dissimulation of and by the Fourfold itself. Our analysis of this dissimulation will center on its most recent form, which Heidegger
calls *Gestell.*

Further elucidation of the nature of the Fourfold must then come
through a characterization of its relation to Heidegger's notion of
historical dissimulation. Otherwise we run the risk of regarding the
Fourfold as a kind of ahistoric or metaphysical entity not subject to
the vicissitudes of time, or as a construct of Heidegger's imagination. Of course, this is far from Heidegger's intention, which is to
accomplish the exceedingly delicate task of reconciling permanence
with change, unity or oneness with diversity, rest with movement,
eternity with time—without reducing either to the other. This task
is not a new one but rather a reappropriation of the ancient effort to
reconcile Parmenides with Heraclitus—or at least the opposition
that the Greeks attributed to these thinkers. It is the effort to recon-

cile 'Being' and 'Time', which is why Heidegger regards himself as meditating on the *'und'* of *Sein und Zeit*. The 'reversal' of *Sein und Zeit* as *Zeit und Sein* has the effect of identifying Being with Time and Time with Being. Their difference dissimulates an identity. This points to the core of Heidegger's positive relation to German idealism, which consists in the refusal to choose between notions that appear, logically, as mutually exclusive opposites. This is one reason why Heidegger valued his work *Identität und Differenz* so highly.[2] The *'und'* of *Identität und Differenz* is, one might argue, the *'und'* of *Sein und Zeit*. It is the *'und'* that is already asked about in Heidegger's original question: "If beings are spoken of with a multiplicity of meanings, what then is the guiding and basic meaning? What does it mean to be?"[3] That is, what is the relation between the one Being and the many beings? What remains or rests amid the flux of meanings or beings? (Note that I say here 'amid' the flux—not 'over' or 'under' or 'against' the flux.) Hence Being *and* Time, or: Identity *and* Difference, or: Clearing *and* Presentness, or: Fourfold *and* History. Again and again the 'and' refers to the precedent community of nature, or identity in the sense of mutual belonging, in what the tradition has held simply distinct and different.

Out of Heidegger's career-long meditation on the nature of this 'and' there finally emerges the notion of the Fourfold as 'illimitable relation' (*unendliche Verhältnis*).[4] Heidegger's awareness of this relation emerges from sustained meditation on history. The Fourfold emerges as the site, ground, or place of history. The Fourfold is the place of the originating 'Event of Appropriation' (*Ereignis*) or 'Gathering' that initiates and sustains history. This Event is at the same time the illimitable relation. Thus we are dealing with a complex of notions: the illimitable relation of the Event of the Fourfold as the place of history.

Yet this notion of the Fourfold as the place of history appears to be grossly inadequate, for history itself appears to have reached the point where the "members" of the Fourfold—Earth, Heavens, Mortals, the Divine—are known for what they really are—poetic, mythical, fictive images. Inasmuch as modern history manages without these images, it would seem that the Fourfold can hardly be the place or site of history. Three of these "members" can still be taken as referring to something real, but only as poetic embellishments of the real: "the Earth" is really nature, "the Heavens" are really the sky or the atmosphere, and "Mortals" are really human beings. Sartre's atheism would seem to be a realistic acknowledgment that reflective thought has reached the stage when it must dispense with the Divine. Heidegger's defense against this line of attack is to be found in his notions of 'privation', 'semblance' or 'dissimulation' or 'blocking' (*Verstellung*), and 'forgottenness'. They account for displacement: the way in which the Place dissimulated its 'original' or 'originary' nature at the 'beginning' (*Anfang*) and in the course of what is called Western history or the Western tradition. The particular character of the *movement* and *direction* of this tradition—as a quest based in a falling and forgetting—is not a sign of the mere absence of the Fourfold or Place but is rather owing to the Fourfold's own self-dissimulation. I construe 'direction' (*Richtung*) as governed by an 'original unity' and the dissimulation of this unity.

Heidegger repeatedly refers to this beginning as 'the first beginning' (*der erste Anfang*) by way of comparison with 'the other beginning' (*der andere Anfang*)—a future and merely "possible" terminus toward whose realization his thinking is "underway."[5] It is his effort to move from our habitual first-beginning modes of thinking toward an other-beginning thinking that largely accounts for the alleged poetic diffuseness of his later essays.

Heidegger was for some years preoccupied with the question of the relation between the first beginning among the Greeks and the possible other beginning, a question that is inseparable from the question of the nature of the Fourfold. The first beginning and the other beginning are identifiable only in relation to each other. What is this relation, and why are the "termini" of the relation—the first beginning and the other beginning—not separately or independently identifiable?

Heidegger's very locution 'other beginning' immediately suggests that the two beginnings are radically, perhaps wholly, different from each other—an impression reinforced by the vehemence with which he appears to criticize the metaphysical thinking of the first beginning. But we shall find that the relation between the two beginnings is one of radical—root—identity, whatever differences there may be in the two "branches" or "beginnings" growing from this common root. We shall see that a great deal is at stake in the resolution of this interpretive problem.[6] The later positions of both

Heidegger and Sartre appear vulnerable to the charge of being utopian philosophies of history that devalue the present relative to a
romanticized past and a romanticized future. We shall need to
know whether this charge is in either case justifiable.

One of Heidegger's chief means of meditating on the relation of
the first beginning, which appears to be past, and the other beginning, or possible future, is analysis of the present epoch, which he
characterizes as the epoch of the *Ge-Stell*. One of his chief means of
analyzing the *Ge-Stell* is, in turn, meditation on the relation of the
Ge-Stell to the Fourfold (*Geviert*).[7]

The term *Ge-Stell*, also written by Heidegger as *Ge-stell* and as
Gestell, is a collective term derived from the verb *stellen*. In his 1956
addendum to *Der Ursprung des Kunstwerkes*, Heidegger writes that
"We must think of 'stellen' in the sense of [the Greek] *thesis* . . .
which means a setting up in the unconcealed. The Greek 'setting'
means placing *[Stellen]*, as for instance, letting a statue be set up."
He argues that for the Greeks 'placing' is also 'letting'. "Setting and
placing here never mean the modern concept of the summoning of
things to be placed over against the self (the ego-subject)."[8] For the
Greeks, in other words, the placing connoted by *thesis*, or by
poiēsis, is not simply a subjective act of will but a 'letting' in the
sense of an act of deference, a kind of compliance. "The Ge-Stell, as
the nature of modern technology, derives from the Greek way of experiencing letting-lie-forth, *logos*, from the Greek *poiēsis* and *thesis*."[9]

In the term *Ge-Stell*, the prefix 'Ge-' indicates a whole range of
possible settings, placings, or layings; I shall translate it by the
Latin prefix 'com'. I shall translate '-Stell' by 'position', and 'posing', from the Latin *ponere*, in accord with Heidegger's observation
that "also correlated with 'to place' and 'to set' is 'to lay'; all three
meanings are still intended jointly by the Latin *ponere*."[10] Thus
'Com-position' will mean the essence of modern technology as a
constellation of ways of placing, positioning, posing, imposing,
disposing, planning, and calculating, which appear as subjective
and willful acts and have thus lost track of their own original source
in a compliant 'letting'. Heidegger also connects *Ge-Stell* with "the
Greek sense of *morphē* as Gestalt"—form or figure.[11] Thus one can
think of the epoch of technology as a subjective composing or
making-conform that has forgotten its real roots in *poiēsis*, form-

ing or composing as an "art" that complies with, or defers to, or lets things lie forth in their own configuration or conformation, that is, in their own proper, fitting, or appropriate place. In this original composing, man is neither merely an active composer nor merely passively composed.[12] He is an active *and* receptive participant in the play of the Fourfold. I shall try, then, to show that for Heidegger the technological epoch of Composition dissimulates this play of the Fourfold by misconstruing placing, setting, and laying in a purely subjective and willful sense. This blocks access to the larger play in which man plays a necessary and active, and yet limited, role. The Composition then shows itself as it really is—as itself a mode of Fourfold-play. The Composition is thus the way in which the Being of beings occurs in the present epoch. This phase of Heidegger's thought is in part a protracted effort to understand the true balance or 'harmony' (*Fuge*) between human activity and the human deference or compliance requisite for the Event of ongoing truth—the Event of an intelligible world. One may regard the Fourfold as a central focus of Heidegger's later thinking, relative to which other aspects of his later thinking may be understood.

II

It will aid the analysis of Heidegger's understanding of the relation of Fourfold and Composition, the relation of the two beginnings, and the correlation of these two relations, if I first outline an interpretation that in important respects differs from my own. The greatest danger is that the interpretation itself will be influenced by the displacement characteristic of the tradition, misrepresenting Heidegger's understanding of the 'contemporaneity' of past, present, and future in the time-play-space that I have called the 'Place'. The interpretation that immediately follows succumbs to this danger in certain respects, particularly its treatment of 'world'.

The early or "first beginning" Greeks experienced themselves as dwelling within and essentially dependent upon a context or "home" out of whose dark and uncognizable recesses all beings come for a time into presence and back into which all beings after a time return. The Greeks understood themselves as "mortals" whose limited but necessary role in bringing beings into presence was to be shared with "the divine," with "the heavens," and with the productive "earth." Man thus understood himself as only one member of a Fourfold, each of whose members participated in the creative Play (*Gevierstspiel*) by which all beings come into presence. Thus the early Greek felt himself a creative-yet-dependent member of a meaningful "World," whose own or proper (*eigentlich*) being was relatedness rather than isolate individuality.

But at the same time, according to this interpretation, Greek thinking contained the seeds of the dissolution of this Fourfold. The very language of Greek thinking increasingly centered the thinker's attention upon present beings to the exclusion of the creative play of the Fourfold or "Worldplay" (*Weltspiel*) in which beings had come to presence. Metaphysics, "explaining Being through a being, instead of 'understanding' the being from Being"[13] or in terms of Worldplay, culminates in the Composition of the present epoch. In this epoch all beings—including ourselves—are man-handled or manipulated for the sake of other beings. All beings compose a ready stock or standing, standardizable, and disposable inventory (*Bestand*) of raw materials whose "value" is determined by the degree to which they serve in the ever-escalating web of means-end relationships by which the human will wills and calculates that endless change called "progress." In this interpretation, at present *there is no World, no Fourfold.* Since present beings are understood solely in terms of other present or past beings, and since nothing "is" other than such beings, there is no context beyond such beings—no "ontological difference." There is no sense in which man is co-participant in a creative Worldplay whereby Things (*Dinge*) come to be, and no sense in which man and Things emerge from and return to a hidden source. There is only Composition and, beyond that, nothing. Composition "rules" (*waltet*) unchallenged. The ancient sense of Place is altogether absent.

Heidegger's thinking, however, taking a hint from the poetic prophecy of Hölderlin, points to a possible future in which the Fourfold would rule, altogether unencumbered by the language and thinking of metaphysics. For this to be a real possibility, man must prepare for the "turn into" (*Einkehr in*) the *other* beginning by coming to understand the present epoch as a lack and a danger, as an epoch in need of "saving" (*Rettung*). Sensitized to the limits and dangers of a willful calculating and manipulating of materials, he may become receptive to the voice of poets who will serve as messengers of new gods. Heeding the message of the new gods, man will newly experience himself as a mortal destined to create, together with the gods, and care for a new dwelling (*Wohnung*) out of the inexhaustible and hidden fullness of the earth and in harmony with the rhythm of the heavens. A prime trait of this new epoch will be man's openness to Things, which he will let speak for themselves rather than reducing their being to that of materiality or instrumentality or calculability. Man will care for Things themselves, which both come to presence in language (as meanings) and transcend the categories and purposes to which man subjects them.

The foregoing interpretation, no doubt, is one to which no student of Heidegger would subscribe in every detail, nor is it one that I reject in every detail. I wish to question it here only insofar as it interprets World and Fourfold as traits of a more or less utopian future that are altogether absent from the present epoch of Composition.

III

Many passages in Heidegger's essays can readily be construed as implying that the Composition of the present epoch and the Fourfold (or World) are mutually exclusive—where either is, the other is not. For example, Heidegger's use of the expressions 'if' or 'when' and 'only when' in certain contexts appears to be evidence for the futurity of the Fourfold, its exclusion from the present Composition. In *TK*, for example, he writes that "When the danger is as danger . . . World comes to pass." [14] This appears to say that until or unless the danger of the Composition is explicitly grasped, there is no World. Similarly, his assertions that World comes to pass "abruptly" and that Being comes "precipitously out . . . of concealment" [15] may suggest that World is a sudden incursion into a worldless epoch. Can these—and many similar—Heideggerian statements be compatible with the presence of World or Fourfold in the present epoch?

Heidegger appears to claim that what rules today is Composition and only that. To speak of something else ruling "behind" it would seem to be just the sort of metaphysical conception he would reject. Yet his discussion of 'dissimulating' (*verstellen*) [16] in Composition shows that Composition is itself the dissimulated appearance of something that does not appear, in accord with his notion that for the most part the phenomenon does not appear.

Heidegger's essay "Die Frage nach der Technik" is in part a meditation on the relation of Composition and *poiēsis*. *Poiēsis* seems to be an *alternative* mode of disclosure to the mode of disclosure of Com-posing ('challenging' or 'provoking'). "The disclosing that altogether dominates modern technology does not display itself as bringing-forth in the sense of *poiēsis*. The disclosing that rules in modern technology is a challenging. . . ."[17] Heidegger further writes: "Com-posing is a fateful manner of disclosing: disclosing by challenging. Disclosing by bringing forth into presence, by *poiēsis*, is likewise a fateful manner of disclosing."[18] Here "likewise" may suggest that challenging and *poiēsis* are mutually exclusive possibilities. Yet Heidegger immediately adds: "But these ways of disclosing are not modes of the same type subsumable under the general concept of 'disclosing'. . . . Disclosing by challenging has its requisite origin in disclosing as bringing forth into presence. But at the same time Com-posing fatefully dissimulates this *poiēsis*."[19] This establishes that the relation of *poiēsis* and challenging is not simply that of alternative possibilities, but that bringing forth into presence, or *poiesis*, is the dissimulated *origin* of the challenge of Composing. But this raises a new question. Is the poetic-but-dissembled origin of challenging simply a *past* origin? Or must 'origin' be construed according to Heidegger's notion of 'contemporaneity' (*Gleichzeitigkeit*),[20] for which it would be a "historiological" (*historisch*) misunderstanding to think of 'origin' as simply "past"? Can it be that "behind" (in the sense of the verbal essence of) the Composition's challenging is a still-ruling poetic origin? Another passage may help answer this question:

Above all the Com-posing covers over that disclosing which, in the sense of *poiēsis*, lets the being that is coming-into-presence come forth into appearance. . . . Where Com-position rules, all disclosing is reduced to assessing materials on hand and insuring their continued availability. Such assessing and insuring no longer permit the appearance of *the very originative process to which they owe their being* [*ihren eigenen Grundzug*], namely, disclosing as such. . . . The Com-position dissimulates the appearing and ruling of truth.[21]

Thus it is established that the Composition dissimulates the source of its own being. But it is only in a very important later essay, "Hölderlins Erde und Himmel," that Heidegger elaborates in any detail just what it is that Composing dissimulates, just what it is that stands "behind" the Composition as its (nonmetaphysical) origin—the Fourfold. Heidegger begins this essay with a reference to the need for a 'conversion': "The conversion to the thoughtful experiencing of the center of the illimitable relation—: out of the Com-position as the self-dissimulating Event of the Fourfold."[22] Later in the essay, Heidegger elaborates the interrelation of Composition, Fourfold, and dissimulation:

> Does Western civilization still exist? It has become Europe. Its technological-industrial dominion by now extends over the entire earth. . . . The illimitable relation of earth and heaven, man and God *seems* destroyed. Or has it never yet appeared out of the gathering of a suitable directive *as* this illimitable relation, purely articulated within our history? Has it never yet become present, never yet been presented as a whole in the highest regions of art? *In that case it could not be destroyed, but at worst only be dissimulated and denied an appearance.* Then it would be up to us to meditate on this denial of the illimitable relation.
>
> What denies *itself* to us thereby approaches us in its own peculiar way. Today such an approach befalls man everywhere, in the form of a challenging that is still rarely thought about. . . . This challenging, present in the calculative disposing of everything that is and can be, *dissimulates* the illimitable relation. What is more, the challenging, which rules in the sovereignty of the essence of modern technology, hides above all else the very source from which the dictatorial force of the challenging receives its direction. What is this source?
>
> It is the center of the whole illimitable relation. It is the pure directive itself.[23]

Heidegger freely translates—in support of the foregoing—Fragment DK 54 of Heraclitus: "A juncture [*Fuge*] that denies itself an appearance rules more powerfully than one that makes an appearance." Heidegger concludes: "The center . . . is the juncture of the relation of the Four, which is hesitant to appear."[24]

These crucial passages argue that the challenging or provoking of the Composition receives its "direction" (*Schickung*) from "the center of the whole illimitable relation," which center or heart of the Fourfold is hesitant to appear—that is, is the self-dissimulating introplay of the Four. The Fourfold is here characterized as what is never destroyed but at most only dissimulates itself by failing to appear overtly. It is what Heidegger elsewhere calls "the remaining" or "the lasting" (*das Bleibende*).[25] "The originary . . . never perishes, is never merely past."[26] The Fourfold-Play is "the originary." "The advance out of the beginning does not abandon the beginning. . . ."[27] To think of beginning (*Anfang*) as past would be to interpret it metaphysically, as one "now-moment" preceding and causing another. "That which, ascertained historiologically, is later—namely, modern technology—is with respect to the essence ruling in it the historically earlier."[28]

It is impossible to overestimate the importance, for the later Heidegger's thinking, of the notion of 'contemporaneity' (*Gleichzeitigkeit*) that the foregoing passages presuppose. A consequence of Heidegger's lifelong meditation on time, 'contemporaneity' is developed out of Heidegger's early analysis of the introplay of the three temporal 'ekstases'.[29] In both its early and later forms, this notion means, in part, that the being which appears to be simply or merely present is, when understood in its 'essencing' (its *Wesen*; its manner of *coming-into*-presence, or, in older terminology, the manner of its "constitution"), found to be co-formed by its 'contemporaneous' or 'simultaneous' relation to all three temporal dimensions. Further, and most important for my interpretation, Heidegger stresses that this analysis applies to *absence* as well as to presence. Therefore he writes that "absence is not nothing, but is rather the presence—a presence that must first be appropriated—of the concealed fullness of what *has* come into being, and thus it gathers what *is* coming into being. . . . This no-more is in itself a not-yet of the disguised advent of its inexhaustible essencing."[30] This passage refers specifically to "the lack of God and of the divine" but it applies equally to the remaining members of the Fourfold and so to the Fourfold as a whole. Heidegger continues, in a passage deserving great stress: "In the directive of Being there is never a mere succession—now Com-position, then World and Thing—but respectively passing-over and contemporaneity of the early and the late."[31]

In what sense is absence the presence of a "concealed fullness"?

In what sense is Composition the "passing-over" or "overlooking" (*Vorbeigang*) of a "contemporary" early and late? The two questions are the same. In effect they ask in what sense Heidegger takes up and transforms Hegel's critique of immediacy. Appearing as merely present, as what simply *is*, the Composition passes over and over-looks the "concealed fullness" out of which it has come to be what it is. For Heidegger what has come to be (*das Gewesene*) first comes to us dissimulated or disguised—as a simple present (for example, as a stock of materials on hand) that lapses into a mere past (*das Vergangene*)—but may later come to us as what it properly (*eigent-lich, eigens*) is "only when" it is first genuinely appropriated by man as coming to him *out of the future:* "true time is ad-vent of what has been." [32] Composition is the present ad-vent of what has been (of the first beginning) in the mode of self-dissimulation of its own beginning, disowning its own source. The other beginning presupposes the recognition of Composition as the absence—which is really the dissimulated presence—of a concealed fullness that is the lasting first-beginning "introplay" (*Spiegelspiel*) of the members of the Fourfold. The Fourfold may yet come to us as an *acknowledged* presence if in the future the lasting first beginning comes to us ex-plicitly (*eigens*) as the other beginning; which means the genuinely appropriated first beginning. For this to occur, man must own up to his ownmost (*eigenst*) essence, which means 'release' (*Gelassenheit*) into what he is already in, but in the mode of appearing not to be in it. His essence is to be a 'mortal', and to be a mortal is to be one member of the Fourfold. What man is already in, in the mode of not being in it, is the introplay of the members of the Fourfold. In other words, man is, in the mode of "passing over" it, coparticipant in the Play of language whereby—even in Com-posing—beings are named or articulated and form a coherent environment of a particu-lar character in which man must live and move. This Play is not simply the play of a present-time Fourfold in a present-time envi-ronment; its locale is the "time-play-space" (*Zeit-Spiel-Raum*) where time is understood as "the ad-vent of what has been." It is there-fore impossible to characterize the Fourfold, its members, or its Play as simply past—as a once-upon-a-time phenomenon—or as simply a future possibility. To do so would be to force the ordinary, and non-Heideggerian, notion of time upon Heidegger's quite dif-ferent notion of the Play of 'true time'.

Composition is thus only the Fourfold's greatest possible self-dissimulation. Therefore the other-beginning directive would be the "conversion" or "retuning" (*Um-stimmung*) of Composing itself, whereby it first becomes understood that Composing is "tuned" or "disposed" (*ge-stimmt, be-stimmt*) by the Fourfold-Play itself. Thereby the Fourfold-Play may come to be 'protected' (*gewahrt, gehütet*). In other words, it may then be understood that the Fourfold-Play dissimulates itself and consequently understood that appearances cannot be taken at face value but are appearances of what does not appear. The other-beginning directive would be the "protecting" of the Fourfold. The Composition-Fourfold relation is the mode of the ontological difference itself in the present epoch. As always for Heidegger, the difference hides an identity; for Composition is the *self*-dissimulated Fourfold *itself*. In protecting the Fourfold as the unseen essencing (*Wesen*) of Composing, the appearances that comprise the Composition would cease to be taken at face value and the epoch of Composition as such would be overcome.

Thus there is always World (Fourfold-Play), which has always dissimulated itself to some degree, but now dissimulates itself maximally (that is, completely) in the epoch of Composition. The very notion of entities occurring without World is foreign to Heidegger's thinking. Entities 'are' only in context (World) and are never self-defining. Expressed differently, the 'as' of language always determines our understanding of entities as the "relation of all relations." [33] Language as the "relation of all relations" is to be associated with the "illimitable relation" (*unendliche Verhältnis*) [34] of the Fourfold. If there is an epoch without World, then World is dispensable—but Heidegger aims to show that all beings stand within its dominion: "at the start and in the course of modern times . . . the entity became a thoroughly graspable object masterable by calculative means. Each time [ancient, medieval, modern] a new and essential World broke forth. . . . Each time an unconcealing of the entity occurred." [35] If Worldplay occurs "at the start and in the course of modern times" then it must be the case that the members of the Fourfold still play. Therefore Heidegger says: "In Worlding is gathered that spaciousness out of which the saving grace of the gods offers or refuses to offer itself. Even the misfortune of the god's failure to appear is a way in which World worlds." [36]

As I have noted, Heidegger states that "the center of the whole illimitable relation . . . is the pure directive itself" and that "The center . . . is the juncture of the relation of the Four, which is hesitant to appear." And in the essay "Die Kehre" he states: "But the overcoming of a directive of Being, in this case the overcoming of the Composition, always eventuates from the advent of another directive. . . ."[37] Correlating these statements, one must conclude that (1) Composition is itself a Fourfold-directive; (2) a directive is only overcome by (remains until it is overcome by) another directive. Thus there is always Fourfold-Play, always a bringing-forth or *poiēsis* (to which the poet's *poiēsis* may or may not cor-respond or be attuned). "But at the same time Com-posing fatefully dissimulates this *poiēsis.*"[38] *Technē*, as the Greeks saw, really belongs to *poiēsis.*[39] The essence of *technē* (and of *Technik*), what "pervasively rules" (*durchwaltet*) it,[40] is *poiēsis* (a mode of Fourfold-Play).

This means that man's essence as the mortal always rules his activities even if thoroughly dissimulated; the heavens always rule, even when dissimulated; and so on. And the Thing is always what it is owing to its essence as a "foured" Thing, even if dissimulated. For example: "The bridge gathers as the overarching crossing in the presence of the divine—whether its essential presence is properly thought and visibly *acknowledged* as in the figure of the saints of the bridge *or rather remains dissimulated or even shoved aside.*"[41] And "were the bridge not a [sc. worlded, foured] Thing, it would never be a mere [sc. present, standing] bridge." The same notion governs Heidegger's assertion that "In order for a man to be blind, he must remain in his essence a being who sees."[42] The essence (*Wesen*) of man, gods, earth, heaven, and Thing always remains, and *Wesen* is here, as always, to be thought verbally, not simply as idea or ideal. The *Wesen* is always that participating in Play by which a being is what it is. The self-dissimulation of *Wesen* occurs in all beings as the ontological difference between their appearance and the nonappearing "source" (*Wesensherkunft*) of that appearance. Com-posing is the uttermost self-denial of and by *Wesen* itself. One can therefore say, paraphrasing *SZ*, that the Fourfold "is something that proximally and for the most part does *not* show itself at all; it is something that lies *hidden*. . . . but at the same time" the Fourfold "is something that belongs to" the Composition, "and belongs to it so essentially as to constitute its meaning and its ground."[43]

To borrow a description used by Heidegger in another context, the events of the epoch of Composition "are only the surface run-offs of a great hidden current, a torrential course that initiates all and traces a path for all." Indeed the original context of this passage is not far removed from the question of the nature of the Composition, since the passage refers to "method" and to the hidden source of "the mysterious power of the rule of method in our time," the time of Composition.[44]

As the self-denying Fourfold, the Composition is the "farness" of what is "nearest." "The Event is the least apparent of all nonapparent things, the simplest of the simple, the nearest of the near and the farthest of the far, *within which we mortals dwell lifelong."* [45] And Heidegger explicitly affirms that Com-posing is governed by this Event (*Ereignis*). "Insofar as it [Com-posing] disposes man, i.e., provokes him to organize everything present as a technological stock of components, Com-posing happens in the manner of Event, though in such a way that it at the same time dissimulates it. . . ." [46] "Every language of man [even, therefore, "the language of Com-posing"] is an event of primordial utterance and as such is essential language in the strict sense, though in varying degrees of nearness to the Event." Furthermore, Heidegger specifically names language—"as the utterance of the World-Fourfold" and "as the World-initiating-utterance"—"the relation of all relations." [47]

I can now summarize, in non-Heideggerian tabular form, the nonapparent and apparent modes of the Fourfold in the present era:

Fourfold	Com-position
Event (gathering, appropriation)	Dis-ownment (disjoining, expropriation)[48]
current	runoff
nonapparent	apparent
the lasting	inconstancy of the constantly new
nearest of the near	farthest of the near
essential language	language of information

The whole possibility of a 'conversion' of Com-posing, or "turn into the Event" (*Einkehr in das Ereignis*), depends on the Fourfold's being the essencing (*Wesen*) of the Composition, the latter's being the dissimulation of the former. *What saves the Fourfold-Play from being merely a fantasied future or a regression to past history is that it is the simple Event that 'lasts', what 'eternally' rules human thought and events, the* Wesen *of all that is.* Heidegger's fundamental argument for the Fourfold is not its desirability but rather its inevitability; the only question of Heidegger's thinking with respect to the future is whether the Fourfold will be 'protected', with all the unforeseeable consequences that might ensue therefrom. The expression 'only when', which at first seemed fatal to interpretation of the Fourfold as 'remaining', refers to that time when the Fourfold is experienced as the *withheld* essence of the Composition, and is thus one example of Heidegger's general notion of the "ad-vent of what has been," as well as of his early [49] and still fundamental distinction between 'phenomenon' on the one hand and 'semblance' on the other. These two notions combine in the following typical passages:

> The coursing can lead us into what belongs to us, into the domain where we already dwell. Then why, one may ask, must we first travel a course toward it? Answer: because we are there, where we already are, in such a way that we are at the same time not there, insofar as we have still not properly appropriated what belongs to our essence. [50]
>   . . . We still do not sufficiently dwell where we really [*eigentlich*] already are. [51]

The step back into the ground of metaphysics, which leads Heidegger to the uncovering of the Fourfold, is the step "back into where we already are." [52] This "where" is the Place displaced, the Fourfold's "time-play-space." In protecting it lies the possibility of an end to man's "flight from his own way of being [*eigenen Wesen*]." [53]

It is the self-dissimulated absent-presence of the Fourfold as the real nature of Com-posing which insures that technology (*die Technik*) is in reality not simply "a means in the hands of man" and which insures that "the semblance of a thoroughgoing humanizing of Being" [54] is only a semblance. In reality the Fourfold, not man alone, composes, disposes, directs, gathers.

It is for these reasons that Heidegger is using the term 'World' (which he has defined as Fourfold-Play) [55] advisedly and not loosely or inconsistently when he speaks of "the technological World." [56] Even in the Composition, "the way of being of man rests on Being-in-the-World." [57]

The other beginning, which initially sounds like a sharp break with "the past," must be thought of primarily in terms of continuity, and only secondarily in terms of discontinuity. In its most important meaning, it is not a new (novel) beginning but rather the possible guarding or protecting of a beginning that is "omnipresent" as the primordial *Grundzug* of all events that come to pass in language. The most accurate characterization of the other beginning is found in Heidegger's expression "the more original origin."[58] The other beginning is the more original or primordial (*anfänglicher*) relation to the lasting (*bleibend*) beginning, while the first beginning was determined by a nonprimordial (*un-anfänglich*) relation to the lasting beginning (the forgetting of Being's self-dissimulation). In other words, 'beginning' (*Anfang*) must come to be understood as "lasting and sustaining origin" (*Ursprung*) rather than simply as a 'start' (*Beginn*) that is left behind. The new is the explicit guarding; the remaining is what is guarded, the 'illimitable' and 'groundless' and 'eternal' Play in which the "more original origin" would play as *self*-guarding. Remembering the illimitable or groundless ground, their place, mortals would no longer seek to ground themselves in a strictly delimitable or absolute ground.

IV

I wish now to ask whether the foregoing interpretation can meet several possible objections to it, and if so, what final conclusions can legitimately be drawn from the interpretation.

The interpretation is compatible with Heidegger's references to the 'abruptness' or unpredictability of the arrival of the other beginning, and with the fact that Heidegger considers the arrival of this other beginning as merely possible, not inevitable. This abruptness and mere possibility refer not to the Event of the Fourfold as such, but rather to a change in its mode of Play.

We have seen that the plausibility of Heidegger's thought is thereby enhanced. Heidegger is saved from the charge of directing us toward a visionary utopia, whose only basis is its similarity to an alleged pre-Socratic outlook, to the extent that he can point to a process of Play that pervasively rules all human experience in and through language, whether explicitly attended to by man or not. If Heidegger's "vision" is of a possible future in which man comes to

terms with what has always already ruled, in which man owns up
to his ownmost mortal way of being, to that extent Heidegger's
view is not utopian in the sense of groundless, but is rather the
calling of attention to an always-ruling "groundless ground" (ab-
gründiges Spiel), Fourfold-Play.

It would seem, however, that if man is already 'the mortal' then
nothing remains to be done—in which case the foregoing interpretation could not account for the stress Heidegger places on preparation for a qualitatively different future. Many passages do indeed
suggest a genuinely different future, for example the following:
"The rational animals must first become the mortals."[59] Does this
not say quite unequivocally that man is at present not the Fourfold-
member 'mortal'? This and similar passages are to be understood in
the spirit of Nietzsche's injunction, "Become who you are!"[60] The
"owned-disowned" (eigentlich-uneigentlich) distinction of SZ,
which, we have seen, is by no means discarded by the later Heidegger, provides support for the claim that man as 'rational animal'
and man as 'mortal' can, and do, characterize one and the same
being. For example, SZ states that "Neither the Self of one's own
Dasein nor the Self of the Other has as yet found or lost itself as
long as it is [seiend] in the modes we have mentioned. In these
modes one's way of Being is that of disowning and failure to stand
by one's Self."[61] Similarly, in WM, "The anxiety is there. Only it is
sleeping. Its breath reverberates constantly through Dasein."[62] The
same may be said of 'the mortal' as "the Self of one's own Dasein"—it is there, but sleeping. Unless the mortal is already there,
he could not be found (or lost). And unless the mortal is already
there, man's experience of himself as 'the mortal' in the other
beginning could be taken as merely personal fantasy, a case of the
human being of the future—or the Heidegger of the present—arbitrarily positing a "new essence" for himself.

What remains to be done is for man to come to terms with his
Wesen—his 'own' relation to language, to Things, to the other
members of the Fourfold. When Nietzsche enjoins man, "Become
who you are!", what remains to be done is "merely" the affirmation
of the necessary (amor fati), yet Nietzsche suspects that great
changes might ensue therefrom. Heidegger's many references to
'release', 'serenity', and 'resignation'[63] are to be understood as references to a kind of affirmation of the necessary. If the other

beginning is a purely speculative hypothesis, a utopian futuristic ideal, and if it is discontinuous with the Composition of the present epoch, then Heidegger's allusions to affirmation of the necessary (and to the 'lasting' and 'eternal') become problematic, if not pointless. If man is not in some sense already the mortal, for example, then it is wholly arbitrary for Heidegger to suggest that man can fulfill his "own essence" in coming to understand himself as the mortal; there would be no reason to suppose that man's self-apprehension of himself in the epoch of Composition as "lord of beings" is not quite as just as Heidegger's characterization of man as "shepherd of Being."[64]

My interpretation may seem "metaphysical" because it speaks of "something else" ruling "behind" the Composition. However it invokes something behind only in the sense in which Heidegger has always distinguished 'essencing' (Wesen, construed verbally) and 'semblance' (which dissimulates its essential origin or Wesensherkunft).

Yet I may seem to put the later Heidegger in the metaphysical position of substituting a permanent substrate of beings (the members of the Fourfold) for his earlier notion of World as a context of meaning (Sein). If for Heidegger 'ground' (Grund) becomes 'abyss' (Ab-grund)[65] it nevertheless remains a 'lasting' Boden, or "home ground," and thus a principle of continuity. Heidegger differs with the metaphysical tradition not in abandoning continuity for radical discontinuity or pure possibility but in reconceiving continuity as the 'introplay' within language of a Fourfold whose members are not externally related as things or simple entities, but internally related as meanings that are the Playground, the inevitable context and source, in which and out of which all historical beings play. Not simply a set of entities,[66] the Play-ground itself plays; but the locale or Place, the time-play-space, remains, and the essential meanings of its four members remain. The Play of Being is "as-play" ('is' is always 'is as'); the four dimensions of the Fourfold mark the 'regions' within which and by reference to which every 'as' is the 'as' that it is (for example, 'as' a standing inventory). This means that the only ground for something being "as it is" is a Playground. If that is a substrate or hypokeimenon, it is a very peculiar sort of hypokeimenon for at least two reasons. First, it is not a thing or set of things so much as a nexus or 'gathering' of meanings. Second, it is a grouping of meanings no one of which is self-defining or self-identical. Rather each is identified solely in the introplay of internal relations with each of the others and insofar as they all gather in identifying the Thing (*das Ding*) in the meaning-Event or primal utterance of identifying and differentiating that is language (the *Sage* of *Sprache*). Heidegger's question is the question whether man will "second," or remember this "priming" (*Ereignis*) in which he already plays.

Putting the matter differently, one may say that Heidegger interprets the Fourfold-Composition relation in light of his own reappropriation of the notion of *sterēsis*—the Aristotelian notion of 'privation' or 'privative mode',[67] which had played an important role in the content and methodology of *SZ* and had served Heidegger as a clue for his delineation of the *A-lētheia-Lēthe* or phenomenon-semblance relation. The notion of privation is of crucial importance for Heidegger as a means of interpreting the ontology of simple 'presentness-at-hand' and its attendant theory of causation. Something that is not a simple material entity—although it *seems* to be only that—but rather a structure of *meanings* can be effective in its "absence," not only despite but because of its absence. And its absence may be proof for it rather than against it. Where one understands "the real" "as" a "stand" of materials, there the "immaterial" origin of the "as" itself will be neither experienced as such nor taken into account, but will be maximally dissembled.

The Composition is in effect a privation or deficient mode of the Fourfold. This means that the Fourfold is still "present in its absence," that it is present *as* its absence, i.e., that the first-beginning Fourfold-Play has itself brought about a situation in which man fails to apprehend the Fourfold-Play itself. But one (namely Heidegger) can see the contemporary effect *of* the first-beginning Fourfold-Play in our absence of awareness of the Fourfold-Play.

This means that we dwell in that epoch in which we are deprived of all awareness of the play of *meanings* in which alone both we and the entities that surround us can come to appear as inherently meaning*less* (or subjectively definable) present-at-hand entities or components at our disposal. Man proposes, man disposes. Our experience of the meaningless is itself the privative (*self*-depriving) play of meanings. In other words, the appearance of Things as meaningless is itself a historical way of meaning, but one in which the play-ful source of meanings remains concealed or dissimulated. Put still differently, the first-beginning directive occurred and does occur now in such a way that language comes to stamp beings as 'real' (*wirklich*) precisely to the extent that they are *deprived* of inherent meanings, since meanings are taken to be subjective and not objective or calculable. But what man does not yet see is that the last consequence of this gradual deprivation of meaning—the Composition's standing stock of components—has no ultimate ground or warrant but is itself a historically conditioned meaning. It is a historically conditioned meaning that, far from being simply "objective" and "independent" of man, *appears only by the suppression of the very meaning-process that has brought it about and that sustains it.* Composing is therefore self-contradictory—self-blocking, self-dissimulating, self-forgetting—since it can appear as it appears only by denying its own essence, origin, or beginning. Heidegger's question with respect to the future then becomes: how would man experience himself and his environment if he were to 'resign' or 'release' himself to, affirm the inevitability of, dwelling expressly (*eigens*) in a World in which he already dwells in the mode of passing-over it?

The career of Heidegger consists in the effort to draw all the consequences of taking meaning into the internal and essential constitution of all beings; and in this sense, it has been argued, he has always been a phenomenologist. From *SZ* forward,[68] Heidegger associates phenomenology with 'possibility', giving rise to the suspicion that he thereby replaces the "universality and necessity" of orthodox phenomenology by pure possibility (nothing)—especially as concerns his view of the future. It would be more accurate to say that he weds 'the possible' to a version of the universal and necessary: there is possibility at all only within and out of the locale or time-play-space of the 'lasting' and 'eternally' playing Fourfold, each of whose possible linguistic plays (directives, *Geschicke*) is undeterminable in advance yet is bound to be determined by the essencing (*Wesen*) of the four members who play. To come back to the necessary is to understand the Composition's standing stock of disposable components as one *possible* Fourfold-Play of language; it may then be possible to move from a static Composition to 'release' into an experience "richer in contingencies."[69] We are confronted in Heidegger with a new reconciliation of possibility and necessity;

its newness is traceable to Heidegger's meditation on what is necessary and what is possible within the old and remaining meaning-
Event that is language.

It may seem, lastly, that Heidegger offers no concrete evidence
that the Fourfold has any effect today. No doubt Heidegger has
spoken of the Fourfold as the essence of the Composition only in a
general way (although more specifically in "Hölderlins Erde und
Himmel" than elsewhere). One can regard this lack of specificity as
either Heidegger's failing or a failing of language. Heidegger, of
course, regarded his thinking as still "underway." But one may
have to allow that not much more *can* be said. If the Fourfold-Play
is really a mirroring *intro*-play of all its members in language and in
relation to Things, the Play cannot be detailed in ordinary language, which would require one to speak of one "factor" at a time,
thus falsifying a 'simultaneous' ('contemporaneous') or 'equiprimordial' four-way (six-way, if one thinks 'language' and 'Thing'
together with the Fourfold) Play of *internal* relations. The notion of
internal relations essentially limits the possibility of a factor analysis. The relation in question is by its nature 'illimitable'.

I nevertheless risk the following highly tentative and incomplete
description of the Fourfold-Play and of the roles of its members.

Every naming-articulating in language (including the Composition's "language of information") takes a stand about what is
named (is interpretive)—a stand that happens through man but is
beyond his control, a stand that says less of what is named than the
entity essentially is and neglects the nature of the process of naming
itself, which first and continuously constitutes beings as beings.
The process of naming whereby Things come to be Things is essentially the process in which a finite being, understanding himself as
finite, dwells with Things in a particular historical way (wondering
about them, using them, looking at them, etc.). This particular way
either recognizes or neglects the fact that they come to be Things for
him only because he dwells, in language, in an articulated region
(time-play-space) that is a 'between' (*zwischen*) whose 'limits',[70]
context, and source are marked by the mortal, the immortal or divine, the inexhaustible earth, and the rhythm of the heavens.
Whether man is explicitly aware of it or not, in naming he has entered:

—a World that surpasses names and on which all names depend, a source not wholly revealable and calculable and not reducible to a ready and standardized stock of materials (Earth);

—a World that, in being beyond mere mute living or animal existence, shares in the 'divine' insofar as its articulation depends upon the gift of a word—*logos*—that we do not invent or simply employ and that transcends the merely transitory muteness of "natural" events (the Divinities);

—a World in which man, through the gift of articulation and articulateness, both becomes consciously mortal and thereby surpasses mere becoming ("has a history" and *is* a history) and in this special sense 'transcends' (that is, understands, articulates, and is disposed by) the very time to which he is essentially in thrall, the very Things that always exceed that to which his limited assertions try to limit them (the Mortals);

—a World in which man himself and everything named are named within the rhythm of the cosmos on which all is dependent but which, through language, becomes at once the region of the lasting, of the new, of the repeatable, and also a mark of human limitation (the Heavens).

In articulation (language and its meaning) all saying and all experiencing thus occur in and are conditioned by a double between—between heavens and earth, between immortal and mortal. As union of thrown givenness and possibility, as union of limited and unlimited, man dwells in a 'between' that originally (i.e., always) is the Fourfold place/event that dissimulates itself, limits as it empowers, closes as it discloses.

In the epoch of Com-posing, man altogether ignores the Place to which he owes all, his ownmost locale. But as this Place is the lasting source (*Herkunft*) of all that phenomenally is, it is inescapable. The only question is whether man will continue to ignore his source, with all the consequences ensuing therefrom. Yet even this ignorance is conditioned by the Fourfold itself; the linguistic Event articulates all but is poorest at articulating itself, because naming (especially, Heidegger suspects, Western naming) appears to name entitatively (nominally) and not verbally and relationally—thus obscuring 'play' and internal relations.

The only question is whether there will be a "turn into"[71] the lasting: "The conversion to the thoughtful experiencing of the center of the illimitable relation—: out of the Com-position as the self-dissimulating Event of the Fourfold."[72]

V

I conclude that the 'first beginning' is the 'other beginning' disowned or disguised. The other beginning could not be a simple reversion to the first beginning, for the other beginning would remember what is forgotten in the first beginning. But since what is forgotten in the first beginning is something that 'remains' and 'rules', the other beginning could not be a novel beginning. As a remembering of the play of "true time," which "rests the same,"[73] the other beginning would be neither a regress nor a progress. It would be the coming on of the past out of the future. It would be "new" as a remembering of the remaining, and it would be "old" as the remaining of what is remembered. It would embody the seer-like wisdom of affirming temporality and mortality as the only possible conditions of truth if there is to be truth at all.

This is Heidegger's final "moment of vision," and it is visionary in its envisagement of a 'simple' truth amid the variety and multiplicity of historical events. Yet it 'renounces' the metaphysical quest for a vision that essentially transcends finite conditions. In chapter 7, I held that for Heidegger Being is appearing in Place. If beings are spoken of with a multiplicity of meanings, the guiding and basic meaning is: showing itself, although mostly as dissimulated, in the time-play-space of the Fourfold. Our history has been sentenced to a dissimulation or displacement of this place and hence of the nature of Being itself. What now appears, under the impress of modern subjectivism, to be a field of components for human composing and disposal is the historical consequence of the self-displacement of Being from the beginning of the tradition on. Speech, thought, and action have appeared as transcendental activities capable of making a meta-physical determination of the nature of their place by attributing the composition or constitution of that place to beings—alternatively to divine, natural, or human beings. The proper future of ontology is not an advance to something essentially new but a remembering of the event of the place in which beings have always appeared and can appear. If beings for the most part have not shown themselves as they are, the remembering of their place brings them into their own original nature. They become what they are. These are "the things themselves" to which phenomenology was to return us. To return to the Place of things themselves is at the same time to recall the original nature of truth, which has been dissimulated as correspondence of linguistic statement and non-linguistic referent. Truth is fundamentally the showing of beings as what they are in their relation to, or centering of, the Fourfold as a time-play-space in language. The locus of Being and Truth is thus neither mortals nor immortals, neither earth nor the heavens, but solely the coming-to-be of things in the introplay of the four. Being is timed, things coming into being and remaining insofar as they are named in a saying that both refers to the named's identity and maintains that identity in the course of time. The difference between name and named, which is necessary if the name is to hold a multiplicity of appearances in unity, dissimulates the identity of name and named, the belonging together of word and earth. This treatment of the interrelation of name and thing stands in stark contrast to Sartre's interpretation of the relation of name and thing, to which we turn now. It is possible that this contrast may shed some light on the relation of language and ontology—one of the most vexing problems in recent philosophy.

10

Language, Action, and the Sartrean Beginning

The question at issue between us, one that often arises in the history of philosophy, is that of the beginning.
—Sartre, *Situations*, I, 226

I HAVE found Heidegger's reappropriation of history to consist in the reconversion of 'space' into 'place', where 'space' is equivalent to the appearance of 'nothing' and 'place' is space restored to its original temporal (always-prior), but nonapparent fullness and concreteness as the linguistic time-play-space of the Fourfold. The course of Western history is then to be regarded as the epochal working out of the consequences of an initial displacement, or forgetting of the event of place. This event is the linguistic articulation of a totality or orientation within which man and things are internally related and therefore locatable, intelligible, and meaningful. At the same time, this event has taken the form of a dissimulation of that totality whereby the tangible and nominable present steals the stage from the imperceptible totality *within* which the tangible and nominable present stands forth 'as such'—that is, as what it is. For Heidegger both the originative articulation and its dissimulation mark man's thoroughgoing indebtedness to language, which is indicated by the characterization of language as the 'house' of Being, including man's Being. Given the centrality of language in Heidegger's "turning thinking," a consideration of Sartre's treatment of language is imperative in any confrontation between the thinking of Heidegger and that of Sartre. Since Sartre does not accord to language the centrality that Heidegger accords to it, his references to it are neither as numerous nor as thoroughly elaborated as are Heidegger's. We shall therefore have to work hard to infer as much of a Sartrean theory of language as is consistent with this essential difference between Heidegger and Sartre.

In examining Sartre's treatment of language in this chapter, we shall find ourselves drawn into his theory of action, his distinction between poetry and prose, and his understanding of what constitutes a true 'beginning'. Consideration of these themes will conduct us naturally toward Sartre's subsequent reappropriation of history (chapters 11 and 12) and then to a final confrontation between the two efforts to reinsert man in his true history (Part IV).

I noted in chapter 7 that Sartre's "espousal of nominalism" would appear to constitute a decisive deficiency from the standpoint of the later Heidegger. If Being is appearing in place, and if that place is linguistically constituted, Being will be inseparable from language. But the espousal of nominalism would suggest that language does not constitute Being at all but is rather an overlay that slides over the surface of beings without adhering to them. If so, both natural being and human being stand essentially outside of language rather than being 'housed' within it. But is this in fact Sartre's view? We look for an answer first to Sartre's late work *L'Idiot de la famille*, then back to *EN* and several of Sartre's literary essays, especially his essay on Brice Parain.

I

In the course of *IF* Sartre writes:

> our espousal of nominalism prohibits classifications: it is necessary to understand . . . all projects . . . on the basis of a complex situation, irreducible to the sum of its elements, which qualifies them by its complexity in the very moment when these projects surpass that situation toward their ends.[1]

If "it is necessary to understand . . . all projects" in this way, it will be necessary to understand the project or quest of Western history in this way, assuming that there is such a pan-cultural project. The project must be understood without resort to the sort of classifications by which linguistic distinctions do violence to a complex situation. Sartre implies that linguistic distinctions run the risk of reducing a complex situation to "the sum of its elements." Yet he does not deny that the situation has "elements." Rather these elements are surpassed toward ends. We know that for Sartre the most fundamental elements of any and every 'situation' are 'surpassed' in the 'project' of their unification. But if the project surpasses the elements, it is nevertheless the opposition of the elements that dictates the need for reuniting them. The elements demand the situation as the surpassing of them.

But are not 'in-itself' and 'for-itself' 'classifications'? Presumably Sartre's espousal of nominalism does not extend to these two linguistic terms. And yet one could argue that the 'in-itself' is precisely a function of nominalism; the view that names and classifications do not really "stick" to things is a premise from which one may conclude that the actual is a region in principle inarticulable, lying beneath all denominations or classifications. But if this is the case, how can one return "to the things themselves"? We have seen that in *La Nausée* Sartre finds that "things are divorced from their names."[2] This is an expression of Sartre's revolt against what may be called "linguistic idealism," the perennial human tendency (which achieves formal expression in philosophical idealism) to reduce things to what man says and wants to say of them. Against this tendency to, and philosophy of, "assimilation, unification, identification," Sartre in his 1939 Husserl essay proclaims a world that is "essentially external to consciousness" but "nevertheless essentially relative to consciousness"—the world of "the tree," "the plain earth," the "Japanese mask" that is inherently "dreadful," and the woman who is inherently "lovable."[3] But, we have seen, this is the 'world' of the 'real', not the region of the 'actual'.[4] It is real, rather than ideal, because it is *grounded in* an inarticulable actuality, i.e., a region beyond all denomination and classification except for the term 'in-itself', actual.

The tree, the plain earth, the dreadful Japanese mask, and the lovable woman are obviously "what they are" in being named, identified, articulated within a world or complex of meanings; they are what they are through internal meaning-relations with a totality of beings. Thus it would appear that in the 'world' of the 'real', Sartre either does not, or cannot consistently, adhere to a nominalism. The 'real' world seems inherently linguistic. It is however, not inconsistent for Sartre to maintain that beings flow beyond and are more than their names or, as Heidegger would put it, have a dimension called 'earth' that is in part 'concealed' even as it is 'revealed'. This would have the effect of obviating a rank idealism while at the same time not treating beings as inherently inarticulable or "essentially devoid of any meaning at all." There is plenty of evidence that epistemologically this is the view that Sartre wishes to espouse.[5] But ontologically and morally he is committed to the priority of the antithetical and *actually* unsynthesizable relata, 'in-itself' and 'for-it-self'. Hence we have observed that in the reflexive movement of ontological and moral analysis the prior "affective-cognitive synthesis"—the real—falls apart. Return to 'the real' then becomes a moral dilemma. Linguistically regarded, this dilemma takes the form of the question, under what circumstances may I legitimately denominate and classify? If in the reflexive-anxious purification "things are divorced from their names," what would a legitimate remarriage be like? In *EN* Sartre's answer would appear to be: approach language playfully. Rather than try to make names and classifications stick to things, regard words as well as meanings as transitory signs and symbols of the inapprehensible, which play over the surface of things without essentially changing them. Avoid verbal violence.

It may be objected that the foregoing characterization seriously underplays the extent to which Sartre espouses a realist theory of meaning, if not a realist theory of language. Sartre does, after all, maintain that "on the level of concrete experience"[6] I encounter "objective meanings" of which I am not the source:

in "my" world, in fact, there exists something other than a multiplicity of possible meanings [*significations*]. There are objective meanings that are given to me as not having been brought to light by me. Although meanings come to things through me, I find myself engaged in an *already meaningful* world that reflects meanings to me that I have not put there. Consider, for example, the vast quantity of meanings, independent of my *choice*, that I discover if I live in a city: streets, houses, stores, streetcars and buses, signs, warning sounds, music on radios, etc. Were I in solitude, I would of course discover the brute and unpredictable existent [*l'existant*]—for example, *this* rock—and I would limit myself to making *there be* a rock—that is, *this* existent *here* and beyond that, nothing. Yet I would nevertheless confer on it the meaning "to be climbed," "to be avoided," "to be contemplated," etc.[7]

The way in which Sartre here distinguishes between the natural object and the artifact deserves notice. In society I encounter entities already designed and designated by others, who leave their meanings behind in these entities. These entities are meaning-beings. But, alone in the country, I encounter a "brute . . . existent" on which, because it is not the vehicle of the Other's meaning, I can freely "confer" meanings in accordance with the particular character of my projects. Because the rock is understood as merely present-at-hand—"*this* existent *here* and beyond that, nothing"—it is possible to fill that "nothing" with *my* meanings. It becomes "my rock." The natural object is the physical vehicle of my metaphysical choice; the artifact is the record of the metaphysical choice of the Other. And insofar as the metaphysical choice of Others is not my metaphysical choice, their artifact is an actual or possible mode of alienation. When I conform to these objective ('real') meanings and directions of Others, "insofar as I obey them, insofar as I fall into line, I submit myself to the goals of a human reality which is *anybody* and I realize them by *anybody's* techniques."[8] I am, in other words, disowned by both the means, or techniques, and the ends ('goals') of the "they." What would in a state of nature be my "hodological space,"[9] where I could follow a "path" (*hodos*) traced out by my own choice of projects in free space, becomes a bound space where I follow paths established by Others. But, since man always already inhabits a social world, he always confronts a world that is already a *totality*, a nothing already filled, a synthesis already made. Sartre here reappropriates Heidegger's notion of the average everyday world of *das Man*.

Since the world thus presents itself as the objective record of the metaphysical projects of others, it would appear that I here encounter "narrow limits to my freedom."[10] Sartre denies this, for my consciousness is a 'surpassing' of the given (including the given, objective meanings of others), a 'detotalizing' of all given totalities. Sartre attempts to demonstrate this surpassing of given meanings by reference to the nature of language.

Sartre's strategy is to stress man's finite freedom in the use of language. If one takes a *word* to be the basic unit of language, such freedom is difficult to establish, for the word seems relatively invariant over long periods of time. If language were only the communication of words, it could be construed as simply the transmission of given, objective meanings. As an example, the word 'rock', in the passage just quoted, seems to convey an inherited, stable, and objective meaning over which the speaker or writer has little control. If language were simply an ensemble of such words, it could be construed as merely the bound expression of the present-at-hand. "But," Sartre argues, "if the phrase or sentence [*la phrase*] pre-exists the word, we are driven back to the *speaker* as the concrete foundation of speech."[11] Why? "The sentence is a [free] project which can be interpreted only on the basis of the nihilation of a given."[12] And if "the sentence is necessary for throwing light on the given and for knowing what to make of the word, the sentence is a moment of the free choice of myself. . . ."[13] The sentence, then, is a surpassing of the word in a project that situates the word in a totality (situation) within which the word is meaningful. "What is primary is the situation on the basis of which I grasp the *meaning* [*sens*] of the sentence. This meaning is not in itself to be regarded as a given, but as an end chosen in a free surpassing of means."[14] Sartre allows that both words and rules or techniques for their use are learned from others,[15] but rather than constituting a limit to his freedom, they are freely appropriated by the for-itself, which affirms them only in the act of surpassing them: "the for-itself can choose itself only beyond particular meanings of which it is not the origin."[16]

Here, as always for Sartre, the disclosure of meaning is ultimately traceable to the 'fundamental project'. It is the goal I have freely chosen that determines the nature of the path I take toward that goal. The end determines all of the means. But as I build my own world, all the materials I have to work with are prefabricated. In order to build at all I must therefore take over these existing materials and make them my own by subordinating them to my own ends. (This is Sartre's version of Heidegger's notion of a "limited submission to beings.")[17] Thus, I must take over words and rules for their usage in order to use them for my own ends.

This is not to say, however, that language can be regarded simply as a set of materials or an instrument. Sartre writes that "We are in language as we are within our bodies. . . ."[18] And: ". . . I am a language, for language is only existence in the presence of another."[19] For Sartre we are "in our bodies" in the mode of *ambiguity*: we are and are not our bodies.[20] Analogously, we are and are not in language. And when Sartre says, "I am a language," 'I' is to be construed as 'ego' (that which I am for others). But as the for-itself is a surpassing of its own body, it is also a surpassing of its own language (and its own being-for-others); if 'I' am a body and a language, 'consciousness' is *not* a body and a language but one step removed (*séparé*) from body and language, as consciousness *of* body and *of* language. Here as always the 'of' means the insertion of a 'nothingness' between consciousness and its object, which guarantees the independence of consciousness from the same objects of which it is inescapably aware. Consciousness is bound to the same objects it freely surpasses. Consciousness perpetually surpasses the for-itself's own language. This means for Sartre that the for-itself is never contained within, or simply determined and defined by, a linguistic totality. Consciousness detotalizes (surpasses) an inherited linguistic totality in the course of achieving its own ends (the 'specification' of its fundamental project).

Since the for-itself's relation to its language is strictly analogous to its relation to its body—a relation of ambiguity—the possible modes of bad faith are in both cases the same. One may in emotion try to fall into complicity with the body, to be only body; one may try to be only one's language, to be wholly governed by it. These are cases of what Alain calls 'magic'—"the spirit dragging among things."[21] It is the self-degradation of consciousness. Conversely, one may try to be pure spirit, "all mind,"[22] or a "beautiful soul" free of embodiment and finite conditions. This has its linguistic analogue in Brice Parain's effort, at one stage in his thought, to take silence—freedom from language—as an ideal.[23] The antidote to both modes of bad faith is "living the ambiguity." In the case of language, this means committing oneself to the inventive reappropriation of the language in which one inevitably finds oneself by 'surpassing' that language toward one's own freely chosen ends. This view of the legitimate employment of language regards it as both what I *am* and at the same time an instrument or means I direct toward an end, or what I desire *to be*. Language is therefore neither thing (totality) nor instrument but the ambiguous relation of the two.

In *QL* this conception of language is developed in a way that will utlimately help us clarify its relation to Heidegger's understanding of language. Restricting himself to the sphere of the writer, Sartre outlines two fundamental attitudes toward language—that of the prose writer and that of the poet.

Poetry is magical. For the poet, that which ontologically belongs to the for-itself as its "instrument"—language—becomes a "structure of the external world." [24] In effect, the poetic attitude collapses the distinction between word and thing. It "considers words as things and not as signs. . . . They are natural things which grow naturally on the earth like grass and trees." [25] For the poet, the word loses its "autonomous function"—that is, its function of pointing *toward* a thing that the word itself is not, and its function of *surpassing* the thing—and is instead "given to him as a material quality." [26] But the poet can regard himself as outside of language only because he has read language into the thing. He then contemplates the word-thing as an independent entity, while in fact "the word . . . reflects back to the poet, like a mirror, his own image." [27] So poetry is a case of "the spirit dragging among things." The poet, in other words, refuses to try to break the unreflective circle of interpretation. "Thus a double reciprocal relation of magical resemblance and signification is established between the word and the thing signified." [28] Poetry is *an immediate synthesis* of word and thing and hence a collapsing of ontologically distinct relata. Sartre describes this "poetic unity" [29] in a way that reminds the reader of Heidegger: the poet "discovers" in words "particular affinities with earth, heavens, water, and all created things." [30] Sartre finds it a sign of the "crisis of language" that the writer at the beginning of this century experienced a "depersonalization . . . in the face of words. . . . They were no longer his . . . but in those strange mirrors heavens, earth, and his own life were reflected; and finally they became the things themselves—or rather the black heart of things." [31]

I interpret this as meaning that for Sartre the "crisis of language" consists in the danger of the reduction of prose to poetry, the loss of the distinction between word and object: the loss of nominalism and the loss of truth. For Sartre the radical distinction between language and things is a condition of truth. If name and thing, sign and referent, are fused and confused, things themselves cannot show themselves as they are. Poetry, therefore cannot discover the true:

> Poets are men who refuse to *utilize* language. Now, since the quest for truth takes place in and by language conceived as a certain kind of instrument, it is unnecessary to imagine that they aim to discern or expound the true. Nor do they dream of

naming the world, and, this being the case, they name nothing at all, for naming implies a perpetual sacrifice of the name to the object named, or, as Hegel would say, the name is revealed as the inessential in the face of the thing which is essential.[32]

Sartre stresses that he is neither criticizing poetry nor requiring that it defer to prose. What disturbs him is the danger of loss of the distinction between prose and poetry. The "crisis" is one in which prose surrenders its identity and proper function to poetry.[33] If poetry is an *immediate* synthesis of language and thing, truth requires a *temporal* utilization of language. The thing, which is not now known, is to be known by the present assertion of a hypothesis that revises or 'surpasses' past assertions. Sartre would no doubt adhere to the traditional view that it is the analytic scission of a prior mythopoetic unity by the early Greek philosophers that establishes the conditions in which truth is ascertainable. Language and object must first be understood to be distinct relata before language can be taken as a set of assertions about the actual, may be checked against the actual, may make hypothetical proposals that are to be verified or disverified. So regarded, language is an instrument for 'surpassing' inherited notions toward the end of true disclosure. Analyzing an inherited unreflective 'unity' or 'synthesis' or 'totality', language as an instrument of knowledge analytically detotalizes this inherited totality into linguistic and nonlinguistic relata in order to effect a retotalizing that is no longer a naïve unity but *a perpetual revision* of the inherited totality—a perpetual oscillation between hypothesis/statement and its referent, each limiting and checking the other. Knowing is a mode of instrumental action and thus is describable by the phrases Sartre reserves for all authentic action: a "surpassing of the given" and a "perpetual" or "permanent revolution."[34] Knowing is in effect a perpetual thrust "meta-" an inherited "physics" in order to reconstitute it "as such and as a totality." Poetry is, on the contrary, the effort to circumvent this perpetual quest in an absolute moment. To the extent that poetry aspires to truth, it is the enemy of truth, for its static, nontemporal, and nonanalytic approach seeks in a magical moment the truth that requires time, technique, and analysis. The price of truth is owning up to consciousness as a 'negation' ('surpassing') of the given, a perpetual resynthesizing of a given totality that is perpetually analyzed. This given totality includes language, which we are both in and beyond. Language is both 'lived' and instrumentally 'surpassed'. On this 'ambiguity' hangs the very possibility of both poetry and prose, both magic and truth.

Sartre in effect holds that poetry and prose are to be understood relative to a perpetual dialectic. Poetry expresses only the moment of totality, as if it were complete and not to be surpassed. Prose expresses the whole movement of detotalizing-negating-surpassing in the thrust toward a new synthesis or totality. If Sartre favors prose, it is because prose expresses the ongoing dialectic of experience and is also one form of that dialectic, while poetry freezes the dialectic. Iris Murdoch writes that "Sartre wishes to do justice to the way in which the mind itself hesitates between monism and dualism—a hesitation which is manifested in real observable modes of experience."[35] Poetry, magic, and unreflective emotion express the moment of monism, totality, affirmation, synthesis, or unity, in isolation from its context of action. Reflection, rebellion, factorial analysis into relata, and psychoanalysis represent the moment of dualism, detotalization, negation, analysis, or disunity, in isolation from its context of action. Action itself is neither permanence nor rebellion but perpetual revolution. It is a detotalizing-retotalizing-detotalizing, etc. toward a goal—the perfected totality, the Parmenidean One—that for society recedes infinitely. Prose, especially the prose of fiction, can express this whole dialectic of action.

Sartre's essay on Francis Ponge makes it clear that Sartre is not antipoetic, provided that the poetic is taken as itself a moment of action. It is indeed "Ponge the poet" who "has laid the foundations of a Phenomenology of Nature."[36] Ponge resists analysis, regarding nature not as a region without human meaning but as a region of meaning-beings: "The thing does not appear to him, as to Kant, as pole X or support of sensible qualities. Things have *meaning* [*sens*]."[37] For a phenomenology of nature "what we find everywhere . . . is ourselves, always ourselves. . . . For man is not assembled within himself but is outside, always outside, from the heavens to the earth. The pebble has an inside, man does not; rather he loses himself so that the pebble may exist."[38] The world of Ponge is one of "human facts," one that is "beyond the distinction of the psychic and the nonpsychic" and is "neither matter nor mind." Like Sartre's description of "the slimy" in *EN*, Ponge's poetry exhibits "an objective structure of the world."[39]. It is a world where things have "unity" rather than being collections of elements,[40] and a world in which things are experienced contextually and relationally—a "world in fusion."[41]

The reader of Sartre's essay who is familiar with Heidegger cannot fail to be reminded of Heidegger's characterization of the primordial unity of Dasein and world. Sartre outlines three additional traits of Ponge's "phenomenology of nature" that remind us all the more forcefully of Heidegger: naming, ekstasis, and love.

1. Ponge believes that "in naming, he fills his office as man." He writes that "naming . . . is the steadfast and definitive union of man and thing, because the nature of the thing is to require a name and the function of man is by speaking to give it a name."[42] So for Ponge "naming, which is the most human of acts, is also the communion of man with the universe."[43]

2. Sartre calls this poetic act of naming an "active contemplation"; it is "the moment of ecstasy in which he is established beyond himself at the heart of the thing. . . ."[44]

3. ". . . Ponge applies without knowing it the axiom which is at the origin of all phenomenology, 'to the things themselves.' His attitude will be love. This love, which permits neither desire, fervor, nor passion . . . is total approbation, total respect, 'extreme care . . . not to obstruct the object'. . . ."[45]

All this might suggest that Sartre, in commending the work of Ponge, is placing himself on the ground of the later Heidegger. But Sartre levels against Ponge the fundamental charge he has leveled against Heidegger. Ponge in effect ignores the *cogito*. He not only revivifies the stone, he petrifies man, dehumanizes him, giving the object preeminence over the subject.[46] Sartre reminds Ponge of his "human power of unification" and of the fact that his contemplative consciousness, "precisely because it is consciousness *of* the world, finds itself necessarily *beyond* the world. . . ."[47] This perennial Sartrean recall to the instantaneous nucleus of consciousness as the pivot of a perpetual detotalizing and retotalizing means that Ponge must understand his work as describing only one moment of an ongoing dialectic. If Ponge has "laid the foundations of a Phenomenology of Nature" by describing the moment of man's unreflective fusion with nature, this moment will serve as the foundation for a prose analysis—that of science, of existential psychoanalysis, of committed literature. This reflective moment negates that poetic fusion, shows its virtuality and transitoriness, and converts man from contemplation of meaning-beings to the exercise of his freedom. Ponge the poet is a revolutionary insofar as he reminds analysis of its foundations in a prior unity that it surpasses, but insofar as Ponge seeks to rest in that prior unity he suppresses the perpetual revolution by which human freedom is affirmed and preserved. Instead of maintaining the ambiguity between monism and dualism, Ponge settles for monism and for rejection of the use of language as an instrument for pointing toward things that *exceed* language and for pointing *beyond* existing conditions to better and truer conditions. Monism is antirevolutionary in that it seeks to hold together the polarities or relata whose separation is a precondition for controlled change, that is, conscious retotalization.

Here, as always, Sartre insists upon both a phenomenological union and its disruption. This ceaseless dialectic can be accounted for, in his view, only by a negating-surpassing consciousness, which is therefore the motor of historical change. For Ponge language is the bond between man and thing; their community of nature is due to the word.[48] For Sartre this "poetic" bond is disrupted by prose and, ultimately, by the very nature of consciousness. Language adheres neither to the thing nor to consciousness. Language inhabits a region *between* consciousness and thing: there is a silence of things and a "silence of consciousness."[49] Poetically and/or unreflectively, thing and word can be experienced as one—as *en-soi-pour-soi* or a mode of the desired union of the in-itself and the for-itself—but prosaically and reflectively thing and word are found to be of differing natures, and the function of the word is restricted to pointing beyond itself to a being of another type. Here we encounter once again the ambiguity previously noted in Sartre's thought. While ontological disunity is uncovered by an analysis grounded in an experiential unity that it surpasses, experiential unity ('reality') is then seen to be grounded in ontological disunity ('actuality' and 'nothing'). One oscillates between an experientially unified ground and an analytically disunified ground, but it is the latter that purifies because it is the latter that is ontologically true. What appeared to be a community of nature turns out to be an artifactual bridge constructed between two silences.

II

Sartre's essay on Brice Parain parallels the essay on Ponge that follows it in *Situations, I.* The essay on Ponge reminds the reader of a level of experience that is preanalytic and "prescientific," in which language and thing cohere, and then proceeds to take this coherence apart. The essay on Parain once again takes this coherence apart by raising the question of *the beginning.* We shall see shortly what this means. But first we note with interest several striking parallels between Parain and Heidegger. These parallels are sufficient to allow us to treat this essay as an indirect critique of certain Heideggerian notions, even it if is unlikely that Sartre so intended it.[50] Among the significant parallels with Heidegger are the following:

1. Parain, as a peasant, has a deep and abiding attachment to the earth, where he feels at home. "The image most deeply rooted in his memory is that of the natural order: the return of the seasons and the birds, the growth of plants and children, the fixed order of the stars and planets."[51] Parain writes, "To a peasant . . . the earth is the intermediary that solidly attaches his thought to his action, that enables him to judge and act. . . ." Coming to the city and its language, its signs, its mechanisms, its anonymity—in short, its artifactuality—Parain experiences a displacement, an uprootedness.[52] "He was stirred, like all men of the 1920's, by a great hostility to mechanism. Behind his ethics and his criticism of language can be seen the pick and spade, the work-bench."[53] It is perhaps worth noting that Parain's temperament is precisely the opposite of Sartre's; Sartre's affinities are with the city and its artifacts, and he is most at home amid words.[54]

2. Parain's thought has a strong affinity with that of Nietzsche. Sartre's own vehement criticism of Nietzsche is no doubt to be explained primarily by Nietzsche's sustained critique of the notion of a transcendental and autonomous consciousness—that consciousness which Sartre holds to be the implicit ground of human experience and the explicit ground of all genuine philosophy.[55] Parain

approves of Nietzsche's critique of the Cartesian *cogito* and also shares the "individualism" of Nietzsche, which Sartre characterizes as "the simple and humble demand of the small agricultural land-owner, who wants to remain his own master" and wants to return men to "the silent and humble order of needs."[56] Like Nietzsche, Parain wants to return to what he calls "the business of man's body. . . . Such is the secret of simple men, of those who, beyond civilization, have retained the same simplicity. It lies in this stub-bornness of the body to love and to beget, to transmit its drive and its joy."[57] Parain wishes to restore man to unity with nature: "In a corner of his mind, there is still a certain nostalgia for the totalitar-ian myth of a harmony that unites the human powers and those of the earth, as the roots of a tree are grounded in the earth that feeds them."[58]

3. In contrast to the grand aspiration of the humanist, Parain in-sists upon observance of man's limits. "Parain . . . bears the marks of his Catholic upbringing. He has no Genevan pride. . . . He did not want to live without limits. Fields have limits. . . . A few acres of land, a decent wife, children, the modest freedom of the crafts-man at work, of the peasant in the fields—in short, happiness. . . . All he wanted was that a more just and paternal organization assign him his place on earth and, by defining him in terms of rigorous co-ordinates, rid him of the need for security, of the 'anxiety that threatened to choke him.' "[59] One finds here a recall to the Greek sense of limit that figures prominently in the thinking of both Nietzsche and Heidegger.

4. Parain's career can be described as a "departure and return." There is first a departure from the "valley" of immediate rapport with the earth, and a climb to the "plateau" where he surveys the common and impersonal rhetoric of man that has forgotten its natu-ral "roots" in "silence." War teaches him "that there were several reasons, that of the Germans, of the Russians, of the French"—several metaphysical options which, rootless and conflicting, can seek dominance only by "a test of force."[60] Parain reacts by a tem-porary plunge into an "authoritarian community of labor," a "prag-matic and relativistic authoritarianism." At this point there is a turn in Parain's thinking; "The rest has been a return."[61]

5. Parain's return is a return to language. "When he finally had to define and fix himself, it was not to the earth that he returned, but

to language." "The reign of the mediating powers and of language, the first of the intermediaries, returns."[62] Words are both "germs of being" and "promises" that "mortgage the future."[63] If we think of 'the future' in Sartre's sense of the term, Parain "does not believe in it."[64] The future for Parain is fated growth of the germ that is engendered in an original "act of naming." Parain writes: "Philosophers have rightly observed that every perception is constituted by a judgment. But have they sufficiently stressed the fact that it is the naming that is the first judgment and that this is the decisive moment of the perception?" Sartre interprets Parain's assertion that I am *"situated in language"* to mean that "man does not create ideas; he assembles them."[65] Thought is ruled by *logos*.[66] Since language is not a free invention of man, Parain concludes that it comes from God.

6. While "Parain has . . . always been concerned with 'preserving the initial anxiety,' " he is nevertheless "convinced that 'man ends with a certain resignation.' "[67] Man's limited role consists in the future actualization of the potential of a few original and elementary words: "Parain's ethics proposes that I beware of words and their magical powers, that I attach myself only to a few of them, the simplest and most familiar, that I speak little, that I name things with caution. . . ."[68] Recalled and resigned to this original and simple situatedness in language, Parain is "humble and assured, clinging to a few sad and simple truths, surveying the plateaux with insolent modesty. . . ."[69]

The reader will have little difficulty in drawing the obvious parallels between the temperaments, careers, and outlooks of Parain and Heidegger. Because of the extensiveness of these parallels, the essay on Parain may offer the best approximation to a critique of the later Heidegger, aside from isolated comments, that we shall have from the pen of Sartre. (It is unfortunately at best only an approximation, for Parain's thought has neither the historical scope, nor the subtlety, nor the radicalness of the later Heidegger's thought.) We therefore turn now to Sartre's critique of Parain with especial interest.

Sartre prefaces his critique by asserting: "I accept roughly the greater part of Parain's analyses."[70] There is a sense in which Sartre in *EN* accepts roughly the greater part of Heidegger's analyses in *SZ*, but we have seen that the resultant position, the whole, is dramatically different. The same is true of Sartre's espousal of Ponge's protophenomenology of nature. One suspects that Sartre's "acceptance" of Parain will be similar. Differentiating between his own position and Parain's, he writes: "The question at issue between us, one that often arises in the history of philosophy, is that of the beginning [*commencement*]."[71] No statement better epitomizes the confrontation between Sartre and Heidegger. The question is that of the beginning of *the ground:* the ground on which analysis is conducted and the ground revealed by that analysis. Parain begins with "needs and speech." That is, his ground is one that is already linguistically articulated, and against it Sartre invokes "the silence of consciousness," which is aware *of* language.[72] Now Parain had argued that in speaking we have entered the order of the impersonal and committed ourselves to universals.[73] Sartre, invoking Kant, asks how this is *possible* and answers that it is a transcendental constitutive consciousness that makes possible the identification and universalization that Parain attributes to language per se. I quote Sartre's argument, which is crucial for the maintenance of his position, at some length:

> Let us grant that, by divine grace, the word "pellet" is preserved and endowed with a kind of permanence and that it is the *same word* that struck me yesterday and that strikes me today. After all, the inkwell, the desk and the tree that I saw a while ago and that I see now are the same. We therefore must admit that even in this unrealizable conjecture, the *external* identity of the word pellet would be of no use to me, for however identical it might be physically, I would still have to recognize it, that is, to extract it from the flux of phenomena and stabilize it. I would still have to refer it to its appearances of yesterday and the day before and establish between these different moments *a synthetic place of identification.*
>
> Of what importance is it that this inkwell is the same outside me? If I have no memory, I shall say that there are ten inkwells, a hundred inkwells, as many inkwells as there are appearances. Or rather I won't even say that there is an inkwell. I won't say anything at all. In like manner for the word "pellet": knowledge and communication are possible only if there is *a* word pellet. But even if the word did exist in the bosom of God, I must produce it by the operation known as "synthesis of identification." And now I realize that *the word had no privileged sta-*

tus. For I must also make the table and the tree and the white worm exist as permanent syntheses of relatively stable properties. It is not by naming them that I endow them with objectivity. But I can name them only if I have [already] constituted them as independent wholes, that is, if I objectify the thing and the word that names it in one and the same synthetic act.

. . . Parain has been mistaken in the order of his thoughts. For if I constitute my experience and my words within this experience, it is not on the level of language but on that of the synthesis of identification that the universal appears.[74]

Sartre's argument is in part very convincing. It is certainly true that no word per se can universalize. In order for a word to stand for a class of beings or for a succession of appearances of a single being, I must understand the word's transferability in time and place. In order to understand its transferability I must understand: (1) the self-identity of the being through time; (2) the distinction between accidental and essential properties of the being, so that I may regard (3) all trees as members of the class of trees despite nonessential differences between members of the class, or (4) all appearances of a tree as appearances of this particular tree.

Each of the foregoing presupposes (5) the reality of the being, independent of my awareness of it, hence (6) the distinction (negation) between myself and the being of which I am aware and the distinction between (*a*) each individual member of a class and (*b*) each class of beings, such that (7) some individuals fall within one class, others not.

My awareness of beings as independent of my awareness of them makes possible an ongoing process of discovery that presupposes (8) that a being may or may not appear when, where, and in the form anticipated, but that (9) if it is to appear as what is anticipated, it must necessarily conform to the traits of the class of which it is a member, must appear in space and time and (10) on appearing, may be said to exist in fact or in bodily presence.

Furthermore (11) if an entity is to appear *as* a certain sort of entity (as self-identical), it must be understood and situated relative to a context in which that particular sort of entity is possible; for example, if a tree is to appear as what it is, it must have its roots in the soil and take nourishment from the elements. This presupposes an understanding that (12) either the being in question conforms to these conditions or else it is a being of another sort.

The understanding of a word as a universal that articulates beings has thus committed us to twelve ways of judging or kinds of synthesis, which are Kant's categories.[75] I have used them here because Sartre's critique of Parain specifically invokes Kant. It is clear that being committed to these categories means being committed to the transcendental unity of apperception[76] whereby a conscious being understands itself as an absolute point of reference around which and relative to which all experienced beings are situated in space and in time. This unity of apperception becomes the "absolute here" of Husserlian phenomenology, around which the world is disposed as a coherent or unified field. The understanding of the world as a unified field of entities *of which* one is aware presupposes the distinction between awareness and its objects.

If we admit this much, we have admitted that the use of words as universals presupposes the laws of logic, for Kant's categories both directly restate and express the implications of the laws of identity, contradiction, and excluded middle. Sartre's point is that the use of words as universals presupposes a complex of mental acts that are acts of understanding brought by us to all words and all assertions. These acts of distinction and synthesis are brought by man to all expressions in language, no matter what particular words are spoken. Therefore, Sartre can conclude that Parain's point of beginning cannot be simply "needs and speech." One cannot characterize the word per se as a universal into which man steps by mouthing it. The word is universal when it is *understood* as such. This understanding cannot be passively received from the word as such but is an *act* of consciousness that both distinguishes and synthesizes what it has distinguished. In short, there is no identity without identification and no universality without universalization.

The foregoing establishes that when I use words as universals I am committing myself to a complex of logical operations that are acts of understanding. Where there is language of the sort that human beings speak, there is logical understanding. But Sartre wishes to go further by asserting the *priority* of logical understanding over language. He argues that consciousness (which for Sartre is basically the logical act of negation) is not in language but beyond it. Here it is Descartes rather than Kant whom he invokes:

when I am conscious of understanding a word, no word is interpolated between me and myself. The word, the single word

in question, is there *before* me, as *that which is understood*. . . .
Otherwise it is merely an idle sound. . . . The effectiveness of
the cogito—its eternity—lies in the fact that it reveals a type of
existence defined as the state of being present to oneself without intermediary. The word is interpolated between my love
and myself, between my courage or cowardice and myself, not
between my understanding and my consciousness of understanding. For the consciousness of understanding is the law of
being of understanding. I shall call this the silence of consciousness. . . . I know what it is that I want to express because I *am* it without intermediary. Language may resist and
mislead me, but I shall never be taken in by it unless I want to,
for I can always come back to what I am, to the emptiness and
silence that I am, through which, nevertheless, there is a language and there is a world.[77]

Against Parain, as against Heidegger, *conscience (de) soi* is the
true beginning, the *fundamentum inconcussum*, the original negation
of being whereby consciousness apperceives itself as nothing, emptiness, silence. There is consciousness *of* language, and consciousness is therefore always one step beyond language. But not beyond
logic, for consciousness *is*, as perpetual 'other-than' and perpetual
'beyond' or 'surpassing', negation, mostly in the form of prereflective nihilation.

This does not mean that consciousness arises without language or
temporally preexists language. In arguing that God is not needed to
account for the origin of language, Sartre writes: "A problem arises
only if man first exists, alone, naked, silent and finished, and if he
speaks only *afterwards*. It is then that we can ask ourselves how he
came to speak. But if I exist originally only by and for the Other
. . . and if the Other is as certain to me as I myself am, then I am a
language, for language is only existence in the presence of another."[78] This is another way of asserting that the 'ambiguity' is
present from the beginning: I am *and* am not language. Origin for
Sartre is not the temporal precedence of consciousness to its objects,
as *EN* makes amply clear. It is the negation *of* objects. Consciousness is presence to objects, including the object: language.

I am in and out of language; the Other is in and out of language,
which is therefore between me and the Other as "the mere surface
of contact between me and the Other."[79] Things as well are in and
out of language:

Language is located *between* stable and concrete objects which have not waited for it in order to reveal [*dévoiler*] themselves (intentional desires, forms of external perception), and human realities who are by nature speakers, and, by virtue of this fact, are located outside speech, for they *attain each other directly* and are thrust together *without intermediary*. Consequently, it can lie, mislead, falsify and make improper generalizations. . . . But there is no metaphysical problem of language.[80]

This passage flatly denies that language is what Heidegger calls "the house of Being." Both human being and environmental being are fundamentally extralinguistic, although they are modes of being that occur to a being, human reality, who is at the same time "in" language. Sartre can maintain that beings are meaningfully apprehended (identified, interrelated, understood) *beyond* language only by asserting that there is an articulation or revealing (*dévoilement*) of beings that is extralingustic. This is furthermore the fundamental articulation, and language is found to be accurate or inaccurate by checking it against this fundamental extralinguistically revealed articulation. (As noted previously, the proper use of words for Sartre consists in pointing *toward* beings that are not themselves essentially linguistic.) This extralinguistic articulation would, however, as a conscious understanding, be a logical articulation.[81] Because human realities "attain each other directly and . . . without intermediary" Sartre can conclude that "there is no metaphysical problem of language." In other words, while language is there from the start as a 'between', this does not prevent an experience of being that is not mediated by language (though it must always, as consciousness *of*, be *logically* mediated).

We are now in a position better to understand what Sartre's "espousal of nominalism" means. The condition for naming a being is that the being be logically understood as an extralinguistic, independent, and self-identical entity, or class of such entities, *to* which a name may be attached or *toward* which a name can point. The name does not constitute, identify, or objectify but rather signifies an entity independently constituted by a silent and immediate understanding. This is the meaning of the passage quoted earlier: "It is not by naming them that I endow them with objectivity. But I can name them only if I have already [*déjà*] constituted them as independent wholes." Sartre goes on to assert that this does not mean that the act of constitutive objectification must temporally precede the act of naming—naming and constituting can be "one and the same synthetic act." Nevertheless the act understands and constitutes the entity directly and immediately as extralinguistic, as beyond the words that I "synthesize" with the object revealed. Sartre in another passage argues that Parain fails to distinguish between 'idea' and 'word' or reduces the idea to the word.[82] The word does not bear the idea or concept but is rather merely a name (the *nomen* of nominalism) that signifies the idea or concept when it is synthetically related to the idea or concept.

But where, for Sartre, is the idea or concept? The essay on Parain does not tell us. If the entity is revealed "without intermediary," what role remains for the idea? If the idea plays any role in the "synthetic act" of objectification, why is it not like the word an "intermediary"? Here we must revert to our analysis of *EN* in chapter 3 at some length if we are to see clearly how Sartre's treatment of concepts or ideas entails a critique of Parain—and indirectly of Heidegger.

III

We saw in chapter 3 that Sartre distinguishes between two functions of consciousness—that of neutrally revealing 'thises' and that of relating 'thises' to each other as meaningful in terms of the projects of consciousness. So the question of the role of the idea is twofold: (1) What is its role in neutral revealing? (2) What is its role in meaningful relating?

In the determination-by-negation that reveals the 'this' as a determinate being, consciousness adds nothing and subtracts nothing, but merely causes the 'this' to appear as a "differentiated form."[83] This is apparently an act of constitution in which constitution must be limited to negation.[84] This negation is twofold. The being that is revealed is distinguished from consciousness itself, and the being that is revealed is distinguished from other beings so as to stand out as self-identical, as what it is and not another thing. This dual act of constitution is of course an act of understanding; the "differentiated form" of the being is understood. This act of understanding is extralinguistic, so we cannot exactly say that the "differentiated form" is, for example, "this rock," even if such naming is simultaneous with the constitutive act. If the being is constituted as formally distinct from other beings, ideation is required. I (pre-linguistically or extralinguistically) grasp the idea that this tree is a different *sort* of thing from the soil in which it is rooted or the stream that runs near it; otherwise tree, soil, and stream are not really formally differentiated as beings distinct from each other.

But to have the idea of different *sorts* of things is already to have invoked universals, or classes of 'thises'. Now unless Sartre were to embrace a realist theory of universals, which he does not do, it would seem that his notion of an act that constitutes 'thises' of differentiated form really requires an *addition*, rather than simply a neutral revealing, by consciousness. It requires the ideas of particular classes of beings, which in turn presupposes the idea of 'class' as such. This means that the act of formal identification of a 'this' is an act of *relating* that invokes other 'thises' in order to establish *this* 'this' as what it is and not another thing. Furthermore, Sartre has argued that the act of identifying a thing must "extract it from the flux of phenomena and stabilize it," which means, he explains, "to refer it to its appearances of yesterday and the day before and establish between these different moments a synthetic place of identification."[85] This once again requires the idea of the thing's essence, such that the thing is identifiable as essentially the same despite accidental differences in its appearances—that is, the notion of the distinction between substance and accident is invoked. (It has already been argued that the use of names as universals presupposes the employment by the understanding of Kant's categories. The same may be said of the prelinguistic use of universals—if there is such a prelinguistic use of universals.)

The foregoing considerations suggest that the two questions I have raised about the role of the idea in neutral revealing are in fact one. The role of the idea in neutral revealing is not really separable from its role in meaningful relating, since the revealing of a this *is* a meaningful relating of the 'this' both to its other appearances and to other 'thises' that are formally different. Further, it would appear that in constituting the 'this' consciousness far exceeds neutral revealing in (1) employing a whole complex of logical operations and categorial distinctions and (2) making a judgment of identification that decides what will count as the essence of the thing as distinct from its accidental traits.

Now it might be objected that we have already gone far beyond what Sartre means by a neutrally revealed 'this'. Sartre could argue that we have put the cart before the horse, for he is the first to maintain that 'thises' are not revealed in isolation but only against the background of a 'world' and its relationships.[86] Very well, we may reply, but what then is to guarantee the *neutral* revealing of the 'this', and what is to guarantee the sharp distinction between the actuality of the thing and the ideal human meanings that relate things meaningfully to each other without entering into their internal constitution? It may help to consider a Sartrean example of a 'this':

> It is in relation to the full moon that the crescent of the moon is determined as *lacking* or as *deprived of*. But at the same time it is revealed as being exactly what it is: that concrete mark in the sky, which has need of nothing [*rien*] in order to be what it is. The same holds for this bud, or for this match which is what it is, whose meaning as being-a-match remains external to it, which *can* to be sure be ignited but which *at present* is this bit of white wood with a black tip. The potentialities of the *this*, though strictly correlated with it, appear as in-itselfs and are in a state of indifference in relation to it.[87]

Several aspects of this passage deserve comment. First, it seems clear that Sartre holds that the crescent is revealed as "what it is" in an act of understanding that at the same time surpasses what the crescent actually is toward the crescent's potentialities; the neutral revealing and the meaningful relating are contemporaneous. In order for there to be a genuine surpassing of the given by the understanding, the given must be understood as "what it is." But it is understood as what it is only if it is meaningfully situated relative to other appearances, past and future, which are *not* what it (now) is. Sartre can be interpreted as saying that the meaningful context of the appearance is a necessary condition for the identification of the appearance as what it is, while this context does not enter into the actual nature of that appearance, since the appearance "has need of nothing in order to be what it is." It needs nothing in order to be a crescent, a bit of white wood with a black tip, an herb that burns, water vapor, or a contingent mass of roots. To take them as *actually* a phase of the moon, the match, the pleasureful tobacco, the cloud pregnant with rain, or the beautiful tree is to allow the mind to drag amid things, to poetize, to seek to realize an impossible union of in-itself and for-itself that Sartre calls 'beauty'.[88] But, one can object, has not Sartre himself maintained that "we in no case get out of an existing world"? Has not Sartre indicated that there is an equivalence of interpretations, such that "an herb that burns" is the *true* appearance only if one has *chosen* a certain particular criterion of objectivity?[89] Indeed, Sartre writes: "To perceive the match as a bit of white wood with a black tip is not to deprive it of all potentiality, but simply to confer on it new potentialities (a new permanence, a new essence). For the this to be entirely deprived of potentialities, I would have to be a pure present, which is inconceivable."[90] Yet this does not mean that the bit of white wood with a black tip is not such; it rather means that I have extended its presently revealed qualities into a permanent nature. "Here again knowledge neither adds nor subtracts anything from being, nor embellishes it with any new quality. It makes being be there by surpassing it toward a nothingness which maintains only negative external relations with it."[91] Clearly the 'this' cannot be a neutral matrix on which any meaning whatsoever may be conferred; the bit of wood with a black tip is not the crescent moon. There is a particular range of equivalences (match; bit of white wood, etc.) that may not be exceeded because it is grounded in the experience of a 'this' whose particular *qualities* are neutrally revealed.

It is qualities, not the 'this,' that limit the range of equivalences. The 'this' has no priority over the other 'structures' of the 'thing': "the this and spatiality, permanence, essence and potentialities." The 'this' has no priority because "the rise of the for-itself makes the thing reveal itself with the totality of its structures." Each structure implies all the others. The 'this' has no priority over essence but rather "presupposes essence and, reciprocally, essence is the essence of this." Sartre concludes, "Thus, there is here no substantial form, no principle of unity to stand *behind* the modes of appearance of the phenomenon. Everything is given at once with no primacy."[92]

This convoluted argument is the consequence of Sartre's assertion of "the undifferentiation of the in-itself."[93] The in-itself is not potentially determinate (has no "substantial form" *potentialiter*)—yet the phenomenon is a "revelation" of being to which consciousness adds nothing. Sartre sees the conscious act of revealing in part as the dividing up of an undivided and timeless plenitude into discrete parts or 'thises' and 'thats'. This negation or insertion of "nothingnesses" between beings *which are actually not beings* but a seamless being, is quantification, and quantity is thus an ideal division.[94] The boundaries of any 'this' are therefore ideal, although being-in-itself submits to these divisive incisions. It follows that the 'this' is not a unit or 'form' of actuality. It further follows that any idea or concept that refers to any such unit or class of such units is ideal. The same holds of any name, which is therefore merely nominal.

But the act of revealing is an apprehension of quality as well as of quantity, and for Sartre quality has a less ideal function than quantity. Indeed quality plays a privileged role as a revealer of being. "The quality is nothing but the being of the *this* when it is considered apart from every external relation with the world or with other *thises*." Not "a simple subjective determination," the quality is "the presence of the absolute contingency of being; it is its indifferent irreducibility." Consciousness is subjected to the "total interpenetration" of the qualities of the 'this'. They cannot be separated from each other without altering the 'this'. The 'this', in fact, *is* its qualities: "it is the form that is color and light."[95] And qualities are always apprehended as qualities of a 'this'. If consciousness has the power to separate a seamless being into beings or 'thises', it must nevertheless suffer the qualities of this ideally bounded this.[96] It is probably not too far-fetched to infer that Sartre thinks that consciousness follows the clue of qualities in surpassing and constituting them as 'thises', and in this limited sense the 'form' of the this is not ideal. To be sure, Sartre writes that "the intuition of the quality is not at all passive contemplation of a given"—yet this is not because consciousness constitutes qualities but rather because "through quality the for-itself makes known to itself what it is not."[97]

It is, in fact, in his description of the "intuition" of quality that the early Sartre's generally "activistic" conception of consciousness most closely approaches the admission of a genuine passivity or unilateral affection.[98] Although Sartre rightly denies that we sense without actively identifying,[99] his theory of quality allows a passive "moment" of this act of identification. It is moreover this passive moment that is the most direct and immediate (as Sartre's term 'intuition' indicates) access to being that consciousness has. Qualities, to be sure, are apprehended as "not me" and "in this sense the quality is a presence perpetually out of reach." But Sartre can add: "We shall best account for the original phenomenon of perception by insisting on the fact that, through its relation to us, the quality stands in *absolute proximity*—it *'is there'*, it haunts us—without either giving itself or refusing itself. . . ."[100]

This at long last enables us to understand fully what Sartre means by the prelinguistic and silent presence of being "without intermediary." It must mean the absolute proximity of the "suffered" quality of the 'this'. It is roughly the pure sensory moment of an act of identification that always exceeds or surpasses that sensory component. Pure sensation is an abstraction, but Sartre also insists that "if the *this* does not include its own abstractions, there is no possibility of subsequently deriving them from it."[101] In *L'Imaginaire* Sartre writes:

> I always *perceive more and otherwise* than I see. . . . Into the very constitution of the (spatiotemporal) object there enters a multitude of empty intentions which do not posit new objects but which determine the present object in its relation to aspects not at present perceived. . . . These diverse kinds of understanding [*connaissances*] come either from a mnemic knowledge or from antepredicative inferences. Yet . . . this knowledge . . . sticks to the object. . . .[102]

I infer that 'seeing' is a "moment" or "component" of a synthetic perceiving. This moment of seeing consists in the suffering of a qualitative *presence* that is abstractly distinguishable from the negating-and-synthesizing intentions that relate this qualitative presence to past and future appearances. Quality is an abstract yet actual component of an act of perception that is always a totality grounded in the referential world and is at the same time that aspect of the perception that grounds the act of perception in an *actual* ground beyond the *world*-ground. Immediately intuited in the midst of mediated and temporal thought, quality is the timeless and unmediated presence of the transphenomenal being of beings.

Sartre's way of philosophizing consists in a constant shifting from the world-ground to the actual ground and back again. He shifts from synthetic totality to a detotalizing analytic of relata, retotalizes the relata, and so forth. When he is defending the charac-

ter of experience as a worldly totality he appears as a crusader returning us "to the things themselves." But when he is analytically
detotalizing that very totality he appears instead as the stern de-
fender of an ontological dualism that finds the drive to totality epistemologically misleading and morally reprehensible. This ambiguous tension, one might argue, is already present in Husserl, insofar
as he seeks to restore totality by means of provisional reductions. It
is present in the early Heidegger, who construes anxiety as a kind
of "lived reduction" that is to return us to totality in the mode of
true resoluteness. The later Heidegger comes to reject the view that
reduction-analysis-anxiety can serve as a means for restoring totality, for it is indebted to the dualism and subjectivism he is combatting. The later Sartre, we shall find, seeks a sort of "provisional
totalizing" in the form of historical revision that remains aware of
its dualistic base.

In response to the questions whose answers I sought in the passage previously cited: (a) what guarantees the *neutral* revealing of
the 'this' is an analysis that reduces the experience of what-is-as-
such-in-the-context-of-totality to its qualitative suchness by bracketing the projected totality within which, nevertheless, the being
has first revealed itself as what it is as such. Thus (b) what guarantees the sharp distinction between the transphenomenal actuality of
the thing and the ideal human meanings that relate the thing to
other things is a reduction to pure qualitative presentness. It is in
this way that Sartre reappropriates Heidegger's distinction in *SZ*
between our *proximal* everyday experience and the *clarification* of
that experience in anxiety and the true retrieve of proximal experience. The 'this' is Sartre's version of the 'present-at-hand' being
when it stands forth in anxiety as without any referential involvement.[103] Thus the proximal ground—the referential totality—is
ironically the inevitable basis of the same anxious experience which
shows that prior ground to be not the *true* ground, which is Dasein
as projector of referential meanings over entities inherently devoid
of meaning. We saw this as a liability and a problem for Heidegger,
given his phenomenological intentions, but a palatable conclusion
for Sartre, given his different intentions.

We can now come back to a previous problem. It would appear, I
argued, that in constituting the 'this', consciousness far exceeds a
neutral revealing in (1) employing a whole complex of logical opera-

tions and categorial distinctions and (2) making a judgment of identification that decides what will count as the essence of the thing, as
distinct from its accidental traits. Sartre's answer must be that these
logical operations and categorial distinctions are at most necessary
conditions for the revelation of a qualitative 'this' which is not essentially or internally modified by them. They are "only ideal mixings of things which leave them completely intact."[104] For example,
the whole-part distinction "ideally mixes" the ensemble of absent
qualities we call a past and future whole or full moon with the
present part moon or crescent, and relates the moon with the sky as
a part situated in the whole sky. These ideal mixings are necessary
conditions for the crescent moon being revealed *as* present—as
'this' entity in *this* (not that) place at *this* time. But these ideal relations leave the actual present crescent moon as an ensemble of qualities intact. There is a Sartrean principle at work here: the conditions of revelation do not modify the qualitative nature of the
phenomenon.[105] Since this is the case, the judgment of identification whereby the thing is first revealed can be said to be neither arbitrary nor distortive.

It will be recalled that we originally distinguished between neutral revealing and meaningful relating in order to ascertain the role
of prelinguistic idea in each. Suppose we take the idea "crescent
moon." It appears to be a universal, in that it refers to any and
every appearance of the moon at a particular stage in a repeated
lunar cycle. We infer that this idea is for Sartre an "ideal mixing"
that is a necessary condition for the appearance of any particular
crescent moon *as* "a crescent moon." It surpasses-and-reveals this
particular crescent moon without altering its present qualities. If
ideationally I understand this particular crescent moon as a member
of a class, I nevertheless at the same time understand the class as
only the ideal sum of these particular appearances. Without the
contingent appearance of these ensembles of qualities I call "crescent moons," there is no universal. That is, I understand the universal as ultimately dependent for its being upon the contingent
qualitative particulars, not the contrary. Thus the universal idea
"crescent moon in general" is not constitutive of any particular
crescent moon as an ensemble of qualities.

One can conclude that for Sartre ideas, concepts, and categories
are *ideal* quantifications, groupings, and relatings of *actual* qualities

in a synthesis of the ideal and the actual that can be called *the real*. The real *is* real because it is grounded in the intuited actual, but is not the actual, insofar as the real is constituted by the ideal, by a projective synthesizing action that perpetually surpasses its actual ground. From the standpoint of projective *action*, therefore, ideas, concepts, and categories enter into the constitution of the real. As they are thus already part and parcel of the real, they may be abstracted out as ideas per se: the idea of the match, the idea of the crescent moon, etc. But they do not stand between me and the real, and they only stand between me and the actual in the sense that they delimit the actual into ideally separated groups of qualities.

Ideas as such—in the sense of concepts, classifications, and categories of things—are abstractions of 'real' distinctions of projective experience that are nevertheless 'ideal' divisions of the 'actual'. When Sartre speaks from the standpoint of the world-ground or 'reality', they have cognitive import; when he speaks from the standpoint of the actual ground or being-in-itself, they do not have cognitive import. The always-prior articulation of the for-itself's environment is ambiguous, since it is perpetually threatened by a shift from unreflective and active involvement in the real to reflective and contemplative analysis of the actual ground of the real, exposing brute quality as a ground that human articulation cannot modify. Such is the consequence of Sartre's reappropriation of the implicit distinction in *SZ* between the proximal ground and the true ground, the proximal beginning and the existentially analyzed beginning.

IV

For a philosopher, everything hangs on where one begins. Will one begin with the perspective of action, with that of contemplation, or with that of poetry? Sartre criticizes Parain (and in our extrapolation, the later Heidegger) for beginning unambiguously with the perspective of action:

> "Words are ideas," he [Parain] writes in *Investigations*, for he has placed himself in a perspective which is already practical and political, as has Heidegger, who refuses to distinguish between the body and the soul, a problem of *contemplative* philosophy, and who would readily say that, from the point of view

of *action*, which is the only real point of view, the soul is the body, and the body the soul.[106]

From this perspective, words flow into action; there is a fusion, a unity, a synthesis of the two. "When the word is a link in a chain— 'hand me the . . . the . . . there!'—it is effaced. One obeys it without hearing it, without seeing it."[107] This, it appears, is what really bothers Sartre. The fusion of word with idea, and of both with actuality, is a confusion of an ontological sort and of a moral sort. One must simply suffer actual qualities but one need not simply suffer words and ideas, inasmuch as they are subject to a reflective and contemplative critique that reveals them as consciously controlled instruments. The shift of perspective from either action or poetry to reflective analysis can distinguish the controllable from the uncontrollable, the possible or ideal from the given or actual, the moral from the natural, the human from the inhuman. Otherwise there is a blind obedience, a suffering of the merely possible as if it were the necessary, a loss of human transcendence. Heidegger, like Ponge and Parain, suppresses the original moment of negation—all the more so in his later thought, where language and thing are explicitly and unambiguously fused. In allowing the spirit to drag amid things, Heidegger stands convicted of the spirit of seriousness, a mode of human play that denies its playfulness, its humanity. The price paid is loss of a perspective from which one might guard oneself against magic, mysticism, mystification, and totalitarianism.

Nevertheless we are always in language, and the act of identification is at the same time an act of naming. What is constitutive, however, is not the naming but the logical organization of intuited qualities as 'thises'. The name merely expresses or points toward a logically constituted 'this'. The name is thus *twice removed* from actuality, for it points toward a 'this' that is already a logical ordering of brute quality. Hence names can only be legitimately regarded as instruments of use in surpassing the real, which is already a surpassing of the actual. This is indicated by the fact that names and individual words are subordinate to the real unit of language, the sentence, which is a project whose goal is the humanization of the actual. When the name is "poetically" regarded as an expression of the actual, the mind has disowned itself (disowned its constitutive function) by dragging amid things in an effort to realize the humanization of the actual immediately—i.e., without instrumental action (or, in Sartre's later thought, without the labor of praxis). Poetry, however, performs a legitimate function when it recalls our attention to the totality or synthesis or world, providing that it acknowledges the fact that consciousness perpetually detotalizes this totality and the fact that the totality of which the poet speaks is already the consequence of a surpassing.

Behind this humanization of the actual, whether instrumental or poetic, stands what Sartre calls "the beginning"—the original confrontation of silent consciousness and inarticulate actuality, between and beyond whose respective silences consciousness by means of logic and language constructs a world.[108] It is the original diaspora of the unrecoverable One into a logical and linguistic articulation and action that seeks recovery of the One. But logical and linguistic action slide across the surface of the actual, without taking root. The true beginning or ground is conscious negation of being.

I can now repeat Sartre's six characterizations of Parain and explicitly construe them as aspects of a hypothetical Sartrean critique of the later Heidegger.

1. Parain (Heidegger) is a peasant, at home in nature, who experiences the artifactual human order as alienation, uprootedness. Sartre: the human project of return to union with its natural conditions is intelligible as an effort to recoup the unity lost by the rise of consciousness as negation of its actual ground. One can therefore understand this project and even sympathize with it. But lucidity requires recognition of its impossibility, because man truly "begins" not in unity but in negation.

2. Parain (Heidegger) espouses Nietzsche's critique of the notion of a transcendental and autonomous consciousness and Nietzsche's correlative recall to the controlling power of the simple natural need to love and beget in a natural rhythm. Sartre: This alleged effort to return man to his true nature is in fact the betrayal of what is genuinely human. It is man's disownment of himself. To define oneself by one's body and its attachment to nature is to seek vainly to suppress the ambiguity of the consciousness/body relation. By suppressing the ambiguity in favor of a mythical natural totality, it succumbs to the "totalitarian danger" inherent in all assertions of

an immediate and unsurpassable totality—namely, the danger of subordination of man to the inhuman, the alienation of his freedom.

3. Parain (Heidegger) surrenders the pride and aspiration of the humanist (and the Protestant) and insists on the observance of strict limits under a paternal organization (like the Catholic) in order to rid himself of the anxiety that had threatened him. Sartre: The recall to man's "beginning" is a recall to anxiety rather than an overcoming of it. The retreat into paternal organizations, which are inherently totalitarian, must be recognized for what it is. It is not a return to natural limits, but man's self-imposition of limits in order to flee an anxiety that nevertheless remains. To accept the inevitable anxiety is to take legitimate pride in one's freedom and to own up to that humanistic aspiration which is the character of consciousness as a project.

4. Parain (Heidegger), having "departed" from the "valley" of his early rapport with the earth, reacts to the conflict between the ungrounded metaphysical truths of nations by temporarily plunging into a "pragmatic and relativistic authoritarianism," followed by an effort to return to his beginnings. Sartre: if one does not like the sociopolitical conditions one finds on the human "plateau," that does not warrant a plunge into authoritarianism, which means one's active assent to alienating sociopolitical conditions. Nor does it warrant a flight back to the "valley," which means one's passive assent to these alienating conditions in one's very effort to escape them.

5. Parain (Heidegger) finally turns to language and construes it as a return, since he holds that an original "act of naming" establishes an orientation that lasts; man's future consists in realizing the "promises" inherent in these original linguistic "germs of being." Sartre: there is language at man's beginning but the beginning is not language. The original articulation is the work of negation. To say that thought is ruled by *logos* therefore must mean not that thought is ruled by a prelogical language but rather that thought is essentially conscious negation and discrimination by negation. Language points toward this articulated order in naming and goes beyond that order in serving as an instrument for expressing that order, for making hypotheses about it, and for trying to change it. *Between* us and others, *between* us and things, language constitutes

neither consciousness nor its objects. Since original negation inserts an impassable nothingness both between consciousness and its objects and between objects of consciousness, language can never fuse the relata it stands between. Thus the real beginning, conscious negation, places strict limits upon linguistic mediation. To say that words are potencies or "germs of being" that originally situate man and determine his path to be that of an actualization of original potencies is to deny man a *human* future. A human future is an open future, a perpetual surpassing of the given, or "permanent revolution." In this perpetual revolution language serves as a means rather than as the determinant of the end.

6. Parain (Heidegger) is convinced that man ends in a certain resignation, humble and assured, attaching himself only to the simplest and most familiar words and to a few "sad and simple truths." From the valley to which he has returned, he surveys the plateaux "with insolent modesty." Sartre: given a phenomenological-ontological analysis of the human condition, one can understand the appeal of resignation and even sympathize with the desire for release from "metaphysical anxiety." Given the diaspora of the One into the articulation of a multiplicity of warring for-itselfs and a multiplicity of discrete environmental beings that can only be synthesized by free metaphysical projects that clash with one another in their competitive rage to fill the nothingness, the desire for a radical simplification is inevitably great. Technological production has no doubt exacerbated this situation by further multiplying the number and variety of artifactual entities that projective experience must somehow master and coordinate. But lucidity requires one to recognize that the existence of a desire for simplification does not entail the possibility of gratifying that desire. Paradoxically, it is the recognition of the impossibility of a real simplification of the human situation that motivates the leap into an alleged simplification. This leap is therefore irrational and magical, succeeding only by suppressing its own premise.

The modesty of resignation is insolent, for it scorns metaphysical solutions to the human situation, while itself being one. It inhabits the plateau it claims to have abandoned, for in no case do we get out of an existing world. If resort to a few sad and simple truths means owning up to the permanently anxious condition of man, all well and good. But if it means an effort to leap out of self-transcending history into a simpler past—and dead—tradition, it is a misunderstanding of history and a betrayal of the human condition. The effort to affirm one's own death in true resoluteness symbolizes this betrayal, because it signifies an attitude that takes termination of surpassing, rather than surpassing, to be the prime index of the human condition.[109] It betrays a desire to assimilate one's life to a dead past. Presenting itself as a projection into the future, it is in fact an effort to see one's life as the finished and simplified whole that it can never be for a self-surpassing consciousness. The only admissible resignation consists in consigning the past to the cemetery, recognizing the irreversibility of time, and living forward. Adherence to a few sad and simple truths and to a few ancient words is the goal (!) of an antirevolutionary ideology that masks its anxiety over the open future by reducing that future to the eternal recurrence of the past. Fascination with things ancient, whether in its Nietzschean form or in other forms, is ready to affirm history only on condition that history is already essentially finished. The "revolution" that seeks to return man to his true beginning is a revolution only if it understands that beginning as the origin of a permanent revolution. To see history as a circle that returns to its point of beginning is to seek to reduce history to the Parmenidean unity of the closed and self-identical sphere, while real history is precisely the diasporatic explosion of that sphere. From Sartre's viewpoint, the greatest irony of Parain's (Heidegger's) affirmation of history and love of fate is that it flees both history and man's fate.

The greatest irony of Sartre's *own* affirmation of history is that he will retrospectively find it to have been conditioned by the very same flight from metaphysical anxiety that he had condemned in others. Sartre will find living the ambiguity, or owning up to one's ownmost way of being, or coinciding with oneself as non-self-coincident, to be far more difficult than he had imagined. In the late forties and fifties he comes to see himself as having reserved to himself a metahistorical vantage point he denied to all others. This recognition will require of him a new effort to situate *himself* within the history within which he had situated everyone else. I turn now to Sartre's effort to reappropriate himself as "wholly a man, made of and by all men, as good as any of them but better than none of them."[110]

11

Sartre's Problem of Action Metaphysically Resolved

The problem is to determine *on what level* we place ourselves in order to define reality.

—Sartre, *CRD*, p. 84 (*SM*, 130)

I

SIMONE DE BEAUVOIR wrote in 1955 that "Sartre's reconciliation of ontology and phenomenology raises difficulties" but that "Sartre is preparing a philosophical work which makes a frontal attack on the problem."[1] In 1947 Francis Jeanson likewise thought that Sartre had a problem, "the ethical problem."[2] The two problems are two aspects of a single problem—the problem of action—and consideration of this problem should facilitate understanding of Sartre's later thought. The two aspects of this problem are indicated by the division of the conclusion of *EN* into two parts: "metaphysical hints" and "ethical perspectives."[3]

In reviewing Sartre's "metaphysical hints" we discovered that from within phenomenological ontology Sartre finds evidence only for a decapitated synthesis, "a passage that is not completed, a short circuit." The quest, announced in the introduction to *EN*, for "the meaning of that being which includes within itself these two radically split regions of being" turns out to be a quest for a metaphysical ideal.[4] A genuine synthesis of these two regions of being appears to be precluded by Sartre's analysis, which breaks up the virtual synthesis of unreflective experience into its irreducible ontological relata. That this represents a problem, and a grave one, is indicated by Sartre's implicit admission that the phenomenological ontology of *EN* has not accounted for the possibility of *action*:

It is after having decided the question of the origin of the for-itself and of the nature of the phenomenon of the world that metaphysics will be able to handle various problems of the first importance, in particular the problem of action. Action is to be considered in fact *simultaneously* on the plane of the for-itself and on the plane of the in-itself, for it involves a project whose origin is immanent but which determines a modification in the being of the transcendent. It would in fact be useless to declare that the action modifies only the phenomenal appearance of the thing: if the phenomenal appearance of a cup can be changed to the extent of annihilating the cup *as* cup, and if the being of the cup is nothing but its *quality*, then the action envisaged must be able to modify the very being of the cup. The problem of action thus requires elucidation of the transcendent efficacy of consciousness and puts us on the path of its true relation, that of being with being. It also reveals to us, owing to the repercussions of the act in the world, a relation of being with being which, while the physicist perceives it in exteriority, is neither pure exteriority nor immanence but rather refers us to the Gestaltist notion of *form*.[5]

This extraordinary passage tells us that Sartre's 722 page work, although it has included a lengthy study of 'doing' and/or 'making' (*faire*), must relegate action to the region of the metaphysical. Action implies a positive relation of interaction between for itself and in-itself, while phenomenological ontology limits the genuine relation of for-itself and in-itself to that of logical negation. If interaction between two factors requires a precedent community of nature between the factors,[6] if 'action' is such an interaction, and if metaphysics alone can conceive, hypothetically, a *positive* relation between in-itself and for-itself, then the apparently simple action of destroying a cup requires a metaphysical foundation. So long as the for-itself lacks such a foundation, its activity will be merely "a surface runoff."[7] One might reasonably suspect that Sartre will, after *EN*, either have to take the leap into metaphysics or modify his conception of phenomenological ontology.

The imperviousness of being-in-itself to human activity is matched by its imperviousness to human meanings. We have observed how, in *La Nausée* and in *EN*, meanings and significations become detached from their referents under the double onslaught of anxiety and analysis. The correlate of the problem of action is therefore the problem of meaning. Might recourse to metaphysics resolve the problem of meaning as well as the problem of action? If so, would not such recourse to metaphysics require a loss of the lucidity attained by phenomenological ontology, a lapse from authentic awareness of the impossibility of a genuine synthesis of in-itself and for-itself?

The references to lucidity and authenticity in this last question already suggest that the metaphysical problem and the ethical problem go together. They represent the two sides of the problem of action. How can one return to the world from reflexive withdrawal in such a way that one's actions will be (1) causally efficacious, will mirror one's purposes, will make a difference to and in being, while being (2) 'lucid' or 'authentic', rather than a self-deceptive and 'degrading' loss of oneself in 'matter' or 'slime'? These are the two aspects of the question we saw emerging at the end of chapter 6, that of the nature of alienation and the possibility of escaping it.

I have in chapter 5 characterized Sartre's implicit ethical response in EN as the religion of artful play, which "lives the ambiguity" by restricting itself to merely symbolic syntheses of ontologically antithetical relata. We saw that, in the section of the conclusion devoted to "ethical perspectives," Sartre proposes as a moral possibility that freedom take *itself* for an end and ideal, as the sole nonalienating and nondeceptive end. This proposal, I argued, is adopted and some of its implications explored in EH and in QL: freedom must be the goal of social action in general and of that particular mode of social action that is prose. I have proposed that the balance of Sartre's career can be seen as the effort to understand what sort of 'situation', and what sort of 'world', would be compatible with the pursuit of freedom as an end and a value.

The solution of the problem of action is therefore the answer to the question asked at the end of EN: "will freedom, by taking itself for an end . . . situate itself all the more precisely and all the more individually . . . ?"[8] The general answer Sartre wants to give is "yes," but this general answer can only be a specific and concrete answer ("precisely and . . . individually"). Ultimately, it must be a *historical* answer, and we must now try to understand why this is so, why and in what sense and to what extent history can resolve what I am calling "the problem of action" in both its aspects. To accomplish this, we must first turn to Sartre's account of "the Other," which in part forms the basis of Sartre's later theory of social action yet must in part be revised if social action is to be able to realize the goals it sets itself.

II

My treatment of Sartre's thought so far has concentrated on the character of the relation of the for-itself to the in-itself in its synthetic and analytic forms. I have given scant attention to the relation of for-itself and Other, thus by implication conforming to the commonly held view that Sartre's early thought is "individualistic"—as well as to Sartre's own retrospective critique of his early thought as under the influence of bourgeois individualism.[9] It is no doubt significant that in *EN* Sartre's chief illustration of a justifiable pursuit is skiing—an individual venture—and that it is the solitary drunkard, not the leader of nations, who serves as a model of lucidity.[10] The human affair thus might seem to be essentially a matter of individually coming to terms with the ambiguity of one's being.

Now it is significant for my study that Sartre arrives at his characterization of the Other and of the for-itself's essential relation to the Other in part through criticism of Heidegger's treatment of the Other.[11] The same consideration governs this aspect of Sartre's critique of Heidegger that has governed his critique of other aspects of his thought—Heidegger suppresses the original negation.[12] How? "Heideggerian *transcendence* is a concept in bad faith."[13] Heidegger's Dasein transcends itself only toward itself, and not in such a way as to encounter a genuine otherness. "What human reality [for Heidegger] in fact reencounters at the inaccessible terminus of this flight beyond itself is still itself: the flight beyond the self is flight toward the self, and the world appears as pure distance between self and self."[14] "At the very heart of its ekstases, human reality [for Heidegger] remains alone."[15] But Heidegger has rightly seen that if there is to be a genuine relation between the self and the Other it must be *internal;* Dasein must be a being that in its being implies the being of Others.[16] If, Sartre argues, the relation is not constituted by its very terms, it will require a witness or "third man" to posit it. The relation will not be possible or explicable on its own terms, by itself, or through its own nature.[17] In other words, Heidegger like Hegel understands that the self in its very way of being depends on the Other. The self would not be what it is without the Other, and this is indicated by the fact that for Heidegger "Being-with" (*Mitsein*) is an existentiale.[18]

But there are two possible sorts of internal relation: internal negation and what might be called "internal community." Heidegger opts for the latter.

> The experiential image which may best symbolize the Heideggerian intuition is not that of conflict but rather that of *the crew*. The original relation of the Other with my consciousness is not the *you* and *me*; it is the *we*, and Heideggerian being-with is not the clear and distinct stance of an individual faced with another individual. . . .[19]

Dasein is thus in its being a member of a community. But how has Heidegger reached this position? "In his abrupt and a bit barbaric fashion of cutting Gordian knots, rather than trying to untie them, he responds . . . with a *definition* pure and simple."[20] It is not a matter of a conjoining that *creates* solidarity, but rather of a conjunction that is posited by Heidegger as solidarity.[21] This conjunction is "abstract" and it "does not escape idealism"; it unifies experience, a priori, like the Kantian concepts.[22] Sartre finds Heidegger both too Kantian and too Hegelian, and one may presumably lay against him the charge Sartre lays against Hegel: "Here, as everywhere, one must oppose to Hegel Kierkegaard, who represents the claims of the individual as such. The individual demands his fulfillment as an individual . . . and not [as] the objective specification of a universal structure."[23] The objectionable universal structure in this case is "Being-with."

In the terminology of *CRD*, Heidegger has "totalized too quickly." Experientially or ontically there are indeed crews, teams, etc.—a variety of forms of communal organization—but is communal being the essential ontological relation of Dasein and Other?

> Why did Heidegger believe he was authorized to pass from this experiential and ontic case of being-with to the position that co-existence is the ontological structure of my 'being-in-the-world'? . . . To what extent does this position preserve the negation that makes of the Other *an other* and that constitutes him as inessential?[24]

These rhetorical questions convey their own answers. Heidegger was not authorized to make this leap from the ontic to the ontological, for the irreducible otherness of the Other is thereby lost. Once again it is a matter of beginning in the right place:

> the only possible point of departure is the Cartesian *cogito*. . . . The *cogito* . . . must throw me beyond it, upon the Other, just as it threw me beyond it upon the in-itself—not by revealing to me an *a priori* structure of myself which would point toward an equally *a priori* Other, but by disclosing to me the concrete and indubitable presence of *this* or *that* concrete Other. . . . In the very depths of myself, I must find . . . the Other himself as not being me.[25]

There follows Sartre's well-known analysis of "the look." If my look at the Other runs the risk of a sort of optical idealism that tends to reduce the Other to an object in *my* visual field (he is intended as *I* intend him), the look of the Other makes me an object in *his* field:

> a spatiality unfolds that is not *my* spatiality, for, in place of a grouping of objects *toward me*, there is an orientation *that flees from me*. . . . It is not I who accomplish this disintegration. . . . the Other is first of all the permanent flight of things toward a terminus . . . that escapes me. . . . The appearance of the Other in the world thus corresponds to a fixed sliding of the whole universe—a decentralizing of the world which undermines the centralizing that I am effecting at the same time.[26]

The look refutes my idealism—and Heidegger's. The Other first appears not as member of the same *category* as me but as the brute *fact* of a negation that is at once both logical and concrete: the Other appears as not-me in appearing as an assault. (Part of the genius of Sartre's empirical descriptions lies in his ability to exhibit the logical structure of concrete experience, which is an aspect of the phenomenological effort to show that structures of *thought* are first and foremost structures of *experience*, that is, are 'intentional' rather than simply 'mental' or 'psychological'. Note, in the foregoing passage, that the appearance of the Other is not primarily a *psychological* trauma; it is the restructuring *of the world*.) In effect, the Other demonstrates his independent status as for-itself by doing to me

and my world what I do to him and his world. We violate or de-
center each other, and we do so not accidentally but in order to
master our environment, to accomplish the fundamental project.[27]
My fundamental project seems to entail the enslavement of the
Other, hence "conflict is the essential meaning of being-for-
Others."[28]

Nevertheless the Other is not only the "alienation of my own
possibilities" but also their "solidification."[29] "Shame reveals to me
that I *am* this being. Not in the mode of having *been* or of having *to*
be, but *in-itself*."[30] Ironically, the Other who spoils my project abets
my project in the act of spoiling it. I am a project to *be* (to be self-
coincident or self-identical rather than ambiguous), and for the
other I *am:* "Thus I who, in so far as I am my possibilities, am what
I am not and am not what I am, behold! *I am* somebody!"[31] But I
am somebody not for myself but for the Other, and to destroy the
Other would be to destroy the being *through whom* I get my being-
in-itself, my identity or "solidity."[32] I *need* the Other, even at the
high price of alienation, and the Other needs me. There is a reciprocal alienation and a reciprocal need, both of which exemplify the
fundamental logical reciprocity of the relation of for-itself and
Other: "apprehension of the Other is . . . an internal negation,
which means a synthetic and active conjunction [*liaison*] of the two
terms, each of which constitutes itself by denying it is the other.
Thus this negative relation will be reciprocal. . . ."[33]

From this fact Sartre draws an important conclusion: "the multiplicity of 'Others' will not be a *collection* but a *totality*—in this respect Hegel is right—since each Other discovers his being in the
Other."[34] By this Sartre appears to mean that the multiplicity of
Others is not an assemblage of identical but atomic units, but rather
a group in which each 'unit' is what it is only in relation to (and
dependence upon) whatever Others exist. A number of originally
separate (atomic) units could *subsequently* be assembled by someone
as a collection—for example, a collection of tables. A 'totality', on
the other hand, is an *original* unity in which each part is what it is
owing to its relation to the other parts. For example, the legs of a
table *are* legs in relation to the top of the table and vice versa. But
a table is, in Sartre's sense of the terms, not simply a "totality' but a
'whole'; a table is looked at by an observer from *beyond* it in such a
way as to constitute it as a finished and complete object. The total-

ity of Others is not such a whole: "this Totality is such that it is impossible in principle to place oneself 'at the point of view of the whole.' "[35] There is no external, absolute, or divine vantage-point from which the social totality can be viewed. It is to be experienced only from the inside—as a leg would see the other legs and top of the table, so to speak. But here my analogy is imperfect, since the parts of the table do not see and constitute each other ('reciprocally') as a totality, but are constituted as a totality only by the external agency of its maker or user or viewer. The look of God is not returned by the object at which God looks, and hence God's relation to the world is not reciprocal. He is not drawn into the totality by looking at it, not made dependent on it or compromised by it.

The fascination of God for Sartre, and according to Sartre for man in general, partly consists in this ability to look without being compromised and without altering the object seen in the very act of seeing it. If Hegel seeks to raise man to this divine vantage point, Kierkegaard (and in effect the early Sartre) answers that "Truth is for God alone,"[36] where 'Truth' means knowledge of the whole as whole, as "system." And we have seen[37] that Sartre appears unwilling to make that leap into metaphysics that attempts to envisage the cosmos *as a whole*, as what-is-as-a-whole, as a universal drama with a single meaning. Insofar as we know, the only teleology, and thus the only meaning, is a human teleology and a human meaning. It is even misleading to speak of a single human teleology, since each individual fundamental project needs to cancel all the others in order to establish itself in the sovereign position from which *its* view of the world cannot be challenged by the view of the Other. So long as there are Others, each of them "detotalizes" or disunifies the totality as it is construed from my vantage point. There are as many centers or orientations as there are for-itselfs, and therefore there is no one center, no one orientation: "this totality . . . is a detotalized totality. Since existence-for-Others is a radical refusal of Others, no totalitarian [*totalitaire*] and unifying synthesis of 'Others' is possible."[38] Here, as always for Sartre, unity has exploded in a diaspora. Consciousness has suffered a Plotinian dispersion into matter and thereby into multiplicity, into a plurality of bodily spatiotemporal standpoints, each of which is haunted by the vision of a "lost" Oneness. Each Other, each local center or orientation, is the frustration of the very Universal Center of which each for-itself, as *itself* a center but a threatened center, has both a tempting foretaste and a need.[39]

One notes the term 'totalitarian' in the last passage cited. Its ideological connotation is very likely intended by Sartre, and the passage may suggest that the impassable internal negation between for-itselfs is an inevitable limit to the possibility of achieving an integrated political whole. Inevitable ontological pluralism seems to mean inevitable political pluralism. The human situation is a sociopolitical pluralism, no matter how hard totalitarian and/or dictatorial theory and practice may try to mask this fact. But, one can ask, may not Sartre's term 'reciprocity' also have an ideological connotation, but one of a more positive sort?

Sartre's notion of 'reciprocity' means both that the Other necessarily violates my totalizing impulse, my effort to center the world on myself, and also that each for-itself, beginning with the situation of 'shame', acknowledges in the Other the same limited centrality that it itself has. May not the same relation to the Other that limits the possibility of totalitarianism (pure political totality) also ground the possibility of pluralistic democracy (limited political totality)? Is it not the case for Sartre that each for-itself needs, in order to "be somebody" objective, the Other who threatens him? Sartre argues against Heidegger: "The we is a particular kind of experience produced in special cases on the foundation of being-for-the-Other in general. Being-*for*-the-Other precedes and founds being-*with*-the-Other."[40] We have already noted Sartre's strictures on the totalitarian tendency of Parain, and we have found significant parallels between the views of Parain and those of the later Heidegger. And we have noted Sartre's early conviction that his description of consciousness can serve as a foundation for an ethics and a politics that are "absolutely positive."[41] We can now construe "absolutely positive" to mean: *not* founded in any alleged metaphysical or theological or a priori (metapositive) unity or whole, any nondetotalized or totalitarian totality. When Sartre argues in *EH* that if God does not exist, man is free,[42] he is arguing that the absence of an a priori whole makes possible *human* totalizing, but with the limitation that such totalizing is at the same time a detotalizing.

If the later Sartre correlates this social totality with history, it is important to recognize that he had already, if only implicitly and formally, made this correlation in *EN*. This becomes clear when the following passages are compared: (1) "the multiplicity of 'Others' will be . . . a *totality* . . . since each Other discovers his being in the Other"; (2) "the springing up of my consciousness into being . . . is at once historization—for I temporalize myself as presence to Others—and a condition of all history. . . ."[43] Each for-itself temporalizes itself, or surpasses its past, as presence to a totality of Others. This means (*a*) that the for-itself must surpass (by challenging or maintaining) a social inheritance; (*b*) that the for-itself surpasses by projecting an ideal future that must affect future Others; (*c*) that the for-itself establishes an identity in the eyes of Others that haunts it (that is, I understand that my acts make me something definite for Others, that I can never directly know this something that I am, but that I must attempt to know it through feedback from Others if I am to have any control over my objective identity). Historization thus means my continual and simultaneous adjustment of my acts to a social past, a social future, and a social present.[44]

But this continual adjustment is not just mine; it is *reciprocity within a totality*. This may perhaps best be understood in terms of the notion of double feedback. I continually readjust my behavior to take into account the reaction of the Other to my behavior while he continually readjusts his behavior to take into account my reaction to his behavior. The social fabric at large is a vast web (totality) of such reciprocating feedbacks, of which double feedback (the interrelation of only two for-itselfs) is only the simplest form; the Other whose view of me concerns me may be a group of Others, or I and the Other may be mutually adjusting our behavior in coordinated response to the behavior of a Third, etc.[45] Furthermore, given the fact of a multiplicty of Others, who have a multiplicity of differing goals ('specifications' of the fundamental project), it would seem inevitable that any adjustment of my behavior to achieve solidarity (being-*with*) with one or more Others will ipso facto achieve a being-*against* certain Others. But I do and must "find my being" or identity in the eyes of both those I am "with" and those I am "against," since I am fundamentally being "for" Others. In other words, the reciprocal negation of for-itself and Other opens up a "space" that may (and must) be filled with both solidarity and violence. Indeed, reciprocity within a totality is itself a simultaneous violence-and-solidarity in the minimal but fundamental sense that *the negation is mutual.*

This reciprocity also means that the totality is rife with ambiguity. If my possibilities are solidified and objectified by being looked at, my possibilities also surpass this objectification, and the same is the case for the Other. Each of us is and is not as he is seen; there is a double solidification and a double desolidification. Each of us materializes and dematerializes for the Other. This perpetual game of hide and seek—now-you-see-me-now-you-don't—makes the social field highly volatile. The social field is at once solid materiality (a field of bodies), ghostly immateriality (a field of consciousnesses), and evanescent syntheses of the material and the immaterial (a field of actions).

Summarizing, the social field is not a whole (or One). Sartre writes:

> It seems that . . . nothingness has slipped into this totality in order to shatter it, just as in the atomism of Leucippus non-being slips into the Parmenidean totality of being in order to make it explode into atoms. Therefore it represents the negation of any synthetic totality in terms of which one might claim to understand the plurality of consciousnesses."[46]

What is "this totality" of which Sartre speaks? As at the very end of *EN*, Sartre toys with a variant of Plotinian metaphysics. If one could stand outside history (that is, outside the temporalization of for-itselfs), might not the multiplicity of negating consciousnesses, which is from our temporal point of view simply a brute and inexplicable fact, be explained as "the scattering of the being-in-itself of a broken totality"?[47] Sartre speculates that "being-for-Others can only be if it *is made-to-be* by a totality that loses itself so that being-for-Others may spring up, and this would drive us to postulate the existence and passion of *mind* or *spirit* [*l'esprit*]."[48] Then the existence of a plurality would not be simply an unintelligible fact. It would have an intelligible origin in a unifying and animating spirit. In the philosophical tradition, this mind explanation probably originates with Anaxagoras, and it profoundly excited the young Socrates as a possible way of reaching the goal of the pre-Socratic quest for cosmic intelligibility. It is significant that Hegel, to whom both the early and the later Sartre owe so much, regards Anaxagorean *Nous* as a crucial advance in the history of thought. Hegel seeks to show in detail, as Socrates and Aristotle saw that Anaxagoras failed to do,[49] how mind can make, and has made, the world intelligible. This requires the correlation of Greek Mind with the self-sacrificing passion of Christian Spirit (*Geist, l'esprit*). Sartre however draws back: "But . . . this being-for-Others can only exist if it admits an incomprehensible external nonbeing which no totality, not even *l'esprit,* can produce or found."[50] Although Sartre does not say so, this amounts to the rejection of Hegelian logic and Hegelian history. 'Mind' for Sartre is totality, and nondetotalized 'totality' is being-in-itself, that which "is what it is," fullness. 'Nonbeing' is by definition external to being, and a being that contained or produced nonbeing would not be a complete being. The idea of being producing nonbeing is therefore contradictory. "Negation cannot affect the nucleus of being of being, which is absolute plenitude and utter positivity."[51] Being itself cannot originate nonbeing, nor are being and nonbeing genuinely synthesizable. "There is nonbeing only on the surface of being."[52] Why, then, the appearance of being in the guise of beings separated by nothingness? One can answer this metaphysical question only by "so it is."[53]

In what sense, then, is the multiplicity of Others a 'totality'? Why is it more than simply a collection of atoms? "The multiplicity of consciousnesses appears to us as a *synthesis*, not as a *collection*. Yet it is a synthesis that is inconceivable as a totality."[54] The sense of 'synthesis' meant here is that which we have seen Sartre employ in describing the "apprehension of the Other" as "an internal negation, which means a *synthetic* and active conjunction of the two terms, each of which constitutes itself by denying it is the other." The multiplicity of consciousnesses is a synthesis in the sense of a web of reciprocal negations. This means that the field of Others is a field of *irreducible* otherness, and in this sense each Other is an atom. Yet we have seen that "each Other discovers his being in the Other." This is to say that man is, as consciousness, being-for-itself and he is, as body, being-for-Others. As being-for-itself-for-Others, he is an atom perpetually recouping and perpetually losing his atomicity. He is a perpetual hemorrhaging of interiority into exteriority and a perpetual surpassing of exteriority by interiority. He is 'ambiguous'. Not only the natural field, and not only the social field, but also each individual can be envisaged as a One in diaspora, a detotalized totality.

Such is the power of negation, by neglecting which Heidegger was able to regard Being-with as an original rather than a founded relation. If, now, being-for is indeed original and also impassable, in what sense can there be "being-with"? If reciprocity is originally and fundamentally mutual negation—my situation is the "death" of yours, yours the "death" of mine—how can it subsequently be cooperation or community? This requires the appearance of "the Third": "With the appearance of the Third I abruptly find my possibilities alienated and discover that the Other's possibilities are likewise dead possibilities. . . . In the world of the Third I suddenly encounter an objective situation-form in which the Other and I will figure as *equivalent* and *solidary* structures."[55]

Sartre gives class consciousness as an example of such solidarity in the face of mutual alienation by a Third who is the master, the feudal lord, the bourgeois, or the capitalist.[56] The ultimate Third, as "he who is Third in relation to all possible groups," would be God, but "since God is characterized as radical absence, the attempt to realize humanity as *ours* perpetually gets renewed and perpetually gets stymied." God therefore represents the purely ideal limit of "an abstract and unrealizable project of the for-itself toward an absolute totalization of itself and of *all* Others."[57]

In any case, such solidarity is not positive community. It is only common or equivalent alienation, the passive suffering of a mutual threat, a common objectification as "us-object." Ironically, solidarity is fundamentally not an overcoming of alienation but rather the mutual suffering of a new alienation.[58] Positive and active solidarity arises only from this negative or passive solidarity: "The oppressed class can . . . affirm itself as we-subject only through relation to the oppressive class and at its expense—that is, by transforming it in its turn into 'they-objects.' "[59]

For Sartre I arrive at the experience of 'we' only by experiencing myself as one of the 'they'. Sartre here reappropriates Heidegger's description of *das Man* in the world of the ready-to-hand. In my everyday existence I repeatedly have to use "instruments" that are designed for "anybody" and "everybody." The subway, maps, exit signs, etc., are designed not for my use but for anybody's use and I use them only by doing what everybody does. "They" designed the subway, for another "they"; in using it I am one of a "they" following a route laid out by another "they." "When I realize my project as but one of a thousand identical projects, all projected by the same undifferentiated transcendence, I experience a common transcendence directed toward a unique end of which I am but an ephemeral particularization. I insert myself into the broad human stream."[60] I enter into a common "rhythm," *our* rhythm. Is this not, for example in "the rhythmic work of a crew,"[61] real being-with? No. Rather than transcending it toward my very own possibilities, I "slur my transcendence together with its transcendence, and my own end . . . is an end of the 'They' that is not distinguished from the characteristic end of the collectivity."[62] In doing so, I may have a psychological feeling of community: "we" are doing something together. But this psychological feeling is merely subjective, by no means necessarily shared, and, far from being a direct being-with-Others, it is merely a by-product of my submission to the same instruments to which the Other is submitting. It is an extremely "unstable" experience, "for it requires particular organizations in the midst of the world and it disappears with those organizations."[63]

The "we-subject" is then "a psychological experience realized by an historical man who is plunged into a universe of work in a society of a specific economic type."[64] Sartre's indirect and subtle *coup de grâce* to Heidegger's *Mitsein* is based on this psychological and socioeconomic interpretation of being-with. It is *the bourgeois* who has a special stake in appealing to an inherent being-with: "he opposes to class solidarity a more spacious solidarity . . . where the worker and the employer are integrated by a *Mitsein* that suppresses the conflict."[65] Thus Heidegger's philosophy is—perhaps unwittingly—implicated in a purely epochal political conservatism, a bourgeois humanism. Heidegger's authentic being-with, as a deliverance from 'theyness', is in fact a move from identification with one 'they' (the oppressed class) to identification with another 'they' (the oppressive class) and thus a rationalization of the status quo. In expressing the ambitions of a class, however, Heidegger's philosophy is performing the function that the later Sartre will hold to be the function of all philosophies.[66] There is no univeral historical or ontological community. "Thus human-reality seeks in vain to escape this dilemma: either one transcends the Other or one lets oneself be transcended by him. The essence of the relations between consciousnesses is not *Mitsein*. It is conflict."[67] Here, as always for Sartre, the Heideggerian precedent community of nature explodes into antitheses. At the level of phenomenological ontology, which for Sartre interdicts real synthesis, conflict is unsurpassable. Will not Sartre have to have recourse to the level of *metaphysics* if he is to justify the possibility of real and efficacious social community?

III

Consideration of being-for-Others has brought us into the arena of history (the for-itself's temporalization in the presence of Others). From the foregoing it is clear that history is for Sartre fundamentally an arena of conflict and alienation. It is not, as for Heidegger, essentially a region of being-with. Furthermore this alienation of individual by individual, of individual by group, and of group by group appears to be irremediable. Just as the origin and goal of being-for-itself in an original and final totality or whole is a mere metaphysical hypothesis for which there is no phenomenal evidence, so the origin and goal of being-for-Others in an original and final totality (Universal Mind or Spirit) is a mere metaphysical hypothesis. What appears, empirically and historically, is only the contingent fact of *detotalized* totality, disharmony, diaspora— without metaphysical ground or rationale. Rather, the for-itself and its history are *haunted* by this absent metaphysical ground or rationale. Just as Cartesian man identifies himself as imperfect only in relation to a Perfect Being,[68] so Sartrean man identifies himself as schizoid, sick, and degraded relative to a speculative once-and-future whole—the One, God, Mind. Yet Sartre writes that "These considerations do not rule out the possibility of an ethics of deliverance and salvation."[69] I have already identified an implicit Sartrean ethic in the form of a religion of artful play that "lives the ambiguity" rather than trying to cancel it. It settles for a merely symbolic metaphysical resolution and is thus a renunciation, insofar as possible, of the metaphysical quest. It refuses to regard either individual temporalization or social and cultural history as a "romance." Reconciled to the impossibility of actual synthesis with being-in-itself, it slides across the surface of being in a symbolic dialectical synthesis. Hegelian progress drops down to symbolic dialectic. The Heideggerian project to achieve a *unified* comprehension of Being is rejected as lying essentially outside the scope of phenomenological ontology, in metaphysics.

The very vehemence of the public and critical response to Sartre's conclusions seems proof of Sartre's delineation of the importance to man of the metaphysical quest. Sartre was proclaimed a nihilist, an inhumanist, a pessimist. After reading *EN*, students committed suicide, clerics chastised, communists attacked.[70] Everyone with any stake in totality—which may be all of us—found *EN* unsatisfactory. It was not long before its author found it unsatisfactory, and in later years he confessed that *EN* was itself motivated by a metaphysical quest[71]—perhaps the best proof of all of the ubiquity and tenacity of this quest.

We know that Sartre responded in *EH* to almost all of the charges laid at his door; existentialism is a humanism, an optimism, a solidaritarian philosophy of human betterment. Two aspects of this response deserve our attention—its invocation of freedom as a goal and the practical inefficacy of this response. Both of these aspects bear on the problem of action with which this chapter began. Both bear as well on the question of what might be called Sartre's "turn" as distinguished from Heidegger's "turn."

We have seen, in chapter 5, that in *EH* Sartre proposes freedom as the sole nonalienating and nondeceptive end or "value." I noted in passing that he does so by grounding his proposal in the "logical virtues" of honesty and coherence. A value is admissible only insofar as it does not contradict the *source* of value, which is freedom itself. But freedom is necessarily thrown freedom, a freedom that temporally-ekstatically surpasses itself toward an end. As freedom is thus necessarily situated freedom, 'situation' will become, ethically regarded, nothing other than the pursuit of freedom *in the world*. It was suggested in chapter 5 that the balance of Sartre's career can be seen as the effort to understand what sort of 'situation', and what sort of 'world', would be compatible with the pursuit of freedom as an end and a value. We also saw that in *QL* Sartre characterizes this 'situation' very broadly as that of perpetual revolution. It is the office of the writer to provoke such revolution by being "in a state of perpetual antagonism toward the conservative forces which are maintaining the balance he tends to upset."[72] By the time of *Les Mots* Sartre has been forced to conclude that words change nothing—an ironic confirmation of his own nominalism.

But practical efficacy had become a problem long before *Les Mots*. I have argued that the return from reflexive withdrawal—from anxiety and analysis—is both a metaphysical and a moral problem. The broad outline of the moral return is given by the proposal of freedom as an end. But this proposal remains abstract. This abstractness can be noted in the 1945 lecture *EH*, where taking freedom as an end suggests little more than an individualistic humanism of a very general and ideal sort; each individual should choose in the knowledge that in so doing he "makes himself" and that he can consistently take freedom as a goal only if he takes that of others as a goal as well.[73] It was with some justice that, in a discussion following the lecture, the French Marxist Pierre Naville reproached Sartre for reviving a lofty "old-time liberalism" that "doesn't admit the truth of history."[74] Naville charged Sartre with an inconsequential "idealism" that "comes out of an arbitrary scorn for things."[75] Though publicly Sartre vigorously defended himself against these charges, there can be no doubt that privately, and at the same time or soon thereafter, he laid roughly these same charges against himself. The proof of this is to be found not only in Sartre's subsequent writings but more immediately in his response to Francis Jeanson's study *Le Problème moral et la pensée de Sartre* (1947).

After an extremely sympathetic exposition of Sartre's thought, Jeanson feels compelled to conclude: "what we fear . . . is that this movement, far from being too dangerous, may lack efficacy."[76] A philosophy that places a premium on self-consciousness and reflexive purification or mediation of the "natural attitude," it is also a philosophy that holds any effort to *remain* in reflexive withdrawal to be inauthentic.[77] Pure unreflective immediacy is inauthentic and alienating; pure reflective mediacy is equally inauthentic. How can one maintain the ambiguity, one's simultaneous in-and-outness, separateness and involvement? The fact is that, thus far, Sartre's thought has been much clearer about the nature of purifying reflection than about the nature of purified involvement. Precisely because of the nature of purifying reflection, in fact, "purified involvement" may appear to be a contradiction in terms. But in fact, for Sartre, neither reflection alone nor involvement alone can be purifying. Reflection per se could be purifying only if man were essentially consciousness. Involvement per se could be purifying only if man were essentially body. If one is to be what one is (ambiguous), reflection must purify involvement and involvement must purify reflection. And yet, thus far, the reflective moment of the dialectic has held the upper hand. It is clear that this one-sided reflexivity must be counterbalanced. *But how?* The needed balance between reflexion and involvement, analysis and synthesis, is rendered all the more problematic by Sartre's own elaborate descriptions of the powerful pull of the bad faith of flight from embodiment on the one hand and flight from consciousness on the other hand. To be sure, he outlines a mode of coordination of the two— symbolic synthesis—but it "lacks efficacy." This is the heart of the dilemma. Assuming that Sartre could offer a specific rather than abstract moral response to a specific contemporary historical situation, would it not remain theoretically impossible for the agent to carry out that response? Synthesis can only be symbolic; genuine modification of the in-itself by the for-itself and genuine social community are by definition impossible within the limits of phenomenonological ontology, for which negation is primary and unsurpassable. But if moral action is merely symbolic, sliding over the surface without leaving a trace, it essentially alters nothing. It "lacks efficacy." This is the problem of action to which I have been calling attention.

Jeanson finds existentialism in 1947 to be "at a dangerous turning point."[78] From its Kierkegaardian beginnings, it has been a peculiarly reflexive philosophy. It withdraws from an "inauthentic" sociopolitico-historical involvement that smothers the sense of individual agency and self-identity, in order that one may in reflexive isolation "authentically" define oneself in terms of freely chosen possibilities. On this view, involvement appears as a threat to *self*-identification. In Hegel, as Kierkegaard saw him, the self seems defined not by itself but by its historical circumstances. Historical necessity eliminates individual possibility.

Consequently, the most critical problem of existentialism has been to find an acceptable way of recommitting oneself to society and history without losing the sense of personal agency and self-direction gained through reflexive separation from society and history. To paraphrase Kant, reflexive separation seems empty; historical immersion seems blind. Sartre is wary of two opposite modes of alienation: solipsism on the one hand, historical immersion on the other. In Jeanson's words:

> The temptation is great to turn either toward a transcendental philosophy ignorant of individual historical situations or toward an exclusive preoccupation with historicity. In this sense we can say that the ambiguity can be maintained to the very end only on condition of realizing some synthesis between radical conversion and historical progress [cheminement] or, to put it another way, between the realism of authenticity in Husserl or even in Heidegger and the realism of History in Marx.
>
> Such no doubt is the prognosis for overcoming the dilemma between individualism and communism.[79]

In a foreword to Jeanson's book, Sartre affirmed that Jeanson had indeed anticipated the direction in which his thought was moving.[80] But, granting the Sartrean need for history, why *Marxian* history? Can Marxian history, or the conflation of Marxian history and Sartrean ambiguity, really solve the moral and metaphysical problem of action? Can it make possible a social action that is anything other than that of individuals in unresolvable conflict with each other? Sartre, who characteristically relegates some of his most revealing assertions to footnotes, writes in a footnote to *CRD:*

> this will to transcend the oppositions of externality and internality, of multiplicity and unity, of analysis and synthesis, of nature and antiphysis, is actually the most profound *theoretical* contribution of Marxism. Yet these are but suggestions to be developed; it would be a mistake to believe the task is easy.[81]

This statement is important in two respects. First, it locates the possible source of genuine correlation between transcendence and historicity in Marxian theory. Second, it locates the most profound theoretical contribution of Marxism in a will (*volonté*) to harmonize oppositions rather than in the accomplishment of this will. One might (correctly) construe the latter to mean that the actual accomplishment of this will requires an existentialist revision of Marxian theory. But it means even more. It signals the entry into Sartrean thought of a moral will to "totalize," to "progress," to harmonize, to take root rather than slide over the surface of nature and history. If there was an "arbitrary scorn for things" (Naville) in Sartre's early thought, it is here challenged by a countervailing will.

For Sartre, the solution to the problem of action cannot be demonstrated or deduced from phenomenological ontology; it must be introduced by an act of will. Here I defer to another important insight of Jeanson. After having outlined the solution to the Sartrean problem I have quoted, Jeanson notes that this does not mean an escape from *conviction*. Rather: "The essential thing is to understand that conviction must not be belief [*croyance*] but rather faith [*foi*], for belief addresses itself to *that which is*—whether in the realm of facts or in that of ideas—and can only be bad faith; but faith concerns *him who exists* and makes his existence his own. . . ."[82]

In other words, bad faith can be exorcised only by faith, not by knowledge or by phenomenological description. This is the case because human being, and everything the human being touches, is antinomic. Man is antinomic: his project is self-contradictory. Being-for-Others is antinomic: as reciprocal negation, it is conflict. World is antinomic: the real is a merely virtual synthesis of a logically contradictory and unsynthesizable plenitude and nothingness. Under the rule of traditional logic to which the phenomenological ontology of *EN* is bound, there are several irreducible antinomies that interdict synthesis. There appears to be only one way out, which is the exercise of *metaphysical* will or 'faith', the regulative use of reason to ground and govern action or practice. But this is not the importation into human activity of an additional, foreign factor. It is the moral reaffirmation of the for-itself's own project, which is a project to achieve synthetic totality, a "totalizing." It is at the same time, we shall see, a revindication of the region of 'the real'—'world'—as the genuinely "concrete." It is fundamentally a matter of *the revindication of teleology*. But it is a revindication solely of the teleology of which we have direct experience, a human teleology and not a divine teleology, and hence this revindication makes only a *limited* recourse to metaphysics.

Sartre's implicit recourse to metaphysical regulation and faith seems to bear an unmistakable similarity to that of both Kant and Kierkegaard. But neither Kant nor Kierkegaard is Marx, and it is Marx whom Sartre now chiefly invokes. Furthermore, *CRD* offers not simply a doctrine of faith but a doctrine of truth. Sartre's "turn" and its resolution of the problem of action is complex; "it would be a mistake to believe the task is easy," he has warned. It requires a complex adjudication of the legitimate claims of Kant, of Hegel, of

Marx, of Kierkegaard, of the early Sartre (and, through the latter, of Descartes, Husserl, Heidegger). Sartre's reassessment of man's place in history necessitates reassessment of existentialism's place in the history of modern philosophy and society. Sartre's turn, like Heidegger's, requires acknowledgment that his early thought was insufficiently aware of its indebtedness to history and the logic of history. It is a matter of recognizing the ironic fact of his having been historical in being antihistorical, the fact of the inherence of his early thought in "our great classical tradition which since Descartes . . . has been completely hostile to History."[83]

Sartre, whose "style" Jeanson has called "a flight forward,"[84] now finds it necessary to go back, to reinsert himself and his thought in the history they were already in. Having promised Camus that he would subject himself to the same harsh criticism to which he had subjected Camus,[85] Sartre writes in Les Mots:

> I could not grant that one received being from without, that it was preserved by inertia, and that the impulses of the mind were the effect of earlier impulses. . . . The past had not made me. On the contrary, it was I, rising from my ashes, who plucked my memory from nothingness by an act of creation which was always being repeated. . . . I had stuffed my soul with the continuous progress of the bourgeois and had turned it into an internal combustion engine. I subordinated the past to the present and the present to the future; I transformed a quiet evolutionism into a revolutionary and discontinuous catastrophism.[86]

A few pages later Sartre writes: "Naturally I'm not taken in. I'm quite aware that we repeat ourselves. But this more recently acquired knowledge undermines my old certainties without quite destroying them."[87] This last observation is not, as might appear, simply the recording of a biographical fact—Sartre's inability to liberate himself altogether from what he calls his "old certainties." These old certainties—bourgeois individualism, revolutionary discontinuity, continuous progress, creation ex nihilo—are being subjected to an Hegelian judgment. They are being taken into history as neither absolutely true nor absolutely false. Sartre's old certainties—his early existentialism—are true as correctives to inherited truths that were themselves correctives. Sartre finds that the price of truth is partiality, is being a 'moment' in a Truth that becomes, that is temporal and historical. Sartre is forced to situate himself in the bacchanalian revel; the drunkard can no longer be solitary.[88] Sartre is a man among men, and men are "madmen."[89] His chief criticism of his early thought is that it took itself to be written from a standpoint of pure transcendence, emancipated by purifying reflection from rootedness in muddy and sticky inertia. Sartre, romantically perched on a private moral and metaphysical eyrie above the revel, looked down on the vain revellers with the cynical detachment of the French moralists. Seeing the human folly whole in its timeless sameness, he was freed of it, saved. With the benefit of hindsight, Sartre sees himself as a complex web of contradictions: an atheist who took "holy orders," a nominalist who "regarded words as the quintessence of things," a critic of romantic linearity whose career would be a linear romance.[90] Even now, hopefully freed of his romanticism, he sees his career as a story, a romance. In *EH* he had declared: "Existentialism is nothing else than an attempt to draw all the consequences of a coherent atheistic position."[91] And in *Les Mots* he writes: "I collared the Holy Ghost in the cellar and threw him out; atheism is a cruel and long-range affair: I think I've carried it through. . . . For the last ten years or so I've been a man who's been waking up, cured of a long, bitter-sweet madness."[92] Autoanalysis has laid bare the motivational source of Sartre's childhood neurosis and its pervasive subterranean influence on him ("the Holy Ghost in the cellar") and has enabled him to renounce the motive and conquer the neurosis, religious idealism.

In his study of Genet in 1952, Sartre had written: "I think, along with many others, that it is necessary to shorten the convulsions of a dying world, to help in the birth of a producing community and to try to draw up, with the workers and militants, the table of new values."[93] The table of *old* values, which he learned at his grandfather's knee, had been a table of bourgeois values guaranteed by religion. Sartre the Marxian revolutionary will "shorten the convulsions of a dying world" by striking at the opiate of that world's masses. Victimized by a world that conditioned him to expect a private salvation—in his case, by words—he will now strive for the establishment of a world in which the realism of salvation by communal work will replace the idealism of salvation by magical and merely verbal flights from reality. The child must be conditioned not to a neurotic escapism but to realistic solution of practical problems common to all men. Sartre will work for a world in which the child, spared the crippling self-centered neurosis of a Sartre, will be freed for the creation of a socialist society. Victorious over a religion that separates men into the saved and the damned, that offers salvation as a consolation prize to society's dispossessed, Sartre at last joins a common humanity.

One is tempted to say: What a story! A gigantic lifelong encounter with religious idealism, culminating in victory—it sounds suspiciously like a *romance*, like evidence of the romantic idealism Sartre thinks he has conquered. But in *Les Mots* Sartre sees and admits this contradiction.[94] It is at just this point that Sartre, like anyone who speaks of himself with real candor, becomes vulnerable to critical assault. The critic will miss the fundamental point of *Les Mots* if he does not interpret it in light of Sartre's *philosophical* turn. Nothing could be easier than to dismiss *Les Mots* by invoking elementary logic: it says nothing because it contradicts itself. "Obviously" Sartre cannot be both romantic and antiromantic, both mad and lucid, both bourgeois and antibourgeois, both existentialist and Marxist.[95] But such arguments presuppose the absoluteness of the very "analytic reason" whose absoluteness Sartre now challenges. It is, in fact, in this challenge that a central aspect of Sartre's "turn" is to be found. We must now examine how Sartre's relocation of himself and his thought within history depends upon an adjustment in his understanding of the logic and rationality of history. From the standpoint of *EN*, this adjustment requires shifting from the level of phenomenological ontology to the level of metaphysics.

IV

Sartre writes in *CRD* that "the problem is to determine *on what level* we place ourselves in order to define reality."[96] There is possible here what might be called a certain metaphysical leeway. From the level of phenomenological ontology in *EN*, 'reality' appears to Sartre as a merely virtual synthesis of relata that are in principle antithetical. If one takes the wholly actual (being-in-itself) and nothingness as the ultimate "elements" of the world, as a "standard," then by comparison with this standard the 'real' is secondary, "merely" real, and efficacious 'action' (alteration or transformation of being) is impossible. But if one exercises metaphysical will or faith one can shift to another level; one can will 'world' or 'the real' as the standard, as one's proper environment. From *this* level, the effort to judge the real by reference to a standard or standpoint external to it will appear as a "flight from reality," a devaluation of the environment in which our lives must be lived. From *this* level, the religion of artful play will appear as escapist, as aestheticism, and an individual ethic of lucidity will appear as abstract and inefficacious.

What happens, then, in the later Sartre is not so much a renunciation of his earlier phenomenological ontology as its reappropriation at another level. It is a matter of a shift of accent necessitated by the move from the level of detached reflection to the level of 'action'. An effort is made to bring to action the results of the earlier reflection, yet the *interpretation* placed on the results of the earlier reflection is modified by its insertion into the now-justified context of action.

Terminologically and actually, 'praxis' establishes the reorientation, the shift of level. We have seen that *EN* was in the last analysis oriented by being-in-itself and being-for-itself, or by being and nonbeing, and not by action; indeed we have seen that action is still an unsolved problem at the end of *EN*. Because action was a problem, no genuine interaction between consciousness and being could be considered. Hence *EN* repeatedly "breaks the circle," or analytically distinguishes between the source of intention in nothingness and the source of thing in plenitude, in such a way that intentional (in both the technical and the ordinary senses of this term) constitution and transformation of the environment are frustrated. All intentional or intended wholes or totalities are ideal, ontologically impossible. There is no integrity because there can be no ontological integration. The completeness of the circle, the One, haunts the for-itself as the impossible terminus of his truncated circular affair with his environment. Circularity thus appears as an impossible effort to transform one's environment by sinking intentionally into it. By contrast we find the following in *CRD:*

> The major discovery of the dialectical experience . . . is that man is "mediated" by things to the exact extent that things are "mediated" by man. We shall have to bear in mind the whole

of this truth, in order to develop all its consequences. It is what
is called dialectical *circularity*. . . .[97]

This mediation, or truly dialectical circularity, can be called 'totalizing' or the making of history by praxis:

> The whole historical dialectic rests upon the individual
> praxis, insofar as the latter is already dialectical—that is, to the
> extent that action is, by itself, the negating transcending of a
> contradiction, the determination of a present totalization in the
> name of a future totality, *the real and efficacious labor upon mat-
> ter*.[98]

One is struck by the phrase "real and efficacious" where one
would expect from the early Sartre "(merely) real and (hence) inefficacious." The passage speaks of the *transcending* of a contradiction. One also notes that Sartre now speaks of man as 'organism'
rather than as 'for-itself'.[99] The term 'organism' implies an integral
whole. In accordance with the shift of stress from man's for-
itselfness to his organic character, the former's 'lack' has become the
latter's 'need'; metaphysical absence has become absence *of food*,[100]
and this latter absence is one which can in principle and often in
practice be filled. The accent now falls more on the "living body"
and "the organic totality" or "living totality"[101] than on the self as
ideal and impossible fusion of consciousness and body. To be sure,
"the organism can act upon the environment only by falling provisionally back to the level of inertia," but it is *the organism* that acts
and its acts are *"inscribed in Being [inscrit dans l'Être]."*[102] The term
'praxis' indicates practical action, the action of an organism in need.
The metaphysical problem of action is resolved by reconceiving action as praxis:

> The organic totality, in order to find its being in nature or to
> protect itself against destruction, must become inert matter, for
> it is as a mechanical system that *it can modify the material envi-
> ronment:* the man in need is an organic totality who perpetually
> makes himself his own tool in the realm of exteriority. The
> organic totality acts upon inert bodies through the intermedi-
> ary of the inert body *which it is*. . . .[103]

In other words, on the level of praxis there is *always already* a
functional unity (organism) of consciousness and body, of thought

and matter. Let us not be misunderstood: this is also the case in *EN*. But in *EN* this prior synthesis becomes, through analysis, both ontologically derivative and a logical and metaphysical problem. The conclusion of *EN* tells us, it will be recalled, that the "problem" of action can only be attacked "after having decided the question of the origin of the for-itself and of the nature of the phenomenon of the world."[104] *CRD* locates the origin of the for-itself in the *organism* as "living body" existing in "dialectical time."[105] *CRD* identifies the world as the practical organization of the inorganic as real meaning-beings, *real fusions* by which meaning has *"come into Being"* and is "engraved into Being."[106] Here Sartre's 'Being' no longer stands outside of time, non-Being has entered Being itself, and what fundamentally governs the characterization of Being is not analysis but praxis. Sartre now shares the common will and faith in praxis. Thus the ontological and metaphysical conditions are met for the operation of dialectic as a totalization that achieves *genuine syntheses* ('affirmations') by negation of ('labor' upon) a negation (inorganic, external 'matter' as needed, scarce, and recalcitrant).

We note, further, that the practical organism—as befits an organism but not a for-itself or a consciousness—has an "interior" or "inside" *in* which there are "immanent" needs, habits, meanings. The organism has material, physiochemical, and biological "structures" and "functions."[107] These structures and functions are however not separate systems but are a functional unity or "living unity" as a temporal activity or transcendence.[108] There is a "cyclical process" of organic self-renewal, "an elementary synthesis of change and identity,"[109] since the organism must change in order to remain the same. That is, the organism must satisfy its present need in order to be in future the totality that it has been. This repeated cycle of self-renewal or repetition "characterizes both biological time and that of the earliest societies."[110] So long as there is no interruption of this smooth recycling, so long as the future is essentially the same as the past, there is no 'History'. History arises when 'scarcity' makes self-renewal, the future maintenance of the organic totality, into a mere 'possibility' and "the possibility of its own impossibility." "This interruption is lived *as a negation,* in the simple sense that the cyclical movement or function reproduces itself to no effect, and by just this denies the identification of future with past. . . ."[111] The contingent fact of scarcity means that "there is not enough for everyone."[112] Unless scarcity is equally suffered by all, relations of production, distribution, and consumption institute radical inequalities between man and man. These inequalities take the form of economic-cultural hierarchies; some men are constituted as "expendable." This violence then breeds counter-violence; groups form to challenge the exploitation and solitude they cannot individually ('serially') counter with any effectiveness. Able to consolidate themselves against the external threat only by the internal violence of the 'oath' and 'terror', the group in time petrifies into an 'institution' that is the 'ossification' of the group-praxis into a thing. The individual now finds himself born into the 'prefabricated' destiny of maintaining the institution for its own sake rather than for the original purpose of gaining, by closing ranks, the restitution that could not be gained serially. The individual now ironically suffers in the institution the serial impotence that the original group had sought to overcome.

Thus the contingent fact of scarcity has initiated both an 'exteriorization' of the interior and a 're-interiorization'.[113] What this essentially means is that the individual organic cycle, which was organically self-sufficient, a self-maintaining cycle within itself ('interior'), has had its smooth repetitive cycle of unimpeded self-renewal exploded by an absence of ready sustenance. There is need of a future essentially *different* from the present. One recognizes in this a reappropriation of Sartre's early vision of the One ("organic" unity) exploded by Nothingness (lack, absence) into spatiotemporal diaspora, a breaking of the original circle or plenitude of being. As a lack of material density (food), the organism experiences its dependence on an environment 'exterior' to it (inert inorganic matter) and must adapt itself to that environment, work it over, in an attempt ('project') to 're-interiorize' the lacked matter. The organism must complete the broken cycle and become once again an internally complete self-renewing cycle. Until and unless this restoration of the cyclic is accomplished, the organism will experience itself as lack of the needed and will experience the spatiotemporal field as a material environment in which it must lose itself (by apprenticing itself, making itself an instrument reworking matter, etc.) in order to recoup itself. History is an odyssey in which the organism wanders in laborious search of its lost self-sufficiency. History is the quest for practical retotalization.

Other organisms have experienced the same explosion of interior cyclic unity at the hands of scarcity. Reappropriating his earlier analysis of being-for-Others, Sartre once again finds conflict to be the essential social relation: the Other and I compete for the scarce. We seek to make each other instruments for our own 'retotalization'. If we form a 'group', this communality or solidarity is owing to our mutual objectification or alienation by a Third (feudal lord, king, factory owner, the bourgeoisie).[114] This community, being non-spontaneous and derivative, is highly unstable; it is maintained only under external threat (mutual threat) or internal threat ('terror'). When finally free of external threat (when the group dominates), the stringent conventions or regulations the group had to invent in order to consolidate itself or conquer its serial impotence outlast inertially their original purpose. These regulations become unjustifiable institutional restrictions upon the individual freedom originally intended by the members of the group.[115]

It would appear that the explosion of individual totalities under threat of scarcity provokes a mutual retotalization that is unstable and transient precisely because this *mutual* retotalization is only a means to *individual* retotalization. The group is but a means to individual ends. Furthermore, it would appear that history is but a repetition of the rise and decay of groups without any real progress being made toward the original purpose of retotalization, which was restoration of the original "prehistoric" unity of the organism. Is not the conclusion of *EN* here reappropriated: metaphysically regarded, the development of history appears as a cosmic drama whose goal is the restoration of an original unity—yet there is no phenomenal evidence for the original unity and no possibility of a final unity?

To read *CRD* this way, one would have to ignore several important considerations. (1) It is not a theory of history but rather a theory of the ideal (abstract) development of "practical ensembles."[116] (2) Its fundamental purpose is to develop a theory of the *intelligibility* of groups.[117] (3) Sartre's thought has shifted from the level of what he had called phenomenological ontology (analysis of phenomena into their irreducible ontological relata) to that of practical totalizing. On this level, we have seen, the old distinction between ontological analysis of human aspiration as logically self-contradictory and metaphysical resolution of the contradiction does not hold. Analysis itself becomes part of the metaphysical quest for totality, the metaphysical quest for totality becomes the historical and material quest, and Sartre is committed to that quest. CRD illustrates this shift of level insofar as it treats human activity as praxis, as real transformation of matter by a material organism. But in its preoccupation with development of a general and abstract theory of the origin, nature and intelligibility of groups, it merely prepares the way for a theory of history; once again, it is necessary that one not "totalize too quickly."[118] The theory of history (CRD, II), like Sartre's announced Ethics, never appeared. And yet, as had been the case with the Ethics, one finds anticipations of it, both in the body of CRD and especially in its preface, QM, for the latter was intended as the preface to the whole of CRD rather than just to volume I. We need to consider next, in chapter 12, these anticipations of a philosophy of history in order better to understand the meaning and direction of Sartre's later ontological thought, its relation to phenomenology, and its relation to Heidegger.

It may first be useful to summarize the ground traversed in this chapter. Sartre had found phenomenological ontology incapable of accounting for instrumental action as genuine modification of the being of externality. He had also found it incapable of justifying efficacious moral and social action, because EN finds interpersonal relations to be limited by an unsurpassable negation that entails unresolvable conflict, and because EN reaches no conclusion as to whether human freedom can and should take itself for an ethical end. But by shifting to the level of metaphysics Sartre seeks to solve both the instrumental and social aspects of the problem of action. At this point he passes beyond phenomenological description and exercises the metaphysical will and faith necessary for committing himself to the practical transformation of the actual that had appeared impossible at the level of phenomenological ontology. The level of 'reality' or practical synthesis takes priority over the level of a 'phenomenology' for which being and consciousness are simply antithetical. This shift of level is a commitment to the logic of praxis as it occurs in concrete history—as contrasted with the abstract and one-sided logic of analysis as it had occurred in the implicitly transhistorical descriptions in *EN*. Furthermore, as chapter 12 will show, the logic of history for Sartre represents a movement toward practical freedom, fully answering Sartre's question as to whether human freedom can and should take itself for an end—a question Sartre had already answered affirmatively, but only individualistically and ahistorically, in *EH* (chapter 6).

The logic of negation had required Sartre's critique of Heidegger's existentiale 'Being-with' as an unjustifiable attempt to define social community (and its attendant Heideggerian notion of a common social 'destiny'), rather than conflict, as ontologically fundamental. It might be thought that Sartre's shift to a genuine logic of synthesis would undercut his critique of Heidegger's Being-with. But it must be recognized that the later Sartre's logic of synthesis, as a dialectical logic, still regards negation as fundamental. Practical synthesis is accomplished by negation of a prior negation. This means that social community is *to be achieved* by the overcoming of social negations, rather than community being an inherent, structural, or definitional trait of the human being, as in *SZ*. This difference once again demonstrates the fundamental gap separating the Heideggerian ontology of precedent community and the Sartrean ontology of dualities or polarities. Methodologically, this gap entails a confrontation between the notion of unmediated identity-and-difference and the notion of dialectical mediation. Is the future to be essentially a coming to terms with what already is, or essentially the filling of a lack?

12

Man's Place in the Spiral: Beyond Atomism

CHAPTER 11 has outlined the nature of the turn in Sartre's later thinking. The present chapter seeks to show the ontological consequences of this shift for the human being, for environmental beings, and for their interrelation. We shall find these consequences in *QM*, *CRD*, *IF*, and in Sartre's philosophically significant self-critique in *Words*. The key consequences are a return to the ordinary, a series of characterizations of the rationality of teleological praxis, and the notion of the spiral as a movement from atomism to totality.

I

The most significant trait of *QM*, despite its elaborate existentialist and Hegelian-Marxian vocabularies, is its labor over the ordinary and the obvious. It is a revindication of the ordinary and the obvious, and this accords with Sartre's new understanding of himself as just a man among men,[1] one who has neither as man nor as philosopher a privileged standpoint. One may regard this insistence on the ordinary and the obvious as scandalous. Surely a philosopher has something better to do than call our attention to what is obvious to the point of triviality. Surely the vocation of both philosopher and scientist is that of taking us *behind* the obvious to its real import. Surely the early Sartre attempted to do so. Surely modern science has shown that real explanation consists in getting behind certain ordinary meanings and ordinary teleology (behind formal and final causation) to real meaning and real action (to material and efficient causation). Surely it would be irrational to attempt a return to naïve and outdated Aristotelian modes of explanation.

Sartre can respond to these charges by pointing out the effect of material and efficient explanation and analytic reasoning on both "the human sciences" and his own early thought. *QM* and *CRD* repeatedly attack the allegedly dominant methodology of the social sciences. Psychology, sociology, anthropology, economics, and history have succumbed to a one-sided reliance on material and efficient causation and analytic reasoning.[2] This has had several consequences: (1) an 'atomism' that regards individuals as discrete units by disregarding the meaning-relations that bind them to each other;[3] (2) an 'inhumanism' that regards man as less than and other than what he is—as a state of matter, a bundle of drives, a merely physiochemical structure, a statistical mean;[4] (3) a 'fetishism' that makes a fetish of human 'products' by seeking to understand man solely in terms of those products and not also in terms of the teleological activity that produced those products;[5] (4) an 'a priorism' or 'formalism' that maps an abstract categorial unity (e.g., 'thing', 'ego', 'mechanism', 'class', 'collective') on individuals or groups without investigating how these individuals and groups came to be as they are.[6]

Sartre's own early thought is not free of these problems and of the method and outlook of which they are consequences. In retrospect his early thought is guilty of a form of atomism; owing to the stress placed on an unsurpassable negation as principle of individuation, individual for-itselfs have no genuine relations, other than negation, with either being-in-itself or other for-itselfs. The 'this', whose problematic nature was explored in some detail in chapter 10, is a consequence of this same atomic tendency in the early Sartre. His early thought is guilty of a form of inhumanism; because of the dominance of analysis over synthesis, the 'world' of the 'real' in which man has to live is treated as essentially and necessarily a region of alienation. His early thought is guilty of a sort of fetishism insofar as it is excessively preoccupied with an abstract reflective freedom isolated from real praxis. His early thought is guilty of 'a priorism' insofar as it takes the abstract categories 'in-itself' and 'for-itself' to be a kind of acid in which all wholes can be dissolved into their elements and insofar as it takes the traditional distinction between philosophy and practice to be self-evidently valid.

To be sure, Sartre already had, and had used, some of the tools necessary for going beyond these problems: intentionality and teleology. What he did not have was freedom from the conditioning of bourgeois culture and its philosophy. Naville was right; Sartre was operating from within an "old time liberalism" that "doesn't admit the truth of history." [7] He now sees that he is *a cultural being* both philosophically and personally. He finds philosophies expressive of, and instruments of, the praxis of a class and he isolates three philosophies in the modern period: "there is the 'moment' of Descartes and Locke, that of Kant and Hegel, finally that of Marx." [8] Each has a relative truth but becomes false if taken as absolute or final. Sartre, in retrospect, appears to locate his early thought in the 'moment' of Kant and Hegel, which is the moment of bourgeois individualism, of encyclopedism, of appeal to an abstract and ideal rational unity and equality of all human beings who nevertheless remain essentially private individuals. This 'philosophy' is true insofar as it challenges the myth of inherent privilege or aristocratic rights, but it is false insofar as it settles for a unity, or universality, and an equality that remain ideal and abstract. The fixed and timeless Kantian categories, the ideal Kantian kingdom of ends, and the abstract rationality of the Hegelian system constitute half-truths that become errors and weapons of conservatism when they are used as means for preventing the achievement of a real and practical unified society of equals.

What Sartre thus discovers is that his early thought was unknowingly repeating an individualistic "idealism" that had been instilled in him as a child and reinforced by his education. [9] A philosophy is "a community of language" and of habits, and in learning the language and habits of his family and peers Sartre lived "the universal as particular" without knowing what he was doing. [10] Both for-itself and in-itself expressed a timeless ontology insofar as they ruled out real change. His implicit ethics was abstract, private, individualistic. His description of being-for-Others acquiesced in the social status quo by regarding real union of for-itselfs as impossible. Regarded methodologically, his philosophy was conservative since it held synthesis to be impossible. Sartre sees this as the real, practical import of a philosophy that had, ironically, taken itself to be "revolutionary." [11] But the genuinely revolutionary philosophy must for Sartre be the most recent, the one that is "simultaneously a totalization of knowledge, a method, a regulative Idea, an offensive weapon, and a community of language" [12] for the rising class, the class suffering injustice.

If we had to select one phrase that best expresses the shift in Sartre's outlook *and* methodology, the insertion of himself and his thought in history, that phrase would be 'practical totalizing'. It is 'totalizing' that characterizes the development of history, and history is the inevitable site of present human experience. The logic of totalizing is dialectical logic, which is essentially Hegelian logic. It is a logic that, in Kant's categorial terminology, understands 'totality' as a real synthesis of 'unity' and 'plurality'. The analytic logic that dominates in pre-Hegelian thought, and in Sartre's early thought, takes its place as a 'moment' of dialectical logic. It is significant that Sartre regards the achieving of an appropriate logic as a 'problem' of existentialism. "Its problem is to discover a supple, patient dialectic which espouses movements as they really are and which rejects the a priori view that all lived conflicts pose contradictories or even contraries." [13]

The logic of *EN* has been neither "supple" nor "patient." It was not supple insofar as it regarded conflicts categorically as cases of unsurpassable contradiction. It was impatient insofar as it jumped out of the real movement of history to a metahistorical vantage point that, with divine impartiality, summarily judged all human striving to be vain. Sartre learned from Merleau-Ponty, who was the immediate catalyst of his conversion to history, the importance of the patience that "keeps digging in the same place." [14] Again, one must not "totalize too quickly"; if there is to be real understanding of man and his history, it will have to be achieved gradually by men within history and not by one man in some suprahistorical moment of individual vision. [15] Truth is historical, it *becomes* true "progressively" by the patient labor of history, by successive reworking of inherited truths that are preserved as partial truths but canceled as absolute truths. The price of a truth remaining "alive" is that it be "surpassed" (*dépassé*), that it surrender its claim to be the whole truth. As one is a man among men, so one's truth is a truth among truths and must take its humble place in "a long labor." [16]

The philosopher must relearn how to be the ordinary man that he is. Sartre relearns his relative and temporal position. He has to conclude that his "philosophy," his existentialism, is only an "ideology," only "a parasitical system living on the margin of knowledge, which at first it opposed but into which today it seeks to be integrated." [17] That is, the individual recognizes his commonness, his place in the social and philosophical community. *And yet* the individual joins the community without surrendering his individuality; if Sartre is "no better than any" he is nevertheless "as good as any."[18] The price he exacts from the philosophy of community, Marxism, for his membership in it is a steep one—that existentialism be "absorbed, surpassed and conserved" in such a way as to become nothing less than "the foundation of all inquiry."[19] Sartre allows in *Les Mots* that he may be playing the game of "loser wins,"[20] and an existentialism that lost its status as 'philosophy' in order to win a place as foundation of all inquiry would be well compensated indeed for its loss of absoluteness. What all this means is that the Marxian 'moment' is not true knowledge of the nature of community until it has sufficiently 'absorbed' and 'conserved' what remains valid in the prior Cartesian and Kantian-Hegelian moments. Real community is a community *of cogitos* and a community *of real individuals* or 'ends' who surpass on their own behalf the very community to which they are necessarily subject: "We affirm the specificity of the human act, which cuts across the social milieu while still holding on to its determinations, and which transforms the world on the basis of given conditions."[21]

In other words, the "totalizing" is ultimately and necessarily that of individual praxis. In accord with the thesis that the nature of the beginning determines the nature of the outcome, Sartre insures that history will be a history of individuals by locating the beginning of history in the *organic individual*. Sartre accomplishes this by a striking transmutation of his early Plotinian tendency.

All Sartre's thought, early and late, is a study of phenomena relative to the One as origin and terminus of a diaspora. In Sartre's early thought, however, the One is only a speculative metaphysical hypothesis. In his later thought the One takes concrete form as the prehistoric organism. The One has become a plurality of Ones that, prior to scarcity, are self-sufficient, not needing a future essentially different than their past. At this point society is repetitive, rather than historical. But once these organisms experience scarcity as a negation of their 'interior' self-sufficiency, they become dependent on an 'exterior' matter and threatened by Others who are likewise dependent on the same limited quantity of external matter. There is then need of a future different than the past; history begins as the quest to gain the scarce, to internalize an external and needed matter. Each organism seeks to negate the original negation, hence to reaffirm its lost oneness. The Other is first the potential negation of my projected reaffirmation. He may, for example, hoard the limited food supply. The field of matter is both a negation of my projected reaffirmation, as the scarce, and the possibility of my projected reaffirmation, as a matter to be internalized or "humanized" or "put to work" on my behalf through labor. The attempted negation of negation through 'interiorization' of 'exteriority' is praxis.[22] These few assertions constitute the core of Sartre's later thought, for in them Sartre has sought to ground the possibility of both history and the understanding of history, while taking history to be the field of a praxis which resolves the problem of action.

These assertions define praxis as both action and comprehension. They define praxis as *logical* action on a matter that itself becomes comprehensible insofar as it is the object of action. They define social action as logical. Thus there is an interior logic of action, and any exteriority that falls within this logic (matter, Others) becomes logically comprehensible.[23] This is to say that intelligibility is grounded in intentionality and in practical teleology. We must note carefully what Sartre has done. He has construed the beginning of history in such a way that history is governed from beginning to end by the quest for totality. Totality, the restoration of the organism's original integrity or cyclic interiority, is the "regulative principle of totalization."[24] It is the organism's practical commitment to this ideal totality that causes the whole field of history and historical experience to appear as, and be comprehensible or intelligible as, stages on the way to totality.[25] In this frame of reference any present will appear as, or be comprehensible as, what it is relative to a past that has been surpassed and a future as yet unattained. This is merely to say that *teleology assembles the field* ("the totalizing activity tightens all the bonds")[26] so that everything past, present, and future means what it means relative to the end at which it is aimed and relative to the original sense of need that provoked one to take action. Hence to understand a particular historical action is essentially to understand where it stands in relation to the need that provoked it and the end that will satisfy the need. "The movement of comprehension is simultaneously progressive (toward the objective result) and regressive (I go back toward the original condition)."[27] This is the essential condition of historical knowledge; praxis *is* comprehension, or understanding what one is doing. Knowing what others are doing or have done is essentially nothing other than imaginatively recapitulating *their* action and comprehension by a progressive-regressive movement that asks what the agent originally needed (regressive aspect) and what he did by way of meeting that need (progressive aspect). Although Sartre's exposition of the "progressive-regressive method" is lengthy and apparently technical, it is fundamentally only a retracing of ordinary, everyday practical reasoning, the commonest thing in the world.

I suspect Sartre regarded it as scandalous that he should have to devote so many drily technical pages to the labor of description and justification of the mode of understanding inherent in the most elementary human practice. This is necessary because of the one-sided dominance of analytic or factorial reason and the mistrust of formal and teleological explanation in post-Cartesian culture. Sartre calls it the "horror of dialectic"[28]—a deeply ingrained mistrust of wholes that have not been reduced to their "molecular" or atomic elements. In philosophy and in science it has taken the form of the search for irreducible self-identical and independent beings—logical and material atoms—of which wholes are only temporary and evanescent syntheses. In social and political philosophy it has taken the form of pluralism and radical individualism. Relations between these material or private units are external—relations of efficient causation.

II

Because ordinary teleological reasoning *is* the commonest thing in the world, Sartre finds it to be the foundation of knowledge, of communication, of all historical understanding. Because "the original dialectical movement" is "in the individual and in his enterprise of producing his life, of objectifying himself,"[29] the following seven ontological and epistemological conditions, upon each of which I shall comment at some length, obtain. They spell out Sartre's conception of the rationality of human praxis and the ontology of beings as conceived from the standpoint of praxis.

1. The temporal, material, and social fields are *coherent*. Past, present, and future have an intelligible coherence as successive phases of praxis. If they lack such intelligible coherence, this lack is understood precisely as a demand for making them coherent. That is, incoherence and unintelligibility are understood to be a *privation*

of coherence, what *resists* praxis ('inertia', 'antidialectic', and the 'opaque').

One's material environment has an intelligible coherence relative to praxis—as a field of instruments of praxis or potential instruments of praxis. Here again, incoherence and unintelligibility are understood as a privation of, and demand for, coherence, unification, totalization, "interiorization."

The field of Others has an intelligible coherence relative to both their praxis and my own. Since our relation is one of reciprocity, the Other and I understand each other both as instruments in each other's practical field and as the pursuit of independent aims. These independent aims limit our reduction to pure instruments. Our *mutual* teleological praxis is understood as the possibility of both conflict and cooperation, of both serial impotence and solidaritarian power. The social field, then, is intelligible as a field of individuals all of whom are of the same teleological character. So the social field from the start and in principle is a community in the minimal sense of a universe or class of beings each of whom is the pursuit of its own organic reintegration. This minimal teleological community is the ground-possibility, or potentiality, of goal-oriented groups of any size up to and including *all* individuals.

2. The field of external and material instruments is intelligible as a field of instruments both for me (or my group) and for the Other (or his group). Thus this field is understood as having more than one meaning and as having contradictory meanings. Incoherence and unintelligibility in the instrumental field are comprehensible as the privation of, and demand for, coherence. Conflicts of ends are *inscribed in matter* by what might be called "practical intentionality"; hence contradiction between projects is at the same time contradiction *in* the material instruments "worked over" by these projects. (There is "dialectical materialism" only insofar as there are individual dialectical praxes.) Hence "subjective" conflicts are objective and material conflicts, and there can be unification of the field of Others only if there is unification of the field of instruments. The field of instruments is a field of "collective objects which people our social field and which may be conveniently called the midworld [*intermonde*]."[30] Sartre here comes explicitly to terms with Merleau-Ponty's criticism that Sartre had discounted the reality of the "midworld" relative to its irreducible components or relata, for-itself and

in-itself; Sartre now writes, "It is no use to try to throw 'collectives' over to the side of pure appearance."[31] Examples of collectives are a church, a bank, a café, a club, a dollar bill, a newspaper, a city— each of which is "a concrete materiality" endowed with a meaning by a group of individuals. Here Sartre offers a remark that, as an acknowledgment of conditioning, is a crucial index of the shift of stress in his later thought:

> it is in terms of his relation with collectives—that is, in his "social field" considered in its most immediate aspect—that man learns to know his condition. . . . Man *at the same time* exists in the milieu of his products and furnishes the substance of the "collectives" which consume him. At each phase of life a short-circuit is set up . . . which contributes to change him on the basis of the material conditions from which he has sprung. The child *experiences more than* just his family. He lives also—in part through the family—the collective landscape which surrounds him. It is . . . the generality of his class which is revealed to him in this individual experience.[32]

Sartre manifests in a number of places a patent anger at collectives. The collective conquers the child before he has had a chance.[33] The collectives to which the child is exposed are an environment to which he must accommodate himself, and relative to which he must identify himself; they are his "milieu." For him they are natural. It is as if they had always been there. He does not know that they are *partializing,* that they are objectifications of and instruments of the praxis and values of a class, that they are the instruments of his indoctrination and habituation. They represent the incursion of irrationality into the child's praxis, inasmuch as he is formed by them without his being aware of their meaning. "All the objects which surround us are signs,"[34] but the child, not knowing this, "lives the universal [only] as particular."[35] By the time he can begin to decipher the signs—to see, for example, that his speech, his clothes, his gestures, his dialect, his favorite haunts set him apart from and against, and superior to or inferior to, others—he is already set against his fellow man. We are "lost since childhood."[36] The collective, then, represents to Sartre the vehicle of a conditioning from which the child never altogether liberates himself, a leaden inertial weight that insures the transmission from generation to generation of the 'violence' of class distinctions between "the good" and "the evil," the saved and the damned. Far from being mere appearance, collectives are bloody instruments; the midworld is a field of battle from which no amount of 'purifying reflection' can liberate one. *No one plays over the surface.* This is the price of Sartre's commitment to the reality of the midworld. One is born into a field of real material contradictions that cannot be privately resolved but only resolved, if at all, by long labor against heavy inertial odds.

One will recall that in Sartre's characterization of the 'problem' of action at the end of *EN* he wrote that action "determines a modification in the being of the transcendent" by "a relation of being with being which . . . is neither pure exteriority nor immanence but rather refers us to the Gestaltist notion of *form.*" [37] The 'collective object' is such a modification in the being of the transcendent and it has the character of a 'form'. A form or *Gestalt* is the recognizable entity it is owing to its referential relation to the 'field' or context in which it is perceived as being. The structure and meaning of the entity is relative to the subject's (perceiver's, agent's) intentions, relative to what he is about; it is constituted by "a relation of being with being." Given his intentions, the subject structures the material before him as a meaningful whole that coheres with other meaningful wholes in the field. Given my hunger and penury, for example, the bank down the street appears as to-be-robbed, an instrument or means to the end of relieving my need. In his *Esquisse,* Sartre wrote that "spontaneous unreflective consciousness constitutes a certain existential level of the world," on which level one "seizes upon the world as a quality of things" by "a pragmatistic intuition of the determinism of the world." [38] In other words, at this level one grasps entities as being in a practical field in which they are practical instruments, which can alter (determine) the practical field if I understand how they function in this field. The bank is, in Sartre's terms, a sign, a collective, an instrument, and a form. It is a collective that has contradictory meanings. For wealthy depositors it is a sign of their economic power and an instrument for securing their future; for penurious robbers, it is a sign of their own disadvantaged estate, of a power they lack, and a potential instrument for the violent restoration of their fair share. The bank is in either case a form; it is a material entity, a building, which is at the same time a *common* meaning (institution for holding and dispersing monies) and *con-*

tradictory meanings (an institution for maintaining my security; an institution that hoards what I lack).

The relation of agent to collective is thus a *formal* relation, that is, a meaning-relation. If it is thought of as simply a relation of efficient causation to a purely material entity it becomes unintelligible and impossible. The human act that "determines a modification in the being of the transcendent"—e.g., robbing a bank—is not essentially that of the bumping of bits of matter; it is the modification of a field of forms (which are also to be sure material) by an intention that means the act as a reorganization of material meanings. It is only possible if the agent or agents and the field acted upon have something in common, a 'midworld': material meaning. Through my material body my intentions modify other materialized intentions and meanings. What action therefore requires is *the phenomenon*, the meaning-being. The sort of being that man can alter by action is a being whose *form* he can alter. Take Sartre's example in *EN* of the destruction of a cup. What I succeed in doing in smashing a cup is not destroying its matter but rather destroying its form—the phenomenal organization of the matter *as* a cup. If the cup is at the start defined nonrelationally as its matter—its pure being-in-itself or pure actuality—then smashing it changes nothing essential, does not and cannot touch its *actuality*. So defined, the cup has no *potential* for destruction. But if the cup is at the start defined *relationally and functionally*, which is to say defined by its 'form', then I can modify it in its very being (*qua* cup).

This simple shift from defining the being of the cup as pure nonrelational matter to defining its being relationally may seem a matter of arbitrary choice. One might say that it really changes nothing. Yet it changes everything, and it can be defended against the charge of arbitrariness by the argument that ordinary experience itself has always already, in practice, "defined" beings in terms of their form. If that is the case, then a purely materialist or nonrelational definition (assuming that such a definition could in fact be utterly nonrelational) serves to undercut the cognitive validity of the 'world' in which man does and must live and undercuts the efficacy of 'action' in that world. Sartre's turn requires a "metaphysical" decision to give ontological status to praxis and its forms. It is such shifts or adjustments of the 'as' of beings, changing nothing and yet changing everything, that Heidegger regards as the essential "decisions" of our history.[39] This particular Sartrean shift, which Sartre thinks of as mandated by the Marxian philosophy of our epoch, would appear to bring Sartre's ontological position much closer to that of Heidegger. It revalidates phenomena.

The field of such meaning-beings is a field of formal causes in formal relations with each other. This field of formal causes, or "collective objects," which appear as what they are relative to final causes or ends (e.g., the cup is *for drinking*), is Sartre's reappropriation of Heidegger's "referential totality." We have seen how, in Sartre's early thought, the referential totality comes apart under the onslaught of anxiety and analysis.[40] This dissolution was confirmed by Sartre's inability in *EN* to validate the 'action' that maintains the referential totality as a meaningful instrumental field of intelligible forms. Sartre's subsequent resolution of the problem of action through praxis serves to reestablish the referential totality—as a "detotalized totality" which is the material embodiment of "collective" meanings that are both common (to groups) and contradictory (insofar as there is a plurality of groups with conflicting intentions). One way of understanding the ideal future Sartre proposes is as a field of material meanings or forms whose formal relation with each other is absolutely coherent, freed of contradictory meanings for different groups or different agents.

In any case, we find a profoundly conservative element here reaffirmed by Sartrean thought—the rehabilitation of the ancient notion of formal cause, which may be said to be a necessary consequence of the phenomenological doctrine of intentionality[41] and of the commitment to teleological explanation.

3. Each human praxis is a project to recoup one's organic integrity by an exteriorization (dependence upon an exterior matter that both subserves and resists his project) whose goal is reinteriorization (making the world "his" or, as Sartre often says, creating a genuinely "human world" in which one's purposes are objectified without alienation).[42] But so long as the world in whole or in part objectively mirrors the purposes of less than everyone, it remains to just that extent an "inhuman world." The objectification-without-alienation attained by some is purchased at the cost of the alienation of others. The alienated others remain a threat to the *total* coherence of those who have achieved a relative objectification-without-alienation. So, given the presence of everyone in a field of

everyone, there is no total coherence or nonalienating totality for anyone as long as there is not coherence for everyone. Therefore the rational ideal term of every individual praxis is communal praxis. This is the rational goal of history, given the nature of *the beginning* of history. It is grounded in, and required by, the teleology of every individual praxis.

4. Rationality is neither a special and derivative nor primarily a subjective activity. Praxis is itself logical and dialectical. "In relation to the given the praxis is negativity; but what is always involved is the negation of a negation. In relation to the object aimed at, praxis is positivity. . . . At once a refusal and a realization, the project retains and unveils the surpassed reality. . . . Thus knowing is a moment of praxis."[43] In other words, the terms of praxis are its starting condition (a need as negation of a totality) and its goal (negation of the original negation). The praxis is thus premised upon the starting condition as the "reason for" the praxis; but the starting condition is the "reason" only when it is known or fixed upon and characterized as both the objective result of prior praxis and the reason for further praxis. In other words, understanding of what remains to be done depends upon estimation of the extent to which past praxis has and has not achieved the objective result at which it aimed. The particular means to be used to reach the objective are continually readjusted in light of a retrospective assessment of the objective results of the praxis up to the present moment. One lives time as a continual course correction by feedback concerning the course actually traveled so far. Praxis is a 'synchronization' (simultaneous adjustment to each other) of the necessarily 'diachronic' (successive) moments of time relative to a projected totality.[44]

5. All praxis is therefore a "totalization in course" that is cumulative in the sense that the 'given' which is at present the "reason for" the action now to be taken is the consequence (whether intended or not) of all prior praxis up to this moment. In "living the universal as particular," the child is in fact mirroring the entire state of society as lived from and through the particular standpoint of the family and collectives that condition him. Since his behavior reproduces the immediately preceding stage of totalization, he is from the start internally related to the whole not merely as its negation but as its reproduction. Something like a Leibnizian monad, he mirrors the whole from a particular spatiotemporal perspective.

This circumstance explains Sartre's claim that "the opaqueness of direct human relations comes from the fact that they are always conditioned by all others."[45] To suppose that one is, or that one is dealing with, a pure individual or a social atom is to be duped. To understand oneself (as Sartre seeks to do in *Les Mots*) or to understand another (as Sartre seeks to understand Genet or Flaubert) is to understand oneself or another as the "interiorization" of the totality and the reappropriation or reliving of this interiorized totality in the individual's praxis. (The gigantic size of Sartre's study of Flaubert, *IF*, is fundamentally attributable not to Sartre's prolixity but to the necessity of comprehending how Flaubert expresses, in his own way and from his own perspective, the whole state of society. Flaubert is, as Sartre says of himself, "made up of all men."[46] This is also why Sartre can say that Genet "holds the mirror up to us: we must look at it and see ourselves.")[47]

6. To reproduce or relive the totality in one's praxis, to preserve it in the act of surpassing it,[48] is not simply to relive a coherent totality. It is to relive contradictions. Since praxis is a surpassing (a detotalizing and retotalizing) of the inherited totality, it is the possibility of resolution (negation) of the very contradictions it relives. But because these contradictions are contradictions of society, and "inscribed" in matter, their resolution cannot be individual and private. As one is a microcosm of the macrocosm, to change the microcosm in any essential way one must change the macrocosm. This requires, as Marx saw, the sort of massive leverage only possible in large political groups. Genet, as the isolated individual his society wants him to be, can only live the human contradiction or else rebel against it inefficaciously. Neither good nor evil is fundamentally in the individual and hence under his control. Good and evil are functions of the totality; the praxis of the dominant class is defined by it as good, and whatever does not accord or cohere with 'good' thus defined is 'evil'. Any totality divided into classes appears to be Manichaean but in reality is not, since 'evil' is only a function of 'good'. Therefore for Sartre one can root out 'the evil' only by rooting out 'the good'.[49] Sartre calls for a totality that is in a sense beyond good and evil. This would be a state of the whole in which there were no contradictions, no loss of individuals in an alienating matter or inertia. It would be in effect a recovery of organic integrity out of a diaspora in which individuals and groups

are set against each other and sunk in evil. We recognize here once again Sartre's Plotinian tendency: evil is the privation of oneness, the explosion of organic unity into apparently atomic plurality by negation, nothingness. Totalization must be a stepwise ("a long work") reascent to unity, the Good.[50] Yet Sartre, of course, is not Plotinus. This unity would be a society of freedoms, of individuals still distinct (separated by logical negation), not a distinctionless or immaterial One.

The foregoing explains the remarkable footnote in *SGCM* in which Sartre in effect renounces his early plan to write an ethics. ". . . Any Ethic which does not explicitly profess that it is *impossible today* contributes to the bamboozling and alienation of men."[51] Given the internal relatedness of the individual to the totality, ethics is possible, as for Aristotle, only within the context of politics. The notion of individual good and evil, or of a private purification or salvation, is a bourgeois mystification. So-called "ethics" is today a luxury only possible for the *soi-disant* Good People.

Sartre would presumably no longer find the ethics of play, which he had illustrated by skiing, to be a viable option at the present time. Sliding playfully over the surface—as in skiing, yachting, or water-skiing—is the sport of the privileged, indulged in primarily by those who hold a disproportionate share of what is scarce. They play while others labor, and their labor maintains the conditions in which the privileged can play. One must rather consent to sink in the mud and slime, to dirty one's clean and innocent hands, as one has in fact already done.

In retrospect Sartre sees that this is not a time for play, but for work. Conversion is no longer a matter of an instant but of a long labor. As for Marx, work must establish the conditions for play in a future "society of freedom." This would be the ideal term of the long labor of surpassing existing contradictions: an actualizing of our common "reciprocity—which is the token of the True."[52] Only in a society where all are actually and not just theoretically free, equal, and fraternal can there be an ethics that can justifiably bind each and every individual to the same moral requirements. A *universal* morality presupposes that "anyone" (*n'importe qui*) and everyone has the "margin of real freedom"[53] requisite for acting without being fated to exploit anyone or be exploited by anyone.

7. Inasmuch as the cumulative objectification of both individual

and group praxis often deviates (as a result of ignorance, inertia, counterfinality, antidialectic) from the objective intended (freedom), the 'given' at any moment is not necessarily more coherent (closer to 'totality') than the given of a prior moment. There may be, and often is, static 'repetition' (mere circularity) or even 'regression' rather than real progress.[54] The reduction of the whole field to coherent totality is a rational and regulative norm of praxis but not a historical inevitability.

These, then, are the consequences of understanding history in light of its beginning, "the original dialectical movement" in which the individual organism becomes dependent on scarce matter to "produce his life," to recoup his organic wholeness or 'interiority'. These considerations will now enable us to comprehend Sartre's characterization of the topology of the individual and his history as a spiral.[55]

III

I have had occasion to comment on the phenomenon of circularity in Heidegger and in the early Sartre.[56] Circularity is originally for Heidegger and Sartre, as phenomenologists, a function of intentionality. It is a matter, Sartre wrote, of "losing oneself in order that the world might be" by "bursting forth" beyond oneself in such a way that one's meanings come back to one as if they were actually "out there," inherent in the material being of the environment, a humanized world. But anxiety and analysis purify one of this naïve unreflective synthesis by provisionally breaking the circle.[57]

In the later Sartre, intentionality has become exteriorization of interiority, one half of a circle whose other half is interiorization of exteriority. The original "closed" circle or organic interiority has been invaded by scarcity so that the organism has had to set out on a quest "outside" itself to "humanize" an environment that, as contest for an insufficient matter, appears as antihuman, as not assimilable to one's praxis. There begins an indefinitely protracted historical quest whose goal is the eventual reclosing of the circle. The original circle becomes a spiral:

> this ceaselessly detotalized and retotalizing totalization is *personalization*. The *person*, in fact, is neither altogether undergone nor altogether constructed. Moreover he *is not* at all or, to put it

differently, he is at each instant only the *surpassed* result of the ensemble of totalizing processes by which we continually try to assimilate the unassimilable. . . . Or rather it is . . . as if each new aggression from the cosmic exterior appeared at the same time as a disparity to be absorbed and as the perhaps unique opportunity to recommence, on new grounds, the great total-ity-concocting which tries to assimilate ancient and indestruc-tible contradictions, that is, to surpass them in a unity which is at long last rigorous—a unity which would be manifested as a cosmic determination. . . . One may envisage the circular movement in a three-dimensional space, as a spiral whose many centers are ceaselessly deviated and ceaselessly rise by executing an indefinite number of revolutions around their starting point. Such is the personalizing evolution, as least up to the moment . . . of sclerosis or regressive involution. In this latter circumstance the movement indefinitely repeats itself by passing the same places again or else is an abrupt fall from a higher revolution to some inferior revolution. But personal-ization is always the surpassing and conserving (assumption and internal negation), at the heart of totalizing project, of what the world has made and continues to make of the individual.[58]

The spiral is one of the clearest and most compact expressions of Sartre's later thought. It expresses man's relation, both retrospective and prospective, to the haunting One. It represents the circle stretched out in three dimensions—an exploded "center" that has to keep on circling, optimally at an ever-higher level, in an effort to reach the ideal future time at which the organism will, as at the beginning, again be in equilibrium or in a stable relation with its environment. Its vertical axis represents the linearity of man's his-torical quest for reunification. Its horizontal axes (each revolution) represent the 'deviations' from strict linearity necessary along the way, the repeated externalizations and internalizations in which man both makes and is made by a material environment that both threatens and supports his project. Thus the inward-and-outward horizontal movement expresses a dialectical mediation. Each out-ward movement at the same time represents an intentionality lived and suffered. Because the line of the spiral is, like that of the circle, continuous and unbroken, it expresses the fact that intentionality is not simply a "bursting forth" *ex nihilo* but a regurgitating of one's inheritance. Because the vertical movement or 'evolution' is entirely composed of 'revolutions', the spiral expresses the fact that real progress, if any, occurs only through a precarious and delicate balancing of repeated alienating submission to inertia and repeated surpassing of this same inertia. It represents, then, the materialization of the existentialist project or the insertion of Sartrean "revolutionary consciousness"[59] into a material history as the price of its efficacy. Because the spiral is fundamentally a movement of human praxis, it represents the fact that there is material evolution or "historical materialism" only relative to man's conscious praxis.

My diagram, "The Spiral of 'Anyone'" attempts at one and the same time (a) to picture the spiral as Sartre describes it; (b) to elaborate imaginatively upon what Sartre explicitly says about it; (c) to treat it in its ideal or truly progressive form. Going beyond Sartre's own indications, it depicts the spiral as progressively *expanding*, in order to convey the sense of totalizing that at the same time progressively masters more of the material context and progressively incorporates and reconciles more partial truths, up to the ideal point, at the top, where the truth is "one" and is embodied in and reflected by a unified and mastered material environment, which supports it. This expansion represents the progressive incorporation of the perspective of the Other into my perspective, up to the point (top) of universal reciprocity. The two diagonal lines diverging from the individual organism (at bottom) toward totality (at top) represent the explosion of an original unity into ideal and material moments that thenceforth require mediation and reconciliation. A philosophy that pursues the left diagonal alone is a reductive materialism, while a philosophy that pursues the right diagonal alone is a reductive idealism. The progressive flattening of the ellipses (revolutions) is intended to suggest a progressive approximating of the moment when the "need" for "vertical" material and cognitive mastery finally disappears. This is the ideal moment when anyone may find *the present*, the horizontal horizon, nonalienating. It is the moment of reciprocating co-sovereignty. It is also the ideal synchrony, or resynchronization, of time in which the three temporal ekstases are reunified without tension. That is, it is the time when anyone can affirm a future that is *essentially the same* as his immediate past.[60]

The ideal terminus of a history that begins with scarcity is the point at which no individual would any longer have to quest to

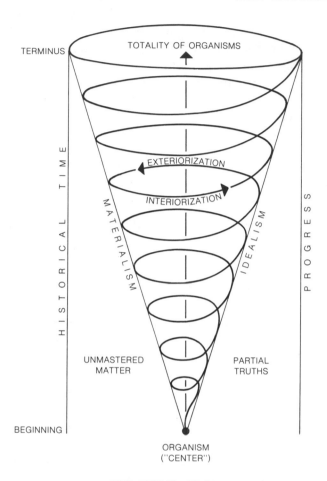

THE SPIRAL OF "ANYONE"

transform a future environment by mastering it, laboring over it, humanizing it, making its conflicting "parts" cohere or co-exist peace-
fully and even playfully with each other as an integrated cosmos
composed of individuals of integrity. Sartre's early cosmic romance
is not over; a few pages before the evocation of the spiral in *IF*
Sartre writes: "In human reality . . . the multiple is always haunted
by a dream or a memory of synthetic unity; hence it is the detotalization itself which demands to be retotalized. . . ."[61] But the later
Sartre, unlike the early Sartre, *assents* to this romantic "demand"
even while fearing the impossibility of its being wholly met. The

perhaps unpayable price of this romantic human quest's being fulfilled is that it take place in hard material conditions. The revolutions no longer leave the past behind but are situated *within* a laborious "evolution." The spiral, which ideally takes the form of a
genuinely progressive Hegelian-Marxian dialectic, is corroded by
antidialectic. There is repetition and even regression: the surpassing becomes a dumb, stifling, and habitual routine (as on the
assembly line) or one abruptly loses the little one has gained (as the
factory shuts down and one eats up one's savings to survive). Or
one finds to one's horror that each "new" phase of one's life is
repeating, in altered circumstances, the archaic gestures of one's
childhood, that one has been all along the unwitting mouthpiece of
a world one never made, that one has "interiorized" and "reex-
teriorized" the violence of one's ancestors as one's own. There are
good reasons for having a "horror of dialectic." The later Sartre
bombards himself with reminders of the "permanence amid the
permanent alteration."[62] He writes that "a life unrolls itself in
spirals; it is always repassing the same points but at different levels
of integration and of complexity."[63] He constantly challenges his
own deep-seated Cartesian drive for simplicity: "everything becomes complex and difficult."[64] His 1946 study of Baudelaire took
only 166 pages; his 1952 study of Genet required 573 pages; his
more recent study of Flaubert consumes 2800 pages and remains, so
to speak, a detotalized totality.

In the preface to this last study Sartre tells us that "empathy" is
"the sole attitude which is requisite for understanding."[65] The long
and difficult work of becoming a "man among men, no better than
any" requires empathy in place of the harsh and summary dis-
missal of "cowards" and "stinkers" for their bad faith and spirit of
seriousness.[66] Sartre becomes one who can offer a "prayer for favorable treatment of Genet."[67] One is inescapably sunk in inertial matter and mud. Sartre can no longer see himself as having any special
metahistorical purity; the former advocate of leaving the past behind without a trace can now say, "I like and respect the humble
and tenacious faithfulness of certain people . . . to their tastes,
their desires, their former plans, to bygone red-letter days; I admire
their will to remain the same amidst change. . . ."[68] Facing his
own mortality, Sartre now criticizes the major premise of his early
critique of Heidegger's conception of death—the view that the for-

itself never encounters its own limits.[69] He can now see that his early penchant for purificatory ascesis was an expression of a bourgeois need to suppress the body.[70] *Les Mots* betrays evidence of tenderness and tolerance of moral weakness uncharacteristic of the early Sartre. The "They" can no longer be simply characterized as a "stream" in which my own ends are alienated; it *is* that, but it is also 'anyone'—including Sartre.[71]

Such is Sartre's new humbleness, and his "pessimism" regarding change and purification. But we should not pass too quickly over Sartre's term 'anyone.' It is both fact and norm. As fact it means that we all have a common plight, inasmuch as we are all stuck, all internally related to a contradictory and alienating totality. But as norm it calls for recognition of this fact, for becoming who we are. That clearly means real historical and social change. The optimism of *EH* is not quite gone; it is chastened, reconciled to "a long labor." Can there be, after all, a Heideggerian "crew" that is more than a "psychological experience"?[72] Has not Sartre's early analysis of "the Other" shown that there is an inevitable political pluralism? Is not reciprocity essentially only a negative relation? Has not *CRD* shown that all groups in time come apart? Yet Sartre can write: "The true problem . . . is less concerned with the past, where recurrence and alienation are encountered in every epoch, than with the future: to what extent will a socialist society banish atomism *in all of its forms?"* [73] If we think through the meaning of Sartre's notion of 'anyone', it implies a positive universality and a positive fraternity. Each of us is essentially interchangeable with every Other; not only is our goal the same (restoration of organic unity), but it cannot be achieved in private, inasmuch as all are alienated and either actually or potentially threatened so long as anyone is alienated and threatened. In addition, each of us has from childhood internalized the social totality, so that in effect all others are in each of us.[74] To change myself is to change the totality, and to change the totality is to change myself. This is the essential consequence of the admission of positive internal relations (through 'interiorization'), which results from Sartre's "metaphysical" shift to "faith" in the level of 'the real' or of 'world'.[75] This shift enables, and requires, Sartre to say: "My sole concern has been to save myself . . . by work and by faith." [76]

Through 'personalization' by interiorization, I *am* the Others, although from my own perspective and in my own unique way. This is a far more intimate relation to the Other than negation, or even likeness. But it is not, like Heidegger's early "Being-with," an a priori or original 'we'. It is a "founded" relation that evolves out of the disruption of the cyclic interiority of organisms with the event of scarcity. Does this not mean that the ideal terminus of history would be a return to unbroken interiority, a radical independence of the Other, a flushing of Others out of my "interior," a restoration of universal privacy? Can one even answer this question in the absence of CRD, II, which was to be a full-fledged study of history, and given Sartre's avowed historical empiricism, which would seem to preclude historical forecasts? What is "the human kingdom" (le règne humain) mentioned in CRD? [77] Perhaps the most one can say at present is that it would in effect be a society of Cartesian cogitos that had, through a Hegelian-Marxian dialectical praxis, succeeded in realizing the material conditions under which the Kantian universal kingdom of equal and sovereign ends has ceased to be a mere materially impossible abstraction. It would be the global maintenance of the material conditions of individual freedom by and for all individual freedoms. It would be the practical realization of human "sovereignty," for which one can find *no ground:*

> There is none *because* there is no need for it: it is simply the univocal relation of interiority of the individual as *praxis* to the objective field he organizes and surpasses toward his own end. . . . Man *is sovereign.* . . . The only limitation of the sovereignty of man over all Others is simple reciprocity. . . . This original relation, when it is lived beyond all institutions, once again constitutes every man as an absolute for any other man whatsoever. . . .[78]

Does Sartre here exhibit a "utopian" commitment to a future whose shape is largely unknowable until we get there? And does it make any sense to speak of a terminus of history in light of Sartre's claim that dialectical totalization never ceases?[79] He leaves open the possibility of "another History, constituted on another basis, with other motivating forces"—"in the event that technical and social transformations should destroy the context of scarcity." Or there might be a post-historical era in which human "temporalization . . . would not take the form of a history."[80]

Despite this uncertainty, or because of it, one can only submit to the working out of one's spiraling 'destiny'[81] in the context of scarcity that happens to obtain at present. Sartre's new humbleness, compassion, and pessimism, consequent upon his recognition of this common destiny, are counterbalanced by a revolutionary zeal and verbal violence directed against those who would impede the effort of "the workers and militants"[82] to advance the long labor imposed by this destiny. This verbal violence reaches perhaps its highest pitch in *QM:*

> What the totalization must discover . . . is the multidimensional *unity* of the act. Our ancient habits of thought risk oversimplifying this unity. . . . The present form of language is hardly fit to restore it. . . . The dialectical knowing of man, according to Hegel and Marx, demands a new rationality. Because nobody has been willing to establish this rationality within experience, I state as a fact—absolutely no one, either in the East or in the West, writes or speaks a sentence or a word about us and our contemporaries that is not a gross error.[83]

In a footnote Sartre adds: "Our present ideas are false because they have died before us."[84] Sartre's early thought was 'false' in this sense because, I have argued, it was too analytic. It arrested the dialectic, taking the "multidimensional *unity* of the act" apart without being able to justify, metaphysically or morally, putting it back together again. Sartre discovers that the essential problem of the thought and praxis of our time is to comprehend how individuality and totality do and can go together. The quest for freedom to which Sartre committed himself in *EH* has turned out to be a quest for totality. No one writes or speaks a word about us that is not a gross error because no one has been willing or able to correlate individuality and totality nonreductively. Sartre sees fragmentation everywhere—individuals, groups, academic disciplines struggling against each other, each claiming absoluteness or totality for itself, and each claiming to find unity or totality in the present or in the past. What all fail to see is that unity and totality are essentially futural. All unity is established in terms of the future, and Sartre's commitment to practical teleology has validated the claims that the future makes on the present. Totality is the "regulative principle of totalization."[85] Sartre's "turn" essentially consists in his *commitment* to this regulative principle that his early thought had already recognized. It is a commitment, we have seen, to the ordinary teleology of individual praxis as intentional surpassing of the past for the sake of an ideal future. What every *individual* ultimately has in common is the need for and quest for *totality*. But, confronted by individual and class dispersion or atomization and a brief lifetime in which to totalize it, he totalizes too quickly. He thus arrives at allegedly finished and final truths that are, according to Sartre, 'dead' or 'false' totalities. Examples abound—the "truths" of religion (including Sartre's early "religion"), the "truths" of existentialism as "philosophy," the "truths" of Stalinist Marxism, the "truths" of American sociology, the "truths" of psychoanalysis—and so on. Everywhere Sartre finds a 'sclerosis' that has resulted in taking the part, the aspect, or the perspective for the Whole. Insofar as each part (each discipline, each group, each life) claims to be or have the Truth, there is conflict and contradiction or, in Nietzsche's expression, "anarchy among the atoms."[86]

Furthermore, a criterion or ground in terms of which one could choose between conflicting claimants to "truth" and "totality" seems to be missing. There is nihilism, the absence of an overarching metaphysical standard. It takes the global form of a conflict between individualistic pluralism and collectivistic totalitarianism. There is no neutral standard, external to both of them, by reference to which one might decide between them or reconcile them.

The "present form of language" must be worked over. Sartre's view of language has not essentially changed. One's relation to language is ambiguous—one is in it *and* beyond it. And yet language is now for Sartre rather more inertial, more of a dead weight, than before. Language is still "a structural ensemble of instruments which one assembles or disassembles in order to produce a signification," but its words are also the bearers of counterfinality as embodiments of 'commonplaces': "The word . . . is an idea already made since it is defined beyond us, through its differences with other words within the verbal ensemble. . . . Thought gets caught in the snare of commonplaces when it believes that it is utilizing them. . . ." Flaubert, for example, "speaks *in* bourgeois."[87] The 'commonplaces' are only commonplaces of particular groups and are not yet a universal language. There is in language, as in other collective objects, an inertial drag that praxis must labor to surpass. The verbal praxis of Sartre's later works is to be seen as such a labor. It is in part an effort to "totalize" the vocabularies of the various partial and partializing 'anthropological' (in English parlance, roughly, "social scientific") disciplines.

Sartre's answer to the aforementioned anarchy among the atoms lies in the character of *individual* human praxis as itself a spiraling *totalizing*. The response to nihilism lies in man himself, in humanism as a "long labor." In other words, the answer lies in recognition of the comprehensibility and real unity of the present as given to it by the future—in effect by nothingness and nihilism themselves. This means that the *absence* of metaphysical totality is the precondition for achieving a genuinely *human* totality and that man must therefore, in effect, altogether embrace nihilism, affirm nothingness as part of Being itself.[88] This means to commit oneself to time and history. Time and history are the invasion of the fullness of Being by nothingness such that totality is always future, to be recouped. Unity and totality are therefore *to be made*. But this making is nothing new. It is what historical praxis has already been doing. To invoke totality is therefore to invoke what man has already done, not to invoke something essentially new. It is to invoke the ordinary as the standard.

IV

Correlating intentionality and teleology, as Heidegger had in *SZ*, Sartre finds the future to be the meaning of the present. It is the future that holds the present together as more than a plurality of atoms. Sartre writes: "A person who from a distance watches a man at work and says: 'I don't understand what he is doing,' will find that clarification comes when he can unify the disjointed moments of this activity, thanks to the anticipation of the result aimed at."[89]

The heart of Sartre's thought lies in this homely example. As praxis is an organizing of the inherited and present environment for the sake of a future end, and as individual human understanding is fundamentally the comprehension of both oneself and one's environment relative to a future end, so all historical action and all historical knowledge are the unification-and-comprehension of the past and present in the reflected light of a projected future. All particulars are comprehensible only as moments of a Whole that *is and is not*. The moment is a moment *of*; the part is a part *of*. The "of" refers to a totality that is imagined, projected, in the making. So long as the logic of analytical reason requires that the future cannot be "in" the present, or that the "meaning" of the part cannot be "in" the whole, or that nothingness cannot be "in" Being, just so long will philosophy and science be unable to know human praxis and hence the nature of history.

It is the simplest and most ordinary human praxis that illustrates, correlates, and justifies intentionality, teleology, and dialectic. The most elaborate philosophical constructions of Descartes, Kant, Hegel, Marx, Kierkegaard, Husserl, Heidegger, and the early Sartre are intelligibly synthesizable and criticizable only by reference to ordinary human activity. It is solely because existentialism calls attention to the elementary teleological, intentional, epistemological, and ontological structure of this activity that it earns the right to serve as an 'ideological' corrective to Marxism. For Sartre, Marxism is itself "the unsurpassable philosophy of our time" only because, we have seen, of its "will to transcend the oppositions of externality and internality, of multiplicity and unity, of analysis and synthesis, of nature and anti-nature."[90]

Sartre subscribes to Hegel's claim that "the truth is the Whole."[91] ". . . The truth must be *one*," Sartre writes, but it must be a "Truth that becomes [*Vérité en devenir*]."[92] He anticipates "the moment when History will have only one meaning."[93] This is the remnant of his old cosmic romance, legitimated by his later faith in the level of 'the real', by dialectic, and by long labor. It is a doubly relative truth or meaning—relative to human praxis and relative to a whole never wholly achieved. But it is not an arbitrary truth, for the very same reasons that it is relative; it grows out of human praxis, it rejects all fixed and unverifiable ahistoric absolutes, and it is patiently and laboriously constructed out of partial truths, developed within history. The alleged absoluteness of these partial truths is guarded against by their incompleteness when judged against the standard of Completeness, Coherence, or Oneness projected by human praxis itself. The infection of Oneness by Nothingness proves to be both an imperfection and the condition that guards against loss of the human in an alien, inhuman, and ahistoric One. Sartre's greatest battle has been to "discard the *purely theological* temptation to contemplate nature 'without foreign addition'."[94] We may, without forcing the issue, call this Sartre's effort to fight his own early attitude of (in Nietzsche's terms) "revenge against time" or to carry out the phenomenological program. This would, abstractly regarded, seem to bring Sartre into greater accord with Heidegger. There is therefore high irony in Sartre's denunciation of Heidegger in CRD for hating man:

> How can one justify *praxis* . . . if one sees in it merely the inessential moment of a radically inhuman process? How can one show it to be a real and material totalization if, through it, what is totalized is Being pure and simple? Man would then become what Walter Biemel, in commenting on Heidegger's works, calls "the bearer of the Opening of Being." This identification is not inapt; if Heidegger has praised Marxism, it is because he sees in this philosophy a way of showing, as Waelhens says of Heideggerian existentialism, "that Being is Otherness in me . . . (and that) man . . . is himself only through Being, which he himself is not." But every philosophy that subordinates the human to the nonhuman—be it an existentialist or a Marxist idealism—has hatred of man as its basis and its consequence; History has proved it in both cases. One must choose: man is from the first himself or he is from the first other than himself. And if one chooses the second doctrine one is nothing but a victim and an accomplice of real alienation.[95]

It is now possible for us to characterize the response of the later Sartre to what he takes to be the position of the later Heidegger. Heidegger, it seems, has succumbed to "the purely theological temptation to contemplate nature 'without foreign addition'." Sartre might well find external confirmation for this assessment in Heidegger's own acknowledgment of the decisive significance of his early theological studies for all of his subsequent thinking.[96] The Holy Ghost remains in Heidegger's cellar.[97] One can imagine Sartre ascribing to Heidegger that "nostalgia for the Whole" which he finds in Flaubert,[98] together with that "horror of dialectic" which prevailed in Sartre's student days.[99] It is a matter of wanting the Whole immediately, without the long labor of realizing it in human and nonalienating form. It is the logical consequence of Heidegger's early bypassing of the logical negation that explodes all Wholes. Had Heidegger recognized the force of negation, he would have had to regard history as a field of contradictions to be resolved by a protracted dialectic. He would have had to conserve Kant's and

Hegel's binding of the human imagination to logic, rather than attempting to bypass Hegelian dialectic. He would have had to understand community as to be made, rather than as an original and constant condition. By assigning to man the passive role of mouthpiece of Being, Heidegger has discounted both the metaphysical possibility and the moral necessity of a human praxis that can and must labor to surmount "real alienation."

These criticisms of Heidegger strongly suggest that Sartre did not read the later Heidegger extensively or carefully. I do not mean to imply that Sartre would have agreed with Heidegger if he had studied his later publications at length. But Sartre's condemnation of Heidegger—that is not too strong a word for his reaction—is overly simple and not meticulously defended, invoking Biemel and Waelhens rather than Heidegger's own works. Sartre ascribes to Heidegger a categorical distinction between the active and the passive—Being is active, man is passive—that clearly does not do justice to the active role played by 'mortals' as members of the Fourfold. Nevertheless it is true, as the *Letter on Humanism* had established, that Heidegger is not a humanist. Mortals are but one of the four members of the Fourfold. Heidegger takes as a dissembling of truth the very post-Cartesian philosophical development that Sartre regards as an essentially progressive approximation to truth. This philosophical development establishes the primacy (or apparent primacy) of subjectivity and technology the actual and rightful determination of the Being of beings by human thinking and praxis. To deny this is for Sartre to deny man his true and rightful role and place. To affirm it is for Heidegger to have succumbed to a semblance of both human Being and the Being of things.

This completes my study of the respective ways in which Heidegger and Sartre came to relocate the human being in a history to which their early philosophies had been insufficiently sensitive—a history that in both cases had conditioned their early thinking. But the two histories are not the same, and Heidegger and Sartre finish their careers farther apart in one fundamental respect than they had been in their early work. Chapter 13 will attempt to show what this fundamental respect is and whether it provides a basis for judging the respective merits of the two ontologies.

IV

Confrontation and Prospect

BY NOW it is clear that the differences between Heidegger and Sartre as ontologists are attributable, in the last analysis, to their notions of 'ground' or 'beginning'. Therefore the final confrontation must center on the question of the validity of their respective notions of ground. It will be argued that the ultimate test of the validity of their respective notions of ground is the ability or inability of these grounds to ground the thought of Heidegger and Sartre themselves in the truth. This test must also serve as a way of deciding whether their ontologies are functions of differing personal attitudes. The conclusions reached by this confrontation should make it possible to take a stand on many of the differences of detail between Heidegger's and Sartre's thought, although such a detailed application of the conclusions of the inquiry lies beyond the scope of the present volume.

The final chapter is limited to a single application of the conclusions reached through confrontation in chapter 13. This study has been concerned throughout to delineate certain contemporary problems of the phenomenological program, which I have construed, with Husserl, as ultimately an ontological program. Chapter 1 traced the rise of phenomenological ontology and formulated three interrelated questions inherited by Heidegger and Sartre from the tradition out of which phenomenology arises: the questions of the beginning, of metaphysics, and of unity. Chapter 14 attempts to show what sort of resolution of these problems the confrontation between Heidegger and Sartre makes possible. This concluding chapter outlines, on the basis of my entire investigation of Heidegger and Sartre, the legacy of the confrontation for a future phenomenological ontology.

13

The Ground and
Truth of Being

As men holding something in their hand sometimes seek what
they're holding, we too didn't look at it but turned our gaze somewhere far off, which is also perhaps just the reason it escaped our
notice.

—Plato, *Republic*, 432d/e

I

WE HAVE followed the course of Heidegger's and Sartre's
thought in detail in an effort to understand how each in his own
way works through the implications of his early ontological problematic. While their early positions are already quite distinct, their
later thought seems to evoke two altogether different worlds. Yet
we have seen in chapter 1 that their original philosophical inheritance is similar. Is the radical divergence between them simply a
sign of speculative imagination falling into unbridled contradictions? Can anything be learned from a comparison of ontologies
that seem different *toto coelo*, rather than simply different in detail?
Is there any basis at all for comparison? It must be emphasized that
in their later writings there are a number of significant respects in
which they agree as ontologists:

1. Ontology is not description of inherent traits of beings-in-
themselves. As Heidegger has come to exorcise the residue of sheer
presentness-at-hand in his early thought—the entity devoid of
meaning—so Sartre has come to qualify the notion of unmediated
actuality in his early thought.

2. Ontology is only possible in relation to the human being.
Being and human thought and attitude are inextricably interrelated
and covariant.

3. Ontology is only possible in relation to 'world'. The sense of
the Being of beings is a function of the sense of their conditions.
Beings are what they are relative to the context of meanings in

which they appear. The nature of beings is functional and relational. Relations enter into the internal nature of beings.

4. Ontology must be temporal. Being is not to be understood apart from time. The nature of beings is to be understood in terms of how they *come* to be what they are. (This is a corollary of 1, above—the critique of Being as sheer presentness.)

5. The sense of Being is epochally conditioned. The epochal character of the sense of Being is due to the splitting of an original unity. At least under conditions now prevailing, the way in which Being appears is historical, meaning that the degree of fullness with which Being (the true nature of beings) shows itself is variable.

6. The degree to which the nature of beings shows itself during the present epoch is only determinable by reference to the true beginning and outcome of an epochal history. Thereby the extent of human "alienation" is determinable.

7. The sense of Being is not determinable apart from formal cause. It cannot be determined solely on the basis of material and efficient cause. Taking the notion of intentionality seriously means the inherence of thought-determinations in beings themselves. Beings are "meaning-beings" or "phenomena."

8. Reality is not to be understood as excluding possibility, nor is perception to be understood as excluding imagination. The possibilities, uses, functions, relations of a thing are to be understood as belonging to the thing. In other words, 'Being' in the traditional modern sense (pure unmediated physical being-in-itself) is conditioned by 'Nothing' (what is "no-thing" or nonmaterial—thought, ideation, what is presently absent).

9. Analytic thinking as an ontological method is to be used with great circumspection (literally). The nature of the thing as found in ordinary experience—as a formal whole—is to be respected and regarded as the essential meaning of the thing. Analysis cannot construct the thing out of its elements or factors, but must regard the elements as aspects *of the thing*. The thing, that is, is to be regarded fundamentally as a whole rather than as simply an additive composite.

If Heidegger and Sartre agree in the foregoing respects, that is no accident. It is the mark of their common post-Kantian inheritance—in which Hegel plays an important role for both Heidegger and Sartre—and more particularly the mark of their common inheritance from *Lebensphilosophie* and from Husserl, and more particularly still the mark of the indebtedness of Sartre to Heidegger. The

extent of this agreement should not be minimized; it is easily overlooked because of the dramatic differences between the two thinkers. The agreement is sufficient to warrant the judgment that Heidegger and the later Sartre both participate in a movement of
thought that can be called "phenomenological ontology," broadly
defined as the effort to understand the phenomenon as a relative
absolute in the sense outlined in chapter 1. While it is possible and
even useful to define phenomenological ontology more narrowly, I
have kept the definition broad in order not to lose sight of (a) a certain linearity amid the flux of post-Kantian ontology, and (b) the
common effort of Heidegger and Sartre to heal what Murdoch has
called a "broken totality, a divided being" by pursuing a "third
way."[1]

II

Beyond the points enumerated above, it is difficult to find agreement between Heidegger and Sartre. In fact their thought appears
to stand in massive and elemental conflict as "a newly rekindled
gigantomachia peri tēs ousias"[2]—providing that the reader is willing to characterize both Heidegger and Sartre as ontological
"giants." It is necessary at this point to formulate as concisely as
possible the fundamental loci of disagreement between the late
thought of Heidegger and Sartre. The following represent fairly obvious areas of conflict:

1. *The province of humanism.* Heidegger's thought is "Being-centered"; Sartre's thought is "man-centered." By 'transcendence' the
later Heidegger meant man's orientation by the Event of gathering,
while Sartre has basically meant by it the orientation of the world
relative to consciousness, its projects and praxis. Hence each finds
the other alienated from the true center. This difference is manifested in their respective treatment of fate and choice, past and future ekstases, remembering and surpassing, thought and action,
nature and artifact, poetry and prose, theism and atheism.

2. *The reading of history.* Heidegger interprets history in terms of
thought, as a movement whose fundamental direction is determined by a forgottenness that provokes a metaphysical quest for an
absolute ground, but that is secretly ruled by another "ground" (the
form of the Event in the first beginning). Sartre interprets history in

terms of praxis, as a movement whose fundamental direction is determined by scarcity of a needed matter, which provokes the formation of groups to secure this matter. In the former case, history is not essentially progressive or constructive; in the latter case it is or can be, although not in a necessary or wholly linear manner. For Heidegger, one cannot properly interpret history by relying on the cumulative truth of philosophies. For Sartre, recent 'philosophy' (that is, the philosophy of Marx) itself embodies such truth as history has thus far attained.

3. *The province of metaphysics.* If metaphysics is defined as reflective determination of the criterion of reality or the Being (nature) of beings by reference to an originative being (such as God, ego, consciousness) that constitutes beings as what they are, Heidegger holds this effort to be impossible. Any such absolute being would be grounded in (understood relative to and within the context of) a world of beings *already* revealed as what they are. Sartre, to the contrary, holds that reflection establishes the conscious practical project as the original metaphysical determinant of the reality or nature of beings. Thus for Sartre the very nature of reality is historically modifiable by human agency, decision, reasoning. For Heidegger, to be sure, mortals participate in the constitution of the nature of reality, but in such a way that their precise contribution is not ascertainable.

4. *The topology of philosophical disciplines.* Heideggerian thought requires a far-reaching reordering of the relations between the fields of philosophy. Ontology grounds (*and* ungrounds) metaphysics and logic. Both epistemology and axiology are fused with ontology, for the Event of Being *is* the disclosure of truth, beauty, and the good (*ēthos* as "abode").[3] Sartre, as just noted, grounds ontology in metaphysics. He grounds logic and epistemology in transcendental consciousness (negation), that is, metaphysically, and subordinates ethics to political philosophy and its praxis as the fundamental plane and orientation of human conduct.

5. *The province of language.* For Heidegger language is primarily the articulation of Being and is therefore a region within which all beings are what they are. Human speech is not essentially the use of an instrument for communication but rather the reevoking of the "utterance" of Being itself. Expressed differently, what accounts for the applicability, correlation, or correspondence of words to things

is that things come into being *in* language—the thing is a "linguistic-thing." For Sartre, the status of language is ambiguous, for man and thing are both in and beyond language. While language is a necessary vehicle for thought, for identification of entities, and for communication, neither thing nor thought is *essentially* linguistic. The thing is articulated or discriminated by thought. To confuse word and thing is to idealize the thing; to confuse language and thought is to reduce the spontaneous synthesizing power of thought to the mechanical mouthing of conventional terms with their baggage of conventional (and ideological) connotations. If language is not criticizable by thought, man is the victim of language. Sartre situates the 'logos' of phenomena in logical thought (negation and synthesis), while Heidegger situates the 'logos' of phenomena in the event of language.

6. *The synchrony of ekstases.* For Heidegger, in the whole of its nature, time rests, or the past comes on as future. This means that the original and originary Event, which is the coming-to-be of beings, keeps on coming ('remains') in essentially the same way (that is, as the round-dance of the Fourfold) in essentially the same space (in the whole of its nature, space rests). But this essential sameness of time and space is epochally dissimulated owing to the forgottenness of the Event and its true character: since the ground is hidden, there arises the quest *for* a ground, namely, for a future place (time-play-space) essentially different from the past place. *SZ* evokes the powerlessness of man to effect an essentially different time and space by appeal to a Being before ('whence') or after (whither') or above ('meta-') his traditional time and space (which he must therefore "resolutely" reappropriate), and so prepares the way for the turn into affirmation of the recurrence of the Same Place as his proper abode, the sole possible region of Being and Truth for mortal beings.

For the later Sartre there is a superficial similarity, for prehistoric time is a time of recurrence of the same (the cyclic repetition of organic self-renewal or "elementary synthesis of change and identity") that is disrupted by unfulfillable need into a quest for an essentially different future. This future would, however, be the restoration of the original condition of nonscarcity. The essential difference between this position and Heidegger's is that the original synchrony or recurrence is actually destroyed rather than dissimulated and hence must be *reconstructed* rather than *remembered*. There is, in addition, a difference of level between these two interpretations of time, for Sartre's original time is "biological" and his historical time "economic," while Heidegger's original time is "mortal" and his dissimulated time is "metaphysical." We shall have to ask whether, when regarded as different levels, these interpretations of time might be reconcilable rather than mutually exclusive.

7. The nature of truth. Heidegger distinguishes between an original truth and a truth of assertions. He holds that the price of assertions' having an intelligible referent is that their referents already be intelligible before we make truth-claims *about* them. They must already have been disclosed as the beings they are. This original disclosure is what the Greek term for truth, *alētheia*, connotes. This term also connotes, he argues, a disclosure that is at the same time a closure—a disclosure or truth that is partial and occurs at the price of 'untruth'. By this Heidegger means that the original disclosure—occurring in language to finite beings—is necessarily relative and contextual.

The early Sartre holds the Cartesian view that the final criterion of Truth is direct intuition. It is a matter of an immediate "seeing," it is extralinguistic, and it is governed by the logical requirement of coherence or consistency. Thus the original locus of truth is transcendental—the cogito—rather than the world. The later Sartre seeks to synthesize this conception of truth with a Hegelian-Marxian conception of truth as progressively achieved through dialectical praxis in history. While the final criterion of truth remains transcendental thought, the inherence of thought in matter owing to transformation of matter by praxis means that praxis and its products can now be understood as 'true' to the degree that they are coherent and 'false' to the degree that they are contradictory. Coherence and contradiction are determined by praxis on the basis of "a new rationality"[4] that tests the human and material environment for the degree to which it mirrors without contradiction the aims of the free project of the conscious organism toward the practical embodiment of its original freedom.

8. Thought versus temperament. We have observed that Heidegger and Sartre are sharply opposed in temperament and life-style. While one might hold this to be an extraphilosophical consideration, we are dealing with thinkers who are indebted to *Lebensphilosophie* and committed to the notion that philosophy is to be situated within history. Both Heidegger and Sartre seem easy prey for sociological analysis: the agrarian mentality vs. the urban-industrial mentality, the intention to live in harmony with nature as opposed to the intention to transform nature. Is their thought any more than a reflection of their circumstances? Heidegger himself said, with reference to himself, "as you began, so you will remain"[5]—but he also sought to distinguish his 'thought' from the 'philosophy' he inherited. Sartre acknowledged that his thought and praxis were molded by a bourgeois culture—but he also believed he had finally freed his thought from that influence. Heidegger found Sartre's philosophy the expression of a metaphysical tradition. Sartre implied that Heidegger's thought expressed and even furthered a cultural alienation. Such considerations provoke the question whether the ontology of either Heidegger or Sartre can claim truth-status.

III

I have outlined certain respects in which Heidegger and Sartre agree and disagree. Essential for the confrontation between them is a closer look at the basis of this agreement and disagreement. This I shall undertake now. I shall then be in a position to offer some reflections on the general nature and prospects of phenomenological ontology (chapter 14).

In Part I my analysis of the two ontological orientations was based on the notions of man's nature (*Dasein; l'être-pour-soi*), ground, and time. Heidegger's and Sartre's respective interpretations of these notions were regarded as determining the fundamental difference between their versions of phenomenological ontology, or their ways of carrying out what I have called the phenomenological program. These notions remained determinative for the mid-career adjustments made by both Heidegger and Sartre, as reflection on the foregoing eight areas of disagreement between them will show. Their respective interpretations of humanism, history, metaphysics, philosophical disciplines, language, interrelation of past and future ekstases, truth, and the relation of thought to its circumstances are determined by their characterizations of the relation of ground to time in and for human experience. And the char-

acter of the relation of ground to time in human experience expresses the time-space within which beings occur as the particular
sorts of phenomena that Heidegger and Sartre construe them to be.
Thus for Heidegger the experience of the phenomenon in its Being
is the lasting Event of the coming-on of the past out of the future in
the Fourfold (ground), as the Fourfold 'assembles' itself or 'centers'
on the 'thing'. For Sartre, however, the experience of the phenomenon in its being is the coming-on of the future totality in the practical field, as praxis (subjective ground) deforms and reforms resisting matter (objective ground). In these contexts the nature and role
of humanism, history, metaphysics, and so forth are determined.

If I am right in arguing that it is the particular relation of ground
to time in and for human experience that determines the distinctive
character of the two ontologies, these then are the notions that must
be critically examined in an effort to assess the relative soundness
of the two ontologies. This is the final point of confrontation.

But carrying out this final confrontation requires that a distinction be made between the *content* of these determinative notions
and the *validity* of the thought that proposes them. In asking about
the truth of any notion or doctrine of ground, one must ask whether
that ground makes possible the independence of thought necessary
for this thought to discriminate between true and false doctrinal
content. Does the Heideggerian or the Sartrean 'ground' ground the
possibility of assessing the truth or falsity of the assertions
grounded in them? I have already raised this question indirectly in
asking whether there is any reason (ground) for regarding the
ontologies of either Heidegger or Sartre as more or other than expressions of their temperaments and circumstances. This question
takes precedence over all others. It means that consideration of the
question of ground is necessarily consideration of the question of
truth. But this consideration cannot take the form of grounding
truth, since the ground of truth would itself in turn have to be established as true, and the grounding-process would recede infinitely. If truth is prior to ground, truth is ungrounded, baseless; if
ground is prior to truth, the ground or basis of truth is not known
to be true. Truth and ground must be the same. Both Heidegger
and Sartre are aware of this old and perhaps obvious requirement.
We must examine how each responds to it.

We first, then, reexamine Heidegger's and Sartre's notions of

truth, in order to be able to ask in the next two sections how the
thought of each is grounded in his notion of truth.

Heidegger accepts the correspondence theory of truth, but he
responds to the traditional difficulty[6] of the theory in accounting for
the possibility of correspondence between two generically different
modes of being—name, concept, proposition (level of language and
thought) on the one hand, thing (level of matter) on the other
hand—by pointing to a more fundamental level of truth where the
thing is one with language and thought. Original truth is the original disclosure of the thing as what it is; if name and thought apply
to the thing, that is because the thing is first encountered or perceived *as* what it is when it is thought and named.[7] All propositions, true and false, refer to a world of things already disclosed.
Propositions do not first disclose the things to which they refer;
there is prior experiential familiarity with the things referred to.
This prior familiarity is at once and inextricably perception,
thought, and naming. Any effort to establish the true nature of
beings propositionally presupposes what it proposes to prove. (I
can propose that "The true nature of tables is so-and-so" only if tables have *already* appeared *as tables*.) But Heidegger does not claim
that such prepropositional truth is total and incorrigible truth, for
all disclosure is at the same time closure. Thus more may be
learned—but always *on the basis of* what is already disclosed.[8] Thus,
again, the past comes on as future. This means that the true
"ground" can never be propositional, that "grounding" has always
already occurred when we make assertions about the world, and
that, like it or not, human thought already inheres in the thing
spoken of. The condition of truth is necessarily finite and relative.[9]

Sartre in his later writings regards truth as a function of historical
praxis (embodied consciousness acting upon matter in a social milieu). Where Heidegger speaks of an original truth, Sartre speaks of
a truth achieved by dialectical mediation. In the manner of Hegel
and Marx, he judges truth relative to a future totality and relative to
the consciousness that desires and proposes this totality. The Truth
(with a capital "T") is the Whole, and it is a *rational* truth. The historical past is therefore the coming on of the future. The historical
past and present represent degrees of privation of an ideal truth
that is implicitly proposed by consciousness at the beginning of
history and more and more widely and self-consciously proposed as

history proceeds. This truth is objectification without alienation—that is, a condition in which one's rational aspirations are mirrored by one's material and social environment rather than negated by it. This Truth must be One or universal, because unless the rational aspirations of 'everyone' are objectified, the world is to that extent irrational or logically internally contradictory. Truth is then the ideal synthesis of all rational wills in a rational environment. The demand for rationality is ultimately traceable to consciousness, conscious of itself as freedom. As negation of Being, separation from its material ground, consciousness makes possible the for-itself's free project toward negation of the original negation *without loss of* the original negation—that is, 'synthesis', in Hegel's sense, of consciousness and its environment. For the later Sartre, this consciousness is the consciousness *of the organism*, and of the organism *in need*, so that the original logico-rational requirement of coherence or wholeness (negation of negation, surpassing of contradictions) takes the specific historical form of negation of material scarcity (lack of what I need in order to objectify or concretely realize my inherent freedom). The relocating of consciousness in the historically needy organism is itself a stage in the realization of Truth because it constitutes a positive relating or synthesizing of consciousness and its environment, as does praxis when conceived as the real interaction of consciousness and its environment through the 'mediation' of the lived body (conscious matter—a 'form').

Sartre's early conception of the for-itself as desire to be God can now be seen as a partial truth. Insofar as it means that man desires Truth in the form of absolute coherence and universal community, an embodiment of the rational absolute, this conception is to be preserved; insofar as it meant deliverance from finite social and material conditions it is to be canceled. Sartre's early conception of conflict as the essential meaning of being-for-Others must likewise be subjected to mediation. Insofar as it means that, historically, scarcity forces individuals and groups to negate each other in the very effort to overcome scarcity, it is to be preserved; insofar as it means that individuals necessarily negate each other in the quest for godlike appropriation of their environment, no matter what that environment may be, it is to be canceled.

Truth, then, is for Sartre a function of the 'whence' (consciousness as original negation, freedom, accompanied by scarce matter as negation of freedom) and the 'whither' (universal communal negation of scarcity).[10] It is a dialectical progression, historical and teleological. It invokes formal cause in the sense that worked-over matter is intelligible as the embodiment of rational praxis, and also as the negation of rational praxis (the counterproductive). The progression of truth is the progressive formal embodiment of ideal truth or rationality. The region of truth is the field between the original negation and its final mediation.

Truth for the later Heidegger occurs nonteleologically between a dark 'whence' and a dark 'whither'. There is therefore no ground fore or aft relative to which the partiality of original truth could be canceled or mediated. Truth fundamentally or originally occurs not by mediation of differences between thought and matter but rather by the unmediated (self-mediating) event of difference-and-identity (a differentiated unity). This means that the thought and matter, subject and object, idea and referent of which the philosophical tradition speaks, can occur as different only if they occur as identity. There is the thought of the thing as opposed to the matter of the thing precisely when the thing materializes as thought. This is what happens in the perception of a mortal in language, for the thing appearing as named is the unmediated unity or togetherness or identity of "thought" and "matter," of "essence" and "existence." This is the "hidden harmony" by which the flux is a unity of the distinct and in which "the same is for thinking as for being."[11] This conception of the groundless ground of truth as the introplay of thought and "matter" in a finite field invokes formal "cause," in the sense that the thing is intelligible "owing to" its *inherent* essence, which is nevertheless *relative to* thought. This is—if only very roughly—comparable to Aristotle's understanding of formal cause or intelligible 'nature' as inherent in the thing. But Aristotle could ultimately account for this inherence of form in matter only by reference to a metaphysical and teleological ground, the First Mover. The true "greatness" of German idealism[12] lies in its notion of the identity-and-difference of thought and being, which prepares Heidegger for the notion of Event. Missing this notion, Aristotle had to invoke a metaphysical explanation for the formal intelligibility of beings. Missing this same "natural" Event, Plato had to invoke the notion of metaphysical forms, man's recollection of them, and the Demiurge's imperfect imposition of them upon a resistant matter, in order to account for the possibility of an intelligible world. Insofar as modern thought has lost confidence in the divine, it has accorded to human praxis and technology the function of the Demiurge and to human reason or imagination the function of generating the forms. In the case of both Plato and Aristotle, the ground of intelligibility had to be displaced into a metaphysical region, and displaced with it was the Good (the original and final source of meaning and intelligibility). Thus the philosophies of Plato and Aristotle have a common root in a missed Event. Missing the "nearest of the near," they had to seek it in the "far," the region of metaphysics. Heraclitus and Parmenides had, in their quite different ways, dimly divined the Event that Plato and Aristotle missed. Truth is a "groundless" (self-grounding) self-lighting rather than an event for which one can find a sufficient reason (*Grund*) in a reflected light cast from a metaphysical source. Phenomena cannot be constructed out of prior causes or factors (the physical and the metaphysical).

From these considerations the following conclusions can be drawn as to the ways in which Heidegger and Sartre identify truth with ground. Heidegger finds *original* truth to be the original-and-remaining disclosure of beings as what they are in the identity-and-difference of thought and referent occurring in language and in experience. This is the ground of all *propositional* truth because the name *already belongs to* the being to which it refers. But in our tradition the difference has hidden or dissimulated the identity, so that a metaphysical cement has seemed necessary in order to guarantee the applicability of thought to beings. Ground and truth thus mean the original union of thought and beings in the Event of Being. In the *apparent* absence of this ground and truth, a metaphysical ground of union of thought and thing must be posited, a "highest" truth or "absolute" ground (divine creation, divine veracity, absolute ego, etc.).

There is thus a forgotten togetherness (union) of thought and beings which nevertheless persists, unnoticed, as thought thinks *about* and makes assertions about beings. Missing this union of thought and beings, thought tries to establish it by positing a metaphysical truth and ground (ground of the intelligibility of beings and possibility of correspondence between assertion and its ref-

erent). But an "other beginning" is possible in which thought remembers its forgotten union with beings. In the former case the
grounding truth must be supplied by metaphysical thought; in the
latter case it is remembered as already there. The original identity-
and-difference occurs in language, but in metaphysics the enclosure
of both thought and beings in language is dissimulated. In summary, any present effort to ground (as in metaphysics) is grounded
in a prior disclosure, which is the original truth.

How does Sartre identify truth with ground? The original negation is the rise of consciousness over against being or the splitting
of unity into difference (which appears to the early Sartre as absolute irreconcilable difference) between thought and matter, being-
for-itself and being-in-itself. There are *two* grounds, for being-in-itself is the source of being, while being-for-itself is the source of
truth as negation of being. Loss of truth is then loss of being-for-itself by sinking into being, loss of freedom and transcendence. The
price of truth is disunity of thought and being, requiring a continual effort at purification from the tendency of thought to fuse itself
with matter in unreflective experience and the spirit of seriousness.
Metaphysics, interpreted as the quest to heal the split by appealing
to an in-itself-for-itself or identity-and-difference, God, is futile.
The later Sartre, however, finds a way to make this metaphysical
move by regarding historical praxis as the progressive reunification
of truth and matter, thought and being-in-itself. Praxis *makes*
being-in-itself 'true'. Praxis transforms an historical noncorrespon-
dence of thought and its referent into a correspondence. The degree
of truth is the degree of correspondence established between free
project and resisting matter. Reason persuades necessity until matter accepts the impress of form. Thus the two grounds, rational free
thought and matter, *become* one at the ideal term of history. At this
point, truth and ground are one. Truth is degree of correspondence
judged relative to an ideal coherence.

Thus the usual pre-Hegelian metaphysical effort to reunify
thought and referent nontemporally and nonhistorically must be
surpassed. Reunification is fully achieved only in a future "society
of freedom" in which 'exteriority' mirrors 'interiority' in such a way
that matter supports the freedom of all. The truth of freedom is materialized. Truth is grounded in matter and matter is grounded in
truth; that is, the environment is, through praxis, rationalized mat-

ter or materialized rationality. Language stands between thought and matter, mirroring neither thought nor matter perfectly,[13] until the union of truth and matter saves language from the dual dangers of reducing matter to ideality or reducing ideality to matter without the necessary mediation of the two across time.

IV

Having established the nature of truth as ground for Heidegger and Sartre, we now confront the question of how these notions of truth ground the assertions made by each of them. The present section concentrates primarily on Heidegger's thought, while the next centers on Sartre's thought. It will be recalled that this question was originally provoked by another: what prevents the content of the thought of either of them from being more than the mirror of his *particular* circumstances, rather than a validly formed truth-claim about the *universal* nature of ontology? Can their assertions be said to be dispassionately proposed autonomous judgments?

It is clear that in neither case are we dealing with 'philosophy' in the traditional sense of autonomous and disengaged transcendental reflection. It is significant that both of them came to disavow the title 'philosopher', Heidegger characterizing himself as a 'thinker', Sartre calling himself an 'ideologist'. These new titles acknowledge two kinds of indebtedness to orientations within which their early 'philosophies' unknowingly stood: in Heidegger's case, the non-metaphysical Event of the Fourfold; in Sartre's case, the philosophical and political praxis of post-Cartesian times. Heidegger and Sartre are writing at a time when—owing to Marx, Darwin, Freud, Nietzsche, Frazer, and others—we have found it impossible to ignore the possible disparity between what we think we mean and what we really mean, whether what we really mean is economic, biological, instinctual, or cultural. Heidegger's violent interpretations of earlier philosophers—and of his own early thought—are in effect depth-analyses that attempt to thrust through an overt metaphysical meaning to a 'directive' dissimulated by the overt meaning. Sartre's analyses of other writers—and of his early writing—attempt to thrust through the overt individual meaning to "projects" that are individual reappropriations of class attitudes. Are these depth-analyses themselves the expressions of unanalyzed depths? It is at

this point, as Husserl saw, that the question of 'foundations' becomes 'critical'. If thought cannot be an absolutely self-grounding
and self-certain arbiter of truth, knowledge seems impossible.

Heidegger's response to this problem differs from Sartre's. He
meditates on the traditional notions of light, illumination, clarity
(the light of the 'heavens') and their relation to the dark and hidden
(the dark recesses of 'earth'). Metaphysics has sought, by going
above (transcending), to bring everything into the light, without
remainder. Presumably Heidegger would associate the complex of
recent efforts to inquire into the hidden depths of human motivation and thought with the epoch of the "consummation" of metaphysics.[14] It is characteristic of this epoch to be "positive." Ostensi-
bly it inquires without the now-dead metaphysical guidelines or
criteria, and hence it sees things as the unidealized, brute, prerational givens they really are. But this antimetaphysical inquiry is
still covertly metaphysical, since it does not 'remember' the Being *of*
beings and hence thinks it is dealing merely with beings per se
(beings apart from the complex of conditions that Heidegger calls
'the Fourfold'). And, paradoxically, the very time when inquiry
thought it had gained access to pure unqualified brute beings with
no meta-physical overlay is the time when inquiry is confronted by
the problem of the relativity of the object of inquiry to the thought,
language, and situation of the inquirer. Hence there arises the peculiar circumstance of inquiry becoming certain of an inevitable uncertainty and, from a necessarily relative position, proposing the
relativity of knowledge as a nonrelative truth.[15]

In this peculiar circumstance, what would it mean to "remember"
the Being of beings? Heidegger's notion of Being means "appearing
in Place." This means that beings have always appeared relative to
their context, which means for Heidegger that they have always
been partial disclosures in thought and language of something that
remains partially hidden. The price of illumination is a surrounding
darkness. The price of human understanding and imagination is
awareness of the 'divine' or metaphysical position of absolute
nonrelative knowledge or total illumination as an ideal that cannot
be achieved by mortal man (hence the gods' true mode of appearing
is 'absence'). Heidegger thinks that in owning up to the necessary
finitude and relativity of human knowledge the first step toward
thrusting through the dissimulation of Being has been taken in

post-Nietzschean thought. But this is not an *achievement* of human thought—whether Nietzsche's or Heidegger's—operating in transcendental and reflective freedom. It is the result of thought having worked through all the consequences of the Greek beginning's forgetting of the relativity of thought to its Place—a forgetting that started Greeks on the 'fated' quest for nonrelative (absolute, unconditioned) knowledge. But the inevitable discovery of the impossibility of completing this quest is only the first step in thrusting through the dissimulation of Being. The second step consists in meditation on the occurrence (Event) of this finite Place as the precondition ('gift') of everything man values. This prepares the way for affirmation of this Place (*amor fati*), caring for it as holy and as source of 'wonder' at the ultimately inexplicable fact that there are beings for us (phenomena) at all. But ours is the time of 'danger' [16] because, while the first beginning directed thought to the quest for an absolute or nonrelative ground, destined to end in nihilism, it did not direct thought to affirm its finite ground. At this point Heidegger seems to see only a *possibility* of such affirmation. [17] There is at this point a certain leeway of attitude, or indeterminacy; nothing can be isolated that would *necessitate* affirmation of the Place.

We can infer, then, that Heidegger understands his thought and his language to be thought in the process of coinciding with itself—owning up to its own nature as owned by Being. This implies that Heidegger does not regard his own thought as operating on a different or higher level or plane than that of Plato, Aristotle, Descartes, Kant, or Nietzsche. His thought is the consequence of theirs. Pursuit of the metaphysical quest up to the point of its self-critique in Kant and his successors is the precondition for being driven back to the beginning of that quest, to what lies "underneath" it, its forgotten source. But Heidegger does not freely and spontaneously discover this forgotten source by pure intuition or ingenious surmise. He is compelled by the contemporary evidence of finitude and relativity (most especially by the failure of Husserl's last-ditch attempt to reach an absolute ground) to ask how the finitude and relativity of understanding can be finitely and relatively explained. His clues have not been invented. He has rather found at the beginning of the metaphysical quest the same union of thought and matter, of language and referent, that has been exposed to contem-

porary man as "the problem of relativity." His "own" thought recalls its own dependence on the Place. He encounters a ground
rather than making one.

It is to these considerations that Heidegger can appeal in seeking
to ground his thought insofar as it can be grounded.[18] His implicit
argument is that his thinking is *claimed* in the same way as any
thinker's thought. His attitude is different in that it responds to this
claim directly, while the thought of metaphysics has not yet similarly responded to that claim. *His thought, then, is fundamentally the
expression of his circumstances.* Yet he does not deny that philosophy
and science can operate at a level where there is reflective entertain-
ment of hypothetical alternatives, critical analysis, logical inference.
He is holding that this same thought, at a deeper level, has as its ultimate referents phenomena that are already, and must already be,
thought and named. That is, free imagination, rational analysis,
and mental invention depart from relative phenomena only in the
end to return to them, since relative phenomena are the original
and ultimate referents of thought. Thought that does not 'remember' this has not "become what it is." Thought can, to be sure, be
the expression of unknown psychic motives, of class behavior, of
cultural or national attitudes and preferences. And these motives,
behaviors, and attitudes can be rationally inquired into. But no
matter what the motive or attitude, this thought is in any case ultimately about phenomena in which thought and language already
inhere.

We can now conclude that Heidegger's thought seeks to validate
itself by regarding itself as *essentially* the expression of a prior and
remaining truth or disclosure. But inasmuch as *all* human thought
is an expression of this same truth, in which it is grounded, the essential difference between his thought and, say, Sartre's (or to some
extent the *early* Heidegger's) is that Heidegger's thought remembers the truth it expresses. The principle of forgetting/remem-
bering serves as the fundamental principle for criticizing, and validating, thought at the level of assertion.

We must be sure to be clear about what this means. It is *not* a discounting of assertions, the truth of assertions, the logic of assertions, the need for reasoning and reflecting. It is a recalling of the
basis (ground) of assertions, which makes it possible for assertions
to be true or false at all. If assertions cannot refer to beings that are

already intelligible as what they are, there is no truth or falsity in assertions and no possibility of judging the truth of Heidegger's and Sartre's assertions when they disagree. Real disagreement presupposes, or is grounded in, a prior community or prior "agreement" at a deeper level. For example, if two people disagree about whether it is the earth or the sun that really moves, that presupposes the prior disclosure of the sun to both disputants as a being, the earth as a being, and the relation of movement between them. Disagreement is always disagreement in detail grounded in a prior truth that is shared by human beings who dwell in the same world, disclosed in naming. To use Aristotle's distinction, the idea of a thing is "separable in statement" from the thing or relation and thus can be used in contradictory assertions (the sun is moving; the sun is stationary), but it belongs to the thing, is "separable only in statement." [19] Nothing in Heidegger's thought says that Heidegger cannot be quite as much mistaken in assertion and as subject to criticism and self-criticism on grounds of logical coherence or empirical correspondence as anyone else. What he writes of is a prior truth. To be sure, he makes assertions about this prior truth. These assertions can and must be judged by whether or not they express adequately their own ground. But any assertions that deny Heidegger's assertions about the ground of assertions must show how *they* can refer to intelligible entities and relations and how *they* can count on the reader or hearer referring to these same intelligible entities. *At this level, truth is the same for Heidegger and for Sartre.* It is in this fundamental sense that Heidegger's thought is grounded in truth (like anyone's) and to that extent validated (like anyone's). But Heidegger's thought is also validated at another level in that it has remembered and so can point to its ground, which at the same time grounds and hence validates the thought even of those who disagree with him. This is the case because, as shown, disagreement presupposes a common truth at a deeper level. Therefore we must conclude that Heidegger's thought is *fundamentally* valid. It is grounded *with awareness* in that prior disclosure that inevitably grounds and orients even philosophies that seek, without owning up to their prior relative and conditioned ground, to establish a transcendental or absolute present ground (for example, Descartes).

Hegel singles out the following passage from Aristotle's *Metaphysics* to serve as epigraph for, and guide to, his *Phänomenologie des Geistes:* "by starting from what is inadequately known, but familiar to us, we can learn to know what is intrinsically intelligible, using what we do know . . . to guide us."[20] Heidegger reappropriates this notion, which stands as motto at the Hegelian beginning of the phenomenological movement as I have broadly defined it. But at the same time he frees this notion from the attempt made by both Aristotle and Hegel to go on and ground this prior and 'familiar' ground in a metaphysical, absolute, and rational ground. He does so because any posited metaphysical ground is already inevitably grounded in the ground of prior familiarity rather than vice versa.

At this point one must raise the question whether Heidegger commits himself to a conventionalism that the grounding of the familiar in an absolute transcendental-rational ground seeks to avoid. Does Heidegger end up in the same position as Nietzsche, who wrote that "every advance in epistemological and moral knowledge has reinstated the Sophists—Our contemporary way of thinking . . . is Protagorean"?[21] Would such a position not be consonant with Heidegger's obvious indebtedness to Nietzsche? Would it not be consonant with Heidegger's notion of a future that would be "richer in contingencies?"[22] Is the "precedent community of nature" merely a conventional community? If so, is not Heidegger's thought in essence nihilistic? This is a critical question.

A Heideggerian response might begin by cautioning against what can be called the fallacy of argument from need. There is a remarkable tendency in human thought, including philosophical thought, to believe that if there is need for an absolute, it must exist. The argument sometimes takes the following form: X cannot be right because his view would lead to conventionalism (or nihilism, or relativism, or absence of standards). That philosophy should be sensitive to human need does not require defense; that philosophy can fulfill that need, however, is not an a priori truth. If Heidegger's notion of primary truth should present problems to a tradition that has in large part been devoted to a quest for absolute truth,[23] that is not in itself a demonstration that Heidegger is wrong.

Second, it must be noted that we live at a time when philosophy and science have themselves conducted us toward a relativist, nihilist, and conventionalist point of view. It is possible that this trend is not simply a mistake. But at the same time Heidegger does not take this point of view at face value. He writes that "it seems as if everywhere man encounters only himself," but he argues that this is only "a last deceptive appearance [Schein]."[24] He does not simply take over Nietzschean nihilism (which even Nietzsche himself saw as only a stage, as I have noted), although this nihilism is not simply "Nietzsche's." Heidegger has a double attitude toward the philosophical tradition—it is often 'right' although not fundamentally 'true'. To determine how it is right is to correlate it with the true. To correlate the tradition with the true is to show how the metaphysical quest *both* expresses *and* dissimulates its own 'origin' or 'ground'.[25] The nihilism in which the metaphysical quest itself terminates is 'right' in two ways. (1) Nihilism expresses the fact that no absolute or unconditioned ground is knowable by man. (2) Nihilism expresses the fact that any ground which can enter human experience will be one in which thought itself already participates and will thus in an important sense be "relative." If one demands the unconditioned, one will end in nihilism owing to one's having begun in a forgetting of the conditionality of one's beginning. But at the same time the metaphysical quest dissimulates the disclosive power of its own ground, which is not something that man can originate. Rather each man is granted the ungroundable 'gift' of an intelligible world ('truth') when he comes into language (that is, when he becomes 'man'). The time of relativism, nihilism, subjectivism, and conventionalism provides the condition for remembering this 'gift' because (a) man can no longer expect deliverance from his age-old mortal and finite condition (this is the real meaning of Nietzsche's "eternal recurrence of the same") and (b) there is thus nowhere to turn for meaning and truth except to his finite world—it is there or nowhere—and (c) there is now no escape from the conclusion that this finite world has been man's true ground all along.

These are the preconditions for man's turning his care and concern wholeheartedly to this finite world, but as we have noted they do not insure this turning. Nietzsche implies that a long cultural deconditioning of the quest for absolutes[26] must occur before real affirmation of the earth (*amor fati*) is possible, and we have observed that Heidegger looks forward perhaps a thousand years.[27] So much may be required to counteract "the argument from need." But even Nietzsche does not see this finite world as 'gift'. He rather sees it as an expression of will to power and is quite committed to the "last deceptive appearance" in which everywhere man encounters only himself. Nietzsche's thought is still subjectivist.

But does all this mean any more than that the time may come when man will affirm conventionalism? A 'convention' is a rule, order, or attitude that is generally agreed to but that is arbitrary in origin. The term 'arbitrary' refers to will and choice. A convention attains its validity from being generally chosen or willed; it is a coming-together of individual wills. The conventional is the nonnatural; the natural is a given, while the conventional is posited within the sphere of the human. It is then clear that conventionalism falls within the orientation called humanism, which Heidegger rejects. Heidegger repeatedly speaks of 'measures' or 'standards' that are not simply human measures or standards.[28] A measure means a stable amount or a delimited and definite reference point. Metaphysics seeks the largest or highest definite reference point in the ultimate 'whence' and 'whither'. The failure of this search leaves only a standing stock of raw materials to be ordered and measured out arbitrarily—by will or choice. But this standing stock is the dissimulated Place of the Fourfold. This Place, not man alone, establishes the measures. The Place *is* the ultimate measure, in the sense of the original *and remaining* reference point, as it assembles upon, around, and in the 'thing'. The regular recurrence of day and night, of the seasons, of birth, growth, maturity, decline and death, of warmth and cold, of water and desert, of mountain and valley, of work and rest, of speech and silence—these are fundamental measures. It is they that form the grounding ethos, the way that is proper for mortals, their own way. It is they that enable man to situate and orient (that is, place) himself in the most fundamental sense, to have familiarity, to belong.

This Place is not 'nature' in the usual sense (hence Heidegger is not a 'naturalist' in the usual sense) since it is a world that is what it is only in language and only for mortals. It is a world of 'phenomena'. These phenomena are not conventional, since they are what they are prior to any act of will or choice. Phenomena are not products of a coming-together (*con-venientia*) of factors that were previously separate. But they are not what they are prior to all thought. In language, thought has contributed to ("played into") their formal intelligibility and definiteness, as has the earth. This is a critical point for ontology and must be considered more closely. Can it be shown that the application of word to thing in naming is more than nominal, hence conventional? Can it be shown that distinctions of thought (concepts, universals) really *belong to* things, rather than being conventional ways of dividing up a seamless matter? If not, Heidegger's version of phenomenological ontology is in serious difficulty.

In answer to these questions, I shall attempt to apply Heidegger's notion of identity-and-difference to the relation between word, thought, and thing.[29] In the process I shall consider how such application of the notion of identity and difference departs from a dialectical account of the word-thought-thing relation; this will facilitate subsequent comparison of Heidegger and Sartre on this point. In my discussion, 'word' is meant to include verbs as well as nouns, and 'thing' is meant to include events and processes as well as entities. If nouns name entities, verbs name events or processes. It is the general relation of name to named that is here in question.

We say that we "make distinctions." One of the most elementary among these distinctions is that between word and thing; word and thing are distinct, even different in kind. Words are for the most part "universals" (at least when paired with their concepts—as when one pairs the mere word "table" with the concept of "table"); things are "particulars." Words pertain to speech; things pertain to reality, materiality, substance, or actuality. Words refer to things; things refer only to themselves. Words are therefore secondary, *post hoc*. The real *hoc*, or the real *hic et nunc*, is the thing. It is obvious that words are and must be independent of things. If word and thing were not different in kind, words could not refer *to* things, and things would not be more than words. All this is elementary and correct; it is 'right'.

Furthermore, it seems that the same is true of the relation between thought and thing. They are and must be distinct, different in kind. The thing is and must be independent of and prior to the thoughts we entertain about it. If we were to advance the thesis that thought and thing are not distinct, we should, correctly, be accused of succumbing to a "poetic" or "primitive" confusion, or a lapse into "mystical" indistinction or inarticulateness, or a relapse into the crassest idealism.

Furthermore, to these distinctions it seems that a third must be added. Despite the affinity between word and thought—both of which are distinguished from the thing as secondary to it and by comparison with it merely mental or ideal or ideational—word and thought are different in kind. A thought, a concept, seems essentially prelinguistic, although the word may refer to a concept and even express it in a statement.

So there seem to be three ontologically distinct kinds of being— that of the word, that of the thought, that of the thing. It appears that both word and thought have only a borrowed being, so to speak: they are "meaningful" or "significant" only if they refer to a thing. They need the thing, but the thing does not need them. This ontological poverty, or dependence of word and thought upon the thing, seems to be reinforced by the commonsensical fact that man depends on things—food, timber, etc.—more essentially than upon either word or idea. To take any other position would be to suppress man's real needs and his real and fundamental dependence on materiality.

These distinctions, then, are not accidental and are not erasable. And if any of these distinctions comes under attack, invocation of elementary logic can easily dispel the attack. A thing is a thing; a word is a word; a thought is a thought; therefore a word is not a thing, nor is a thought a thing, nor is a word a thought. The law of identity maintains beings as what they are, in their distinctness from each other. The price of being able to relate beings to each other is that they first be maintained in their difference from each other, that their distinct identities be maintained and preserved against any thoughtless attempt to con-fuse them with each other. Thus Gilbert Ryle rightly warns against "category mistakes."[30] By the reflective exercise of one's analytic powers, isolating differences in kind, one protects philosophy and culture against the collapse of distinctions. Having done so, one is in a position to relate these distinct beings to each other by an exercise of one's powers of synthesis; one points out which words properly correspond to which concepts, and which concepts properly correspond to which things. The exercise of these analytic and synthetic powers goes by the name of dialectic. Dialectic works with, or uses, distinctions.

Now when Heidegger states that dialectic is not fundamental or that the rule of logic is not absolute, this seems patently wrong.[31] And when he asserts that distinct kinds of being are 'the same' even though 'different', this seems to confirm his mistake.[32] Heidegger apparently succumbs to the nihilistic loss of all distinctions foretold by Nietzsche. Logic and commonsense seem to be undermined. Yet Heidegger asserts that he is not in a position to undermine these distinctions, and that he would not if he could.[33] The absoluteness or fundamentality of these distinctions has in fact *never existed*, yet this has prevented neither these distinctions nor the logic that "supports" them from being preserved. There is in fact always a community already between these "dialectical polarities" or distinct "opposites." Heidegger expresses this in *EM* by saying that there is "an initial [*anfänglichen*] inner union between thinking and Being itself," a union that he speaks of as a "harmonia."[34] Harmony is a tension in which "opposites" are together in their apartness. The originary unity is a togetherness in apartness and an apartness in togetherness. Earth and thought are certainly distinct, yet they belong together and from the beginning play into each other as Intelligible Earth. In this notion one hears echoes of both Heraclitus and Hegel. Heidegger seems to be espousing precisely a dialectic, an interplay of oppositions. These opposites or polarities seem to be dualities, yet Heidegger seems to claim to have escaped both dialectic and dualism.

It is not a question of escaping either dialectic or dualities but rather of recollecting their origin in "the same." Let us take an ordinary philosophical case—that of universals and particulars. We say that universals and particulars are "opposites," opposed in their natures, yet we invoke them together. The particular, we say, is just the individual itself. The universal goes far beyond that particular or indeed beyond any particular. The universal does violence to the particular, in the sense that it departs from the particular, seems perhaps to ignore the uniqueness of the particular, seems to subsume the particular by force under a generality. The particular, for its part, resists this universalization by remaining a mere particular, an irreducible particular, in some ways a unique particular. There is tension, *polemos*, between them. But each requires the other in order to be what it is. The particular tree is what it is—a tree—with reference to the universal, treeness. It owes its very appearing *as* a particular, even unique, tree to the violence done it by the universal; it is as it is *in* itself only in light of what is *beyond* itself; its showing itself as what it is—a tree—depends on its place or situatedness within the universal. On the other hand, the universal is what it is only by reference to particular trees—it is the treeness *of* trees. Universal and particular are what they are—are distinct—only by playing into each other and out of each other. They are the same *and* different, unity and disunity. The harmony or equilibrium in which there appears tree as tree is extremely delicate, precarious. It requires what Heidegger has called "restraint."[35] Particular and universal must each defer and yield to the other while at the same time preserving their difference or independence. In our thinking the precarious balance is generally upset; particulars go their own way and universals are reached only by sloppy generalization from particulars or habitual association of particulars. Or so empiricists maintain. Universals go their own way and dictate to particulars, regardless of how they first appear, their real natures or essences. Or so rationalists maintain. In either case there seems no mutual deference, no restraint, no harmony. And logic requires that one choose between sameness and difference; things that are distinct cannot enter into each other and yet remain distinct. The original 'gathering' seems dispersed—beings are only beings, thought is only thought.

Why is this original unity any different from Hegel's 'concrete universal'? In part it is different because Hegel regards the concrete universal as an achievement, a final result of dialectical becoming, of logical negation and affirmation. According to Heidegger, what happens at the very beginning and ever since is that meaning and the meant are simultaneously the same and different. There is *an unmediated difference of the same.* If there were no original togetherness of meaning and the meant, a sameness of nature, then it would never be possible subsequently to relate them. Because there has occurred a forgetting of this original union, we are now confronted with an essentia and an existentia that appear to have nothing to do with each other, that appear unrelatable, or relatable only by man's willful, arbitrary, and conflicting imposition of essences upon existents. There appear to be only particular existents surrounded by nothingness, a free field for the imposition of essences at will, the situation known as nihilism. What needs to be remembered is that this free field has already been filled and that if it had not been, the allegedly pure particulars would not and could not be intelligible as the particulars they are.

The foregoing means that neither universal nor particular precedes the other. Neither is the ground of the other. "Everything happens together."[36] This happening requires language. The naming of a thing is simultaneously perceiving a thing (a 'particular') and thinking its kind or type (a 'concept'). It is to name the thing as the sort of thing it is. *The "genius" of the name is that it holds the universal and the particular as one, refers and defers to both.* But it does not do so by a dialectical synthesis of a universal previously thought and a particular previously sensed. When a child first hears a name with understanding, he first experiences, or sees understandingly, the thing (particular existent) as what (universal essence) it is (the being in its Being). Thus idea and thing happen together in language. The thing named is neither subjective nor objective, neither form nor matter, neither idea nor sense-datum, neither essence nor existence, but both, and only as both is it the thing (phenomenon). This means that its structure and properties are neither simply material nor simply ideational, but both. This is the case because thought has deferred to sensing and sensing has deferred to thought, simultaneously. That is, the structure and properties of a thing are traits of the phenomenon named.[37]

The phenomenon is thus the ground of subsequent distinctions between the concept and the matter, the essence and the existence, both of which are *of* the thing. The thing cannot be dialectically reconstructed or synthesized by a regressive movement that goes back to its original discrete or atomic elements (thought, matter, name) because each element is what it is only in relation to the others, and these relations occur simultaneously.

Through this original 'sameness' or identity the thing comes into presence as what it is and remains—that is, gains its own identity and is hence self-identical. But here the Platonist, the Kantian, or the Husserlian is likely to raise a serious question. If the concept, essence, or universal does not have an absolute transcendental origin that guarantees its permanence, cannot the very nature of the thing change in time? Heidegger's response might be as follows. First, philosophical inquiry has not been able to demonstrate an absolute transcendental origin of essences. Second, if essences are transcendental and absolute in origin, the consequence is an idealism in which the thing is reduced to the idea of it, or a dualism in which there is no real community of nature between the essence and the existent to which it is supposed to apply. Third, given the foregoing considerations, one is left with the original unity of essence and existent being—in the naming of the perceived—as the real source of the identity of the thing through time, rather than as a threat to its self-identity.

On the other hand, Heidegger might continue, one has to face the fact that this identity has no absolute and eternal guarantee. Thought *does* overreach the particular when a certain series of particulars receives the same name and essence. The particulars of this group, class, or genus are the same *and* different, and we inevitably encounter limiting cases where the particular barely belongs under the name and concept, where the "family resemblance"[38] among particulars is strained to the breaking-point. This is not to be denied and is not rectifiable by any spurious effort to make names more univocal. Language and things are inherently ambiguous;[39] the extension of the name and concept is necessarily fuzzy at the edges; language by nature does violence. But this is the price of there being an intelligible world. Disclosure is also closure. This contingency must simply be faced.

The very condition of a thing having self-identity through time is that its 'nature' or 'essence' cannot be transcendentally fixed and its boundaries thus absolutely determined. One can only say that in attentive naming the "free ranging" of conceptual imagination is restrained by the sensing of "material structures" (Earth), although the disclosure of these structures in thought is the closure of them as they would perhaps appear to a god. The god who would create the world of things with fixed boundaries once and for all is 'absent', although the 'holy' gift of an intelligible world ('illuminated' by the 'heavens') is evident when mortals realize that in language their transcendental imagination has participated in the constitution of the very world to which they are subject. Thus there is a finite transcendence in the experiencing of phenomena as what they are that recognizes its power and the limitation of its power by reference to the gods above and the mute but supporting Earth below. Man's quasi-theological power (imagination, conceptuality) is limited by the Earth but given its subject matter by the Earth.

Distinctions and determinations are therefore given their relative permanence both by the relative constancy of the name and by the deference of the concept to such structures as Earth may possess.

The constraint of the Earth is indicated by the fact that a child in taking over an inherited name understands its extension when he "gets the idea" of the thing named in *seeing* the traits of that kind of thing. This means that the transcendental power of his imagination is limited by its formation of a concept that must apply to a particular range of sensible traits, and that does not overstep these boundaries by including things called by other inherited names.

There is thus a relative constancy of distinctions or "fundamental measures," which is what I set out to show. To demand greater constancy would be to try to abrogate the conditions under which there is constancy (self-identity, "permanence of substance") at all. The laws of logic are grounded in this primary constancy, in the *logos* which is the original saying-and-laying (*legein*) of the phenomenon *as* what it is (phenomeno-logy). In other words, the power of logic (including dialectic) to identify and distinguish, to synthesize and analyze, to require identity and avoidance of contradiction, is premised on the original disclosure of phenomena and the thought of them as identical *and* as different. If thought as identifying and distinguishing did not already inhere *in* phenomena, there would be no ground for the applicability of logic *to* phenomena. Thus the very possibility of a logic of beings is grounded in a primary level of truth where the logical requirement of identity *or* difference does not hold—a level at which thought and thing are *both* the same and different. This represents the limit of applicability of logic as well as its warrant. *The price of thought's applying to things is that thought belong to things.*

I set out in this section to show how Heidegger's conception of truth grounds the ontological assertions Heidegger makes. This question was provoked by another. Is Heidegger's thought more than the mirror of his *particular* circumstances rather than a validly formed truth-claim about the *universal* nature of ontology? I have argued that Heidegger's notion of primary truth grounds the possibility of the applicability of any assertions whatsoever to phenomena. It therefore refers and defers to a level of primacy and universality that prevents it from being merely the mirror of his particular or idiosyncratic circumstances. Since primary truth is the precondition for either idiosyncratic or nonidiosyncratic assertion, the assertion of it is therefore nonidiosyncratic. Such assertion does not try to *establish* a priori the nature of truth in all possible worlds; it *defers* to the truth that always already grounds it in this world. It shows that any doctrine of truth that tries to be self-grounding at the level of assertions cuts itself off from its own phenomenal ground.

V

How does Sartre's conception of truth ground his own ontological assertions? His response to this problem, Heidegger would argue, is one that remains at the upper or metaphysical level. Sartre writes that "So long as thought watches over its own movement, all is truth or a moment of truth . . . as a real factor in historical evolution. . . . Our present ideas are false because they have died before us." [40] What does this mean? The movement of thought is for Sartre a surpassing of its past, even if that surpassing takes the form of 'repeating' the past in new circumstances. [41] A thought that watches over its own movement looks for the dialectical nature of the movement of surpassing by a regressive and a progressive analysis. It recognizes negation of inherited negations as forming higher truth. It recognizes that mere repetition of past thought is false because it carries over unchanged into present circumstances a thought that was true only for past circumstances that praxis has already altered. For example, to advocate bourgeois ethics today is to commit oneself to an individualism at a time when social praxis is surpassing bourgeois individualism in the direction of socialism, owing to the contradictions inherent in bourgeois individualism. It is therefore to fail to recognize the fact that one's attitudes are necessarily 'interiorized' class attitudes: one's thought is 'false' because it sees itself as espousing a neutral individualism in which all individuals are already free and equal. It fails to see that free and equal individuality has been 'taken up' (*aufgehoben* in Hegel's sense) into a social philosophy which realizes that free and equal individuality is a rational ideal that must be practically realized rather than a present objectified or materialized fact. The movement of thought is thus 'true' when it is in the process of negating the contradictions it inherits. It recognizes these contradictions by looking for the dominant thought inherited, for social struggle on the part of groups disinherited by this inheritance, and for a philosophy that calls for a solution to this contradiction by proposing a new social order.

But Sartrean rationality requires still more than this. It requires the recognition of truths that, if partial, are nevertheless permanent truths. Thus existentialism, while ceasing to be a particular inquiry, will become the foundation of all inquiry. A free project of the negating-surpassing consciousness is a permanent or universal truth. How is it known to be so? Through Sartre's early philosophical analyses, primarily in *TE* and *EN*. These analyses establish that consciousness is the negation of being that projects toward an ideal synthesis of thought and its objects—a humanizing of its environment. The later Sartre comes to see that in history this projecting consciousness takes the essential form of economic praxis. But the ultimate ground of this praxis and of all thought is negation of being by a consciousness that is aware of itself as lack and projection toward what it lacks. Beings (phenomena) are matter in process of being transformed by the consciousness of an organism projecting teleologically toward a final complete unity of thought and matter (matter as perfect mirror of human aims).

Sartre's critique of Marxian thought for neglecting the project of free consciousness is a case of thought "watching over its own movement": Marxian thought had failed to take up "the Cartesian moment" into its surpassing, thus "totalizing too quickly." Sartre's self-critique is also a case of thought watching over its own movement: his early thought had failed to take up the present Marxian moment into its surpassing and had thus merely 'repeated' a variant of the Cartesian moment.

Thus what proximately grounds Sartre's assertions is the historical field of praxis that his assertions both express and surpass. These assertions are true insofar as they express the complex present synthesis of past and formerly contradictory truths. (And they are false insofar as they fall short of an ideal truth that is 'one'.) But what originally guarantees that historical praxis is indeed the field of "Truth that becomes"[42] is its termini—the original negation and the anticipated ultimate condition that will have synthesized the negation. This means that the ultimate ground of truth is the project of free consciousness to negate a negating matter by making it support practical freedom.[43] Does this mean that truth is really a transcendental condition imposed upon matter by consciousness? The criterion of truth is objectification of freedom, materialized freedom, practical freedom. Does this not mean that truth is the assessment of the world relative to a criterion of truth proposed by transcendental consciousness? In what sense then do the distinctions that consciousness finds in the world really *belong to* the world? This question requires exploration if we are to understand (*a*) to what, ontologically, Sartre's assertions really refer, and (*b*) how his view of the original constitution of the phenomenon relates to Heidegger's.

We have seen that in *CRD* Sartre argues for what he calls "dialectical circularity" as the "major discovery of the dialectical experience"; "man is 'mediated' by things to the exact extent that things are 'mediated' by man."[44] We saw that this differs from the early Sartre, for whom there is no genuine mediation of externality. But this mediation is not like Heidegger's unmediated identity-and-difference. Even for the prehistoric 'organism' there is rather at first pure difference—matter as negation of conscious praxis and conscious praxis as negation of matter. The totalizing movement of history and *historical* truth is grounded in this dialectical circularity. But this is not a *reciprocal* dialectic,[45] not a true double mediation. The negation is originally traceable to consciousness; matter becomes a negation only in relation to human freedom's project. Sartre rightly cannot make matter per se a negating because matter is not, like conscious praxis, a teleological surpassing. If he did so, he would fall back into an indefensible dialectic of matter (pre-existentialized "dialectical materialism").

What the foregoing argues is that the meaning of matter is defined by praxis. The fundamental meaning of matter is its negation of the practical project or its facilitation of the practical project (objectification without alienation). The prehistorical organism of *CRD* can 'repeat' without having to 'totalize'.[46] In each case its surpassing is able to negate the negation successfully—that is, to continue to make matter conform to the organism's praxis (hunger is negated by ready supply of food, and without depriving the Other of food). It is the logic of teleology that determines the meaning of the environment. This practical field, as noted in chapter 12, is reminiscent of Heidegger's referential totality, whose ready-to-hand meanings are ultimately traceable to Dasein as the ultimate "for-the-sake-of-which." But it will be remembered that Heidegger's referential totality was liable to a kind of disintegration in anxiety—in the appearance of the entity in its sheer presentness-at-hand, "devoid of meaning," its sheer material otherness. We saw in this a danger to the phenomenological program of reuniting meaning and Being. If the attempt is made to define the meaning of all beings relative to human purposes as their "baseless basis," phenomena threaten to lose their integral identity and fall apart into "what-being" (essence, defined relative to Dasein's projection) and "that-being" (sheer existence). I have interpreted the later Heidegger as finding this to be a consequence of the residual metaphysics of SZ, the attempt to ground phenomena in Dasein.[47] The later Heidegger preserves the integral identity of the phenomenon by what is in effect a reappropriation of the notion of a "precedent community of nature" between man and thing at a level deeper than that of praxis— the original event of the phenomenon in language. In carrying this out, the notion of unmediated or immediate identity-and-difference is necessary.

Sartre remains on the metaphysical level that the later Heidegger finds grounded in a precedent ground. Logic, now in the form of a dialectic of organic praxis, retains its primacy for Sartre. Even in the prehistorical organism the meaning of beings is determined by negation and its surpassing. The fundamental ontological unit is the conscious organism, as a 'One', which successfully reduces 'exteriority' (needed matter) to 'interiority' by negating its negation. The orienting center is the original prehistorical One whose historical negation (through scarcity) requires the project toward a final "unity which would be manifested as a cosmic determination"[48]—that is, the restoration of unbroken organic 'interiority' through the total determination of matter by praxis. This would be a 'cosmic' objectification of freedom in which matter no longer negates freedom but rather supports it.

Thus the identity of meaning and Being, which Heidegger finds always already given, must for Sartre be created by historical praxis. The phenomenon in its 'true' integral identity ("the truth must be one")[49] occurs only at the end of history. I have called this the project of humanism. At its completion, reason has successfully persuaded necessity; matter has taken the impress of intentionality (formal cause) and of rational desire or practical need (final cause) without remainder.

I have raised these considerations in an attempt to understand to what Sartre's assertions really refer, the truth in which they are grounded. As it is a truth of praxis, the only real meaning of phenomena is their praxis-meaning. Even when phenomena refuse to conform to praxis, their meaning is practical—that of 'counterfinality'.[50] As counterfinal, the phenomenon means precisely the not-yet-finalized. But these are still *general* meanings, categorial meanings. The particular counterfinality is, say, a bank, which symbolizes unequal distribution of wealth, which means the not-yet of objective freedom for all practical organisms. Sartre is beyond doubt right in arguing that a phenomenon such as a bank is a 'collective' form whose nature is determined teleologically and referentially or contextually. The bank is a phenomenon that is what it is in its very Being only in relation to human being, and it is through a temporal, progressive-regressive comprehension that I understand what it is in terms of the purposes it serves. This confirms the phenomenological-ontological view that the Being of a being is to be understood temporally, in terms of its coming-into-being in a manner beyond that of mere material and efficient causation, and in relation to human thought.

Thus, Sartre's assertions about a phenomenon (such as a bank) are grounded in truth in the sense that they represent a practical organism situating itself relative to an environment that has been constituted by and for practical organisms. This prior practicalization of nature accounts for the possibility of making reference to an intelligible world. Praxis, then, would appear to be the self-grounding origin of truth. What could a Heideggerian interpretation possibly add? Recourse to a more "primordial" level of truth would seem to be superfluous. What could it conceivably add to say that a bank is a dissimulated assembling of the Fourfold? Cannot Sartre with perfect justice say that this would be a mystification, serving only to darken what is already quite clear?

A Heideggerian response to this challenge would be prefaced by wholehearted agreement with the Sartrean analysis of a bank as only comprehensible temporally, teleologically, formally, and contextually. This may serve to remind us that there are significant respects in which Heidegger and Sartre agree; I have enumerated nine of these respects at the start of this chapter. But a Heideggerian response would add that human praxis is nevertheless grounded in a deeper ground. To grasp this, one must rethink the question of the conditions under which something like a bank

comes to be what it is. One notes that the foregoing Sartrean analysis makes no reference to language, yet the analysis is in language
and makes reference to phenomena by naming them.

Now Sartre might counter that surely a bank is a bank regardless
of what it is called. Although one must of course use a word in
order to refer to the phenomenon, clearly the bank is a creation of
the practical working-over of matter by embodied and purposive
thought and not *essentially* a grammatical or nominal entity. Not
only that, but the name may even hide the bank's meaning, as
when a bank belonging to only a few is called "The People's Bank."
If the name is necessary in order to provide a common reference
point for the bank itself and my idea of it, surely that does not make
the name *constitutive* of either the bank itself or my idea of it, nor
does the fact that I and the Other must share the word 'bank' in
order to be able to talk about banks make the name constitutive.

But is this really the case? The bank comes to be as bank only for
beings who speak in language. Why? The name is one, a unit, and
without this unit there is no unity of particulars on the one hand
(all banks as members of the class of banks) and no concept on the
other hand (the essence holding together the particular and even
diverse ideas of properties of banks). The name, *as unit*, holds both
a complex of sensible particulars and a complex of ideas in an immediate triple unity: that of particular and particular, of idea and
idea, and of particular and idea. The name holds them in identity
despite their differences.

This unity, in which thing belongs to idea and idea belongs to
thing, does not preexist the name. Nor does the name simply *accom-
pany* the unity of idea and particular. The name neither follows nor
simply accompanies the perception of the thing as what it is.[51] The
thing is perceived *as* what it is when it is named, because only then
"is there"[52] the single 'it' that is at the same time (a) a self-identical
unity persisting through change of properties and of perspectives;
(b) a member of a class of beings relative to which it is the *kind* of
thing it is; (c) an unmediated or immediate unity of sensation and
thought. All the sensible properties of the thing and all the conceptual ideas of the thing and its properties are held in the perception
of one enduring self-identical phenomenon by the word. It is the
original unifying unit.

This naming of which Heidegger writes is not simply an ancient beginning but the beginning of the mortal experience of each of us as a child. The world forms itself around the young child as he hears words, gifts received by his parents and passed on to him as gifts. The child does not perceive things as they are prior to his coming into language, nor does he create the language in which things come to be what they are. He listens to words and must learn what these words bespeak. When in a dawning comprehension he "gets the idea" of what he is looking at and hearing the name of, then the thing itself shows itself as what it is: *a* tree, *a* building, *a* growing or decaying, etc. It is perceived (literally *and* intuitively) as the particular it is when it shows itself in its true boundaries (as having class identity and as having specific difference, etc.). In this disclosing of the thing in its true nature—its coming into its own—there play simultaneously sensing, imagining, conceptualizing, retaining, "protaining." All these are centered on the emerging thing. It is the name that holds them together in one experience because the name belongs *both* to the present perceived thing, to the absently present (remembered, anticipated) enduring thing and other things of the same nature, and to the concept of the thing that is both *in* the thing perceived and transferable to (belonging to) other things not present. The thing as named thus "gathers", or assembles in one place, the present and other times and places. There occurs the lighting of the world of such things as the Place of all places and times. Out of the original experience of the thing as what it is there comes the possibility of disassembling the thing into its "components": its matter, its form, its idea, its name, its pure nonrelational particularity, its efficient cause. But all of these only come to be thought separately by abstraction from (on the ground of) the thing itself in its original seamless unity as named.

This means that, in language, the thing named assembles *and* brings into their difference:

—the "matter" of the thing, its independence, with its own structures, together with our bodily sensing (Earth);[53]
—the "idea" of the thing, the imaginative and conceptual ranging beyond the moment in memory and anticipation, and beyond sensation into the sensible and universal, up to the limits imposed by finitude (mortals);
—the "holding" of the thing in an ongoing light by a cosmic har-

mony whose ultimate source is beyond mortal knowledge (heavens);

—the "word" of the thing as a gift that is first received rather than invented, as the coming at once of the unity of the intelligible world, transcendence of sheer finitude, and awareness of finitude (the gods).

These gather as the Place and *its* things. The Place is where things belong—that is, where they first come into their own, their proper being. But they are expropriated by the same thought that depends for its being on this Place. Under the onslaught of a thinking that seeks a ground in *one* of these essential beings alone ("matter," "idea," cosmos, the gods)—in what become material, formal, final, or efficient causes—the Place and its originary Event are dissembled and apparently disassembled. They can be reassembled only by thinking back to their original (and remaining) introplay, not by any 'progressive' attempt, dialectical or otherwise, to synthesize them. The world is not fundamentally an artifact under the hand of man, not a series of raw materials to be efficiently manipulated and impressed with form until they finally compose a totality. This humanistic and technological program flees its own ground and truth.

I return now to the example of the bank. The bank appears as an artifact. And it is. It is a 'collective form', but it collects more than human wills and is more than an objectification of wills. The mortals who invest or save in the bank are beings whose dwelling in language and thought is the *possibility* of the complex of written and computerized accounts as well as the possibility of accumulation of capital. These enduring records exemplify in the language of numbers and symbols the power of the word to hold the moments of time together in an enduring meaning. Only in the relative constancy of language do past, present, and future assemble as a continuous story, with a beginning and an end: for example, the "savings of a lifetime" as the fruit of labor, the presence of security, and the promise of rest.

The mortals who bank measure themselves against the gods. One who banks on immortality, for example, may not lay up wealth where moth and rust corrupt. One may claim divine right to mundane riches denied to other people. Or one may find hoarding of resources vital because this life is all there is. Or one may find the absence of divine right the sign of the equality of all men and the sign of the freedom of man to do what he will with the earth, to master it for his own ends. But if man's image of the gods is the sign of his power to think beyond the moment, to transcend imaginatively toward the eternal and the one, he owes this power to the Event of disclosure in language. The very Event that is the source of his knowledge and power is beyond his knowledge and power, an unaccountable gift. If oneness, harmony, intelligibility *are* divine,[54] as the condition for everything human beings value, that divinity is manifested only in the thing named, the order of the phenomenal world, and this Place is thus holy.

The bank is supported by the Earth, which is not *fundamentally* a negation of the banker's or builder's praxis, to be transformed by another negation, but rather the provider of the site for any venture and any edifice. The earth also gives the variety of materials out of which the venture and its edifice are made—not basically as raw materials but as intelligible things: the gold of the valley, the wood of the forest, the stone of the ridge. These "natural resources" are gifts of the earth, whose essential meaning and nature are prior to and support for the practical uses they come to serve. They must be intelligible as what they are in order to serve any of a variety of human purposes.

The bank is lighted by the heavens, which are not *fundamentally* atmospheric conditions to be shut out by the architect but the ongoing harmony of light and darkness, the illuminated space within which alone the architect can build and the banker can work. The bank's electric light and air-conditioned air are reappropriations of the natural light and air, and not original inventions. Only those who have had disclosed to them what light and air are are granted the power to adapt them to their purposes.

The main thrust of the foregoing "poetic" grounding of the building and functioning of a praxis-phenomenon, the bank, is that any practical truth created by transformation of matter is grounded in and presupposes a precedent truth. This precedent truth is not owing to the logic of dialectical negation but to the Event of the word (*logos*) as the coming on of an intelligible world in which alone there can be dialectical praxis. This does not necessarily mean that the event of an intelligible world precedes praxis chronologically. It means that praxis as conscious negation of matter cannot fully account either ontologically or epistemologically for the occurrence and intelligibility of the objects of praxis.

While I have used an artifact, a bank, as a vehicle for showing the partiality of Sartre's attempt to ground the phenomenon in praxis, Sartre's position is even more problematic when applied to wholly nonartifactual or noninstrumental beings. There is no way to account for the phenomenon of tree *qua* tree, or river *qua* river, by dialectical combination of matter and conscious negation, that is, by praxis. Sartre's early inability to make thought successfully (actually) combine with being-in-itself in order to form 'the real' is not altogether overcome by his turn to dialectical analysis and his will to take the level of the 'real' as primary. Because he still regards consciousness as ground and source of distinctions, even though these distinctions are now "etched" into the matter of the world itself in embodied praxis, he has no way of taking the natural phenomenon as disclosing *its own* structures and properties. Because he wants to ground distinctions in man, he cannot start with the experience of the phenomenon *as truth*, only subsequent to which do the conceptual and the natural appear as opposites seeming to require synthesis.

In the terms of *SZ*, Sartre's phenomenon as a function of praxis is conceived in terms of a dialectical transformation of the 'present-at-hand' (resistant matter) into the 'ready-to-hand' (matter subserving the ends of praxis). If these were the only characterizations of the phenomenon available to Heidegger in *SZ*, he had nevertheless written: "Perhaps even readiness-to-hand and equipment have nothing to contribute as ontological clues in interpreting the primitive world." He wrote darkly of an "understanding of Being" that "can remain neutral. In this case readiness-to-hand and presence-at-hand have not yet been distinguished."[55] It is now clear that these passages look forward to an original disclosure of the phenomenon that is approached neither from a transcendental pole (praxis, interiority, use; essence) nor from an immanent pole (exteriority, external materiality; existence). Rather, a prior original disclosure is the ground of both approaches—the phenomenon within language as immediate identity-and-difference of the "transcendental" and "immanent" factors or aspects that subsequently are derived from it and that dissimulate their original identity.

Sartre's assertions about the original ground and truth turn out to be the mirror of a particular epochal environment after all—that of metaphysics—rather than a properly grounded universal ontology. The attempt to ground the phenomenon in the ego, cogito, or subject in any of its forms overlooks the unity of the phenomenon and, by apparently freeing thought from its original tie to the phenomenon, leaves thought vulnerable to epochal, hypothetical, and speculative interpretations of the nature of the phenomenon. The reason Sartre experienced a metaphysical leeway between taking the level of the 'actual' as ontological and taking the level of the 'real' as ontological is that he was not compelled by "the things themselves."

VI

It is necessary to conclude that the truth to which Heidegger refers is prior to the truth to which Sartre refers. They occur at different levels and are different in that one grounds the other. The intelligible world grounds praxis and its logic; praxis and its logic cannot of themselves generate an intelligible world. But this difference of level suggests that one might not have to choose between Heidegger's truth and Sartre's truth—providing that Sartrean truth were not to claim to be primary truth.

Yet this leaves open the question of the precise extent to which admission of a prior truth might require modification of Sartre's humanism, his philosophy of history, and his conception of the epistemological and practical powers of dialectical reasoning. This question lies beyond the scope of my study, except insofar as I must respond to it in summarizing Heidegger's and Sartre's versions of phenomenological ontology in the next and last chapter.

14

The Direction of
Phenomenological Ontology

WITH DETERMINATION of the ground of the phenomenon, the question of the nature of phenomenological ontology is essentially answered. Phenomenological ontology is revalidation of the phenomenon through consideration of the place and the way in which beings come into their Being. From the nature of this ground as Place a number of consequences follow for the future conduct of phenomenological and ontological inquiry. I should like to conclude this study by spelling out some of these consequences, to each of which a section of the chapter will be devoted. With the help of our interpretations of Heidegger and Sartre, it should be possible to pass judgment upon the importance and durability of some of the traits of post-Copernican ontology outlined in chapter 1. This will at the same time provide an occasion for further evaluation of the relative merits of Heidegger's and Sartre's orientations.

I

Interaction between two factors requires a precedent community of nature between the factors.

This Aristotelian notion has proven to be crucial for my interpretation of the nature and truth of the phenomenon. It expresses the principle that beings cannot be successfully interrelated unless they already have something in common. Chapter 1 attempted to show that in post-Copernican thought there occurs what Murdoch has called "a broken totality, a divided being." It is evident in Cartesian dualism and in the ensuing long history of efforts to heal that dualism. These efforts have been of essentially two kinds: (1) The two poles or kinds of being have been reunited by reduction of one to the other. Given a dualism between thought and entities or subject and object, one attempted to define entity or object relative to thought through an idealism that ran the risk of reducing the entity

to thought or to a subjective appearance. Or one attempted to define the subject and his thought relative to the object through a realism or materialism that ran the risk of reducing the subject and his
thought to matter. (2) Recognizing the reductiveness of the foregoing attempts, one reunited the two poles by reference to a third factor, God. God is the substance of which thought and object are two
modes; or the divine mind is a historical process of reconciling all
dualities; or God is the object of a faith in his power to resolve rationally unresolvable contradictions. But this second or nonreduc-
tive solution requires the invocation of a metaphysical being whose
existence is indemonstrable. Whitehead correctly delineated this
problematic situation:

> The seventeenth century had finally produced a scheme of
> scientific thought framed by mathematicians, for the use of
> mathematicians. The great characteristic of the mathematical
> mind is its capacity for dealing with abstractions; and for elicit-
> ing from them clear-cut demonstrative trains of reasoning, en-
> tirely satisfactory so long as it is those abstractions which you
> want to think about. The enormous success of the scientific ab-
> stractions, yielding on the one hand *matter* with its *simple loca-
> tion* in space and time, on the other hand *mind*, perceiving, suf-
> fering, reasoning, but not interfering, has foisted onto
> philosophy the task of accepting them as the most concrete ren-
> dering of fact.
>   Thereby, modern philosophy has been ruined. It has os-
> cillated in a complex manner between three extremes. There are
> the dualists, who accept matter and mind as on equal basis,
> and the two varieties of monists, those who put mind inside
> matter, and those who put matter inside mind. But this jug-
> gling with abstractions can never overcome the inherent confu-
> sion introduced by the ascription of *misplaced concreteness* to
> the scientific scheme of the seventeenth century.[1]

The only recourse is to challenge the dualism at its roots by showing that the distinction it makes is not ultimate. Subject and object
or thought and entity have been mistakenly defined as pure opposites. For Descartes, *res cogitans* and *res extensa* are defined precisely
as mutually exclusive—each is what the other is not. Their logical
relation is one of negation. Spinoza asserts that *all* determination is
negation. What must be shown is that thought and entity arise

together as the same *and* different. Neither is the result of the other, nor are both the poles of some third factor. In human experience of entities, the structure of thought and the structure of thing have already commingled.

Because Husserl in effect takes the origin of the structure of entities to lie in thought, he misses this precedent community of nature. Because Sartre takes the origin of the structure of entities to lie in negation, he misses the precedent community of nature. What is requisite is seeing that the linguistic distinction between thought and its referent is not characterizable by the logic of negation. When a thing is originally named, it comes simultaneously into being *as* thought and *as* thing. From thenceforth, the thought is that of the thing and the thing is that of the thought.

If phenomenological reduction is construed as recourse to transcendental thought as the true ground, in the sense that it regards the nature (essence, essential structure) of beings as originally constituted by a priori thought, then the common ground between thought and beings will be missed and the nature of beings will be ideal, rather than inherent in beings themselves.

If community of nature must be made historically by practical transformation of inert matter, the precedent unity of nature between thought and beings, in which beings have already been disclosed as what they are, is overlooked.

II

Inquiry and knowledge are grounded in what is already familiar, and this is ontologically real.

This principle means that the familiar is more than a starting point in the sense of the "proximal and for the most part" experience of *SZ* or the level of "the real" in *EN*. As the very subject matter that inquiry investigates and comes to know more about, the familiar world is inevitably the true world. This does not mean, however, that this familiar world is necessarily recognized in its true nature and role by either philosophy or science. Hence Heidegger can at one and the same time, from *SZ* forward, both attack familiarity and defend it. He claims that what is "nearest" is "farthest" in the sense that philosophy and science have not ceded validity to the same world of phenomena in which they inevitably orient themselves; any effort to ground the familiar in a prior ground is itself inevitably grounded in the familiar. Therefore a protracted effort at revalidation of the familiar is called for. The commonplace becomes the Common Place. Because this effort has to take the form of a going back into the *ground* of metaphysics, Heidegger's thought often gives the impression of cutting behind the familiar in quest of a mystical ground in relation to which the ordinary and familiar would be mere appearance. This is perhaps the most widespread of all misinterpretations of Heidegger's thought. His effort is rather to call attention to the familiar world itself as "wondrous" and "holy" when it is no longer devalued by reference to a transcendent ground or the quest for such. This, to be sure, has to be accomplished by pointing to another ground that has been hidden, but this "groundless ground" is nothing other than the event and place of disclosure of phenomena themselves, the familiar world. If the familiar then appears in its essential *un*familiarity,[2] this only means in its true inexplicable and ungroundable wonder, the wonder that there are beings at all, given as an intelligible realm to human beings.

Because the familiar world is not absolutely grounded, it is necessarily a *relative* world and an *incomplete* world from the standpoint of the epistemological quest for absolute knowledge. This quest appears to give the true "measure." Because thought inheres in any disclosed being, however, the ideal of disclosure of a being unqualified or unmediated by thought is impossible. This frustrates the possibility of truth only if truth is defined as correspondence of pure thought and pure being (the unqualified and nonrelational entity). What is called for is *a reversal of attitude* in which phenomenal disclosure is defined as primary truth. This amounts to an affirmation of the truth of ordinary experience—an affirmation that experience necessarily makes but in which modern philosophy and science allow experience to place little confidence.

The conflict between this tradition and the effort to revalidate the phenomenon is illustrated by the early Sartre's oscillation between the phenomenon or ordinary experience and the phenomenon as analytically factored. Sartre subsequently appears to affirm the field of relative phenomena as true unreservedly—but only on the condition that the partiality of their truth ("untruth") be capable in principle of being progressively overcome in history. But this is possible only if truth is defined as absence of impediment to (negation of) the human desire for oneness. In the end, therefore, Sartre's later thought seeks to idealize the phenomenon rather than affirming its essential and necessary incompleteness. In this respect he seeks to salvage the Hegelian quest for the absolute. The later Heidegger seeks to free philosophy and culture from this metaphysical and teleological quest, which cannot affirm the phenomenal world in and for itself but only insofar as it subserves human ends. This is not an ideological matter for Heidegger; it is a matter of allowing the phenomenon its full natural weight as a being whose original nature exceeds and grounds the uses to which it may be put and whose intelligibility is not reducible to the degree to which it becomes an unimpeding instrument or artifact.

III

Language is the medium of Being and not a consequence of it or merely an instrument for its expression.

The naming word belongs to the phenomenon, which would not be what it is without its name. In the naming of the thing seen, all its structures—natural, perceptual, conceptual, or practical—are one, so that the thing is as seen and as thought. The name is thus enabled subsequently to serve for the thing itself, the thing as now perceived, the concept of the thing, the image of the thing, the function of the thing. The name is proper to them all inasmuch as all arise together. As named by one name, the thing endures as what it is, seen and unseen, remembered and anticipated.

Proximally and for the most part, the thing appears in its self-identity without its Being (its *place* and *way* of appearing) showing itself. Name and thought, being unseen and hence *different* from the thing seen, do not ordinarily show themselves in their hidden *identity* with the thing. Insofar as access to the entity is held to occur through preverbal and preconceptual sensing, the perhaps natural tendency of sight to miss the inherence of thought in the thing seen is compounded, and the way and the place are doubly hidden. It is therefore a main task of present thought to remember the original (and lasting, although dissimulated) unity of thought and thing in language. This is to struggle against the identification of Being with *Vorhandenheit*, or its dialectical opposite, the identification of Being with idea (pure a priori thought or concept). In this effort, the difference between word, thought, and thing is not denied or collapsed into a mystical unity. Rather it is to be seen that the self-identity of the phenomenon depends as much on the difference between word and thought and thing as on their unity; word and concept must transcend their unity with the entity presently seen in order that this entity may be the same as its past and future appearances, and in order that the thing may be the constant referent of thought and speech *about* it.

If the natural tendency of the entity named is to dissimulate its relations and hence to appear as a relationless internal or immanent self-identity, this is also true of the way in which the name itself (or the concept itself) appears. Its original way of being is to be the name (or concept) *of the thing*, but it appears as if it were what it is simply in and of itself. Only because of this dissimulation is it possible to regard name (or concept) as merely nominal (or merely conceptual), or as arbitrary or conventional in origin.

Language can express entities, can speak correctly or falsely of entities, only because of the original union of language, thought, and thing. Language can distort the nature of entities not because entities are prelinguistic but because the word is different from the entity as well as at one with it. The *fundamental* corrective to the use of the word as a distorting instrument consists in remembering the phenomenon to which it belongs as dependent upon the word, and also as exceeding its self-disclosure (being incompletely, although truly, revealed).

Sartre is rightly wary of the power of words to conceal and to distort. Even in their original disclosive function, words are a kind of violence. Sartre regards the doctrine of nominalism not only as true but as a necessary safeguard against verbal and ideological mystification. He rightly warns against the dangers of a linguistic idealism that reduces things to words. Like Plato, he does not believe that poetry can also express the true—at least in present social conditions.

Heidegger's association with the poetry of Sophocles, Hölderlin, Rilke, Hebel, and George appears to mark him as an irrationalist, even though he can point to the poetry of Parmenides as a decisive formative force in the determination of Western philosophy. But Heidegger is no more than Plato committed to the notion that all poetry expresses truth and all rationality error. It is rather a matter, as always with Heidegger, of exploring the original nature of disclosure and intelligibility as such. This exploration shows that the world of intelligible beings is disclosed as such neither in a passive looking nor in an active conceptualizing, nor in a dialectical interplay of these opposites. The world is disclosed in an event that is an inextricable and unfactorable fusion or "juncture" of sensing, thinking, and naming. This original unity of the passive (*pathos*) and the active (*poiēsis*), of undergoing and making, of deference and violence, is the primary way of "seeing." Seeing is primarily the unity of two "founded modes" of seeing that we tend to think of separately: passively looking ("I see it") and actively construing ("I see what you mean"; "I perceive that you're right"). Seeing is primarily seeing something *as* what it is, and this is indivisibly sensing *and* understanding the thing as named, and doing so primarily in the normal course of experience and praxis. This is the ground and referent of subsequent inspection of or subsequent reasoning about, rather than a condemnation of either empirical or rational inquiry. At the same time it marks the limits of empirical or rational inquiry in that neither is self-grounding. (This notion is pursued further in the next section.)

Original disclosure is thus "poietic" in the sense that it founds an intelligible world and so also the exercise of clear eye and independent reason upon the world. The writing of poetry by poets is most profoundly disclosive when it remembers and evokes anew this original founding, when it does not simply treat words as basically signs or tools but "hears" what words evoke. So heard, words evoke the way and the illumined place of articulation, understanding, inspection, and reasoning as the fundamental gift.[3]

IV

An original identity both grounds dialectic and limits its powers of analysis and synthesis.

The term 'dialectic' meant to the Greeks both 'language' or 'speech' and 'conversation' or 'discourse', including logical-rational discourse designed to elicit a conclusion. In either case it implied a back-and-forth spatial or temporal movement across or between (dia-) two speakers or two ideas or positions. In German idealism

after Kant it means the confrontation of opposed notions in a movement toward a truth that embraces both of them. 'Dialectic' thus
suggests two discrete poles that are to be harmonized by a subsequent movement. Language, when thought of as dialectic, is the
medium of this movement, lying between the two poles as a common medium for the expression of both. If these poles are construed as logical opposites, as antithetical, the law of excluded middle would appear to forbid their harmonization until or unless a
reform of traditional logic is effected.

In post-Kantian idealism such a reform is attempted through a
rethinking of the fundamental logical notion of identity. But this rethinking does not center upon the notion of identity in the abstract;
it centers on a particular identity that is nevertheless regarded as
the most fundamental identity—that of thought and being. We have
observed that it is this identity that Hegel regards as "the most interesting idea of modern times."[4] The attention of Fichte, Schelling,
and Hegel centers upon this particular identity because after Kant
there is access to beings only through the conditions of thought.
Therefore there is no access of thought to beings as such unless
there is a unity of thought and beings, but rather only the "broken
totality" of which Murdoch has spoken. Yet the thought of the subject is clearly *different* from the matter of the object. The task of German idealism thus becomes, Heidegger writes, that of rethinking
identity "as the belonging together of the different in one or, more
generally, as the oneness of a one and an opposition."[5] German
idealism, however, understands this "union of union and nonun-
ion" (Hegel) metaphysically—as explicable in terms of beings (ego,
will, God) and in terms of dialectical logic.

Freed of its metaphysical and of its dialectical form, the notion of
the unity of identity and difference becomes a decisive consideration for Heidegger. It is a key to the character of the event of Being
and a key to the character of the self-dissimulation of Being in the
history of philosophy. The event of Being is the simultaneous happening of identity and difference as a unity, but this inner unity of
identity and difference dissimulates itself because what shows itself
in this event is beings. Beings appear as self-identical, as what they
are simply in and by themselves. But they are what they are in
themselves—self-identical—owing to a hidden union with the different. This means that identity and difference are not pure oppo-

sites; a being has an intelligible identity (shows itself *as* what it is) when the 'as' comes to pass. Thus "tree *as* tree" means a relation of tree to itself which is other than that of *empty* identity: it is tree in its treeness (in its Being). This difference between the tree and its Being *is* the tree *in* its very own Being. But the inner union of the being with its Being is concealed precisely because the Being that allows a being to be identified as tangibly and visibly there is not tangibly and visibly there. What exist are beings. When the Greeks first raise the question of how beings come to be, they therefore seek to account for beings in terms of beings. The Being of beings is ascribed to beings (water, air, thought, idea, atom, God). Something *different* from the beings to be accounted for is sought, in *other* beings. Thus the union of identity and difference is concealed. It can be remembered only when the quest to account for the Being of beings in terms of beings is exhausted—that is, when the Being of beings can be thought as not itself a thing or entity. It is to be thought as an event in which the being is revealed in its identity when what is different from itself, its *as*, is one with it.

This event must not be thought of as the joining of two different beings—entity and thought—through dialectical combination or synthesis. Entity as entity and thought as thought cannot *be* prior to the event of Being itself. The event in which the entity comes into being is the event in which thought comes into being.[6] Thought *as* thought is thought as a kind of entity—an identifiable being. But precisely in appearing in their own different kinds of being, thought and physical thing conceal their inner union. Thought and entity come to be as what they are (in their different identities) when they come to be as one.

Insofar as dialectic means the synthesis of preexisting opposites or poles, it cannot account for Being because it misses the union in which these opposites *are* at all. Insofar as dialectic seeks to comprehend a unity of thought and beings by analyzing it—by taking it apart into its elements and rejoining them rationally ("justifying" the unity) by showing what is contributed to the unity by each element—it misses the nature of the original unity. It seeks to know the precise role played by each element in the unity, while the elements come to be only in the unity itself and do so without a reason. Insofar as dialectic seeks the common ground of these elements in a third thing (for example, God, or the descent of God into

the world), it invokes something *in* Being rather than accounting for
the Being that this being, like all beings, is in.

The analytic and synthetic interrelation of beings cannot account
for the Being that the beings referred to are already in. Insofar as
transcendental phenomenology is a dialectical procedure that seeks
the Being or intelligible nature of beings in a polar relation between
a being (ego or its thought) and other beings (object, referent), it
again invokes something in Being rather than taking into account
the Being in which these beings are. This is why the phenomenological reduction cannot account for and justify the life-world; it
seeks to account for Being by reference to beings and it seeks to reassemble unity out of its elements. These elements, however, already *are* in and through a unity that is not their combination but
their origin.

Sartre looks to an existentialized dialectic to reassemble historically a lost unity of conscious organism and environment. This dialectic is, on the one hand, a process of responding to the contingent
facts of scarcity and unequal distribution of matter. It is, on the
other hand, the condition of truth and intelligibility, for Sartre has
come to regard truth as a function of economic (in a broad sense)
praxis. The question of the possibility of a dialectical overcoming of
scarcity lies beyond the scope of this study. The equation of this
economic process with truth is an artificial narrowing of the region
of truth as such to the subregion of practical truth. This is possible
only because Sartre grounds truth in conscious praxis, ruling out in
advance a truth that is not so grounded. He thereby overlooks what
I have called primary truth, the disclosing of beings of *any* region,
including, but not limited to, the practico-economic region. This
oversight is owing to two features of dialectical procedure: (*a*)
grounding the Being of beings in a being (in this case, the practical
organism as prehistoric unity or disrupted historical unity of project
and matter) and (*b*) regarding unity as the interplay of discrete elements (in this case, matter and the conscious project that negates
it). What this dialectic misses is its own ground in a unity of
thought and entity that is prior to negation, an identity of these opposites. A remembering of this precedent and lasting unity limits
the extent to which the Being of beings can be dialectically transformed or reconstituted out of its elements. Thus a regressive movement cannot isolate thought and matter as pure opposites (and

hence ground the Being of beings or of truth in either one of them
or in both) and a progressive movement cannot convert their opposition into a synthesis. Sartre's early dialectic of in-itself and for-
itself conditions his whole career by posing, as the *goal* of personal
and historical desire, a union and a truth that *already* grounds in-
itself and for-itself.

V

*Internal relatedness requires modification of the notions of inten-
tionality and circularity.*

The notions of intentionality and circularity suggest a relation of
self to environment other than that of simple mutual externality. As
Sartre has noted, intentionality implies a "bursting forth" of
thought and emotion into the world such that experience is not
primarily or essentially experience of internal ideas and feelings—
representations and reactions—but direct experience of the world.[7]
According to Merleau-Ponty, it revalidates "a direct and primitive
contact with the world" by "endowing that contact with a philosophical status."[8] But we have seen, from chapter 1 forward, that
this most fertile of phenomenological notions raises a severe problem when it is interpreted by reference to traditional ontology and
its logic. Because ontology traditionally holds beings to be simply
internally self-identical or 'atomic', they are and must be what they
are *in themselves*. They thus fulfill the Parmenidean requirement of
constant presentness: "it is." In addition, the modern ontology of
Vorhandenheit requires that an entity in itself be understood as "devoid of meaning"—as pure physical externality. As soon as these
ontological requirements are applied to the notion of intentionality,
the "intentional unity" of the phenomenon—the union of essence
and existence—is split asunder. The consequence is existentialism.
In holding that "existence precedes essence," existentialism merely
reverses the doctrine that essence precedes existence, thus maintaining the polarity of essence/existence rather than showing the
oneness of essence and existence. It is for this reason that I hold existentialism to be incompatible with the phenomenological effort to
revalidate the 'phenomenon' or immediate unity of essence/exis-
tence, meaning/being. If Heidegger has resolved this problem, it is
by the exercise of a habit for which Sartre criticized him—cutting

Gordian knots rather than untying them.[9] But, in my judgment, that is the only way the problem can be resolved. It cannot be resolved by a dialectical procedure that retains the notion that essence/existence, meaning/being, thought/matter are fundamentally polar opposites but that regards them as reconcilable through time and praxis. The cleft between them is a wound that time cannot heal, for neither time nor praxis can create a community of nature where none already exists.

I have argued that the notion of circularity represents for the earlier Heidegger a way of uniting meaning and entity. Rather than, in reduction, tracing meaning to a transcendental source in the intentions of an ego or consciousness, one must regard man at any given moment as having to experience a world qualified by prior intentions ('projections'), so that at no point[10] is man in a position spontaneously to originate meanings *de novo* and impose them upon a bare existentia. The meanings one finds in present experience of entities already reside there owing to a prior projection, and one can therefore locate an absolute beginning of these meanings neither in any present thought nor in the entity. Yet Heidegger subsequently judges that "talk of a circle always remains superficial,"[11] since the circle is still essentially a polar notion referring to an intercirculation between experiencer and experienced, or meaner and meant, in which the former is the "baseless basis" of meanings. The experiencer must to be sure "repeat" meanings that have been "handed down" to him, but the suspicion remains that these meanings ultimately originate in transcendental intentionality and in free projection—even though not in a specifiable present or individual intention, perhaps in a collective conventional intention, such as the traditional will of a nation or a linguistic group.

Heidegger comes to see that the notion of circularity does not sufficiently modify the *transcendental*-phenomenological construing of intentionality as ego-originated. Hence it does not overcome the tendency of transcendental phenomenology to split the unity of the phenomenon by grounding meaning metaphysically in the ego, thus leaving the entity in itself as bare existentia. The problem is ultimately resolved only by the notion of the Event of identity-and-difference, which defers to the phenomenon itself as the real locus of meaning. Meanings and their referents, beings, are "different," as is indicated grammatically by the phrase "the meaning *of* entities." The meaning is not the entity. And yet it is the meaning *of* the entity—the meaning belongs to the entity. In this latter sense the meaning is the very "identity" of the entity. Thus meaning-essence/thought and being/existence/thing are and must be internally related; if they are only joined subsequently and synthetically they do not "by nature" *belong* together. The relation is closer than that of a diachronic circularity in which an intentional act would qualify an entity that would in turn be perceived as so qualified, this perception further qualifying subsequent intentional acts, and so forth.

What role then remains for intentionality? That of a co-constitutor of phenomena whose precise contribution to the character of phenomena can never be specified. For to specify the precise contribution made by intentional acts to the character of phenomena would mean once again to factor the phenomenon into its atomic constituents—the mental component vs. the external material component—and hence to destroy the unity of the phenomenon and the claim of experience to truth. It cannot be done because, as we have seen, the necessary referent of such factors—what they are factors *of*—is a prior phenomenon, the character of whose very factors is owing to the whole and indivisible phenomenon itself. Intentional acts have real constitutive efficacy only if they belong to beings so inextricably that neither the being nor the intention can be separately specified.

VI

Ontology requires readjustment of the doctrine of causation in modern thought.

The quest for pure, unqualified, nonrelative and nonrelational physical externality has entailed a critique of formal and final causation. Where mathematical physics has served as the model of inquiry into the real, formal and final causation have appeared as subjective and human qualifications or misconstructions of the world. The real world consists exclusively of quanta of matter or energy, whose changes of quality or place are attributable solely to states of matter or energy as efficient causes. To understand this material-efficient order as a region of formal causation would be to confuse the region of ideation, definition, hypothesis—the region of mind—with the region of nature. To understand this order as a region of final cause would be to fail to observe that all effects are attributable to efficient causes preceding these effects in time.

Phenomenological ontology in effect rehabilitates Aristotle's fourfold doctrine of causation.[12] In so doing, it does no more than explicitly reaffirm the formal and final causation covertly relied upon by the very sciences that have rejected them. To experience any entity as the kind of thing it is is to understand its form, in the sense of its nature or kind, its essence or definition. This is primarily not a matter of synthesizing a sensory appearance with a separate mental idea; it is a matter of directly *seeing* the entity as what (the *kind* of thing) it is. The seeing and the understanding coincide and are a single act of recognition; the form is in that which is seen. If the entity is, like the atom, not literally seen but rather inferred, it is nonetheless identified by its formal cause—its kind, essence, or nature. Formal cause is a condition of the intelligibility of anything whatsoever; and the condition for this intelligibility being the intelligibility *of the thing itself* is that the thing's formal cause not be simply and solely a mental construct that is either prior or posterior to the experience of the thing. The phenomenon itself is formal.

This does not commit one to the Aristotelian doctrine of fixed natural genera and species. Rather it reconfirms our existing and inevitable commitment to the "formal" (or conceptual and "intentional") content of both ordinary and scientific experience. In other words, the form to which both Heidegger and Sartre call attention is not the form of an allegedly pure external entity; it is the form of the phenomenon, which is as we have seen an entity that is neither a simple actuality nor a simple ideality but instead an "introplay" of "the actual" and "the ideal."

We have observed the role of final cause in Heidegger's treatment of the ready-to-hand and in Sartre's treatment of objects of praxis. This rehabilitation of final causation does not entail reverting to the ancient and medieval conception of the cosmos as teleological. It does, however, mean that the entire ranges of phenomena classifiable as artifacts and actions are intelligible (are experienceable as what they are) only if reference is made to their final cause. It is impossible, for example, to know what either a computer or the act of programming a computer is, apart from reference to the end for the sake of which this entity was made and for the sake of which it is programmed. If the same claim cannot be made for those phenomena classifiable as natural or nonartifactual, it is nonetheless true that natural phenomena are experienced as what they are only within the temporal and teleological experience of man.

It is under the foregoing conditions that there is knowledge of material and efficient causes. Any material or efficient cause is itself a form and is intelligible within the temporal and teleological order of human experience. Material cause specifies an aspect of the phenomenon—either the sheer fact of its externality and givenness or its material composition, if it is material, or both. Efficient cause specifies one cause of the phenomenon but cannot account for the phenomenon in the absence of formal cause and additionally, in the case of the artifact, final cause. This is only to reaffirm that the phenomenon is a *"relative* absolute" or a "meaning-being."

VII

Being is only properly understood in terms of coming-to-be (time and place).

We have observed that both Heidegger and Sartre wage war against the perceptual or ontological atom, or the alleged discreteness of the present moment. The enemy is the Eleatic notion that being excludes becoming—that what-is is constant or timeless internal self-identity. There seems the best of warrant for the Eleatic view. Unless a being has an identity that outlasts change, the world becomes unintelligible flux. Unless a being is what it is in and by itself, it will lose its identity. If it is defined by its relations to *other* beings, it will cease to be what it is in *itself*. The price of self-identity would therefore seem to be that a being be unconditioned, or not relative to its environment.

Insofar as Heidegger and Sartre understand beings to be doubly relative or doubly conditioned—relative to and conditioned by both other environmental beings and by the experiencer—they may be suspected of having relinquished the conditions under which there may be an intelligible world. Yet I have interpreted them as seeking precisely to maintain the world's intelligibility. Neither of them is a "Heraclitean" in the popular sense of that term. As had Husserl, both of them see clearly that in an era of nihilism, subjectivism, and relativism, the battle for intelligibility is the fundamental battle. It is the struggle for "the thing itself," on whose successful resolution hangs the meaning and truth of all theoretical and practical activity.

They have both learned the lesson of Hegel: one conquers a problematic inheritance not by rejecting it out of hand but by working it through. The Eleatic condition for intelligibility cannot simply be rejected—nor can relativism and its problem of unintelligibility simply be rejected. But we have seen that in certain respects Heidegger and Sartre adjust the claims of Eleaticism and relativism differently. If both insist that beings are intelligible only relative to time and place, for Heidegger the "beginning," "perduring," and "coming on" of that time and place bring intelligibility, while for Sartre its "end" brings intelligibility. Yet Heidegger's "beginning" and Sartre's "end" are both unions in which man plays a necessary part and is no innocent bystander, no mere spectator. For Heidegger, man finds that he has always already participated in the "round-dance" or "play" that is the Event of World; for Sartre, man is already engaged in the practical/rational remaking of matter.

In both cases, the identity of beings is relative to time; what a being is is understood in terms of its manner of coming-to-be. A phenomenon that comes-to-be in the Fourfold-Event *or* in human praxis gains its identity in part owing to the human temporal ekstases. They let the phenomenon stand forth in its constancy or self-identity by understanding the phenomenon of the present moment as the same as the phenomenon remembered and the phenomenon anticipated. The "overreaching" power of imagination and conceptuality "inform" the phenomenon presently seen with that totality of traits, remembered and anticipated, without which it could not now be experienced as the whole and the identity it is. The past and future are thus *in* the present phenomenon. The present is a constancy only relative to a past and a future and to an ekstatic being who grasps past-present-future in their simultaneous or contemporaneous presence, assembled in a present phenomenon. Thus the experience of presence, permanence, constancy, identity—the Eleatic experience—is itself a "timing" or "synchrony," an internal relation of the three temporal ekstases. So the presentness or identity of phenomena is owing to a double relativity, a double conditioning, or a double contextuality: their relation to past and future phenomena and their relation to the being who in overreaching the present lets the present stand forth *as* the present. Being is in Time. Time is in Being.

The notion of timeless being is a privation of the phenomenon. It abstracts permanence out of the time in which permanence occurs. The semblance of timeless permanence is facilitated by the self-dis-simulating character of Being or "timing". Both entity and essence give themselves out in a dualistic culture as independent of each other and independent of time—the former as a natural permanence independent of changes in human conceptualization, the latter as a conceptual or ideational permanence independent of changes in natural process.

VIII

History is the region of ontological alienation and of its possible over-coming.

Sartre has written of the need to "discard the *purely theological* temptation to contemplate nature 'without foreign addition.' " [13] I have at several points observed that philosophy frequently seeks to establish the powers and limits of man by comparing him with God. If God is taken as a model for knowledge of the real, then human knowledge of the real will either be impossible or will require that man raise himself to the standpointless standpoint or nonperspectival *theōria* of God. In Parmenides' *Proem* and sub-sequently in Plato, Plotinus, Descartes, and Spinoza, knowledge of the real requires a reflective purification of mortal conditions as the price of contemplation of the real *sub speciē aeterni*, "without foreign addition," absolutely, unconditionally. If Hume and Kant argue the impossibility of an epistemological escape from finite conditions, Hegel represents the final attempt of philosophy to raise itself to the absolute, but by going *through* finite conditions, rather than by purifying itself of them by a "shot out of a pistol." [14] How-ever, this requires the notion of Spirit as the identity of divine and human minds. Given the questionableness of this speculative no-tion of Spirit, in the wake of Hegel either the notion of absolute knowledge is surrendered and yields to skepticism and nihilism, [15] or the effort is made to show that an environment that, to be sure, cannot be known immediately can in time be reshaped into a mirror of human designs through praxis. Both these post-Hegelian tendencies share the premise that man begins with an alien environment, and hence that experience of the real and the true is essentially futural.

With respect to this premise, Heidegger and Sartre divide, but not unequivocally, since they both find man in some sense historically "alienated" from the real and both find their own early thought conditioned by this alienation. The mode of alienation is the same for both of them insofar as it represents an historically "broken totality" or loss of unity. The mode of alienation differs insofar as Heidegger regards the broken totality as a semblance while Sartre regards it as real. If it is semblance, then history is the dissimulated record of unity or Being and a future overcoming of alienation would consist in coming to terms with a unity that already is. If this alienation is real, then history is the record of the diaspora of a prehistoric organic oneness or interiority into a schism between interior project and external matter that negates it, and a future overcoming of alienation would consist in a humanization of matter through praxis.

Heidegger's reading of history is conservative where Sartre's is radical, for Heidegger holds that no revolutionary praxis can hope to bring about an ontological union since that union already occurs and must be remembered and affirmed. At the same time, Heidegger's reading of history is radical where Sartre's is conservative, for Heidegger holds that the entire history of "ontologic" on which Sartre builds is but a semblance of Being and Logos. Heidegger is thus both more profoundly conservative and more profoundly revolutionary than Sartre, for Heidegger's 'remembering' is a 'saving' of the tradition through its 'destruction'—a conserving of a hidden union by a revolutionary critique of its cultural and philosophical manifestations or dissimulations. Heidegger is a cultural revolutionary; Sartre is a revolutionary primarily in one region of culture, politics. The implications of Heideggerian thought for Sartrean politics are difficult to fathom; Heidegger's critique of culture is so wide ranging, and so relatively new, as to make deductions regarding practical consequences of its widespread acceptance difficult at the present time.[16] Sartre has, to be sure, implicated Heidegger in a reactionary antihumanism, but only by misinterpreting Heidegger as having reduced man to an altogether passive mouthpiece of

Being. Heidegger's later thought transcends the humanism/antihumanism and agent/patient distinctions in holding mortals to be active coparticipants in a Fourfold activity centered not on themselves but on the thing. The grounding activity of Dasein in *SZ* is sublimated, so to speak, by a "shift of accent" in the later Heidegger but not altogether rejected. If Heidegger regards history as essentially the history of Being rather than as essentially the history of man, it must be remembered that "there is" Being only insofar as mortals participate in this Event.

I have shown in chapter 13 how Sartrean thought is grounded in a prior truth rather than being self-grounding. For this reason, Sartre's humanistic philosophy of praxis is alienated from its own basis—a mode of alienation not recognized by Sartre. Heidegger's recognition of the event of truth or phenomenal intelligibility in a precedent community of nature, or event of identity-and-difference, is a fundamental reassessment of man's relation to the past. It takes account of the fact of ontological alienation in our culture but establishes the possibility of its overcoming by showing that the ontological unity sought is not contingent upon an ideal and hypothetical humanization of the earth but upon a remembering of what has already happened. Contrary to what some of its critics have claimed, it does not call for an impossible utopian future that would turn history upside down. It calls for a coming to terms with what has been and remains.

IX

Metaphysics historically seeks its own dissimulated ground and unity. The grounds sought by metaphysics are already present.

In 1929, Heidegger described metaphysics as "a questioning above and beyond the region of beings for the purpose of reappropriating it as such and in its wholeness for conceptual understanding."[17] Metaphysics seeks the ground, or Being, of beings— their essence, meaning, nature, intelligibility, and value. The standing premises of metaphysics have been that this essence is not at first given and hence must be sought, and that the ground sought is itself a being. The fact that the enquirer must go above and beyond beings in search of their ground suggests that this ground is separate from beings. Ascesis, katharsis, paideia, reflection, epochē—forms of the discipline of method—are prerequisite for reaching it. This method extends from Pythagoras and Parmenides down to Husserl's reduction, Heidegger's authentic repetition of disowning average everydayness in Division II of *SZ*, and Sartre's purifying existential psychoanalysis in *EN*.

In *SZ*, this method discloses Dasein as "groundless ground." Dasein has always already taken over being a ground by projecting the Being of beings, which are in themselves "devoid of meaning." In Sartre's reappropriation of Heidegger, the for-itself fills the "holes in being"—opened up by its own negation—with projective meaning. Thus human intentionality, in the form of care or fundamental project, is seen as performing the metaphysical grounding and unifying function. We have traced the processes by which both Heidegger and Sartre subsequently find these formulations inadequate. Both retrospectively judge themselves to have been insufficiently sensitive to the force of history, and both decipher its influence in their early work.

Heidegger finds his early thought to be under a historical 'directive' of Being in a 'first beginning' that dissembles itself in hiding the identity of meaning and beings while manifesting only their difference. A 'remembering' of this first beginning reveals that the union of meaning and beings that metaphysics seeks is already there. Therefore Heidegger calls for an 'other beginning' that would renounce the metaphysical quest and own up to the "hidden juncture" or identity of the different already present in the first beginning.

Sartre finds his early thought conditioned by a bourgeois individualism rooted in pre-Hegelian philosophy and culture. Its ontology regards beings as atomic or private; its logic regards relations between these beings as one of nonsynthesizable negation. This atomic and nondialectical view is one consequence of the rupture of a cyclic prehistoric organic praxis that provokes a competition of groups for matter and the rise of philosophies as expressions of partial truths, the truths of groups. The quest of history is for a restoration of organic praxis and a single comprehensive or synthetic truth.

There is a sense in which Sartre resembles Heidegger in locating the truth in a lost beginning that future history must recover. But the beginnings are different, and in one the truth is dissembled and remains, while in the other it is genuinely lost. It seems to us that if there is a truth that is genuinely lost, it is a practical truth that is not truth as such or as a whole. It will be recalled that Sartre criticizes Parain for condemning man to "a few sad and simple truths" and that he elsewhere criticizes "commonplaces."[18] Despite his commitment to the common man, and despite his elaborate defense of ordinary praxis, it remains an essential part of Sartre's attitude to mistrust the ordinary and the commonplace. This attitude, first evident in *La Nausée*, is characteristic of existentialist metaphysics: the region of existence lacks a grounded order and essence, which it is the task of practical will or faith to supply. Man must make or posit an intelligible whole where none is given. The romance of a cosmic drama, struggling toward recouping a lost One that haunts man in its absence, remains. Existence is measured against the desired ideal and found grossly lacking.

There is no gainsaying the importance of the ideal as a goal of and stimulus to cultural and practical advancement, and there is no denying the dangers of acquiescence in the ordinary and commonplace. But the ideal cannot be equated with the truth as such. Such an equation has two consequences—the reduction of the past to untruth and the requirement that truth be complete in order to count as truth. Sartre can anticipate a *total* truth, which is "one" and the single truth of history,[19] only by making truth altogether a function of human praxis. Given the inevitable relativity of truth to the experiencer, there can be total truth only if existence is finally totally transformed by human praxis so as to leave no residue of the unknown and uncertain. This means the final reduction of beings to praxis-beings without residue. So far as a residue of resistant or counterpractical matter remains, the truth is to that extent an unfulfilled but legitimate demand.

The alternative is to regard truth as necessarily accompanied by untruth; in Heidegger's terms, disclosure is inevitably at the same time a closure. This means that beings are inevitably irreducible to our experience and knowledge of them. Total truth is an illusion of metaphysics. It would be illusory to succumb to the sleight of hand of simply redefining truth as practical truth in order to try to do away with the inevitability of untruth or incomplete knowledge. The price of taking the phenomenon to be truly disclosed is the admission that the truth is inevitably partial; if the phenomenon can

be totally revealed, this can only be by a reduction of being-in-itself
to being-for-us that deprives beings of all otherness by reducing
them to ideality. This is the "Fichtean" danger of Sartre's program;
it can succeed only by reducing nonego to ego—the reduction of nature to ideality. In the end, Sartre is unwilling to settle for human
limitation; the demand for a single truth of man, a total humanization of the earth, is the apparently nontheological residue of the
quest of Fichtean and Hegelian idealism for the raising of man
through praxis to the position of God. The Holy Ghost remains in
Sartre's cellar.

Trite, trivial, and obvious though they may seem, one must remember "the sad and simple" commonplaces that the metaphysical
romance obscures. No doubt there are gross untruths in the region
of the polis and its praxis. No doubt they should be rectified. But
they must not be allowed to hide the larger truth of the region of
physis. *There is* an intelligible world of sun and earth, of seasons, of
birth and death, of forests, seas, mountains, and plains. It is the
site and ground of praxis, of metaphysics, and of existentialism. To
remember it is to mark the limitation of praxis, for it is the necessary ground of a praxis that must either defer to it or lose its own
ground and support. To remember it is to mark the limitation of
metaphysics, for it is a region that has not had to wait for metaphysics to make it intelligible but is rather the unacknowledged
context in which metaphysics inevitably situates all its inquiries. To
remember it is to mark the limitation of existentialism, for commonplace experience already experiences, even if it does not acknowledge it, the union of existence and essence that existentialism
finds lacking.

X

*The ground of values is the value of the ground. The realization of this
is the end of nihilism.*

I have defined nihilism as appearance in space, or displacement
of beings from the Place and its relations within which beings have
their intelligibility or meaning.[20] In nihilism beings appear independent of place, as standing in and by themselves (*selb-ständig*).
The foregoing critique of atomism, of *Vorhandenheit*, of the notion of
the relationless, nonlinguistic, and nonconceptual entity, has established the meaning of Being as appearing in Place. The phenom-

enological program to revindicate the phenomenon must complete itself in the remembering of the Place. The quest for the ground of beings both completes and limits itself in the remembering of the Event of the thing in language as the precedent and mutually qualifying union, in perception, of thoughtful and natural determinations.

This Place and its Event are the conditions of the possibility of any experience and knowledge of beings as what they are. To discount these conditions is ultimately to discount the experience and knowledge that depend upon them. This is why the history of metaphysics terminates in nihilism. In displacing into the future and the transcendent the conditions of the possibility of experiencing beings in their true or essential natures, it begins by making unintelligible its own experience of and talk of the very beings whose real natures it wishes to find.

The Place and its Event are the ground not only of truth but of value. The quest for absolute, nonrelative, unconditioned value, like the quest for absolute truth, is displacement of the conditions under which there is and can be value. Value resides neither primarily in man nor primarily in nature but in their precedent union. The Place of truth is the Place of value. This means that value, like truth, centers in the thing, the phenomenon. The valuable *is* the true—that is, what has primary value is the intelligible world itself, the ungroundable "gift" of an illuminated region or "clearing" standing out from a surrounding darkness. Man has always already in care played his mortal role in the illuminating of the Earth. His proper response to the Place is owning up to this care, that is, explicitly affirming the Event of the Place as the originally good and beautiful—what originates, founds, and grants him a world at all. The primary evil is destructive violence against the Place, vengeance against time and place, because this attitude displaces the source of the true, the good, the beautiful.

Intentionality becomes care, and care becomes love. "Authenticity" becomes a becoming what one is by owning up to, or remembering and hence preserving, the Place as what mortals have always already cared for and loved. This love has been widely dissimulated in metaphysics and nihilism; man has *not* become what he is insofar as he has quested for release from the very conditions in which he can be and can quest at all. A consistent love is love of mortal fate, love of the earth.

Here Husserl and Nietzsche meet—at first sight the most improbable of companions. The phenomenological program completes itself in love of mortal and earthly fate. Nietzsche did not have the notions of intentionality and phenomenon that would have enabled him to surmount his naturalistic metaphysics of the will to power and carry out consistently his effort to pass beyond both a subjectivism and an objectivism. Husserl did not participate in Nietzsche's thoroughgoing critique of the history of metaphysics and its quest for transcendental essences and grounds. The union of Husserl and Nietzsche in Heidegger is analogous to the precedent community of nature in the sense that it represents a wedding of the same apparently irreconcilable opposites—transcendental origination and natural origination, idealism and naturalism, the primacy of the cogito and its constant essences and the primacy of nonrational natural becoming. Each of these dualities dissimulates a prior identity.

The price of such a union is no doubt high—absence of a guarantee of eternal or universal and necessary essences, incompleteness and relativity of truth, renunciation of the quest for absolute grounds. But if this union is, in fact, the precedent basis of our world, objections to it are invalidated. Such objections presuppose that to which they object, the intelligible Place in which objections are possible at all. It is at this point that the question of *attitude* that I have repeatedly raised becomes critical. In the Socratic attitude, in the Cartesian epochē, and in Husserlian reduction, one suspends commitment pending the achievement of absolute certainty about one's grounds. In the metaphysical attitude, all precedent commitments are disarmed and the past is judged by criteria proposed by the present and the future. In a pure existentialism, ultimate grounds are chosen by an act of will or faith, and ontology is accordingly a function of attitude. In the metaphysical attitude, it is impossible to allow and defer to a precedent ground. When Heidegger writes that "metaphysics may remain," [21] what he probably means is that the Place cannot guarantee that there will in future be an attitude of remembering, deference, and love favorable to its preservation. "Revenge against time and its 'it was' " may prevail.

The foregoing ten features of phenomenological ontology have enabled us to answer the three critical questions proposed at the end of chapter 1 as the problematic ontological inheritance of Heidegger and Sartre from their philosophical predecessors:

1. *Where does and can one begin in order to arrive properly at an ontology?* One cannot really begin anew or construct an ontology on the basis of either a transcendental or a natural ground. Ontology must essentially consist in a remembering of a precedent Event and Place in which phenomena, the fundamental ontological entities, have come into being and can alone come into being.

2. *Can ontology avoid recourse to metaphysics?* Unless ontology avoids recourse to metaphysics, it can end only in skepticism, nihilism, mere speculation, or mere faith, rather than in the genuine intelligibility of beings. Ontology can avoid recourse to metaphysics by recalling the hidden yet phenomenal ground of metaphysics itself.

3. *Can the phenomenon be a genuine unity of thought and Being?* It can be only if it is seen to be so already and if this seeing is taken as the experience of an original and remaining whole. The effort to construct and justify such a unity out of prior discrete elements can only dismember the very unity it wishes to establish.

In the end, it is a matter of recognizing and honoring one's prior commitments, commonplace though they be.

Notes

PREFACE

1. See, for example, Oskar Becker, "Heidegger und Wittgenstein," in Pöggeler, ed., *Heidegger*; Morris, *Sartre's Concept of a Person*; Mays, ed., *Linguistic Analysis and Phenomenology*; Cowley, *A Critique of British Empiricism*; Erickson, *Language and Being*.

2. Iris Murdoch (*Sovereignty of Good*, pp. 34–35) has already found Hampshire, Hare, and Ayer, as well as Sartre, to be "existentialist."

3. In *W*, pp. 145–94.

4. See, e.g., *CRD*, I, 248.

5. ". . . The atheistic existentialists, among whom I class Heidegger" (*EH*, p. 17 [15]). Yet Sartre had earlier understood Heidegger to be trying to "reconcile his humanism with the religious sense of the transcendent." (*EN*, p. 122 [80]). Note also Sartre's association of Heidegger with humanism.

6. *M*, pp. 210–11 (252–53).

7. See esp. the pieces from *Les Temps Modernes* translated as *The Ghost of Stalin* and *The Communists and Peace* (*S*, VI and VII).

8. See esp. Heidegger's concluding remarks in a 1969 television interview in Wisser, ed., *Martin Heidegger im Gespräch*, p. 77.

9. See *M*, esp. pp. 211–12 (253–54).

10. See *W*, p. 191 (300): "Thus thinking is an acting, but an acting which is at the same time superior to all praxis." We shall find that the term 'thought' has rather different connotations for the two thinkers.

11. Heidegger, e.g., *SZ*, p. 183 (227). Cf. Heidegger's association of truth with *Raub* (rape, robbery), ibid., p. 265 (222).

12. See, for example, Werner Marx, *Reason and World*, pp. 46–61.

1. THE PROBLEM OF PHENOMENOLOGICAL ONTOLOGY

1. Murdoch, *Sartre*, p. 55.

2. Ibid., p. 54.

3. Randall, (*Career of Philosophy*, I, 309–10) points out that there is another way to look at this shift: the universe at large, not just the earth, is henceforth man's home. Even on this interpretation, however, the earth loses its privileged position as an orienting center. The center is everywhere and nowhere.

4. Aristotle, *Metaphysics,* 1029b10 (*Aristotle's Metaphysics,* translated by Richard Hope, p. 134).

5. Walter Biemel, "The Development of Husserl's Philosophy," in Elveton, ed., *Phenomenology of Husserl,* p. 169.

6. Descartes, *Meditations,* II.

7. Ibid., VI; *The Principles of Philosophy,* LX.

8. Descartes, *Meditations,* VI.

9. Ibid., II; *The Passions of the Soul,* I.50, III.211–12.

10. Descartes, *The Principles of Philosophy,* IV.301.

11. Descartes, *Rules for the Direction of Mind,* III; *Meditations,* I.

12. Descartes, *The Principles of Philosophy,* Author's Letter to the Translator.

13. See Hume, *A Treatise of Human Nature,* esp. Book I, Part IV, Section VII.

14. Kant, *Critique of Pure Reason,* A183/B227; A189/B232; A265/B321; A277/B333.

15. E.g., Heidegger, *Nietzsche,* I, 476; 115; *EM,* pp. 29, 34 (32, 37).

16. Kant, *Critique of Pure Reason,* B145–49.

17. Ibid., e.g., A35–36/B52.

18. Ibid., A84–85/B116–17.

19. Hegel, *Phenomenology of Mind,* esp. pp. 218–27, 803–8; *The Philosophy of History,* esp. pp. 318 ff.

20. Hegel, *Lectures on the History of Philosophy,* III, 230.

21. James, *Pragmatism,* p. 64.

22. Kierkegaard, *Philosophical Fragments,* p. 12.

23. Nietzsche, *Werke in drei Bänden,* III, 774–75 (*Will to Power,* pp. 26–27).

24. E.g., ibid., III, 483 (*Will to Power,* p. 312): "Being—we can have no idea of it apart from the idea of 'living'—How can anything dead 'be'?"

25. Ibid., II, 323 (Kaufmann, *Portable Nietzsche,* p. 171).

26. Ibid., II, 479 (Kaufmann, ibid., p. 351).

27. Ibid., II, 839: "the human will needs a goal—and it would sooner will *nothingness* than *not* will at all"; III, 895 (*Will to Power,* p. 330).

28. Ibid., II, 959 (Kaufmann, *Portable Nietzsche,* p. 481).

29. Ibid., III, 665, 882, 862 (*Will to Power,* pp. 20, 8, 328).

30. Ibid., III, 557 (*Will to Power,* p. 14).

31. Ibid., III, 856 (*Will to Power,* p. 39).

32. Ibid., III, 763, 555 (*Will to Power,* pp. 313, 302–3).

33. Ibid., III, 719 (*Will to Power,* p. 321).

34. E.g., Husserl, *Idea of Phenomenology,* p. 4 and passim.

35. Husserl, *The Crisis,* p. 115.

36. Cf. Husserl, *Cartesian Meditations,* p. 21: ". . . I can enter no world other than the one that gets its sense and acceptance or status [*Sinn und Geltung*] in and from me, myself. . . . Thus the being of the pure ego and his *cogitationes,* as a being that is prior in itself, is antecedent to the natural being of the world. . . . Natural being is a realm whose existential status [*Seinsgeltung*] is secondary; it continually presupposes the realm of transcendental being."

37. Husserl, *Ideas*, §§ 49, 50, 55. See Rudolf Boehm, "Husserl's Conception of the 'Absolute' " in Elveton, ed., *Phenomenology of Husserl*, pp. 174–99; esp. pp. 184–85.

38. Husserl, *Ideas*, p. 168. Quoted by Boehm, "Husserl's . . . 'Absolute'," p. 185.

39. Husserl, *Cartesian Meditations*, p. 155. Italics, in part, deleted.

40. Husserl, *Paris Lectures*, p. 23. Italics deleted.

41. Husserl, *Ideas*, p. 126. Quoted by Boehm, "Husserl's . . . 'Absolute'," p. 191.

42. Merleau-Ponty, *Phénoménologie de la perception*, pp. ii–iii (*Phenomenology of Perception*, pp. viii–ix).

43. Ibid., p. i (vii).

44. Husserl, *The Crisis*, p. 59. Italics added.

45. Ibid., p. 179.

46. Ibid., p. 173, p. 156.

47. Ibid., pp. 155–56.

48. Ibid., p. 188, p. 192, p. 99, p. 259.

49. Ibid., p. 71 and § 15, entire.

50. Ibid., p. 181.

51. Leibniz, *Principes de la nature et de la grâce fondées en raison*, § 7, in Leibniz, *Philosophical Papers and Letters*, ed. Loemker, II, 1038. Quoted by Elveton, *Phenomenology of Husserl*, p. 202.

52. Husserl, *Ideas*, §§ 149, 150; *Paris Lectures*, pp. 16–17; *Cartesian Meditations*, §§ 37, 64; *The Crisis*, § 49.

53. Husserl, *The Crisis*, p. 181.

54. Hegel, *Phenomenology of Mind*, pp. 781–82.

55. Husserl's *Crisis*, written from 1934 to 1937, does not, of course, form part of the philosophical work drawn upon by the early Heidegger—except insofar as *The Crisis* mirrors the earlier *Lebensphilosophie* of Dilthey.

56. Sartre, *EH*, pp. 26–37 (21–27).

Part I. Introduction

1. *BH*, p. 159 (280). Note the ambiguity of the wording of this passage, which could be read as asserting both that *SZ* was subject to the forgottenness of Being and that *SZ* was already aware of this forgottenness.

2. See esp. chapters 4 and 6.

3. See *BH*, pp. 159–61 (280–81).

2. Dasein, Ground, and Time in <u>Sein und Zeit</u>

1. *SZ*, p. 60 (87).

2. Ibid., p. 129 (167).

3. Ibid., p. 48 (74). Contrast the interpretation of Bernd Magnus, in *Heidegger's Metahistory of Philosophy*, p. 133: ". . . Heidegger viewed Being as dependent upon man, *Dasein* in 1927. . . ."

4. *BH*, p. 160 (280). See Heidegger's reference to "the transformation of man into his Da-sein" in *WM*, p. 33 (337). See also his reference to "the *Dasein* in man" in *KPM*, p. 213 (244).

5. *SD*, p. 81. See Richardson, *Heidegger*, p. x.

6. *SZ*, p. 13 (34).

7. Ibid., p. 394 (446); *SD*, p. 90.

8. *SZ*, pp. 67 ff. (96 ff.) and *passim*.

9. Among other things, of course. Here I am isolating those aspects of the *Phänomenologie* that seem to me especially decisive for the development of what has come to be called "the phenomenological movement."

10. The phrase is A. N. Whitehead's.

11. Again the phrase is Whitehead's. See, e.g., *Science and the Modern World*, pp. 179 ff. The doctrine is anticipated in the cosmologies of Spinoza and Leibniz.

12. Whitehead, *Science and the Modern World*, p. 180.

13. Ibid., pp. 72 ff.

14. See Husserl, *Ideas*, § 80; *Paris Lectures*, esp. p. 8 ("I am the ego in whose stream of consciousness the world itself . . . first acquires meaning and reality"); *Cartesian Meditations*, § 58, esp. p. 136. But, on the 'life-world' as 'ground', see *The Crisis*, pp. 48–49, 59.

15. *SZ*, p. 358 (410). See also p. 147 (187): "we have deprived pure intuition [*Anschauen*] of its priority, which corresponds noetically to the priority of the present-at-hand in traditional ontology."

16. *SZ*, p. 132 (170).

17. Thus Gérard Granel has argued that what unites Husserl and Heidegger—despite all their differences—is a quest that is for both of them "the fundamental struggle": "the struggle against *Vorhandenheit*." ("Remarques sur le rapport de *Sein und Zeit* et de la phénoménologie Husserlienne," in Klostermann, ed., *Durchblicke*, pp. 350–68; esp. p. 358.) Otto Pöggeler can, with some justification, argue that Heidegger "gives up" phenomenology—insofar as phenomenology is oriented toward beings and the allegedly invariant essences of beings. Yet Pöggeler allows that the later Heidegger's notion of 'world' in a sense completes the phenomenological program: "This world—the fourfold of earth and heaven, the divine and the mortal—is however what phenomenology sought under the rubric of the 'natural world' and what the metaphysics of metaphysics sought under the rubric of the 'ground' of Western thought: the originary, out of which all thinking is *what* it is and *how* it is." (*Der Denkweg Martin Heideggers*, pp. 234–35. See also pp. 79, 166.) Cf. Richardson, *Heidegger*, p. 627: "Heidegger's perspective from beginning to end remains phenomenological."

18. *SZ*, p. 38 (62). On Husserl's own association of phenomenology with ontology, see *Cartesian Meditations*, p. 155; *Paris Lectures*, p. 23.

19. *SZ*, p. 145(186): "werde, was du bist!" See *Also sprach Zarathustra*, p. 4. Teil: "Werde, der du bist!" (Nietzsche, *Werke in drei Bänden*, II, 479.) It is possible that Heidegger intentionally makes the relative pronoun neuter to coincide with the presexual nature of Dasein. The notion goes back at least as far as Pindar, whom Heidegger quotes in *EM*, p. 77 (86): "Through learning, may you come forth as he whom you are."

20. See, e.g., *SZ*, p. 148 (188); p. 287 (333).

21. Ibid., p. 190 (235).

22. Ibid., p. 232 (275); p. 53 (78); pp. 42–43 (68).

23. Ibid., e.g., p. 87 (121).

24. Ibid., p. 146 (186–87). A crucial aspect of Heidegger's critique of Husserl occurs three paragraphs later, when Heidegger contends that this transparent sighting precedes (and grounds) Husserl's pure intuition (*Anschauen*) and intuition of essences (*Wesensschau*).

25. *SZ*, p. 87 (120–21). Note here Heidegger's special sense of a priori: "always already" (*immer schon; je schon*). I shall consider its significance later in this chapter.

26. Ibid., p. 64 (92).

27. Ibid., e.g., p. 154 (196).

28. Hence Heidegger can speak of Dasein moving *out* of itself *into* itself (see *SZ*, p. 178 [223]). But this is not to be conceived in terms of ordinary physical location. Heidegger warns: "In French Dasein gets translated as *être-là*, as for example in Sartre. But thereby everything which was won in *Sein und Zeit* by way of a new position is lost. Is man there [*da*] in the way a chair is? . . . Dasein does not mean being-there and being-here [*Dort- und Hiersein*]. . . . The *Da* is the clearing and openness of beings, which man endures." (*Heraklit*, p. 202.) This warning should be borne in mind as one reads my interpretation of 'Dasein'. I am not suggesting that Dasein exists at two points in ordinary space but rather that Dasein, as "context," transcends any such simple location. Thus Heidegger can write that "Dasein *is* its world existingly" (*SZ*, p. 364 [416]).

29. *SZ*, p. 38 (63).

30. Cf. Justus Buchler's distinction between the "imminent proceptive domain" and the "gross proceptive domain" in *Toward a General Theory of Human Judgment*, chap. 1.

31. *SZ*, p. 364 (416). See Biemel, *Martin Heidegger*, p. 40: "Dasein develops a relation to itself."

32. *SZ*, pp. 137–38 (177).

33. Ibid., p. 137 (176). Heidegger italicizes the sentence as a whole.

34. Ibid., p. 133 (171–72). Heidegger alternatively groups *Verfallen* together with these three, as a fourth mode of disclosure (pp. 334–35 [384]), and in one case replaces *Rede* by *Verfallen* (p. 349 [400]). This shift is discussed by Pöggeler (*Denkweg*, p. 210) and by Biemel (*Martin Heidegger*, p. 61).

35. *SZ*, pp. 132–33 (171). Translation modified.

36. Ibid., p. 53 (78): "The compound expression 'Being-in-the-world' indicates in the very way we have coined it, that it stands for a *unitary* phenomenon. This primary datum must be seen as a whole."

37. *De Anima*, 429b25 (McKeon, *Basic Works of Aristotle*, p. 591).

38. *SZ*, p. 132 (170). Heidegger goes on to qualify this assertion carefully. It is misleading, since it covertly assumes the entities (subject and object) between which this 'between' lies.

39. "Lichtung und Answesenheit": *SD*, p. 80.

40. *WM*, p. 42.

41. *SZ*, p. 133 (171).

42. I am not claiming that all this is immediately clear from a reading of *SZ*, but only that with the help of the author's later clarification it becomes possible to regard this as what he meant but failed to convey clearly. The later writings of Heidegger are—despite their alleged muddiness—to a considerable extent efforts at clarification of his earlier work and its intention. Heidegger's later interpretations of *SZ* are to be seen as his effort to interpret himself in much the same way he interprets other thinkers: by seeking to elucidate the thinker's ownmost thought, which he himself was not wholly able to express. For a close study of Heidegger's later analyses of *SZ*, see von Hermann, *Die Selbstinterpretation Martin Heideggers*.

43. *SZ*, p. 365 (417). It should be noted that 'world' is not, strictly speaking, simply identical with the 'there'. A distinction between the two is suggested by the wording of the following passage (*SZ*, p. 365 [416]): "In the disclosedness of the 'there' the world is disclosed along with it." The 'there' is Dasein's Being, while world is one of the *existentialia* of Dasein. That is, the whole of Dasein is Being-in-the-world, where a distinction can be made between 'Being-in' and 'world'. World is a project of Dasein. World is 'there' but is not *the* 'there'. I interpret this as meaning that a relative sort of distinction must be made between the ground and the grounding process. Dasein as a whole is "ground grounding," two aspects of which are 'Being-in' (grounding) and 'world' (ground). Being-there (Da-sein) as a whole, as ground-grounding, means Dasein's having to be its own ground. Dasein has to *be* the 'there'. If world were simply the 'there', this would leave out of account the *Being* of the 'there', Dasein's having to be the 'there'. The 'there' is always worldly, but it includes the awareness of, and projection of, the world.

44. Ibid., p. 329 (377).

45. Ibid., p. 332 (381).

46. Ibid., pp. 107–8 (142–43). Note that Heidegger does not say that Dasein 'intends' or 'experiences' spatiality; he says that Dasein *is* spatial. (I shall not treat here Heidegger's grounding of spatiality in temporality.)

47. *SD*, p. 24 (23). Cf. *SZ*, p. 367 (418).

48. *SD*, p. 24 (23). *Ort* is the term here translated as 'Place'.

49. *WM* (Einleitung), p. 202. Heidegger's terms here are *Stelle* and *Ortschaft*.

50. I have coined this term to indicate a unity of functions that are internally related, as opposed to an ordinary 'interplay' between functions that are originally separate and only subsequently come into relation ('external relation') with each other. The functions or factors are nevertheless relatively distinguishable from each other. The relation is one of oneness *and* difference, a notion that will be explored in some detail in later chapters of this volume.

51. *SZ*, p. 362 (414).

52. Ibid., p. 150 (191–92).

53. Ibid., p. 153 (195).
54. Ibid., p. 161 (203).
55. Ibid., p. 162 (205). Italics added.
56. Ibid., p. 169 (213). Italics added. Cf. p. 43 (69).
57. Ibid., p. 235 (278). Translation modified.
58. Ibid., pp. 43, 53, 331–32, 352 (69, 78, 380, 403). Cf. p. 191 (235).
59. Ibid., p. 130 (168). Translation modified.
60. Ibid., p. 179 (224). Translation modified. Cf. p. 371 (422): "Every-dayness is determinative for Dasein even when it has not chosen the 'they' for its 'hero'."
61. Ibid., p. 345 (396).
62. Ibid., p. 356 (407).
63. Ibid., p. 352 (403–4).
64. Ibid., pp. 350–51 (401–2).
65. Ibid., p. 351 (402).
66. Ibid., p. 183 (228).
67. Kierkegaard, *Concluding Unscientific Postscript*, pp. 169 ff., 122.
68. *SZ*, p. 186 (230). Italics deleted.
69. Ibid., p. 188 (233). Italics, in part, deleted.
70. Ibid., p. 189 (233).
71. Heidegger claims that the emergence of the entity as bare *vorhanden* does not entail loss of its prior everyday *zuhanden* character or of its worldly character. Cf. *SZ*, pp. 65, 74 (93–94, 103–4).
72. *SZ*, p. 188 (232).
73. Ibid., p. 192 (236). The reader should bear in mind that chapter 4 will both flesh out and modify the treatment of nihilism given here.
74. *SZ*, pp. 286–87 (333).
75. I am here drawing freely on the argument of *WM* and *WG*, both written in 1928.
76. Heidegger's own *KPM* lends some credence to this interpretation, especially in its implication that Heidegger is carrying out the temporal-historical freeing of Kant from himself in the way in which Hegel *ought* to have revised Kant. See *KPM*, esp. pp. 127 ff., 219–22 (144 ff., 251–55). Cf. *SZ*, p. 427, note 4 (499, note xvi). Michael Gelven's *A Commentary on Heidegger's "Being and Time"* finds a close bond between Heidegger and Kant. See, e.g., p. 50: "like categories, the existentials are necessary ways in which the mind operates." For the antithetical view, see John Macquarrie, *Martin Heidegger*, p. 13: "the existential analytic will not describe universal 'properties', but simply possible ways in which the *Dasein* may exist. These possible ways of existing, Heidegger calls the *existentialia*." For my part I understand the *existentialia* as what might be called "inevitable possibilizers." In characterizing the status of the *existentialia*, a phrase used in another connection by Heidegger is suggestive: "basis of possibility and mode of necessity" (*KPM*, p. 202 [231]).
77. *KPM*, pp. 214–15 (246). Translation modified.
78. Ibid., pp. 210–11 (241–42). Translation modified.

79. *SZ*, p. 354 (405). Translation modified.

80. Ibid., p. 134 (173). For the notion of groundless ground (or baseless basis), see ibid., pp. 283–85 (328–31).

81. Ibid., p. 284 (330). Note that Heidegger speaks of "Being-a-ground" not as an assumption of power or self-will but as recognition of Dasein's powerlessness. "Dasein is not itself the ground of its Being, inasmuch as this ground first arises from its own projection; rather, as Being-its-Self, it is the Being of its ground." (*SZ*, p. 285 [330]; translation modified.) This has to be understood in light of Dasein's *temporal* structure; Dasein cannot be the ground/basis *of* its Being, because it has always to take over a grounding-function which is its very temporal Being, or way of Being. Dasein does not preexist its way of Being so as to be able to found or ground it.

82. Ibid., p. 35 (59).

83. Ibid., p. 338 (387–88).

84. Ibid., p. 347 (398). Italics deleted.

85. Cf. *SZ*, p. 270 (315): "Dasein exists as a potentiality-for-Being which has, *in each case*, already abandoned itself to definite possibilities." (Italics added.) Cf. p. 222 (264–65): "*Because Dasein is essentially falling, its state of Being is such that it is in 'untruth'*. This term, like the expression 'falling', is here used ontologically. . . . To be closed off and covered up belongs to Dasein's *facticity*. In its full existential-ontological meaning, the proposition that 'Dasein is in the truth' states equiprimordially that 'Dasein is in untruth.' " Many passages in *SZ* suggest the pervasiveness and inevitablity of the tendency to falling. It is, and apparently must be, the normal condition of Dasein. It is even the condition in which the disclosure of beings generally occurs. Heidegger goes so far as to say that "Temporality is essentially falling" (*SZ*, p. 369 [421]) and that falling "constitutes *all* Dasein's days in their everydayness" (p. 179 [224]; italics added).

86. Ibid., p. 134 (173).

87. Ibid., p. 310 (358).

88. Ibid., p. 371 (422).

89. Ibid., pp. 144, 188 (183, 232).

90. Ibid., pp. 325–26 (373). Translation modified.

91. *WG*, p. 44 (104–5).

92. Ibid., pp. 45–46 (108–9).

93. Heidegger says that "we shall not give the answer to our leading question as to the meaning of Being in general." (*SZ*, p. 17 [38].) It is worth noting that there is a possibility that *SZ* was published in 1927 without Division 3 of Part I and Part II not because Heidegger at that time thought that he had reached an impasse but rather for professional and extraphilosophical reasons. Heidegger had to publish when he did in order to qualify for the post at Marburg formerly held by Nicolai Hartmann. (See *SD*, pp. 87–88.) On the other hand, Heidegger states (in retrospect, 1963) that "the path of questioning" that he was following "was longer than I had suspected." (*SD*, p. 87.)

94. *SZ*, p. 329 (377). Translation modified.

95. Ibid., p. 35 (59). Translation modified; italics deleted.

3. L'Être-pour-soi, Ground, and Time in
L'Être et le Néant

1. Biemel, *Jean-Paul Sartre*, p. 21; de Beauvoir, *Prime of Life*, p. 282.
2. *EN*, pp. 30–34 (lxiv–lxix).
3. *SZ*, p. 35 (60). Italics deleted.
4. *EN*, p. 342 (282). Cf. p. 502 (430): "a general theory of being . . . is the very goal we are pursuing." See also p. 34 (lxix).
5. Just as *Dasein* is not 'man', but rather man's Being, so Sartre's *l'être-pour-soi* is not man but rather man's Being—although Sartre occasionally slides over the distinction, and translations can mislead in this regard. (For example, on p. 520 of *Being and Nothingness* the translator has written "the for-itself—i.e., man" where the French text [p. 603] has simply *le pour-soi*.) Like Dasein, the for-itself is not simply present-at-hand as a self-contained being but is ekstatically dispersed. But, unlike *Dasein*, it has a self-transcending 'instantaneous nucleus', 'consciousness', which ties it more closely to traditional conceptions of 'man' than Heidegger intends *Dasein* to be. And Sartre's frequent use of the adjective *humain* in *EN* (as in the assertion "Le monde est humain," *EN*, p. 270) suggests that Sartre finds little to criticize in the term. (In chapter 6 I shall consider Sartre's and Heidegger's respective stands on "humanism.") Hana has argued, rightly I think, that Sartre tends to collapse his own distinction between the for-itself or *way of being* of the conscious human being, and consciousness itself (*Freiheit und Person*, p. 4; pp. 26–28). Cf. *EN*, p. 111 (70): "we can at this juncture handle the ontological investigation of consciousness, not as the *totality* of the human being, but as the instantaneous *nucleus* of this being." (Italics added.)
6. *EN*, p. 12 (xlviii).
7. Ibid., pp. 15–16 (*li–lii*).
8. Ibid., p. 17 (*liii*).
9. Ibid., p. 24 (*lix*).
10. Ibid., p. 27 (*lxii*).
11. Ibid., p. 28 (*lxiii*).
12. Ibid., p. 29 (*lxiv*). Here and elsewhere Sartre's term *l'être* is ambiguous, since it can mean both 'a being' and 'being' in the sense of "the nature of a being" or "being as such." Where Heidegger's German always distinguishes between the two—"Das Seiende, dem es in seinem Sein um dieses selbst geht" (*SZ*, p. 42)—Sartre writes "un être pour lequel il est dans son être question de son être" (*EN*, p. 29). Also cf. *SZ*, p. 42 with *EN*, p. 21. Sartre has available to him the term *l'étant* to translate Heidegger's *das Seiende*, yet he prefers to use the terms *l'être, la chose*, or *l'existant* to refer to beings at what Heidegger calls the "ontic" level. In *CRD* (e.g., p. 357) Sartre sometimes capitalizes (*Être*) to distinguish between beings and Being, but usually does not in *EN*. I have adopted the convention of translating Heidegger's *das Seiende* as 'being', 'a being', 'beings', 'entities', or 'what-is'

(depending on the context), reserving 'Being' for his term *Sein*. If Sartre does not capitalize *être* when he speaks of "the being of a being" or "the being of beings," and if he uses *être* both for beings and for their being, this must be intentional on his part. It may signify a rejection or reformulation of Heidegger's "ontological difference"; use of the same term for beings and their being may imply a judgment that Heidegger has distinguished too sharply between beings and their being. In translating and commenting on *EN*, I have therefore respected Sartre's usage, leaving the word 'being' uncapitalized.

13. *L'Imagination* (1936); *L'Imaginaire* (1940).

14. *I*, pp. 233–39 (265–73).

15. Ibid., p. 234 (*268*).

16. Ibid., p. 235 (*269*).

17. Ibid., p. 234 (*268*).

18. Ibid., p. 233 (266).

19. *EN*, p. 270 (218). Cf. p. 77 (40): "In anxiety I discern myself . . . as unable to make the meaning of the world come to it except through me."

20. *I*, p. 235 (*269*).

21. *EN*, p. 148 (*104*).

22. Ibid., p. 381 (*318*).

23. *I*, p. 236 (*270*).

24. *EN*, p. 228 ff. (*180* ff.).

25. ". . . This being is . . . the transphenomenal being of phenomena and not a noumenal being hidden behind them." (*EN*, p. 29 [*lxiv*].)

26. *EN*, p. 128 (*85*).

27. Ibid., pp. 54–55 (*18–19*). Italics added.

28. One must bear in mind Sartre's frequent argument to the effect that if the being of consciousness is anything in addition to negativity, consciousness then becomes 'opaque' and ceases to *be* consciousness. (E.g., *EN*, p. 80 [42].) But one must also bear in mind that consciousness is not "the *totality* of the human being" but rather "the instantaneous *nucleus* of this being." (Ibid., p. 111 [70].) A 'totality' for Sartre is always a synthetic whole— something that is *made* to be, like 'the world', out of disparate elements. Thus consciousness is only the intantaneous nucleus of the human being as an ekstatic unity (whole) that is *more than* consciousness yet that is, owing to consciousness itself, always a 'detotalized totality', a whole that fails to coincide with itself in the simple identity of pure presentness.

29. *EN*, p. 57 (*21*).

30. Ibid., pp. 44–45 (*9–10*); pp. 245–46 (195–96).

31. Ibid., p. 57 (*21*). But cf. p. 52 (*16*): "there is nonbeing only on the surface of being." The Jamesian (and Nietzschean) metaphor of the serpent has more dignity than the Sartrean metaphor of the worm. One of the consequences of the dominance of negation in Sartre's ontology is the special language of *EN*. Taking the book as a linguistic whole, one can hardly fail to see it as a vast pageant of negative terms. These terms seem to express certain common themes, such as infection, degradation, and disintegration.

They suggest that the for-itself has infected the world with its distinctive sickness, spoiling the perfection of pure being. Is this of philosophical importance, or is it the intrusion of Sartre's temperament into his ontology? De Beauvoir notes, "I knew how readily Sartre's imagination tended toward disaster." (*Prime of Life*, p. 170.)

32. Ibid., p. 129 (77).

33. Ibid., pp. 32–34; 119 (*lxvi–lxviii; 77*).

34. Ibid.

35. Ibid., p. 34 (lxviii).

36. Ibid., p. 32 (lxvi), p. 589 (507).

37. Ibid., p. 34 (lxviii).

38. *SZ*, p. 38 (62). Heidegger's and Sartre's treatments of *existentia* and *essentia* will be compared in chapter 6.

39. *EN*, pp. 228–35 (180–86).

40. Ibid., p. 232 (*183*).

41. Ibid., e.g., p. 375 (*312*); pp. 567–68 (*487*).

42. *WM*, p. 30 (*333*). Sartre of course also has in mind the Gestaltist notion of "hodological space" and Husserl's notion of presentation by "profile" (*Abschattung*).

43. See *QL*, p. 90 (*39*): "This landscape, if we turn away from it, will wallow unwitnessed in its dark permanence."

44. See *EN*, p. 234 (*185*): "we cannot imagine that the for-itself effects *distorting* [*déformantes*] synthetic negations between the transcendents which it is not." (Italics added.)

45. *PH*, pp. 31–35.

46. *SZ*, p. 34 (58).

47. *PH*, p. 34 (5).

48. *EN*, p. 375 (*312*). Italics, in part, added.

49. Ibid., e.g., p. 720 (625).

50. Ibid., p. 233 (*184*). Italics, in part, added.

51. Ibid., p. 234 (*185*).

52. Ibid., pp. 119–20 (77). Italics, in part, added. This argument raises a serious question as to whether the phenomenological program can be carried out without a modification of the traditional principle of identity. See chapter 14.

53. Ibid., pp. 142–144 (*98–99*). Cf. Heidegger, *SZ*, p. 70 (100): "The wood is a forest of timber, the mountain a quarry of rock; the river is waterpower, the wind is wind 'in the sails.' " (Also see Heidegger's treatment of the relation of 'nature' and 'landscape' in *EHD*, p. 21.) To be sure, Sartre can and does similarly characterize the phenomenal environment. What is in question is the relative degree of 'reality' accorded to this phenomenal environment by the two thinkers, and ultimately the degree of constitutivity accorded to internal relations by the two thinkers.

54. *EN*, p. 228 (*179*).

55. Ibid., p. 232 (*183*).

56. Ibid., p. 429 (*362*).

57. Ibid., p. 588 (506). Italics, in part, added.
58. Ibid., p. 590 (508–9). Italics, in part, added.
59. Ibid., pp. 670–671 (581–82). Italics, in part, added.
60. Ibid., p. 687 (597). Italics, in part, added.
61. Ibid., p. 691 (600). Italics, in part, added.
62. Ibid., pp. 694–97 (603–5). Here, as elsewhere, Sartre intends *il y a* ("there is") as a translation of Heidegger's *es gibt*. Cf. *EN*, p. 305 (248).
63. For a fuller analysis of the role of magic in Sartrean thought, see Fell, *Emotion in the Thought of Sartre*, passim.
64. See *SZ*, p. 65 (93–94).
65. *EN*, p. 232 (183).
66. Cf. *EN*, p. 51 (15): "Being is empty of all determination except identity with itself. . . ."
67. Hartmann, *Sartre's Ontology*, p. 43.
68. Cf. Spiegelberg, *Phenomenological Movement*, II, 489: "Perhaps the most appropriate way of characterizing Sartre's position would be to call it a combination of a phenomenalism of essences with a realism of existence." On the "ideal status" of meaning, cf. Hartmann, *Sartre's Ontology*, p. 106 and passim.
69. *EN*, p. 30 (lxiv–lxv). Sartre here argues that any mode of being simultaneously "manifests" and "veils" being.
70. See *I*, p. 98 (104) and Fell, *Emotion in the Thought of Sartre*, pp. 38–44.
71. *EN*, p. 687 (597). The question of alternative or "equivalent" apprehensions of the "same" being will be further explored in chapter 10.
72. See Fell, *Emotion in the Thought of Sartre*, pp. 15–18 and passim.
73. *EN*, pp. 656 ff. (568 ff.).
74. Ibid., p. 650 (563).
75. Ibid., e.g., p. 669 (580).
76. See *SZ*, e.g., p. 291 (337).
77. *EN*, pp. 255–68 (204–16).
78. Ibid., p. 259 (208).
79. Plato, *Timaeus*, 37D (*Plato's Cosmology*, translated by F. M. Cornford, p. 98).
80. *EN*, p. 12 (xlviii).
81. Ibid., pp. 201–18 (155–70).
82. Ibid., p. 253 (202).
83. Ibid., p. 689 (599). It should be noted that Sartre raises the possibility of an alternative approach, which tends "to confer being on the for-itself without detour." I shall consider it in chapter 5.
84. Ibid., p. 139 ff. (95 ff.).
85. Ibid., p. 159 (116).
86. Ibid., p. 163 (119).
87. Ibid., pp. 161–62 (117–18).
88. Cf. *EN*, p. 162 (118).
89. Ibid., p. 70 (33).
90. If the past is a humanized actuality, is there not a sense in which

man adds to the plenitude of being? If so, can it still be maintained that the for-itself adds *nothing* to being? In becoming past, 'nothing' (possibility) becomes 'something'.

91. *EN*, p. 161 (117).

92. Ibid., p. 188 (*142*).

93. *SZ*, p. 329 (378).

94. Jeanson, *Le Problème moral et la pensée de Sartre*, p. 340.

95. *SZ*, p. 407 (459). Cf. p. 338 (387), where the privileged experience known as "the moment of vision" is called a 'Present'.

96. *EN*, pp. 616 ff. (533 ff.).

97. Ibid., p. 188 (*142*). Italics, in part, added.

98. Ibid.

99. Ibid., pp. 721–22 (627).

100. Cf. *TE*, pp. 84–85 (103–4); *EN*, p. 26 (lxi).

101. *EN*, p. 381 (318).

102. *La Nausée*, pp. 161–71 (170–82).

103. *PH*, p. 34 (5).

104. *EN*, pp. 712–13 (*618–19*).

105. Ibid., p. 713 (*619*).

106. Ibid., p. 714 (*620*).

107. Ibid., pp. 716–17 (622). Italics, in part, added.

108. Ibid., p. 719 (624).

109. Cf. *De Anima*, 429b25.

110. *TE*, p. 64 (82).

111. *EN*, p. 232 (183).

112. Ibid., p. 711 (*617*).

113. Ibid., p. 713 (*619*).

114. Ibid., p. 714 (*620*).

115. See ibid., p. 697 (605).

116. *EN*, p. 715 (*621*): "There would be . . . no sense in asking what being was *before* the appearance of the for-itself. Nevertheless metaphysics must try to determine the nature and meaning of this *prehistoric process and source of all history*" (italics added).

117. Ibid.

118. *WM*, p. 15 (*344*).

119. *EN*, e.g., pp. 50–51 (15), undifferentiated plenitude; p. 116 (74), decompression of plenitude; p. 118 (76), the self vanishing into identity; p. 182 (136–37), diaspora, ekstasis, ontological mirage of the self, quasi-multiplicity of being; p. 243 (193), all negation is ekstatic; p. 252 (201), diaspora; p. 306 (249), Platonic ekstasis; p. 667 (578), emanation; pp. 671, 672 (582, 583), emanation; p. 680 (590), creation as emanation; p. 689 (599), action as emanation; p. 712 (618), emanation; pp. 718–20 (624–25), disintegrated oneness. (I am indebted to Ch. Perelman for the notion of interpreting *EN* by reference to Plotinus.)

120. See Sartre's reference to the "explosion" of the Parmenidean totality of being in the atomism of Leucippus, *EN*, p. 362 (300); the multiplicity of

'thises' are in effect the irreducible atoms of Sartre's ontology, and are a multiplicity that arises out of undifferentiated plenitude by "ekstatic nega-tion." See also Sartre's analysis of the fundamental human tendency to fill holes, as it expresses itself in the child: "He aspires to the density, the uni-form and spherical plenitude of Parmenidean being" (EN, p. 705 [613]). Cf. Hartmann, Sartre's Ontology, p. 35: "This characterization of being reminds us, even down to details, of Parmenides' account of being."

121. EN, p. 715 (620–21). Italics, in part, added. At one point Sartre presents this metaphysical hypothesis as if it were a fact: "The for-itself is the in-itself losing itself as in-itself in order to ground itself as conscious-ness." (EN, p. 124 [82].)

122. Ibid., p. 717 (623). Italics, in part, added. If metaphysical cosmology is given a "Kantian" status by Sartre, we are perhaps justified in hearing an echo of Vaihinger's als ob in Sartre's repeated appeals to an "as if" cosmol-ogy.

123. Ibid., p. 719 (624): "une dualité tranchée."

124. Cf. EN, pp. 243–44 (193–94): "The existent does not possess its es-sence as a present quality. It is the very negation of essence: the green is never green. Instead the essence comes to the existent from the ground of the future, as a meaning that is never given and that always haunts it. It is the pure correlate of the pure ideality of my negation." Thus a genuine "fusion of essence and existence" is "impossible."

125. EN, p. 719 (625). Italics, in part, added. This is "the monism of the phenomenon," which, according to the first paragraph of EN, has been the goal of "modern thought." In that same paragraph Sartre asks whether modern thought has reached this goal (EN, p. 11 [xlvii]). In light of the conclusion of EN, the answer must be a qualified no. Sartre's conclusion re-affirms the ambiguity already present in the following passage from the in-troduction: "despite the fact that the concept of being has the peculiarity of being split into two incommunicable regions, it is necessary to explain how these two regions can be placed under the same rubric. This will require examining both these types of being, and it is evident that we can only truly grasp the meaning of either of them if we can establish their true con-nections [rapports] with the notion of being in general and establish the relations [relations] which unite them." (EN, p. 31 [lxv].)

126. Ibid., p. 718 (623).

127. Ibid., p. 34 (lxix).

128. Ibid., p. 719 (625).

129. That in-itself and for-itself—rather than phenomenon and world—are for Sartre the genuine and irreducible ontological relata is especially clear in the following assertion: "For ontology, the only regions of being that can be elucidated are those of the in-itself, the for-itself, and the ideal region of the 'cause of itself.' " (EN, p. 719 [624].) Analytically regarded, phenomenon and world, as attempted fusions of the irreducible ontological regions, are impossible attempts to inhabit the 'ideal'—and impossible—region of "cause of itself." (Regarded epistemologically, phenomenon and

world are ideal—and impossible—syntheses of idealism and realism.) For-itself and in-itself have the character of "natural" (given) being, relative to which phenomena have merely "artifactual" status. Therefore, we can second Simone de Beauvoir's admission that "Sartre's reconciliation of ontology and phenomenology raises difficulties" (*Privilèges*, p. 271). But at the same time she notes that "Sartre is preparing a philosophical work which makes a frontal attack on the problem." Since de Beauvoir wrote these remarks in 1955, the philosophical work she is presumably referring to is Sartre's *QM*, published in 1958. In chapter 12 I shall consider whether this work or *CRD*, begun in 1958, solves the problem of integrating ontology and phenomenology.

4. NOTHING AND WORLD: THE NEED FOR THE TURN

1. *SD*, p. 31.
2. *N*, II, 194–95. ('Subject', Heidegger argues, means 'ground'; cf. *SG*, p. 23.) I infer that *SZ* remained "subjectivist" insofar as it could be construed as treating Dasein as a final ground, and in this sense as 'subject'.
3. From the orientation of *SG*, Heidegger's early thinking is still in danger of *Gründenwollen*, the will to ground.
4. *SD*, p. 34.
5. *SZ*, p. v (17). Cf. *WW* (3d ed.), p. 27 (323): "Every sort of anthropology and all subjectivity [*Subjectivität*] of man as subject has . . . in *Sein und Zeit* already been left behind." Here Heidegger is speaking of the *intention* of *SZ*, whereas in *N*, II, 194–95, he is speaking of its effect.
6. Cf. *SD*, pp. 31–32.
7. Cf. Fell, "Sartre's Words," esp. pp. 427–34.
8. I make no pretense of offering here a definitive analysis of the immediate circumstances of the turn or *Kehre*. Although Heidegger reportedly became impatient with all the talk about it, I suspect that it will be some time before the circumstances and dating of the *Kehre* are fully known. Both Pöggeler and Richardson, whose studies of the development of Heidegger's thought are of primary importance, assume without adequate evidence that the *Kehre* begins in 1930–31. This is a common view, based upon the *published* content of *WW*. This lecture, originally delivered in 1930, was only published in 1943, after considerable reworking. Walter Schulz, citing a stenographic transcript of the original Marburg lecture, argues that in important respects its content antedates the *Kehre* (Schulz, in Pöggeler, *Heidegger*, p. 115). The correct dating of the *Kehre* is of more than historical importance. It is of philosophical importance since some critics of Heidegger have used his rectoral addresses of 1933–34 to discredit his entire philosophical position. But until the initiation of the *Kehre* is correctly dated, there remains a definite possibility that Heidegger's rectoral addresses do not mirror his mature thought. (They may not, for that matter, accurately mirror his early thought.) There even remains the possibility that Heidegger's experiences as rector themselves contributed to the shift in his thinking. (For a balanced estimate—amid a welter of slander—of Hei-

degger's attitude and conduct as rector of the Albert-Ludwigs-Universität, see Beda Allemann, "Martin Heidegger und die Politik," in Pöggeler, *Heidegger*, pp. 246–60).

9. *SZ*, p. 344 (394–95).

10. Ibid., p. 356 (407).

11. Von Hermann, *Die Selbstinterpretation Martin Heideggers*, p. 42.

12. *SZ*, p. 270 (315).

13. Ibid., p. 384 (436).

14. Cf. J. W. Miller, "The Ahistoric and the Historic," in Ortega y Gasset, *History as a System*, pp. 237–69. Miller's treatment of Eleaticism has significant affinities with Heidegger's critique of the notion of atemporal presence.

15. See *KPM*, esp. p. 37 (37).

16. Here, as elsewhere, I am treating temporality and historicality as essentially the same. See *SZ*, p. 332 (281): "The *temporalization-structure* of temporality . . . reveals itself as the historicality of Dasein." Also cf. p. 382 (434): "the Interpretation of Dasein's historicality will prove to be, at bottom, just a more concrete working out of temporality."

17. *SZ*, pp. 384–85 (436).

18. Ibid., p. 386 (437–38): "Repetition does not let itself be persuaded of something by what is 'past,' just in order that this, as something which was formerly actual, may recur."

19. Ibid., pp. 386–87 (438–39). Italics, in part, added.

20. *EN*, pp. 543–46; 555 (465–67; 475). Sartre's notion of "radical conversion" is examined in chapter 5.

21. *SZ*, pp. 385–86 (437–38). Translation slightly modified.

22. Following my conception of the *existentialia* as "inevitable possibilizers" (chapter 2).

23. *SZ*, pp. 187–88 (231–33).

24. Kierkegaard, *Fear and Trembling and The Sickness unto Death*, pp. 168–75.

25. The later thought of Sartre is likewise in important respects a mediation of Hegel and Kierkegaard. Cf. Fell, "Sartre as Existentialist and Marxist," passim.

26. *EN*, pp. 305–7 (248–50).

27. *SZ*, p. 88 (122).

28. Ibid., pp. 207–8 (251).

29. Ibid., p. 208 (251–52).

30. *EN*, p. 305 (248). This is one of Sartre's most fundamental criticisms of Heidegger; Sartre's own use of *l'être* for both ontological and ontic being probably symbolizes his effort to surmount the difficulty alluded to.

31. *WM*, p. 32 (336–37).

32. Ibid., p. 33 (337); p. 32 (336). One is immediately reminded here of Sartre's "purifying reflection" and "radical conversion."

33. Ibid., p. 32 (335–36).

34. Ibid., p. 41 (348).

35. Ibid., p. 32 (336).
36. Ibid., p. 42 (349).
37. Ibid., p. 38 (344).
38. Ibid., p. 33 (337). Italics added.
39. Ibid., p. 33 (338).
40. Ibid., p. 35 (340).
41. Ibid. Italics added.
42. Ibid., pp. 35–36 (340–41): "But what does it mean to say that this primordial anxiety occurs only in rare moments? Nothing other than that the nothing is proximally and for the most part dissembled [*verstellt*] in its primordiality. . . . In one way or another we completely lose ourselves amid beings." I resist the temptation to elaborate further the analogy, though it is a fruitful one in the context of Heidegger's thought. In a tribute to Heidegger on his eightieth birthday, his brother Fritz wrote to him: "perhaps you may only be thoroughly understood long after the Americans have built a colossal supermarket on the moon." (*Martin Heidegger zum 80*, p. 63.) Heidegger might argue that the moon voyages symbolize the essential meaning of the meta-physical quest, in both its positive and negative aspects.
43. WM, p. 34 (339).
44. Cf. SZ, p. 16 (37).
45. This is an inevitable corollary of the doctrine of internal relations. That is: if beings are what they are in their Being by reference to each other (i.e., by reference to other beings), they are not themselves by reference to a metaphysical Being that is not their own but beyond them as transcendent. I am going to hold that the early Heidegger imperfectly realizes this truth.
46. WG, p. 50 (118–19).
47. WM, p. 38 (343): "Die Hineingehaltenheit des Daseins in das Nichts auf dem Grunde der verborgenen Angst macht den Menschen zum Platzhalter des Nichts."
48. Once again, a thesis of Sartre's comes inevitably to mind: the idea of man as the plugger of the hole in being.
49. WM, p. 41 (348).
50. EN, p. 708 (615).
51. WM, pp. 35–36 (340–41).
52. Ibid., p. 42 (349). I have preserved part of Hull and Crick's translation.
53. I have used the language of Paul Tillich here. See *The Courage to Be*, esp. pp. 37, 139.
54. WM, p. 37 (343). Cf. Nietzsche, *Also Sprach Zarathustra*, in *Werke in drei Bänden*, II, 380: "Schöpfer-Begier" (*The Portable Nietzsche*, p. 236: "creative longing").
55. Schulz, in Pöggeler, *Heidegger*, pp. 115–16. Schulz claims that Heidegger's characterization of Dasein as *ohnmächtig* becomes, after the *Kehre*, the precondition for Dasein's openness to the power of Being. See SZ, p.

384 (436). Dasein's "supreme power" (*Übermacht*) consists in its reappropriation of its "powerlessness" (*Ohnmacht*).

56. *SZ*, p. 35 (59); p. 222 (264); p. 354 (405).

57. *WM*, p. 36 (*340–41*).

58. For this sense of 'interpretation', see *SZ*, pp. 148 (188–89).

59. *SZ*, p. 343 (393).

60. But Heidegger problematically adds: "and certainly the ontology of Thinghood does even less." (*SZ*, p. 113 [82].)

61. *SZ*, p. 152 (193). Translation slightly modified. On the primordiality of the present-at-hand, see *WG*, p. 43 (100–1).

62. In addition to Schulz's "Über den philosophiegeschichtlichen Ort Martin Heideggers" (in Pöggeler, *Heidegger*), see Löwith, *Heidegger*, esp. p. 24; Ott, *Denken und Sein*, esp. pp. 73–82.

63. *WM*, p. 35 (*340*). Italics added.

64. Ibid., p. 40 (*346–47*).

65. Ibid., p. 40 (*347*).

66. This by no means excludes Heidegger's subsequent assertion of the relativity of Dasein to Being.

67. *WM*, p. 39 (346).

68. *SZ*, pp. 220–22 (263–65).

69. *WG*, pp. 53–54 (126–29).

70. See Granel, "Remarques," in Klostermann, ed., *Durchblicke*, p. 358.

71. Nietzsche, *The Will to Power*, aphorisms 7, 12, 16, 20.

72. Cf. *SZ*, p. 203 (247): "both change and persistence belong, with equal primordiality, to the essence of time."

73. *SZ*, pp. 68–69 (97–98).

74. Ibid., p. 70 (99). Italics added. Cf. p. 76 (106): "only on the basis of the phenomenon of the world can the Being-in-itself of entities within-the-world be grasped ontologically."

75. Ibid., p. 69 (99).

76. Cf. Macomber, *Anatomy of Disillusion*, esp. pp. 24–51.

77. *WM*, p. 38 (*344*). Italics added.

78. *SZ*, p. 70 (100). Cf. Merleau-Ponty, *Phénoménologie de la perception*, p. iii (ix). I forebear speaking here of the historical character of the notion of 'nature'.

79. *SZ*, p. 388 (440).

80. Ibid., p. 71 (101).

81. Ibid., p. 44 (70). Translation slightly modified.

82. Ibid., p. 88 (121). Translation modified. (Macquarrie and Robinson's translation distinguishes the two categories more sharply than the original does.) At *SZ*, p. 364 (415), Heidegger speaks darkly of a "neutral" understanding of Being in which "readiness-to-hand and presence-at-hand have not yet been distinguished. . . ." With this passage one may compare pp. 50–51 (76) and p. 82 (113), where Heidegger refers briefly to primitive experience. Does Heidegger mean to say that 'primitive phenomena' (p. 51) are "neutrally" apprehended? He asserts: "Primitive Dasein often speaks to us more directly in terms of a primordial absorption in 'phenomena' (taken in

a pre-phenomenological sense)" (p. 51). Does this mean that the circularity of understanding is more easily seen in the primitive than it is in later thinking that thinks it has overcome this circularity by analyzing 'the phenomenon' into 'subjective' and 'objective' components? Heidegger leaves the matter unclarified.

83. *WM*, p. 32 (336).

84. Cf. *SZ*, p. 149 (190): "This grasping which is free of the 'as', is a privation of the kind of seeing in which one *merely* understands. It is not more primordial than that kind of seeing, but is derived from it."

85. Ibid., p. 151 (193). Kurt Jürgen Huch (*Philosophiegeschichtliche Voraussetzungen*, esp. pp. 37–39) attempts to demonstrate that Heidegger, in holding meaning to be an *existentiale* of Dasein, situates himself on the ground of modern subjectivism and nominalism.

86. Heidegger will later, correlating meaning and language, write: "When we walk to the fountain or through the forest, we are always already walking through the word 'fountain' or through the word 'forest', even if we do not say these words or think about linguistic matters." (H, p. 286.)

87. This is the impasse of Platonism—an impasse still present in Descartes, and more recently in Karl Jaspers' notion of the 'cipher'.

88. *SZ*, p. 152 (193); p. 153 (194). Italics added.

89. Ibid., p. 65 (93–94); p. 74 (104).

90. As in Sartre—and in Kant. Cf. *KPM*, pp. 112–16 (124–29).

91. Thus it is the possibilizing ground for the fact that "natural events . . . can break in upon us and destroy us." (*SZ*, p. 152 [193].)

92. *SZ*, p. 134 (173).

93. Ibid., p. 188 (232).

94. Ibid., p. 394 (446).

95. Ibid., p. 392 (444).

96. Ibid., p. 285 (331).

97. Ibid., p. 343 (393).

98. Ibid., p. 337 (387).

99. Ibid., p. 391 (444).

100. *KPM*, p. 213 (244). Italics added.

101. *WM*, p. 37 (343).

102. *SZ*, p. 310 (358); *WM*, p. 37 (342).

103. Nietzsche, *Werke in drei Bänden*, II, 301, 445, 826.

104. *WM*, p. 37 (343).

105. See Heidegger's treatment of "pure intuition" in *KPM*, esp. pp. 130 ff. (148 ff.). If "our mode of cognition is not ontically creative" (p. 71 [76]), nevertheless it is asserted that transcendental imagination is *ontologically* "creative" (pp. 112–13 [125]).

106. Regardless of whether this unconditioned being is conceived as God or as transcendental ego.

107. Sartre himself retrospectively recognizes this. See *M*, p. 210 (252): "I gaily demonstrated that man is impossible."

108. E.g., *SZ*, p. 88 (122).

109. Ibid., p. 391 (443).

110. Ibid., p. 396 (448).

111. See, e.g., *VA*, p. 229: "verändert das Denken die Welt"; *W*, p. 191 (300): "So ist das Denken ein Tun. Aber ein Tun, das zugleich alle Praxis übertrifft."

112. In the Epilogue to *WM* (1943), Heidegger denies that the implications of the lecture are nihilistic (p. 45 [352]). But he attempts to show this by invoking in the Epilogue a conception of language that is not invoked by the lecture itself. One can only say that if this was Heidegger's position in 1929, he failed to communicate it; and I am arguing that, whatever his intention, the lecture, without the retrospective guidance provided by the Epilogue and the Introduction (1949), is *inherently liable* to a "nihilistic" interpretation.

113. *SZ*, p. 128 (166).

114. Ibid., p. 391 (444). This notion reappears with renewed force in Heidegger's later critique of the epoch of the *Gestell*.

115. Ibid., p. 43 (69); p. 191 (235–36).

116. Why, then, would the *Kehre* have been made to appear as an event of 1930? I raise the possibility, again without evidence, that Heidegger may have wished to avoid giving the impression that political considerations could redirect "thought." Thought must redirect politics. If this outrageous hypothesis should stimulate closer study of the immediate circumstances surrounding the *Kehre*, it will have been an outrage worth perpetrating.

117. *KPM*, pp. 118, 142, 152–53, 179 (134, 161, 173, 202).

118. Ibid., p. 70 (75). Translation revised. Further, at p. 220 (252), Heidegger appears to equate "what-being" with "possibility."

119. *SZ*, p. 161 (203–4).

120. Cf. von Hermann, *Die Selbstinterpretation*. Von Hermann succeeds in isolating ten significant "shifts of accent" in Heidegger's "turn."

121. *SG*, p. 184.

122. *WG*, p. 39 (88–89). In this same place Heidegger uses the phrase *der ursprüngliche Entwurf* (der Möglichkeiten des Daseins), which is probably the source of Sartre's expression *projet fondamental* (see *EN*, part IV). And in Sartre's reappropriation of Heidegger, the disjunction between meaning and *existentia* is explicitly realized: "In choosing ourselves we choose the world—not in its texture as in-itself but in its meaning." (*EN*, p. 541 [463].) It is significant in this regard that de Waelhens can hold that pp. 161–66 (170–77) of Sartre's *La Nausée* "translate with matchless power and clarity the central experience of Heidegger's whole philosophy" (*La Philosophie de Martin Heidegger*, p. 367. See also p. 366). The passage in question, from which de Waelhens quotes extensively, is that in which Sartre elaborates upon the disjunction between meaning and *existentia*: "The words had vanished and with them the significance of things, their methods of use, and the feeble points of reference which men have traced on their surface." (*La Nausée*, p. 161 [171].) De Waelhens finds the philosophy of Heidegger to be a nihilistic "exaltation of contingency" (pp. 356, 360).

123. The present-at-hand, as we have seen, is never worldless, but its significance is variable. Division II thus relativizes the readiness-to-hand referentiality of Division I.

124. To be sure, Heidegger warns that "the significance relationships which determine the structure of the world are not a network of forms which a worldless subject has laid over some kind of material." (SZ, p. 366 [417].)

5. THE ETHICS OF PLAY AND FREEDOM: CONVERSION

1. EN, p. 11 (xlvii).

2. Ibid., p. 542 (464); pp. 638–42 (553–56).

3. Ibid., p. 720 (625).

4. Cf. EN, pp. 295–96 (239–40); pp. 669–70 (580–81).

5. Ibid., p. 614 (531). In a subsequent passage Sartre softens the apparently personal accusation of insincerity; speaking of Heidegger's classifications of "authentic project" and "inauthentic project of the self," Sartre writes that "such a classification is infected with an ethical concern by its very terminology, despite its author's intention" (EN, p. 651 [564]). I shall have occasion in chapter 6 to comment on Sartre's and Heidegger's respective classifications or typologies of the regions of Being and regions of philosophy (e.g., theory/praxis; ontology/metaphysics/ethics; etc.).

6. Thus I cannot agree with those who argue that Sartre is more faithful to Husserl's program than Heidegger is.

7. WM, p. 41 (348).

8. Nietzsche, Werke in drei Bänden, I, 48 (Birth of Tragedy, p. 51). Cf. the related remark of Sartre in TE, pp. 42–43 (59): "Reflection 'poisons' desire. . . . My reflective life 'by nature' poisons my spontaneous life."

9. De Beauvoir, Pour une morale de l'ambiguité, p. 66 (46): ". . . Being and Nothingness is in large part a description of the serious man and his universe." Cf. S, IV, 196 (234), where Sartre can be construed as characterizing EN as, at least in part, an "eidetics of bad faith."

10. EN, p. 111 (70).

11. Ibid., p. 484 (412).

12. Although it has become common to say that Sartre never published his long-promised ethics (EN, p. 722 [628]), it might be more accurate to say that he was publishing it all along—at least until 1952, when he reached the self-critical conclusion that an ethics cannot be written today (SGCM, p. 177 [186]).

13. See, e.g., EN, pp. 64 (28), 83–84 (44–45), 127–28 (84–85), 140 (96), 144 (100), 149 (104), 151–52 (108–9), 176 (131), 181 (135), 194–96 (148–49), 241 (192), 540 (462), 543–46 (465–67), 555 (475), 560 (480), 661 (573).

14. EN, p. 176 (131).

15. Ibid., p. 64 (28).

16. Ibid.

17. Ibid., p. 144 (100).

18. Ibid., pp. 83–84 (44–45). Italics, in part, added.

19. Ibid., p. 83 (*44*).
20. Ibid., pp. 127–28 (*85*).
21. Ibid., p. 127 (84).
22. *TE*, p. 24 (40).
23. See *EN*, pp. 222 ff. (173 ff.).
24. Ibid., pp. 195–196 (*149*). Italics added.
25. Ibid., p. 221 (173).
26. Ibid., e.g., pp. 133–34, 708 (90, 615).
27. Ibid., p. 544 (*465*). Italics deleted.
28. Ibid., p. 97 (*58*).
29. F. Jeanson bases his interpretation of Sartre on this notion. See *Le Problème moral et la pensée de Sartre*, passim. For Sartre's own understanding of the notion, see *EN*, p. 138*n* (94*n*).
30. *EN*, p. 544 (*466*); cf. p. 560 (480).
31. Ibid., p. 167 (123).
32. Ibid., pp. 545–46 (*467*). Italics, in part, added.
33. Ibid., p. 95 (56).
34. *SZ*, e.g., p. 310 (358).
35. *EN*, p. 661 (*573*).
36. The progressive-regressive method (or analytic and synthetic activity) remains a fundamental Sartrean technique. See *CRD*, pp. 41–42 (*SM*, pp. 51–52). Cf. *EN*, p. 537 (460).
37. *EN*, p. 182 (136).
38. Ibid., p. 249 (199).
39. Ibid., p. 208 (161).
40. Ibid., p. 540 (462).
41. Ibid., p. 84 (45).
42. Ibid., p. 720 (626).
43. See *EN*, p. 560 (481); pp. 643 ff. (557 ff.); and Fell, "Sartre's Theory of Motivation," esp. pp. 29–32.
44. *EN*, p. 77 (*39–40*). Note the association of 'value' (*valeur*) and 'meaning' (*sens*) in this passage. It is in taking an end as a value that the world appears as meaningful.
45. Ibid., p. 76 (*38*).
46. Ibid., p. 642 (*556*).
47. *SZ*, p. 344 (394).
48. See *SZ*, p. 152 (194); *WG*, p. 53 (126–29).
49. *EN*, p. 69 (*32*).
50. In *TE* Sartre had already advanced the idea of regression to the instantaneous nucleus as a moral experience. Describing a lasting hatred, Sartre writes: "If I limited it to what it is, to something instantaneous, I could not even speak of hatred anymore. . . . But precisely by this refusal to implicate the future [i.e., by this refusal of the refusal of the instant], I would cease to hate." (p. 46 [62].) In this work Sartre had already conceived of his theory of "absolute consciousness" as "a philosophical foundation for an ethics and a politics which are absolutely positive." (p. 87 [106].)
51. *EN*, p. 140 (*96*).

52. Ibid., p. 69 (32).

53. Ibid., p. 70 (33).

54. Ibid., p. 125 (83).

55. "*Nature naturée*": probably a reference to Spinoza's *natura naturata*. In play, man is in effect *natura naturans*, making his own nature, a semidivine activity of imaginative freedom.

56. *EN*, pp. 669–70 (*580–81*). Italics, in part, added.

57. See ibid., pp. 111, 484 (70, 412).

58. See *M*, esp. pp. 79, 96, 208–11 (97, 118, 249–53).

59. *EN*, p. 670 (581).

60. See *KPM*, pp. 70, 112–13, 118, 142, 152–53, 179 (75, 125, 134, 161, 173, 202).

61. *EN*, pp. 670–71 (*581–82*). Italics added.

62. Ibid., p. 671 (*582*).

63. Ibid.

64. Ibid., pp. 672–74 (*583 84*). Italics, in part, added.

65. *La Nausée*, pp. 161–71 (170–82). Cf. *M*, p. 210 (251): "I *was* Roquentin."

66. *EN*, p. 669 (581).

67. See *EN*, p. 111 (70); cf. Heidegger's *Hebel der Hausfreund*, p. 28, where Heidegger invokes Hebel's claim that "we are plants."

68. *EN*, p. 671 (582).

69. *La Nausée*, p. 159 (169).

70. *SZ*, p. 152 (193).

71. Cf. *EH*, p. 75 (*49*): "Moral choice must be compared to the construction of a work of art."

72. *EN*, pp. 696–704 (605–12).

73. *M*, p. 198 (237–38).

74. See chapter 3, above.

75. *PH*, p. 34 (5).

76. Sartre, as is well known, reappropriates Heidegger's notion of Being-toward-death in such a way that meaningful death in effect becomes continuous, or a constantly encountered and surpassed limit, while one's ultimate death becomes meaningless because it is a limit never encountered. See *EN*, pp. 615–38 (531–53).

77. *EN*, p. 615 (531).

78. See *M*, p. 197 (237): "each instant repeated the ceremony of my birth. . . ."

79. For Sartre's critique of the ego, see esp. *TE*, pp. 37 ff. (54 ff.). For his critique of ego-emotions, see ibid., pp. 45–51 (61–68); *EN*, pp. 209–18 (162–70). For his characterization of emotion as a fall into complicity with the flesh that "degrades," see *Esquisse d'une théorie des émotions*, esp. pp. 53 ff. (75 ff.). For his analysis of self-degradation by incantation, magic, and sorcery, see *Esquisse*, pp. 54–60 (77–86); *I*, p. 161 (177) and passim; *EN*, pp. 217–18 (169–70). For his critique of beauty as a vain ideal, see *EN*, pp. 244–45 (194–95).

80. *EN*, pp. 721–22 (*626–28*). Italics, in part, added.

81. Since "play is rarely pure of all appropriative tendency" (*EN*, p. 670 [581]) and "the original project . . . is a project of appropriation" (697 [605]). But in another passage Sartre appears to make a categorical connection between play and appropriation: "Art, science, play are activities of appropriation—in some cases wholly so, in other cases partially so—and what they want to appropriate, through and beyond the concrete object of their quest, is being itself: the absolute being of the in-itself." (p. 675 [585].)

82. On the distinction between freedom as a given and freedom as a goal, see Fell, "Sartre's Theory of Motivation," pp. 33–34, and *Emotion in the Thought of Sartre*, pp. 176–79.

83. *EN*, p. 670 (581). In de Beauvoir's interpretation of radical conversion, the fundamental project remains, but is stoically defused: "Existential conversion . . . merely obviates all possibility of failure by refusing to set up as absolutes the ends toward which my transcendence throws itself, and by considering them in their relation to the freedom which projects them." (*Pour une morale de l'ambiguité*, p. 21 [14].) Cf. *EH*, p. 49 (34): "we shall limit ourselves to counting solely upon what depends on our will." Also cf. *S, X*, 135 (5): "I have always had sympathy for the Stoics."

84. *I*, p. 113 (122).

85. *QL*, p. 85 (35n). Cf. *EH*, pp. 82–83 (54): "the ultimate signification of the acts of men of good faith is the quest for freedom as such."

86. Since 'freedom' is selected by Sartre as an admissible value on the ground that it is the only value compatible with lucid self-awareness and the avoidance of self-contradiction, it could be argued that Sartre's whole ethical program hangs on an unexamined or allegedly self-evident premise or value—that of lucidity. Sartre appears to recognize this dependency in *EH*, pp. 81–82 (53–54). His ultimate appeal is to lucid and logical self-consistency, "coherence," "honesty," and the avoidance of the "self-contradictory."

87. See *EN*, pp. 694–95 (*603*): "In each apprehension of quality, there is . . . a metaphysical attempt to escape our condition."

88. Ibid., p. 542 (*464*).

6. HUMANISM: THE LECTURE AND THE LETTER

1. *PH*, p. 33 (5).

2. *EH*, pp. 82–83 (*53–54*).

3. Ibid., p. 84 (*55*).

4. Ibid., p. 17 (*15*).

5. For passages that either are or could be construed as critical of certain *aspects* of traditional theology, see *SZ*, pp. 48–49 (74); 229 (272); 248 (292), 268n (313n), 275 (320), 427n (279n).

6. *SZ*, p. 10 (30); pp. 48–49 (74). The publication of Heidegger's 1927 lecture "Phänomenologie und Theologie" confirms this construction of his early stance toward theology, granting Heidegger's assertion that the lecture was not subjected to substantial revision in the intervening years.

7. *WM*, p. 42 (349).

8. *EH*, pp. 33–34 (25). Cf. *SZ*, e.g., p. 356 (407).

9. *EN*, p. 122 (*80*).

10. *EH*, p. 93 (*60*).

11. Ibid., p. 36 (26–27).

12. Ibid., p. 21 (*18*). One will, however, recall Sartre's sharp criticism of Dasein as a notion that suppresses an original negation.

13. See *SZ*, p. 329 (378); *EN*, p. 188 (142).

14. *EH*, p. 22 (*18*). Italics added. The construction to be placed on *après* at the end of this passage is indicated by the term *ensuite* in the second sentence.

15. Ibid., pp. 23–24 (*19*). Italics added. On Sartre's careful distinction between 'choice' and 'will', and between the 'spontaneous' and the 'voluntary', see Fell, *Emotion in the Thought of Sartre*, pp. 96–101; Fell, "Sartre's Theory of Motivation," pp. 32–33.

16. *EN*, pp. 516 ff. (441 ff.).

17. Ibid., pp. 560–561 (480–481).

18. Ibid., p. 544 (*466*).

19. It is therefore no accident that in Sartre's hands the injunction "Become what you *are!*" is rendered as "I must become what I *was*" (*EN*, p. 172 [127]). The futurizing present is always separated from the past by a negation.

20. *EH*, p. 17 (*15*).

21. *EN*, p. 72 (*35*). One should note that *Wesen* is generally construed verbally by Heidegger and nominatively by Sartre. Hence Heidegger does not restrict *Wesen* to the past; cf. his notion of *An-wesen*, the "coming on" of essence (e.g., *H*, pp. 319 ff.).

22. *EN*, p. 655 (568).

23. Ibid., p. 547 (*468*). Sartre is here referring to Adam, and, strictly speaking, the assertion would apply only to Adam or to the child in his adamic state.

24. Ibid., p. 243 (193). Translation slightly modified.

25. Ibid., p. 244 (*194*).

26. *SZ*, p. 43 (68): "der Vorrang der 'existentia' vor der essentia."

27. *EH*, p. 64 (*43*). For Sartre's elaboration of this thesis, see *Esquisse*, pp. 7–19 (*1–21*); *I*, pp. 13–29, 79–92 (3–21, 81–96); *TE*, pp. 13–37, 74–87 (32–54, 93–106); *EN*, pp. 14–23 (l–lviii), and esp. p. 23 (lviii): "the absolute is defined by the primacy of existence over essence."

28. *Esquisse*, p. 14 (*13*). Sartre here already recognizes that "a truly positive study of man in situation should first of all have had to elucidate . . . being-in-the-world" (17 [*18*]).

29. *TE*, pp. 13–18 (32–35).

30. Ibid., p. 79 (*99*).

31. Ibid., p. 19, p. 78 (36, 98). It is worth noting that Sartre writes "*individuated* and impersonal" (ibid., p. 78 [98]); cf. *SZ*, p. 187: "Die Angst *vereinzelt* das Dasein." (Italics added.) For both Heidegger and Sartre anxi-

ety becomes the key to their versions of the phenomenological reduction, which reduces 'man' to his ownmost individualized and individuated essence, which is ordinarily dispersed or 'lost' in flight from itself.

32. *WM*, p. 28 (*330*).

33. Ibid., p. 29 (*331*). Translation slightly modified.

34. *EN*, pp. 54–55 (18–19). Sartre does not, however, hold that this original negation is an "act of reason."

35. *WM*, pp. 36–37 (*342*). I translate *löst sich auf* by "loses its footing," rather than by the more obvious "is disintegrated" or "is dissolved"; the latter translations, out of context, suggest that Heidegger is out to denigrate 'logic', whereas his intention is only to challenge its primordiality.

36. *N*, II, 178–79.

37. Hegel, *Phenomenology of Mind*, pp. 80, 85–86, 679.

38. I locate this reformation of logic, which can itself be said to preserve *and* cancel the traditional logic of noncontradiction and principle of identity in their ontological application, in the notion of immediate identity as potential contradiction and that of synthesis as mediation of contradiction. This means at the same time that (*a*) an entity is what it is only relationally, by internal relation to other entities; (*b*) Being and Nothing are thus not mutually exclusive but dialectically synthesizable. Cf. Hegel, *Science of Logic*, I, Book I, § 1; *Phenomenology of Mind*, e.g., p. 68; *Lectures on the History of Philosophy*, I, 73: "The external is not the true relation; it will disappear."

39. Hegel, *Phenomenology of Mind*, pp. 149–60.

40. *N*, II, 194–95; *SD*, p. 34.

41. *KPM*, p. 179 (202).

42. *SZ*, p. 41 (67). For Sartre's interpretation of Heidegger's 'mineness', see *Esquisse*, pp. 13–14 (12–13).

43. Although Heidegger does not quite put it this way, it seems that a primary reason for the forgottenness of the ontological is that it is not "there" in bodily, perceptible, tangible presence. An embodied perceptual being naturally centers its attention on perceivable bodies.

44. I am here recapitulating the conclusions of chapter 4.

45. Heidegger dates the letter "Autumn 1946" (*W*, p. 397). It was published on neutral ground, in Bern, in 1947, together with *Platons Lehre von der Wahrheit*, but was also published separately in Frankfurt during the same year.

46. Personal contact between Heidegger and Sartre has been minimal. Contat and Rybalka's chronology of Sartre's life lists only one meeting of the two (*Les Écrits de Sartre*, p. 34)—a brief encounter in December 1952, presumably that mentioned by de Beauvoir (see the next note).

47. De Beauvoir, *Force of Circumstance*, pp. 288–89. Italics added.

48. Richardson, *Heidegger*, p. 671.

49. A phrase used in another connection by Heidegger in *W*, p. 147.

50. *BH* refers to previous correspondence between Heidegger and Beaufret (*BH*, p. 194 [301–2]).

51. *Platons Lehre von der Wahrheit,* in *W,* pp. 142–143 (269–70). We have seen that in his lecture Sartre defends subjectivity as a necessary ground of truth.

52. *BH,* pp. 159–60 (279–80).

53. Ibid., p. 159 (280).

54. *WM,* p. 41 (348).

55. I leave open for the moment the question whether the later Heidegger altogether succeeds in renouncing this transcendental-metaphysical standpoint.

56. *SZ,* p. 9 (29).

57. More than once in *EN* Sartre accuses Heidegger of bad faith. E.g., Heidegger employs positive terms that "hide" implicit negations (54 [18]); Heidegger's 'transcendence' is a concept that is "in bad faith" (306 [249]); Heidegger's expressions *eigentlich* and *uneigentlich* are "not very sincere" (614 [531]); Heidegger's treatment of 'Being-toward-death' indulges in "hocus-pocus" (*tour de passe-passe:* 617 [533–34]); Heidegger disclaims interest in the very ethics he is trying to ground (122 [80]).

58. It is of course important not to confuse Sartre's quite intentional revisions of *SZ* in *EN* with misreadings of *SZ.* The chief evidence for the conclusion that Sartre studied *SZ* rather thoroughly is the vulnerability of *SZ,* at certain critical points, to a Sartrean interpretation, as I have tried to show in chapters 3 and 4.

59. See Löwith, *Heidegger;* esp. p. 21. Löwith, incidentally, holds that Sartre's interpretation of the early Heidegger is not a misreading of Heidegger's position at that time (ibid., pp. 24, 76).

60. *WM,* Epilogue, p. 51 (360). *Schleier,* here translated as "veil," also carries the sense of "pretense," and can thus be associated with Heidegger's notion of semblance or dissimulation (*Verstellung*).

61. *BH,* p. 164 (283).

62. Ibid., p. 165 (283); cf. *EH,* p. 36 (26–27). See also *VA,* p. 35 (*TK,* p. 27), where Heidegger argues that in the present epoch (*Gestell*) the directive (*Geschick*) of Being dissimulates itself in giving "the appearance that everything one encounters exists only insofar as it is a human artifact. . . . Accordingly it looks as if man everywhere encounters only himself."

63. See *VA,* p. 183 (184).

64. *BH,* p. 165 (283).

65. Ibid., pp. 157, 167, 180 (279, 285, 293).

66. Ibid., p. 190 (299): "Nihilation is essentially [*west*] in Being itself and by no means in the Dasein of man, insofar as this is thought as subjectivity of the *ego cogito*"; p. 194 (302): there is no "absolute knowledge."

67. Ibid., p. 166 (284): "Es gibt, anfänglicher gedacht, die Geschichte des Seins, in die das Denken als Andenken dieser Geschichte, von ihr selbst ereignet, gehört."

68. Ibid., p. 170 (287).

69. Ibid., pp. 166, 170 (284, 287).

70. Here Marx—but not Heidegger—would add: and establish the ob-

jective conditions within which all free subjects can play out their wills.

71. *BH*, p. 170 (*287*): "Was Marx . . . von Hegel her . . . erkannt hat.
. . ." Cf. *W* (*Hegel und die Griechen*), pp. 260–61: "Marx and Kierkegaard are, against their own intentions, the greatest of the Hegelians." Eckhard Heftrich shows how important Hegel had become for Heidegger by 1946 ("Nietzsche im Denken Heideggers," in Klostermann, ed., *Durchblicke*, esp. pp. 339–40).

72. *H*, p. 298. Italics added. Cf. Heftrich, "Nietzsche im Denken Heideggers," p. 340.

73. See *EN*, pp. 128, 54–55 (*85, 18–19*).

74. *BH*, p. 152 (*275*). I translate *Rückgang* by 'recursion' to indicate a retracing or reappropriation of the 'course' (*Gang, Weg, Strom*) of the history of thought.

75. But not as a fixed *hypokeimenon;* rather as a continuing event of historizing itself. See chapter 9.

76. *BH*, p. 184 (*295*).

77. Ibid., p. 193 (*301*).

78. *SZ*, p. 308 (*355*); *EM*, pp. 29–30 (*32*).

79. *BH*, p. 168 (286).

80. Ibid., p. 182 (*294*).

81. Ibid., p. 156 (*278*). On 'actuality' in *EN*, see chapter 3.

82. I.e., the nonbeing of its own being ('ambiguity').

83. *EN*, p. 22 (*lvii*): "la conscience existe par soi." Italics added.

84. Ibid., p. 22 (*lviii*). Italics, in part, added.

85. Ibid., p. 127 (*84*).

86. *TE*, p. 64 (*82*).

87. Sartre argues that "Choice and consciousness are one and the same." (*EN*, p. 539 [*462*].)

88. *EN*, p. 23 (lviii).

89. *KPM*, p. 202 (*231*).

90. *WHD*, p. 162 (*161*). Translation slightly modified. See also *N*, II, 399 ff.

91. *BH*, p. 158 (*279*).

92. Ibid., p. 164 (*283*).

93. Ibid., p. 179 (*292*).

94. See *KPM*, pp. 152–53 (*173*).

95. *I*, pp. 82, 98, 113 (*85, 104, 122*).

96. For elaboration and documentation of Sartre's interpretation of the perception-imagination relation, see Fell, *Emotion in the Thought of Sartre*, pp. 35–44. For the interrelation of rationalism and romanticism in Sartre's thought, see Murdoch, *Sartre*, passim.

97. It can be argued that imagination employs logical, linguistic, and ontological distinctions even in its freest exercise. It is hardly formless.

98. *H*, p. 286.

99. *BH*, p. 168 (*285*).

100. *SZ*, p. 222 (*264–65*).

101. Cf. Aristotle, *Metaphysics*, 1029b5 ff. Employed by Hegel as epigraph for *The Phenomenology of Mind*. Cf. *US*, p. 127 (33), where Heidegger refers to "the originarily familiar" (*anfänglich Vertraute*) as what "becomes known only at the last." It is important to distinguish here, as *SZ* already does, between "the familiar" in the sense of the well known (*SZ*, p. 194 [239]: *Bekannten*) and the "primordially familiar" (*SZ*, p. 86 [119]: *ursprünglich vertraut*). Heidegger repeatedly seeks to take the reader behind the familiar in the sense of the publicly common or well known to the familiar in the sense of the intimate (a connotation of *vertraut*) or closest, yet forgotten. The former dissimulates and blocks access to the latter. The former is common in the sense of trivially obvious, while the latter is common in the sense of being always there, behind the "idle talk" that trips along inconstantly from one well-known commonplace to another. The "primordially familiar" is also common in the sense of what one is intimately joined with because there is a community of nature (common ground, common place) between Dasein and what is familiar to Dasein. The term of Aristotle's that I have translated as 'familiar', *gnōstos*, can connote that which is commonly known and that which one understands through direct acquaintance with it.

102. *BH*, p. 180 (293).

103. Chapters 7, 8, 9, below, may be taken as in part an effort to defend this particular construing of Heidegger's notion of *Rettung*, a term that might ordinarily be translated as 'salvation'.

104. *EH*, p. 105 (69).

105. *BH*, p. 182 (295).

106. See *SZ*, pp. 294–95 (340–41); p. 306n (496).

107. *BH*, p. 184 (295). In *SZ* Heidegger had already raised this question in his outline of problems of Cartesian ontology to be handled in the unpublished Division III of Part One: "4. Why has recourse been taken to the phenomenon of value when it has seemed necessary to round out such an ontology?" The answer is hinted at in a previous question: "1. Why was the phenomenon of the world passed over at the beginning of the ontological tradition which has been decisive for us. . . ?" (*SZ*, p. 100 [133]). The implication is that value is in some sense already immanent in 'world', but that when world is forgotten, the ontic ("physical") environment appears as *lacking* value, which must therefore be metaphysically added to it.

108. *BH*, pp. 184–85 (295–96).

109. Ibid., p. 185 (296).

110. Ibid.

111. Ibid., p. 186 (297).

112. De Beauvoir, *The Prime of Life*, p. 107.

113. De Beauvoir, in Contat and Rybalka, *Les Écrits de Sartre*, p. 418. This is, of course, also accorded literary expression in *La Nausée*.

114. *M*, esp. pp. 194–98 (233–38). This also is exemplified in *La Nausée*.

115. I take my license to correlate the personal and the philosophical Sartre from the fact that he has himself done so, covertly in *La Nausée*,

overtly in *M*. *M* shows that Sartre has come to recognize that the notion of a 'radical conversion', which was to deliver one from the metaphysical quest for an ideal being, was ironically itself in the service of this metaphysical quest.

116. Sartre, *AR*, p. 235 (161); *SGCM*, pp. 320–24 (346–50). Sartre's treatment of Nietzsche, even in 1952, is "subjective" and "psychoanalytic," whereas Heidegger's treatment of Nietzsche is "historical."

117. *BH*, p. 193 (301). I am deferring until chapter 9 fuller treatment of Heidegger's view of the present epoch as Being's utmost self-dissimulation.

118. Ibid., p. 190 (299).

119. See de Beauvoir, *Force of Circumstance*, pp. 288–89.

120. *BH*, pp. 189–91 (298–300). Cf. *US*, p. 60 (178), where "the bad" or "the malevolent" (*das Bösartige*) is identified as "the destructive" (*das Zerstörerische*).

121. *BH*, p. 182 (294).

122. Ibid., p. 148 (272–73).

123. *VA*, pp. 115 ff. (422 ff.).

124. *SZ*, p. 222 (265).

125. Ibid., p. 121 (157).

126. Heidegger had asserted in *SZ* that "a 'ground' becomes accessible only as meaning, even if it is itself the abyss of meaninglessness." (p. 152 [194].) The force of this claim only becomes clear after the initiation of the *Kehre*.

127. *BH* makes a point of acknowledging "the essential help of phenomenological vision" (*BH*, p. 187 [297]). It is my judgment that Heidegger has by no means left phenomenology behind and that the *Kehre* is the precondition for completion of the phenomenological program as I have defined it.

128. Here Heidegger is reappropriating *SZ*, pp. 274–89 (319–35).

129. The terminology invoked here by Heidegger is not to be thought of as a "hangover" or remnant of Christian theology. It is rather to be understood as evidence of Heidegger's effort to reappropriate the fundamental meaning of the phenomenon of religion in human history, which he takes to be remembering of the gift of Being-in-the-world, or what is prephenomenologically called "the gift of life itself," as owing to an ultimately unknown source. This means that for Heidegger the Sartrean understanding of religion as the quest for cancellation of mortal-finite-temporal conditions is a derivative or privative interpretation of the phenomenon, grounded in the forgetting of a 'gift' already dispensed to 'mortals'. Chapter 8 explores the question of the later Heidegger's "theology."

130. The commonly heard assertion that Heidegger is not really concerned with *Mitsein* seems to me entirely mistaken.

131. *M*, p. 200 (241).

132. "À propos de l'existentialisme: Mise au point" (1944), in Contat and Rybalka, *Les Écrits de Sartre*, pp. 653–62. Sartre writes (p. 654): "Heidegger was a philosopher well before being a nazi. His adherence to Hitlerism can

be attributed to fear, perhaps to opportunism, certainly to conformism. It is not pretty, I admit. But the following is enough to invalidate your lofty reasoning: 'Heidegger,' you say, 'is a member of the National Socialist Party, therefore his philosophy must be nazist.' The one is not the other. Heidegger has no character, that's true; can you venture to conclude from this that his philosophy is merely an excuse for his cowardice [lâcheté]? Don't you know that some men happen not to attain the eminence of their works? . . . And why bring Heidegger into this matter anyway? If we discover our own thought by reference to the thought of another philosopher . . . does that mean we espouse all his theories?" For Sartre's delineation of 'cowards' (les lâches), see EH, p. 84 (55).

133. Sartre, "Merleau-Ponty vivant," pp. 367–68 (314–15). See also S, IX, 52, where Heidegger's conception of Being is called "an alienation" that is also found in the late Merleau-Ponty "to a certain extent." Cf. Merleau-Ponty's treatment of identity and difference, openness upon the world, chiasm, and intertwining in his posthumously published Le Visible et l'invisible.

PART III, INTRODUCTION

1. SZ, pp. 152–53 (193–95).

2. Jeanson, speaking of two themes of La Nausée, "the theme of salvation by ethical conversion and that of wresting oneself from contingency through the rigor of the work of art," argues that both themes exhibit a "contempt for our genuinely historical dimension." (Sartre, pp. 35–36.)

3. See Jaspers, Nietzsche, pp. 211–28, 318, 329–30. This should by no means be regarded as a problem for philosophy alone. The descriptions attempted by the physicist, the sociologist, the historian, or the psychologist require the same validating grounds as those of the philosopher. (Thus for Husserl the 'crisis' in the foundations of philosophy is equally a crisis in the foundations of all the sciences.)

4. Hegel, Lectures on the History of Philosophy, III, 231.

7. THE NATURE OF THE PLACE: EARTH AND LANGUAGE

1. So Heidegger writes that "In Plato and Aristotle we encounter the words on and onta as concepts. From these the later terms 'ontic' and 'ontological' are formed." (H, p. 317.) This is presumably one of the cases in which Heidegger has found the language of SZ still "metaphysical" (see SD, p. 31). The Kehre requires a new sensitivity to the way in which language both evokes and conceals the directive [Geschick] of Being.

2. SZ, p. 8 (28). Cf. p. 152 (194): "All interpretation . . . operates in the fore-structure. . . . Any interpretation which is to contribute understanding must already have understood what is to be interpreted."

3. Ibid., p. 8 (28).

4. US, p. 151 (51).

5. W. J. Richardson (Heidegger, p. 570) translates Geviert as 'quadrate'. While one might be tempted to suggest that Heidegger has thus succeeded in "squaring the circle," this would overly geometricize his thought.

6. *Die Frage nach dem Ding,* p. 188 (242).

7. Ibid., p. 188 (243).

8. Ibid., p. 189 (243–44). Heidegger's expression *"ein* Wesen des Menschen" (*H,* p. 310) suggests the possibility of a change in man's essence.

9. Heidegger offers a catalog of historical modes of 'presence' in *SD,* p. 7. The history of modes of presence is elaborated in *N,* II, 399–480.

10. *Die Frage nach dem Ding,* p. 31 (41).

11. Ibid., p. 163 (210).

12. Ibid., p. 110 (141).

13. Ibid., p. 164 (211).

14. I have in mind here Heidegger's many assertions to the effect that man is distant from himself but can become who he is (e.g., *EM,* p. 53 [58]), as well as his many catalogs of the epochal determination of human being, as *zōon echon logon, mens humana, ego cogito, Bewusstsein,* etc. (e.g., *N,* II, 399–480).

15. *SZ,* p. 152 (193).

16. To be sure, the later Heidegger associates a *perennial* anxiety with wonder, but I submit that this is a qualitatively different anxiety than that of *SZ* and *WM.*

17. *EM,* pp. 10 ff. (11 ff.).

18. It perhaps goes without saying that here Heidegger reappropriates his early notion of *Sein zum Tode,* now freed of its residual indebtedness to the "heroic" Baconian-Cartesian view of man as finite master of nature and the Christian view of man as fallen and abandoned in a region where he is primarily not at home (see *WM,* p. 32 [336]).

19. *H,* p. 31 (43).

20. Kant, *Critique of Pure Reason,* A183/184; A265; A277.

21. Ibid., B509.

22. See Pöggeler, *Denkweg,* p. 255. Pöggeler is here drawing on the unpublished *Beiträge zur Philosophie* (1936–38). Cf. *H,* pp. 37 ff.; *EM,* pp. 47–48 (51–52).

23. *SZ,* pp. 188–89 (233–34).

24. The *Kehre* should probably be thought of as a continuing process, not simply a one-time event. In fact, Heidegger's own conception of time requires that any significant event in thinking be a long coming-to-itself after its mere 'start' *(Beginn)*. It must also have been "prepared for," and in chapter 2 I have tried to interpret *SZ* as just such an implicit anticipation of the *Kehre.*

25. Werner Marx (*Heidegger und die Tradition,* pp. 188, 194) notes that in Heidegger's late works the notion of 'strife' has been supplanted by notions such as 'play', 'round dance', etc. See also Heidegger's dissatisfaction in 1956 with the role that had been played by 'decision' in *Der Ursprung des Kunstwerkes* (Reclam edition, p. 100 [87]).

26. *Rede* is of course referred to extensively in *SZ;* it is underdeveloped only in the sense that it remains unclear in *SZ* what 'true' *(eigentlich) Rede,*

in its full concreteness, would be like. For what may possibly be conceived as Heidegger's own expression of dissatisfaction with his treatment of *Sprache* in *SZ*, cf. *US*, p. 93 (7).

27. *SZ*, p. 161 (203–4). Italics deleted.

28. See chapter 9, § III. See also Heidegger's treatment of *Fug* (joint, order) in relation to Heraclitus' *hen* and *synapsies* in *Heraklit*, esp. pp. 38–39, 92, 154, 214 ff., 233, 247, 248, 255.

29. *SZ*, p. 33 (56).

30. Ibid., p. 161 (204). Italics added.

31. Erickson, *Language and Being*, p. 107.

32. *SZ*, p. 160 (203). Italics, in part, deleted.

33. Ibid., p. 161 (204).

34. Ibid., p. 165 (209).

35. Ibid., p. 161 (204).

36. Ibid.

37. Sartre retrospectively criticizes himself for the linguistic idealism of taking words for things, losing himself in a world of words. See *M*, p. 117 (141–42).

38. *SZ*, p. 349 (400).

39. Ibid., p. 350 (401).

40. Ibid., pp. 32 ff. (56 ff.). And language is of course at the same time the *sharing* of articulation with other *Dasein* in 'communication' (ibid., p. 162 [205]).

41. See *La Nausée*, p. 159 (169).

42. *WG*, p. 39 (88–89).

43. In its inception, then, phenomenology is already historical in orientation, and Heidegger reappropriates this necessary togetherness of phenomenology and history.

44. Heidegger's critique of Hegel falls outside the scope of my study. For this critique, see esp. *KPM*, pp. 179, 220 (202, 252–53); *H*, pp. 117–92 (27–154); *N*, I, II, passim; and *W*, pp. 255–72; "Die onto-theo-logische Verfassung der Metaphysik" (in *ID*), entire. This critique has largely overshadowed the positive relation between the thought of Hegel and that of Heidegger. The sighting of this connection has also been hindered by the popular view of Heidegger as an existentialist, where 'existentialism' means in part a rebellion against all that "Hegelianism" stood for. In *EM*, pp. 34–35 (37), Heidegger hints at his positive relationship to Hegel, presumably, among others: "It was not German idealism that collapsed; rather the age was no longer strong enough to stand up to the greatness, breadth, and originality of that spiritual world, i.e., truly realize it." Heidegger "realizes" German idealism by a "violent" reappropriation that finds its phenomenological drive for unification of Being and appearance to be at one and the same time the beginning of the consummation of the metaphysical quest (and hence another symptom of the forgetting of the underlying unity of Being and appearance) *and* a major step toward a remembering of

the historical unity of Being and appearance, and of Being and thought. For Heidegger's evaluation of German idealism see also *Schellings Abhandlung über das Wesen der menschlichen Freiheit*, passim.

45. *EM*, pp. 94, 100, 98 (104, 110, 108). These pages rank among the most important in the whole of Heidegger's published work.

46. See *SZ*, p. 407 (459).

47. Cf. *EM*, p. 100 (110), where Heraclitus is paraphrased: "Men. . . . thrash about amid beings, always supposing that what is most tangible is what they must grasp, and thus each man grasps what is nearest to him." (Translation modified.) Cf. p. 101 (112): "Being is not tangible." (*Sein ist nicht greif- und tastbar.*)

48. *EM*, pp. 33–34 (36).

49. Ibid., p. 65 (71).

50. Ibid., p. 68 (75).

51. Ibid., p. 69 (77).

52. Ibid., p. 69 (76).

53. Ibid., p. 70 (77). Translation modified.

54. I am using 'place' both to refer generally to Heidegger's many terms for the intelligible environment (e.g., *Lichtung, Wohnung, Heimat, Haus, Raum, Stelle, Stand, Lage, Bereich, Ort*), and subsequently to refer specifically to "the one place" (*HEH*, pp. 32, 39), the Place of the Fourfold.

55. Place, provisionally characterized as "worlded earth," will subsequently become the Fourfold's "time-play-space."

56. *EM*, p. 139 (152).

57. Ibid., (*a*) pp. 10, 108–10 (11, 119–21); (*b*) p. 139 (152); (*c*) pp. 88 ff. (98 ff.); (*d*) p. 80 f. (89 f.); (*e*) p. 74 (82); (*f*) pp. 149–52 (164–67).

58. Ibid., p. 72 (80).

59. *IF*, I, 686: "notre parti pris de nominalisme nous interdit les classifications. . . ."

60. *Der Feldweg*, passim.

61. *VA*, pp. 272–73; *EHD*, p. 55.

62. *WM*, p. 32 (336).

63. *H*, pp. 198, 248.

64. *EHD*, p. 120: "das Darstellen des Bleibenden."

65. See Pöggeler, *Denkweg*, p. 248: "there can be no doubt that Hölderlin's poetry provided him [Heidegger] with the decisive impetus for regarding the world as the Fourfold of divinities and mortals, earth and heaven." See also Allemann, *Hölderlin und Heidegger*.

66. *EHD*, p. 117.

67. Ibid., p. 38.

68. E.g., *EHD*, p. 38; *Der Feldweg*, pp. 4–5; *SD*, pp. 41, 55 (41, 51).

69. *EHD*, p. 38.

70. *BH*, p. 159 (280); Richardson, *Heidegger*, pp. xvi–xvii.

71. *EHD*, p. 87.

72. Ibid., p. 83. Heidegger, to be sure, identifies "the sailors" of Hölderlin's poem as the future Germanic poets (p. 82), not as Western man per se.

Yet it is man as such who "dwells poetically on this earth" (p. 84). Thus the poets are not to be construed as a class of beings apart, a species of the genus homo, but rather as man in his essential nature. This essential nature is for the most part dissimulated, and man appears to be essentially "the rational animal," "homo faber," etc.

73. Ibid., p. 23.

74. Heidegger's "other beginning" (chapter 9) does not cancel or replace the historical "first beginning."

75. US, p. 213 (106).

76. EHD, p. 137: "zu ruhen, d.h. zu bleiben."

77. Ibid.: "Das Bleiben im Eigenen ist der Gang an die Quelle. Sie ist der Ursprung, dem alles Wohnen der Erdensöhne entspringt. Das Bleiben ist ein Gehen in die Nähe des Ursprungs."

78. US, p. 198 (92).

79. For Heidegger's understanding of the notion of a standing stock (Bestand) of materials, a form of Vorhandenheit, see chapter 8, §§ II, III.

80. Nietzsche, Werke in drei Bänden, III, 882 (Will to Power, p. 8). See Heidegger, Heraklit, pp. 142–43.

81. Yeats, "The Second Coming," in Collected Poems, p. 184.

82. EHD, p. 87: "Die Heimat ist der Ursprung."

83. Ibid., p. 23.

84. Hence Heidegger's reference to Hölderlin's words: "in the beginning the spirit is not at home, not at the source." (EHD, p. 85.)

85. See EN, p. 253 (202–3).

86. Heidegger expresses this by saying that beings do not occur without Being. E.g., ID, p. 62 (64): ". . . Being does not leave its own place and go over to beings, as though beings were first without Being and could be approached by Being subsequently."

87. WM, p. 41 (348).

88. SD, p. 45 (42).

89. EHD, p. 59: "den Bereich aller Bezirke."

8. MAN'S PLACE IN THE FOURFOLD: BEYOND DISPLACEMENT

1. See Aus der Erfahrung des Denkens, p. 23: "die Topologie des Seyns." See also Pöggeler, Denkweg, pp. 280–99.

2. SD, p. 81 (74).

3. H, p. 37 (48–49). Italics added.

4. VA, pp. 275–82; TK, pp. 43–45.

5. SZ, pp. 28–31 (50–55).

6. E.g., WM, Epilogue, p. 49 (358).

7. See Pöggeler, Denkweg, pp. 229, 234, 255.

8. N, II, 354.

9. SD, p. 80 (73), "Lichtung und Anwesenheit."

10. The overriding importance of challenging this view is indicated by the uncharacteristic air of impatience and exasperation exhibited in the following passage from EHD, p. 21 (255): "How much longer? How much

longer are we going to think that there was first of all a nature in itself and a landscape in itself, which subsequently became mythically colored with the aid of 'poetic experiences'? How much longer are we going to bar ourselves from experiencing beings as they are [*das Seiende als seiend*]?"

11. *SD*, p. 45 (42).

12. Afterword to Reclam Edition of *Der Ursprung des Kunstwerkes*, p. 100 (87); italics deleted.

13. *EM*, e.g., pp. 47–48 (51–52), 110–28 (121–41).

14. *BH*, p. 185 (296).

15. See *WM*, p. 26 (328).

16. E.g., *TK*, pp. 37–38.

17. *N*, II, 300–1.

18. *Hebel der Hausfreund*, pp. 28–29.

19. See *EHD*, p. 36.

20. *HEH*, p. 33.

21. *SD*, pp. 5–6, 8, 18–19, 43 (5–6, 8, 17–19, 40).

22. *SG*, p. 69; *SD*, p. 56 (52).

23. See *WM*, p. 22; p. 42 (349).

24. *SZ*, p. 38 (63). What "makes possible" is no longer a cluster of existentialia or ontological characteristics that make possible existentiell acts and ontic beings, and it is no longer simply a transcendental imagination. It is rather the "it gives" of the Event (*Ereignis*).

25. Chapter 9 analyzes this notion of the proper future as a reappropriation of the past in more detail.

26. *US*, p. 213 (106).

27. The word 'place' comes from the Greek *plateia*, associated in Greek with *hodos* ('way' or 'course').

28. *VA*, p. 179 (181).

29. *HEH*, p. 27. Commenting on Heidegger's commentary, Hartmut Buchner writes, "We believe that here Heidegger has with utter simplicity said of death the utmost that is to be said and that on this statement hangs all understanding of the Heideggerian notion of death." ("Review of J. M. Demske, *Sein, Mensch und Tod*," p. 194.)

30. *SZ*, p. 35 (59).

31. *US*, p. 259 (128). The passage refers to *Ereignis*, which is the Event of the Place.

32. *VA*, p. 195 (221). Cf. Vycinas, *Earth and Gods*, p. 232.

33. *Gelassenheit*, p. 15 (48). Heidegger is here once again commenting on Hebel's term 'ether'.

34. Hegel, "Fragment of a System," in *On Christianity*, p. 312.

35. *CRD*, e.g., pp. 119, 148, 176.

36. *Hebel der Hausfreund*, p. 29.

37. *VA*, p. 179 (180). I.e., out of the "round dance" of the members of the Fourfold.

38. Ibid., p. 176 (178). 'Self-united' means not grounded in any prior ground, original, yet not itself bounded (*unendlich*) so as to be determinable

relative to what it is *not*. This is Heidegger's reappropriation of his own early notion of a groundless ground (*SZ*, pp. 283–86, 306 [328–32, 354]; *WG*, pp. 53–54 [126–29]; cf. *SG*, pp. 184–85), and is in effect his resolution of the traditional problem of a first cause vs. an infinite regress. The Fourfold or Place of Event is, so to speak, an "infinite first cause." It is self-limiting or self-bounding. These limits or bounds give the 'measure' (*Mass*) or "outline" the Place within which both things and human beings are understood to be. Heidegger's notion of "self-clearing Alētheia" is another way of speaking of the same Event.

39. *VA*, p. 177 (*178–79*).

40. Ibid.

41. See my remark, above, on the danger of triviality inherent in phenomenology.

42. See "*Zur Seinsfrage*," in *W*, passim.

43. *H*, pp. 296 ff.

44. Ibid., p. 339.

45. Ibid., p. 322.

46. Ibid., p. 320.

47. Ibid.

48. Ibid., p. 323. This gives Heidegger's thinking a limited similarity to "process philosophy." See the use made of Whitehead in chapter 2.

49. Heidegger identifies "the need for dwelling" (*Wohnungsnot*) "as *the* need" (*VA*, p. 162 [161]).

50. See chapter 6, § II.

51. *VA*, p. 76.

52. *TK*, pp. 40 ff.

53. Merleau-Ponty, *Primacy of Perception*, pp. 26–27.

54. See chapter 9, entire.

55. e. e. cummings, *1 × 1*, p. 14.

56. *SG*, p. 187.

57. *VA*, p. 197 (222).

58. Schweitzer, *Quest of the Historical Jesus*, p. 403. Heidegger, as a close student of theology, was probably familiar with this work, written by Sartre's great uncle.

59. *VA*, p. 195 (*220–21*).

60. Ibid., p. 197 (223).

61. *H*, p. 322.

62. See *EN*, pp. 653–54, 670 (566–67, 581) and *VA*, p. 195 (221).

63. See *EHD*, p. 38.

64. *N*, I, 51–53.

65. See Merleau-Ponty, *Phénoménologie de la perception*, Preface. I have tried elsewhere to spell out in some detail how a particular area, the psychological study of emotion, is grounded in this original truth (Fell, "The Phenomenological Approach to Emotion").

66. On the correlation of beauty with the true and with coming-to-presence on the earth, see *EHD*, pp. 126–27. In contrast, Sartre holds that

beauty is an ideal state of the world, an "impossible fusion . . . of essence and existence"; "the beautiful. . . . haunts the world as an unrealizable" (*EN*, pp. 244–45 [*194–95*]). In *I*, p. 245 (*281*), following an analysis of listening to Beethoven's Seventh Symphony, Sartre concludes that "the real is never beautiful. Beauty is a value that applies solely to the imaginary and entails the nihilation of the world in its essential structure." A much later reference to a Beethoven symphony, in *S*, X, 172 (*40*), demonstrates just how ideal beauty is for Sartre: "I don't think anyone has really been able to compose symphonies; they're difficult. . . . Not even Beethoven. Though if I had to name one, I'd say the Ninth was almost a beautiful symphony."

67. *VA*, p. 179 (*181*).

68. Hegel, *Lectures on the History of Philosophy*, III, 230. In Heidegger's version, the identity of Being and thinking cannot mean the identity of substance and subject.

9. HEIDEGGER'S NOTION OF TWO BEGINNINGS

1. An earlier version of this chapter appeared in *The Review of Metaphysics*, 25, no. 2 (1971), 213–37. Professor Heidegger made the following comment on the paper (personal communication of March 24, 1972): "Sie sind auf der richtigen Spur; denn: 'der andere Anfang' ist kein zweiter, sondern der *eine* erste u. einzige, dieser jedoch auf eine andere Weise—nämlich aus der sich lichtenden *Alētheia* als solcher." ("You are on the right track, for 'the other beginning' is not a second beginning, but rather the *one* first and only beginning—yet in another manner, namely from the self-clearing *Alētheia* as such.")

2. Cf. Heidegger's remark to Joan Stambaugh, *Identity and Difference*, p. 7. Heidegger's *Schellings Abhandlung über das Wesen der menschlichen Freiheit* sheds considerable light on the extent of continuity between the consideration of the theme of identity and difference in German idealism and in Heidegger.

3. *SD*, p. 81 (*74*).

4. E.g., *HEH*, p. 17. *Unendlich* is translated as 'illimitable' rather than 'infinite' to forestall its confusion with the ordinary mathematical, metaphysical, and cosmological connotations of 'infinite'. Heidegger does not mean *unendlich* as the logical opposite of *endlich*. He means by *unendliche Verhältnis* a complex relation or 'junction' that is illimitable by man, in the sense that it is an internal relation that cannot be analyzed in such a way as to determine or limit the precise contribution made by each member of the relationship.

5. On the first and other beginning, see *N*, I, 259, 364, 390, 395, 470, 480, 547, 626, 656–57; II, 29, 201–2, 279, 471, 481; *EM*, pp. 29–30 (*32*).

6. The most trenchant discussions of the two beginnings are offered by Werner Marx, *Heidegger und die Tradition*, esp. pp. 183–237 (183–241); and Dieter Sinn, "Heideggers Spätphilosophie."

7. See esp. *VA*, pp. 13–44, 145–85 (143–86); *US*, pp. 22 ff., 211–16, 263 ff. (199 ff., 104–8, 131 ff.) and *passim*; *HEH*, pp. 17–39; *TK*, entire. I shall capi-

talize in translation several of Heidegger's terms as a constant reminder that he is employing these terms in a manner not always congruent with ordinary usage. Extensive commentary on *Ge-Stell* and *Geviert* may be found in the works of Marx and Sinn cited in the preceding note; in Pöggeler, *Denkweg*, pp. 236–67; in Vycinas, *Earth and Gods*, pp. 224–37; and in Mehta, *Philosophy of Martin Heidegger*, pp. 205–23.

8. *Der Ursprung des Kunstwerkes* (Reclam ed.), pp. 95–96 (82). Translation slightly modified.

9. Ibid., p. 98 (84). Translation slightly modified.

10. Ibid., p. 95 (82).

11. Ibid., p. 97 (84). Translation modified.

12. The composer Gustav Mahler wrote in 1900, "I'm coming increasingly to realize that it's not man who composes but man who is being composed." (H.-L. de La Grange, *Mahler*, I, 585.) Significant affinities exist between Mahler and Heidegger. Mahler underwent a shift from a sort of creative violence to an attitude of resignation, had an ambivalent attitude toward Nietzsche (ibid., pp. 101, 671), read and reread Angelus Silesius (p. 101), preferred Hölderlin among the romantics (p. 102), celebrated the childlike innocence of the creator (p. 656), and wrote that "the life of men . . . appears to hang on the protection of higher beings, including Earth, who is certainly one of them" (p. 579). With a few exceptions (e.g., the Kreutzer address in *Gelassenheit*, pp. 9–26 [43–57] and reference to a Mozart quintet's intimations of mortality in "Hans Jantzen dem Freunde zum Andenken," p. 20) there is a perhaps surprising paucity of references to music in Heidegger's published work.

13. *W*, p. 342.

14. *TK*, p. 42; see pp. 40–45.

15. *VA*, p. 180 (182); *TK*, p. 43.

16. For Heidegger's early treatment of dissimulation (or semblance), see *SZ*, pp. 29–31, 35 ff. (51–54, 59 ff.). Heidegger implies that, under the influence of "ancient ontology," the phenomenon's semblance has come to be taken for the phenomenon itself. For Heidegger's later treatment of dissimulating in the Com-position, see "Die Frage nach der Technik," in *VA*, pp. 13–44, *TK*, pp. 5–36, and "Hölderlins Erde und Himmel." Heidegger's term *verstellen* means both "to block" or "obstruct" and "to dissemble" or "dissimulate." Thus a semblance, when taken as the phenomenon itself, blocks access to the phenomenon, which has dissimulated or dissembled itself.

17. *VA*, p. 22.

18. Ibid., pp. 37–38.

19. Ibid., p. 38.

20. See *VA*, 183 (185); *N*, II, 481.

21. *VA*, p. 35 (italics added).

22. *HEH*, p. 17: "Die Umstimmung in die denkende Erfahrung der Mitte des unendlichen Verhältnisses—: aus dem Ge-stell als dem sich selbst verstellenden Ereignis des Gevierts."

23. Ibid., pp. 35–37. Italics, in part, added.

24. Ibid., pp. 37–38. With this should be compared Heidegger's treatment of *synapsies* (Heraclitus, Fragment DK 10) in *Heraklit*, pp. 214–19.

25. E.g., *Der Feldweg*, pp. 4–5; *Hebel der Hausfreund*, p. 8.

26. *N*, II, 481: "Das Anfängliche . . . vergeht nie, ist nie ein Vergangenes."

27. Ibid., II, 488.

28. *VA*, p. 30.

29. See *SZ*, pp. 328 ff. (376 ff.).

30. *VA*, p. 183 (*184*).

31. Ibid., p. 183 (*184–85*).

32. *US*, p. 57 (*176*).

33. Ibid., p. 215 (*107*).

34. *HEH*, e.g., p. 17.

35. *H*, p. 64 (*77*).

36. Ibid., p. 34 (*45*).

37. *TK*, pp. 38–39.

38. *VA*, p. 38.

39. Ibid., pp. 20, 42.

40. Ibid., p. 13.

41. Ibid., pp. 153–54 (*153*). Italics, in part, added.

42. Ibid., p. 203 (*203*).

43. *SZ*, p. 35 (59).

44. *US*, p. 198 (92).

45. Ibid., p. 259 (*128*). Italics added.

46. Ibid., p. 263 (*131–32*): "insofern es den Menschen stellt, d.h. ihn herausfordert, alles Anwesende als technischen Bestand zu bestellen, west das Ge-stell nach der Weise des Ereignisses und zwar so, dass es dieses zugleich verstellt. . . ."

47. Ibid., pp. 264, 215 (*133, 107*).

48. *Enteignis;* see *SD*, pp. 23, 44.

49. *SZ*, pp. 31, 35–36 (54, 59–60).

50. *US*, p. 199 (*93*).

51. *ID*, p. 25 (*33*).

52. *US*, p. 208 (*101*).

53. *N*, II, 395.

54. *TK*, p. 37; *N*, II, 452.

55. See *US*, pp. 22 (*Poetry, Language, Thought*, p. 199), 215 (*107*).

56. See, e.g., *ID*, p. 25 (*34*); *US*, p. 212 (*105*).

57. *BH*, p. 181 (*293*).

58. *N*, II, 471: "der anfänglichere Anfang."

59. *VA*, p. 177 (*179*).

60. Nietzsche, *Werke in drei Bänden*, II, 479. See *SZ*, p. 145 (186).

61. *SZ*, p. 128 (166). Translation slightly modified.

62. *WM*, p. 37 (*343*).

63. *Gelassenheit, Heiterkeit, Verzicht.* See, e.g., *Der Feldweg*, pp. 5–7.

64. *BH*, p. 172 (*288*).

65. *SG*, pp. 60, 162, 184–85.

66. Ernst Tugendhat (*Der Wahrheitsbegriff bei Husserl und Heidegger*, pp. 400–1) argues that since World is for the later Heidegger the play space *of beings* (the "members of the Fourfold"), this rules out Heidegger's earlier conception of World as the play space of " 'meaning' and 'possibilities'." This interpretation fails to see (1) that the 'beings' of the Fourfold are not beings in the usual sense but rather what might be called "meaning-be-ings"; (2) that the "center" (*Mitte*) of the Fourfold-Play or World-Play is an introplay of meanings in which alone, or as which, the members of the Fourfold themselves come into being. Heidegger is not to be caught in the position of saying either that meanings precede and ground beings or that beings precede and ground meanings—both of which are for him "meta-physical" modes of thought.

67. *Privation, privativ, defizient, defizienter Modus.* See *SZ*, pp. 20, 29, 57, 61, 75, 120 (42, 51, 83, 88, 106, 157), etc. For Heidegger's examination of Aristotle's treatment of *sterēsis*, see *W*, pp. 364–71.

68. *SZ* (1927), pp. 38, 394 (63, 446); *SD* (1969), p. 90 (82).

69. *Gelassenheit*, p. 61 (82).

70. In Heidegger's Greek-inspired interpretation of 'limit' (*peras*): "Limit is respectively the bounding, de-termining [tuning], that which gives sta-bility and constancy, that through which and in which something begins and is." (*W*, p. 339.) This 'limiting" process is itself illimitable, or not pre-cisely describable or knowable. It is possible that Anaximander's term *apeiron* carries this "epistemological" connotation—'the illimitable' by mor-tals.

71. See *SD*, p. 45 (42): "Einkehr in das Ereignis."

72. *HEH*, p. 17.

73. See *US*, pp. 57, 213, (177, 106); *H*, p. 322; *EHD*, pp. 120, 137.

10. Language, Action, and the Sartrean Beginning

1. *IF*, I, 686. Sartre's *La Nausée*, at the other end of his career, may be seen as a veritable phenomenology of nominalism.

2. *La Nausée*, p. 159 (169).

3. *PH*, pp. 31–35 (4–5).

4. See chapter 3, section II.

5. See Van de Pitte, "Sartre as Transcendental Realist," pp. 22–26.

6. *EN*, p. 592 (510).

7. Ibid., p. 592 (510–11).

8. Ibid., p. 593 (511).

9. See *Esquisse*, pp. 42, 47 (57, 64–65).

10. *EN*, p. 593 (511).

11. Ibid., p. 598 (515).

12. Ibid., p. 598 (516).

13. Ibid.

14. Ibid., p. 600 (518).

15. Ibid., p. 602 (519).

16. Ibid., p. 602 (520).

17. *WM*, p. 25 (327). It is what I have called a "Baconian-Cartesian" and a "humanistic" reappropriation of Heidegger, in that it envisages man as a project to master nature or the given by a disciplined appropriation of it for his own ends. But I have also noted a "Hellenistic" strain in *EN*: Sartre's recognition of the vanity of the fundamental project, i.e., the severe limits of the human effort to achieve its own ends.

18. *QL*, p. 71 (20). Cf. *EN*, p. 442 (374): "The problem of language is exactly parallel to the problem of the body. . . ." See also *S*, IX, 40.

19. *AR*, p. 237 (163).

20. *EN*, p. 368 (305).

21. *AR*, p. 222 (151).

22. *EN*, p. 95 (56).

23. *AR*, pp. 194–207 (129–39).

24. *QL*, p. 65 (13).

25. Ibid., p. 64 (12–13).

26. Ibid., p. 66 (15). Cf. *S*, IX, 53, where Sartre describes the word as a "worked matter . . . historically produced and remade by me" rather than as matter per se. Because language is "practico-inert," to regard it as simply independent of me is "an alienation" (ibid., pp. 40, 52).

27. *QL*, p. 67 (15).

28. Ibid., p. 66 (14).

29. Ibid., p. 68 (16).

30. Ibid., p. 65 (14).

31. Ibid., p. 67 (16). Translation slightly modified.

32. Ibid., pp. 63–64 (12).

33. Iris Murdoch (*Sartre*; esp. pp. 26–36) describes the particular literary movements that for Sartre constitute this crisis.

34. *QL*, pp. 129–30, 196 (81–82, 159).

35. Murdoch, *Sartre*, pp. 59–60.

36. *HC*, p. 293.

37. Ibid., p. 279. Cf. *SGCM*, p. 283 (304): "Things signify [*signifient*] nothing. But each of them has a meaning [*sens*]. By *signification* is meant a particular conventional relation which takes a present object as the substitute for an absent object. By *meaning* I refer to the participation of a present reality, in its very being, in the being of other realities, present or absent, visible or invisible, up to and including the universe itself [*de proche en proche à l'univers*]. Signification is conferred on the object from beyond it by a signifying intention, while meaning is a natural quality of things. The former is a transcendent reference [*rapport*] between one object and another, while the latter is a transcendence which has fallen into immanence. Signification can prepare for an intuition . . . meaning is by nature intuitive." Thus Sartre writes that a meaning is a "syncretic unity" (p. 285 [306]). It refers to that ontological level which Sartre calls 'the real'.

38. *HC*, p. 291.

39. Ibid., pp. 289–90. Cf. *EN*, p. 708 (615).

40. *HC*, p. 281.

41. Ibid., p. 276.

42. Ibid., p. 264.

43. Ibid., p. 266.

44. Ibid., pp. 266–67.

45. Ibid., p. 263.

46. Ibid., pp. 283, 269, 259.

47. Ibid., pp. 281, 289.

48. In addition, of course, Ponge is a materialist who defines man as a *thing;* this materialistic community of nature is effectively criticized by Sartre (ibid., esp. pp. 287–88; *CRD*, pp. 123–26).

49. *AR*, pp. 196–97 (130–31); 235 (161).

50. On the question of Sartre's familiarity with the *Kehre* writings of Heidegger available to him at roughly this time, see chapter 6, esp. § I. Heidegger's reflections on language were of course published for the most part after 1944. It may or may not be significant that the Parain essay contains a number of more or less parenthetical references to Heidegger.

51. *AR*, p. 213 (144). Translation slightly modified. On the question of the relation between Heidegger's social and geographical origins and his thinking, see Beda Allemann, "Martin Heidegger und die Politik," in Pöggeler, ed., *Heidegger*, pp. 255 ff.; Palmier, *Les Écrits politiques de Heidegger*, pp. 13–33 and passim; Schwan, *Politische Philosophie im Denken Heideggers*, pp. 187–88. Needless to say, I am not attempting a sociological reduction of Heidegger's thinking. But neither can one rule out in advance the relevance of his personal, social, geographical, and political situation to the effort to understand his thinking. The same is true in the case of Sartre.

52. *AR*, pp. 195–97, 217 (130–31, 147).

53. Ibid., p. 194 (129).

54. See de Beauvoir in Contat and Rybalka, *Les Écrits de Sartre*, p. 418, and the analysis of Sartre's *Words* in chapters 11 and 12.

55. Sartre can therefore say, quite flatly, "We know that Nietzsche was not a philosopher." (*AR*, p. 235 [161].) Cf. Heidegger, whose reading of *EN* led him to conclude that "Sartre is a good writer but not a philosopher." (*Le Figaro Littéraire*, 4.11.50; quoted by Philip Thody in *Jean-Paul Sartre*, p. 254.) See also *SGCM*, pp. 320–24 (346–50).

56. *AR*, pp. 212, 213 (143, 144).

57. Ibid., p. 214 (145).

58. Ibid., p. 217 (147).

59. Ibid., pp. 215–16 (146–47). I hesitate to ascribe to Heidegger—the later Heidegger at least—a desire for "paternal organization."

60. Ibid., p. 197 (131).

61. Ibid., p. 207 (139).

62. Ibid., p. 217 (147). We have seen that for Heidegger the return to language does not preclude a return to earth. This return to earth, of course, is

not in Heidegger's case a return to his early philosophy, in which the notion of 'earth' is absent except for passing references such as *SZ*, p. 198
(242–43).

63. *AR*, pp. 222, 224 (151, 152).

64. Ibid., p. 212 (143).

65. Ibid., p. 220 (150).

66. See Colin Smith's interpretation of Parain's *Recherches sur la nature et
les fonctions du langage* in *Contemporary French Philosophy*, pp. 136–39. See
also Sartre's characterization of Parain's *Essai sur le logos platonicien* in *EN*,
pp. 598–99 (516–17). Parain has posited "an impersonal life of the logos,"
making of language "a language which speaks all by itself." Parain has
forgotten that language, a technique, requires a speaker, just as any technique requires a technician. What "directs" is the agent, not his instruments. See also *IF*, I, 623: "Flaubert does not believe that *one speaks: one
is spoken*." Flaubert thinks that "the verbal materiality organizes itself in a
semi-externality and produces a *thought-matter*." In one sense Flaubert is
right—words are bearers of a counterfinality—but it is necessary to add that
"we surpass them toward a thought which is ever new to the extent that we
utilize them." Cf. *SGCM*, p. 239 (255), where Sartre, noting that to Genet
events seem to have a meaning (*sens*), argues that Genet ignores the sort of
experience of the 'absurd' described by Camus. "In Camus' eyes, the light
crust of signification sometimes melts, uncovering [*dévoilent*] the brute reality that signifies nothing. . . . The metaphysical intuition of the absurd
leads to nominalism; that of Genet orients him toward a vague Platonic realism." (But cf. Sartre's distinction between 'meaning' and 'signification' in
SGCM, p. 283 [304].)

67. *AR*, p. 226 (154).

68. Ibid., p. 225 (154).

69. Ibid., p. 217 (147).

70. Ibid., p. 231 (158).

71. Ibid.

72. Ibid., p. 235 (161).

73. Ibid., p. 225 (153).

74. Ibid., pp. 233–34 (160–61). Italics, in part, added.

75. See *Critique of Pure Reason*, A80/B106. My discussion invoked the
twelve categorial judgments in the following order: (1) categorical judgment
of relation; (2) limiting judgment of quality; (3) universal judgment of
quantity; (5) affirmative judgment of quality; (6) negative judgment of quality; (7) particular judgment of quantity; (8) problematical judgment of modality; (9) apodictic judgment of modality; (10) assertoric judgment of modality; (11) hypothetical judgment of relation; (12) disjunctive judgment of
relation. The categorial concepts thus invoked are: (1) substance and accident; (2) limitation; (3) totality; (4) unity; (5) reality; (6) negation; (7) plurality; (8) possibility/impossibility; (9) necessity/contingency; (10) existence/
nonexistence; (11) causality and dependence; (12) community.

76. Ibid., A105–108, B129–146.

77. *AR*, pp. 235–36 (161–62). Translation slightly modified.

78. Ibid., p. 237 (162–63).

79. Ibid., p. 237 (163).

80. Ibid., p. 241 (166). Italics added; translation modified.

81. I have tried to show elsewhere that Sartre regards ordinary experience as a logical and pragmatic experience, a standard behavior from which emotional or irrational conduct represents a departure or debasement. See Fell, *Emotion in the Thought of Sartre*, esp. chapters 1, 5, 8.

82. *AR*, p. 241 (166). See p. 248, where this deficiency is ascribed to both Parain and Ponge. Cf. *IF*, I, 637: Flaubert "has no means of distinguishing thought, as a synthetic and constructive activity, from language. . . . Gustave abandons himself . . . to words."

83. *EN*, p. 232 (*183*).

84. Ibid., p. 241 (*191–92*): "What Husserl calls *categories* (unity-multiplicity-relation of whole to part . . . etc.) are only ideal mixings of things that leave them completely intact, neither enriching nor impoverishing them by one iota." The implication is that otherwise categories become cases of "the mind dragging amid things."

85. *AR*, p. 233 (160).

86. *EN*, p. 348 (198).

87. Ibid., p. 246 (*196*). Italics, in part, added.

88. Ibid., pp. 244–45 (194–95).

89. Ibid., pp. 687, 375 (*597, 312*).

90. Ibid., pp. 246–47 (*196*).

91. Ibid., p. 247 (*197*).

92. Ibid., p. 248 (*197–98*).

93. Ibid., pp. 32–33 (lxvii).

94. Ibid., pp. 240–41 (191).

95. Ibid., pp. 235–36 (186).

96. Sartre has not explained, however, how qualities are originally discriminated—an insoluble problem so long as the actual is construed as wholly indeterminate.

97. *EN*, p. 236 (*187*).

98. For Sartre's view of the privileged role of intuition as irreducible source of evidence, see esp. *TE*, p. 17 (35); see also *EN*, pp. 220–21 (172).

99. *EN*, pp. 377 ff. (314 ff.).

100. Ibid., pp. 236–37 (187). Translation modified. Wilfrid Desan identifies Sartre as "a realist concerning 'quality.' " (*The Tragic Finale*, p. 52.) If Desan means that Sartre is a realist with respect to the apprehension of 'real' qualities, he is undoubtedly right. If, however, he means that Sartre is a realist with respect to the apprehension of 'actual' qualities, he may not technically be correct. See *EN*, p. 695 (*603–4*), where Sartre claims that "we can grasp quality *only as a symbol* of a being which entirely escapes us, even though it be entirely there before us." If Sartre means that we inevitably surpass the neutrally revealed qualitative component of experience in interpreting it as a symbol of the whole of being, then Desan is right. But if

Sartre means that particular qualities (already subjected to numerical/quantitative separation from an indeterminate being) can only serve as symbols of a wholly indeterminate and inapprehensible quality, pure materiality, then Desan would seem to be wrong. I frankly hedge my bets by claiming only that Sartre's analysis of quality represents his closest approach or approximation to a direct realism.

101. *EN*, p. 239 (*189*).

102. *I*, pp. 156–57 (*172–73*). Cf. p. 135 (*147*): "We have seen that *the sensible element as such* [*l'élément proprement sensible*] is framed by a protention and by a retention." (Italics added.)

103. See *SZ*, p. 343 (*393*).

104. *EN*, p. 241 (*191–92*).

105. Nevertheless, the for-itself may, in accordance with the particular aims of its project, convert certain qualities into essences, regarding the rest as accidents.

106. *AR*, p. 193 (*128*). Italics added.

107. Ibid., 197 (*131*).

108. By 'original' is not meant that at some point in time consciousness confronts actuality without at the same time being in a human world. What is meant is that consciousness is always aware of itself and of transphenomenal being as the irreducible relata in a negative relation to each other.

109. See chapter 5, § IV, where Sartre's early "religion of artful play" is interpreted as the explicit living of a *continual* dying of the past that therefore frees the future from the inertia of the past.

110. *M*, p. 213 (*255*).

11. Sartre's Problem of Action Metaphysically Resolved

1. De Beauvoir, *Privilèges*, p. 271.

2. Jeanson, *Le Problème moral*.

3. *EN*, pp. 711, 720 (*617, 625*).

4. See chapter 3, § IV.

5. *EN*, pp. 719–20 (*625*). At the end of Part Three, Sartre had criticized Heidegger for altogether neglecting the fact that the for-itself is "the being by whom ontic modifications supervene on the existent qua existent." This modification Sartre characterizes as "*acting*—that is . . . modifying the in-itself in its ontic materiality, in its 'flesh'." (*EN*, p. 503 [*430*]) The reader expects that the ensuing Part Four will show how action, so defined, is possible. But it does not. It offers "a broad sketch for the study of action" (*EN*, p. 507 [*431*]) but not a thoroughgoing study of action itself. Hence the passage from the conclusion I have just quoted. See *EN*, p. 588 (*506*) (action cannot *condition* beings but only reveal them) and p. 590 (*508–9*) (beings are thus designated but not *formed*). In *Sens et non-sens* (pp. 125–26 [*72*]), Merleau-Ponty had called attention to the problem: ". . . *L'Être et le néant* . . . remains too exclusively antithetic: the antithesis of my view of myself and another's view of me and the antithesis of the *for itself* and the *in itself* often

seem to be alternatives instead of being described as the living bond of communication between one term and the other. . . . He [Sartre] is putting off the study of the 'realization' of nothingness in being—which is action and which makes morality possible—until some other time."

6. Cf. *De Anima*, 429b25.

7. *EN*, p. 714 (620).

8. Ibid., p. 722 (628).

9. *M*, passim.

10. See *EN*, pp. 672–74, 721 (583–84, 627).

11. Ibid., pp. 301–7 (244–50).

12. Ibid., pp. 54–55 (18–19).

13. Ibid., p. 306 (249).

14. Ibid.

15. Ibid., p. 307 (250). Sartre concludes that "Heidegger does not escape idealism." This suggests a liability of *SZ* that we encountered in chapter 4.

16. *EN*, p. 303 (247).

17. Ibid., p. 286 (231).

18. *SZ*, p. 114 (149), p. 118 (155).

19. *EN*, p. 303 (246).

20. Ibid., p. 301 (244).

21. Ibid., p. 304 (247).

22. Ibid., p. 304; p. 306 (248, 249).

23. Ibid., p. 295 (239). We shall see how Sartre, in *CRD*, continues to adjudicate the claims of Hegel, and of Marx as well, by appealing to Kierkegaard.

24. *EN*, p. 304 (247).

25. Ibid., pp. 308–9 (251).

26. Ibid., pp. 312–13 (254–55).

27. Ibid., p. 432 (364): "My project of recovering myself is, fundamentally, a project of reabsorbing the Other."

28. Ibid., p. 431 (364). Cf. p. 502 (429).

29. Ibid., p. 321 (263).

30. Ibid., p. 320 (262).

31. Ibid., p. 322 (263).

32. Ibid., p. 329 (270).

33. Ibid., p. 309 (252).

34. Ibid.

35. Ibid. The distinction is between *totalité* and *tout*.

36. Kierkegaard, *Concluding Unscientific Postscript*, p. 97. Consideration of the position and powers of God often serves in philosophy and in human culture at large as a means of establishing the position and powers of man. This phenomenon may seem obvious, commonplace. But insofar as phenomenology attempts to vindicate the commonplace, it may be a phenomenon of some importance.

37. Chapter 3, §IV.

38. *EN*, pp. 309–10 (252).

39. It should be noted here that the for-itself's totality is exploded or de-totalized not only by Others but by the 'ambiguous' situation of the individual for-itself. See, e.g., *EN*, p. 309 (252): "cette totalité—*comme celle du Pour-soi*—est totalité détotalisée" (italics added).

40. *EN*, p. 486 (*414*).

41. *TE*, p. 87 (*106*).

42. *EH*, pp. 21, 35–36 (*18, 26–27*).

43. *EN*, pp. 309, 342 (*252, 282*).

44. Little attention is paid to history as such in *EN*, and the conclusions I am here drawing are therefore largely inferential. Part of Sartre's subsequent readjustment to his own past will consist in recognizing the necessity of an explicit and thoroughgoing study of historization and history.

45. *CRD* considers a variety of such forms of reciprocity.

46. *EN*, p. 362 (*300*). Translation slightly modified.

47. Ibid., p. 361 (*300*).

48. Ibid., p. 362 (*301*).

49. Plato, *Phaedo*, 97B/98E; Aristotle, *Metaphysics*, A, 985a18.

50. *EN*, p. 362 (*301*).

51. Ibid., p. 50 (*15*).

52. Ibid., p. 52 (*16*). Italics deleted.

53. Ibid., p. 363 (*301*).

54. Ibid.

55. Ibid., p. 489 (*417–18*).

56. Ibid., pp. 492–93 (*420–21*).

57. Ibid., pp. 494–95 (*423*). Cf. Heidegger's own characterization of the gods as absent, e.g., *VA*, p. 197 (*222*).

58. Thus it "corresponds to a mere enrichment of the original proof of the for-Others" rather than being a new and positive type of being (*EN*, p. 502 [*429*]).

59. Ibid., p. 494 (*422*).

60. Ibid., p. 496 (*424*).

61. Ibid., p. 497 (*424*).

62. Ibid., p. 497 (*425*).

63. Ibid., p. 498 (*426*).

64. Ibid., p. 502 (*429*).

65. Ibid., p. 501 (*429*).

66. See *CRD*, pp. 15–17 (*SM*, 4–7). It should also be noted that Sartre criticizes Lukács for holding that "Heidegger's existentialism is changed into an activism under the influence of the Nazis." To the contrary, Sartre argues, "Heidegger has *never* been an 'activist'—at least not as he has expressed himself in his philosophical works." (*CRD*, p. 34 [*SM*, 37–38].)

67. *EN*, p. 502 (*429*).

68. Descartes, *Meditations*, III.

69. *EN*, p. 484 (*412*).

70. For a record of some of the reactions to *EN*, see de Beauvoir, *Force of Circumstance*, esp. pp. 38 ff, 141–43.

71. See *M*, esp. pp. 79, 96, 208–11 (97, 118, 249–53).
72. *QL*, p. 129 (81); see also pp. 130, 196 (82, 159).
73. *EH*, pp. 78, 83 (51, 54).
74. Ibid., pp. 107, 115 (70, 75).
75. Ibid., p. 124 (81).
76. Jeanson, *Le Problème moral*, p. 294.
77. Ibid., p. 288.
78. Ibid., p. 287. Some of the analysis that follows is drawn from my papers, "Sartre as Existentialist and Marxist" and "Sartre's *Words*."
79. Jeanson, *Le Problème moral*, p. 287.
80. Ibid., p. 12.
81. *CRD*, p. 61 (*SM*, 87).
82. Jeanson, *Le Problème moral*, p. 287. See Sartre's reference to his own present "faith" at the conclusion of *M* (p. 212 [255]).
83. *S*, IV, 113 (*Situations*, 93).
84. Jeanson, *Le Problème moral*, p. 340; the expression comes from *M*, p. 160 (193).
85. *S*, IV, 122 (*Situations*, 101).
86. *M*, pp. 197–98 (237–38). Where relevant, I shall correlate Sartre's philosophy with passages in his autobiography. This is a matter of following out Sartre's own insertion of both philosophy and himself into history, and in such a way as to regard individuals as themselves conditioned by and expressions of the philosophy of the epoch in which they live.
87. Ibid., p. 201 (241).
88. See Hegel, *Phenomenology of Mind*, p. 105.
89. *M*, pp. 213, 54 (255, 69).
90. Ibid., pp. 208, 117, 96 (250, 141–42, 117–18).
91. *EH*, p. 94 (60–61).
92. *M*, pp. 210–11 (253).
93. *SGCM*, p. 192 (202).
94. *M*, pp. 211–12 (254).
95. A considerable literature has already grown up written by critics who seem to have decided a priori that the later Sartre must be *either* an existentialist *or* a Marxist. Against those who hold that the later Sartre has swallowed up Marxism in existentialism, one can bring Sartre's argument for the view that Marxism is "the unsurpassable philosophy of our time" (*CRD*, p. 9 [*SM*, xxxiv]). Against those who hold that Sartre has betrayed his own existentialism, one can bring Sartre's argument that in return for surrendering its autonomy existentialism "will become the foundation of all inquiry" (*CRD*, p. 111 [*SM*, 181]).
96. *CRD*, p. 84 (*SM*, 130).
97. Ibid., p. 165 (Cumming, ed., *Philosophy of Jean-Paul Sartre*, p. 428). Hereinafter, the pagination in parentheses for translations of *CRD*, except where preceded by *SM*, will refer to the Cumming volume.
98. Ibid., pp. 165–66 (428). Italics added; Sartre's italics deleted; translation slightly modified.

99. Ibid., e.g., pp. 166 ff. (429 ff.).

100. Ibid., p. 166 (429).

101. Ibid., pp. 166, 167 (429, 430).

102. Ibid., p. 168 (431); p. 297. Cf. EN, pp. 50, 52 (15, 16).

103. CRD, p. 167 (430). Italics, in part, added.

104. EN, p. 719 (625).

105. CRD, p. 167 (430–31).

106. Ibid., pp. 245–46 (452): "Matter alone carries meanings. It retains them in itself, like engravings, and gives them their real effectiveness . . . man's projects are engraved in Being . . . they *come into Being.* . . . Through transubstantiation, the project that our bodies engrave in the thing assumes the substantial characteristics of that being. . . . Meanings . . . modify the whole of the material universe. This means both that they have been engraved into Being, and that Being has been poured into the world of meanings." Thus (p. 249 [453]) "it is not the understanding that solidifies meanings [*significations*], it is Being."

107. Ibid., pp. 166–68 (428–32).

108. Ibid., pp. 167–68 (431–32).

109. Ibid., p. 168 (431).

110. Ibid.

111. Ibid.

112. Ibid., p. 204 (435).

113. Cf. HC, p. 291: "The pebble has an inside, man does not."

114. See CRD, e.g., pp. 388–89.

115. Ibid., pp. 577 ff.

116. CRD, I, is titled "Théorie des ensembles pratiques."

117. Ibid., p. 753 (482): "What concerns us is the general problem of intelligibility."

118. CRD, p. 38 (SM, 45). I.e., without sufficient regressive analysis. Cf. CRD, pp. 86–87 (SM, 133–35).

12. Man's Place in the Spiral: Beyond Atomism

1. M, p. 213 (255).

2. See, e.g., CRD, pp. 39–40, 50–56, 95–99 (SM, 48, 68–78, 150–57).

3. Ibid., e.g., pp. 26–27 (SM, 25); 153, 332–33.

4. Ibid., e.g., p. 109 (SM, 178–79).

5. Ibid., e.g., pp. 28, 99, 100–1 (SM, 27, 158, 161).

6. Ibid., pp. 80–86 (SM, 123–33).

7. EH, p. 124 (81).

8. CRD, pp. 15–17 (SM, 4–7).

9. See M, esp. p. 96 (117–18).

10. CRD, pp. 17, 45 (SM, 6, 58).

11. M, pp. 196–98 (236–38).

12. CRD, p. 17 (SM, 6).

13. Ibid., p. 82 (SM, 126). Translation modified. This passage, in context, is directed at the inflexibility of Stalinist Marxist "idealism."

14. "Merleau Ponty vivant," p. 373 (*Situations*, 322).

15. Hence Sartre writes that there is no "Philosophy"—only "philosophies" (*CRD*, p. 15 [*SM*, 3]).

16. *CRD*, p. 71 (*SM*, 106).

17. Ibid., p. 18 (*SM*, 8).

18. *M*, p. 213 (255).

19. *CRD*, p. 111 (*SM*, 181).

20. *M*, p. 212 (254).

21. *CRD*, p. 63 (*SM*, 91).

22. Ibid., pp. 165–68, 202–3 (428–34). Sartre stresses that scarcity does not *necessarily* initiate a historical development.

23. Minimally as the negation of my praxis or as the bearer of contradictory significations.

24. *CRD*, p. 138 (422).

25. The "act in process. . . . delineates a practical field which . . . is the formal unity of the whole which is to be integrated." (*CRD*, p. 138 [422]; italics deleted.) ". . . Each praxis, insofar as it is a radical unification of the practical field, already delineates in its relation to all the others the project of the unification of all" (ibid., p. 198.)

26. *CRD*, p. 139 (422).

27. Ibid., p. 97 (*SM*, 154).

28. Ibid., p. 22 (*SM*, 17). In this respect Sartre has become profoundly critical of Cartesian method.

29. Ibid., p. 101 (*SM*, 161). See p. 106 (*SM*, 171): "The dialectic itself . . . is the development of praxis. . . ."

30. Ibid., p. 55 (*SM*, 76). See also pp. 306 ff.

31. Ibid., p. 57 (*SM*, 80). See "Merleau-Ponty vivant," p. 324 (*Situations*, 255): "At heart, I was a throwback to anarchy, digging an abyss between the vague phantasmagoria of collectivities and the precise ethic of my private life."

32. *CRD*, p. 56 (*SM*, 78–79).

33. *M* offers many illustrations from Sartre's own childhood.

34. *CRD*, p. 97 (*SM*, 155). See "Merleau-Ponty vivant," p. 354 (*Situations*, 296): "we discovered, astounded, that our conflicts had, at times, stemmed from our childhood, or went back to the elementary differences of our two organisms. . . ."

35. *CRD*, p. 45 (*SM*, 58).

36. Ibid., p. 49 (*SM*, 65).

37. *EN*, p. 720 (625).

38. *Esquisse*, p. 42 (56–57).

39. Although Heidegger does not regard them as individual and voluntary decisions. See, e.g., *EM*, pp. 29, 34, 84, 128 (32, 37, 93, 141).

40. Cf. chapter 3, esp. § II. But see also *EN*, p. 503 (430): Sartre thinks Heidegger has neglected action! Whether this is the case depends, it seems to me, on whether the Sartrean interpretation of the early Heidegger is adopted or not, as well as on the question whether action is to be characterized in terms of logical negation.

41. See Sartre's interpretation of "the laws of form as studied by Köhler

478 NOTES: MAN'S PLACE IN THE SPIRAL

and Wertheimer" in terms of the doctrine of intentionality, in *I*, pp. 47–55, 156–57 (42–52, 172–73). See also *Esquisse*, pp. 28 ff. (33 ff.).

42. *CRD*, e.g., pp. 62, 64, 95 (*SM*, 89, 93, 150).

43. Ibid., p. 64 (*SM*, 92).

44. Ibid., pp. 155–56, 507–8, 754–55.

45. Ibid., p. 57 (*SM*, 80). Translation modified.

46. *M*, p. 213 (255).

47. *SGCM*, p. 550 (599).

48. See, e.g., *CRD*, pp. 68–69 (*SM*, 100–1).

49. *SGCM*, esp. pp. 33–35, 146–148, 192 (28–30, 152–53, 202–3).

50. Sartre writes (*SGCM*, p. 177 [186]) that it is a matter of a Hegelian *Aufhebung* of Good and Evil, not of a "Parmenidean" *cancellation* of Evil. Yet the 'good' and 'evil' to be surpassed are in a real sense for Sartre *both* functions of a more primary good and a more primary evil, which are unity and disunity. In this connection I find provocative Howard Burkle's view that "seriality and fusion would be the *yin* and *yang* of Sartre's political *Tao*. . . . They would, in a sense, be good and evil contesting for dominance. The closer a society approaches to pure seriality, the more inhumane and more ripe it is for overthrow; and the more it retains of the pattern of pure fusion, the more humane and worthy it is to be preserved. In this case Sartre has not only a social ideal but a principle of social evil. Seriality and fusion are evil and good, respectively" (Howard R. Burkle, "Sartre's 'Ideal' of Social Unity," in Warnock, ed., *Sartre*, p. 332). It might, however, be argued that fusion is not the ultimate "good" for Sartre, because it is a closing ranks against an enemy, an "evil," and is still therefore a group-formation which has to declare some sector of the world as evil. The ultimate good for Sartre would be a *universal* actualization of reciprocity which, as the group of the whole, or the disappearance of groups, would not need to close ranks against any enemy.

51. *SGCM*, p. 177 (186).

52. *IF*, I, 622. See p. 816 on reciprocity as "the fundamental relation between men."

53. *CRD*, p. 32 (*SM*, 34). Italics deleted.

54. *IF*, I, 657.

55. For Sartre's handling of the notion of the spiral, see, e.g., *CRD*, pp. 71 ff., 308 (*SM*, 106 ff.); *IF*, I, 657–65. Cf. the notion of the *tourniquet*, "Merleau-Ponty vivant," pp. 362, 364, 372 (*Situations*, 307, 311, 321).

56. See chapter 3, § III; chapter 7, § I.

57. Cf. chapter 5, esp. § II.

58. *IF*, I, 656–57.

59. For the early Sartre it is individual consciousness that is revolutionary, not society. Much later Sartre said: "*L'Être et le Néant* traced an interior experience, without relating it to the exterior experience . . . of the petty-bourgeois intellectual that I was. . . . Thus, in *L'Être et le Néant*, what you could call 'subjectivity' is not what it would be for me today: the small margin [*décalage*] in a process by which an interiorization re-exteriorizes itself in an act." (*S*, IX, 102.)

60. See *CRD*, pp. 167–68 (431–32). Of course, my diagram, like any diagrammatic representation of ideas and their interrelation, is inevitably partial and misleading. It could have been constructed differently—e.g., by showing the return of the organism (at the top) to a point, its organic center. Furthermore it does not distinguish between the successive, and partial, lives of individuals who neither begin at the bottom of the diagram (of history) nor attain the top. The greatest danger of this diagram is that it will suggest that history is a "hyperorganism" over and above individual praxes. My description of the relation of the individual to the totality as that of 'microcosm' to 'macrocosm' earlier in this chapter similarly runs the risk of falsely implying that the 'macrocosm' or 'totality' is a kind of hyperorganism. Any totality for Sartre is relative to individual praxes, and only has "a life of its own" (which, as source of alienation, it really has) insofar as praxes have endowed it with that life. For Sartre's critique of the notion of 'hyperorganism', see *CRD*, p. 432.

61. *IF*, I, 653.

62. *CRD*, p. 72 (*SM*, 107).

63. Ibid., p. 71 (*SM*, 106).

64. Ibid., p. 79 (*SM*, 120).

65. *IF*, I, 8.

66. See *EH*, pp. 82–83 (53–54).

67. *SGCM*, p. 536 (584).

68. *M*, p. 199 (239).

69. "Can anyone imagine how secure I felt? Chance events did not exist. . . . I, the predestined one, would never encounter any." (*M*, p. 194 [234]; see also pp. 162–65, 208 [195–98, 249–50].)

70. See *CRD*, p. 717. On Sartre's early penchant for ascesis and mortification, see chapter 5.

71. See *EN*, p. 496 (424). For Sartre's early use of 'anyone', see *EN*, p. 593 (511). For his later use of the term, see *CRD*, pp. 141–43 (424–27). The linguistic parallel is not exact: the earlier expression is "une réalité humaine *quelconque*," while the later term is "n'importe qui."

72. See *EN*, pp. 497, 502 (425, 429).

73. *CRD*, p. 349. For Sartre's handling of atomism, see pp. 144, 153 ("the atomism of analytic Reasoning"), 332–33 ("social atomism" and "human molecule"; atomicity as alienating), 686 ("molecular exile"), 741–42 ("positivist atomization"), 746. The corrective is indicated by "*monism* of interpretation" (115).

74. See *M*, p. 208 (249–50), where Sartre writes of his "fellowmen" that, after his death, he will be "present in every one of them just as the billions of dead . . . are present in me."

75. Cf. chapter 11, § III.

76. *M*, p. 212 (255).

77. *CRD*, p. 377.

78. Ibid., p. 588. This passage is perhaps the clearest and boldest reaffirmation of humanism to be found in Sartre's later writings.

79. See, e.g., *CRD*, pp. 132, 176*n*, 665.

80. Ibid., p. 202 (433).

81. Ibid., e.g., pp. 631, 644. Sartre holds open the possibility of "the future as common freedom and no longer as destiny" (733).

82. See *SGCM*, p. 192 (202).

83. *CRD*, p. 74 (*SM*, 111).

84. Ibid.

85. Ibid., p. 138 (422).

86. Nietzsche, *Werke in drei Bänden*, II, 917.

87. *IF*, I, 622–24. See also pp. 637, 783, 879. Sartre has of course testified in *M* to his own early victimization by words. See also *CRD*, p. 126: "The ambiguity of language comes from the fact that words designate objects on the one hand and their concepts on the other hand." See also p. 176: "It *is true* that most people express themselves in discourse according to the rules of analytic rationality: but this does not mean that their *praxis* is not conscious of itself. . . . Praxis . . . does not necessarily express itself in words. In fact, *knowledge* appears as the disclosure [*dévoilement*] of the perceptual and practical field by the end, i.e., by the future non-being. . . . But this disclosure *remains practical* and cannot fix upon itself in a society which . . . still confuses knowledge with its contemplation." See also p. 249 (language as "material"); p. 303*n* (language as "field"); pp. 440–41 ("oath" as both word and praxis).

88. See *CRD*, esp. pp. 245–46 (452).

89. Ibid., p. 98 (*SM*, 157).

90. Ibid., pp. 61, 9 (*SM*, 87, *xxxiv*).

91. Hegel, *Phenomenology of Mind*, p. 81.

92. *CRD*, pp. 755, 11.

93. Ibid., p. 63 (*SM*, 90). Italics deleted.

94. *CRD*, p. 248.

95. Ibid. The references are to Walter Biemel, *Le Concept de monde chez Heidegger*, pp. 85–86, and to Alphonse de Waelhens, *Phénoménologie et Vérité*, p. 16. Sartre further quotes Biemel to the effect that in the writings after *SZ* "Heidegger begins with Being in order to reach an interpretation of man." Sartre comments: "This method is comparable to what we have called the materialistic dialectic of the external: it also begins with Being (Nature without foreign addition) in order to reach man. . . ." See *CRD*, p. 731: "dialectical rationality . . . requires . . . the fundamental priority of constituted praxis over Being. . . ." On Heidegger's handling of Marx, see chapter 6, § II and Gajo Petrovic, "Der Spruch des Heidegger," in Klostermann, ed., *Durchblicke*, pp. 412–36.

96. See *US*, p. 96 (10): "Without this theological background I should never have come upon the path of thinking. But origin always comes to meet us from the future." With this statement should be associated Heidegger's invocation of Hölderlin a few pages earlier (p. 93 [6]): "For as you began, so you will remain."

97. See *M*, p. 210 (253).

98. *IF*, I, 562.

99. *CRD*, p. 22 (*SM*, 17).

13. THE GROUND AND TRUTH OF BEING

1. See Murdoch, *Sartre*, pp. 54–55.

2. *SZ*, p. 2 (21).

3. Heidegger is of course no longer committed to the term 'ontology', because of its metaphysical connotations. My use of the term 'disclosure' here does not entail explicit disclosure; here, as elsewhere for Heidegger, the phenomenon for the most part does not show itself as it is.

4. *CRD*, p. 74 (*SM*, 111).

5. *US*, p. 93 (7).

6. See, for example, Ewing, *Fundamental Questions of Philosophy*, pp. 60–61, 63–64, 66.

7. More technically expressed, the "apophantic 'as' " presupposes the "hermeneutic 'as'." See *SZ*, pp. 158–59 (201–2).

8. This is the essential meaning of Heidegger's claim in *SZ* that present experience and thought are always grounded in a prior "projection" in which Dasein has already given itself "ekstatically" to the world (i.e., has already in "lived intentionality" or 'Care' endowed entities with thought). See *SZ*, e.g., pp. 87, 137–38, 211–12 (120–21, 177, 254–55). *Present* thought can never overtake what past thought has already committed one to; hence present thought can never begin from scratch, *ex nihilo*, and ground itself.

9. The early Heidegger approaches this marriage of thought and thing primarily from the side of thought; the later Heidegger seeks not to give undue emphasis to the "human" aspect of the thing but rather to take it as the unity it is.

10. Or at least universal communal negation of the unequal sharing of scarcity. Sartre is ambiguous on this point. On the 'whence' and 'whither' or 'prae' and 'post', see Kierkegaard, *Philosophical Fragments*, p. 12.

11. The implied reference is of course to Heidegger's reappropriation of Heraclitus and Parmenides. The preceding sentences perhaps help to show why Heidegger "considered *Identity and Difference* to be the most important thing he has published since *Being and Time*." (Joan Stambaugh, in *Identity and Difference*, p. 7.)

12. *EM*, pp. 34–35 (37).

13. Sartre regards language as a material (words, sounds) vehicle of thought (ideas, concepts), which is therefore subject to the opposite "mystifications" of reducing matter to ideas (idealism) or losing idea in matter (poetry). See chapter 9, passim, and *CRD*, p. 77 (*SM*, 115): "The idea is the man himself externalizing himself in the materiality of language."

14. See, e.g., *N*, II, 20–29.

15. Thus appearing to confirm Nietzsche's prediction that science was entering the time when it would "bite its own tail." (Nietzsche, *Werke in drei Bänden*, I, 87 [*Birth of Tragedy*, 95].)

16. See *VA*, pp. 34–36.

17. See esp. *TK*, passim.

18. I state here "insofar as it can be grounded" because of the apparent proneness of Heidegger's orientation to a conventionalism. This will be discussed below.

19. Aristotle, *Physics*, 193b; cf. *De Anima*, 431b.

20. Aristotle, *Metaphysics*, 1029b10 (*Aristotle's Metaphysics*, translated by Richard Hope, p. 134).

21. Nietzsche, *Werke in drei Bänden*, III, 757 (*Will to Power*, p. 233).

22. *Gelassenheit*, p. 61 (82).

23. It should be noted that much of John Dewey's critique of "the quest for certainty" in his work of the same name would readily be agreed to by Heidegger.

24. *VA*, p. 35.

25. In the sense of the express-and-dissimulate notion that was developed in the course of chapter 9.

26. Nietzsche calls it a going forward "step by step further into decadence" (*Werke in drei Bänden*, II, 1019 [*Portable Nietzsche*, p. 547]).

27. Wisser, ed., *Martin Heidegger im Gespräch*, p. 77.

28. E.g., *VA*, pp. 194–204.

29. In *ID*, Heidegger speaks of "the mediation within identity" (p. 34 [41]) as the event in which the difference between beings and their ground (Being) first occurs, so that henceforth the ground may be specified as thought (e.g., by Hegel; ibid., p. 54 [57]). But what remains hidden is the event of the "difference as difference"—i.e., the original differentiation, which is a differentiation of "the same," i.e., of what "belong together," namely man and Being (pp. 23–24 [32]). My specific application of identity-and-difference to the word-thought-thing relation goes somewhat beyond what Heidegger has written and should therefore be judged not by whether it transcribes more or less literally what Heidegger has said, which it clearly does not, but rather by whether it is in the spirit of what Heidegger has said about the role of language in the disclosure of beings. But see esp. *EM*, pp. 60–64 (67–70).

30. Ryle, *The Concept of Mind*, esp. pp. 16–23.

31. See *WD*, pp. 74, 100–1 (79–80, 154–157).

32. See *ID*, p. 18 (27).

33. See *BH*, pp. 176–83 (290–95).

34. *EM*, pp. 91, 102 (101, 112).

35. Ibid., p. 100 (111).

36. *H*, p. 322.

37. If I have belabored this point, it is because it seems to me the heart and soul of Heidegger's later thought, and because most of the literature on Heidegger has insufficiently explicated it.

38. Wittgenstein, *Philosophical Investigations*, I, sect. 67.

39. For Heidegger's notion of 'ambiguity' (*Zweideutigkeit*, *Mehrdeutigkeit*), see, e.g., *N*, I, 168–70, 342–43 and D. Sinn, "Heidegger's Spätphilosophie," esp. pp. 173–74.

40. *CRD*, p. 74 (*SM*, 111).

41. See *M*, p. 96 (117–18); *IF*, I, 656–57; *CRD*, p. 72 (*SM*, 107).

42. See *CRD*, pp. 755, 11.

43. See ibid., p. 101 (*SM*, 161): "If we refuse to see the original dialectical

movement in the individual and in his enterprise of producing his life, of objectifying himself, then we shall have to give up dialectic or else make of it the immanent law of History." Cf. p. 96 (*SM*, 153): "this knowing is simply the dialectical movement which explains the act by its terminal signification in terms of its starting condition."

44. Ibid., p. 165 (428).

45. Of man and things. Reciprocality for Sartre refers to the relation of man and *Other*.

46. See *CRD*, pp. 168, 204 (431, 435).

47. This is of course an oversimplification. In Part I, I have also stressed the other side—the extent to which *SZ* is already on the way to overcoming this metaphysical problem.

48. *IF*, I, 656–57.

49. *CRD*, p. 755.

50. Ibid., e.g., pp. 202, 258, 352, 372, 750, 754.

51. I am referring to ordinary sense-perception, which Heidegger, in his intentness upon 'thought', is sometimes said to have overlooked. Cf. the remarks of J. M. Edie in J. Kockelmans, ed., *On Heidegger and Language*, pp. 266–67.

52. The reference is to Heidegger's 'es gibt'.

53. Heidegger does not endorse the form-matter or idea-matter dualities. I am employing them *with qualification* as part of an effort to call attention to such ties as exist between Heidegger's thought and philosophical thought. But 'Earth' is a much richer notion than 'matter', and 'thought' is a much richer and indeed different notion than 'form' or 'idea'.

54. In the sense that mortals have perenially attributed to the gods originating power, cosmic design, light or illumination.

55. *SZ*, pp. 83, 364 (113, 415).

14. The Direction of Phenomenological Ontology

1. Whitehead, *Science and the Modern World*, pp. 81–82.

2. As in 'anxiety', in 'remembering', and in uncovering a phenomenon that has been dissembled.

3. It might be argued that Heidegger thus recalls the common root of the Hebraic conception of the revelatory power of the word and hearing and the Greek conception of the revelatory power of light and vision. Both *Sprache* and *Lichtung* are essential to Heidegger's understanding of the character of disclosure. The thing comes to light in being called something, in the word.

4. Hegel, *Lectures on the History of Philosophy*, III, 230.

5. Heidegger, *Schellings Abhandlung*, p. 93.

6. I am not stressing language in this section, but it should be noted that the event of Being here spoken of is the event of the saying of the 'as' of the being, the saying of a word that is the union of thought and entity, i.e., *meaning* the thing, saying the thing in its meaning.

7. Sartre, *PH*, pp. 32–33 (4–5).

8. Merleau-Ponty, *Phénoménologie de la perception,* p. i (vii).

9. See *EN,* p. 301 (244).

10. With the possible exception of anxiety; see chapter 4, § II.

11. *US,* p. 151 (51).

12. For Heidegger's analysis of the doctrine of the four causes, see *TK,* pp. 7–11.

13. *CRD,* p. 248.

14. Hegel, *Phenomenology of Mind,* p. 89.

15. I include in this tendency Kierkegaardian thought and its progeny, since its premise is an epistemological skepticism and nihilism that are not resolved epistemologically but rather by an act of faith. A nontheological analogue is Santayana's "animal faith."

16. Heidegger's sympathetic treatment of Marx is of course a matter of record. I do not find the implication of the later Heidegger's thought in any particular political tendency persuasive.

17. *WM,* p. 15 (344).

18. See *AR,* p. 217 (147); *IF,* I, 623.

19. *CRD,* pp. 156, 755.

20. See chapter 7, § III.

21. *SD,* p. 45 (42).

Bibliography

ONLY WORKS cited in the text and/or notes are listed here. For a complete bibliography of works by and about Heidegger to 1967, see Hans-Martin Sass, *Heidegger-Bibliographie*. For a complete bibliography of works by Sartre to 1973, see Michel Contat and Michel Rybalka, *The Writings of Jean-Paul Sartre*.

WORKS OF HEIDEGGER CITED

Einführung in die Metaphysik. Tübingen: Max Niemeyer Verlag, 1953. *An Introduction to Metaphysics.* Translated by Ralph Manheim. Garden City, N. Y.: Doubleday, 1961

Aus der Erfahrung des Denkens. Pfullingen: Günther Neske Verlag, 1954

Erläuterungen zu Hölderlins Dichtung. Frankfurt am Main: Vittorio Klostermann, 1951.

Der Feldweg. Frankfurt am Main: Vittorio Klostermann, 1953.

Die Frage nach dem Ding. Tübingen: Max Niemeyer Verlag, 1962. *What Is a Thing?* Translated by W. B. Barton, Jr., and Vera Deutsch. Chicago: Henry Regnery, 1967.

Gelassenheit. Pfullingen: Günther Neske Verlag, 1959. *Discourse on Thinking.* Translated by John M. Anderson and E. Hans Freund. New York: Harper and Row, 1966

"Hans Jantzen dem Freunde zum Andenken." In *Erinnerung an Hans Jantzen.* Freiburg: Eberhard Albert, 1967.

Hebel der Hausfreund. Pfullingen: Günther Neske Verlag, 1957.

Heraklit: Seminar Wintersemester 1966/1967. With Eugen Fink. Frankfurt am Main: Vittorio Klostermann, 1970.

"Hölderlins Erde und Himmel." *Hölderlin Jahrbuch,* 11 (1958–60), 17–39.

Holzwege. Frankfurt am Main: Vittorio Klostermann, 1950. Essays cited, together with their pages:

"Hegels Begriff der Erfahrung," pp. 105–92. *Hegel's Concept of Experience.* New York: Harper and Row, 1970.

"Nietzsches Wort 'Gott ist tot,' " pp. 193–247.

"Der Spruch des Anaximander," pp. 296–343.

"Der Ursprung des Kunstwerkes," pp. 7–68. "The Origin of the Work of Art." In *Poetry, Language, Thought*. Translated by Albert Hofstadter. New York: Harper and Row, 1971.

"Wozu Dichter?," pp. 248–95.

Identität und Differenz. Pfullingen: Günther Neske Verlag, 1957. *Identity and Difference*. Translated by Joan Stambaugh. New York: Harper and Row, 1969.

Kant und das Problem der Metaphysik. Frankfurt am Main: Vittorio Klostermann, 1951. *Kant and the Problem of Metaphysics*. Translated by James S. Churchill. Bloomington: Indiana University Press, 1962.

Martin Heidegger zum 80. Geburtstag von seiner Heimatstadt Messkirch. Frankfurt am Main: Vittorio Klostermann, 1969.

Nietzsche. 2 vols. Pfullingen: Günther Neske Verlag, 1961.

"Phänomenologie und Theologie." *Archives de Philosophie*, 32, no. 3, (1969), 356–94.

Zur Sache des Denkens. Tübingen: Max Niemeyer Verlag, 1969. *On Time and Being*. Translated by Joan Stambaugh. New York: Harper and Row, 1972.

Der Satz vom Grund. Pfullingen: Günther Neske Verlag, 1957.

Schellings Abhandlung über das Wesen der menschlichen Freiheit (1809). Tübingen: Max Niemeyer Verlag, 1971.

Sein und Zeit. 9th ed. Tübingen: Max Niemeyer Verlag, 1960. *Being and Time*. Translated by John Macquarrie and Edward Robinson. London: SCM Press, 1962.

Die Technik und die Kehre. Pfullingen: Günther Neske Verlag, 1962.

Unterwegs zur Sprache. Pfullingen: Günther Neske Verlag, 1959. *On the Way to Language*. Translated by Peter D. Hertz. New York: Harper and Row, 1971. Contains all essays except "Die Sprache," "Language," which is translated in *Poetry, Language, Thought*. Translated by Albert Hofstadter. New York: Harper and Row, 1971.

Der Ursprung des Kunstwerkes. Introduction by Hans-Georg Gadamer. Stuttgart: Philipp Reclam Jun., 1965. In *Poetry, Language, Thought*. Translated by Albert Hofstadter. New York: Harper and Row, 1971.

Vom Wesen des Grundes. 5th ed. Frankfurt am Main: Vittorio Klostermann, 1961. *The Essence of Reasons*. Translated by Terrence Malick. Evanston: Northwestern University Press, 1969.

Vorträge und Aufsätze. Pfullingen: Günther Neske Verlag, 1954. Essays cited, together with their pages:

"Aletheia" (Heraklit, Fragment 16), pp. 257–82.

"Bauen Wohnen Denken," pp. 145–62. "Building Dwelling Thinking." In *Poetry, Language, Thought.* New York: Harper and Row, 1971.

". . . dichterisch wohnet der Mensch . . . ," pp. 187–204. ". . . Poetically Man Dwells . . . ," in *Poetry, Language, Thought.*

"Das Ding," pp. 163–85. "The Thing," In *Poetry, Language, Thought.*

"Die Frage nach der Technik," pp. 13–44.

"Logos" (Heraklit, Fragment 50), pp. 207–29.

"Überwindung der Metaphysik," pp. 71–99.

"Wer ist Nietzsches Zarathustra?" pp. 101–26. "Who is Nietzsche's Zarathustra?" Translated by Bernd Magnus. *The Review of Metaphysics,* 20, no. 3 (1967), 411–31.

Vom Wesen der Wahrheit. 3d. ed. Frankfurt am Main: Vittorio Klostermann, 1954. "On the Essence of Truth." Translated by R. F. C. Hull and Alan Crick. In *Existence and Being.* Chicago: Henry Regnery, 1949, pp. 292–324.

Was heisst Denken? Tübingen: Max Niemeyer Verlag, 1961. *What is Called Thinking?* Translated by Fred D. Wieck and J. Glenn Gray. New York: Harper and Row, 1968.

Was ist Metaphysik? 9th ed. Frankfurt: Vittorio Klostermann, 1965. "What is Metaphysics?" Translated by R. F. C. Hull and Alan Crick. In *Existence and Being.* Chicago: Henry Regnery, 1949, pp. 325–49; Epilogue, pp. 349–61.

Wegmarken. Frankfurt am Main: Vittorio Klostermann, 1967. Essays cited, together with their pages:

"Brief über den Humanismus," pp. 145–94. "Letter on Humanism." Translated by Edgar Lohner. In W. Barrett and H. D. Aiken, eds., *Philosophy in the Twentieth Century.* New York: Random House, 1962. Vol. III.

"Einleitung zu Was ist Metaphysik? Der Rückgang in den Grund der Metaphysik," pp. 195–211. "The Way Back into the Ground of Metaphysics." Translated by Walter Kaufmann. In Kaufmann, ed., *Existentialism from Dostoevsky to Sartre.* New York: Meridian, 1957.

"Hegel und die Griechen," pp. 255–72.

"Kants These über das Sein," pp. 273–307.

"Platons Lehre von der Wahrheit," pp. 109–44. "Plato's Doctrine of Truth." Translated by John Barlow. In W. Barrett and H. D. Aiken, eds., *Philosophy in the Twentieth Century.* Vol. III.

"Vom Wesen und Begriff der *Physis:* Aristoteles' Physik B, 1," pp. 309–71.

"Zur Seinsfrage," pp. 213–53.

WORKS OF SARTRE CITED

Critique de la raison dialectique (précédé de Question de Méthode). Vol. I. *Théorie des ensembles pratiques*. Paris: Gallimard, 1960. Preface translated by Hazel E. Barnes as *Search for a Method*. New York: Knopf, 1963. Selections translated by Starr and Jim Atkinson in R. D. Cumming, ed., *The Philosophy of Jean-Paul Sartre*. New York: Random House, 1965.

Esquisse d'une théorie des émotions. Paris: Hermann, 1960. *The Emotions: Outline of a Theory*. Translated by Bernard Frechtman. New York: Philosophical Library, 1948.

L'Être et le Néant: Essai d'ontologie phénoménologique. Paris: Gallimard, 1943. *Being and Nothingness: An Essay on Phenomenological Ontology*. Translated by Hazel E. Barnes. New York: Philosophical Library, 1956.

L'Existentialisme est un humanisme. Paris: Les Éditions Nagel, 1946. *Existentialism*. Translated by Bernard Frechtman. New York: Philosophical Library, 1947.

L'Idiot de la famille: Gustave Flaubert de 1821 à 1857. 3 vols. Paris: Gallimard, 1971.

L'Imaginaire: Psychologie phénoménologique de l'imagination. Paris: Gallimard, 1940. *The Psychology of Imagination*. Translation anonymous. New York: Philosophical Library, 1948.

L'Imagination. Paris: Presses Universitaires de France, 1963. *Imagination: A Psychological Critique*. Translated by Forrest Williams. Ann Arbor: University of Michigan Press, 1962.

"Merleau-Ponty vivant." *Les Temps Modernes*, 17, nos. 184–85 (1961), 304–76. (Reprinted in *Situations*, IV, q.v.) "Merleau-Ponty." In *Situations*. Translated by Benita Eisler. New York: George Braziller, 1965, pp. 225–326.

Les Mots. Paris: Gallimard, 1964. *The Words*. Translated by Bernard Frechtman. New York: George Braziller, 1964.

La Nausée. Paris: Gallimard, 1938. *Nausea*. Translated by Lloyd Alexander. Norfolk: New Directions, n.d.

Saint Genet, comédien et martyr. Paris: Gallimard, 1952. *Saint Genet: Actor and Martyr*. Translated by Bernard Frechtman. New York: George Braziller, 1963.

Situations, I. Paris: Gallimard, 1947. Essays cited, together with pages:
"Aller et retour," pp. 189–244. "Departure and Return." In *Sartre, Literary and Philosophical Essays*. Translated by Annette Michelson. London: Rider, 1955.
"L'Homme et les choses," pp. 245–93.

"Une Idée fondamentale de la phénoménologie de Husserl: L'Intentionnalité," pp. 31–35. "Intentionality: A Fundamental Idea of Husserl's Phenomenology." Translated by Joseph P. Fell. *The Journal of the British Society for Phenomenology*, 1, no. 2 (1970), 4–5.

Situations, II. Paris: Gallimard, 1948. "Qu'est-ce que la littérature?" *Literature and Existentialism.* Translated by Bernard Frechtman. New York: Citadel Press, 1962.

Situations, IV. Paris: Gallimard, 1964. Essays cited, together with pages:

"Merleau-Ponty," pp. 189–287. "Merleau-Ponty." In *Situations.* New York: George Braziller, 1965.

"Réponse à Albert Camus," pp. 90–125. "Reply to Albert Camus." In *Situations.* New York: George Braziller, 1965.

Situations, VI. Paris: Gallimard, 1964. Includes "Les Communistes et la Paix." *The Communists and Peace.* Translated by Martha H. Fletcher. New York: George Braziller, 1968.

Situations, VII. Paris: Gallimard, 1965. Includes "Le Fantôme de Staline." *The Ghost of Stalin.* Translated by Martha H. Fletcher. New York: George Braziller, 1968.

Situations, IX. Paris: Gallimard, 1972. Essays cited, together with pages:

"L'Écrivain et sa langue," pp. 40–82.

"Sartre par Sartre," pp. 99–134.

Situations, X. Paris: Gallimard, 1976. Includes "Autoportrait à soixante-dix ans," pp. 133–226. In *Life/Situations.* Translated by Paul Auster and Lydia Davis. New York: Pantheon, 1977.

La Transcendance de l'ego: Esquisse d'une description phénom-énologique. Paris: Librairie Philosophique J. Vrin, 1965. *The Transcendence of the Ego.* Translated by Forrest Williams and Robert Kirkpatrick. New York: Noonday Press, 1957.

OTHER WORKS CITED

Allemann, Beda. *Hölderlin und Heidegger.* 2d ed. Zurich and Freiburg: Atlantis Verlag, 1954.

Aristotle. *The Basic Works of Aristotle.* Edited by Richard McKeon. New York: Random House, 1941.

——*Metaphysics.* Translated by Richard Hope. New York: Columbia University Press, 1952.

Barrett, William, and Henry D. Aiken, *Twentieth Century Philosophy.* 3 vols. New York: Random House, 1962.

Beauvoir, Simone de. *Force of Circumstance*. New York: Putnam's, 1964.

—— *Pour une morale de l'ambiguité*. Paris: Gallimard, 1947. *The Ethics of Ambiguity*. Translated by Bernard Frechtman. New York: Philosophical Library, 1948.

—— *The Prime of Life*. Translated by Peter Green. Cleveland: World, 1962.

—— *Privilèges*. Paris: Gallimard, 1955.

Biemel, Walter. *Le Concept de monde chez Heidegger*. Louvain: Nauwelaerts, 1950.

—— *Jean-Paul Sartre in Selbstzeugnissen und Bilddokumenten*. Reinbek: Rowohlt Taschenbuch Verlag, 1964.

—— *Martin Heidegger in Selbstzeugnissen und Bilddokumenten*. Reinbek: Rowohlt Taschenbuch Verlag, 1973.

Buchler, Justus. *Toward a General Theory of Human Judgment*. New York: Columbia University Press, 1951.

Buchner, Hartmut. "Review of J. M. Demske, *Sein, Mensch und Tod*." *Philosophisches Jahrbuch*, 74 (1966–67), 191–94.

Contat, Michel, and Michel Rybalka. *Les Écrits de Sartre*. Paris: Gallimard, 1970. *The Writings of Jean-Paul Sartre*. Translated by Richard C. McCleary. Evanston: Northwestern University Press, 1974.

Cowley, Fraser. *A Critique of British Empiricism*. London: Macmillan, 1968.

Cumming, Robert D., ed. *The Philosophy of Jean-Paul Sartre*. New York: Random House, 1965.

cummings, e. e. *1 ×1*. New York: Holt, 1944.

Desan, Wilfrid. *The Tragic Finale*. New York: Harper Torchbooks, 1960.

Descartes, René. *The Philosophical Works of Descartes*. Translated by E. S. Haldane and G. R. T. Ross. 2 vols. Cambridge: Cambridge University Press, 1969.

Elveton, R. O., ed. *The Phenomenology of Husserl: Selected Critical Readings*. Chicago: Quadrangle, 1970.

Erickson, Stephen. *Language and Being: An Analytic Phenomenology*. New Haven: Yale University Press, 1970.

Ewing, A. C. *The Fundamental Questions of Philosophy*. New York: Collier Books, 1962.

Fell, Joseph P. *Emotion in the Thought of Sartre*. New York: Columbia University Press, 1965.

—— "Heidegger's Notion of Two Beginnings." *The Review of Metaphysics*, 25, no. 2 (1971), 213–37.

—— "The Phenomenological Approach to Emotion." In D. K. Candland et al., *Emotion*. Monterey: Brooks/Cole, 1977.

—— "Sartre as Existentialist and Marxist." *Bucknell Review*, 13, no. 3 (1965), 63–74.

—— "Sartre's Theory of Motivation: Some Clarifications." *The Journal of the British Society for Phenomenology*, 1, no. 2 (1970), 27–34.

—— "Sartre's *Words*: An Existential Self-Analysis." *The Psychoanalytic Review*, 55, no. 3 (1968), 426–41.

Gelven, Michael. *A Commentary on Heidegger's "Being and Time."* New York: Harper Torchbooks, 1970.

Hana, Ghanem-Georges. *Freiheit und Person: Eine Auseinandersetzung mit der Darstellung Jean-Paul Sartres*. Munich: Verlag C. H. Beck, 1965.

Hartmann, Klaus. *Sartre's Ontology: A Study of "Being and Nothingness" in the Light of Hegel's Logic*. Evanston: Northwestern University Press, 1966.

Hegel, G. W. F. *Lectures on the History of Philosophy*. Translated by E. S. Haldane and F. H. Simpson. 3 vols. London: Routledge and Kegan Paul, 1955.

—— *On Christianity: Early Theological Writings by Friedrich Hegel*. Translated by T. M. Knox. Edited by Richard Kroner. New York: Harper Torchbooks, 1961.

—— *The Phenomenology of Mind*. Translated by J. B. Baillie. New York: Macmillan, 1931.

—— *The Philosophy of History*. Translated by J. Sibree. New York: Dover, 1956.

—— *Science of Logic*. Translated by W. H. Johnston and L. G. Struthers. 2 vols. New York: Macmillan, 1929.

Holz, Hans Heinz. *Jean-Paul Sartre: Darstellung und Kritik seiner Philosophie*. Meisenheim: Westkulturverlag Anton Hain, 1951.

Huch, Kurt Jürgen. *Philosophiegeschichtliche Voraussetzungen der Heideggerschen Ontologie*. Frankfurt am Main: Europäische Verlagsanstalt, 1967.

Hume, David. *A Treatise of Human Nature*. Oxford: Clarendon Press, 1965.

Husserl, Edmund. *Cartesian Meditations: An Introduction to Phenomenology*. Translated by Dorion Cairns. The Hague: Martinus Nijhoff, 1960.

—— *The Crisis of European Sciences and Transcendental Phenomenology: An Introduction to Phenomenological Philosophy*. Translated by David Carr. Evanston: Northwestern University Press, 1970.

—— *The Idea of Phenomenology.* Translated by William P. Alston and George Nakhnikian. The Hague: Martinus Nijhoff, 1964.

—— *Ideas: General Introduction to Pure Phenomenology.* Translated by W. R. Boyce Gibson. New York: Macmillan, 1931.

—— *The Paris Lectures.* Translated by Peter Koestenbaum. The Hague: Martinus Nijhoff, 1964.

James, William. *Pragmatism: A New Name for Some Old Ways of Thinking.* New York: Longmans, Green, 1949.

Jaspers, Karl. *Nietzsche: An Introduction to the Understanding of His Philosophical Activity.* Translated by Charles F. Wallraff and Frederick J. Schmitz. Tucson: University of Arizona Press, 1965.

Jeanson, Francis. *Le Problème moral et la pensée de Sartre.* Foreword by Jean-Paul Sartre. Paris: Éditions du Seuil, 1965.

—— *Sartre* ["Les Écrivains devant Dieu"]. Paris: Desclée de Brouwer, 1966.

Kant, Immanuel. *Critique of Pure Reason.* Translated by Norman Kemp Smith. New York: St. Martin's, 1965.

Kaufmann, Walter. *Existentialism from Dostoevsky to Sartre.* 1st ed. New York: Meridian, 1957.

Kierkegaard, Søren. *Concluding Unscientific Postscript to the Philosophical Fragments.* Translated by David F. Swenson and Walter Lowrie. Princeton: Princeton University Press, 1944.

—— *Fear and Trembling and The Sickness unto Death.* Translated by Walter Lowrie. Garden City, N.Y.: Doubleday, 1954.

—— *Philosophical Fragments or a Fragment of Philosophy.* Translated by David F. Swenson. Princeton: Princeton University Press, 1936.

Kirk, G. S. and J. E. Raven. *The Presocratic Philosophers.* Cambridge: Cambridge University Press, 1962.

Klostermann, Vittorio, ed. *Durchblicke: Martin Heidegger zum 80. Geburtstag.* Frankfurt am Main: Vittorio Klostermann, 1970.

Kockelmans, Joseph J., ed. *On Heidegger and Language.* Evanston: Northwestern University Press, 1972.

La Grange, Henry-Louis de. *Mahler.* Vol. I. Garden City, N.Y.: Doubleday, 1973.

Leibniz, G. W. *Philosophical Papers and Letters.* Edited and translated by Leroy E. Loemker. Chicago: University of Chicago Press, 1956.

Löwith, Karl. *Heidegger: Denker in dürftiger Zeit.* Göttingen: Vanderhoeck and Ruprecht, 1965.

Macomber, W. B. *The Anatomy of Disillusion: Martin Heidegger's Notion of Truth*. Evanston: Northwestern University Press, 1967.

Macquarrie, John. *Martin Heidegger*. London: Lutterworth Press, 1968.

Magnus, Bernd. *Heidegger's Metahistory of Philosophy*. The Hague: Martinus Nijhoff, 1970.

Marx, Werner. *Heidegger und die Tradition*. Stuttgart: W. Kohlhammer Verlag, 1961. *Heidegger and the Tradition*. Translated by Theodore Kisiel and Murray Greene. Evanston: Northwestern University Press, 1971.

—— *Reason and World: Between Tradition and Another Beginning*. Translated by T. V. Yates and R. Geuss. The Hague: Martinus Nijhoff, 1971.

Mays, Wolfe and S. C. Brown, eds. *Linguistic Analysis and Phenomenology*. Lewisburg: Bucknell University Press, 1970.

Mehta, J. L. *The Philosophy of Martin Heidegger*. New York: Harper Torchbooks, 1971.

Merleau-Ponty, Maurice. *Les Aventures de la dialectique*. Paris: Gallimard, 1955.

—— *Phénoménologie de la perception*. Paris: Gallimard, 1945. *Phenomenology of Perception*. Translated by Colin Smith. London: Routledge & Kegan Paul, 1962.

—— *The Primacy of Perception*. Translated by James M. Edie et al. Evanston: Northwestern University Press, 1964.

—— *Sens et non-sens*. Paris: Nagel, 1948. *Sense and Non-Sense*. Translated by H. L. Dreyfus and P. A. Dreyfus. Evanston: Northwestern University Press, 1964.

—— *Le Visible et l'invisible*. Paris: Gallimard, 1964. *The Visible and the Invisible*. Translated by Alphonso Lingis. Evanston: Northwestern University Press, 1968.

Morris, Phyllis Sutton. *Sartre's Concept of a Person: An Analytic Approach*. Amherst: University of Massachusetts Press, 1976.

Murdoch, Iris. *Sartre: Romantic Rationalist*. Cambridge, England: Bowes and Bowes, 1953.

—— *The Sovereignty of Good*. New York: Schocken, 1971.

Nietzsche, Friedrich. *The Birth of Tragedy and The Genealogy of Morals*. Translated by Francis Golffing. Garden City: Doubleday Anchor, 1956.

—— *The Portable Nietzsche*. Edited and translated by Walter Kaufmann. New York: Viking, 1954.

—— *Werke in drei Bänden*. Edited by Karl Schlechta. 3 vols. Munich: Carl Hanser Verlag, 1956.

—— The Will to Power. Edited by Walter Kaufmann. New York: Random House, 1967.

Ortega y Gasset, José. History as a System. Translated by Helene Weyl. Afterword by John William Miller. New York: Norton, 1961.

Ott, Heinrich. Denken und Sein. Der Weg Martin Heideggers und der Weg der Theologie. Zurich: EVZ-Verlag, 1959.

Palmier, Jean-Michel. Les Écrits politiques de Heidegger. Paris: Éditions de l'Herne, 1968.

Plato. Phaedo. Translated by R. Hackforth. New York: Liberal Arts Press, n.d.

—— Plato's Cosmology: The Timaeus of Plato. Translated by F. M. Cornford. New York: Bobbs-Merrill, n.d.

—— The Republic of Plato. Translated by Allan Bloom. New York: Basic Books, 1968.

Pöggeler, Otto. Der Denkweg Martin Heideggers. Pfullingen: Verlag Günther Neske, 1963.

——, ed. Heidegger: Perspectiven zur Deutung seines Werks. Cologne: Kiepenheuer und Witsch, 1969.

Randall, John Herman, Jr. The Career of Philosophy. Vol. 1. New York: Columbia University Press, 1962.

Richardson, William J. Heidegger: Through Phenomenology to Thought. The Hague: Martinus Nijhoff, 1963.

Ryle, Gilbert. The Concept of Mind. London: Hutchinson's University Library, 1949.

Sass, Hans-Martin. Heidegger-Bibliographie. Meisenheim: Verlag Anton Hain, 1968.

Schwan, Alexander. Politische Philosophie im Denken Heideggers. Cologne: Westdeutscher Verlag, 1965.

Schweitzer, Albert. The Quest of the Historical Jesus: A Critical Study of Its Progress from Reimarus to Wrede. Translated by W. Montgomery. New York: Macmillan, 1950.

Sinn, Dieter. "Heideggers Spätphilosophie." Philosophische Rundschau, 14 (1967), 81–182.

Smith, Colin. Contemporary French Philosophy. London: Methuen, 1964.

Spiegelberg, Herbert. The Phenomenological Movement. 2 vols. The Hague: Martinus Nijhoff, 1960.

Thody, Philip. Jean-Paul Sartre: A Literary and Political Study. New York: Macmillan, 1960.

Tillich, Paul. The Courage to Be. New Haven: Yale University Press, 1952.

Tugendhat, Ernst. *Der Wahrheitsbegriff bei Husserl und Heidegger.* Berlin: Walter de Gruyter, 1967.

Van de Pitte, M. M. "Sartre as Transcendental Realist." *The Journal of the British Society for Phenomenology,* 1, no. 2 (1970), 22–26.

Von Hermann, Friedrich Wilhelm. *Die Selbstinterpretation Martin Heideggers.* Meisenheim: Verlag Anton Hain, 1964.

Vycinas, Vincent. *Earth and Gods: An Introduction to the Philosophy of Martin Heidegger.* The Hague: Martinus Nijhoff, 1961.

Waelhens, Alphonse de. *Phénoménologie et Vérité.* Louvain: Nauwelaerts, 1965.

——— *La Philosophie de Martin Heidegger.* Louvain: Institut Supérieur de Philosophie, 1942.

Warnock, Mary, ed. *Sartre: A Collection of Critical Essays.* Garden City, N.Y.: Doubleday, 1971.

Whitehead, Alfred North. *Science and the Modern World.* Cambridge: Cambridge University Press, 1926.

Wisser, Richard, ed. *Martin Heidegger im Gespräch.* Freiburg and Munich: Verlag Karl Alber, 1970.

Wittgenstein, Ludwig. *Philosophical Investigations.* Oxford: Basil Blackwell, 1953.

Yeats, W. B. *The Collected Poems of W. B. Yeats.* New York: Macmillan, 1955.

Index

Abandonment: in Heidegger, 52, 56, 100; in Sartre, 153

Abode: historical, 171; language as, 176; *ēthos* as, 177–78, 365, 382; devaluation of, 180; event of, 204

Absence: and negation, 72; of ground, 163; *see also* Presence

Absolute, the, 21, 236, 387–88; Descartes on, 4–5; the relative, 7, 15, 19, 84, 172, 364, 415; Nietzsche on, 15–17; Husserl on, 18–20, 285; Heidegger on, 53, 189, 227, 235, 376–77; plenitude as, 76; for-itself as, 90, 159, 171–72, 184, 285, 353; in Hegel, 105, 202, 417; truth as, 157, 234; as measure, 235, 404; Merleau-Ponty on, 237

Abyss, 139–40, 261

Action: cannot condition existence, 77; ground of, 123; as surpassing of given, 276; and reality, 296–97, 472*n*5; as praxis, 298, 326–30; as metaphysical problem, 302–4, 318–27, 337, 341; inscribed in Being, 326; as multidimensional unity, 337, 354, 390–400, 422; as metaphysical, 365, 374; logic of, 367, 371; as subjective ground, 369; defined, 472*n*5; as unification of field, 477*n*25; and language, 480*n*87

Actuality, 13, 362; and possibility, 33, 41, 59, 78–79, 102, 181; as presentness, 51; and potentiality, 76, 80, 290–92; and materiality, 78, 223; and reality, 78–81, 89, 270, 279, 295–96, 400; and time, 84, 472*n*108; and meaning, 102, 414; and intentionality, 142; humanization of, 151; and *existentia*, 171; and quality, 293, 471–72*n*100; and form, 342

Affectivity, 12, 81–82, 88–89, 151; and degradation, 179; *see also* Hatred; Love; Magic; Passion

Ahistoric, the, *see* History

Alain, *see* Chartier, Émile

Alētheia, 218, 262, 463*n*38, 464*n*1; *see also* Truth

Alienation, 183, 298–300, 304, 316, 364; Sartre on, 150, 184, 272, 308, 314, 319–20, 333, 343–44, 349, 358–59, 457*n*133; Marx on, 170; by nature, 196; and beginning, 363; objectification without, 371, 392; Heidegger and Sartre on, 418–19; *see also* Composition; History, epochal

Allemann, Beda, 441–42*n*8, 460*n*65

Ambiguity: of world, 73, 142; of for-itself, 135, 156, 313–14; and play, 142, 304; and fundamental project, 149; and language, 273–74, 277, 286, 355, 388, 480*n*87, 482*n*39; maintaining the, 279, 301, 318–20

Amor fati, 13, 15–16, 62, 103, 110, 146, 183, 195, 260, 301, 381; as *amor potestatis*, 123–24; as affirmation of place, 377, 423; and phenomenology, 424

Analysis: as factoring, 8, 106, 159–60, 200, 302, 338, 409; in Hegel, 12; in Sartre, 75–76, 82, 89, 129, 132, 137, 230–31, 269–80 *passim*, 293–94, 296, 324, 347; in Heidegger, 188, 200, 232; in Pascal, 236–37; as condition of truth, 276; balance of synthesis and, 319, 357; as moment in totalizing, 330, 335; as disassembling, 396; limits of, 407

Anaxagoras, 312–13

Anaximander, 234, 467*n*70

Anger, 180; *see also* Hatred

Animal, the, 213, 218, 260, 265

Anselm, Saint, 68

Anthropology, 63, 65, 67, 157, 333, 356

Anthropomorphism, 11

Antinomies, resolution of, 321; *see also* Metaphysics; Synthesis

Anxiety (or anguish): in Kierkegaard, 13, 54; in Heidegger, 54–56, 99, 107–10, 126, 216, 260, 294; and nothing, 107–8, 163–64, 173–74, 216; and motivation, 123; in Sartre, 138–40, 299, 347; threatens phenomenological program, 160, 193, 199–200, 343, 392–93; shift in sense of, 193

'Anyone', 344, 346, 352, 371, 479*n*71

Apodicticity, 18

Appearance, 33, 303; in Nietzsche, 16; and ground, 46; in Heidegger, 46, 256; as displacement, 203–4; *see also* Phenomenon

A priori, 431*n*25

Arbitrary, the, *see* Conventionalism; Will

Aristotle, 3, 20, 42, 56, 76, 80, 90, 100, 106, 177, 178, 262, 313, 332, 346, 372–73, 379–80, 401, 414, 455*n*101, 457

Art: in Sartre, 144–48, 449*n*71, 450*n*81, 457; in Heidegger, 191; *see also* Music; Poetic, the

Articulation, 44, 47–48, 182, 196–205, 225, 365; and time-space, 113, 127; naming and, 231–32, 264–65, 268, 270; extralinguistic but logical, 287–88; *see also* Determination; Discourse; Distinctions; Juncture; Meaning

Artifactual, the, 118, 145, 179, 271–72, 280, 397, 405, 414–15; phenomena as, 147; as alienating, 298; omnipresence of, 453*n*62; *see also* Instrumentality

Artistry, symbolic, 144–46

'As', *see* Being, and the 'as'

Assembling, 102, 205, 282; teleology as, 337; by language as instrument, 355; dialectic as, 410; *see also* Gathering; Synthesis

Assertions: grounded by Heidegger, 242, 378–79, 389–90; grounded by Sartre, 390–94; *see also* Truth, propositional

Atheism, 156, 239, 246, 323, 427*n*5

Atomism, 188, 198, 312, 313, 333, 338, 352, 355–56, 387, 415, 420, 479*n*73

Attitude: historical shifts in, 7; natural, 17, 18, 21, 25, 93, 318; naiveté as, 21, 22, 24; question of, 24; anxiety and, 107, 301; love as, 180; metaphysical, 237; Sartrean, 280, 323, 436–37*n*31; Heideg-

gerian, 282, 378, 469*n*51; Sartrean and Heideggerian compared, 367–68; leeway of, 377, 424; reversal of, 404; vengeance as, 423, 424

Attunement, 63; *see also* Disposition

Augustine, Saint, 230

Authenticity, 39, 423; falling and, 50–51, 304; as ethical term, 130, 453*n*57; as escape from bad faith, 131; as owning up to ambiguity, 135, 138, 301; as coming on of what has been, 254; and involvement, 318–21; *see also* Owning up

Autonomy: ego and, 60; freedom and, 62; *see also* Freedom; Thinking

Bacon, Francis, 144, 458*n*18, 468*n*17

Basis, *see* Foundation; Ground

Baudelaire, Charles, 351

Beauty: as impossible fusion, 156, 291, 463–64*n*66; as coincidence of actual and possible, 211; love and, 235–37; original, 242, 423; and truth, 463–64*n*66

Beauvoir, Simone de, 66, 131, 179, 185, 302, 437*n*31, 441*n*129, 450*n*83, 474*n*70

Beethoven, Ludwig van, 464*n*66

Befindlichkeit, see Attunement; Disposition

Beginning: Greek, 22, 25, 36, 246, 372–73, 377; question of, 25, 30, 243, 268, 280, 283, 425; always-prior, 45–46, 48, 481*n*8; no absolute, 53; instant as, 135; Cartesian, 189, 307; Hegelian, 201; first, as appropriated, 254, 259, 266, 374, 420, 464*n*1; and origin, 259; as negation of being, 298, 300; in organic individual, 336; of epochal history, 363, 364; and language, 395–96; *see also* Ground

Being: as noumenal, 10; identity of thought and, 10–12, 23, 90, 219–20; as transcendental, 14–15; and time, 14–16, 26, 64, 66, 72, 87, 238, 245, 327, 356, 363, 415–17; as independent, 19, 38, 77; as natural, 20; as self-identity, 24, 338; as forgotten, 30, 168–69, 408–9; and ground, 33, 87, 283, 369–75; and meaning, 35; as oneness, 38, 50–51, 92, 156, 336; meaning as truth of, 47, 176; as presentness, 60, 64, 111–12, 119, 216, 362–63; levels of, 89, 92, 341–42; general theory of, 90, 93, 97, 209, 216, 266; as split, 93, 374, 393, 440*n*125; as dissimulated, 98, 168–71, 204–5, 359, 408–9; and nothing, 108, 127, 180, 188, 238, 363, 452n38; as finite, 113; as referential, 117, 362–63; as actuality, 172, 362; as 'what' and 'that', 173, 194, 393, 446n118; as enabling power, 181; and the 'as', 203–4, 255, 261, 342–43, 409; as appearance in place, 204, 266, 376, 422; place and manifold uses of word, 209; as coincidence of actual and possible, 211; as presence in worlded earth, 216; absolute contingency of, 292; acts inscribed in, 326, 476n106; as place and way, 405; not tangible, 460n47; priority of praxis over, 480n95

Being-for-itself: as relation, 77; as factor in synthesis, 82; nucleus of, 83–84, 171, 435n5; as flight forward, 86; as ambiguous, 135, 156; in question, 149; as actuality, 171; problem of origin of, 302–3, 312–13, 327; as historizing, 311; haunted by the One, 325, 411, 421; becomes organism, 326–29, 336, 371, 392, 477n34; as personalizing, 347–48, 352–534 grounded in prior unity, 411

Being-for-Others, 334, 353; language and, 286; as conflict, 308, 316, 320–21, 331, 339; founds Being-with, 310

Being-in itself, 66, 399; as absurd, 16; as nonrelational, 38, 76, 342; as undifferentiated plenitude, 72, 313, 328; as nontemporal, 72, 83–84, 327; excludes potentiality, 76; and meaning, 77–78, 303, 446n122; as ground, 87, 296; as readiness-to-hand, 116–17; as substance, 142; as identity, 175; as linguistic being, 176; as function of nominalism, 270; grounded in prior unity, 411; as materiality, 472n5

Being-with-Others, 100–1; Sartrean critique of, 305–10, 331, 353; as 'we', 306, 310; implies common destiny, 331; see also Community

Beings (or entities): as devoid of meaning, 112, 120, 163, 216, 411, 420; as nonreferential, 223; as praxis-beings, 421; see also Meaning-being; Phenomenon; Thing

'Between', 42–43, 190, 192, 239–40, 287, 299–300; see also Relation

Biemel, Walter, 3–4, 358, 359, 431n31, 480n95
Biology, 375
Bracketing, see Reduction
Buchler, Justus, 431n30
Buchner, Hartmut, 462n29
Bultmann, Rudolf, 222
Burkle, Howard R., 478n50

Calculation, 240, 247, 255
Camus, Albert, 322, 470n66
Care, 50, 52–53, 200, 420; and love, 182, 242, 423; as preservation of place, 229
Categories: Kantian, 8, 17, 161, 284–85, 306, 334, 470n75; projection of, 49; as historical, 112, 126–27, 144, 161, 175; of presentness and readiness, 119–20; as ideal mixings, 295, 471n84; see also Distinctions
Cause, 34–35, 91, 397, 484n12; formal, 10, 341–43, 363, 372, 393; meaning and, 35, 44, 332, 413–15; first, 57, 112–13, 372–73, 463n38; self-, 110, 148, 172, 440n129; material, 145; final, 145, 309, 316, 343, 393; psychic, 154; action as, 303–4; efficient, 338
Center, 18, 396, 427; Nietzsche on, 14, 211; Yeats on, 211; place as, 235; as juncture of the Four, 252; of illimitable relation, 252; for-itself as, 307, 309–10, 348; Heidegger vs. Sartre on, 364; organism as, 393; as introplay, 467n66
Challenging (or provoking), 251, 252
Chartier, Émile [pseud. Alain], 274
Choice: in existentialism, 54, 63; Heidegger on, 56, 62; Sartre on, 75, 77, 89, 136, 138, 151, 172, 272, 291; distinguished from will, 154–55; as absolute, 172
Circle, 11, 20; Nietzsche on, 15; Heidegger on, 36, 48–50, 216; Sartre on, 139, 149, 275, 325–26, 392; accounts for unity of ground, 162; challenges dominance of presentness, 189; not originary, 189, 192, 243, 412–13; dialectical, 326; as repetition, 347; as function of intentionality, 347
Circuit of selfness, 69, 81; breaking, 84–85, 139, 164, 275, 325; as short circuit, 93; see also Circle
Circularity, see Circle
Circumspection, 36, 59

Classification, 269, 271; *see also* Articulation; Determination; Universals

Clearing, 42, 99, 104–5, 169; and time, 36; as self-clearing, 44, 463*n*38, 464*n*1; as nothing, 114; as general and particularized, 122, 203; anticipated by Kant, 190; and Event, 218–21; and intelligibility, 221, 423

Cogito, 11, 278, 281, 336, 353; as instantaneous, 132; as certain, 157; Sartrean modification of, 159, 172; ontological and existential, 172; as true beginning, 186, 307, 367, 400; as prior to word, 285–86

Collectives, 340–43, 394, 397

Commonplace, the, 228, 473*n*36; and community of nature, 178–79, 214; as holy, 223; as snare, 355, 421; as ground, 404, 422, 425; and the familiar, 455*n*101

Communication, ground of, 50, 225

Community, 101–3, 335–36, 371–72; of inheritance, 122–23; synthetic, 196; internal, 306; subjective, 315; producing, 323; as achievement, 331; of language, 334; social field as, 339

Community of nature, 20, 91, 114–15, 178, 183, 245, 401–3; Husserl on, 20; Aristotle on, 42, 56; Dasein as, 46; and the familiar, 56, 455*n*101; threatened, 90, 160–64, 392–93; nihilism and, 114–15; ontological difference and, 120; between statement and referent, 176–77; necessary for phenomenological program, 188, 199; and circle, 188–89, 243; and *physis*, 196; between language and articulation, 199–201; aspects of, 205; as hidden ground of metaphysics, 214; between understanding and nature, 219–20; requisite for action, 303; between individuals, 315–16, 379; *see also* Identity; Union; Unity

Components, *see* Composition; Factors; Stock, standing

Composition (*Gestell*), 42, 188, 198, 207, 247–66 *passim*; as dissimulation of Fourfold, 248, 252, 254–55; *see also* Analysis; Synthesis; Totalizing

Comprehension, *see* Thinking; Understanding

Concealment, 4, 9, 61, 81, 250, 376; language and, 173–74; evil and, 181; earth and, 232; death and, 233; tangibility and, 409; *see also* Dissimulation; Forgottenness

Concept, *see* Category; Idea; Universals

Concreteness, misplaced, 402

Conditioning, 15, 17, 166–67, 241, 243, 340, 415–17

Conflict, *see* Being-for-Others

Connection, hidden, 44; *see also* Juncture

Conscience, call of, 99

Consciousness: in Husserl, 19; as negation, 29, 82, 157, 171, 374, 391; in Sartre, 67–71, 131–32, 170–73, 301, 330, 341; as Demiurge, 84; instantaneous nucleus of, 131–39, 155, 278, 448*n*50; as ekstasis, 132; as dyad, 133–34; as certain, 157; as impersonal, 158; as logical, 158, 286, 365, 371; Heidegger on, 170–71; contingent being of, 172; as cause of itself, 172; as true beginning, 286, 399; problem of efficacy of, 303

Constancy: Heidegger and Sartre on, 125

Constitution, *see* Determination; Language; Thinking

Contemporaneity, *see* Time

Context, 38, 42–43, 106, 203, 226, 284, 290, 362–63, 367, 394, 416, 431*n*28; *see also* Ground; Place; Totality; World

Contradiction: Kierkegaard on, 13; overcoming, 321–24, 326, 339

Conventionalism, 11, 126, 366, 380–83, 406, 412

Conversion: radical, 103, 107, 131, 138–39, 320, 450*n*83, 456*n*115; as valid coordination, 139; as play, 141; as willing freedom, 152; out of Composition, 252, 255; as long labor, 346; *see also* Salvation

Copernicus, 2–3, 6, 16, 24, 401

Correspondence, *see* Truth

Corruption: and authenticity, 131, 141, 144–46, 346, 351; language of, 436–37*n*31

Cosmology, 91–93, 129–30, 150, 229, 309, 329, 348, 350, 357, 393, 414, 421, 440*n*122; *see also* Metaphysics; Neoplatonism

Courage, 110, 115

Creation: of ground by idealism, 23; in projection, 122, 222; and longing, 124; and sliding, 143–44

cummings, e. e., 237

Danger, the, 223, 236, 241, 249, 250, 377

Darwin, Charles, 375

Dasein: as unity, 29, 55–56, 159; as place, 31, 45–48, 56, 97; and man, 31–32; as way, 32, 46–47; as 'there', 40–48, 229, 431*n*28, 432*n*43; as ground, 41, 99, 420, 434*n*81; as historical, 46, 101; as nullity, 56–57; and negativity, 71, 158–59; as metaphysics, 110, 130, 166, 213, 216; and consciousness, 132–33; as subject, 167; and things correlatively dissembled, 191–92; sublimated, 419; primitive, 444*n*82

Death: Heidegger on, 59–60, 100, 227–29, 233–38; Sartre on, 86, 148, 227–28, 301, 351–52, 449*n*76, 479*n*74; as continuous, 148

Decadence: Nietzsche on, 14

Deception: Heidegger and Sartre on, 98

Decision, 7, 24, 104, 106, 122, 458*n*25; metaphysical, 13, 127–28, 342, 365; moral, 129–31, 138; choice and, 154–55; as resolution of dualism, 167; and language, 199

Demiurge: consciousness as, 84; man as, 142, 145, 373

Democritus, 188

Desan, Wilfrid, 471–72*n*100

Descartes, René, 1, 3–6, 10–11, 20, 21–22, 58, 66, 77, 132–33, 143, 144, 157, 159, 171–72, 186, 189, 202, 281, 285–86, 307, 316, 322, 334, 336, 338, 351, 359, 367, 379, 391, 401–2, 417, 424, 458*n*18, 468*n*17

Destiny, *see* Directive

Determination: in Husserl, 19–20; in Sartre, 73–83, 283–88, 336, 359, 471–72*n*100; in Heidegger, 203–4, 234, 483*n*6; relational, 342, 362–63; cosmic, 348; in Spinoza, 402; *see also* Articulation; Classification; Distinctions

Devaluation, *see* Value

Dewey, John, 482*n*23

Dialectic, 13, 42, 213–14, 230–31, 239, 384–87, 477*n*29; grounded in identity, 108, 407–11; of subject, 159, 338, 482–83*n*43; frozen by poetry, 277; of union and its disruption, 279; symbolic, 316–17; real, 330–31, 335; horror of, 338, 351, 358–59

Diaspora: temporality as, 86–87, 137, 301; as negation of the actual, 212; action as,

298; as articulation, 300; as dispersion into matter, 309; as detotalized totality, 312–14, 316, 328; and scarcity, 336–37; and reintegration, 345–46, 418

Difference: hides identity, 46, 229, 245, 255, 384–85, 405; of meaning and beings, 120; ontological, threatened by dualism, 128, 167, 408–9; unmediated, 217, 221, 386; collapsed by poetry, 275; for prehistoric organism, 392; of the same, 482*n*29; *see also* Identity

Dilthey, Wilhelm, 20, 429

Directionality, *see* Space

Directive (or destiny), 100–1, 103, 122, 126–27, 180, 192, 223, 240, 252, 255, 256, 263, 375; and contemporaneity, 253; Composition as, 256

Disclosure, 39–40, 42, 46, 48, 63–64, 399, 483*n*3; by consciousness, 72–90 *passim*; and closure, 114, 121, 168, 181, 233–36, 251–52, 367, 370, 388, 421–22; and prior familiarity, 121, 370, 378–79, 404; by *poiēsis*, 251; prior to language, 287–88; grounds inquiry, 407

Discourse: and meaning, 127; and subject/object distinction, 162; and language, 173–74, 198, 223

Discovery: Galilean, 3–4; projection and, 48–49; meaning and, 121; *see also* Disclosure

Disownment, *see* Displacement; Owning up

Displacement, 3, 48, 55, 246–67 *passim*; in metaphysics, 14–16, 179, 204–5, 212–14, 235–37, 422–23; as historical direction, 223, 266; as Fourfold's self-dissimulation, 244

Disposition (or state-of-mind), 42, 255, 257

Dissimulation, 46, 60–61, 65, 117, 250–67 *passim*, 359, 376–77, 465*n*16; Being's self-, 98, 168–71; of phenomenon's meaning, 192; and language, 198–99, 267, 374; of place, 206–7, 397; of identity by difference, 220, 229, 373, 399, 405–6, 408–9; in Composition, 251–52; in first beginning, 420; of the familiar, 455*n*101; *see also* Concealment; Forgottenness; Semblance

Distance, 47, 239–40; *see also* Near, the

Distinctions: basis of human/natural, 162;

Distinctions (*Continued*)
  logico-linguistic, 173–75; dissimulated source of, 177, 230–31, 399; in poetry, 275; between word, thought, and thing, 383–89; relative constancy of, 388–89; *see also* Articulation; Categories; Determination
Divine, the (or divinities): as Fourfold-member, 222, 238–42, 265; shows itself as unknown, 239, 241; as making possible, 398; *see also* God; Gods, the; Religion; Theology
Doxa, 22
Dualism, 1–2, 8, 23–24, 53–54, 65, 277, 387–88, 417; Cartesian, 3–4, 401–2; Husserlian, 19–20, 294, 403; metaphysical resolution of, 93, 321, 324–25, 328; danger of in *SZ*, 128, 167; Sartrean, 294
Dwelling, 171, 178, 210, 238, 257, 258, 264; as unity of life and death, 233, 235

Earth: Nietzsche on, 14; Heidegger on, 47, 195–97, 265, 385, 469–70n62; Sartre on, 143–44, 275, 280–81; not a noumenon, 195; worlded, 200, 206, 216–18; heavens and, 218–19, 376; as the sensible, 224; as limitation, 388–89, 423; as making possible, 398, 465n12
Efficacy, problem of, *see* Action
Ego, 213, 243, 408; as ground, 5, 11, 22, 26, 57–58, 373, 400, 428n36; as absolute here, 18; *see also* Subject
Einstein, Albert, 93, 236
Ekstasis: in Heidegger, 45, 46, 61, 64, 86, 133, 153–54, 243, 253, 305; in Sartre, 73, 86, 152, 154; joy and pain of, 124; and instant, 131–39; of naming, 278
Eleaticism, 100, 102; and nihilism, 115–16; as condition of intelligibility, 415–16
Elements, *see* Factors
Emanation, 77, 92, 142, 145
Embodiment, 74, 179, 273–74, 281, 296, 298, 319, 326–27, 352, 367, 371, 396
Emotion, 158, 179, 277, 463n65, 471n81
Empathy, 182, 183, 351
Empiricism, 5–6, 229–30, 353, 386
Endowing, meaning-, *see* Intentionality
Entities, *see* Beings
Epochē, see Reduction
Epochs, *see* History

Equanimity, 52, 61; *see also* Stoicism
Equiprimordiality, 217, 264
Erickson, Stephen A., 198
Essence, 26, 215, 289–91; Kierkegaard on, 13; Husserl on, 18, 19, 20, 40; in existentialism, 24, 54, 99, 156, 172–73, 421, 438n68; Heidegger on, 37–40, 166, 173, 253, 451n21; nothing belongs to, 112; as metaphysical, 127–28; impossible fusion of existence and, 156; as 'me', 156; granted by love, 180–81; dissimulated, 204, 256; as aspect of an identity, 220, 232, 372, 386–88; as commonplace, 228
Eternity, *see* Time
Ethics, 236, 239, 282; Sartre on, 130–31, 310, 316–17, 390, 447n12, 477n31; ambiguity as premise of, 138, 304; and play, 141; logical ground of, 175; source of as *ēthos*, 177–79; problem for Sartrean, 302–4; as positive, 310; impossible today, 346; and regression to nucleus, 448n50
Ethos, see Abode
Event (*Ereignis*), 44, 57, 245, 364, 369; as understanding of place, 204; and clearing, 218–21; as making possible, 226–27, 397–98, 423, 462n24; as linguistic articulation, 232, 265, 268, 483n6; Composition and, 252, 257; as missed, 265, 372–73, 397; and *ēthos*, 365; and identity, 408–9; and groundless ground, 462–63n38
Evil: as matter, 145, 148; rests on anger, 180; as loss of empathy, 182–83; as hatred, 235, 423; as class-distinction, 340–41, 345–46; as seriality, 478n50; *see also* Hatred
Existence: Kierkegaard on, 13; in Husserl, 19–20; in existentialism, 24, 54, 99, 438n68; as *Existenz*, 39; as *existentia*, 72–73, 87–90, 127–28, 142, 171–73, 204, 221, 227, 412, 446n122; precedes essence, 156, 172, 411; as consciousness-of-being, 172; as dissimulated Being, 204; as aspect of an identity, 232, 372, 386–88; as negation of essence, 440n124
Existentialia, 39, 306, 462n24; and the existentiell, 50–51, 104, 106, 128, 161–62; as possibilizers, 101–2, 161, 433n76; as historical, 166
Existentialism, 24, 30, 54, 152–84 *passim*,

355; essence in, 24; and nihilism, 56; and freedom, 63, 152; and phenomenology, 93, 411; as liability of SZ, 99, 104, 112, 164; problem of authenticity in, 319–21; atheistic, 323; logic of, 335; and Marxism, 336, 349, 357, 391; and metaphysics, 421–22, 424
Experience, ordinary, 2–4, 6, 24, 363, 404; in Heidegger, 37–38, 193, 422; in Sartre, 88–90, 136, 307, 332, 356, 471n81

Factoring, see Analysis
Factors (or elements, relata), 13, 56, 264, 275, 278; interaction between, 42, 90; ideal and real as, 106; Dasein and present-at-hand as, 160; as components, 188, 257, 339, 396; original unity of, 205, 363, 409–11, 413; as preexisting their relation, 214, 373; for-itself and in-itself as, 271, 339–40; as interdicting action, 303, 324–25; see also Analysis
Faith: in Kierkegaard, 13, 484n15; in existentialism, 24, 54, 424; and ground, 26; bad, 131, 135, 137, 139, 141, 150, 274, 305, 351; good, 152; Heidegger on, 153; in later Sartre, 321, 352, 357, 475n82
Falling, 50, 55–56, 59–61, 179, 431n34, 458n18; intentionality as, 82–83, 85, 88; the unreflective as, 85; temporality essentially, 434n85
Familiar, the, 24, 48, 55–56, 300; Aristotle on, 3, 177, 380, 455n101; Nietzsche on, 16; Merleau-Ponty on, 21; priority of, 120–21, 370, 403–5; Hegel on, 177, 201, 380; two senses of, 455n101; see also Near, the
Fate: in Nietzsche, 13–16, 181; in Heidegger, 61–62, 101, 220, 235, 251, 377; in Sartre, 184, 301, 354, 480n81
Favor, see Gift
Fetishism, 333
Fichte, Johann Gottlieb, 9, 20, 408, 422
Field, 43, 48, 49, 64, 206, 214, 216, 337, 477n25; see also Clearing; Place; Totality
Finality, see Teleology
Finitude, 13, 14, 58, 113, 194–95, 241, 370, 371, 376, 381; and transcendence, 213, 228; see also Death; Limit; Mortality; Transcendence
Flaubert, Gustave, 345, 351, 358, 470n66, 471n82

Forgottenness, 42; of identity, 46–48, 220, 386; in SZ, 56, 98, 166; as necessary, 58–61, 111, 126; in nihilism, 115, 193; in metaphysics, 168–69, 181, 202–14, 364, 376–77; and making-present, 202; types of, 205; of plàce, 268, 377; and tangibility, 452n43; see also Concealment; Displacement
Form, 18, 19, 363, 374, 414–15; ego as origin of, 26; Sartre on, 77, 288–92, 303, 341–43, 371, 394, 397, 472n5; Heidegger on, 247–48, 483n53; Platonic, 372–73; and intentionality, 477–78n41
Foundation: Descartes on, 4–5, 159; ego as, 5; Husserl on, 22–23, 376; Heidegger on, 33, 98, 126; Sartre on, 172; see also Beginning; Ground; Origin
Fourfold, 206, 221–43, 244–67 passim, 366, 376; circle and, 189; Hölderlin and, 208, 460n65; as community of nature, 232, 245; Composition as self-dissimulation of, 252; originary play of, 253; activity of mortals in, 254, 359, 388, 419; protecting of, 255, 258; as ground, 260, 430n17, 462–63n38; as making possible, 397–98
Frazer, James G., 375
Freedom, Heidegger on, 56, 62, 100–1, 109; Sartre on, 69, 77, 272, 298–99, 371; for the ground, 109; as play, 141; as end, 141, 148–51, 152–53, 304, 317, 331, 353, 450n86; as ground of values, 152, 317; practical, 331, 390–94; society of, 346, 374
Freud, Sigmund, 14, 375
Functionalism, 341, 342, 363
Future: primacy of, 86, 154, 322; past comes on as, 183, 226–27, 237, 254, 331; human, 300; as locus of unity, 354; requisite for comprehension, 356–57; richer in contingencies, 380; see also Time

Galileo, 2–4, 7, 21
Gathering, 202, 232, 245, 396–97; as forming of juncture, 198, 204; of universal and particular, 386; see also Assembling; Event
Gelven, Michael, 433n76
Genet, Jean, 323, 345, 351, 470n66
George, Stefan, 406

Gift: *noema* as, 22–23; of intelligibility, 194, 218, 226, 381, 396, 407, 423; fragility of, 238; as precondition, 377; and religion, 456n129

God, 9–10, 26, 178, 282, 310, 473n36; as nonfinite standpoint, 7, 156, 195, 213, 218, 309; death of, 15, 207; ground as, 20, 57, 316, 365, 373, 374, 402, 409; nothing and, 109; as *ens causa sui*, 110; Being of, 114, 153; project of being, 142, 241, 371; as ultimate Third, 314

Gödel, Kurt, 236

Gods, the, 373; as present, 194, 223, 239, 253, 376; and world, 255, 388; and word, 397–98

Goethe, Johann Wolfgang von, 224

Good, the: and love of place, 235, 242; as class distinction, 340–41, 345–46; as original, 423; in later Sartre, 478n50

Grace, 180–81, 183, 255, 283

Granel, Gérard, 430n17

Ground, 11, 242, 283; Descartes on, 4–5; ego as, 5, 18, 22, 26; absent, 12, 163, 193; Nietzsche on, 14; Husserl on, 18, 20–23, 33; phenomenon's, 27, 38, 67, 109, 294; Being and, 33, 169, 482n29; place as, 42, 178, 226–27, 242, 366; common, 42–43, 56, 178, 179, 403; groundless or null, 44, 57–63, 99, 115, 259, 260, 261, 372, 404, 420; laying of, 58–59; freedom and, 62–63, 109, 374; actuality as, 78, 87–90, 293–94, 296; unity of thought and existence as, 106, 372 74, 387–90; finite, 113, 370; as earth, 196–97; extralinguistic, 200; Fourfold as, 260, 369, 388, 430n17; of inquiry, 336; sovereignty has no, 353; praxis and matter as, 369, 374, 390–94; as familiar, 370, 404; in Plato and Aristotle, 372–73; split and reunified, 374–75; of in-itself and for-itself, 411; subject as, 441n1; *see also* Cause; Foundation; Reason

Guilt, 60

Hana, Ghanem-Georges, 435n5

Harmony, 248, 372, 385–86; as restraint, 386; and heavens, 396–97

Hartmann, Klaus, 80, 438n68, 440n120

Hatred: of time, 16; as true evil, 235; of man, 358; as instantaneous, 448n50

Heavens, the, 14, 376; and world, 218, 388; and the imperceptible, 224; and measurement, 229; as making possible, 230, 398; as Fourfold-member, 238–41, 265, 396–97; Sartre on, 275

Hebel, Johann Peter, 224, 232, 243, 406

Heftrich, Eckhard, 454n71

Hegel, Georg Wilhelm Friedrich, 2, 9–14, 15, 23, 24, 27, 34, 42, 54, 70–71, 80, 105, 116, 156, 158, 160, 161, 170, 177, 186, 190, 193, 201–2, 230, 234, 235–36, 243, 254, 276, 306, 308, 312–13, 316, 322, 334, 335, 336, 351, 354, 357, 359, 370–71, 379–80, 385, 386, 390, 405, 408, 416, 417–18, 422, 452n38, 459n44, 478n50, 482n29

Heidegger, Fritz, 443n42

Heidegger, Martin: and existentialism, 29, 54, 99, 104, 111–12, 152–84 *passim*, 358; intention of in *SZ*, 30, 63, 65, 97–98, 164, 167, 174, 199, 216, 294, 432n42; and the turn, 30, 44, 65, 95, 97–98, 125–28, 164–70, 194, 200–4, 208, 220, 241, 375, 434n93, 441n8, 446n116, 457, 458n24; and phenomenology, 33, 38, 65, 183, 223, 228, 243, 263, 393, 430n17, 456n127, 459n43; centrality of forgetting and remembering for, 59, 98, 221; and metaphysics, 93, 97–98; self-critique of *SZ*, 97–98, 160, 182–83, 189, 229, 362, 393, 420, 458n18, 459n26; and Sartre on deception, 98; and National Socialism, 103, 126, 441–42n8, 456–57n132, 474n66; critique of Sartre, 106, 165–84, 205–6, 390, 431n28, 469n55; and nihilism, 112, 125–26, 199; and Sartre on constancy, 125; rejects *cogito*, 132; and theology, 153, 222–23, 226, 358, 450nn5–6, 456n129, 480n96; visited by Sartre, 165; epistemological status of thinking of, 169, 369–400 *passim;* and mysticism, 210, 241; as seer, 227, 233, 234, 237, 266; extent of ontological agreement with Sartre, 362–63, 394; extent of disagreement with Sartre, 364–68, 418–19, 420–22; critique of Hegel, 459n44; and Sartre on beauty, 463–64n66

Heisenberg, Werner, 236

Heraclitus, 22, 178, 194, 196, 206, 244, 252, 373, 385, 415, 459n28, 460n47

'Here': absolute, 18, 285; 'there' and, 42, 46–47, 60–61, 65

Heroism, 103, 106, 114–15, 433n60

Hiddenness, see Concealment

Historicality, see Dasein

Historicism, 125

History, 24, 111, 147–48; decisions in, 7, 126–28; Nietzsche on, 14–16; 'man' in, 32, 190–91; temporality and, 46, 353; metaphysics and, 91, 124, 150–51, 166–67, 205–14, 330; anxiety and, 99, 123–24, 301; the ahistoric and, 100, 115–16, 124, 166, 331, 335; repetition and, 103, 125, 327, 390; nature and, 111–12, 119; philosophy of, 151, 168–69, 201, 247, 330; as actualization of potentialities, 161; of Being, 168–69, 363; epochal, 168–69, 174, 193, 205, 207, 241, 268, 400; Marxian view of, 170, 320; dissimulation in, 202–5, 262–63, 408–9; displacement in, 206, 223; origin of, 211, 327–28, 336–37, 392–93; as direction, 246; consciousness as motor of, 279, 391; as region of alienation, 316, 319–20, 327–29, 417–19; as retotalization, 329; another, 353; single truth of, 357, 391; Heidegger vs. Sartre on, 364–65

Hobbes, Thomas, 6

Hölderlin, Friedrich, 208–12, 225, 227, 239–40, 406, 460n65, 461n84, 465n12, 480n96

Holy, the: and love, 180; and the common-place, 223, 404; as time-play-space, 226–27; and death, 237–38; as intelligible world, 388, 398

Homecoming, 124, 171, 209–10, 212

Horizon, 13, 50, 203

Huch, Kurt Jürgen, 445n85

Humanism, 30, 63, 152–84 passim, 212, 240–41, 281, 299, 359, 382, 393; religion of, 141–42, 147, 179; attributed to Heidegger, 153–56, 164, 315; not fundamental, 162, 397; begins with Plato, 165; Marx's, 170; abstract, 318; Heidegger vs. Sartre on, 364, 418–19

Hume, David, 5, 7, 417

Husserl, Edmund, 3–4, 7–8, 9, 17–23, 26, 33, 35, 36, 38, 40, 53, 75, 82, 88–89, 93, 107, 118, 129, 132–33, 134, 146–47, 157, 170, 171, 186, 243, 285, 294, 361, 363, 376, 377, 387, 403, 415, 420, 424, 428n36, 457

Idea: as transcendental, 36; as aspect of an identity, 220; synthetically related to word, 288; and 'this', 288–89; as ideal distinction, 296; separable only in statement, 379; falsity of present, 390; in Fourfold, 396; see also Thinking; Universals

Idealism, 67, 70, 80–81, 104–6, 116, 162, 349, 387, 401–2; of meaning based on realism of existence, 73, 193–94, 200; linguistic, 144, 199, 270, 406, 459n37, 481n13; imputed to Heidegger, 306, 358; imputed to Sartre, 318, 334; religious, 323

Idealism, German, 8–9, 43, 245; Husserl's, 18–19, 24, 88; power of ego in, 23; Leibniz's, 91; true greatness of, 243, 372; dialectic in, 407–8; Heidegger on, 408, 459–60n44, 464n2; see also Hegel

Ideality: in Kant, 8; in Hegel, 10; in Husserl, 18, 20; in Sartre, 73, 76, 90, 92–93, 295, 337, 375, 421, 463–64n66; of relations, 105; in Heidegger, 128, 396, 414; in Pascal, 237

Identification, see Articulation; Determination

Identity: of being and thought, 10–12, 23, 54, 219–21, 243, 373, 408–11, 464n68, 464n2; and difference, 27, 46, 162, 217, 229–31, 372, 383–89, 399; in Kierkegaard, 54; and plenitude, 76; as stasis, 87; of thing and name, 225, 267; and change as synthesis, 327, 366; of truth and ground, 369–75; created by praxis, 393; role of language in, 395–96; requires difference, 406; and contemporaneity, 416; in first beginning, 420; see also Difference; Union; Unity

Ideology, 375, 405; existentialism as, 335, 357

Idols, 114, 126, 242

Illimitable (in-finite), the, 233, 245, 252, 264, 464n4, 467n70

Illumination, see Lighting

Imagination, 142, 373, 378; as negation, 68–69; in perception, 81, 363; in history, 126–27, 161, 229–30; and categories,

Imagination (*Continued*)
    161, 175; bound to logic, 359; power and
    limitation of, 388–89, 396, 445*n*105,
    462*n*24; as overreaching, 416; and
    beauty, 464*n*66
Immediacy (the unmediated), 34, 38, 89,
    254
Immortal, the, 227, 229
Individualism: in Sartre, 305–6, 320, 334,
    345–46, 390; and original dialectic, 338
Inert, the, 326
Infinite, the, *see* Illimitable, the
Inheritance, 102–3, 146, 311, 363; owning
    up to, 116, 126; modification of, 122–23,
    335, 348–49, 416
Instant, the, 131–39; as nucleus, 83, 86–87,
    135; and radical conversion, 103, 131,
    135–39; as refused, 133, 139, 155, 159,
    212, 448*n*50; as opening, 134; as
    modification of project, 135, 155
Instrumentality: and the primitive,
    111–12; Being of, 116–19; of language,
    224, 275–76; of man, 326, 328–29, 339;
    and problem of action, 330, 341–43; and
    the noninstrumental, 399, *see also* Ar-
    tifactual, the
Intelligibility, 43, 44, 47–49, 88, 329, 367,
    370–73, 379–80; problem of, 26–27; pro-
    jection and, 49–50, 356–57; freedom
    and, 62–63; metaphysics and, 92, 195,
    312–13; ontological difference and,
    120–21; and anxiety, 193; and language,
    197–200, 225–26, 381; and Event,
    218–21, 233, 404; and praxis, 337–47; of
    assertions, 378–79; and formal cause,
    414; battle for, 415–16, 476*n*117
Intentionality, 343, 363, 414; in Husserl,
    19, 22–23, 412; in Heidegger, 37, 48, 243,
    412–13; in Sartre, 75, 81–83, 88, 142, 152,
    293, 307, 325, 333, 337, 339, 357, 393,
    411, 477–78*n*41; as exteriorization, 347;
    in spiral, 348; in Merleau-Ponty, 411;
    and metaphysics, 420
Interaction, *see* Introplay; Relation
Interiority/exteriority, 313, 328, 336–37,
    393, 478*n*59; in spiral, 348–53; united,
    374–75
Interpretation: projection and, 36, 49–50;
    naming and, 264, 275; equivalence of,
    291; monism of, 479*n*73
Introplay, 48, 131; of ekstases, 53, 64, 161,

    163, 253; of matter and thought, 225,
    372, 414; as mirror-play, 232, 254; of
    Fourfold-members, 253, 397; limits
    factor-analysis, 264; *see also* Relation,
    internal
Intuition: Descartes on, 4–5; Kant on, 6;
    Husserl on, 17–18, 23, 36, 40; Heidegger
    on, 36–37, 40–41, 430*n*15, 431*n*24; Sartre
    on, 157, 292–93, 296, 341, 367, 471*n*98;
    see also Seeing
Inversion, Nietzsche on, 14–16
Involvement: of ready-to-hand, 111; am-
    biguity and, 318–19; *see also* Action;
    Return

James, William, 11, 72
Jaspers, Karl 445*n*87
Jeanson, Francis, 302, 318–22, 448*n*29, 457
Joining: meaning and beings, 128; past
    and future, 136; *see also* Juncture;
    Synthesis
Joy, 61–62, 124
Juncture: dissembled, 198, 252, 420; as
    prior unity, 214, 225, 407; in Heraclitus,
    459*n*28; illimitable relation as, 464*n*4;
    see also Articulation; Identity; Unity

Kant, Immanuel, 6–9, 17, 22, 35, 58, 70, 91,
    100, 106, 114, 126, 161, 175, 190–93, 195,
    206, 213–14, 277, 283, 284–85, 306, 321,
    334, 335, 336, 353, 358, 363–64, 377, 387,
    408, 417, 433*n*76
Kehre, see Heidegger, and the turn
Kierkegaard, Sóren, 2, 12–13, 24, 54,
    104–5, 130, 193, 306, 309, 319, 321,
    481*n*10, 484*n*15
Knowledge: and metaphysics, 5–6; condi-
    tions for, 7, 19, 36, 242; and certainty,
    157, 207; and idea, 296; and ontology,
    365; and relativity, 376; and the uncon-
    ditioned, 417, 484*n*15; and language,
    480*n*87; and dialectic, 483*n*43; *see also*
    Disclosure; Intelligibility; Intuition;
    Thinking; Understanding
Köhler, Wolfgang, 477*n*41
Kreutzer, Conradin, 465

Language, 127, 480*n*87; metaphysical, 97,
    165, 220; as arrival of Being, 173; and
    discourse, 197–98; and nihilism,
    199–200; of Being, 220; as relation of

perceptible and imperceptible, 224–25, 231; dissimulates unity, 231, 242–43, 406; as saying/evoking/utterance, 232–33, 257, 262; of death and love, 243; as relation of all relations, 255, 257; Sartrean conception of, 269–301 *passim*, 355, 470*n*66, 471*n*82; as a community, 334, 459*n*40; and utterance of Being, 365; Heidegger vs. Sartre on, 365–66; and perception, 372, 387, 395; and identity, 373–74, 387, 395–96; inheres in phenomenon, 378; as distorting, 406, 481*n*13

Lebensphilosophie, 20–22, 196, 235, 363, 368

Leibniz, Gottfried Wilhelm, 23, 91, 107, 344, 430*n*11

Legislation (by thought), 8, 17, 20; *see also* Idealism; Idealism, German

Leucippus, 312, 439*n*120

Level, problem of, *see* Reality, problem of level for defining

Life-world (*Lebenswelt*), *see* World

Lighting: and clearing, 44, 53; and darkness, 74, 233–34, 242, 398, 423; groundless, 373; and heavens, 376; and word, 483*n*3

Limit: death as, 59–60, 207, 233–35, 237–38, 351–52; freedom and, 62–63, 353; actuality as, 89; empowers, 238; and humanism, 240–41, 281, 299; of place, 264; God as, 314; Earth as, 388–89; defined, 467*n*70; *see also* Illimitable, the; Measure

Location, simple, 35, 40, 43, 102, 402, 431*n*28

Locke, John, 6, 24, 334

Logic: of consciousness, 158, 365; rule of challenged, 159, 207, 220, 384–85; and imagination, 161; and language, 173–75, 285–86; rejection of Hegelian, 313; revision of traditional, 321, 335, 408, 452*n*35, 452*n*38; of praxis, 330–31, 344, 367, 392–93; limit and warrant of, 389; *see also* Analysis; Dialectic; Negation; Synthesis

Logos: in Husserl, 19; and language, 174–76, 265, 282, 299, 366; and Composition, 247; and logic, 389, 398

Love: in Nietzsche, 16, 281, 424; Stoicism and, 144–45, 183; and the holy, 180; and care, 182, 242, 278; as ekstasis, 183; as *amor fati*, 183; of place, 235–36, 423; ideal unity of, 236–37; intentionality and, 270; *see also* Amor fati

Löwith, Karl, 112, 453*n*59

Lucidity, 87, 89, 131, 139, 140, 150, 298, 304, 450*n*86; as play, 141–42, 145; grounded in logic, 174; and individualism, 305; as inefficacious, 325

Lukács, Georg, 474*n*66

Macquarrie, John, 39, 42, 50, 433*n*76

Magic, 78, 148, 158, 175–76, 297, 300; emotion as, 179; poetry as, 274–75

Magnus, Bernd, 429

Mahler, Gustav, 465*n*12

Man: relational Being of, 29–30; as 'human reality', 31, 155; situated, 43–44; as ass, 85, 212; as absolute, 184, 353, 399; as epochally defined, 190–91, 458*n*14, 461*n*72; as shepherd of Being, 261; as 'anyone', 314–15, 352; as madman, 323

Manichaeanism, 345

Marcel, Gabriel, 152

Marx, Karl, 170, 183, 193, 320–24, 345, 346, 351, 354, 370, 375, 391, 480*n*95, 484*n*16

Marx, Werner, 427*n*12, 458*n*25, 464*n*6

Marxism, 320, 343, 355, 365; view of history in, 170; existentialism conserved in, 336, 357; praised by Heidegger, 358

Mastery: Descartes on, 5; Heidegger on, 52–53, 60–62, 241; Sartre on, 143–46, 349, 468*n*17; *see also* Power; Will

Materialism, 349, 392, 402, 469*n*48, 480*n*95

Matter, 8, 11, 19–20, 23, 26, 230, 262, 304; Sartre on, 78, 143, 339, 476*n*106; as evil, 148; synthesis of immaterial and, 312, 349; efficacious labor on, 326–30, 367; as scarce, 328, 336–37; as objective ground, 369, 374; and thought as identity, 372, 387; praxis defines meaning of, 392; as Earth, 396, 483*n*53; simple location of, 402; *see also* Receptacle

Meaning, 24, 43, 56, 277; Nietzsche on, 14–17; Merleau-Ponty on, 21; Husserl on, 22, 412; problem of, 26; constitution and, 34, 77–78, 113–14; ground and, 61, 97, 151, 163, 294; negation and, 73, 392; existence and, 77–79, 127–28, 163;

Meaning (*Continued*)
  metaphysics and, 92–93, 113–14,
    166–67, 303, 342; of beings, 97, 111–12,
    216, 262–63, 411–13; variability of, 104,
    125–28, 203, 271; and discourse, 127,
    197–201; comes from myself, 138,
    445*n*85, 446*n*122; as symbolic, 145, 271;
    source and receptacle of, 167; as truth of
    Being, 176; the meaningless as, 182,
    262–63; and the 'as', 203–4, 261–63,
    342–43, 409; as placement, 205, 266; lit-
    eral and figurative, 219, 231; and word,
    224–25; as chosen, 273; as end, 273,
    470*n*66; as external to 'this', 290; en-
    graved into Being, 327, 339, 476*n*106;
    and value, 448*n*44; as transcendence fal-
    len into immanence, 468*n*37
Meaning-being, 35, 41, 43–44, 64, 97, 151,
    263, 277, 363; as linguistic, 137, 199–200;
    as identity of the different, 220; as so-
    cial, 272; as object of action, 342; as rela-
    tive absolute, 415; *see also* Phenomenon
Measure/measurement, 46–47, 235, 382,
    389, 404; subject and object as, 213–14;
    heavens as, 229, 239–40; earth as,
    231–32, 240; death as, 238; divinities as,
    239–42; actual and nothingness as, 324;
    and bounds of Fourfold, 463*n*38; *see also*
    Limit
Mediation, 71, 325–27, 331, 370–72,
    374–75, 386, 392, 482*n*29; *see also* Dialec-
    tic; Synthesis
Merleau-Ponty, Maurice, 21, 75, 184,
    236–37, 335, 339, 411, 457*n*133, 472–73*n*5
Metaphor, 197, 219
Metaphysics: Kant on, 6, 13; Kierkegaard
    on, 13; Nietzsche on, 14–16; question
    of, 25–26, 243; meaning and, 57; as will
    to ground, 57–59, 110, 317, 419–22;
    Sartre's phenomenology and, 90–93,
    276, 302–4, 312–13, 321, 330, 336, 352;
    anxiety and, 107; necessity of, 126; as
    quest for beauty, 156, 237; begins with
    Plato, 165; distinguished from ontol-
    ogy, 166; as *Dasein* itself, 166, 213, 216,
    393; as ancient ontology, 169; as rage,
    181; as displacement, 204–5, 207,
    235–37; as quest for place, 212; may per-
    sist, 214, 424; explains Being through a
    being, 249, 266, 408–9; of action, 276;
    becomes historical, 330; Heidegger vs.

Sartre on, 365, 400, 405; and missed
    Event, 372–73, 408–9; grounded in the
    familiar, 380, 422
Method: Cartesian, 4–5, 189; Husserlian,
    18, 19; rule of, 257, 419–20; Sartrean,
    334–35; progressive-regressive, 337–38;
    Heideggerian, 480*n*95
Midworld, 78, 339, 341
Miller, John William, 442*n*14
Mind, 224, 230; two views of, 137; hesi-
    tates between monism and dualism,
    277; as metaphysical totality, 312–13,
    316; non-interfering, 402
Moment of vision, 52, 61–62, 101, 103, 125,
    131, 266
Monism, 3, 214, 277, 402; of phenomenon,
    129; as antirevolutionary, 279; of in-
    terpretation, 479*n*73
Mood: as disclosive, 42; equanimity as,
    52; anxiety as privileged, 56; *see also*
    Affectivity; Disposition
Moral, the: phenomenological ontology
    and, 27; existential psychoanalysis and,
    89–90, 137–38, 271, 318–20; play and,
    141, 297, 346; *see also* Ethics
Mortality: Nietzsche on, 16; and earth,
    218–19, 423; as condition of truth, 266;
    and knowledge, 417; *see also* Death;
    Mortals, the
Mortals, the, 194, 219; as Fourfold-
    member, 206–7, 222, 229, 237–38, 265,
    359, 419; as plants, 224, 232; as essence
    of man, 254; as dissimulated, 256; and
    finite transcendence, 388, 396–97; as
    making possible, 397; as poets, 461*n*72
Motion (or movement), 123–24, 144, 244,
    246
Motivation, 123–24, 149
Mozart, Wolfgang Amadeus, 465*n*12
Murdoch, Iris, 1–2, 6, 277, 364, 401, 408,
    427
Music, 464*n*66, 465*n*12
Mystery, *see* Secret
Mysticism, 165, 180, 210, 211, 241, 297,
    404, 406

Names, 219, 264–65; things divorced
    from, 144, 199, 270–71; as aspects of
    identities, 220; as junctures, 225, 387; as
    inessential, 276; as instruments, 297;
    and disclosure, 370; as uniting units,

395, 405; *see also* Language;
Nominalism; Word

Nature: being of, 3–5, 19–20, 26–27,
118–19; meaning and, 43, 112, 219–20,
413–15, 461–62n10; situated, 44; escaped, 144, 179; as *physis*, 194; as
displaced *physis*, 207; phenomenology
of, 277, 437n53; without foreign addition, 480n95

Naville, Pierre, 318, 320, 333

Near, the, 16, 46, 202, 212, 228, 237, 257,
373, 403

Negation: in Sartre, 68–73, 82, 90, 184,
212, 229, 297, 327, 336–37, 344, 390–93,
398–99; and ground, 71, 183–84, 365,
374; ideality of, 73, 76, 90; as external
relation, 76–77, 313, 319; and consciousness, 157–59, 371; dependent on
nothing, 158–59, 234; Spirit and, 170;
and closure, 181; as freedom from fate,
184; determination as, 234, 288, 402–3;
suppressed by Heidegger, 297, 305,
358; internal, 308, 313, 348; of negation,
327, 331; unity prior to, 410

Negatités, 72

Neoplatonism, 91–92, 309, 336, 346, 348,
439n119

Newton, Isaac, 230

Nietzsche, Friedrich, 12, 13–17, 24, 38, 62,
115, 130, 146, 149, 170, 179, 181, 186,
211, 235, 260, 280–81, 298, 355, 358, 375,
377, 380–82, 385, 424, 456n116, 465n12,
469n55, 481n15

Nihil, see Nothing

Nihilation: in Sartre, 69, 73, 90, 136, 286;
in Heidegger, 108, 112, 180

Nihilism, 56, 104, 355–56, 380–81, 386,
415, 484n15; Nietzsche on, 14–16, 385;
as historical, 16, 115, 168, 193, 423;
heroic, 111, 114–15; *SZ* and, 112,
125–28, 199–200, 209–10, 446n122; *EN*
and, 151; and dissimulated place,
179–80, 207, 238, 422–23; revenge in,
181–82; result of rage for ground, 195,
377; and language in *SZ*, 199; as appearance in space, 204; and Platonism, 231,
417; *WM* and, 446n112

Noema, 23, 46, 134

Nominalism, 176, 199–200, 206, 231,
269–70, 288, 318, 323, 406, 445n85,
467n1, 470n66

Nothing (or nothingness): Nietzsche on,
15; Leibniz on, 23; problem of, 26;
Heidegger on, 52, 58, 99, 106–15,
158–59, 168; Sartre on, 72, 73, 86,
134–36, 155, 300, 313; and anxiety,
107–8, 173–74, 216; in Being of beings,
112, 237–38, 356, 363, 452n38; grounds
negation, 158–59; as veil of Being, 168;
and the 'as', 203–4; place dissimulated
as, 207, 268; infects Being, 211; death as
shrine of, 233–34, 237–38; shatters totality, 312

Noumenon, 10, 17, 70, 190–94, 195, 213

Novelty, 49, 208–9, 227, 237

Nucleus, *see* Instant

Object: possibility of, 43; as present entity, 105; oneness of subject and, 162; as
privative mode of thing, 243, *see also*
Beings; Present-at-hand, the

Objectivity, 79, 242–43; choice and, 75,
291, *see also* Knowledge

Obvious, the, 46, 228, 237, 332

Oneness, *see* Diaspora; Identity; Neoplatonism; Origin; Monism; Unity

Ontic, the, 7, 10, 13, 22, 44, 97, 161–62,
162–63, 188; passage from ontological
to, 106, 128; metaphysical preoccupation with, 169; generalization from, 306

Ontology: problems of modern, 1–2,
23–30; phenomenological, 10, 16, 27, 29,
67, 91, 117, 130, 302, 316, 317, 329–30,
364, 401–25; Nietzsche on, 14–17; Husserl on, 19, 21, 430n18; regional, 21; ancient, 33, 40, 44, 50, 53, 60, 98, 127–28,
166; fundamental, 33, 98; and
metaphysics, 113–14, 243, 425, 481n3;
as description, 130; of actuality, 151,
235, 334, 400; of praxis, 338–47, 391–400;
see also Being; Phenomenology

Opening: the instant as, 134; of/to Being,
181, 184, 233, 358; and language, 224;
and imagination, 230; *see also* Clearing

Ordinary, the, *see* Experience, ordinary;
Familiar, the

Organism, *see* Being-for-itself

Orienting, 36, 48, 137; *see also* Center;
Context; Measure

Origin, 14, 19, 363; Husserl on, 22;
Heidegger on, 39–40, 42, 44, 109, 125,
171, 209, 259; disclosedness as, 42; as

Origin (*Continued*)
  belonging together of the distinct, 205,
  206; and the remaining, 211, 251–53,
  480n96; as Event, 218, 221; and beginning, 259; Sartre on, 286; and the familiar, 455n101; *see also* Beginning;
  Ground

Ott, Heinrich, 112, 222

Owning up, 39, 50–51, 61, 103, 122, 126,
  178, 260; in Nietzsche, 15; in Marx and
  Heidegger, 170; to common place, 178;
  as remembering of place, 226, 423; and
  disowning, 237–38, 241–42, 254; in
  Sartre, 301; Heidegger's thinking as,
  377; *see also* Authenticity; Remembering

Parain, Brice, 274, 280–88, 296–301, 310,
  421, 470n66

Parmenides, 3, 8–9, 92, 206, 230, 234, 244,
  277, 301, 312, 372–73, 406, 411, 420,
  440n120, 478n50

Pascal, Blaise, 236–37

Passion: of humanizing world, 89, 131;
  man as unavailing, 110; love as, 182;
  metaphysics as vain, 205; spirit as,
  312–13

Past, the: as essential future, 48, 62–63,
  183, 254; in existentialism, 54; as death,
  86, 301; as common, 101–3; as surpassed, 301, 322; remembering of, 419;
  as enlarged plenitude, 438–39n90

Perception: Sartre on, 74, 79, 175–76, 179,
  293; and prior intelligibility, 205; and
  sensible Earth, 224–25; Heidegger on,
  224–25, 228–32, 483n51; and naming,
  282, 370, 372, 387, 395–96; imagination
  inheres in, 363

Perelman, Chaim, 439n119

Permanence, 179, 244, 416–17; of form, 26;
  of existentialia, 166; as synthetic, 284;
  amid alteration, 351; relative, 388–89

Perspective, 60, 296–97, 417

Petrarch, 230

Petrović, Gajo, 480n95

Phenomenology: and Kant, 6; in Hegel,
  10, 201–2, 380; Husserl's, 17–23, 25, 26;
  as movement or program, 29, 33, 38, 47,
  57–58, 80, 93, 127–28, 160, 188, 193, 195,
  201, 223, 236, 243, 389, 424–25; and
  metaphysics, 91, 93, 117, 302–4, 316–17,

330, 424–25; and existentialism, 93, 411;
  as synthesis or union, 151, 160, 163; and
  anxiety, 160–64, 392–93; of nature,
  196–97, 277–78; as remarriage of meaning and perception, 205; as statement of
  the obvious, 228; reconciling ontology
  and, 302, 411; reconciling action and,
  320–21, 330; and temporality, 394;
  transcendental, 410; and history,
  459n43; *see also* Heidegger, and
  phenomenology; Sartre, and
  phenomenology

Phenomenon, 26–27, 65, 231–32, 363,
  382–83, 425; as real, 7–8, 17, 76; as union
  of idea and matter, 8–10, 26, 225,
  387–90; as identity, 10–11; as disclosure
  of Being, 26–27, 399; as split, 37, 47, 54,
  393; as hidden, 61; as synthesis, 73,
  92–93, 188; and actuality, 79–81, 88, 91,
  195, 440–41n129; as world, 93; and
  nothing, 108; as present-at-hand, 111,
  118–19; as ready-to-hand, 116–19; dual
  Being of, 119–22; monism of, 129; substance as being of, 142; as plaything,
  147; presupposed and forgotten by science, 191, 402–3, 413–15; dissimulated
  as devoid of meaning, 192, 231; and
  language, 199–200, 225, 395–96, 405–7;
  as 'thing', 206, 225; roles of earth and
  heavens in, 231–32; as ground of
  analysis, 232; as precedent community,
  242; as object of action, 342, 394, 399; as
  ultimate referent of thought, 378, 389;
  as truth, 399, 404; as incomplete, 405,
  421–22; dissimulates its relations, 406;
  as locus of meaning, 412–13; and value,
  423; primitive, 444n82; *see also*
  Meaning-being; Thing

Philosophy, 469n55, 477n15; dialectical,
  42; Hellenistic, 146; rule of logic in,
  159; topology of fields of, 177–78, 365;
  early Greek, 194, 259, 276; as wisdom,
  228, 266; as praxis, 334; and ideology,
  335, 375; as title disavowed, 375; relative autonomy of, 378; role of God in,
  417

Physical, the, *see* Matter; Present-at-
  hand, the

Physics, 3–5, 93, 113, 178, 207, 223, 236,
  413

Physis: ground and, 178; separation of

meaning and, 179–80; as source, 194, 422; as strife of earth and world, 196; becomes nature, 207

Pindar, 430n19

Place: in Nietzsche, 14–16; in Heidegger, 31, 38–39, 42, 46–48, 55–56, 59, 63–64, 109, 204, 265, 460n54; as time-space, 113, 207; as playspace, 126, 224, 254; as common, 178, 209, 214, 223, 404; remembering of, 183, 207–8; Being as appearing in, 204, 225–27, 376; dissimulated, 207, 212, 265, 366; of all places, 214, 396–97; of truth, 215; clearing and, 218–21; synthetic, 283; affirmation of, 377; as measure, 382; as holy, 398; as gift, 407; as making possible, 423; *see also* Abode; Reality; Space; Time

Plato, 14, 92, 165, 177, 178, 215, 230, 231, 362, 372–73, 387, 406, 417, 457, 470n66

Play: in Sartre, 139–46, 304, 325, 341, 346; strips real of its reality, 141; versus love, 145; linguistic, 225; Fourfold as, 232, 254–55; as appropriative, 450n81

Plenitude, 72, 76, 77, 85, 89, 92, 328; as nucleus of being, 313

Plotinus, 91, 145, 230, 309, 312, 336, 346, 417, 439n119

Poetic, the, 223, 224–25, 245–46, 251, 297, 406–7, 481n13; as magical synthesis, 274–75; as the Mortal, 461n72

Pöggeler, Otto, 430n17, 441n8, 458n22, 460n65

Poiesis, 225, 247, 251, 256, 407

Politics: Nazi, 103, 126, 474n66; and perspective of action, 296; totalitarian, 297–99, 309–10; pluralistic, 310; foundation of, 310, 448n50; bourgeois, 315, 322, 323, 333–34, 338, 352, 355, 390, 478n59; liberal, 318; as context of ethics, 346, 365; in Heidegger and Sartre, 418–19; *see also* Individualism

Ponge, Francis, 277–80, 297

Possibility: phenomenology and, 33; *Dasein* as, 39–41, 59–60, 99–100; Place as, 63–64, 263–64, 397–99, 423; existentialia and, 101–2; nothing and, 108, 112; recurrence of, 123–24; essence as, 173, 446n118; Being as quiet force of, 181, 226; imagination of, 229–30; death as, 237; inheres in reality, 363; *see also* Existentialia; Event; Power

Potentiality: as magical, 76; constitutes world, 77–78; and actuality, 80, 290; unlimited, 241

Power: and powerlessness, 9, 51–53, 60–63, 78, 99–101, 124, 328–29, 366, 397–98, 443–44n55; will to, 16; ego's, 23; and freedom, 62–63, 100–1; and nihilism, 111; as possibility, 123–24, 181; human and divine, 124, 142, 242, 388, 417, 473n36; Being as, 181; of unification, 278; *see also* Mastery; Possibility; Will

Prae and *post*, *see* Whence and whither

Praxis, *see* Action

Precedent, the, *see* Community of nature; Prior, the

Presence, 36–37, 44, 51, 87, 220–21; as criterion of Being, 60, 64, 109, 111, 202, 216, 363; and readiness, 105, 119, 399; without involvement, 111–12, 163, 216, 223, 294; of consciousness, 172; of phenomena, 218; absent, 228–29, 234, 238–39, 253, 258, 262–63, 363, 396; bringing forth into, 251

Presence-at-hand, struggle against, 115, 128, 160–64, 166–67, 202–3, 234, 243, 399, 405–6, 411, 422

Present, the: as allegedly pure, 37, 254; as relation, 83, 227, 416, 481n8; as nonbeing, 86, 135; as locus of instant, 135; as foreground, 227; as ideal, 349; *see also* Time

Present-at-hand, the, 238–39; as Being of beings, 119, 216; as unintelligible, 121, 127; as a meaning, 182; as standing stock, 254, 262; 'this' as, 294; *see also* Present, the

Presupposition, 49; of things themselves by science, 191; *see also* Projection

Primitive, the, 21, 399, 411; and readiness-to-hand, 111–12; past as, 240; and *Dasein*, 444–45n82

Primordial, the, *see* Origin

Prior, the, 37–38, 42–43, 99, 101, 106, 159, 162, 268; and the turn, 125; in Kant, 161; *see also* Beginning; Community of nature; Time

Privation (or privative mode), 223, 229, 243; as semblance, 244, 262–63, 417; as incoherence, 338–39, 370–71

Progression (or progress): repetition not,

Progression (*Continued*)
103; and regression, 132, 139, 156, 206, 266, 337–38, 394; unity prior to, 159, 410–11; unlimited, 240–41, 249; relation of will and faith to, 320–21; not inevitable, 347; in spiral, 347–56; of truth, 372; toward unity, 374; *see also* Totalization

Project, fundamental: specification of, 107, 138, 311; radical modification of, 135; as plugging hole in being, 211, 420; as determining meaning, 273; as mastering, 308

Projection, 20, 43, 45, 113, 412; and circularity, 36; categorial, 49; common, 101; of God as ground, 110; of world over beings, 127–28, 200; as realizing synthesis, 296; as humanization, 343, 391; *see also* Intentionality

Proof, ontological, 68, 73

Prose, action and, 274–77, 279, 304

Protagoras, 380

Protention, 396, 472*n*102

Psychoanalysis, existential: as moral description, 137–38, 148; as regression, 139, 279; and atheism, 323–24; as method, 420

Psychologism, 17, 157

Psychology, 12, 307, 315, 333, 378; phenomenological, 66; grounded in anthropology, 157; Gestalt, 303, 437*n*42

Pure, the: Dasein as, 107; Being as, 436–37*n*31; *see also* Reflection, purifying

Purification, *see* Reflection, purifying

Pythagoras, 230, 420

Quality, 75, 77, 78, 151, 291–97, 471*n*96, 471*n*100; as symbol of being, 78, 450*n*87; as loved, 236; as being of entity, 303

Randall, John Herman, Jr., 427

Rationalism, 386

Readiness-to-hand, *see* Artifactual, the; Instrumentality; Presence

Realism, 162, 402; Sartre and, 67, 73, 74–75, 80, 88, 271, 320–24, 470*n*66, 471–72*n*100; Heidegger and, 105–6, 193–94

Reality: phenomenon as, 8, 17, 26, 363; Husserl on, 18; problem of level for defining, 25, 324–25, 352; meaning and,

41, 468*n*37; Sartre on, 69–83, 89, 141, 270, 279, 296, 321, 330, 338–43, 365, 399; Heidegger on, 105–6; as totality of significations, 151; as never beautiful, 464*n*66

Reason: sufficient, 12, 23, 373; Greek, 22; ultimate, 57; dependent on nothing, 158–59; regulative use of, 195, 213–14, 322, 337, 347, 354; dialectical, 214, 230, 338–47, 367, 370–71, 390–400, 480*n*95; without, 225–26; dominance of analytic, 338, 357, 480*n*87; relation of phenomena to, 378, 391; *see also* Analysis; Cause; Ground; Synthesis

Receptacle, 26, 167; *see also* Demiurge; Matter

Reciprocity, 90, 101, 308–10, 311, 339, 392, 478*n*52, 483*n*45; as token of the true, 346; in spiral, 349; as limitation of sovereignty, 353; as the good, 478*n*50

Recollection, 13, 177; *see also* Remembering

Recurrence: eternal, 16, 123–24, 301; freedom and, 62–63; ground as, 64; of place, 366; *see also* Return

Reduction: phenomenological, 17–18, 19–23, 25, 37, 93, 188, 403, 420, 424; as cutting symbolic ties, 79; anxiety as lived, 107, 294, 451–52*n*31; and lifeworld, 410

Reference, 34, 41, 72, 76, 102, 117, 223, 293, 343, 446*n*122; *see also* Relation

Reflection: purifying, 82–85, 131, 137–51, 154–55, 346, 352, 417; as withdrawal, 88–89, 129, 318–19

Regression, *see* Progression; Psychoanalysis, existential

Relata, *see* Factors

Relation: Nietzsche on, 16–17; problem of, 23–24, 26–27; external, 27, 34, 76, 77; internal, 27, 34–36, 41, 56, 74, 97, 102, 105, 127, 190, 199, 201–3, 261–65, 305, 352, 411–13, 416; Being and, 29–30, 75–83, 216, 362–63; unity and, 31; negation as, 73, 82, 308, 333; synthetic, 88–90; of spirit and sensible in language, 224; in Fourfold, 232–33, 255–56; illimitable, 245, 252, 264, 464*n*4; of all relations (language), 257; formal, 341; *see also* Dialectic; Difference; Identity; Mediation; Negation; Synthesis

Relativity: of known to knower, 6–7, 376; of phenomenon to thought, 26–27, 372; and groundless ground, 60, 404; in perception, 75; of Being of beings, 113, 362–63; and inheritance, 116; and truth, 121, 236, 388–89; in experiment, 207; as union of thought and matter, 377–78; as problem, 380–81, 415–16

Release, 226, 254, 260, 263; see also Renunciation; Resignation

Religion: Sartre and, 141–48, 304, 323–24, 325, 355; and death, 148, 242; Heidegger and, 222–23, 242, 456n129; see also Salvation; Theology

Remaining, the: remembering, 208–9, 241–42, 266; space and time as, 226–27; Fourfold as, 253, 382, 416

Remembering, 42, 46–48, 58–61, 124, 376; thinking as, 169–70, 203, 221; phenomenology as, 183; of past as essential future, 202; of place, 206–9, 259, 423–25; as recall to the remaining, 207–8, 266; of original relation, 219, 410; of the gods' transcendence, 242; of prior truth, 378; of prior ontological union, 418; see also Recollection

Renunciation: of Eleatic ideal, 115–16; of appropriation, 148; of absolute grounds, 243, 424

Repetition, 25, 50, 101–3; future as, 48, 125, 322; remembering as, 171; as way back, 189; time of earliest societies as, 327, 336, 392; in spiral, 348, 351; as method, 420; see also Recurrence; Return

Res, 4

Resignation, 236, 260, 263, 282, 300–1, 465n12

Resoluteness, 99, 101, 106

Rest; see Remaining, the; Time

Retention, 396, 472n102

Return: Husserl on, 21–22; Sartre on, 281–82, 299; see also Conversion; Homecoming; Sartre, and problem of withdrawal and return

Revealing, see Disclosure

Revenge against time, 242; metaphysics as, 181; evil as, 235

Revolution: and evolution, 116, 348–49; reflective, 131, 139; in Heidegger, 177, 237; permanent, 276, 277, 300, 317, 322, 334; in Heidegger and Sartre, 418

Richardson, William J., 430n17, 441n8, 457n5

Rilke, Rainer Maria, 406

Robinson, Edward, 39, 42, 50

Romanticism, 175, 316, 323–24, 350–51, 357, 421, 422

Roots, 218, 320, 323; Sartre on, 143–44, 171, 281; Heidegger on, 213, 231–32; Hebel on, 224

Ryle, Gilbert, 384

Sacred/secular, 14, 177, 223

Salvation, 100, 235, 341; Sartre on, 131, 141, 148, 316, 323–24, 346, 352, 457; Heidegger on, 177, 226, 242, 249

Same, the; see Identity

Santayana, George, 89, 484n15

Sartre, Jean-Paul: first contact with Heidegger, 66; and phenomenology, 66–67, 72, 75, 80, 89–93, 129–30, 293–94, 302, 316, 321–25, 329–30, 430n17; reappropriation of Heidegger, 67, 69, 81, 82–83, 88, 91, 103, 110, 116, 128, 130, 131, 138, 146, 147, 149, 151, 153–56, 159–61, 163–64, 167, 272, 273, 294–96, 314, 343, 420, 431n28, 435–36n12, 446n122, 449n76; critique of Heidegger, 71, 78–79, 86–87, 105, 106, 130, 132–33, 158–59, 165, 184, 282–88, 296–301, 305–7, 310, 315–17, 353, 358–59, 411–12, 418–19, 453n57, 457n133, 472n5, 473n15, 480n95; and metaphysics, 90–93, 316, 330, 352; and Neoplatonism, 91–92, 309, 312, 346, 350, 436–37n31; and existentialism, 93, 318–24, 335, 391, 475n95; and problem of withdrawal and return, 95, 129–31, 149, 152, 271, 302–4, 317–21, 334, 351–52, 354–55; projected Ethics of, 141, 149, 330, 346, 447n12; religion of, 141–42, 179, 246, 323–24, 355, 422; visits Heidegger, 165, 452n46; nominalism of, 176, 206, 231, 269–301 passim, 467n1; horror of commonplace in, 179, 421; on Heidegger's character, 184, 456–57n132, 474n66; self-critique of early philosophy, 301, 317–18, 322–31, 333–36, 346, 351–52, 357–58, 362, 375, 392, 420, 441n129, 459n37, 477n31, 479n69; style of, 322; extent of ontological agreement with Heidegger, 362–63,

Sartre, Jean-Paul (*Continued*)
394; extent of disagreement with
Heidegger, 364–68, 418–19, 420–22;
epistemological status of thinking of,
369–400 *passim;* and Stoicism, 450*n*83

Saying, *see* Language

Scarcity, 327–29, 336–37, 349–50, 353–54,
365, 371–72, 410, 477*n*22

Schelling, Friedrich Wilhelm Joseph von,
9, 408

Schopenhauer, Arthur, 14

Schulz, Walter, 111, 112, 441*n*8, 443*n*55

Schweitzer, Albert, 239, 463*n*58

Science, natural, 17, 191; and the familiar,
16, 24; and life-world, objectivity of, 75,
79; implicit metaphysics of, 113, 236;
relative autonomy of, 378;
seventeenth-century, 402; causation in,
413–14; *see also* Physics

Secret, 226, 233–34; *see also* Concealment

Seeing: in Husserl, 18, 36–37, 40; in
Heidegger, 36–37, 39–41, 61–62; as
passive-active, 407; and concealment,
409; as formal, 414; grounds pure intuition, 431*n*24; *see also* Circumspection;
Intuition; Perception

Selbständigkeit, see Existence; Substance

Self: as place, 59–60; loss of, 134, 150, 304,
319; *see also* Being-for-itself; *Dasein;*
Subject

Semblance, 60–61, 201, 244, 258, 262, 418;
of things in science and technology,
191–92; of timeless being, 417; and veil,
453*n*60; *see also* Dissimulation

Sensation, 37, 177, 224, 237, 293, 395–96,
405, 472*n*102

Seriality, 328, 329, 478*n*50

Seriousness, spirit of, 82, 89, 138, 140–41,
297, 351

Shame, 308

Signification, 197, 340–41, 355, 468*n*37,
470*n*66; *see also* Meaning; Reference

Silence: of things, 279; of consciousness,
279, 283, 286–87; in Parain, 281; of beginning, 298

Silesius, Angelus, 465*n*12

Simple, the, 33, 44, 197, 204, 207, 209, 257,
266, 282, 300–1, 351, 421

Simultaneity, *see* Time

Sinn, Dieter, 464*n*6, 482*n*39

Site, *see* Place

Situation, 149–50, 317

Smith, Colin, 470*n*66

Sociology, 333, 368, 469*n*51

Socrates, 312–13, 424

Solidarity, 306, 312–15

Solipsism, 55, 320

Sophocles, 406

Source, *see* Origin

Sovereignty, 309, 349, 353

Space, 23, 36, 42, 110, 126; and directionality, 47; and place, 47, 204, 268, 366; as
ideal, 76; and nihilism, 204; as empty,
240; hodological, 272, 462*n*27; of the
Other, 307

Speculation, 91, 129–30, 195, 196, 239, 261,
316, 336, 400, 417

Spiegelberg, Herbert, 438*n*68

Spinoza, Benedictus de, 14, 402, 417,
430*n*11, 449*n*55

Spiral, the, 347–51

Spontaneity, 18, 144, 154

Sport, 142, 305, 346

Stambaugh, Joan, 464*n*2, 481*n*11

Standard, *see* Measure

State-of-mind, *see* Attunement; Disposition

Stock, standing, 211, 223, 249, 254, 263,
382; *see also* Composition

Stoicism, 100, 144, 450*n*83

Strife, 196, 221–22, 458*n*25

Subject: ground as, 5, 11–12; in Descartes,
11, 159; as arbiter, 12, 18; in Kierkegaard, 12, 104; in Husserl, 18; in
Hegel, 23; in Heidegger, 32, 43, 104–5,
162; possibility of, 43; in Sartre, 159; *see
also* Ego

Subjectivism, 11, 30, 48, 104, 125, 247–48,
294, 382, 415, 441*n*2, 445*n*85; as revenge
against time, 181; as displacement, 207,
242, 263, 266

Subjectivity: Nietzsche on, 16; Husserl
on, 18, 22–23; Kierkegaard on, 54; Sartre
on, 75, 132–33, 153, 157, 359, 478*n*59;
Heidegger on, 98, 165, 207; liberated by
play, 141, 144; attributed to *SZ*, 153–54;
as starting point, 156; of values, 207

Substance, 6–7, 9–10, 11, 389; Kant on,
7–8, 195; Hegel on, 23, 159; Heidegger
on, 36; Sartre on, 77, 78, 89–90, 92, 142,
159

Surpassing: consciousness as, 69, 132,

279, 371; of classifications, 269; language as, 276; of truths, 335; praxis as, 390–94

Symbol, 89, 271; quality as, 78–81, 471*n*100; play and, 140–43, 304; synthesis as, 142–45, 316–17

Synchrony, *see* Time

Synthesis, 7, 293, 409; Hegelian, 27; totality as, 69, 73; ideality of, 76, 90, 92, 302, 440–41*n*129; the real as, 78; affective-cognitive, 81; factoring of, 82; morality of, 89–90, 140–42, 318–20; grounded through analysis, 129; symbolic, 142–46, 304, 319; as goal of man, 148; as beauty, 156; limited by negation, 158, 175; poetic, 275–77; of identification, 283; perceptual, 293; as negation of negation, 327, 331, 371; of change and identity, 327, 348–51, 366; of universal and particular, 387

Tangible, the, 202–5, 232, 268, 409, 460*n*47

Technology, 191, 252, 256, 359, 373; Composition as nature of, 247–48, 397

Teleology: Husserl on, 22; Sartre on, 92, 150–51, 309, 332–33, 337, 343, 357, 372, 391–94; revindication of, 321, 414–15

Temperament, *see* Attitude

Temporality, *see* Time

Terror, 194, 329

Thales, 3

Theology: of death of God, 14–15, 207; revitalization of, 153; ground of, 178; of Fourfold, 222–23, 238–42; temptation of, 357–58, 417; *see also* God; Gods, the

'There': 'here' and, 40–48, 431*n*28; ground as, 97; intelligibility of, 197; world and, 432*n*43; *see also* Clearing; Place; World

Thesis, 247

Thing: as negation of essence, 156; as historical, 190–91; revealed in Fourfold, 206, 221, 232, 256, 388–89; as community of perceptible and imperceptible, 225; as linguistic, 262, 366, 370, 395–96; *see also* Meaning-being; Phenomenon

Thing-in-itself, 9, 24, 195; Nietzsche on, 16; Heidegger on, 105

'Things themselves', 21, 33, 37–38, 65, 129, 278, 294, 400, 416; missed by science and technology, 191; missed by

Kant, 193; located in Fourfold, 267; and classification, 270

Thinking: Descartes on, 4–5, 10, 202; transcendental, 8–9, 11, 17, 186, 266, 367; constitutive, 8–9, 17–20, 33, 37, 283–96, 359; quasi-theological power of, 9, 23, 25–26, 388; Hegel on, 10; Husserl on, 17–23, 471*n*84; as ground, 26, 482*n*29; limited knowledge of role of, 37; autonomy of, 184, 186, 375, 378; as silent saying, 224; inheres in Being, 243, 363, 367, 370; structures of as structures of experience, 307; practical, 338–47, 390–400; and matter as identity, 372, 387, 470*n*66; as expression of circumstances, 378; relation of thing to, 383–89; mathematical, 402, 413; as over-reaching, 416; as acting, 427; distinct from language, 471*n*82; *see also* Intentionality; Reason; Remembering; Understanding

'Third', the, 27, 305, 311, 314, 329, 409–10

'This', 74, 76, 81, 88, 90, 108–9, 288–95, 297

Thrownness, 39, 60, 232; *see also* Finitude; Power, and powerlessness

Tillich, Paul, 222, 443*n*53

Time, 23, 36, 48, 369; and Being, 14–16, 64–65, 72, 106, 127, 327, 394, 415–17; and eternity, 26, 84, 227, 417; ekstases of, 45–46, 366, 416; as temporality, 46, 64, 90; and place, 47, 63–64, 396–97; as horizon, 50; of the world, 83; Heidegger vs. Sartre on, 86, 366–67; as now-sequence, 154, 161, 163, 253; revenge against, 181, 358, 423–24; as coming on of past in future, 183, 254, 349, 369, 370; essentially rests, 210–12, 227, 266, 366; diachronic and synchronic, 218, 344, 349, 413; contemporaneity of, 227, 234, 248, 251, 253, 264, 416; as surpassing, 301; dialectical, 327; and Eleaticism, 415–17; *see also* Future; History; Past; Present; Surpassing; Totalizing

Time-space, *see* Place

Topology, 14, 179, 207, 242; of metaphysics, 177–78, 207; versions of in Heidegger, 215–27; in later Sartre, 347–51; Heidegger vs. Sartre on, 365; *see also* Place

Totalitarianism, *see* Politics

Totality (or whole), 27, 397, 418; broken,

Totality (*Continued*)
1, 312; Hegel on, 10, 308; Kierkegaard on, 13; Heidegger on, 35–36, 43, 107, 122, 294; Sartre on, 69–74, 75, 151, 308–9, 316, 325, 337, 343, 370; instant and, 83; detotalized, 87, 293–94, 309–13, 316, 347–48, 436*n*28; historical character of, 111–12, 392–93; as imperceptible, 268; in poetry, 277; organism as, 326; as regulative principle, 354, 356–57; *see also* World

Totalization: in Hegel, 10; in Sartre, 70, 156, 294, 298, 314, 321, 329; practical, 335; *see also* Progression

Tradition: interpretation and, 36; metaphysics of, 57

Transcendence: Nietzsche on, 14–15; Husserl on, 21–22, 25; consciousness and, 68, 71, 283–84; world as, 126–28; finite, 213, 218, 225, 232, 387–88, 396–97; Heidegger vs. Sartre on, 305, 364; synthesis of historicity and, 320; *see also* Projection; Surpassing

Transparency, 39–40, 88

Transphenomenality, 67–68, 116, 293–94

Trivial, risk of the, 228, 234, 237

Truth, 54, 215, 234; as given and as result, 3; as correspondence, 42, 267, 370, 373–74, 379, 404; of Being, 47, 169, 176; as subjectivity, 54; as perspectival, 60; and untruth, 114, 235–36, 404–5, 421–22, 434*n*85; *cogito* as absolute, 157; language and, 171, 370; primary, 218, 242, 370, 373–74, 389–90, 404, 410; dissimulated origin of, 251, 372–74; metaphysical, 309; is the Whole, 309, 357, 370–71, 421; that becomes, 322–23, 334–35, 349, 391; Heidegger vs. Sartre on, 367, 378, 400; and ground, 369–75, 390–400; propositional, 370, 373, 378–79; as function of praxis, 370–72, 374, 390–400, 410; partiality of, 372; and error, 379; levels of, 400; and rape, 427; *See also* *Alētheia*; Disclosure

Tugendhat, Ernst, 467*n*66

Turn, *see* Heidegger, and the turn; Sartre, and problem of withdrawal and return

Unconditioned, the, 113, 115, 124, 193, 227, 235, 381, 417, 423

Understanding, 49–50, 71, 243; finitude of, 121; kills action, 130; and consciousness, 132; and identity, 219–20, 284; and heavens, 224, 230; as ekstasis, 243; and Being, 249; categories of, 284–85; praxis as, 337–38, 344; requires empathy, 351; requires future, 356; as neutral, 399, 444*n*82; as seeing, 414; *see also* Projection; Thinking

Undifferentiation, 72–74, 80, 126, 142

Unification, *see* Project, fundamental; Synthesis; Totalization

Union: immediate, 6, 386; of idea and matter, 9, 470*n*66; in Hegel, 10, 230, 408; of thought and Being, 10–11; in Kierkegaard, 13; in Nietzsche, 17; of essence and existence, 37–38, 160, 440*n*124; symbolic, 145; of Being and meaning, 216; as ground of analysis, 232; as project, 269; in naming, 278; of thought and beings, 373–74, 409, 481*n*9; as relativity, 377–78; as harmony, 385; dissimulated as goal, 411, *see also* Identity; Relation; Synthesis; Unity

Unity: as prior, 8, 42–46, 106, 159, 373–74, 418–19, 425; Husserl on, 20; of life-world, 25; question of, 26–27, 31, 243; *Dasein* as, 46, 159; Kierkegaard on, 54; of in-itself and for-itself, 90–93; Hegel on, 125; of noetic and noematic, 134; with matter, 143–44; prelogical, 159; threatened by anxiety, 160–64, 200; and circularity, 162, 275, 325; problem of resolved, 199–200, 242–43, 326–27; of the different, 205, 372–74, 482*n*29; of earth and heavens, 231; as poetic, 275, 278; prehistoric, 327–29, 410, 418; as the good, 346; dream of synthetic, 350, 410; of the act, 354; of individual and totality, 354–55; historically split, 363; role of language in, 395–96, 405; of practical field, 477*n*25; *see also* Identity; Juncture; Relation, internal; Synthesis; Union

Universals: and things, 231, 383–89; in Sartre, 283–85, 289, 295, 340

Utopianism, 247, 250, 259–61, 353, 419

Vaihinger, Hans, 440*n*122

Validity, 369–80, 403–4

Value: and devaluation, 14, 235, 404, 423;

Nietzsche on, 14–17; problem of, 24; in existentialism, 54; ekstasis as origin of, 138–39; *ens causa sui* as, 148; freedom as ground of, 148, 152, 317; freedom as, 150, 304; subjectivity of, 207; as goal, 211, 237–38; as determined by progress, 249; place as ground of, 422–23; immanent in world, 455n107; *see also* Beauty; Good, the

Violence, 180–82, 222, 271, 312, 328, 340–41, 354, 385, 406, 407, 423, 465n12

Virtual: phenomenon as, 26, 188; world as, 82, 89, 127, 146, 321; relatedness as, 89; synthesis of actual and intentional, 139; unreflective synthesis as, 302

Voluntarism, 98, 104, 223; *see also* Will

Von Hermann, Friedrich Wilhelm, 99, 432n42, 446n120

Vorhandenheit, see Presence-at-hand, struggle against; Present-at-hand, the

Waelhens, Alphonse de, 358, 359, 446n122

Way: *Dasein* as, 32, 47; all is, 210, 227

Wertheimer, Max, 478n41

Whence and whither, 13, 14, 59, 99, 366, 371–72, 382, 481n10

Whitehead, Alfred North, 34, 35, 402

Whole, *see* Totality

Will, 26, 52, 98, 397–98, 399; to power, 16; in existentialism, 54, 154–55, 424, 450n83; in metaphysics, 110, 127, 223, 236–37, 321, 325, 424; world of arbitrary, 126, 167, 199–200, 342, 382, 386; to will, 241; in Composition, 247–49; of Marxism, 320, 357; rational, 371; *see also* Power

Withdrawal, *see* Action; Reflection,
purifying; Return; Sartre, problem of withdrawal and return

Wittgenstein, Ludwig, 388

Wonder: and anxiety, 107, 193–94, 458n16; and language, 200, 226; and Event, 226; and beauty, 242; and gift, 377; of the commonplace, 404

Word, 269–300 *passim*; as medium, 176, 224, 405–7; dissembles own assembling, 205; as the sensible sense, 224; and earth, 267; magical power of, 282; changes nothing, 317–18; as bearer of counterfinality, 355; correspondence of thing and, 365–66; and thing, 383–84; as gift, 397; and significance, 446n122; as worked matter, 468n26; designates object and concept, 480n87; *see also* Names

World: life-, 4, 20–22, 25, 410; phenomenal, 7–8, 15; mundane, 15; as ground, 22, 55, 68, 97–98, 182, 200, 296; as prior to subject and object, 42–46; as in-itself, 50; as world, 63, 126, 200; as synthesis, 69, 142, 298, 321, 327; as ideal, 81; as humanized actuality, 85; as metaphysical, 93, 216–18, 352; common, 101–3, 306; as nothing, 106, 126; stability of, 111–12, 115, 125–28, 250, 307–8; as projected over beings, 127–28, 196; little reality to, 141; as articulation of earth, 196; as named earth, 200; and heavens, 218; as Fourfold-Play, 255; problem of nature of, 302–3; and 'there', 432n43; *see also* Totality

Worldhood: as existentiale, 40; and relations, 105

Yeats, William Butler, 211